COMPLETE EDITION

Computers Are Your Future

2006

BILL DALEY

Upper Saddle River, New Jersey

Computers Are Your Future 2006
Complete edition / Bill Daley

Executive Editor, Print: Stephanie Wall
Executive Editor, Media: Jodi McPherson
Vice President/Publisher: Natalie E. Anderson
Acquisitions Editor: Melissa Sabella
Project Manager, Editorial and Media: Jodi Bolognese
Editorial Assistants: Alana Meyers, Sandra Bernales, Bambi Marchigano, Brian Hoehl
Developmental Editor: Christine Wright
Senior Marketing Manager: Emily Williams Knight
Marketing Assistant: Lisa Taylor
Managing Editor: Lynda Castillo
Senior Project Manager, Production: April Montana
Production Assistant: Sandra Bernales
Manufacturing Buyer: April Montana
Senior Media Project Manager: Cathleen Profitko
Design Manager: Maria Lange
Art Director: Blair Brown
Cover Design: Blair Brown
Interior Design: Quorum Creative Services
Composition: Quorum Creative Services
Full-Service Project Management: Bookmasters, Inc.
Photo Research: Shirley Webster
Cover Printer: Phoenix Color
Printer/Binder: R. R. Donnelley

Credits and acknowledgments borrowed from other sources and reproduced, with permission, in this textbook appear on appropriate page within text (or on pages C.1–C.11).

Microsoft® and Windows® are registered trademarks of the Microsoft Corporation in the U.S.A. and other countries. Screen shots and icons reprinted with permission from the Microsoft Corporation. This book is not sponsored or endorsed by or affiliated with the Microsoft Corporation.

Pearson Education LTD.
Pearson Education Singapore, Pte. Ltd
Pearson Education, Canada, Ltd
Pearson Education–Japan

Pearson Education Australia PTY, Limited
Pearson Education North Asia Ltd
Pearson Educación de Mexico, S.A. de C.V.
Pearson Education Malaysia, Pte. Ltd

10 9 8 7 6 5 4 3
ISBN 0-13-148801-5

To Sharon

Thank you for your love and unending support.

You are my sweetie, my partner, and my best friend.

I love you with all that I am.

—Bill

Acknowledgments

I am grateful for the assistance of the reviewers of this edition:

Judith F. Bennett, Sam Houston State University
Kristen H. Callahan, Mercer County Community College
Annette Duvall, Albuquerque Technical Vocational Institute
Linda Foster-Turpen, Albuquerque Technical Vocational Institute
Jonathan Hill, Pace University
Cheryl Jordan, San Juan College
Darrel Karbginsky, Chemeketa Community College
Pat R. Ormond, Utah Valley State College
Jennifer Pickle, Amarillo College
Diane Stark, Phoenix College

My deepest thanks also to the reviewers of the seventh edition:

Gary R. Armstrong, Shippensburg University
Wayne E. Ballentine, University of Houston, Downtown
Judith F. Bennett, Sam Houston State University
Deborah Buell, University of Houston, Downtown
Judy Cestaro, California State University, San Bernardino
Joseph DeLibero, Arizona State University
Annette Duvall, Albuquerque Technical Vocational Institute
Deena Engel, New York University
Tracey L. Fisher, Butler County Community College
Linda Foster-Turpen, Albuquerque Technical Vocational Institute
Susan Fry, Boise State University
Marta Gonzalez, Hudson County Community College
Cheryl Jordan, San Juan College
Bhushan Kapoor, California State University at Fullerton
Trudy McNew Gift, Hagerstown Community College
Diane Stark, Phoenix College
Mary Ann Zlotow, College of DuPage

Additional thanks to supplement authors Tony Nowakowski, LeeAnn Bates, and Susan Herrington.

I have been so fortunate to work with people who are at the top of their profession!

My most heartfelt appreciation goes to Jodi Bolognese, who was the Editorial Project Manager for this book. Her greatest attribute is that she always does what she says she's going to do, and usually does it sooner than promised. What a dream it has been to work with Jodi! Special thanks go to Christine Wright, Development Editor. Christine provided expert advice and insight into how to better organize and describe the content of the book. She helped with the research and brought many years of professional experience to the project. Marian Wood made a significant contribution by writing the Impacts and Currents features in each chapter. Thanks, too, to Jason Wertz for writing the Concept Tips at the end of each chapter. April Montana, Senior Project Manager of Production, saw the book through the complex production process with the coolness and calmness that comes only from a consummate professional. I also sincerely appreciate the artistic flair with which Debbie Iverson of Quorum Creative Services rendered the text, photos, and artwork. Jennifer Welsch and the dedicated folks at BookMasters provided the best copyediting and proofreading an author could hope for. Their attention to detail has helped ensure that you are reading the cleanest textbook on the market today. Shirley Webster, Photo Researcher, worked long, arduous hours researching the photos. She is a joy to work with and has provided photos that accurately depict the topics in the text. Jodi McPherson was my Executive Editor. She believed that I could write this book before I knew it was a possibility. Thank you, Jodi, for believing in me and for your unabashed support of my work. Finally, I would like to express my deepest appreciation to everyone in my Prentice Hall family. Quality comes from caring; Prentice Hall is a company of people who care.

—Bill Daley

Preface

A Reference Tool for Today's Students

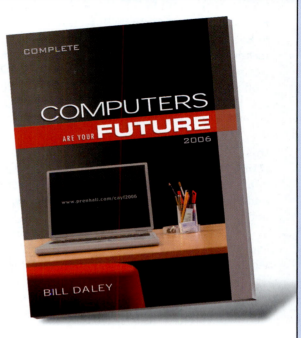

You want a book that addresses the everyday needs of the students you teach. Today, students aren't wowed by technology—it's part of their daily lives. From the time they were in grade school, they have looked at a computer like a toaster—just another common home appliance. This book has been revised so that it matches what we believe they already know with what you've told us they should know. This new edition can serve as a reference tool without being overwhelming or intimidating.

Today's students want a practical "what it is" and "how it works" approach to computers, with less explanation of "why." We've applied this approach to each chapter and Spotlight in this edition. For example, Spotlight 3 clearly identifies the different types of home networks that are available and explains how to set one up.

Today's students also want practical tips that help them understand chapter concepts. We've added a new feature, **Concept Tips**, at the end of each chapter. It serves as a one-page mini-reference tool on topics such as how to capture a screenshot and how to back up data.

You wanted the new edition to be more current and modularized than the seventh edition—but without forcing changes in the way you teach your course. In response, we've significantly reorganized the table of contents, cut redundancy across chapters, and added more Spotlights to deliver smaller chunks of information to give you more flexibility.

You wanted a text-specific, interactive Web site that enhances your students' learning with valuable additional resources and practice exercises—and for your students to be led intuitively to key information that is concise, intelligent, and clearly laid out. Wait until you experience what we've created! Now available as an annual edition, *Computers Are Your Future 2006* brings new and updated coverage; new Spotlight, Currents, and Impacts features; and an updated accompanying Web site. This text is ready for the challenge of teaching even your most diverse class—without sacrificing quality, integrity, or choice. *Computers Are Your Future 2006* comes in two versions—Introductory (Chapters 1–9) or Complete (Chapters 1–14)—to meet the needs of your classroom.

Spotlight sections cover the practical as well as the innovative in various subject areas. For example, ethics, home networks, file management, and buying and upgrading a computer system focus on the practical, whereas Microsoft Office, multimedia devices, and emerging technologies cover innovation in software, hardware, and technology for the future. We've added reinforcing exercises at the end of each Spotlight.

Impacts and **Currents** features focus on cutting-edge computer technology as well as controversial topics that relate to students' lives. Students are introduced to thought-provoking bites of information that will stimulate class discussion or team debates on all aspects of technology's impact on life today. These features examine technical issues in computing as well as the societal implications of computing resulting from emerging technologies, security, crime, and ethics.

Teamwork exercises have been added to this edition. These end-of-chapter activities reinforce chapter concepts by requiring students to work in teams to conduct research and interviews and to create group papers and presentations.

TechTV links and references appear in every chapter. TechTV provides Web-based videos that are current, rich, and interesting. These are the same videos found on the 24-hour G4TechTV cable news channel. Cutting-edge topics covered include ethics, e-commerce, security, privacy, wireless communications, home networks, and multimedia devices.

The chapters have been significantly reorganized and updated. Chapter 1 has been revised to engage the student and to provide a vivid outline of the book's content. The Internet and World Wide Web content has been moved up in the text to Chapter 2 and is followed by a Spotlight on e-commerce. Information on wired and wireless communication has also been moved up in the text, to Chapter 3, and is followed by a new Spotlight on home networks. Chapters 4 and 6 have been revised and updated. Chapter 5 now includes material on multimedia software, which was formerly found in a Spotlight section. Chapters 7 through 9 have been heavily revised, and additional coverage of privacy, security, and intellectual property issues has been included. Chapters 10 through 14 have been updated to include the latest in careers, programming, data and systems management, and enterprise computing.

New! Concept Tips

The Concept Tips at the end of each chapter present guidelines

on how to complete different computer-related tasks. Each Concept Tip

serves as a one-page mini-reference tool. The following list shows

the Concept Tip presented at the end of each chapter:

CHAPTER 1   **Transporting Your Data**
CHAPTER 2   **Creating an E-mail Filter to Fight Spam**
CHAPTER 3   **How to Find Wireless Hot Spots**
CHAPTER 4   **Viruses: How to Tell If Your System Is Infected**
CHAPTER 5   **Capturing a Screenshot and Sending It as an E-mail Attachment**
CHAPTER 6   **CPUs—What's the Difference?**
CHAPTER 7   **Backing Up Your Data**
CHAPTER 8   **Choosing an ISP**
CHAPTER 9   **How to Hide from Pop-up Ads**
CHAPTER 10   **Ethics: Patents and Copyright Issues**
CHAPTER 11   **Programming with Alice**
CHAPTER 12   **Exploring Web Databases**
CHAPTER 13   **Using the SDLC to Buy a Computer**
CHAPTER 14   **Setting Up a Video Teleconference**

For the Instructor

INSTRUCTOR'S RESOURCE CENTER DVD-ROM

The new and improved Prentice Hall Instructor's Resource Center on DVD-ROM includes the tools you expect from a Prentice Hall Computer Concepts text, such as:

- An Instructor's Manual in Word and PDF formats
- Solutions to all questions and exercises from the book and Web site
- Customizable PowerPoint slide presentations for each chapter
- Animations depicting computer concepts
- TechTV videos
- An image library of all of the figures from the text

The DVD-ROM is an interactive library of assets and links. It can be used to create custom "index" pages that can be used as the foundation for a class presentation or an online lecture. You can navigate through this DVD to collect the materials that are most relevant to your interests, edit them to create powerful class lectures, copy them to your own computer's hard drive, and then upload them to an online course-management system.

ONEKEY

OneKey, available at **www.prenhall.com/onekey**, offers you the best teaching and learning resources all in one place. OneKey for *Computers Are Your Future 2006* is all your students need for anywhere, anytime access to your course materials conveniently organized by textbook chapter to reinforce and apply what they've learned in class. OneKey is all you need to plan and administer your course through Blackboard, WebCT, or CourseCompass. With OneKey, all of your instructor resources are in one place, maximizing your effectiveness and minimizing your time and effort. OneKey for convenience, simplicity, and success . . . for you and your students.

TESTGEN SOFTWARE

TestGen is a test generator that lets you view and easily edit test bank questions, transfer them to tests, and print the tests in a variety of formats best suited to your teaching situation. Powerful search and sort functions enable you to easily locate questions and arrange them in the order you prefer.

QuizMaster, which is also included in this package, enables students to take tests created with TestGen on a local area network. The QuizMaster utility built into TestGen enables instructors to view student records and print a variety of reports. Building tests is easy with TestGen, and exams can be easily uploaded into WebCT, Blackboard, or CourseCompass.

TRAIN AND ASSESS IT: HANDS ON TRAINING AND ASSESSMENT SOFTWARE

Prentice Hall offers performance-based training and assessment all in one product—Train & Assess IT, available at **www.prenhall .com/taitdemo**. The training component offers computer-based training that students can use to preview, learn, and review Microsoft Office application skills. Whether delivered via the Web or CD-ROM, Train & Assess IT offers interactive computer-based training to augment classroom learning. Built-in prescriptive testing suggests a study path based not only on student test results, but also on the specific textbook chosen for the course. The assessment component offers computer-based testing that shares the same user interface as Train & Assess IT. The assessment component can be used to evaluate a student's knowledge about specific topics in Word, Excel, Access, PowerPoint, Outlook, the Internet, computing concepts, Windows, and several key computer graphics software packages. It uses a task-oriented environment to demonstrate students' proficiency as well as comprehension of the topics. Train & Assess IT also allows professors to test students out of a course, place students in appropriate courses, and evaluate skill sets.

TOOLS FOR ONLINE LEARNING

COMPANION WEB SITE

This text is accompanied by a companion Web site at **www.prenhall.com/cayf2006**. This new site offers an interactive study guide, downloadable supplements, additional Internet exercises, TechTV videos, Web resource links such as Careers in IT and crossword puzzles, plus technology updates and bonus chapters on the latest trends and hottest topics in information technology. Links to Web exercises will be updated frequently to ensure accuracy.

ONLINE COURSEWARE

CourseCompass

CourseCompass, available at **www.coursecompass.com**, is a dynamic, interactive online course-management tool powered exclusively for Pearson Education by Blackboard. This exciting product allows you to teach market-leading Pearson Education content in an easy-to-use, customizable format.

Blackboard

Prentice Hall's abundant online content, combined with Blackboard's popular tools and interface, results in robust Web-based courses

that are easy to implement, manage, and use—taking your courses to new heights in student interaction and learning. Blackboard can be accessed at **www.prenhall.com/blackboard**.

WebCT

Course-management tools within WebCT, available at **www.prenhall.com/webct**, include page tracking, progress tracking, class and student management, a grade book, communication tools, a calendar, reporting tools, and more. GOLD LEVEL CUSTOMER SUPPORT, available exclusively to adopters of Prentice Hall courses, is provided free of charge upon adoption and provides you with priority assistance, training discounts, and dedicated technical support.

TECHTV

Formed by the May 2004 merger of G4 and TechTV, G4TechTV is a 24-hour television network that is  plugged into every dimension of games, gear, gadgets, and gigabytes. Headquartered in Los Angeles, the network features original programming on the passions and lifestyles of the gamer generation. To learn more, visit **www.g4techtv.com** or contact your local cable or satellite provider to get G4TechTV in your area.

For the Student

Welcome to *Computers Are Your Future 2006*! The following pages are designed to help you get the most out of the course material and make the learning process rewarding. We call your attention to areas that may help you as you read through the book. Please read on, and enjoy!

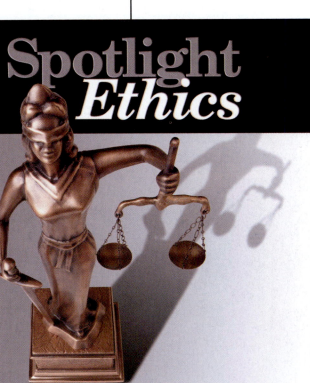

SPOTLIGHT sections highlight important ideas about computer-related topics and provide in-depth, useful information to take your learning to the next level.

Spotlight Ethics

What's the difference between unethical and illegal? WHEN USING COMPUTERS, AND ESPECIALLY THE INTERNET, YOU MAY HAVE TO FACE THIS QUESTION ON A DAILY BASIS. HAVE YOU DOWNLOADED ANY MUSIC RECENTLY? DID YOU PAY FOR THAT MUSIC? WHAT ABOUT THE DVD MOVIE (OR COMPUTER GAME) YOU WATCHED (OR PLAYED) AT YOUR FRIEND'S THIS WEEKEND? DID HE BUY IT OR ILLEGALLY COPY IT? WAS IT A VIOLENT GAME? HAVE YOU EVER THOUGHT ABOUT WHO OWNS THE WORD-PROCESSING SOFTWARE YOU USE IN YOUR COLLEGE COMPUTER LAB? WHAT IS YOUR SCHOOL OR COMPANY'S POLICY ON ACCEPTABLE COMPUTER USE? PERHAPS YOU'VE WRITTEN A RESEARCH PAPER RECENTLY THAT INCLUDED MATERIAL YOU COPIED FROM A WEB SITE. OR, PERHAPS YOU'VE POSTED A NASTY COMMENT ABOUT SOMEONE ON A DISCUSSION BOARD OR SENT A NASTY E-MAIL. HOW CAN YOUR BEHAVIOR ON THE JOB CROSS THESE LINES? *ETHICS* HAS OFTEN BEEN DESCRIBED AS WHAT WE CHOOSE TO DO WHEN NO ONE IS WATCHING. IN OTHER WORDS, WE CHOOSE TO BEHAVE IN AN ETHICAL WAY BECAUSE WE COULDN'T LIVE WITH OUR CONSCIENCE OTHERWISE. IT'S NOT ABOUT WHETHER WE'LL GET CAUGHT. THAT'S THE ILLEGAL PART.

THIS SPOTLIGHT EXAMINES SOME OF THE MOST COMMON ISSUES IN COMPUTER ETHICS, FROM ETHICAL DILEMMAS, WHERE THE DIFFERENCE BETWEEN RIGHT AND WRONG ISN'T SO EASY TO DISCERN, TO LEGAL MATTERS, WHERE RIGHT AND WRONG IS DETERMINED BY LAW.

Figure 1A *Computers cause new ethical dilemmas by pushing people into unprecedented situations.*

Computer Ethics for Computer Users

It isn't always easy to determine the right thing to do. Even when you know what's right, it's not always easy to act on it. Peer pressure is a tremendous force. Why should you be the one to do the right thing when everyone else is getting away with using copied software and music files?

Computers cause new ethical dilemmas by pushing people into unprecedented situations (Figure 1A). Computer ethics uses basic ethical principles to help you make the right decisions in your daily computer use. Ethical principles help you think through your options.

35

Milestones

The Drive Toward Smarter Cars

IMPACTS

Cars are getting smarter all the time, thanks to computer technology. And the auto industry is just beginning its drive toward smarter cars. The OnStar system, installed in some General Motors cars, can give you verbal directions and display maps using GPS navigation software. In an emergency, you can reach an OnStar representative by pressing a cell phone button on the dashboard. If you accidentally lock yourself out, OnStar can remotely unlock the car doors. Can't find your car in a vast parking lot? OnStar can flash the headlights or sound the horn to show you the way. And if your car is stolen, OnStar can track its location for police.

Smarter cars are on the way that will alert you about a possible front or rear collision, monitor your health, offer real-time weather and traffic updates, and keep your car at a safe distance from others. Ford is testing a voice-activated computer system that will announce instructions to bypass traffic jams and flash safety alerts on the dashboard display. Also in testing are night-vision displays projected on the windshield to help you see ahead on dark roads and digital adaptive headlights that aim the beams into a turn when you steer around a corner.

Not too far in the future, you may insert a smart card into your car's dashboard to automatically move the driver's seat to your preferred position, set the interior temperature, or download digital music files for your listening pleasure. Your car's computer will read the car's maintenance history on the smart card and let you know when repairs are needed. The smart card will store your address book and transfer numbers to your cell phone to place calls quickly via voice activation. The goal is to make your driving experience safer and easier, but will you need another driver's education class to master all this new technology? Steer your Web browser to **www .delphi.com/products/ auto/safety/** to find out more about advanced safety systems (Figure 7.23).

FIGURE 7.23 With the industry's most extensive portfolio of safety products and an in-depth understanding of vehicle systems integration, Delphi is revolutionizing onboard vehicle safety.

IMPACTS boxes in each chapter illustrate thought-provoking cultural, ethical, and societal implications of computing.

FLOPPY AND ZIP DISKS AND DRIVES

Like removable hard disks, floppy and Zip disks are forms of near-online, or secondary, storage. A **floppy disk** (also called a **diskette**) is a portable storage medium that contains a circular plastic disk coated with a magnetically sensitive film, the same material that's on a cassette tape. A **floppy disk drive** is a device that enables a computer to read and write data to floppy disks. In desktop computer systems, a floppy disk drive is internal or mou...

Emerging Technologies

Wearables: The Fashion of Technology

CURRENTS

After getting dressed in the morning, you head down the street in your "wearables." As you walk to the library, you use your wrist pad to e-mail a friend, asking her to meet you for lunch later. At the library, the network automatically recognizes you by your ring. You search your pocket for your stylus, find it, point at a library computer screen, and the computer acknowledges you. You use your monocle to access your documents. You open one and jot notes by waving your pen in the air. As you leave the library, you call three of your friends and visually chat together through your monocle and earpiece until your next class. Your wearables seamlessly connect you to a network throughout your day.

Sound intriguing but unbelievable? Some of these technologies already exist. Xybernaut makes wearable computers equipped with Optimus software to link firefighters and other emergency workers by voice and video to each other, to their supervisors, and to local hospitals. Users wear a light, portable CPU (on a belt or in a vest) and either tap a wrist-mounted keyboard or give voice commands through the microphone on the head-mounted display screen. Not only can they check for information over the Internet, they can send or receive e-mails and access applications and files on the server.

Most wearable technologies have been incorporated into headsets and glasses, backpacks and fanny packs, rings and wristbands, and multipocketed pants (Figure 7.19). Now wearables with even more possibilities are on the way. "Smart thread" fiber, similar to nylon, conducts electricity and can be woven into clothing with computer-like abilities to connect soldiers or emergency workers with command centers. "Smart skin" material, studded with microsensors, can be made into gloves or suits that send a signal when industrial workers or astronauts are exposed to toxic chemicals.

If you don't need all the functions of wearables, you might get "chipped" by having a microchip implanted in your arm. Already, members of exclusive European beach clubs are getting chipped to enter the VIP lounge or pay for a drink simply by waving to the electronic receiver. Will getting "chipped" catch on as the next high-tech fashion with function?

FIGURE 7.19 Most wearable technologies have been incorporated into headsets and glasses, backpacks and fanny packs, rings and wristbands, and multipocketed pants.

CURRENTS boxes in each chapter examine cutting-edge issues in computing and computer technology.

TECHTALK margin notes define commonly used computer jargon.

DESTINATIONS margin notes direct you to related Web sites where you can explore chapter topics in more depth.

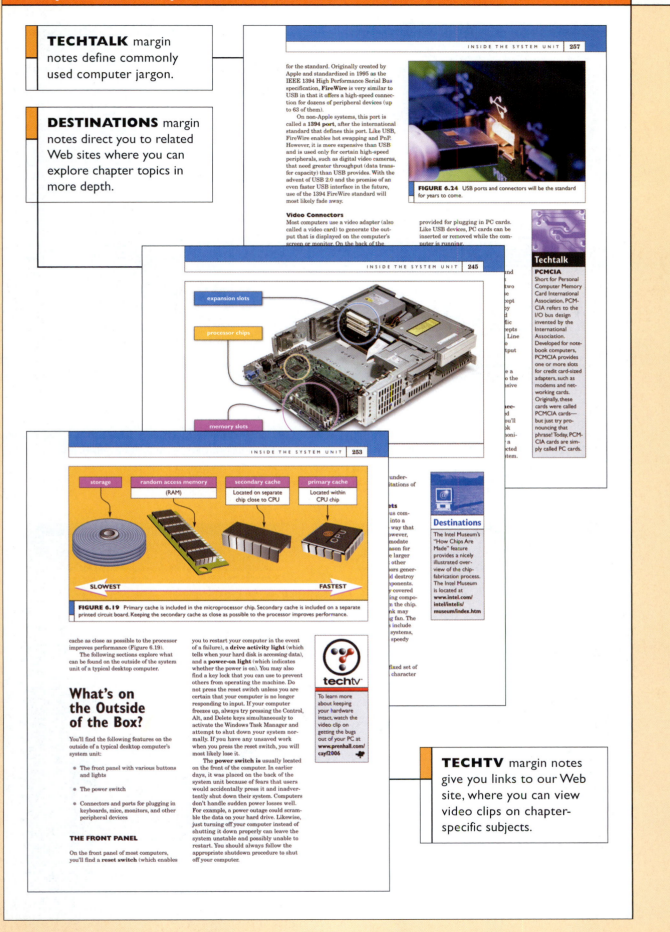

INSIDE THE SYSTEM UNIT | 257

for the standard. Originally created by Apple and standardized in 1995 as the IEEE 1394 High Performance Serial Bus specification, **FireWire** is very similar to USB in that it offers a high-speed connection for dozens of peripheral devices (up to 63 of them).

On non-Apple systems, this port is called a **1394 port**, after the international standard that defines this port. Like USB, FireWire enables hot swapping and PnP. However, it is more expensive than USB and is used only for certain high-speed peripherals, such as digital video cameras, that need greater throughput (data transfer capacity) than USB provides. With the advent of USB 2.0 and the promise of an even faster USB interface in the future, use of the 1394 FireWire standard will most likely fade away.

FIGURE 6.24 USB ports and connectors will be the standard for years to come.

Video Connectors

Most computers use a video adapter (also called a video card) to generate the output that is displayed on the computer's screen or monitor. On the back of the ...

provided for plugging in PC cards. Like USB devices, PC cards can be inserted or removed while the computer is running.

Techtalk

PCMCIA
Short for Personal Computer Memory Card International Association, PCMCIA refers to the I/O bus design invented by the International Association. Developed for notebook computers, PCMCIA provides one or more slots for credit card–sized adapters, such as modems and networking cards. Originally, these cards were called PCMCIA cards—but just try pronouncing that phrase! Today, PCMCIA cards are simply called PC cards.

INSIDE THE SYSTEM UNIT | 245

expansion slots

processor chips

memory slots

INSIDE THE SYSTEM UNIT | 253

| storage | random access memory (RAM) | secondary cache Located on separate chip close to CPU | primary cache Located within CPU chip |

SLOWEST   FASTEST

FIGURE 6.19 Primary cache is included in the microprocessor chip. Secondary cache is included on a separate printed circuit board. Keeping the secondary cache as close as possible to the processor improves performance.

Destinations

The Intel Museum's "How Chips Are Made" feature provides a nicely illustrated overview of the chip-fabrication process. The Intel Museum is located at **www.intel.com/intel/intelis/museum/index.htm**

cache as close as possible to the processor improves performance (Figure 6.19).

The following sections explore what can be found on the outside of the system unit of a typical desktop computer.

What's on the Outside of the Box?

You'll find the following features on the outside of a typical desktop computer's system unit:

- The front panel with various buttons and lights
- The power switch
- Connectors and ports for plugging in keyboards, mice, monitors, and other peripheral devices

THE FRONT PANEL

On the front panel of most computers, you'll find a **reset switch** (which enables

you to restart your computer in the event of a failure), a **drive activity light** (which tells when your hard disk is accessing data), and a **power-on light** (which indicates whether the power is on). You may also find a key lock that you can use to prevent others from operating the machine. Do not press the reset switch unless you are certain that your computer is no longer responding to input. If your computer freezes up, always try pressing the Control, Alt, and Delete keys simultaneously to activate the Windows Task Manager and attempt to shut down your system normally. If you have any unsaved work when you press the reset switch, you will most likely lose it.

The **power switch is** usually located on the front of the computer. In earlier days, it was placed on the back of the system unit because of fears that users would accidentally press it and inadvertently shut down their system. Computers don't handle sudden power losses well. For example, a power outage could scramble the data on your hard drive. Likewise, just turning off your computer instead of shutting it down properly can leave the system unstable and possibly unable to restart. You should always follow the appropriate shutdown procedure to shut off your computer.

techtv

To learn more about keeping your hardware intact, watch the video clip on getting the bugs out of your PC at **www.prenhall.com/cayf2006**

TECHTV margin notes give you links to our Web site, where you can view video clips on chapter-specific subjects.

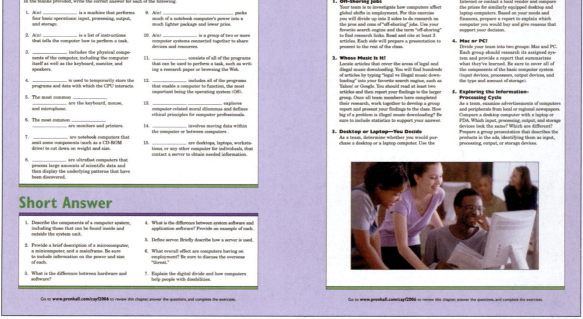

---

26 COMPUTERS ARE YOUR FUTURE 2006

What You've Learned

COMPUTERS AND YOU

- A computer is a machine that performs four operations: input, processing, output, and storage. These four operations are called the information-processing cycle.

- A computer system is a collection of related components that have been designed to work together. It includes both the computer's hardware (its physical components such as the computer, keyboard, monitor, speakers, and so on) and software (the programs that run on it).

- In a typical computer system, a keyboard and a mouse provide input capabilities. Processing is done by the microprocessor (CPU) and RAM (random access memory). You see the results (output) on a monitor or printer. A hard disk is typically used for long-term storage.

- Spell checking a word-processed document is a good example of the information-processing cycle. The input consists of the original document, which contains spelling mistakes. When the computer processes the document, it detects and flags possible spelling errors by checking every word in the document against a massive spelling dictionary. Output consists of a list of words that the spell checker is unable to find in its dictionary. User interaction is required to confirm whether the apparent misspelled words need to be corrected. The user saves the corrected document to storage for future use.

- There are two major categories of computers: computers for individuals and computers for organizations. Types of computers for individuals include personal computers (PCs), desktop computers, notebooks, subnotebooks, laptop computers, handheld computers (PDAs, pen computers and tablet PCs), all-in-one computers, network computers (NCs), and Internet appliances. Types of computers for organizations include servers, minicomputers, mainframes, and supercomputers.

- Responsible computing requires that you understand the advantages and disadvantages of using the computer. Advantages include speed, memory, storage, hardware reliability, and accuracy. Disadvantages include information overload, the expense of computer equipment, data inaccuracy, and dependence on unreliable software.

- Using hardware and software involves some risk. It is important to pay attention to the proper care and use of hardware to avoid damage to the equipment and potential computer-related injuries. Recognize that all programs contain errors that typically cause programs to run slowly or other inconveniences.

- Computers can be misused or used to benefit individuals and society. Examples of misuse include distributing personal information without permission, exposure to unwanted solicitations, viruses, and illegitimate copying of software and music. Benefits include using computers to assist those with disabilities or no access.

- Although computers are creating new job opportunities, they're also shifting labor demand toward skilled workers, particularly those with computer skills. As a result, skilled workers earn more, while unskilled workers' wages have stagnated over the past 20 years. Computers and technology also affect employment through automation, outsourcing of jobs overseas, or the total elimination of job categories.

- Being a responsible computer user means knowing how your computer and Internet usage affects others in your school, family, community, and the environment. Using recycled paper, fairly sharing access to public resources, properly disposing of computers and peripherals, being aware of computer and Internet overuse, and staying informed about changing technology demonstrate responsible computer use.

Go to www.prenhall.com/cayf2006 to review this chapter, answer the questions, and complete the exercises.

CHAPTER 1 **27**

Key Terms and Concepts

Go to www.prenhall.com/cayf2006 to review this chapter, answer the questions, and complete the exercises.

END-OF-CHAPTER MATERIAL includes updated multiple-choice, matching, fill-in, and short-answer questions, as well as Web research projects so you can prepare for tests.

---

30 COMPUTERS ARE YOUR FUTURE 2006

Fill-In

In the blanks provided, write the correct answer for each of the following.

1. A(n) _____ is a machine that performs four basic operations: input, processing, output, and storage.

2. A(n) _____ is a list of instructions that tells the computer how to perform a task.

3. _____ includes the physical components of the computer, including the computer itself as well as the keyboard, monitor, and speakers.

4. _____ is used to temporarily store the programs and data with which the CPU interacts.

5. The most common _____ _____ are the keyboard, mouse, and microphone.

6. The most common _____ are monitors and printers.

7. _____ are notebook computers that omit some components (such as a CD-ROM drive) to cut down on weight and size.

8. _____ are ultrafast computers that process large amounts of scientific data and then display the underlying patterns that have been discovered.

9. A(n) _____ packs much of a notebook computer's power into a much lighter package and lower price.

10. A(n) _____ is a group of two or more computer systems connected together to share devices and resources.

11. _____ consists of all of the programs that can be used to perform a task, such as writing a research paper or browsing the Web.

12. _____ includes all of the programs that enable a computer to function, the most important being the operating system (OS).

13. _____ explores computer-related moral dilemmas and defines ethical principles for computer professionals.

14. _____ involves moving data within the computer or between computers.

15. _____ are desktops, laptops, workstations, or any other computer for individuals, that contact a server to obtain needed information.

Short Answer

1. Describe the components of a computer system, including those that can be found inside and outside the system unit.

2. Provide a brief description of a microcomputer, a minicomputer, and a mainframe. Be sure to include information on the power and size of each.

3. What is the difference between hardware and software?

4. What is the difference between system software and application software? Provide an example of each.

5. Define server. Briefly describe how a server is used.

6. What overall effect are computers having on employment? Be sure to discuss the overseas "threat."

7. Explain the digital divide and how computers help people with disabilities.

Go to www.prenhall.com/cayf2006 to review this chapter, answer the questions, and complete the exercises.

CHAPTER 1 **31**

Teamwork

1. Off-Shoring Jobs
Your team is to investigate how computers affect global shifts in employment. For this exercise you will divide up into 2 sides to do research on the pros and cons of "off-shoring" jobs. Use your favorite search engine and the term "off-shoring" to find research links. Read and cite at least 3 articles. Each side will prepare a presentation to present to the rest of the class.

2. Whose Music Is It?
Locate articles that cover the areas of legal and illegal music downloading. You will find hundreds of articles by typing "legal vs illegal music downloading" into your favorite search engine, such as Yahoo! or Google. You should read at least two articles and then report your findings to the larger group. Once all team members have completed their research, work together to develop a group report and present your findings to the class. How big of a problem is illegal music downloading? Be sure to include statistics to support your answer.

3. Desktop or Laptop—You Decide
As a team, determine whether you would purchase a desktop or a laptop computer. Use the Internet or contact a local vendor and compare the prices for similarly equipped desktop and laptop computers. Based on your needs and finances, prepare a report to explain which computer you would buy and give reasons that support your decision.

4. Mac or PC?
Divide your team into two groups: Mac and PC. Each group should research its assigned system and provide a report that summarizes what they've learned. Be sure to cover all of the components of the basic computer system (input devices, processors, output devices, and the type and amount of storage).

5. Exploring the Information-Processing Cycle
As a team, examine advertisements of computers and peripherals from local or regional newspapers. Compare a desktop computer with a laptop or PDA. Which input, processing, output, and storage devices look the same? Which are different? Prepare a group presentation that describes the products in the ads, identifying them as input, processing, output, or storage devices.

Go to www.prenhall.com/cayf2006 to review this chapter, answer the questions, and complete the exercises.

Table of Contents

At a Glance

INTRODUCTORY EDITION

COMPLETE EDITION

(handwritten margin notes:) 44 32 pgs · 50 pp. · 34 pp. · 44 · 52 · 46 · 44 · 44

Table of Contents

Computers Are
Your Future

2006

What You'll Learn . . .

- Define the word computer and name the four basic operations that a computer performs.

- Describe the two main components of a computer system: hardware and software.

- Provide examples of hardware devices that handle input, processing, output, and storage tasks.

- Give an example of the information-processing cycle in action.

- Discuss the two major categories and the various types of computers.

- Explain the advantages and disadvantages of computer usage.

- Understand the risks involved in using hardware and software.

- Recognize the ethical and societal impacts of computer usage.

- Discuss how computers affect employment.

- List ways to be a responsible computer user.

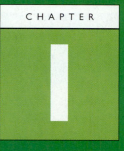
Computers & You

You're here. Your computer's here. Out there's the Web. What do you need to know to get from here to there? You may be thinking "not much" or "quite a bit." You may never have actually used a computer, but you've probably seen ads for computers on television or you may know people who regularly use them. Or, you might have used a computer for ages. You've explored the Web and are at least familiar with the Internet. You "instant message" friends and family, download music files, and burn CDs every day. You've been there and done that. What more could you possibly need to know? What more is there to know? You might be able to perform all of these tasks. But your future isn't just about performing tasks. That's part of it, but hardly all of it. Your future is about having choices and making decisions.

The reason to learn more about any subject is to equip yourself with the knowledge and skills you will need to make informed decisions. Some decisions you

FIGURE 1.1 Computers were once considered to be tools for an information age. Today, they are simply a part of our everyday environment.

FIGURE 1.2
Workers with computer and Internet skills tend to make more money and have more satisfying careers than workers without such skills.

make will be major life decisions; others will have minor consequences. But there will always be facts to gather, opinions to hear, and choices to weigh.

Learning about and understanding computers and technology will help you make informed choices. How can you judge the direction and speed at which technology is moving? What knowledge do you need to capitalize on technological advancements? What current knowledge about your life can you use for perspective?

Think about the changes that have occurred as a result of technological innovation during the most recent 40 years. When your parents were born, there were no telephone answering machines, no cell phones, no handheld calculators, and no personal computers. People wrote letters by hand or with a typewriter, kept track of numbers and data in ledgers, and communicated in person or through the use of the telephone. In fact, telephones were physically connected—there were no wireless phones until the 1970s or cell phones until the 1980s.

In the 1980s, only the U.S. government and colleges and universities were able to access the Internet (including e-mail); cell phones were just coming into use; and fax machines were the fastest way for most people to share documents across

great distances. The World Wide Web would not come into existence until 1993. Today, millions of people use the Internet every day, not only in their professional lives, but also in their personal lives. Cell phones are a seemingly necessary part of everyday life; fax machines are becoming obsolete; and e-commerce—which didn't begin until 1995—generated more than $4 billion in transactions last year.

Today, it's becoming harder and harder to find an activity that doesn't involve computers and technology (Figure 1.1). Clearly, you'd be wise to learn all you can about computers, the Internet, and the World Wide Web. You should know how to use a computer, the Internet, and popular software such as word-processing and spreadsheet programs. Computer and Internet skills are needed to succeed in almost every occupational area. Studies consistently show that workers with computer and Internet skills tend to make more money and have more satisfying careers than workers without such skills (Figure 1.2).

But skills alone aren't enough. To be a fully functioning member of today's computerized world, you need to know the concepts that underlie computer and Internet technologies, such as the distinction between hardware and software

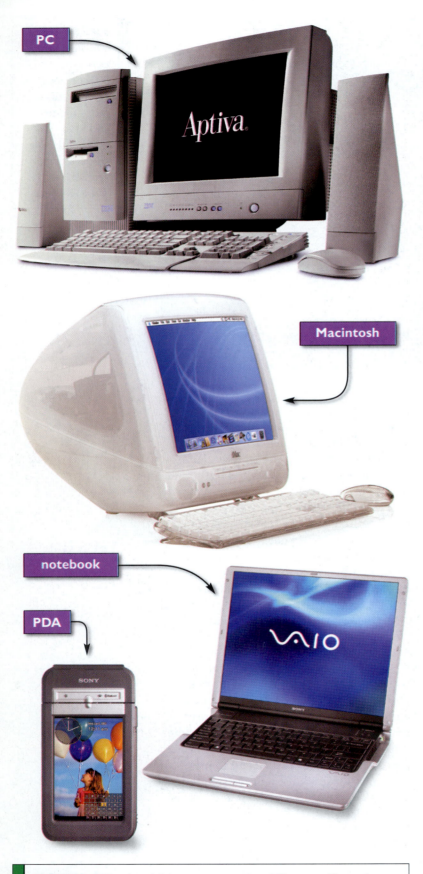

FIGURE 1.3 In addition to possessing skills, you will need to make decisions about technology.

and how to manage the plethora of files that are created each day. As computers and the Internet play an increasingly direct and noticeable role in our personal lives, balancing their proper and improper use also becomes increasingly difficult. Should you shop on the Internet on company or school time? Is your credit card information, Social Security number, or personal communication safe from intrusion or misuse? In the past, the only way to shop during work or school was to leave the premises, and the only time you needed to worry about your personal information was if your wallet or mail were stolen!

You also will need to know enough to make decisions about what types of technology to use, whether in your personal or your professional life (Figure 1.3). How much power and speed do you need to perform everyday tasks? How soon do you need it? What will a more powerful and faster computer enable you to do better? What types of technology tools do you need? Do you need advanced training or just enough for a beginner? This text provides answers to these questions as well as the knowledge and skills required to make informed decisions about technology in all areas of your life. Once you understand these concepts, you'll be able to:

- Decide whether to purchase new equipment or upgrade specific components

- Judge the likely impact of computer innovations on your personal and business life

- Sort through the difficult ethical, moral, and societal challenges that computer use brings

The more you work with computers, the deeper and richer your understanding of computers and technology will become. Instead of being intimidated by new technologies, you will become quietly confident in your abilities. As your confidence and knowledge grow, you will become more and more adept in your use of computers. Let's first start out by describing the machine that's at the center of what you need to know.

Computer Fundamentals

Learning computer and Internet concepts is partly about learning new terms. So let's start with the most basic term of all—*computer*.

UNDERSTANDING THE COMPUTER: BASIC DEFINITIONS

A **computer** is a machine that performs four basic operations: input, processing, output, and storage (Figure 1.4). Together, these four operations are called the **information-processing cycle**. Input, processing, output, storage—that's what computers do. The processing function relies on input; output depends on the results of processing; and storage is where output may be kept for later use. Because these operations depend on one another, the information-processing cycle is always performed in order.

You'll often hear the term *computer system*, which is normally shortened to *system*. This term is more inclusive than *computer*. A **computer system** is a collection of related components that have been designed to work together. These components can be broken down into two major categories: hardware and software. A computer system's **hardware** includes the physical components of the computer, including the system unit itself, as well as

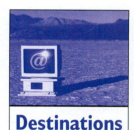

Destinations

To learn about the development of computers over time, see the "Timeline of Computer History" at **www.computer.org/computer/timeline/**

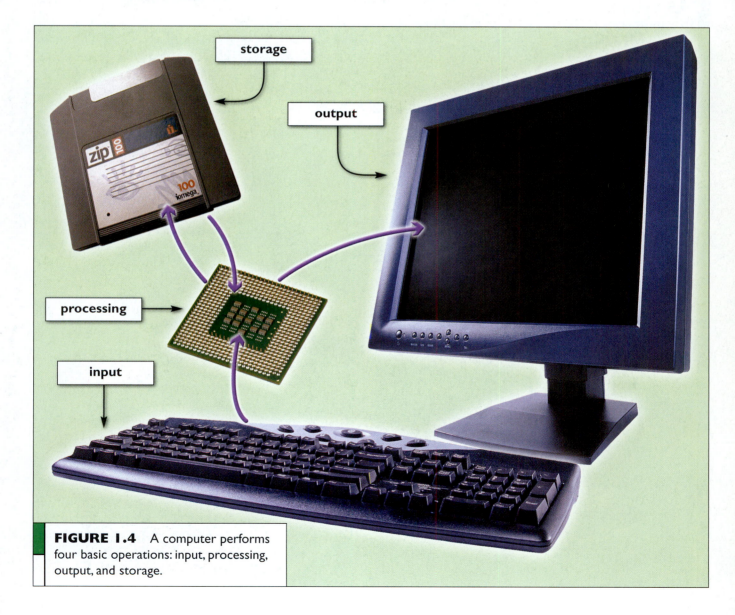

storage

output

processing

input

FIGURE 1.4 A computer performs four basic operations: input, processing, output, and storage.

FIGURE 1.5
The Hardware Components of a Typical Computer System

- **a** Keyboard
- **b** Monitor
- **c** Mouse
- **d** System unit
- **e** CD-ROM and/or DVD-ROM drives
- **f** Floppy disk drive
- **g** Microphone
- **h** Speakers
- **i** Printer
- **j** External modem
- **k** Network interface card

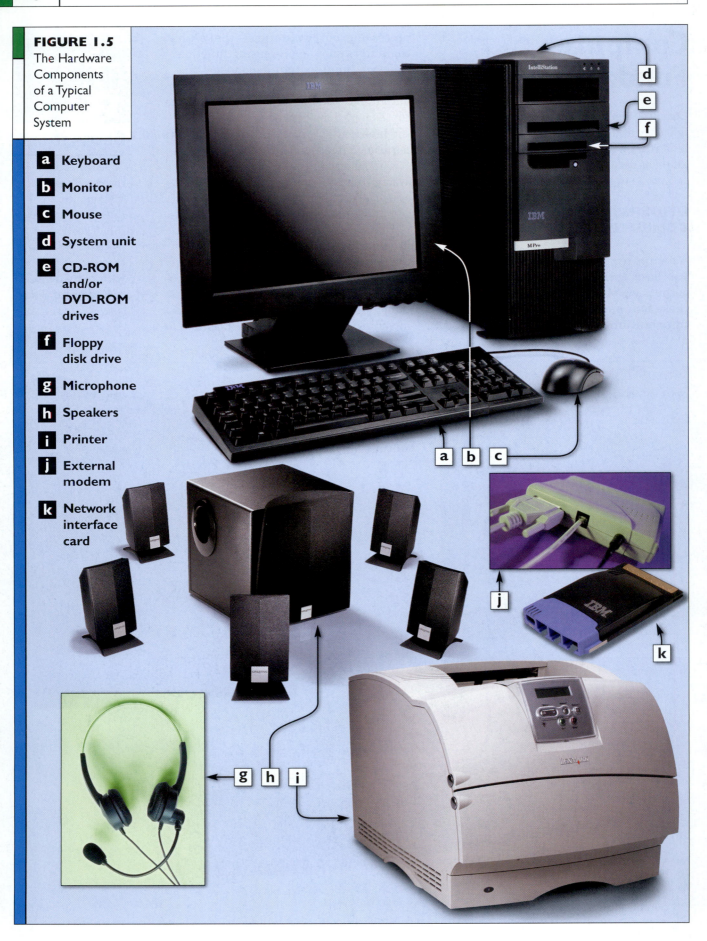

keyboards, monitors, speakers, and so on (Figure 1.5).

In order for a computer system's hardware to function, a computer needs a program. A **program** is a list of instructions that tells the computer how to perform the four operations in the information-processing cycle to accomplish a task. **Software** includes all of the programs that give the computer its instructions. You can divide software into two categories: system software and application software. **System software** includes all of the programs that help the computer function properly. The most important type of system software is the computer's operating system (OS), such as Microsoft Windows. Other parts of the system software include system utilities such as Help and antivirus programs. **Application software** consists of all of the programs you can use to perform a task, including word-processing, spreadsheet, database, presentation, e-mail, and Web browser software.

To better understand how computer system components are interrelated, you might compare a computer system with an aquarium. The computer hardware is like the fish tank, the operating system is like the water, and the software applications are like the fish (Figure 1.6). You wouldn't put fish in an empty aquarium. Fish can't survive without water, just as software applications can't function without an operating system. And without the water and fish, an aquarium is an empty box, just like computer hardware isn't much use without an operating system and applications.

Hardware = fish tank

Operating system = water

Software applications = fish

FIGURE 1.6
A computer system is like an aquarium.

Now that we have the basic terms under our belt, let's take a closer look at the operations in the information-processing cycle (input, processing, output, and storage) and at the hardware devices involved in each step.

INPUT: GETTING DATA INTO THE COMPUTER

In the first operation, called **input**, the computer accepts data. The term **data** refers to unorganized raw facts, which can be made up of words, numbers, images, sounds, or a combination of these.

Input devices enable you to enter data into the computer for processing. The most common input devices are the keyboard and mouse (Figure 1.7). Microphones, disk drives, and devices such as scanners and digital cameras offer other ways of getting data into the computer.

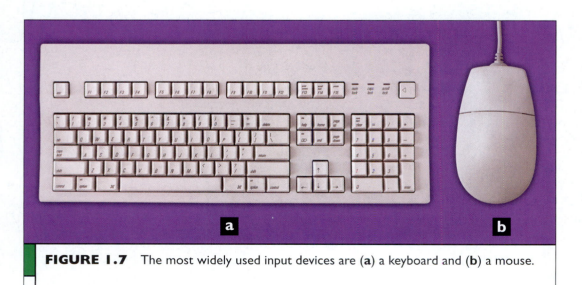

FIGURE 1.7 The most widely used input devices are (**a**) a keyboard and (**b**) a mouse.

PROCESSING: TRANSFORMING DATA INTO INFORMATION

In the second operation, called **processing**, computers transform data into information. **Information** is data that have been simplified and organized in a way that people can use. During processing, the computer's processing circuitry, called the **central processing unit** (**CPU**) or **microprocessor** (or just **processor** for short), performs operations on the input data (Figure 1.8). The processor is located within the computer system's case, also called the **system unit**.

Even though the CPU is often referred to as the "brain" of the computer, computers don't really "think" at all. They are only capable of simple, repetitive processing actions organized into an algorithm—a series of steps that result in the solution to a problem.

Because the CPU needs to juggle multiple input/output requests at the same time, it uses memory chips to store program instructions and data. Memory is essential to the smooth operation of the CPU. A typical computer includes several different types of memory, but the most important of these is **random access memory** (**RAM**), which temporarily stores the programs and data with which the CPU interacts.

FIGURE 1.8
The CPU (microprocessor or processor) performs operations on input data.

OUTPUT: DISPLAYING INFORMATION

In the third operation, called **output**, the computer provides the results of the processing operation in a way that people can understand. **Output devices** show the results of processing operations. The most common output devices are monitors and printers, or, if the computer is processing sounds, you may hear the results on the computer's speakers (Figure 1.9).

STORAGE: HOLDING PROGRAMS AND DATA FOR FUTURE USE

In the fourth operation, called **storage**, the computer saves the results of processing to be used again later. **Storage devices** hold all of the programs and data that the computer system uses. Most computers are equipped with the following storage devices: a hard disk drive, a floppy disk drive, and a CD-ROM drive and/or DVD-ROM drive (Figure 1.10). These devices are commonly not removable and are mounted inside the system unit.

Although communications hasn't traditionally been a part of the information-processing cycle, it can be considered an additional step in the process.

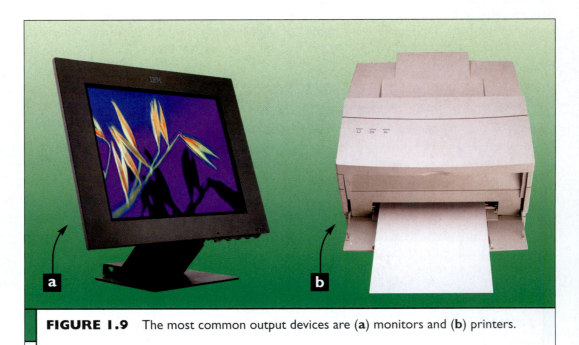

a   **b**

FIGURE 1.9   The most common output devices are (**a**) monitors and (**b**) printers.

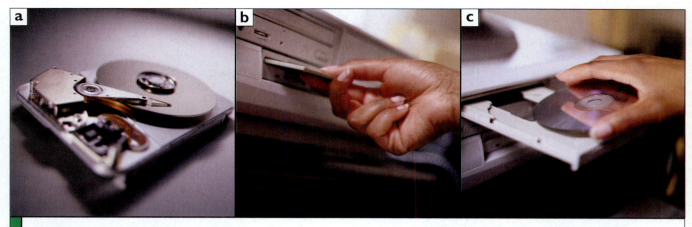

FIGURE 1.10   The most common storage devices are (**a**) hard disk drives, (**b**) floppy disk drives, and (**c**) CD-ROM or DVD-ROM drives.

COMMUNICATIONS: MOVING DATA BETWEEN COMPUTERS

Communications, which is often the fifth operation in the information-processing cycle, involves moving data within the computer or between computers. To move data between computers, communications devices are necessary. **Communications devices** enable computers to connect to a computer network. A **network** is a group of two or more computer systems connected together, usually for the purpose of sharing input/output devices and other resources.

Most computers are equipped with a **modem**, a communications device that enables the computer to access other computers and the Internet via telephone lines, cable, and even wireless connections (Figure 1.11). Most modems are housed inside the system unit.

Now that you understand how hardware and software work in the information-processing cycle and where they are located in a typical computer system, let's look at an example of how the computer uses the basic functions of input, processing, output, and storage.

THE INFORMATION-PROCESSING CYCLE IN ACTION

Even if you haven't wondered what goes on "behind the scenes" when using a computer, the following example illustrates your role and the computer's role in each step of the information-processing cycle (Figure 1.12).

- **Input**. You've just finished writing a research paper for one of your classes. You think it's probably riddled with misspellings and grammatical errors, so you run your word-processing program's spell checker on it. In this example, your entire word-processed document is the input.

- **Processing**. A spell checker makes use of the computer's ability to perform very simple processing operations at very high speeds. To check your document's spelling, the program begins by constructing a list of all of the words in your document. Then it compares these words, one by one, with a huge list of correctly spelled words. If you've used a word that isn't in the dictionary, the program puts the word into a list of apparent misspellings.

Techtalk

peripheral
A computer device that is not an essential part of the computer; that is, any device that is not the memory or microprocessor. Peripheral devices can be external, such as a mouse, a keyboard, a printer, a monitor, an external Zip drive, or a scanner, or internal, such as a CD-ROM or CD-RW drive or a modem.

FIGURE 1.11   A modem is a communications device.

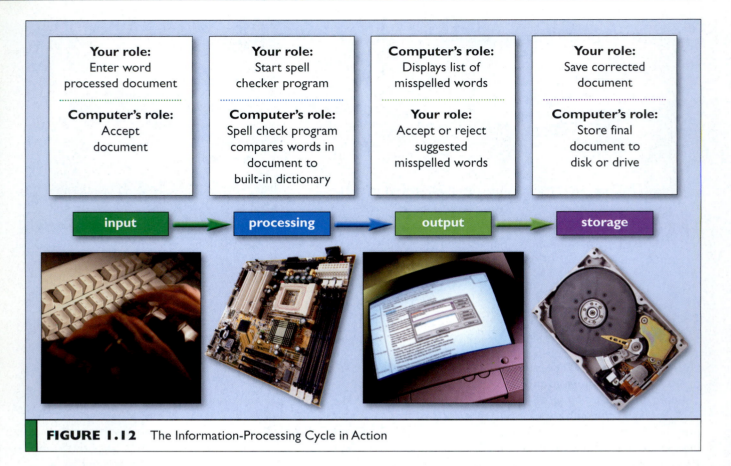

Your role: Enter word processed document	Your role: Start spell checker program	Computer's role: Displays list of misspelled words	Your role: Save corrected document
Computer's role: Accept document	Computer's role: Spell check program compares words in document to built-in dictionary	Your role: Accept or reject suggested misspelled words	Computer's role: Store final document to disk or drive

input → processing → output → storage

FIGURE 1.12   The Information-Processing Cycle in Action

Destinations

To learn more about the information-processing cycle, go to **www.pcguide.com/ intro/works/ example.htm**

Note that the computer isn't really "checking spelling" when it performs this operation. The computer can't check your spelling because it doesn't possess the intelligence to do so. All it can do is tell you which of the words you've used aren't in the dictionary. Ultimately, only you can decide whether a given word is misspelled.

- **Output**. The result of the processing operation is a list of apparent misspellings. The word *apparent* is important here because the program doesn't actually know whether the word is misspelled. It is able to tell only that these words aren't in its massive, built-in dictionary. But many correctly spelled words, such as proper nouns (the names of people and places), aren't likely to be found in the computer's dictionary. For this reason, the program won't make any changes without asking you to confirm them.

- **Storage**. Once you've corrected the spelling in your document, you save or store the revised document to disk.

In sum, computers transform data (here, a document full of misspellings) into information (a document that is free of misspellings).

Up to this point, we've been talking about computers in general. We now need to examine the specific types of computers used in a wide variety of tasks and job situations.

Types of Computers

Computers come in all sizes, from large to small. It's convenient to divide them into two categories: computers for individuals and computers for organizations. Computers for individuals are mainly designed for one user at a time. They process and store smaller amounts of data and programs, such as a research paper or a personal

IMPACTS

Ethical Debates

Digital Piracy: What's the Big Deal?

Most of us wouldn't consider walking into a store and stealing a laptop computer. But when it comes to software (or music or videos) for that laptop, well that's a different story. How many people do you know who have "borrowed" (that means stolen!) software, downloaded movies from the Web, shared music files with friends, or illegally burned copies of music CDs? If you ask around, you'll find that you're surrounded by people who don't think it's a big deal to steal digital data, even though U.S. companies lose an estimated $23 billion through digital piracy every year.

What's the big deal? It may be that when you buy a computer or a CD, you buy a physical, tangible item that you then own. But when you buy software, you're only purchasing the right (or a license) to use the software, not the copyright. So, if you install software on your computer and then install it onto a friend's computer, you're stealing. And if you download music or videos off the Web without paying, you're stealing just as if you grabbed a DVD off the shelf in a store without paying. You may not see it that way, but the companies creating and distributing the software and other digital data do, as does the law (Figure 1.13).

It's tempting to steal software or music. Consider a school system with 1,000 computers, all of which need to have Microsoft Word. Legitimate licensing could amount to quite a hefty bill. Do you think it's okay for a school system to have unlicensed software on its computers? After all, the software is benefiting students. If you think the law bends for schools—and many school administrators do—think again. These same administrators may one day be holding letters from software companies requesting an inspection to determine whether pirated software is running on the school's machines. If piracy is discovered, a school can face steep fines.

What if the school system buys just 500 copies of the software instead of the full 1,000? They're still paying for a lot of software, why should they pay for it all? Do a quick calculation and you'll find that this kind of rationalization is expensive. If the value of each copy is $50, the school is actually stealing $25,000 worth of software. Multiply that to include other schools in the district, state, country, and world, and suddenly billions of dollars of programs are being stolen.

You may think it's no big deal to download a new song off the Web or to burn a copy of your friend's CD or DVD. Who isn't tempted by an apparent freebie (especially college students trying to pinch a penny)? But what about the artists who wrote or performed the song, the record company that produced the song, the programmers who worked on the software, and all the other people down the line who rely on honest consumers to purchase their products? They lose money every time somebody illegally copies their software, music, or movies—and that translates into higher prices for everyone who buys these items legitimately.

Will you get caught if you make illegal copies? Maybe not. But technology offers us many ethical choices, and in the long run, digital piracy hurts us all.

The unauthorized reproduction or distribution of this copyrighted work is illegal. Criminal copyright infringement, including infringement without monetary gain, is investigated by the FBI and is punishable by up to 5 years in federal prison and a fine of $250,000.

FIGURE 1.13 Music and movie companies are using an FBI warning logo to warn users against illegally copying digital data. Offenders can face $250,000 in fines and up to 5 years in prison if caught and convicted.

techtv

To learn more about digital piracy, see the video clip at **www.prenhall.com/cayf2006**

PC or microcomputer

handheld computer

laptop

workstation

FIGURE 1.14 Computers for Individuals

Web page (Figure 1.14). In contrast, computers for organizations are designed to meet the needs of many people concurrently. They process and store large amounts of data and more complex programs, such as all the research papers for every class on campus or the school's entire Web site (Figure 1.15). Computers are also categorized by power (their processing speed) and purpose (the tasks they perform).

COMPUTERS FOR INDIVIDUALS

A **personal computer** (**PC**), also called a microcomputer, is designed to meet the computing needs of an individual. The two most commonly used types of personal computers are Apple's Macintosh systems and the more numerous IBM-compatible personal computers, which are made by manufacturers such as Dell, Gateway, Sony, HP, and many others. These PCs are called "IBM-compatible" because the first such computer was made by IBM. The price range of personal computers has steadily dropped to between $300 and $3,000, even as they have become more powerful and useful.

Designed for use at a desk or in an office environment, a **desktop computer** is a personal computer that runs programs to help individuals accomplish their work more productively or to gain access to the Internet. Dell is the leading producer of desktop computers.

A **notebook computer** is small enough to fit into a briefcase and is portable, because many people need a computer to travel with them. Many notebook computers are as powerful as desktop computers and include nearly all of a desktop computer's components, such as speakers, a CD-ROM drive, and a modem. Notebook computers are generally manufactured by the same companies as desktop computers. Some of the most popular notebook computers are Dell's Inspiron series, Toshiba's Satellite and Tecra series, IBM's Thinkpad, HP's Pavillion, and, for Mac lovers, the Apple iBook. They range in price from $900 to over $3,000.

Laptop computers are like notebook computers except that they are a bit too large to fit into a briefcase. The most popular maker of laptop computers is IBM with models that range in price from $700 to as much as $3,000. Fewer laptops are being sold now that the smaller notebooks have become so powerful.

Subnotebooks are notebook computers that omit some components (such as a CD-ROM drive) so as to cut down on weight and size. A significant advantage of subnotebooks is that some of them weigh less than three pounds. For example, the newest Sony Vaio subnotebook weighs only 1.7 pounds and is less than 1 inch thick. One disadvantage of subnotebooks is that users must often carry along external disk drives and their attendant wiring. A subnotebook might be used by a UPS driver or by salespeople whose specific computing needs do not require all of the peripherals and accessories that are available with desktops, notebooks, and laptops. The top manufacturers of subnotebooks are Sony and Panasonic. Subnotebooks range in price from $1,300 to $2,500.

A **tablet PC** is a type of notebook computer that has an LCD screen that the user can write on using a special-purpose pen or stylus. The user's handwriting is converted to standard text through handwriting-recognition software or it can remain as handwritten text. Tablet PCs also typically have a keyboard and/or a mouse for input. HP's Compaq brand is the most popular, with prices ranging from $1,000 to over $3,900. Toshiba and Acer are two other brands in the top 10 manufacturers. Tablet PC prices will come down as they become more accepted in the marketplace and their production numbers increase.

Personal digital assistants (**PDAs**), sometimes called **handheld computers**, pack much of a notebook's power into a much lighter package and lower price (between $350 and $700). Most PDAs include built-in software for scheduling appointments and sending and receiving e-mail. **Pen computers** accept handwritten input. The Palm series, Sony's CLIE series, HP's iPAQ series, and BlackBerry are the most popular PDAs.

All-in-one computers, such as the Apple iMac, are essentially a monitor with everything else built in. The only external devices are a keyboard and a mouse. The microprocessor, memory, storage, and speakers are all contained within the monitor case. This design may be the wave of the future. The Gateway Profile, the Sony Vaio W, and a relatively new player—the Pelham Sloane PS1500—are all major players in the all-in-one market. All-in-one computers cost about the same as other desktop PCs, ranging from $1,400 to $2,300.

Network computers (**NCs**) and **Internet appliances** provide much of a personal computer's functionality but at a lower price. These computers are designed to connect to a network, such as the Internet. In the consumer market, NCs such as MSN TV enable consumers to use their televisions to connect to the Internet. Because they have limited memory, disk storage, and processing power, NCs rely on computer networks for their power and software. Popular in the mid to late 1990s, they haven't been able to achieve much of a hold in the marketplace.

Professional workstations are powerful tools for engineers, architects, circuit designers, financial analysts, and other professionals who need exceptionally powerful processing and output capabilities. HP dominates the workstation market. It produces workstations that range in price from $1,000 to over $7,000, making workstations the most expensive type of computer made for individuals.

COMPUTERS FOR ORGANIZATIONS

Servers are computers that make programs and data available to people who are connected to a computer network. They are not designed for individual use and are typically centralized or operated from one location. Users connect to the network on **clients**, which can be desktops, laptops, workstations, or any other computer for individuals, to contact the server and obtain the needed information. This use of remote or off-site clients and centralized servers is called **client/server computing**. It plays an important role in today's businesses. Servers can be as small as a microcomputer or as large as a mainframe. The top three server manufacturers are IBM, Sun Microsystems, and Dell. Servers typically cost between

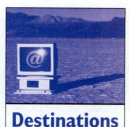

Destinations

To learn more about the different types of computers, go to **computer.how stuffworks.com/ question543.htm**

server

minicomputer (midrange server)

mainframe

supercomputer

FIGURE 1.15   Computers for Organizations

$1,000 and upwards of $30,000, but HP UNIX servers run from $100,000 to over $1 million!

Minicomputers, also referred to as **midrange servers**, are midsize computers that handle the computing needs of a smaller corporation or organization. They enable dozens, hundreds, or even thousands of users to connect to them simultaneously through PCs or terminals. **Terminals** are basically computers that lack processing capabilities. They simply receive input via a remote keyboard and display output on a monitor. Minicomputers can be slightly larger than microcomputers or as big as a washing machine. In recent years, the minicomputer market has waned.

Mainframes are designed to handle huge processing jobs in large corporations or government agencies. For example, an airline may use a mainframe to handle airline reservations. Some mainframes are designed to be used by hundreds of thousands of people at the same time. People connect to mainframes using terminals or PCs. Mainframes are usually stored in special, secure rooms that have a controlled climate. They are manufactured by firms such as IBM, Honeywell, and HP/Agilent, cost hundreds of thousands to millions of dollars, and are very powerful.

Supercomputers are ultrafast computers that process large amounts of scientific data and then display the underlying patterns that have been discovered in the data. In 2000, IBM announced that it had built a supercomputer capable of executing 12 trillion calculations per second. Known as the ASCI White, the supercomputer covers an area the size of two basketball courts and is used by the Department of Energy. In March of 2002, Japan's NEC Corporation announced it had created an even faster supercomputer. The system, known as "the Earth Simulator," takes up the space of four tennis courts and is said to be five times faster than the ASCI White. A supercomputer's price tag is also large—from $1 million to $20 million.

Now that you know the variety of computers available, let's look at how their use has an impact on you as an individual and on society in general.

Computers, Society, & You

A computer can work with all types of data. That is the first major reason for its remarkable penetration into almost every occupational area and nearly two-thirds of U.S. households. While it is true that computers are becoming commonplace, computers and the Internet aren't readily accessible in some segments of society. Computer and Internet use cuts across all educational, racial, and economic boundaries, but there are still inequities.

The higher your education level, the more likely you are to own a computer and have Internet access. Although less than 25 percent of people in the United States have college degrees, these folks account for more than one-half of those with computers and Internet access. Those with only a high school diploma or less comprise only 19 percent of computer owners with Internet access.

Do race and income make a difference with regards to computer ownership and Internet use? African-American households are much less likely to have computers and Internet access than white households in the same income bracket. In households with incomes over $100,000, 80 percent own a computer, whereas in households with incomes under $30,000 only 25 percent own a computer. This disparity in computer ownership and Internet access is known as the **digital divide**. Studies have shown that the digital divide is shrinking due to government programs to bring computing access to all citizens.

Computers enable us to collect, organize, evaluate, and communicate information. Although computers are merely a tool, we can use them for a variety of common activities to make our daily lives easier (Figure 1.16). Instead of going to a record store at the mall to buy CDs for your music collection, you can now use your computer to buy them from an online store. To organize your music collection before computers, you would have to physically sort through and arrange the CDs on your shelf. With a computer, you can organize your CDs, individual songs, or whole categories of music however you wish and reorganize them periodically with much less time and little effort. You can use your computer to find free reviews of new CDs; before you would have to buy a magazine or newspaper to find those reviews. And instead of calling your

FIGURE 1.16 Computers enable us to collect, organize, evaluate, and communicate information.

friends or family to share this information (or writing and mailing a letter!), you can use e-mail to send the reviews directly to their computers within the hour.

Computers also help us to be more productive and creative, reducing the amount of time spent on tedious tasks. A good example of this is using a word-processing program to create a term paper. The computer provides the student with spelling and grammar help and formatting suggestions and also makes it easy to include graphics. Without a computer, the student would need volumes of dictionaries and encyclopedias, not to mention style guides and other special resources, along with extra time to gather and go through all of these sources.

Computers not only help us perform individual activities more efficiently and effectively, they also help us work, teach, and learn better together. Computers facilitate collaboration with others to solve problems. For instance, computers are increasingly part of law enforcement activities. Police use computers to collaborate with one another to be better informed about criminals and crime scenes. When a police officer stops a car, the officer types the car's license plate number into the computer in the patrol car. The license plate number calls up the registered owner's name, both of which can then be checked against the National Crime Information Center database for wants and warrants. All of this can be accomplished before the officer ever gets out of the patrol car. In another instance, GM engineers work collaboratively with fellow engineers overseas to design the next year's line of cars. They send electronic documents to each other, or use the Internet to hold online design meetings.

Computers also facilitate learning and bolster critical thinking through the use of computer-based study guides, problem sets, and educational games. For instance, a CD-ROM that offers tutorial training might have been provided with one or more of your textbooks. Or, you might visit this book's Web site, **www.prenhall.com/cayf2006**, to browse the learning aids provided.

A student group uses computers to do research on the Internet and then collaborates by sharing data with each other. Group members work together to develop a presentation and then use e-mail to share their ideas about how the presentation should look. They then use the computer to produce their paper and presentation as well as charts and exhibits.

Even though computers offer us many advantages in today's hectic world, the responsible computer user should also be aware of both the advantages *and* the disadvantages of computer use.

ADVANTAGES AND DISADVANTAGES OF USING COMPUTERS

A computer system conveys certain advantages, such as speed, memory, storage, hardware reliability, and accuracy, to its users. However, with these advantages come some disadvantages (Figure 1.17) of computer use, including information overload, the expense of computer equipment, data inaccuracy, and an increasing dependence on unreliable software. Computer technology is growing at such an incredible rate that we are spending more and more time just trying to keep up.

A computer processes data at very high speeds. The most brilliant human mathematicians can perform only a few operations per second, whereas an inexpensive computer performs hundreds of millions—even billions—of them in a second.

According to one recent estimate, humans will create more information in the next 3 years than they have in all the previous centuries of our existence on this planet. In fact, people are generating so much information today that they often succumb to *information overload,* feelings of anxiety and incapacity experienced when people are presented

FIGURE 1.17 Advantages and Disadvantages of Computer Use

Advantages	Disadvantages
Speed	Information overload
Memory	Expensive
Storage	Data inaccuracy
Hardware reliability	Software unreliability

with more information than they can reasonably handle.

Computers store and recall enormous amounts of data in a variety of formats, including words, graphic images, and video clips. Even an inexpensive desktop computer can store and provide quick access to a 32-volume encyclopedia, the entire collected works of Shakespeare, a world atlas, an unabridged dictionary, and much more. This computing power enables users to increase productivity, to gain ideas and insight through collaboration with others, and solve real-world problems.

How do computers help us perform these tasks so quickly? The answer is RAM. Although RAM can provide very fast access to resources, it's also expensive. As a result, most computers are equipped with just enough RAM to hold programs and data while the computer works with them, but no more. In addition, programs and data in RAM can be lost if the power is switched off. The alternative is storage devices, which are typically much slower than RAM, but offer increased storage capacity at a more affordable price.

Not only do they hold and generate huge amounts of information, computers are exceptionally reliable and accurate, too. Even the least expensive PCs perform several million operations per second, and can do so for years without making an error caused by the computer's physical components. For example, you can equip a computer to transcribe your speech with an accuracy of 95 percent or more—which is better than most people's typing accuracy. In fact, almost all "computer errors" are actually caused by flaws in software or mistakes in the data people supply to computers. Computers store these mistakes for long periods of time and then replicate the errors with amazing speed.

Even though computers have strengths and weaknesses, there are additional points to consider in your quest to become a responsible user.

DON'T BE INTIMIDATED BY HARDWARE

Many people feel threatened by computers because they fear that computers are too complicated. But without humans, computers have no intelligence at all. The processing operations they perform are almost ridiculously simple. The average insect is a genius compared with a computer.

There is nothing scary about computer hardware. Without a person and a program to tell it what to do, the computer is no more frightening—or useful—than an empty fish tank.

Computer hardware components should be treated with the same care as any other electronic device. Be mindful that electronic devices are sensitive to dust, moisture, static electricity, and magnetic interference. To maintain a safe working environment for you and your hardware, you should heed the following advice (Figure 1.18):

- Do not overload electrical outlets by plugging too many devices into the same outlet.

- Do not position hardware equipment so it can fall or cause accidents.

- Leave plenty of space around hardware for proper air circulation to prevent overheating.

- Make sure computer cables, cords, and wires are fastened securely and not strung haphazardly or left lying where you could trip over them or where they could cause a fire.

FIGURE 1.18
A messy computer environment is an unsafe one.

Destinations

Ergonomics is an important issue for many computer users. To learn more about ergonomics, go to **computer.how stuffworks.com/ search.php?terms =ergonomics**

Although you shouldn't be intimidated by hardware, you should be aware that using it for long periods can result in injuries or health conditions such as eye, back, and wrist strain.

To prevent injuries from happening, you should be aware of the available ergonomic computer products as well as healthy computing practices. If something is **ergonomic**, it means that the product matches the best posture and functionality of the human body (Figure 1.19). For example, prolonged keyboard use can cause **carpal tunnel syndrome** (also known as cumulative trauma disorder or repetitive strain injury). This type of injury is caused by repeated motions that damage sensitive nerve tissue in the hands, wrists, and arms. Sometimes these injuries are so serious that they require surgery. To help prevent these problems,

ergonomic keyboards, such as the Microsoft Natural Keyboard, keep your wrists straight, reducing (but not eliminating) your chance of an injury. Even hotel chains such as Marriott advertise to business travelers that they provide ergonomic desk chairs along with free high-speed Internet access.

In addition to using ergonomically designed equipment, you can promote a safe and comfortable computer environment by arranging your chair, lighting, and computer equipment properly and using antiglare computer screens. You should also take periodic breaks from working at your computer to rest your eyes and stretch your legs.

Treat the physical components of your computer with respect and you will get the most return for your money and health.

Computer hardware can be amazingly reliable, but software is another matter.

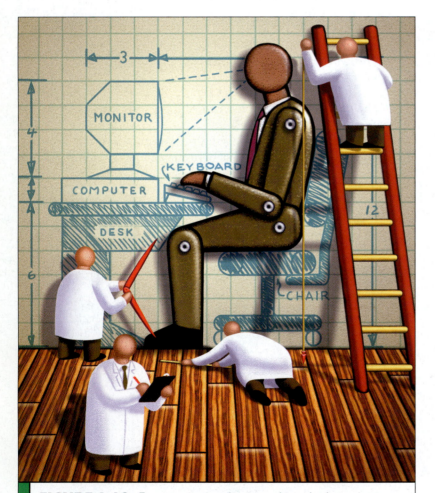

FIGURE 1.19 Ergonomics involves matching the best posture and functionality of the human body to the physical characteristics of various devices.

RECOGNIZE THE RISKS OF USING FLAWED SOFTWARE

All programs contain errors, and this is why: Computers can perform only a limited series of simple actions. Many programs contain millions of lines of programming code (Figure 1.20). In general, each line of program code tells the computer to perform an action, such as adding two numbers or comparing them. Consider this: The program that allows you to withdraw cash from an ATM contains only 90,000 lines of code. But when you file your taxes, the IRS program that gives you your refund contains 1,000 times that— 100 million lines of code!

With so many lines of code, errors inevitably occur—and they are impossible to eradicate completely. On average, commercial programs contain between 14 and 17 errors for every thousand lines of code. This means that an ATM is likely to have 1,350 errors in its code, and the IRS program code might have as many as one and a half million or more errors! Thankfully, most errors simply cause programs to run slowly or to perform unnecessary tasks, but some errors do cause miscalculations or other inconveniences.

Another phenomenon worth mentioning is that the more lines of code you add, the more complex the program becomes—

and the harder it becomes to eradicate the errors. Because every computer program contains errors, all computer use entails a certain level of risk. A bug might occur when you least expect it and cause your computer to freeze up. You may be forced to restart your computer, losing your unsaved work.

The foregoing explains why it's not a good idea to put off writing a paper until the night before your assignment is due. Bugs in a word-processing program aren't usually life threatening, but computers are increasingly being used in mission-critical and safety-critical systems. Mission-critical systems are those essential to an organization's viability, such as a company's computerized cash register system. If the system goes down, the organization can't function—and the result is often a very expensive fiasco. A safety-critical system is one on which human lives depend, such as an air traffic control system or a computerized signaling system used by high-speed commuter trains. When these systems fail, human lives are at stake (Figure 1.21). Safety-critical systems are designed to much higher quality standards and have backup systems that kick in if the main computer goes down.

The disturbing thing about computers isn't the computers themselves but

FIGURE 1.20	Programs often contain millions of lines of code	
Program	**Lines of Programming Code**
Bank ATM	90,000
Air traffic control	900,000
Microsoft Windows 98	18 million
Microsoft Windows 2000	27 million
Microsoft Office XP	35 million (estimated)
Internal Revenue Service (IRS)	100 million (all programs)

what people might do with them—which leads to ethics.

TAKE ETHICS SERIOUSLY

Ethics is the behavior associated with your moral beliefs. You have learned what is right and wrong from your parents, teachers, and spiritual leaders. By this stage of your life you know what is right

Techtalk

bug
An error or defect in software or hardware that causes a program to malfunction. The term is derived from an incident in the very early days of computing when pioneer programmer Grace Hopper witnessed a moth fly into the computer she was manipulating, which caused the program to crash.

FIGURE 1.21 Even with its flaws, the air traffic control system has a remarkable safety record.

and wrong. It is important for you to recognize that the power of computers and the Internet is a relatively new ethical realm. In fact, a new branch of philosophy called **computer ethics** deals with computer-related moral dilemmas and defines ethical principles for computer professionals.

Responsible computing requires that you understand the advantages and disadvantages of using a computer as well as the potential harm of computer misuse. Every day there are stories in the news of people misusing computerized data. Names and e-mail addresses are distributed freely without permission or regard for privacy. Viruses are launched against unsuspecting victims. Credit card information is stolen and fraudulently used. Computerized dialing machines call thousands of households an hour offering unwanted solicitations. Children and women are stalked. Pornography abounds. Illegitimate copies of software are installed every day. Professional musicians lose tens and hundreds of thousands of dollars a year in unpaid royalties due to sharing programs and digital copying. Homework assignments are copied and then modified to appear as though they are original work. The Internet is a hotbed of illicit and sometimes illegal content. The list of ethical considerations goes on and on.

Computers are very powerful tools. They can be used to magnify many aspects of our lives, including unethical behavior. The Spotlight following this chapter provides an in-depth discussion of computer ethics. But computers and the Internet can also be used to improve our lives, resulting in positive impacts on society.

SOCIETAL IMPACTS OF COMPUTER USE

Almost everyone has been affected by computers and the Internet. Although most people are able bodied, consider the effect of technologies that support or provide opportunities to the disabled and disadvantaged (Figure 1.22). As a part of the Americans with Disabilities Act of 1990, your school must provide computer access to people with disabilities. A college's computing services department must provide special software, such as speech-recognition software, to help people with vision impairments use computers. Input and output devices specifically designed for the physically disabled can be installed or existing devices can be modified to accommodate users with hearing or motor impairments. Home and school computers equipped with speech-recognition software can help children and those with learning disabilities learn to read.

Computers are also helping stroke victims to lead more independent lives. From robotic treadmills to muscle stimulators to therapy that involves playing video games, computers are giving many patients hope of almost full recovery of their former abilities.

In schools, students can use computers to take advantage of inexpensive training and learning opportunities. **E-learning** is the use of computers and computer programs to replace teachers and the time–place specificity of learning. People also can access computers and the Internet from libraries, Web cafes, and public Internet centers to look for work or access online training and résumé-creation tools.

FIGURE 1.22 Major advances have been made in speech-recognition software and other technologies, enabling people with hearing or speech impairments to communicate with others using their computers. In this example, renowned physicist Stephen Hawking, who suffers from Lou Gehrig's Disease, uses a computer to help him speak.

THE EFFECT OF COMPUTERS ON EMPLOYMENT

Although computers are creating new job opportunities, they're also shifting labor

Hello, ASIMO: Meet a Computer-Powered Robot

CURRENTS

Computers & Society

From fire fighting to fetching eyeglasses, Honda's ASIMO (Advanced Step in Innovative Mobility) robot could one day take on dangerous tasks as well as everyday functions such as lifting items or opening doors. ASIMO is a 4-foot-tall humanoid robot powered by several computers (carried in a backpack), specialized software, and 26 motors (Figure 1.23).

Sound like science fiction? ASIMO is very real, the result of two decades of research and experimentation by Honda engineers. Unlike the clunky robots of yesterday, this humanlike robot has highly flexible arms, legs, and neck so it can move around much like we do under its own power.

FIGURE 1.23 Honda's ASIMO Robot

And because it's programmed to maintain proper posture and balance as it moves, ASIMO can easily and effortlessly walk up and down stairs, step in any direction, and check around corners.

Think of the possibilities. Computer-powered robots like ASIMO could become helpful assistants to people with physical disabilities—turning lights on and off, finding and moving household objects, opening and closing doors, and taking care of dozens of other daily tasks. Walking independently—with or without packages in hand—they could also guide people through buildings and streets.

Of course, ASIMO is still a work in progress. Behind the scenes, Honda's engineers are continuing to refine the robot's computers, software, and physical structure. As they gain more experience and produce more robots, the price will drop below the $1 million mark (although for $152,000, you can rent one for a year). Meanwhile, ASIMO has demonstrated its capabilities at industry meetings and even served brief stints as an attention-getting greeter for other companies.

Looking ahead, as Honda perfects the technology, such robots may become commonplace as stand-ins for scientists, fire fighters, and police officers facing risky situations. ASIMO robots might shift dangerous chemicals from one storage place to another or climb several flights of stairs to position fire-fighting equipment inside a burning building. Or, they might act as the eyes and ears of emergency personnel, exploring the scene of a natural disaster, gathering data about the extent of the damage, and helping to carry out rescue missions. You may never meet ASIMO, but sometime in the near future, your life might change because of such computer-powered robots.

techtv

To learn more about Honda's ASIMO robot, see the video clip at **www.prenhall.com/ cayf2006**

demand toward skilled workers, particularly those with computer skills. As a result, skilled workers earn more; wages paid to unskilled workers have stagnated over the past 20 years. As a consequence, the gap between the rich and the poor has widened as educated, skilled workers have taken advantage of new technology-based

FIGURE 1.24 Computer-guided robots are taking over many of the manufacturing jobs that people once held.

opportunities. Computer skills have never been more important to a person's future.

Technology is also eliminating some jobs through **automation** (the replacement of human workers by machines). One purpose of advanced technology is to free people from drudgery and make workflow more efficient. However, the result is that fewer workers may be required to perform a task. For instance, computer-guided robots are taking over many manufacturing jobs that people once held (Figure 1.24).

The jobs most likely to be eliminated by computers involve repetitive, semi-skilled tasks. For example, the U.S. Postal Service eliminated nearly 100,000 jobs once held by workers who read and sorted envelopes. Today, automated equipment does most of this work with little, if any, human intervention.

However, computers can also eliminate other types of jobs, even those in the computer and technology industry itself. Many low-skilled and skilled technology jobs, such as technical support personnel and even programmers, are being shipped overseas to countries such as Malaysia, China, and India. According to the U.S. Bureau of Labor Statistics, as of December 2003, almost 200,000 U.S. technology jobs have been

outsourced to foreign countries since 2000. Forrester Research states that by 2015, 3.3 million U.S. technology jobs could be lost to workers overseas.

Structural unemployment results when advancing technology makes an entire job category obsolete. Structural unemployment differs from the normal up-and-down cycles of layoffs and rehires. People who lose jobs because of structural unemployment are not going to get them back. Their only option is to retrain themselves to work in other careers.

Consider this: half of all the jobs that will be available in 10 years don't even exist today. So who will survive—and flourish—in a computer-driven economy? The answer is simple. The survivors will be people who are highly educated, who know that education is a life-long process, and who adapt quickly to change. Being a responsible computer user is just as important.

BEING A RESPONSIBLE COMPUTER USER

How can you become a responsible user of computers and the Internet? Knowing how your computer and Internet usage affects others in your school, family, community, and the environment is a start. Don't hog public computer resources. If you are using a computer and Internet connection at a library or in a wireless hot spot, don't download or upload large files. Be considerate of others who might be sharing the same connection. Responsible users help the environment by recycling paper and printer cartridges (Figure 1.25).

A larger concern is what should be done with hardware that has reached the limits of its usefulness. Should you simply throw old hardware in the garbage? What about the hazardous materials that are contained in the monitor and the system unit? The National Safety Council estimates that there will be 500 million obsolete computers by the year 2007. Because of the phosphor and lead used in monitors, California and Massachusetts now prohibit the dumping of monitors with household waste. They also prohibit the dumping of monitors in landfills or incinerating them. So what's to be done? Responsible users will look for computer and electronics equipment disposal and recycling companies in their areas or check state and federal Web sites, such as the U.S. Environmental Protection Agency Web site, (**www.epa.gov**), for tips on computer disposal. Some schools have computer disposal guidelines for discarding old computers.

Another way to solve the disposal problem and to give back to your community is by donating old computer equipment to local charities that could refurbish it to help new users learn the basics. Who knows, you might even donate a little of your time to help!

Being a responsible user also means being aware of how computers and Internet use can impact your own well-being and personal relationships. Researchers at Carnegie Mellon University were surprised to find that people who spent even a few hours a week on the Internet experienced higher levels of depression and loneliness than those who did not. These people interacted with other Internet users online, but this interaction seems to have been much shallower than the time formerly spent with friends and family. The result? According to these researchers, Internet use leads to unhealthy social isolation and a deadened, mechanized experience that is lacking in human emotion. Interestingly, other studies show just the opposite. These studies demonstrate that there is no difference in socialization between those who use the Internet and those who do not. So, who is right? It will take years of studies to know. But for now, keep in mind that computer and Internet overuse may promote unhealthy behaviors.

Staying Informed About Changing Technology

It is important to stay informed about advances in technology. One benefit of staying informed is getting the latest product upgrades. Upgrading the software on your computer helps you enjoy the most current features the software manufacturer has to offer. Staying informed also helps you thwart the latest computer viruses from invading and harming your computer. Viruses wreak havoc on computers every day. By knowing all you can about the latest viruses and how they're spread, you can prevent your computer from getting infected.

One constant in today's changing technology is the steady advance of computing power. Faster processors and cheaper storage mean that next month's computer will be more powerful than this month's computer. You can take advantage of this fact by upgrading your hardware every 2 to 3 years.

You can stay informed about the latest technology by reading periodicals; reviewing Web sites such as **cnet.com**'s Buzz Report; subscribing to online newsletters, e-mail updates, and publications; and reading technology columns in your local newspaper.

FIGURE 1.25
Recycling paper and using recycled paper helps the environment.

What You've Learned

COMPUTERS & YOU

- A computer is a machine that performs four operations: input, processing, output, and storage. These four operations are called the information-processing cycle.

- A computer system is a collection of related components that have been designed to work together. It includes both the computer's hardware (its physical components such as the computer, keyboard, monitor, speakers, and so on) and software (the programs that run on it).

- In a typical computer system, a keyboard and a mouse provide input capabilities. Processing is done by the microprocessor (CPU) and RAM (random access memory). You see the results (output) on a monitor or printer. A hard disk is typically used for long-term storage.

- Spell checking a word-processed document is a good example of the information-processing cycle. The input consists of the original document, which contains spelling mistakes. When the computer processes the document, it detects and flags possible spelling errors by checking every word in the document against a massive spelling dictionary. Output consists of a list of words that the spell checker is unable to find in its dictionary. User interaction is required to confirm whether the apparent misspelled words need to be corrected. The user saves the corrected document to storage for future use.

- There are two major categories of computers: computers for individuals and computers for organizations. Types of computers for individuals include personal computers (PCs), desktop computers, notebooks, subnotebooks, laptop computers, handheld computers (PDAs, pen computers and tablet PCs), all-in-one computers, network computers (NCs), and Internet appliances. Types of computers for organizations include servers, minicomputers, mainframes, and supercomputers.

- Responsible computing requires that you understand the advantages and disadvantages of using the computer. Advantages include speed, memory, storage, hardware reliability, and accuracy. Disadvantages include information overload, the expense of computer equipment, data inaccuracy, and dependence on unreliable software.

- Using hardware and software involves some risk. It is important to pay attention to the proper care and use of hardware to avoid damage to the equipment and potential computer-related injuries. Recognize that all programs contain errors that typically cause programs to run slowly or other inconveniences.

- Computers can be misused or used to benefit individuals and society. Examples of misuse include distributing personal information without permission, exposure to unwanted solicitations, viruses, and illegitimate copying of software and music. Benefits include using computers to assist those with disabilities or no access.

- Although computers are creating new job opportunities, they're also shifting labor demand toward skilled workers, particularly those with computer skills. As a result, skilled workers earn more, while unskilled workers' wages have stagnated over the past 20 years. Computers and technology also affect employment through automation, outsourcing of jobs overseas, or the total elimination of job categories.

- Being a responsible computer user means knowing how your computer and Internet usage affects others in your school, family, community, and the environment. Using recycled paper, fairly sharing access to public resources, properly disposing of computers and peripherals, being aware of computer and Internet overuse, and staying informed about changing technology demonstrate responsible computer use.

Go to **www.prenhall.com/cayf2006** to review this chapter, answer the questions, and complete the exercises.

Key Terms and Concepts

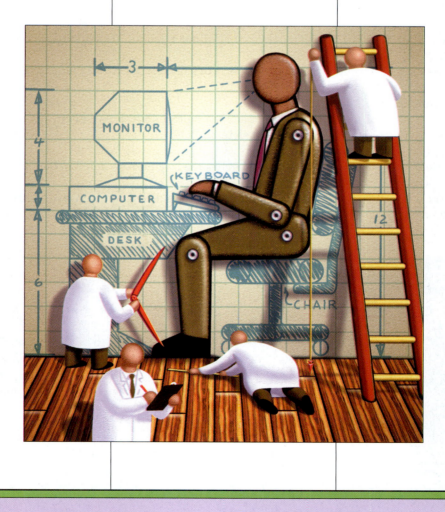

Matching

Match each key term in the left column with the most accurate definition in the right column.

_____ 1. ergonomic

_____ 2. pen computer

_____ 3. carpal tunnel syndrome

_____ 4. personal computer

_____ 5. automation

_____ 6. all-in-one computer

_____ 7. central processing unit (CPU)

_____ 8. Internet appliance

_____ 9. terminal

_____ 10. data

_____ 11. e-learning

_____ 12. desktop computer

_____ 13. output

_____ 14. information

_____ 15. structural unemployment

a. performs operations on input data

b. remote keyboard and display unit

c. unorganized raw facts

d. computers with minimal memory, disk storage, and processing power that connect to a network

e. organized, useful, and/or meaningful facts

f. accept handwritten input

g. a computer that is essentially a monitor with everything else built in

h. the replacement of human workers by machines

i. the use of computers and computer programs to replace teachers and the time–place specificity of learning

j. a personal computer designed for use in an office environment

k. a computer that is designed to meet the computing needs of an individual

l. the result of advancing technology making an entire job category obsolete

m. the product matches the best posture and functionality of the human body

n. repeated motions that damage sensitive nerve tissue in the hands, wrists, and arms

o. the results of processing operations

Multiple Choice

Circle the correct choice for each of the following.

1. What are the four basic operations of the information-processing cycle?
   a. processing, communication, storage, data creation
   b. input, processing, output, storage
   c. input, output, storage, communication
   d. input, printing, storage, retrieval

2. Which of the following is a common input device?
   a. keyboard
   b. printer
   c. disk drive
   d. monitor

3. Which of the following is *not* an output device?
   a. monitor
   b. speakers
   c. printer
   d. mouse

4. Which of the following is *not* a storage device?
   a. floppy drive
   b. DVD-ROM
   c. microphone
   d. hard disk

5. Which type of memory temporarily stores the programs and data with which the CPU interacts?
   a. read only memory
   b. random access memory
   c. refreshable auxiliary memory
   d. read alone memory

6. Which of the following is a computer that processes huge amounts of data within a large organization?
   a. notebook computer
   b. mainframe computer
   c. minicomputer
   d. desktop computer

7. What does the acronym PDA stand for?
   a. personal data aid
   b. professional digital attachment
   c. personal digital assistant
   d. programmable data acquisition

8. Which device enables the computer to access other computers and the Internet via telephone lines?
   a. server
   b. keyboard
   c. hard disk
   d. modem

9. Which of the following computers is designed for individual use while travelling?
   a. workstation
   b. laptop
   c. server
   d. personal computer

10. Which of the following devices allows you to write on the screen with a special pen or stylus?
    a. tablet PC
    b. notebook
    c. subnotebook
    d. laptop

Fill-In

In the blanks provided, write the correct answer for each of the following.

1. A(n) _____ is a machine that performs four basic operations: input, processing, output, and storage.

2. A(n) _____ is a list of instructions that tells the computer how to perform a task.

3. _____ includes the physical components of the computer, including the computer itself as well as the keyboard, monitor, and speakers.

4. _____ is used to temporarily store the programs and data with which the CPU interacts.

5. The most common _____ _____ are the keyboard, mouse, and microphone.

6. The most common _____ _____ are monitors and printers.

7. _____ are notebook computers that omit some components (such as a CD-ROM drive) to cut down on weight and size.

8. _____ are ultrafast computers that process large amounts of scientific data and then display the underlying patterns that have been discovered.

9. A(n) _____._____ packs much of a notebook computer's power into a much lighter package and lower price.

10. A(n) _____ is a group of two or more computer systems connected together to share devices and resources.

11. _____ consists of all of the programs that can be used to perform a task, such as writing a research paper or browsing the Web.

12. _____ includes all of the programs that enable a computer to function, the most important being the operating system (OS).

13. _____ _____ explores computer-related moral dilemmas and defines ethical principles for computer professionals.

14. _____ involves moving data within the computer or between computers.

15. _____ are desktops, laptops, workstations, or any other computer for individuals, that contact a server to obtain needed information.

Short Answer

1. Describe the components of a computer system, including those that can be found inside and outside the system unit.

2. Provide a brief description of a microcomputer, a minicomputer, and a mainframe. Be sure to include information on the power and size of each.

3. What is the difference between hardware and software?

4. What is the difference between system software and application software? Provide an example of each.

5. Define server. Briefly describe how a server is used.

6. What overall effect are computers having on employment? Be sure to discuss the overseas "threat."

7. Explain the digital divide and how computers help people with disabilities.

Teamwork

1. Off-Shoring Jobs

Your team is to investigate how computers affect global shifts in employment. For this exercise you will divide up into 2 sides to do research on the pros and cons of "off-shoring" jobs. Use your favorite search engine and the term "off-shoring" to find research links. Read and cite at least 3 articles. Each side will prepare a presentation to present to the rest of the class.

2. Whose Music Is It?

Locate articles that cover the areas of legal and illegal music downloading. You will find hundreds of articles by typing "legal vs illegal music downloading" into your favorite search engine, such as Yahoo! or Google. You should read at least two articles and then report your findings to the larger group. Once all team members have completed their research, work together to develop a group report and present your findings to the class. How big of a problem is illegal music downloading? Be sure to include statistics to support your answer.

3. Desktop or Laptop—You Decide

As a team, determine whether you would purchase a desktop or a laptop computer. Use the Internet or contact a local vendor and compare the prices for similarly equipped desktop and laptop computers. Based on your needs and finances, prepare a report to explain which computer you would buy and give reasons that support your decision.

4. Mac or PC?

Divide your team into two groups: Mac and PC. Each group should research its assigned system and provide a report that summarizes what they've learned. Be sure to cover all of the components of the basic computer system (input devices, processors, output devices, and the type and amount of storage).

5. Exploring the Information-Processing Cycle

As a team, examine advertisements of computers and peripherals from local or regional newspapers. Compare a desktop computer with a laptop or PDA. Which input, processing, output, and storage devices look the same? Which are different? Prepare a group presentation that describes the products in the ads, identifying them as input, processing, output, or storage devices.

On the Web

1. Owning the Music

Go to **www.apple.com/itunes**, **www.napster.com**, and **www.kazaa.com** to learn more about legal music downloading. You may visit other sites as well. For each site, answer the following questions: What is the price per song? How is the site funded? What process ensures that the music you are downloading is legal? Is illegal downloading possible? Write a one-page report that addresses these questions.

2. Servers: Network Workhorses

Use Google (**www.google.com**) or **www.howstuff works.com** to locate information on servers and the work they perform. Write a one-page report that summarizes what you've learned.

3. Hunting for Easter Eggs

Easter eggs are special, fun screens or information that software developers put into commercial versions of software. Many different programs include Easter eggs. You can find out about Easter eggs at "The Easter Egg Archive" (**www.eeggs.com**). Using the information from the Web site, can you locate any Easter eggs in the programs on your computer? How difficult is it to display Easter eggs in some programs? Which Easter eggs surprised you the most? Prepare a presentation on the information you found.

4. Supercomputers—Super Fast!

Compared with other types of computers, supercomputers are very few in number. Some major universities (such as the University of Tokyo), specialized governmental agencies (such as NASA), and businesses (such as Verizon) use these extremely fast and expensive computers. Visit the list of the world's most powerful computing sites at **www.top500.org** for other types of organizations, agencies, and companies that have supercomputers. Write a brief report that summarizes the following:

- What is the minimum processing speed needed to be included in this list?
- What type and speed of supercomputers are used by:
  - George Lucas's Industrial Light and Magic (ILM) company to make movie special effects?
  - CitiBank to maintain its many accounts?
  - AOL to maintain its vast databases?
  - the FBI to maintain its records?

5. International News—the Big Picture

People use media such as radio, television, newspapers, and, of course, the Internet to obtain information about current events. The Internet Public Library maintains a worldwide list of newspapers at **www.ipl.org**. International students attending schools in the United States can use this site to read (in their native languages) about events that are happening in their home countries. U.S. students can use this site to read (in English) about global political, financial, or cultural events from the perspective of other nations. Prepare a report that includes reasons why someone would read foreign newspapers as well as the headline or lead story in the following newspapers:

- The *Cape Argus*, published in Cape Town, South Africa
- The *Viet Nam News*, published in Hanoi, Vietnam
- The *Buenos Aires Herald*, published in Buenos Aires, Argentina
- The *Moscow Times*, published in Moscow, Russia
- The *Kuwait Times*, published in Kuwait City, Kuwait

Transporting Your Data

The computer ate my homework! One of the best ways to avoid this problem is to stop using floppy disks. You invest a lot of time and energy in your education, and it is worth a few extra dollars to adopt some of today's improved storage solutions to transport the fruits of your labor. Here's a brief overview of some of the products to use instead of floppy disks, as well as some techniques for minimizing the risk of data loss no matter what type of storage you choose.

Some major computer manufacturers, such as Dell and Apple, have already done away with floppy disk drives in most, if not all, of their new products. You can expect floppy disk drives to disappear from new PCs over the next few years. Why are floppy drives disappearing? Although both floppy drives and disks are cheap to manufacture, they are prone to errors and hold a measly 1.4 megabytes (MB) of data, barely enough space to hold half of your favorite song in MP3 file format.

One of the most popular new products is the USB keychain drive (Figure 1.26). This drive is small enough to carry in your pocket but holds the same amount of data as 11 to 365 floppy disks. USB keychain drives can be purchased from any retailer that sells computers and related peripheral devices. Prices usually start in the $20 range for the smaller 16- to 32-MB drives and increase as the amount of storage increases.

If you've recently purchased a PC, your computer probably came with a rewritable CD drive (CD-RW). This drive stores up to 700 MB of data on inexpensive, rewritable CDs. Unlike regular recordable CDs, rewritable CDs can be reused many times. The process of "burning" data to a CD can be time-consuming though, so this may not be the best solution if you're in a hurry. Also keep in mind that not all computers have a CD-RW drive.

Another solution for transporting files between different computers is e-mail attachments. If you have an e-mail account that is accessible using a Web browser (such as AOL, Hotmail, Yahoo! Mail, and so on), simply send an e-mail to yourself with the file attached. Keep

FIGURE 1.26 USB Keychain Drive

in mind that your mail provider may not process large attachments, so you should read your provider's terms of service carefully and send some test messages before relying on this method.

Here are some general tips when using any form of portable storage:

- **No two disk drives are the same. When using a floppy or Zip disk, always use the same computer in labs, at work, or at home. Your disks may fail to store data when you use many different disk drives.**

- **To maximize the life of any disk, always transfer the files you will be working on to the hard drive of the computer, and then transfer them back to the disk when you are done. Some applications create backup files while you work on a file, putting undue stress on the disk.**

Whether you decide to use USB keychain drives, CD-RWs, e-mail attachments, or floppy disks, be sure to transport your data safely!

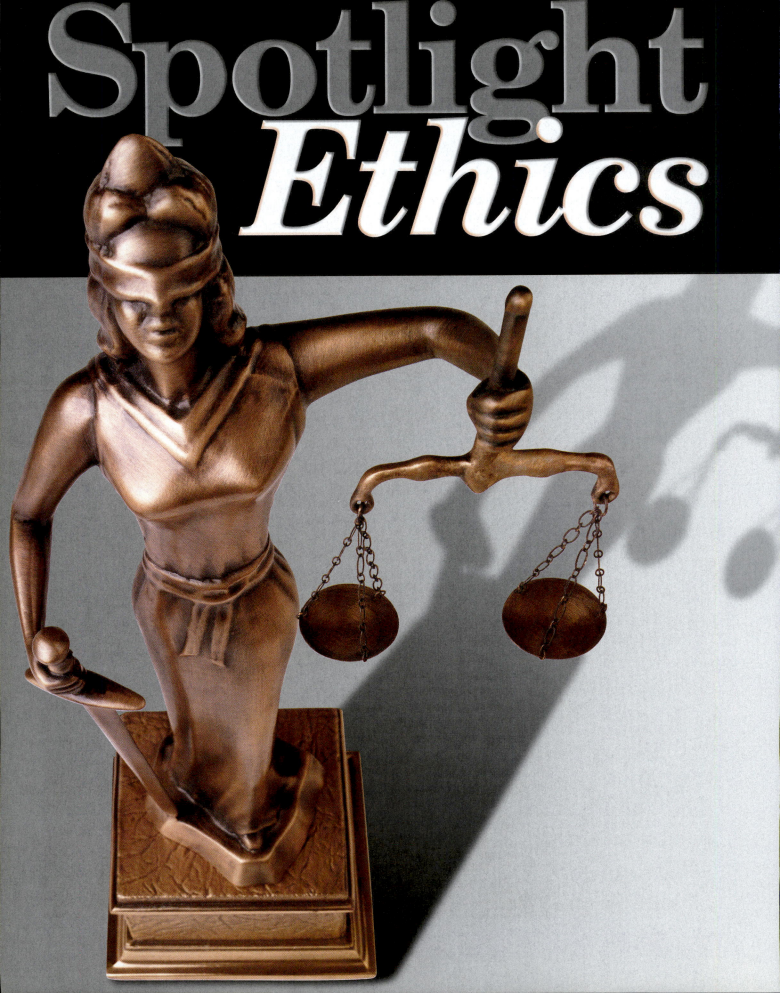

Spotlight
Ethics

What's the difference between unethical and illegal?

WHEN USING COMPUTERS, AND ESPECIALLY THE INTERNET, YOU MAY HAVE TO FACE THIS QUESTION ON A DAILY BASIS. HAVE YOU DOWNLOADED ANY MUSIC RECENTLY? DID YOU PAY FOR THAT MUSIC? WHAT ABOUT THE DVD MOVIE (OR COMPUTER GAME) YOU WATCHED (OR PLAYED) AT YOUR FRIEND'S THIS WEEKEND? DID HE BUY IT OR ILLEGALLY COPY IT? WAS IT A VIOLENT GAME? HAVE YOU EVER THOUGHT ABOUT WHO OWNS THE WORD-PROCESSING SOFTWARE YOU USE IN YOUR COLLEGE COMPUTER LAB? WHAT IS YOUR SCHOOL OR COMPANY'S POLICY ON ACCEPTABLE COMPUTER USE? PERHAPS YOU'VE WRITTEN A RESEARCH PAPER RECENTLY THAT INCLUDED MATERIAL YOU COPIED FROM A WEB SITE. OR, PERHAPS YOU'VE POSTED A NASTY COMMENT ABOUT SOMEONE ON A DISCUSSION BOARD OR SENT A NASTY E-MAIL. HOW CAN YOUR BEHAVIOR ON THE JOB CROSS THESE LINES? *ETHICS* HAS OFTEN BEEN DESCRIBED AS WHAT WE CHOOSE TO DO WHEN NO ONE IS WATCHING. IN OTHER WORDS, WE CHOOSE TO BEHAVE IN AN ETHICAL WAY BECAUSE WE COULDN'T LIVE WITH OUR CONSCIENCE OTHERWISE. IT'S NOT ABOUT WHETHER WE'LL GET CAUGHT. THAT'S THE ILLEGAL PART.

THIS SPOTLIGHT EXAMINES SOME OF THE MOST COMMON ISSUES IN COMPUTER ETHICS, FROM ETHICAL DILEMMAS, WHERE THE DIFFERENCE BETWEEN RIGHT AND WRONG ISN'T SO EASY TO DISCERN, TO LEGAL MATTERS, WHERE RIGHT AND WRONG IS DETERMINED BY LAW.

Figure 1A *Computers cause new ethical dilemmas by pushing people into unprecedented situations.*

Computer Ethics for Computer Users

It isn't always easy to determine the right thing to do. Even when you know what's right, it's not always easy to act on it. Peer pressure is a tremendous force. Why should you be the one to do the right thing when everyone else is getting away with using copied software and music files?

Computers cause new ethical dilemmas by pushing people into unprecedented situations (Figure 1A). Computer ethics uses basic ethical principles to help you make the right decisions in your daily computer use. Ethical principles help you think through your options.

ETHICAL PRINCIPLES

An **ethical principle** defines the justification for considering an act or a rule to be morally right or wrong. Over the centuries, philosophers have come up with many ethical principles. For many people, it's disconcerting to find that these principles sometimes conflict. An ethical principle is only a tool that you can use to think through a difficult situation. In the end, you must make your choice and live with the consequences.

Three of the most useful ethical principles are:

- *An act is ethical if, were everyone to act the same way, society as a whole would benefit.*

- *An act is ethical if it treats people as an end in themselves, rather than as a means to an end.*

- *An act is ethical if impartial observers would judge that it is fair to all parties concerned.*

If you still find yourself in an ethical dilemma related to computer use even after careful consideration of these ethical principles, talk to people you trust. Make sure you have all the facts. Think through alternative courses of action based on the different principles. Would you be proud if your parents knew what you had done? What if your action was mentioned in an article on the front page of your local newspaper? Always strive to find a solution you can be proud of.

FOLLOWING YOUR SCHOOL'S CODE OF CONDUCT

When you use a computer, one of the things you will need to determine is who owns the data, programs, and Internet access you enjoy. If you own your computer system and its software, the work you create is clearly yours, and you are solely responsible for it. However, when you use a computer at school or at work, it is almost always the case that whatever work you create on their computer system is their property. In short, you have greater responsibility and less control over content ownership when you use someone else's system than when you use your own.

Sometimes this question isn't just an ethical one, but a legal one. But how companies and schools enforce computer usage rules tends to vary. So where can you, the college computer user, find guidance when dealing with ethical and legal dilemmas? Your college probably has its own code of conduct or **acceptable use policy** for computer users. It is usually available on a Web page associated with your school's computing center (Figure 1B). You might call the help desk at your computing center and ask for the Web site address of the policy or request a physical copy of it. Read the policy carefully and follow the rules.

- **Respect yourself.** If you obtain an account and password to use the campus computer system, don't give your password to others. They could do something that gets you in trouble. In addition, don't say or do anything on the Internet that could reflect poorly on you, even if you think no one will ever find out.

- **Respect others.** Obviously, you shouldn't use a computer to threaten or harass anyone. You should also avoid using more than your share of computing resources, such as disk space. If you publish a Web page on your college's computers, remember that your page's content affects the college's public image.

- **Respect academic integrity.** Always give credit for text you've copied from the Internet. Obtain permission before you copy pictures. Don't copy or distribute software unless the license specifically says you can.

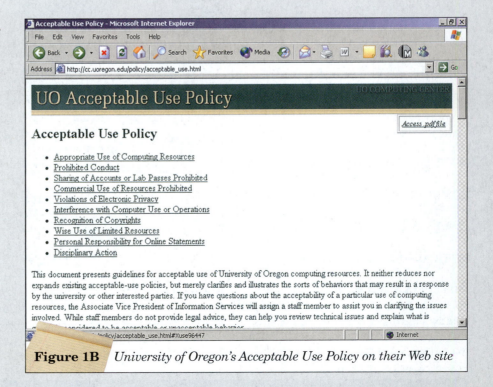

Figure 1B *University of Oregon's Acceptable Use Policy on their Web site*

TEN COMMANDMENTS FOR COMPUTER ETHICS

The Computer Ethics Institute of the Brookings Institution, located in Washington, D.C., has developed the following "Ten Commandments" for computer users, programmers, and system designers:

1. *Don't use a computer to harm other people.*

2. *Don't interfere with other people's computer work.*

3. *Don't snoop around in other people's files.*

4. *Don't use a computer to steal.*

5. *Don't use a computer to bear false witness.*

6. *Don't copy or use proprietary software you have not paid for.*

7. *Don't use other people's computer resources without authorization or proper compensation.*

8. *Don't appropriate other people's intellectual output.*

9. *Do think about the social consequences of the program you write or the system you design.*

10. *Do use a computer in ways that show consideration and respect for your fellow humans.*

NETIQUETTE

General principles such as the "Ten Commandments for Computer Ethics" are useful for overall guidance, but they don't provide specific help for the special situations you'll run into online—such as how to behave properly in chat rooms or while playing an online game (Figure 1C). As a result, computer and Internet users have developed a lengthy series of specific behavior guidelines called **netiquette** for the various Internet services available (such as e-mail, mailing lists, Usenet, Internet Relay Chat (IRC), and online role-playing games), that provide specific pointers on how to show respect for others—and for yourself—while you're online.

Here's a sample, based on Arlene Rinaldi's "Netiquette Home Page" (**www.fau.edu/netiquette/net/netiquette.html**) and other Internet sources:

- **Mailing lists.** After you join a mailing list, read the discussion for a couple of days to see what kinds of questions are welcomed and how to participate meaningfully. If the list has a FAQ (Frequently Asked Questions) document posted on the Web, be sure to read it before posting a question to the list; it may already have been answered in the FAQ. Bear in mind that some people using the list may not speak English as their native tongue, so don't belittle people for spelling errors. Don't post inflammatory messages; never post in anger. If you agree with something, don't post a message that says "Me too"—you're just wasting everyone's time. If you need to unsubscribe from the list, don't post messages requesting that somebody do this for you; find out how to send the correct command to the list server.

- **E-mail.** Check your e-mail daily and respond promptly to the messages you've been sent. Download or delete messages once you've read them so that you don't exceed your disk-usage quota. Remember that e-mail isn't private; you should never send a message that contains anything you wouldn't want others to read. Always speak of others professionally and courteously; e-mail is easily forwarded, and the person you're describing may eventually see

Figure 1C *Netiquette offers guidelines for how to behave properly in chat rooms or while playing an online game.*

the message. Check your computer frequently for viruses that can propagate via e-mail messages. Keep your messages short and to the point; focus on one subject per message. Don't type in all capital letters; this comes across as SHOUTING. Spell check your e-mail as you would any other written correspondence, especially in professional settings. Watch out for sarcasm and humor in e-mail; it often fails to come across as a joke. Be mindful when you request a return receipt; some people consider this to be an invasion of privacy.

- **Internet Relay Chat (IRC).**
Learn what commonly used IRC abbreviations such as BRB (Be Right Back) mean so that you don't pester others to explain them. In a new channel, read the posts to the discussion for a while so you can figure out how to join in meaningfully. Don't flood the channel with text so that others can't communicate and lay off the colors, beeps, and scripts that interfere with the flow of dialogue. Don't harass other users with unwanted invitations. If somebody tells you to type in a command, don't do it—it may be a trick. Learn how to use the ignore command if someone is bothering you.

Besides respectful use of Internet services, playing computer games is another area where you might face ethical dilemmas.

COMPUTER GAMES: TOO MUCH VIOLENCE?

Computer gaming isn't universally admired. More than one-third of all games fall into the action category; among these, the most popular are so-called "splatter" games, which emphasize all-out violence of an especially bloody sort. Parents and

Figure 1D   *Computer games are becoming increasingly violent.*

politicians are concerned that children who play these games may be learning aggressive behaviors that will prove dysfunctional in real life—and they may be right.

In one study, 210 college students were observed before and after playing an especially violent computer game. Researchers found the students were more hostile and reacted more aggressively after playing the game. Another study found that young men who played violent computer games during their teenage years were more likely to commit crimes.

Fears concerning the impact of violent computer games were heightened by the Columbine High School tragedy in 1999, in which two Littleton, Colorado, teenagers opened fire on teachers and fellow students before committing suicide. Subsequently, investigators learned that the boys were great fans of splatter games such as Doom and Quake, and may have patterned their massacre after their gaming experiences.

Still, psychologists disagree on the effect of violent computer games. Some point out that they're little

more than an extension of the World War II "combat" games that children used to play on street corners before the television—and the computer—came along. Others claim that violent video games provide an outlet for aggression that might otherwise materialize in homes and schools.

One thing's for certain: Computer games are becoming more violent. In the past few years, the video game industry has released a slew of new titles that offer a smoother gaming experience, particularly when a player is connected to the Internet in multiplayer mode—and, of course, much more realistic portrayals of violent acts (Figure 1D).

So who's responsible? Is it the software manufacturers who create the programs? Is it the consumers who purchase and use the programs? Parents certainly have a responsibility over what their children do, but what about you—do you make "good" decisions when it comes to exposure to violence? More importantly, is there anything you can do about it? Refer back to the "Ten Commandments for Computer Ethics," especially numbers 9 and 10.

Now that you know about the ethical issues individuals face, let's take a look at how organizations deal with computer ethics.

Computer Ethics for Organizations

Every day, newspapers carry stories about people getting into trouble by using their computers to conduct personal business while they're at work. In many cases, the offenders use company computers to browse the Web and send personal e-mail on company time or to commit crimes such as cyberstalking or distributing pornography. Although most companies have an acceptable use policy for computers, you should be aware that using a computer for non-business-related tasks is generally banned within an organization. You should check with your system administrator, supervisor, or human resources department to obtain a copy of the company's acceptable use policy.

But that's just individuals' behavior while at work. What ethical responsibilities do the companies themselves have? To serve its customers and the public effectively, a business or organization must protect its data from loss and damage and from error and misuse.

Protecting data from loss is often simply a matter of following proper backup procedures. **Backup procedures** involve making copies of data files to protect against data loss or damage from natural or other disasters. Without backup procedures, an organization may place its customers' information at risk (Figure 1E). What would happen to a bank, for example, if it lost all of its data and didn't have any backups?

Data errors can and do occur. It is the ethical responsibility of any organization that deals with data to ensure that its data are as correct as possible. Data that haven't been properly maintained can have serious effects on the individual or organization it relates to.

Data misuse occurs when an employee or company fails to keep data confidential. A breach of confidentiality occurs when an employee looks up data about a person in a database and uses that information for something other than what was intended. For example, some IRS employees routinely looked up the tax returns of neighbors and celebrities. Such actions are grounds for termination.

Companies may punish employees for looking up customer data, but many of them think nothing of selling it to third parties. A mail-order company, for example, can gain needed revenue by selling customer lists to firms marketing related products. Privacy advocates believe that it's unethical to divulge customer data without first asking the customer's permission. These advocates are working to pass tougher privacy laws, so the matter would become a legal concern, not an ethical one.

As an employee, what can you do to stop companies from misusing data or to protect your customers' privacy? Often, there's no clear-cut solution. If you believe that the way a company is conducting business poses a danger to the public or appears to be illegal, you can report the company to regulatory agencies or the press, an action called **whistle-blowing**. An organization called the Business Software Alliance (BSA) helps to combat software piracy by educating the public and businesses about the legal and safety issues regarding commercial software use. You can even fill out a confidential piracy-reporting form on their Web site at **www.bsa.org/usa/ report/Reporting-Form.cfm**. But what if your whistle-blowing causes your company to shut down, putting not only you, but all of your coworkers out of work? As this example illustrates, codes of ethics don't solve every ethical problem; however, they at least provide solid guidance for most situations.

Figure 1E *A backup system can help protect a business's information assets. It would be unethical not to keep regular backups, because the loss of the company's data could negatively impact the stakeholders in the business.*

Computer Ethics for Computer Professionals

No profession can stay in business for long without a rigorous (and enforced) code of professional ethics. That's why many different types of professionals subscribe to ethical **codes of conduct**. These codes are developed by professional associations, such as the Association for Computing Machinery (ACM). Figure 1F is an excerpt from the Code of Ethics of the Institute for Certification of Computing Professionals.

THE ACM CODE OF CONDUCT

Of all the computing associations' codes of conduct, the one developed by the ACM is considered the most innovative and far-reaching. According to the ACM code, a computing professional:

1. *Contributes to society and human well-being*

2. *Avoids harm to others*

3. *Is honest and trustworthy*

4. *Is fair and takes action not to discriminate on the basis of race, sex, religion, age, disability, or national origin*

5. *Honors property rights, including copyrights and patents*

6. *Gives proper credit when using the intellectual property of others*

7. *Respects the right of other individuals to privacy*

8. *Honors confidentiality*

CODES OF CONDUCT AND GOOD PRACTICE FOR CERTIFIED COMPUTING PROFESSIONALS

The essential elements related to conduct that identify a professional activity are:

- *a high standard of skill and knowledge*

- *a confidential relationship with people served*

- *public reliance upon the standards of conduct in established practice*

- *the observance of an ethical code*

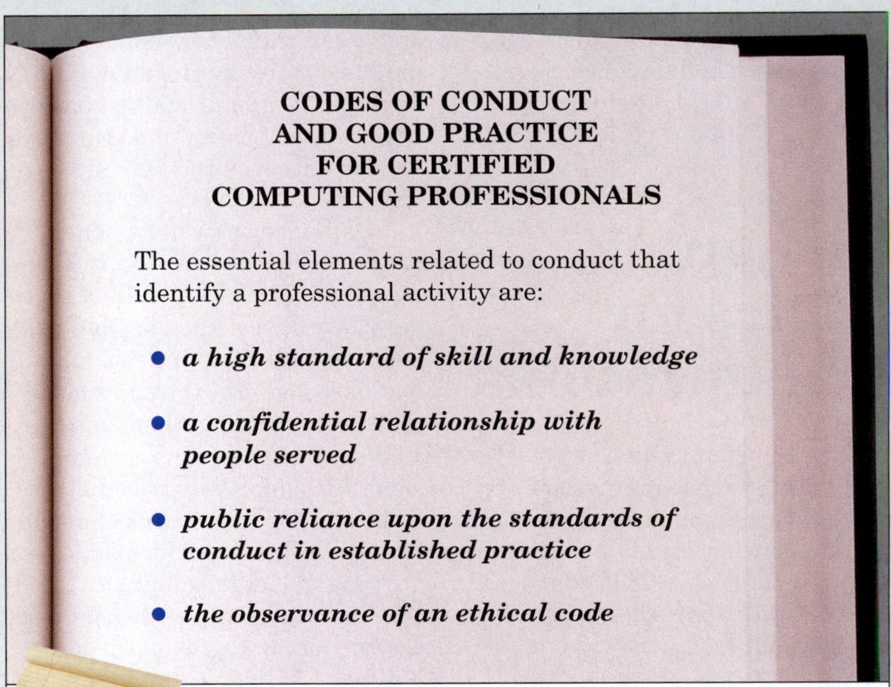

Figure 1F *Excerpt from the Code of Ethics of the Institute for Certification of Computing Professionals*

Like other codes of conduct, the ACM code places public safety and well-being at the top of the list.

SAFETY FIRST

Computer professionals create products that affect many people and may even expose them to risk of personal injury or death. Increasingly, computers and computer programs figure prominently in safety-critical systems, including transportation monitoring (such as with air traffic control) and patient monitoring in hospitals (Figure 1G).

Consider the following situation. An airplane pilot flying in poor visibility uses the computer or autopilot to guide the plane. The air traffic control system is also computer based. The plane crashes. The investigation discloses minor bugs in both computer programs. If the plane's computer had been dealing with a person in the tower rather than a computer, or if the air traffic control program had been interacting with a human pilot, the crash would not have

occurred. Where does the liability lie for the loss of life and property?

Experienced programmers know that programs of any size have bugs. Most complex programs have so many possible combinations of conditions that it isn't feasible to test for every combination. In some cases, the tests would take years; in other cases, no one could think of all the possible conditions. Because bugs are inevitable and programmers can't predict all the different ways programs interact with their environment, most computer experts believe that it's wrong to single out programmers for blame.

Software companies are at fault, too, if they fail to test and document their products. And the organization that buys the software may share part of the blame if it fails to train personnel to use the system properly.

At the core of every computer code of ethics, therefore, is a professional's highest and indispensable aim: to preserve and protect human life and to avoid harm or injury. If the public is to trust

Figure 1G *Computer professionals create products that affect safety-critical systems, including transportation monitoring (such as air traffic control) and patient monitoring in hospitals.*

computer professionals, they must have the ethics needed to protect our safety and welfare—even if doing so means the professional person or the company they work for suffers financially.

Unlike the ethical dilemmas we've discussed up to now, right and wrong are more easily defined when it comes to matters of the law.

It's Not Just Unethical, It's Illegal, Too

What else can cause problems for computer users? Let's start with something that gets many college students into serious trouble: plagiarism.

PLAGIARISM

Imagine the following scenario. It's 4 A.M., and you have a paper due for your 9 A.M. class. While searching for sources on the Internet, you find a Web site with an essay on your topic. What's wrong with downloading the text, reworking it a bit, and handing it in? Plenty.

The use of someone else's intellectual property (their ideas or written work) is called **plagiarism**. Plagiarism predates computers; in fact, it has been practiced for thousands of years. But computers—and especially the Internet—make the temptation and ease of plagiarizing even greater. It's not only very easy to copy and paste from the Internet, but some sites are actually set up specifically to sell college-level papers to the lazy or desperate. The sites selling the papers aren't

guilty of plagiarism, but you are if you turn in the work as your own.

Plagiarism is a serious offense. How serious? At some colleges, the first offense can get you thrown out of school (Figure 1H). You might think it's rare for plagiarizers to be caught, but the truth is that college instructors are often able to detect plagiarism in students' papers without much effort. The tip-off can be a change in the sophistication of phraseology, writing that is a little too polished, or errors in spelling and grammar that are identical in two or more papers. Software programs are available that can scan through text and then compare it against a library of known phrases. If a paper has one or more recognizable phrases, it is marked for closer inspection. Furthermore, even if your actions are not discovered now, someone could find out later, and the evidence could void your degree and even damage your career.

The more well known you are, the more you're at risk of your plagiarism being uncovered. Take noted historian and Pulitzer Prize–winning author Doris Kearns Goodwin, for example. In 2002, she was accused of plagiarizing part of her best-selling 1987 book *The Fitzgeralds and the Kennedys*. Although she claimed her plagiarizing was inadvertent and due to inadequate research methods, she suffered a significant decline in credibility and even felt obligated to leave her position at the PBS news program NewsHour with Jim Lehrer. It took 15 years for Goodwin's plagiarism to come to light.

Plagiarism is a unique offense because it's both unethical and illegal: the unethical part is the dishonesty of passing someone else's work off as your own; the illegal part is taking the material without permission. Plagiarizing copyrighted material is called **copyright infringement**, and if you're caught, you can be sued and may have to pay damages in addition to compensating your victim for any financial losses due to your theft of the material. Trademarks, products, and patented processes are also protected. If you're tempted to copy anything from the Web, bear in mind that the United States is a signatory to international copyright regulations, which specify that an author does not need to include an explicit copyright notice to be protected under the law.

Does this mean you can't use the Internet source you found? Of course not. But you must follow certain citation guidelines. In college writing you can make use of someone else's effort if you use your own words and give credit where credit is due. If you use a phrase or a few sentences from the source, use quotation marks. Attach a bibliography and list the source. For Internet sources, you should list the Web site's address or Uniform Resource Locator (URL), the date the article

Figure 1H *At some colleges, plagiarism can get you thrown out of school on the first offense.*

was published (if available), the date and time you accessed the site, the name of the article, and the author's name. You can usually find a link at the bottom of a Web site's home page that outlines the owner's copyright policy. If not, there is usually a "contact us" link that you can use to contact the owner. You cannot assume that it is legal to copy content from a Web site just because you cannot find a disclaimer.

You'll often hear people use the term **fair use** to justify illegal copying. The fair use doctrine justifies *limited* uses of copyrighted material without payment to or permission from the copyright holder. This means that a *brief* selection from a copyrighted work may be excerpted for the purposes of commentary, parody, news reporting, research, and education. Such excerpts are short—generally, no more than 5 percent of the original work—and they shouldn't compromise the commercial value of the work. In general, the reproduction of an entire work is rarely justifiable by means of the fair use doctrine.

As a responsible computer user, you should worry about not only

wrongly using someone else's words, but also the content you create yourself. The written word carries a lot of power. If those words are untrue, you could be crossing into dangerous, and illegal, territory.

LIBEL

The power of computers and the Internet as a means of communication makes them ripe for involvement in libel. In the United States, **libel** is the publication of a false statement that injures one's business or personal reputation. A plaintiff who sues for libel must prove that a false statement caused injury and demonstrate some type of resulting damage. This could include being shunned by friends and associates or the inability to obtain work because potential employers believed the false accusations. Some states allow for a jury to assess damages based generally on harm to the person's reputation. It is in your best interest to ensure that any electronic publication statement you make about an individual or a corporation is truthful.

SOFTWARE PIRACY

Here's another common situation. You need to have Microsoft Office 2003 for your computer class. A friend has a copy that she got from her mom's office. You've just installed a copy on your computer. Have you done something wrong? Yes, of course you have! In fact, so has your friend. It is illegal for her to have a copy of the software from her mom's office in the first place.

Just like written works, most computer software (including computer games) is copyrighted, which means that you can't make copies for other people without infringing on the software's copyright. Such infringements are called **software piracy** and are a federal offense in the United States (Figure 1I).

How serious is software piracy? The information technology industry loses billions of dollars a year because of piracy. If you're caught pirating software, you may be charged with a felony. If you're convicted of a felony, you could spend time in jail, lose the right to vote, and ruin your chances for a successful career.

When you purchase commercial software you're really purchasing a **software license**, which generally grants you the right to make backups of the program disks and install the software on multiple machines as long as you're only using one copy of the software at a time. Providing the program to others or modifying the program's function is not allowed.

Free programs that users can copy or modify without restriction are called **public domain software**. However, don't assume that a program is public domain unless you see a note (often in the form of a "read me" text file) that explicitly identifies the file as being copyright free.

Unlike public domain software, you can't copy or modify **shareware** programs without permission from the owner. You can almost always find the owner and licensing information by accessing the Help menu

Figure 1I *The Software & Information Industry Association (SIIA) is trying to raise consciousness about software piracy.*

or by locating and reading a "read me" file that is usually placed in the same directory as the program. You may, however, freely copy trial or evaluation versions of shareware programs. When the evaluation period expires, you must pay a **registration fee** or delete the software from your computer.

Other programs qualify under the provisions of the Free Software Foundation's **General Public License (GPL)** which specifies that anyone may freely copy, use, and modify the software, but no one can sell it for profit.

Organizations with many computers (including colleges) also have to be concerned about software piracy. A **site license** is a contract with the software publisher that allows an organization to use multiple copies of the software at a reduced price per unit. Taking copies outside the organization usually violates the contract.

Software manufacturers are working very hard to develop **copyright protection schemes** to thwart the illegal use of their programs. Although early versions of these schemes caused slowdowns on legitimate users' machines, recent versions do not. Increasingly, software is becoming **machine dependent**. This means that the program captures a machine ID during the installation process and writes that ID back to the installation disc or to the software company's server during a mandatory online registration process. Should you attempt to install the program on another machine, the code will be checked and the installation will terminate.

How can you tell whether you're guilty of software piracy? All of the following actions are illegal:

- *Incorporating all or part of a GPL program in a commercial program that you offer for sale.*

- *Continuing to use a shareware program past the evaluation version's expiration date without paying the registration fee.*

- *Violating the terms of a software license, even if you've paid for the program. For example, if you have copies of the same program on your desktop and notebook computers but the license forbids this, you would be in violation of the license.*

- *Making copies of sitelicensed programs that you use at work or school and installing them on your home computer.*

- *Giving or selling copies of commercial software to others.*

Do you have pirated programs on your computer? The police aren't likely to storm into your residence hall and take you away, kicking and screaming. Most software piracy prosecutions target individuals who are trying to distribute or sell infringing copies or companies that have illegally made multiple

Figure 1J *Bands like Metallica fought to have illegal downloads banned from the Internet. In 2000, Metallica sued Napster, a once-popular site for free music downloads. Thanks to lobbying by Metallica and other musicians, consumer consciousness has been raised to understand that it is wrong to obtain music files without paying for them.*

copies for their employees. If you have any pirated software, you should remove these programs from your computer right away. And in the future, consider whether your actions constitute software piracy before the software is installed on your computer. If you still don't see the need to delete pirated software from your computer, consider this: it's very, very wise to become accustomed to a zero-tolerance approach to pirated software. If you're caught with an infringing program at work, you could lose your job. A company can't risk retaining employees who expose the firm to prosecution.

FILE SHARING: MUSIC, MOVIES, AND MORE

You may have heard that it's okay to download a copyrighted MP3 file as long as you keep it for no longer than 24 hours, but that's false. If you upload music copied from a CD you've paid for, you are violating

the law. You can't justify spreading a band's copyrighted music around by saying it's "free advertising;" if the group wants advertising, they'll arrange it themselves (Figure 1J). And don't fall into the trap of thinking that sharing MP3s is legal as long as you don't charge any money for them. Any time you're taking royalties away from copyright holders, it's illegal.

Increasing numbers of Internet users seem to believe that sharing illegally made copies of copyrighted music is permissible because so many people are doing it, especially on college campuses. At the University of Oregon, a student was charged with criminal copyright infringement—a federal crime—after making thousands of MP3s available on his Web site. He faced potential penalties of up to 3 years in prison and $250,000 in fines. At Carnegie Mellon University, 71 students were disciplined for posting illegally duplicated music files on their sites.

Spotlight Exercises

1. Have you ever made a copy of software that you've bought for yourself? Did you ever give a copy of it away? What are your feelings about software piracy? Do you own or have access to a CD burner? What are your thoughts about burning copies of software installation or other CDs? Ask 4 or more other students these same questions and write a report that summarizes your findings.

2. A music fan sets up a Web site about his favorite band. On his site, he posts photos he's downloaded from other sites, as well as the song lyrics of all the band's songs. He doesn't obtain permission for the photos or lyrics, but figures this is fine because his site only serves to promote the band he loves. Write a brief essay on whether he acted ethically or not and provide support for your position.

3. Online file-sharing sites continue to be popular Internet attractions. Detractors claim that such sites make it easy for users to violate copyright laws. The sites themselves claim that they don't support copyright violations; they simply allow users to share files. Are the users who exchange files on such sites acting ethically? What about those who want to prevent such sites from existing at all? Go to the Web sites for Napster.com, KaZaa.com, or Morpheous.net to learn about their different schemes for allowing the copying of music and video files while still protecting copyright. Write a short paper that describes the scheme of the site you chose.

4. An employee at a small nonprofit organization often uses her home computer to do work for her organization. In order to complete her work from home, she copies the software program she uses at work to her home computer. The only time she ever uses the software is when she is performing work for the organization. Is what she has done unethical or illegal? Defend your position in a brief essay.

5. A computer tech person working at a campus repair center finds child pornography on a computer he is repairing. He knows that possession of child pornography is illegal and that he should contact the authorities. However, he also knows he shouldn't have been looking at the contents of the customer's hard drive so closely, and that he may lose his job if his employer finds out he did. He doesn't report his discovery to the police. Instead, he permanently erases all the files containing child pornography from the customer's hard drive. What do you think is wrong with this situation?

6. Working with one or more of your classmates, find and report the following: Obtain a copy of your institution's "acceptable use" policy for computers. What restrictions does the institution place on your computer use that you might not apply when using your own computer or a commercial Internet connection? What are the advantages of connecting to the Internet through an institution instead of through a commercial connection? Are there time restrictions? Are there volume restrictions? Are there any content restrictions? Are there ethical concerns when using the school's system that you wouldn't have if you were using your own system?

online

domain
.com
commu
downloading
ital transerline
.net

web

.com
download
ital transfe
.net
or
web

The Internet & the World Wide Web

Destinations

If you'd like to learn about Internet history, the best place to start is the Internet Society's "Internet Histories" page at **www.isoc.org/ internet/history**. The Internet Society is an organization for professionals who are interested in supporting the Internet's technical development.

Techtalk

Internet2 (I2)
The Internet2 (I2) project is a collaborative effort among more than 120 U.S. universities, several U.S. government agencies, and leading computer and telecommunications companies. The I2 project is developing and testing high-performance network and telecommunications techniques. These improvements will eventually find their way to the public Internet.

As you may already know, the **Internet** is a global computer network made up of thousands of privately owned computers and networks, and it's growing rapidly. Today, hundreds of thousands of networks and nearly 50 million computers of all types and sizes are directly connected to the Internet. According to one estimate, the total amount of information available on this worldwide network doubles each year. But defining the Internet as a fast-growing global network understates its significance.

The Internet was originally planned to be nothing more than a communication and file-exchange network for academics and government agencies. However, it has become a medium for discovering and exploring information that even novices can enjoy (Figure 2.1). Today, we're witnessing the birth of the first major mass medium since television; more than 70 percent of U.S. residents are Internet users. What's more, the Internet isn't simply a new mass medium; it's the *first* mass medium that involves computers and uses digitized data. And it's more interactive than TV, radio, and newspapers, which limit user interaction to content consumption. With the Internet, people can create information as well as consume it. For this reason, it's the first truly democratic mass medium, one that allows anyone to add their own content to the growing mass of information available online.

Most college students have used the Internet—it's hard to imagine students these days not having heard of a Web page, a URL, or a Web link. But no matter how familiar you think you are with this part of the Internet, this chapter will help you fully understand the concepts behind the Web and Web browsers. In addition, this chapter will show you how to use the Web effectively for research and how to evaluate the quality of the information you retrieve.

Now that you know what the Internet is, let's explore how it works and how it is used.

How the Internet Works

The Internet is best thought of as *the* overarching network of networks. In this network of networks, every connected computer can directly exchange data with any other computer on the network. The Internet is also referred to as **cyberspace**—territory that isn't an actual, physical place and that is only accessible with computers. The networks that make up the Internet are maintained by large organizations, such as corporations and universities, as well as by service providers that sell Internet subscriptions to the public (Figure 2.2).

INTEROPERABILITY

The Internet does more than merely allow any one of millions of computers to exchange data with any other. It enables any connected computer to *operate* a remote computer by sending commands through the network. One key to the Internet's success is called **interoperability**, the ability to work with a computer even if it is a different brand and model. This remarkable characteristic of the Internet comes into play every time you use the network. When you access the Internet using a Macintosh, for example, you contact a variety of machines that may include other Macintoshes, Windows PCs, UNIX machines, and even mainframe computers. You don't know what type of computer you're accessing, however, and it doesn't make any difference (Figure 2.3).

The Internet's interoperability helps explain the network's popularity. No network could match the Internet's success if it forced people to use just one or two types of computers. Many home computer users have PCs, but others have Macintoshes or other types of computers or communications and browsing devices. Many businesses

FIGURE 2.1 The Internet is rich with informative and entertaining sites.

FIGURE 2.2
Networks and computers connected to the Internet are maintained by corporations, universities, and Internet service providers.

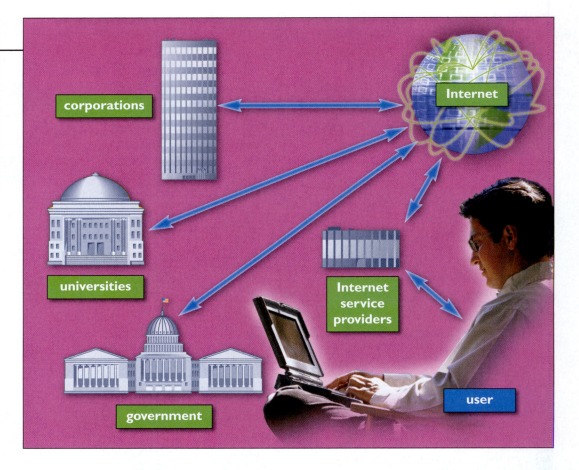

FIGURE 2.3
The interoperability provided by the Internet removes the distinctions among different hardware and operating systems, allowing users on different computers to work with each other.

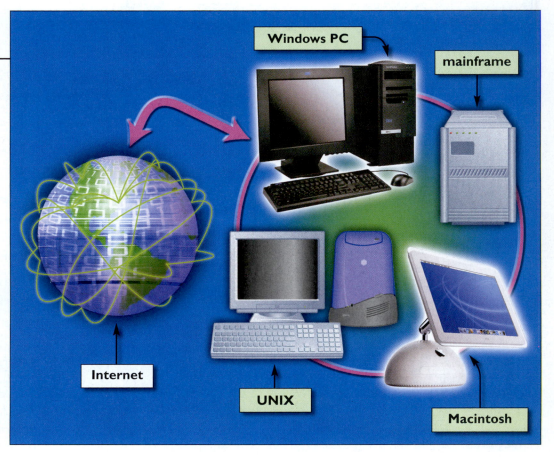

have invested haphazardly in Windows PCs, UNIX workstations, and Macintoshes only to find that, in the absence of the Internet, these computers don't work together well. The Internet enables these computers to exchange data and even to control each other's operations.

Now that you've learned about how the Internet works, the next section explores how you go about getting online.

Accessing the Internet: Going Online

When you access the Internet, it is referred to as *going online*. You need two things in order to go online: an Internet account and a method of connecting or gaining access. How do you get both of these? By contacting an Internet service provider.

INTERNET SERVICE PROVIDERS AND ONLINE SERVICES

Internet service providers (ISPs) are companies that sell Internet accounts, which usually include a user name and a password. They primarily offer access to home and business users. AT&T, Verizon, and other phone companies are considered to be ISPs. An **online service** is a for-profit firm that provides a proprietary network (use is limited to authorized subscribers only) that offers e-mail, chat rooms, discussions, and fee-based content, such as magazines and newspapers (Figure 2.4).

So what's the difference between an ISP and an online service, such as MSN or America Online (AOL)? Not much anymore. As the Internet grew in popularity during the late 1990s, online services began to offer Internet access in an attempt to keep existing customers and attract new ones. While retaining their proprietary network and custom content, they have become ISPs.

To enable users to access the Internet, ISPs distribute software that runs on users' computers, makes the connection, and guides them through the available content and activities. These various providers usually charge a monthly fee for Internet access, but you can sometimes obtain free trial accounts for a certain number of days or hours.

ISPs have several roles and responsibilities. They are responsible for providing and maintaining a connection to the Internet. It might help to think of an ISP as an on-ramp to a highway. When you want to travel that highway, you must first get on the highway via one of its on-ramps. ISPs must also support the hardware and software needed to service that connection. They need to protect their site and network from external threats such as viruses, hacker attacks, and other illegal activities. And, finally, they should provide 24-hour customer service and technical support.

The second decision you need to make is how you will access the Internet (Figure 2.5). Your choices typically include the following options:

- **Dial-up access.** Most home users still connect to the Internet using a dial-up connection, which requires a modem and a telephone line. With this method, your computer is directly connected to the Internet, but it's usually only temporarily connected. That is why you sometimes get bumped off or disconnected

Destinations

Explore the Internet's physical structure at "An Atlas of Cyberspace," located at **www.cyber geography.org/ atlas/atlas.html** This site is maintained by Martin Dodge of the University of London's Centre for Advanced Spatial Analysis.

FIGURE 2.4 America Online is an online service.

Destinations

Looking for an ISP? A good place to start is "The List" (**www.thelist.com**), which is a buyer's guide to ISPs. You can search for an ISP by area code or country.

when online. Dial-up access is typically the most affordable option for many people (ranging from $4.95 up to $25 a month), as well as the least trouble-some, because most homes have at least one phone line. But dial-up is also the slowest type of Internet access.

- **Digital Subscriber Line (DSL).** Available in many urban areas, DSL connections offer high-speed access and a permanent online connection. One drawback of DSL is that service doesn't extend more than a few miles from a telephone switching station or central office (CO). Although this distance is being extended, DSL service remains unavailable in some rural areas. DSL can also be a bit pricier than dial-up, ranging from $30 to $60 a month.

- **Cable and satellite access.** Cable TV companies are increasingly offering Internet access at speeds much faster than that of dial-up access. Satellite access enables fast downloads but requires a phone line and a modem for uploading data. Like dial-up, these access methods give your computer a temporary connection. Cable access typically costs about the same as DSL, whereas satellite access runs from $60 to over $100 per month.

- **Network access.** If the company you're working for has a network or if you're attending a university that provides Internet access in residence halls, you can access the Internet by means of the network. Network access is much faster than dial-up access, but the performance you experience depends on how many other network users are trying to access the Internet at the same time. With net-work access, your computer probably has a permanent connection. Network access is usually free for users; the company or university foots the bill.

Many ISPs also provide direct connections on special leased lines for businesses and large organizations.

Now that you understand the various ways to access the Internet, let's differentiate the Internet from its most popular entity, the World Wide Web.

The Internet and the Web: What's the Difference?

What's the difference between saying "I'm on the Internet" versus "I'm on the Web"? Although many people talk as if the

---

FIGURE 2.5 **Types of Internet Access**

Type	Price Range per Month	Speed of Access (receiving data)	Advantages	Disadvantages
Dial-up	$5 to $25	Slow (56 Kbps)	Availability	Slow speed Reliability
DSL	$30 to $60	Medium (256 to 1,500 Kbps)	Speed Reliability	Availability High user cost
Cable	$30 to $60	Fast (1.5 to 3 Mbps)	Speed Reliability	Availability High user cost
Satellite	$60 to $100	Medium (700 Kbps)	Availability Speed	High user cost Reliability
Network	Usually free to the user	Fast (1.5 to 45 Mbps)	Low user cost Speed	Availability

products
www.consumerreports.org

medicine
www.alternativemedicine.com

news
abcnews.go.com/flash/

FIGURE 2.6 Each day, millions of Internet users turn to the Web to research products, medical advice, and current events.

Internet and Web are the same thing, they aren't. As we learned earlier, the Internet is a network through which any computer can directly access any other and exchange data. The **World Wide Web** (or **Web** or **WWW**) is a portion of the Internet that contains billions of documents. The Web *uses* the Internet as its transport mechanism, but it's a separate entity. The Internet is the physical connection of millions of networks, whereas the Web is an information resource that enables millions of Internet users to research products, medical advice, current events, and much more (Figure 2.6).

Who owns or controls the Internet and the Web? No one. The Internet is made up of thousands of privately owned computers and networks, all of which agree to follow certain standards and guidelines and share resources on the network. A variety of organizations are responsible for different aspects of the network. For example, the World Wide Web Consortium (W3C) based

FIGURE 2.7
A Web site's home page is displayed automatically when you enter the site at its top level.

in Cambridge, Massachusetts, issues standards related to all aspects of the Web.

What else can you find on the Web? You've probably visited many Web sites by now or at least seen them advertised on TV or in periodicals or heard about them on the radio. A **Web site** is a location that is accessible from the Internet and makes Web pages available. A **Web page** is any document on a Web site that includes text, graphics, sound, animation, or video. Web sites are collections of related Web pages. A Web site typically contains a **home page** (also called an **index page**), which is a default page that's displayed automatically when you enter a site at its top level. Figure 2.7 shows the home pages for several Web sites.

It's amazing to think that the Web's billions of documents are almost instantly accessible by means of the computer sitting on your desk. More than 300,000 new Web pages appear every week. The Web is also appealing because of its graphical richness, which is made possible by the integration of text and graphics. Increasingly, Web pages are as well designed as the pages of commercial magazines, and they often feature fonts of the quality you'd associate with desktop publishing.

In the following section, you'll learn how all of these pieces work together on the Web, starting with the concept of hypertext.

THE HYPERTEXT CONCEPT

The Web's billions of documents are created using hypertext. **Hypertext** is a method of preparing and publishing text that is ideally suited to be read with a computer. With hypertext, the *sequence* of the information— the order in which it is read—is determined by the reader. You can think of hypertext as active text. That is, the text you read is linked to text or graphics that are contained within the document you are reading or in other documents in cyberspace. Hypertext works by means of hyperlinks. **Hyperlinks** (also called **links**) are words that you can click to bring another document into view (Figure 2.8).

In addition to being a global hypertext system, the Web is a distributed hypermedia system. A **distributed hypermedia system** is a network-based content development

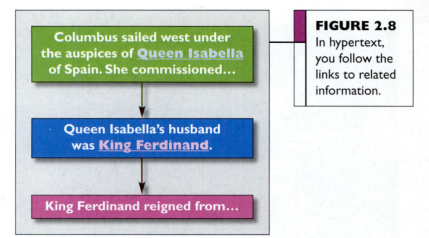

FIGURE 2.8
In hypertext, you follow the links to related information.

system that uses multimedia resources, such as sounds, movies, and text as a means of navigation or illustration. In this system, the responsibility for creating content is distributed among many people. And the more people who create content, the easier hypertext development becomes. For example, if someone has created a document about Queen Isabella and another person has created a document about King Ferdinand, you can link to these documents instead of writing them yourself.

The Web's distribution of content-creation responsibilities does have a drawback: You can link to any page you want, but you can't guarantee that the page's author will keep the page on the Web. The author can delete it or move it, and the author isn't under any obligation to notify other authors who have included links to the page. For this reason, **dead links** (also called **broken links**), which are links to documents that have disappeared, are common on the Web.

Now that you understand hypertext, let's move on to what enables us to use it: browsers and servers.

WEB BROWSERS AND WEB SERVERS

The first graphical Web browsers (which make hypertext become "live" on your computer screen) were developed in 1994. A **Web browser** is a program that displays a Web document and enables you to access linked documents. Figure 2.9 illustrates how to connect to the Web via your browser.

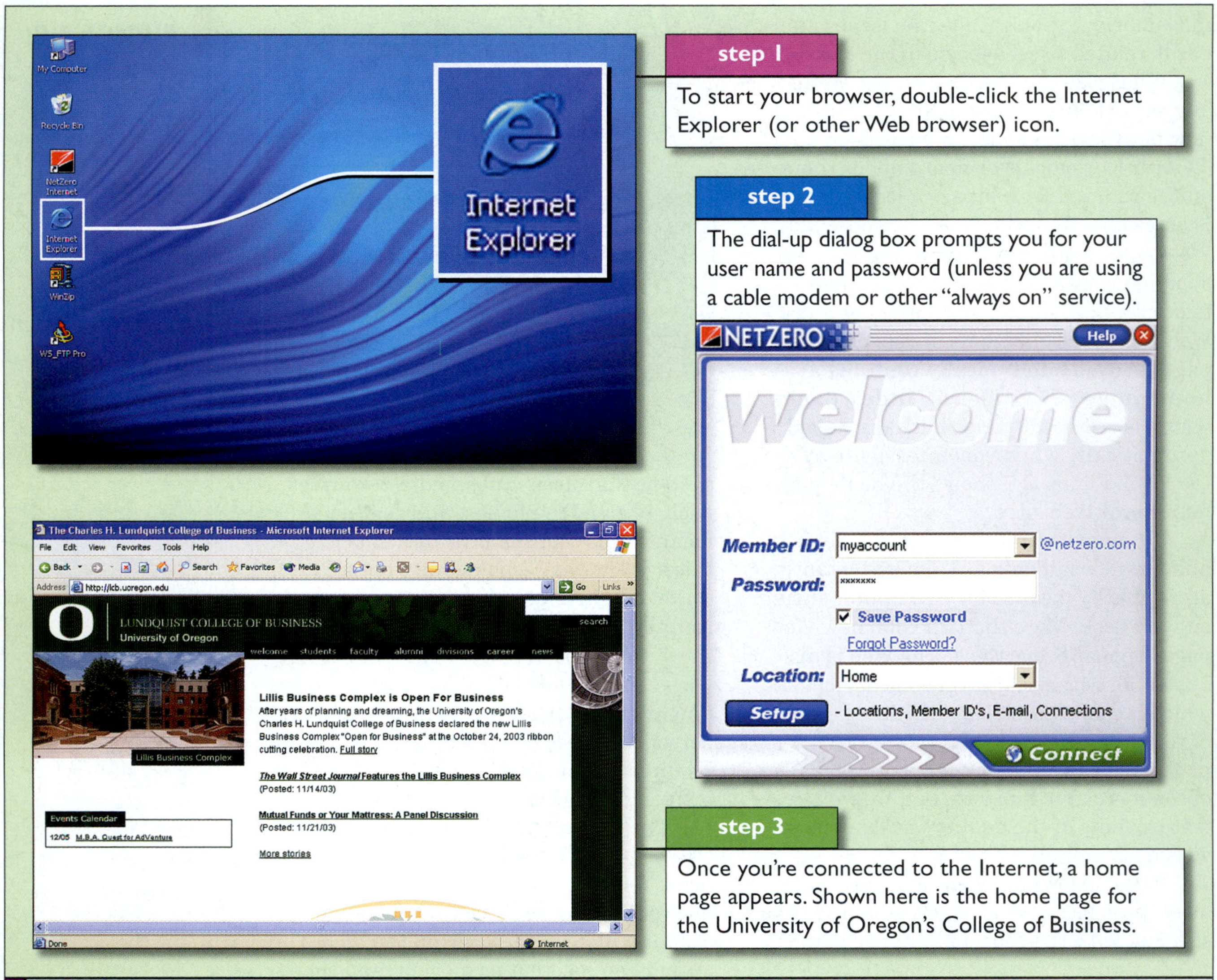
step 1
To start your browser, double-click the Internet Explorer (or other Web browser) icon.
Internet Explorer
step 2
The dial-up dialog box prompts you for your user name and password (unless you are using a cable modem or other "always on" service).
NETZERO
Help
welcome
Member ID:
myaccount
@netzero.com
Password:
Save Password
Forgot Password?
Location:
Home
Setup
- Locations, Member ID's, E-mail, Connections
Connect
step 3
Once you're connected to the Internet, a home page appears. Shown here is the home page for the University of Oregon's College of Business.
The Charles H. Lundquist College of Business - Microsoft Internet Explorer
http://lcb.uoregon.edu
LUNDQUIST COLLEGE OF BUSINESS
University of Oregon
Lillis Business Complex is Open For Business
Lillis Business Complex
Events Calendar

FIGURE 2.9 The following steps show how to connect to the Web via your browser icon.

The first successful graphical browser, called Mosaic, helped launch the Web on the road to popularity. Developed by the National Center for Supercomputing Applications (NCSA) at the University of Illinois, Mosaic was followed by two commercial products, Netscape Navigator and Microsoft Internet Explorer, which have since captured virtually the entire browser market (Figure 2.10).

Both major browser programs use similar features, such as navigation buttons, a program icon, an address toolbar, and a status bar, as shown in Figure 2.10. When you first install a browser, it usually defaults to the home page of the company that owns it (Microsoft or Netscape). You can either keep this as your home page, which will be displayed each time you start your browser, or you can change the browser's default home page, also referred to as customizing your browser. You can find the default home page settings in Internet Explorer under the Tools, Internet Options menu (Figure 2.11).

Browsers view and act upon documents that are created using hypertext. It is the browser that allows the text and graphics on a hypertext document to be active. In short, browsers are meant to work with Web pages. Sometimes you need to upgrade your browser to the latest version so that you can fully enjoy the features of a Web site. New Web page creation software is being developed all the time—and sometimes older browsers don't have the capability

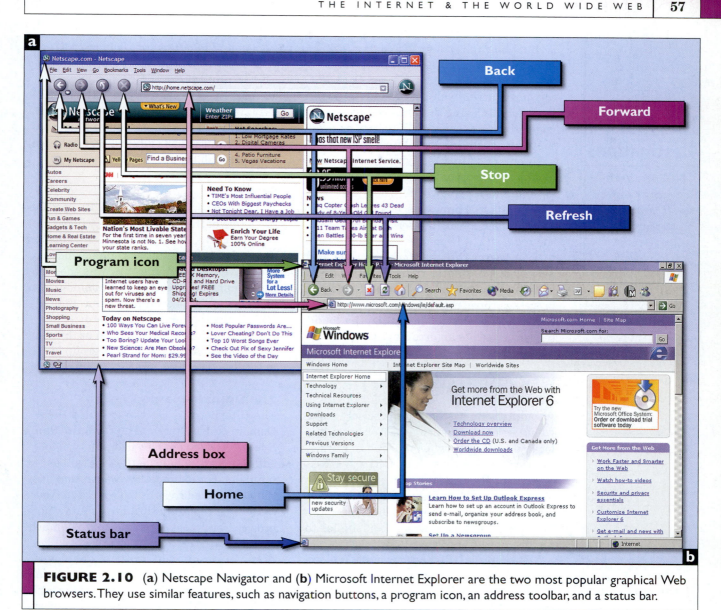

FIGURE 2.10 (a) Netscape Navigator and (b) Microsoft Internet Explorer are the two most popular graphical Web browsers. They use similar features, such as navigation buttons, a program icon, an address toolbar, and a status bar.

of displaying the newest features or animations. Browsers use *plug-ins,* which are software programs that allow you to derive the full benefits of a Web site, such as sound or video. If a Web site requires a plug-in to function properly, there will usually be a link on the home page that directs you to the plug-in download site.

Another feature that browsers share is the ability to cache or store Web page files and graphics on your computer. When you browse a Web page the first time, it is stored on your hard drive in a specially assigned storage space. This allows Web pages to be retrieved faster the next time you want to browse them because they don't have to be transferred across the Internet. The positive aspect of this feature

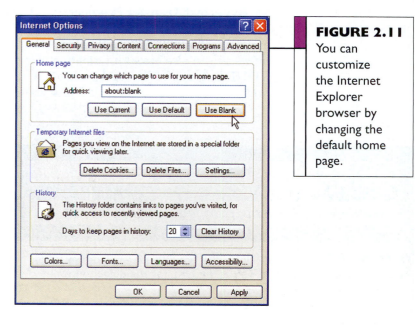

FIGURE 2.11
You can customize the Internet Explorer browser by changing the default home page.

Destinations

The Opera Web browser is known for its advanced cross-platform technology for desktop computers, mobile phones and other products. To find out more details about Opera, visit **www.opera.com**

is that you can retrieve Web pages faster; the downside is that a Web page you retrieve from your hard disk may not be the most current version of the Web page. Occasionally using the Refresh button on your browser's toolbar will help to ensure that you are viewing the latest content.

Content on the Web is made available by means of more than 1 million Web servers located all over the world. When you click a hyperlink, the browser sends a message to a Web server, asking the server to retrieve the requested information and send it back to the browser through the network. A **Web server** is a computer running server software that accepts requests for information, processes those requests, and sends the requested documents. If the file isn't found, the server sends an error message.

WEB ADDRESSES (URLs)

An addressing system that precisely states where a resource (such as a Web page) is located is necessary for the Web to work. This system is provided by URLs. A **URL** (**Uniform Resource Locator**) is a string of characters that precisely identifies an Internet resource's type and location. You've seen plenty of URLs, which look similar to the one shown in Figure 2.12.

A complete URL has four parts: protocol, server, path, and resource name.

Protocol

The first part of a complete URL specifies the **Hypertext Transfer Protocol** (**HTTP**), the Internet standard that supports the exchange of information on the Web. Most browsers can also access information using FTP (File Transfer Protocol) and other protocols. The protocol name is followed by

a colon and two forward slash marks (//). With most Web browsers, you can omit the *http://* protocol designation when you're accessing a Web page, because the browser assumes that you are browsing hypertext Web pages. For example, you can access **http://www.prenhall.com/cayf2006** by typing **www.prenhall.com/cayf2006**.

Server

The second part of a complete URL specifies the name of the Web server on which the page is located. Early Web servers adopted the name "WWW," but as time has passed, the convention of using WWW as the Web server name has become less common. Also included in the second part of a complete URL is the top-level domain name. The **domain** is the extension (such as .com or .edu) representing the type of group or institution that the Web site represents.

The Domain Name System

The Internet uses a system called the Domain Name System. The **Domain Name System** (**DNS**) enables users to type an address that includes letters as well as numbers. For example, **www.msn.com** has the numeric address *207.68.172.246*. You could type the numeric address into your browser, but most of us find that it's much easier to use text names. A process called **domain name registration** enables individuals and organizations to register a domain name with a service organization such as InterNIC. You may use your favorite search engine to search for domain name registration to find other sites that provide this service.

Domain names can tell you a great deal about where a computer is located. For Web sites hosted in the United States, **top-level domain** (**TLD**) **names** (the *last* part of the domain name) indicate the type of organization in which the computer is located (Figure 2.13). Outside the United States, the top-level domain indicates the name of the country where the computer hosting the Web site is located, such as .ca (Canada), .uk (United Kingdom), and .jp (Japan).

Path

The third part of a complete URL specifies the location of the document on the server. It contains the document's location on the computer, including the names of

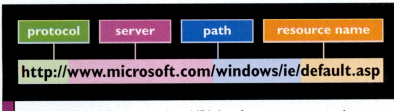

FIGURE 2.12 A complete URL has four parts: protocol, server, path, and resource name. This is the URL for the default Internet Explorer home page.

FIGURE 2.13 Common Top-Level Domain Names

Top-Level Domain Name	Used By
.com	Commercial businesses
.biz	Businesses
.edu	Educational institutions
.info	Information
.gov	Government agencies
.pro	Professionals
.mil	Military
.aero	Flying
.net	Network organizations (such as ISPs)
.coop	Cooperatives
.org	Nonprofit organizations
.museum	Museums
.name	Names

subfolders (if any). In the example in Figure 2.12, the path to the default.asp file on the Web server at **www.microsoft.com** is **/windows/ie/default.asp**.

Resource Name

The last part of a complete URL gives the filename of the resource you're accessing. A resource is a file, such as an HTML file, a sound file, a movie file, or a graphics file. The resource's extension (the part of the filename after the period) indicates the type of resource it is. For example, HTML documents have the .html or .htm extension.

Many URLs don't include a resource name because they reference the server's default home page. If no resource name is specified, the browser looks for a file named

default or *index*—a default page that's displayed automatically when you enter the site at its top level. If it finds such a file, it loads it automatically. For example, **www.microsoft.com/windows/ie** displays the default Internet Explorer home page. Other URLs omit both the path name and the resource name. These URLs reference the server's home page. For example, **www.microsoft.com** displays Microsoft's home page on the Web.

BROWSING THE WEB

Once you have installed browser software and are connected to the Internet, you're ready to browse the Web. To access a Web page, you can do any of the following (Figure 2.14):

- **Click a hyperlink.** Hyperlinks are usually underlined, but sometimes they're embedded in graphics or highlighted in other ways, such as with shading or colors. To tell whether a given portion of a Web page contains a hyperlink, position your mouse pointer over it and watch for a change in the pointer's shape. Most browsers indicate the presence of a hyperlink by changing the on-screen pointer to a hand shape.

- **Type a URL in the Address box (Internet Explorer) or Location box (Netscape Navigator).** You don't need to type http://. Watch for spelling errors, and don't insert spaces. A common mistake is typing a comma instead of a period to separate the components of a URL.

- **Click a button on the Links toolbar.** Both major browsers come with predefined links on a toolbar, which contains buttons linked to Web pages. You can customize this toolbar by adding pages that you frequently access.

As you browse the Web, your browser keeps a list of the Web pages you've accessed called the **history list**. If you'd like to return to a previously viewed site and can't find it by clicking the Back button, you can

Destinations

For more information on domain names, visit the Internet Corporation for Assigned Names and Numbers (ICANN) at **www.icann.org**

Techtalk

spiders
The Web contains more than just a vast network of information links. "Spiders" exist there, too. A spider is a small piece of software that crawls around the Web, picking up URLs and information on the pages attached to them.

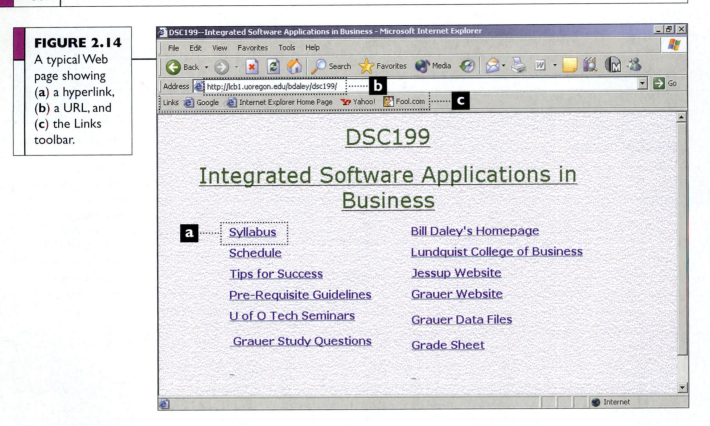

consult the history list and choose the page from there. You'll soon find some Web pages you'll want to return to frequently. To accomplish this easily, you can save these pages as Favorites (Internet Explorer) or Bookmarks

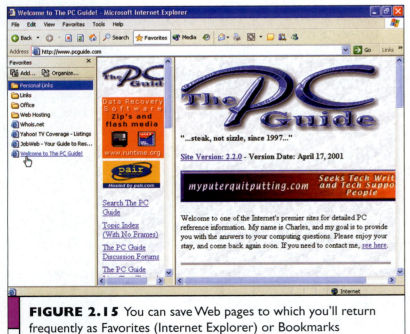

FIGURE 2.15 You can save Web pages to which you'll return frequently as Favorites (Internet Explorer) or Bookmarks (Netscape Navigator).

(Netscape Navigator) (Figure 2.15). After you've saved these pages as Favorites or Bookmarks, you'll see the names of these pages in the Favorites or Bookmarks menu.

Uploading and Downloading
After you have browsed the Web and accessed various Web pages, you may want to try downloading or uploading data. With **downloading**, a document or file is transferred from another computer to your computer. With **uploading**, you transfer files from your computer to another computer.

You should exercise caution when downloading files of unknown origin from the Web. If you download software from a site that doesn't inspect files using up-to-date antivirus software, you could infect your computer with a virus. Most Internet users believe that it's safe to download software from Web sites maintained by software companies. However, be aware that many viruses are spread in the data files of popular programs, such as Microsoft Word or Excel. If you download data files, be sure to check them with an antivirus program.

Now that you understand the basics of the Internet and Web, let's examine how to conduct research on the Web.

IMPACTS

Emerging Technologies

Wiki, Weblog, Moblog: Sharing Information—Fast

Want to share information fast? A wiki, a Weblog, or a moblog may be in your future. A wiki (short for *wiki-wiki,* the Hawaiian word for fast) is a simple Web page on which any visitor can post text or images, read previous posts, change posted information, and track earlier changes. No elaborate coding needed—just click to post, click to refresh the page, and you're done. If a visitor changes what you've posted and you don't like the change, just click to revert back to the original. Next time you're online, surf over to **www.wikipedia.org**, which is an open-content encyclopedia. People can add new encyclopedia entries and edit entries that others have created.

Because wikis are so convenient and easy to use, they're catching on in the business world. Employees at Stata Labs, a software company, can post questions and comments on a corporate wiki so that technical staff and managers can offer solutions and suggestions. For example, when an employee posted a request for help with a problem, an executive read the message and posted an idea that turned out to be the solution. This had a ripple effect: Other Stata employees read the posts, recognized that they had similar problems, and tried the suggested solution. If everything had been discussed in e-mails instead of being posted on the wiki, no one else would have picked up on the solution.

Another way to share information online is via a Weblog (also called a blog). A Weblog is the Internet equivalent of a journal or diary. Bloggers post their thoughts and opinions, along with photos or links to interesting Web sites, for the entire world to see. Of the 5 million blogs on the Web, some are meant for family and friends, some offer running commentary on politics and other timely topics, and others are written by employees about their employers and other subjects. Blogs by Microsoft employees (see **blogs.msdn.com**) have a loyal following because of their insightful observations and tech know-how. Visit **www.blogsearch engine.com** to search for blogs by subject and to read FAQs about blogging (Figure 2.16).

If you snap a digital photo with your camera phone and send it from the phone to your blog, you're building a moblog (short for mobile Weblog and pronounced "moe-blog"). Any time you post words or images to a blog from a cell phone, PDA, or other mobile device, you're moblogging. From quickie notes to photos on the fly, moblogs give you a chance to speak your mind and provide a window on your world even when you're not in front of your computer. Moblog, Weblog, or wiki— the choice is yours.

FIGURE 2.16 Searching for and browsing blogs can be both entertaining and educational.

For information about some of the tools you can use to start a Weblog, view the video clip at **www.prenhall.com/ cayf2006**

Techtalk

clickstream

As you click from site to site on the Web, you leave a clickstream in your wake. A clickstream is the trail of Web links that you have followed to get to a particular site. Internet merchants are quite interested in analyzing clickstream activity so they can do a better job of targeting advertisements and tailoring Web pages to potential customers.

Finding Information on the Web

Although browsing by means of hyperlinks is easy and fun, it falls short as a means of information research. Web users soon find themselves clicking link after link, searching for information that they never find. If you can't find the information you're looking for after a bit of browsing, try *searching* the Web. You've no doubt heard of Google, Yahoo!, AltaVista, and Lycos. Although these and other Web search tools are far from perfect, knowing how to effectively use them (and knowing their limitations) can greatly increase your chances of finding the information you want.

Most search sites offer a **subject guide** to the Web, grouping Web pages under headings such as business, news, or travel (Figure 2.17). These guides don't try to include every Web page on the World Wide Web. Instead, they offer a selection of high-quality pages that the search site believes represent some of the more useful Web pages in a given category. If you're just beginning your search for information, a subject guide is an excellent place to start.

USING SEARCH ENGINES

If you can't find what you're looking for in a Web subject guide, you can try searching databases that claim to index the full Web. Called **search engines**, these sites don't actually maintain databases of every Web page in existence, but the leading ones have indexed about one-third of them (Figure 2.18). Google accounts for 34 percent of the search site market, followed by Yahoo! at 28 percent, AOL at 16 percent, MSN at 15 percent, and others making up the remaining 6 percent. That's an enormous pool of information, and chances are that by using these search engines, you'll find information relevant to the subject you're looking for.

To use a search engine, type one or more words that describe the subject you're looking for into the search text box and click Search (or hit Enter). Generally, it's a good idea to type several words (four or five) rather than just one or two. If you only use one or two words, the Web search will produce far more results than you can use.

Why do search engines sometimes produce unsatisfactory results? The problem lies in the ambiguity of the English language. Suppose you're searching for information on the Great Wall of China. You'll find some information on the ancient Chinese defensive installation, but you may also get the menu of the Great Wall of China, a Chinese restaurant; information on the Great Wall hotel in Beijing; and the lyrics of a song titled "Great Wall of China" by Billy Joel.

Specialized Search Engines

Full Web search engines generally don't index specialized information such as names and addresses, job advertisements, quotations, or newspaper articles. To find such information, you need to use **specialized search engines**. Examples of such specialized search engines include CareerBuilder.com, a database of over 400,000 jobs, and Infoplease.com, which contains the full text of an encyclopedia and an almanac (Figure 2.19).

You can save the results of your searches—the Web pages you visit by following the results links of a search engine—to your hard drive by using your browser's

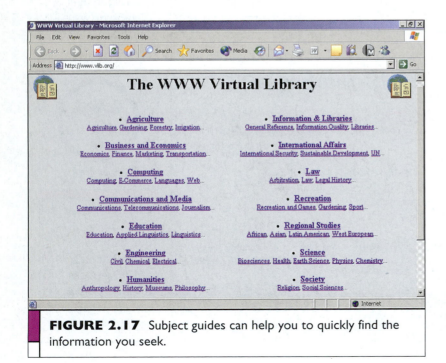

FIGURE 2.17 Subject guides can help you to quickly find the information you seek.

File, Save As menu sequence. If you don't want or need the entire Web page, you can right-click on the various elements of the page and choose from a variety of options (Save, Print, Copy). You can also use your mouse and cursor to highlight and then copy text on a Web page for pasting into a word-processing file or other document. Sometimes you might want to view a Web page that you've saved *offline*; that is, without connecting to the Internet. This is easily accomplished by opening your browser and then choosing the File, Open menu sequence. Simply browse through your folders and files to locate the file of interest and then open it.

Search engines are not the only way to find information on the Web. You can also go to the sites of online services such as MSN, AOL, and Yahoo! These sites are also referred to as portals. A **portal** is a gateway that provides a conveniently organized subject guide to Internet content, fast-breaking news, local weather, stock quotes, sports scores, and e-mail (Figure 2.20). Portal sites usually use indexes and lists of links to provide you with a jumping off place for your search.

Some Web sites have their own site search engines. You will often find this feature on the site's home page. It is usually a clearly marked box into which you type the keywords of what you are looking for. Some home pages will have a Search icon or button that will take you to the site's search page.

FIGURE 2.18 Google is the most popular search engine.

USING SEARCH TECHNIQUES

By learning a few search techniques, you can greatly increase the accuracy of your Web searches. One problem with search engines is that each uses its own unique set of **search operators**, which are symbols or words used for advanced searches. A trend toward standardization, however, means that some or all of the following techniques will work with most search engines. To find out which search operators to use with a given search engine, look for a link on the search engine's home page that will take you to a page explaining which ones to use in your searches.

To learn how to get the most out of your Google searches, view the video clip at **www.prenhall.com/cayf2006**

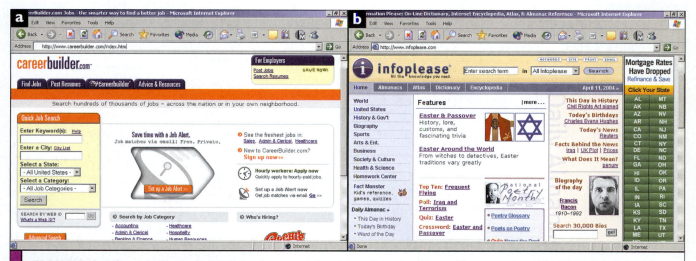

FIGURE 2.19 **(a)** CareerBuilder.com is a specialized search engine that adds more than 110,000 job listings each week. **(b)** Infoplease.com, another specialized search engine, contains the full text of an encyclopedia and an almanac.

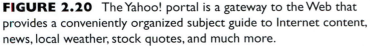

FIGURE 2.20 The Yahoo! portal is a gateway to the Web that provides a conveniently organized subject guide to Internet content, news, local weather, stock quotes, and much more.

states that you don't want a page retrieved unless it contains the specified word. By listing several key terms with this search operator, you can exclude many pages that don't contain one or more of the essential terms. The following, for example, will retrieve only those pages that contain all three of the words mentioned:

kittens+care+Siamese

If the list of retrieved documents contains many items that you don't want, you can use the **exclusion operator**, which is generally a minus (–) sign. For example, the preceding search retrieves many classified ads for Siamese kittens. You can exclude them by prefacing the term *classified* with the exclusion operator, as follows:

kittens+care+Siamese–classified

Wildcards

Many search engines enable you to use wildcards. **Wildcards** are symbols such as ? and * that take the place of one or more characters in the position in which they are used. Wildcards help you improve the

Destinations

Try out and compare some up-and-coming search engines by visiting Vivisimo at **vivisimo.com**, Topix at **www.topix.net**, and Feedster at **www.feedster.com**

Inclusion and Exclusion

With many search engines, you can improve search performance by specifying an **inclusion operator**, which is generally a plus (+) sign (Figure 2.21). This operator

FIGURE 2.21 The results of searching for kittens+care+Siamese.

accuracy of your searches. In the preceding example, many unwanted pages contain the word *classifieds* and aren't excluded by the singular *classified*. The following example using the asterisk (*) wildcard excludes any document containing the words *classified* or *classifieds*:

–classified*

Phrase Searches

Another way to improve the accuracy of your searches is through **phrase searching**, which is generally performed by typing a phrase within quotation marks. This tells the search engine to retrieve only those documents that contain the exact phrase (rather than some or all of the words anywhere in the document). Using the phrase "the care of Siamese kittens" will return approximately the same results as using the inclusion operators discussed earlier.

Boolean Searches

Some search engines enable you to perform Boolean searches. **Boolean searches** use keywords (AND, OR, and NOT) to link the words you're searching for. By using Boolean operators, you can gain more precise control over your searches. Let's look at a few examples.

The AND, OR, and NOT Operators When used to link two search words, the AND operator tells the search service to return only those documents that contain both words (just as the plus sign does). For example, the search phrase *kittens* AND *care* returns only those documents that contain both terms. You can use the AND operator to narrow your search so that it retrieves fewer documents. Searching for *kittens* AND *care* AND *Siamese* will return the same result as shown in Figure 2.21.

If your search retrieves too few documents, try the OR operator. For example, the search phrase *kittens* OR *Siamese* retrieves documents that contain either or both of these words. So, you will receive information on all kittens and information on all things Siamese. (Most search engines will return both without the OR operator.)

To exclude unwanted documents, use the NOT operator. This operator tells the search engine to omit any documents containing the word preceded by NOT (just as

the minus sign does). For example, the search phrase *kittens* NOT *cats* retrieves pages that mention kittens, but not those that mention cats.

Using Parentheses Many search engines that support Boolean operators enable you to use parentheses, a process called *nesting*. When you nest an expression, the search engine evaluates the expression from left to right, and the material within parentheses is resolved first. Such expressions enable you to conduct a search with unmatched accuracy. Consider this example:

(growth OR increase OR development) NEAR (Internet or Web)

This search retrieves any document that mentions the words *growth*, *increase*, or *development* within a few words of *Internet* or *Web*.

EVALUATING INFORMATION

After you've found information on the Web, you'll need to evaluate it critically. Anyone can publish information on the Web; Web pages are not subject to the fact-checking standards of newspapers or magazines let alone the peer review process that safeguards the quality of scholarly and scientific publications. Although you can find excellent and reliable information on the Web, you can also find pages that are biased and self-serving.

Rules for Critically Evaluating Web Pages

As you're evaluating a Web page, carefully note the following:

- Who is the author of this page? Is the author affiliated with a recognized institution, such as a university or a well-known company? Is there any evidence that the author is qualified with respect to this topic? A page that isn't signed may signal an attempt to disguise the author's lack of qualifications.

- Does the author cite his or her sources? If so, do they appear to be from recognized and respected publications?

Destinations

To learn more about search engines and their specialized capabilities, go to **searchenginewatch .com/reports/ index.php**

- Who provides the server for publishing this Web page? Who pays for this page?

- Does the presentation seem balanced and objective, or is it one-sided?

- Is the language objective and dispassionate, or is it strident and argumentative?

- What is the purpose of this page? Is the author trying to sell something or push a biased idea? Who would profit if this page's information was accepted as true? Does the site include links to external information, or does it only reference itself?

- Does the information appear to be accurate? Is the page free of sweeping generalizations or other signs of shoddy thinking? Do you see many misspellings or grammatical errors that would indicate a poor educational background?

- Is this page up-to-date? When was it last updated?

In the next section, you will explore the practical applications of Web research to both the work and school environments.

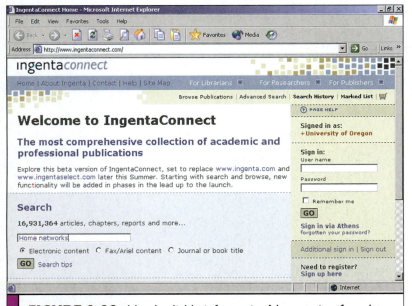

FIGURE 2.22 Need reliable information? Ingenta is a free database service you can use to search for high-quality articles from more than 28,000 published magazines and journals.

USING THE WEB FOR SCHOOLWORK

Finding information on the Web can help you as a consumer. But how can it help you as a student? The following sections provide some helpful hints.

Authoritative Online Sources

Some respected magazines and journals have established Web sites that enable you to search back issues, giving you the best of both worlds—the power and convenience of the Internet, plus material that is more reliable than the average Web page.

Locating Material in Published Works

Remember that the Web is only one of several sources you can and should use for research. Your best sources of information are respected publications, which you'll likely find in the library. As institutions have begun to offer distance learning courses, student access to library materials has become a critical issue. Because students may not be able to visit an institution's library physically, how can they access relevant materials? You can use the Internet to locate publications and then obtain them from your college's library. Check your library's home page to find out what Internet services are available. In addition to standard card-catalog information—such as author, title, and publication date—you can often access full-text versions of books and periodicals online. Some libraries provide these materials directly, whereas others use a third party to provide these services. You can almost certainly access and search your library's inventory of books and can often order them online. The library's books and articles search engine will allow you to search by author, title, and/or key term. Sometimes you can access the online materials from off campus as well as on campus. Materials may be accessible only to faculty and students or they may also be available to the general public.

Also, visit Ingenta (**www.ingentaconnect.com**), a free database service that enables you to search for high-quality articles from more than 28,000 published magazines and journals (Figure 2.22). After you search, you'll see article lists and titles. You can then obtain the source from the library or online.

Citing Online and Offline References

Citing your work is an important way to honor copyright and avoid accusations of inappropriate behavior or plagiarism. Because citing Internet-based sources is not the same as citing traditional references, visit UC Berkeley's "Library style" site at **www.lib.berkeley.edu/TeachingLib/ Guides/Internet/Style.html** to learn how to properly cite online and electronic resources. You should know how to cite Web sites, e-mail messages, and online databases. When citing electronic resources, it is important to include the date the site was last accessed. Unlike the written and published word, electronic words are time sensitive.

Now that you're familiar with how to find and evaluate information on the Web, let's look at some of the Internet's most useful services.

Exploring Internet Services

An **Internet service** is best understood as a set of standards (protocols) that define how two types of programs—a client, such as a Web browser that runs on the user's computer, and a server—can communicate with each other through the Internet. By using the service's protocols, the client requests information from a server program that is located on some other computer on the Internet.

To make use of the most popular Internet services, you need several client programs. That's why the two leading browsers, Netscape Navigator and Microsoft Internet Explorer, are available as part of software suites that include several popular clients in addition to the Web browser. Figure 2.23 lists the clients available in both suites as well as the services they support. Most Internet users obtain additional client software to make use of services that these suites don't support, such as Internet Relay Chat (IRC).

FIGURE 2.23 Clients Available in Popular Browser Suites

Client	Microsoft Internet Explorer Suite	Netscape Communicator
Web browser	Internet Explorer	Netscape Navigator
E-mail	Outlook Express	Netscape Messenger
Usenet	Outlook Express	Netscape Collabra
Internet telephony	NetMeeting	Netscape Conference

E-MAIL: STAYING IN TOUCH

The most popular Internet service is e-mail (Figure 2.24). **E-mail** (short for **electronic mail**) is a software application that enables you to send and receive messages via networks. E-mail is fast becoming indispensable for individuals as well as businesses. It is evolving into a unique communications medium—it can be as formal as a letter or as informal as a phone call. E-mail is well on its way to replacing the postal system as the medium of choice for interpersonal written communication.

When you receive an e-mail, you can reply to the message, forward it to someone else, store it for later action, or delete it. In addition to sending text messages, you can include an e-mail attachment. An **e-mail attachment** is any computer file such as a word-processed document or a photo that is included with an e-mail message. If you receive an e-mail message containing an attachment, your e-mail program displays a distinctive icon, such as a paper clip, informing you that the message contains an attachment. E-mail usually

FIGURE 2.24
E-mail is the most popular Internet service.

arrives at the destination server in a few seconds. It is then stored on the server until the recipient logs on to the server and downloads the message.

To send an e-mail, you need to know the recipient's e-mail address. An **e-mail address** is a unique cyberspace identity for a particular recipient that follows the form **myname@someserver.com**. The components of an e-mail address are the user name, the name of the server that is hosting the e-mail service, and the top-level domain that identifies the type of institution that the provider is. For instance, you can send mail to the president of the United States at the e-mail address **president@whitehouse.gov**. In this instance, the user name is "President," the server is "Whitehouse," and the type of domain is ".gov" (for government). You can often tell quite a bit about someone just by reading their e-mail address!

E-mail has many benefits. It is inexpensive, fast, and easy to access from almost any Internet-connected computer. People can also use e-mail to collaborate with others quickly and efficiently. It also creates an electronic paper trail that documents both the timeliness and content of past communications (Figure 2.25).

The benefits of e-mail are tempered by some potential problems that you should be aware of. Sometimes e-mail systems fail to properly send or receive mail. Attachments may not be delivered or they may be blocked by e-mail system administrators as potentially unsafe. Messages can become corrupted and may not display properly. Sometimes, if you don't regularly check your mail, your inbox may overflow, which causes any messages received past the overflow point to be bounced out of the box and never delivered.

Perhaps the worst things that can happen with e-mail is for you to hastily send a message that you later wished you hadn't or to use the "Reply All" or "Forward" feature to send inappropriate or irrelevant mail messages that can embarrass you or that inconvenience the receiver.

Spam: Can It Be Stopped?

Many e-mail users receive unsolicited e-mail advertising called **spam**. In fact, according to recent estimates as much as 60 percent of all e-mail is spam. This mail is sent by spammers, businesses or individuals that specialize in sending such mail. Spammers believe that they're doing only what direct marketing mail firms do: sending legitimate advertising. But they don't acknowledge a crucial difference between unsolicited postal advertising and spam.

FIGURE 2.25
E-mail has many benefits. It is inexpensive, fast, and easy to access. It enables people to collaborate with others and creates a paper trail of past communications.

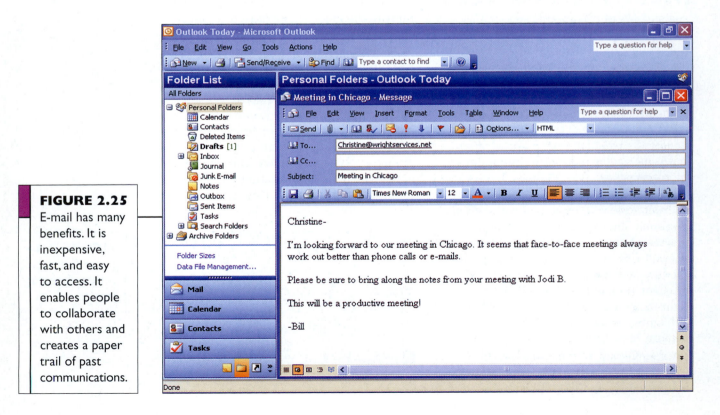

With postal advertising, the advertiser pays for the postage. With spam, the recipient pays the postage in the form of Internet access fees. According to a coalition of ISPs, every Internet user is paying an average of $2 per month in additional fees because of costs directly attributable to the activities of spammers.

Most Internet users detest spam, and some find it so annoying that they stop using the Internet. For businesses, spam is a costly nuisance. On several occasions, gigantic numbers of spam messages have overwhelmed mail servers, resulting in impaired service for legitimate, paying customers.

In most cases, little or nothing of worth is being peddled: pornographic Web sites, phony get-rich-quick scams, bogus stock deals, rip-off work-at-home schemes, health and diet scams, and merchandise of questionable quality.

Can you filter out spam? You can try. Most spam, however, originates from a new account, which is almost immediately closed down after the service provider receives hundreds of thousands of outraged complaints. The spammer just moves on to a new account. One thing you can do to help prevent spam is to avoid posting your e-mail address in any public place. In fact, you should be very selective in providing your e-mail address to anyone. Businesses such as SpamCop protect users against spam for a fee. In addition, software alternatives such as Spam Buster by Contact Plus Corporation and Spam Killer by McAfee let you set rules to limit your inbox spam. Free software such as MailWasher and Mailshell can help you clear spam automatically from your system (Figure 2.26). Some e-mail providers offer on-site spam-filtering services that try to filter out spam before it is even sent to your mailbox, but so far there is no way to get rid of spam entirely.

Don't reply to spam or request to be "removed" from a spammer's mailing list. All that does is verify to the spammer that your e-mail address is valid. A mailing list consisting of validated addresses is much more valuable than a "dirty" list, so all that will happen is that you'll get even more spam.

Increasingly, state and federal legislatures are attempting to pass laws against spam. Bills have been introduced in Congress, and the Senate's "CAN SPAM" act is aimed at deceptive e-mails, unsolicited

FIGURE 2.26 Antispam software, such as MailWasher, can often be downloaded for a free trial.

pornography, and marketing. With regards to such legislation, the Direct Marketing Association (DMA), an advocacy group for both online and offline direct marketers, believes that the appropriate solution is an "opt-out" system in which spammed e-mail users can request that the sender remove their names from the mailing list—but that's just what e-mail users have been trained not to do due to fear that they'll receive even more spam than before. In addition, efforts to outlaw spam run afoul of free speech guarantees under the U.S. Constitution's First Amendment, which applies to businesses as well as individuals. States that outlaw spam, as Washington State did, may find that their laws are thrown out of court because they inhibit interstate commerce. One solution under consideration is a Congressional measure that would give ISPs the right to sue spammers for violating their spam policies.

For now, one thing's for sure: If you haven't been spammed yet, you will be.

INSTANT MESSAGING: E-MAIL MADE FASTER

What's faster than e-mail and more convenient than picking up the phone? **Instant messaging (IM) systems** alert you when a friend or business associate who also

FIGURE 2.27

Instant messaging is a popular way for Internet users to exchange near real-time messages. An IM system alerts you when someone you know who also uses the IM system is online. You can then contact this person and exchange messages.

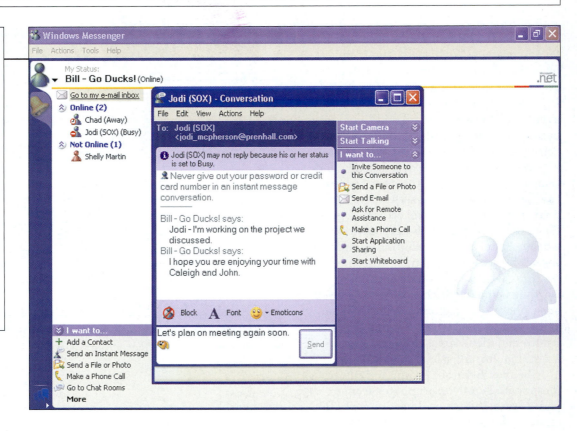

Destinations

To get started with IRC, visit the IRChelp Help Archive at **www.irchelp.org**. You'll find lots of information devoted to making your IRC experience a rewarding one.

uses the IM system (a buddy or contact) is online (connected to the Internet). You can then contact this person and exchange messages and attachments, including sound files (Figure 2.27).

To use IM, you need to install instant messenger software from an instant messenger service, such as AOL's Instant Messenger or Microsoft's Windows Messenger, onto your computer. You can use IM systems on any type of computer, including handhelds. Many IM services also give you access to information such as daily news, stock prices, sports scores, and the weather. You can also keep track of your appointments. At this time, there is no standard instant messaging protocol, which means that you can send messages only to people who are using the same IM service that you are.

An increasing number of businesses and institutions are trying out IM services, with mixed results. On the one hand, IM is a novel and convenient way to communicate. On the other hand, voice communication is faster and richer. Until we can type faster than we can speak, and until we can include timing, inflection, and feeling in the typed word, phone and face-to-face communications will continue to be best.

Another threat to the use of IM is a phenomenon known as *spimming*. Spimming is to IM as spam is to e-mail. Some aggressive spimmers learned how to take over one IMer's contact list—threatening a company's entire IM system!

INTERNET RELAY CHAT: TEXT CHATTING IN REAL TIME

Internet Relay Chat (**IRC**) is an Internet service that enables you to join chat groups, called **channels**, and participate in real-time, text-based conversations (Figure 2.28). Each text message is prefaced by the participant's nickname. Normally, your messages are seen by everyone in the channel, but it's possible to send a whisper, which is seen only by the one person to whom you send it.

Sometimes chat rooms aren't friendly places. You may encounter various sorts of antisocial behaviors, including **flooding** (sending repeated messages so that no one else can get a word in edgewise) and **nuking** (exploiting bugs that cause your computer to crash). Bear in mind, too, that some of the "people" in channels aren't people at all, but rather miniprograms called **bots**. Bots are illegal on some servers, but on others they're

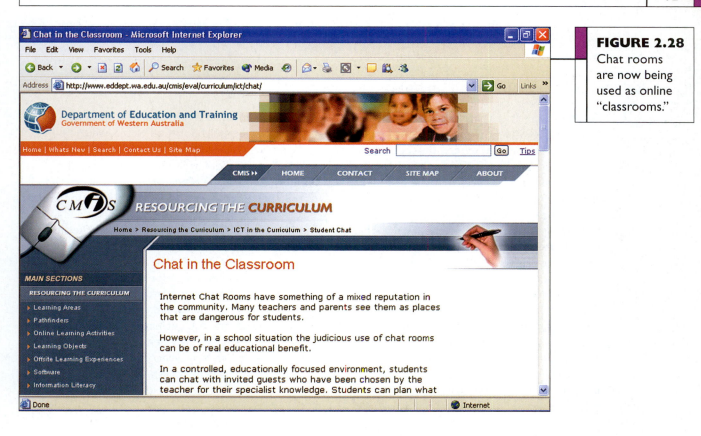

FIGURE 2.28
Chat rooms are now being used as online "classrooms."

used to greet newcomers (and sometimes to harass them). Also, every channel has a channel operator who can kick you out of the channel for any reason, or none at all.

FILE TRANSFER PROTOCOL: TRANSFERRING FILES

File Transfer Protocol (FTP) is one way that files can be transferred over the Internet. With FTP client software such as WS FTP Pro, you can transfer files to and from an FTP server. FTP can transfer two types of files: ASCII (text files) and binary (program files, graphics, or documents saved in proprietary file formats).

In most cases, you need a user name and a password to access an FTP server. However, with **anonymous FTP**, files are publicly available for downloading. It's called *anonymous* FTP because you log on by typing the word *anonymous* instead of a user name and you supply your e-mail address as your password. The leading Web browsers, Microsoft Internet Explorer and Netscape Navigator, support file downloading from anonymous FTP sites, so you don't need any special skills to use anonymous FTP (Figure 2.29). Downloadable files are listed

as hyperlinks; when you click such a hyperlink, downloading begins automatically.

You can easily download publicly accessible files by using a Web browser, but in some cases you'll need an FTP client to upload files. If you'd like to publish your own

FIGURE 2.29 You can use your favorite browser to execute FTP operations. In this instance, Internet Explorer is used to access a remote server.

CyberAngels: Protecting Children in Cyberspace

CURRENTS

Internet Security

Are there angels in cyberspace? A couple in Fanwood, New Jersey, has a ready answer to this question: Yes! After their computer-addicted 13-year-old daughter ran away from home, the parents began to suspect that she had fled to the residence of an adult man who had been romancing the child online. They then contacted CyberAngels (**www.cyberangels.org**), a voluntary organization of thousands of Internet users worldwide (Figure 2.30). The group's purpose: to protect children in cyberspace.

CyberAngels was founded in 1995 by Curtis Sliwa, who also started the Guardian Angels (the volunteer organization whose members wear red berets as they patrol inner-city streets). A radio call-in program host in New York, Curtis received a call from a woman who wanted to know what he would do to keep the Internet safe. Understanding the potential danger for

kids, Curtis asked a few Guardian Angels to create a cyberneighborhood watch, which he called CyberAngels.

Today, CyberAngels volunteers scour the Internet for online predators, cyberstalkers, and child pornographers, and they've been responsible for a number of arrests. The Cybermoms and Dads group monitors chat rooms, a favorite Internet hangout of adults hoping to entice kids into sexual liaisons. Its elite Net Patrol unit includes trained investigators who search for missing children, identify online sexual predators, locate and expose child pornography sites, and help police prosecute sexual predators. Each volunteer snares as many as four cyberstalkers a week. As Internet usage has expanded, so has CyberAngels. Now its services are available in English, French, Dutch, and Spanish, and it has brought its Children's Internet Safety Program to thousands of schoolchildren across the United States.

CyberAngels has been praised not only by the thousands of families it has assisted, but by civic leaders and community groups as well. Although some people lump the group with those intent on imposing Internet censorship, CyberAngels believes in a self-regulating Internet without further censorship. Also, CyberAngels works with Interpol and other law enforcement agencies to have suspects arrested, unlike groups that try to trap cyberpredators on their own, vigilante style. In the end, CyberAngels stresses that the Internet will be safer if more parents supervise their children's online activities.

And what about the New Jersey couple? Their daughter is home and safe thanks to the CyberAngels who successfully used their network to identify the child's online contact.

FIGURE 2.30 Perhaps you would consider becoming a CyberAngel— check out their Web site for more information.

Web pages, you'll need to use FTP to upload your pages to your ISP's server so that your pages are available to other Internet users.

USENET: JOINING ONLINE DISCUSSIONS

Usenet is a worldwide computer-based discussion system accessible through the Internet. It consists of thousands of topically

named **newsgroups**, which are discussion groups devoted to a single topic. Each newsgroup contains articles that users have posted for all to see. Users can respond to specific articles by posting follow-up articles. Over time, a discussion thread develops as people reply to the replies. A **thread** is a series of articles that offer a continuing commentary on the same general subject.

Usenet newsgroups are organized into the following main categories:

FIGURE 2.31   Standard Newsgroup Subcategories

Subcategory Name	Description of Topics Covered
comp	Everything related to computers and computer networks, including applications, compression, databases, multimedia, and programming
misc	Subjects that do not fit in other standard newsgroup hierarchies, including activism, books, business, consumer issues, health, investing, jobs, and law
sci	The sciences and social sciences, including anthropology, archaeology, chemistry, economics, math, physics, and statistics
soc	Social issues, including adoption, college-related issues, feminism, human rights, and world cultures
talk	Debate on controversial subjects, including abortion, atheism, euthanasia, gun control, and religion
news	Usenet itself, including announcements and materials for new users
rec	All aspects of recreation, including aviation, backcountry sports, bicycles, boats, gardening, and scouting

- **Standard newsgroups.** You're most likely to find rewarding, high-quality discussions in the standard newsgroups (also called world newsgroups). Figure 2.31 lists the standard newsgroup subcategories.

- **Alt newsgroups.** The alt category is much more freewheeling. Anyone can create an alt newsgroup (which explains why so many of them have silly or offensive names).

- **Biz newsgroups.** These newsgroups are devoted to the commercial uses of the Internet.

To access Usenet, you use Usenet client software that often comes with most browser suites to communicate with a Usenet server and to post your own messages. But be careful what you post on Usenet. When you post an article, you're publishing in the public domain. Sometimes articles are stored for long periods of time in Web-accessible archives.

Also, be aware that you'll be expected to follow the rules of **netiquette**, guidelines for good manners when you're communicating through Usenet (or any Internet service). For example, some Usenet clients enable you to post messages using formatting, but this is considered bad manners because people who have text-only clients see a lot of meaningless formatting symbols. If you violate netiquette rules, you may receive **flames** (angry, critical messages) from other newsgroup subscribers.

LISTSERV: ELECTRONIC MAILING LISTS

A **listserv** manages electronic mailing lists of e-mail addresses. Eric Thomas developed the program in 1986 for BITNET. Similar in many ways to newsgroups and forums, a listserv automatically broadcasts messages to all individuals on a mailing list. However, because the listserv messages are transmitted as e-mail, only individuals who are subscribers to the mailing list can view the messages. Most colleges and universities manage listservs. The most common listserv program is called Majordomo, which is distributed as freeware.

What You've Learned

THE INTERNET & THE WORLD WIDE WEB

- The Internet is *the* network of networks. The Internet allows every connected computer to directly exchange data with any other computer on the network. It enables any connected computer to *operate* a remote computer by sending commands through the network. The Internet is able to work this way because of interoperability, the ability to work with a computer even if it is a different brand and model.

- Users access the Internet by way of a public or private Internet Service Provider (ISP). Public providers include libraries and schools; private providers are those who provide access for a fee. You can connect to your ISP by way of a telephone modem, a Digital Service Line (DSL) connection, a cable modem, a satellite connection, or a network connection (schools and businesses that maintain constant access to the Internet usually have such connections).

- Whereas the Internet is a global computer network that connects millions of smaller networks, the World Wide Web is a global system that contains billions of hypertext documents and uses the Internet as its transport mechanism. Millions of users turn to the Web to research current events, general information, product information, scientific developments, and much more.

- With hypertext, related information is referenced by means of links instead of being fully explained or defined in the same location. On the Web, authors can link to information created by others.

- A Web browser is a program that displays a Web document and enables you to access linked documents. A Web server is a computer that retrieves documents requested by browsers.

- A URL consists of a protocol (such as http://), a server (such as www), a path (such as /windows/ie), and a resource name (such as default.htm). To access a Web page, you can click a hyperlink, type a URL into a browser's Address box, or click a button on the Links toolbar.

- Web subject guides index a limited number of high-quality pages, whereas search engines enable you to search huge databases of Web documents.

- Most Web searches retrieve too many irrelevant documents. You can improve search results by using inclusion and exclusion operators, phrase searches, and Boolean operators. Search operators such as the + and – signs or the Boolean AND or OR operators can help to limit the results of your search to the particular thing you are interested in.

- To evaluate any information you find on the Web, you should question the Web page author's credentials and purpose for publishing the page. Other criteria are whether reputable sources are cited, who provides or pays for the server that hosts the page, and whether the content seems biased, inaccurate, or out-of-date.

- Popular Internet services include e-mail and instant messaging (IM) for sending messages, Internet Relay Chat (IRC) for text chatting, File Transfer Protocol (FTP) for file exchange, Usenet for joining discussion groups, and listserv for broadcasting content to subscribers.

Key Terms and Concepts

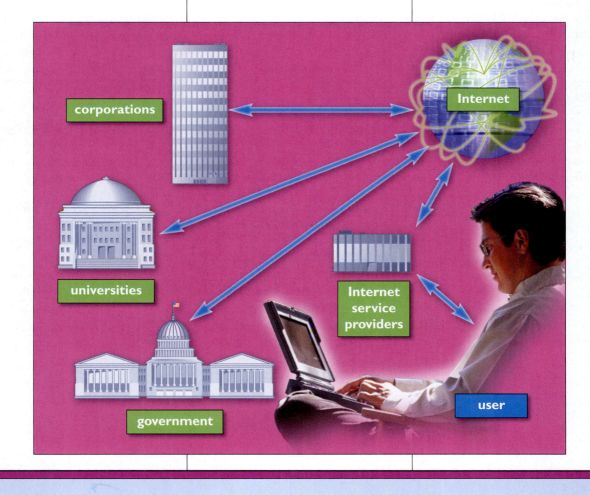

Matching

Match each key term in the left column with the most accurate definition in the right column.

_____ 1. Internet

_____ 2. domain

_____ 3. interoperability

_____ 4. top-level domain name

_____ 5. newsgroups

_____ 6. thread

_____ 7. hypertext

_____ 8. netiquette

_____ 9. online service

_____ 10. flame

_____ 11. Web server

_____ 12. Web site

_____ 13. Internet Relay Chat (IRC)

_____ 14. Internet service

_____ 15. downloading

a. guidelines for good manners when communicating via Usenet or any other Internet service

b. a discussion group devoted to a single topic

c. a global computer network with hundreds of millions of users worldwide

d. indicates the type of organization or country in which a Web site computer is located

e. the process of transferring a document or file from another computer to your computer

f. angry, critical messages from newsgroup subscribers

g. a for-profit firm that provides a proprietary network which offers e-mail, chat rooms, discussions, and fee-based content, such as magazines and newspapers

h. an Internet service that enables a user to join chat groups

i. the ability to work with a computer even if it is a different brand and model

j. a series of articles that offer a continuing commentary on the same general subject

k. the extension (such as .com or .edu) representing the type of group or institution that a Web site represents

l. a computer running software that accepts Web page requests

m. a set of standards (protocols) that define how a Web browser and a server communicate with each other through the Internet

n. a collection of related Web pages

o. a method of preparing and publishing text that is ideally suited to be read with a computer

Multiple Choice

Circle the correct choice for each of the following.

1. When evaluating the information on a Web page, which criteria is *not* as important as the others?
   a. Who is the author?
   b. Does the author cite any sources?
   c. Who provides the server for publishing the Web page?
   d. What is the Web page address?

2. Which of the following is a client program?
   a. hypertext
   b. Internet address
   c. Web browser
   d. search engine

3. You would use this type of Boolean operator to keep certain values out of the search results.
   a. inclusion (+)
   b. exclusion (–)
   c. *
   d. ?

4. When a Web browser accesses a Web site, which page is displayed automatically?
   a. directory page
   b. home page
   c. catalog page
   d. development page

5. Which of the following alerts you when someone you know is online?
   a. client software
   b. Internet Explorer
   c. online services
   d. instant messaging (IM) system

6. Which of the following provides the slowest Internet access?
   a. dial-up
   b. Digital Subscriber Line (DSL)
   c. cable
   d. network

7. Links to documents that have disappeared are known as what?
   a. unknown links
   b. tenuous links
   c. hyperlinks
   d. dead links

8. What enables users to type an Internet address that includes letters as well as numbers.?
   a. domain name system
   b. unicode
   c. registry domain
   d. INCA

9. When using a search engine, a minus sign is an example of what?
   a. an exclusion operator
   b. an addition operator
   c. a mathematical operator
   d. an inclusion operator

10. A complete URL does *not* contain which of the following?
    a. protocol
    b. server
    c. path
    d. author

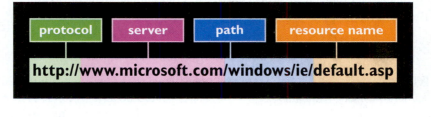

Fill-In

In the blanks provided, write the correct answer for each of the following.

1. A(n) _____ is a string of characters that precisely identifies an Internet resource's type and location.

2. A(n) _____ is a gateway that provides a conveniently organized subject guide to Internet content.

3. The _____ is a portion of the Internet that contains billions of documents.

4. _____ is the Internet standard that supports the exchange of information on the Web.

5. _____ provides a way for users to transfer files via the Internet.

6. _____ is unsolicited and unwanted e-mail.

7. _____ _____ _____ are companies that sell Internet accounts, which usually include a user name and a password.

8. _____ is exploiting bugs that cause your computer to crash, an antisocial behavior associated with IRC chat rooms.

9. A process called _____ enables individuals and organizations to register domain names with organizations such as InterNIC.

10. The Web is a(n) _____, a network-based content development system that uses multimedia resources, such as sounds, movies, and text as a means of navigation or illustration.

11. If you can't find what you are looking for using a Web subject guide, you can try a _____, a database that indexes many Web pages.

12. A browser's _____ records the Web pages that you've accessed.

13. _____ are underlined or highlighted words that you can click to bring another document into view.

14. A _____ _____ uses key words such as AND, OR, and NOT.

15. _____ is performed by typing several words of interest within quotation marks.

Short Answer

1. Describe your experiences with the Internet. Specifically, identify the browser and e-mail software applications that you have used. Have you used other Internet-related software? If you have, describe these applications.

2. Explain the difference between downloading and uploading files. Have you used the Internet to transfer files? What types of files did you transfer? What type of software did you use?

3. Do you submit any of your assignments electronically? That is, have you submitted an assignment to a "drop box," in the body of an e-mail message, or as an e-mail attachment? If you have, describe the method, the assignment, and the course in which you used electronic submissions.

4. What are some rules of thumb for evaluating content on the Web?

5. Now that you have completed this chapter, you should be able to conduct more effective searches. List three search engines that you frequently use and explain why you prefer these search engines over others.

Go to **www.prenhall.com/cayf2006** to review this chapter, answer the questions, and complete the exercises.

Teamwork

1. University Internet Access

Universities usually provide on-campus Internet connections along with free technical support. Some schools, such as Rutgers University in New Jersey, even provide students in on-campus housing with special cable channels that broadcast live review sessions for chemistry classes as well as other classes. In Penn State dorms, students have access to and can download (legally!) streaming music files that the school provides. But what if you live off campus? Contact your institution's computing services and see if they provide off-campus Internet connections. If they do provide this connectivity, do students pay an extra fee for this service, or is it funded by general student fees? If your school does not provide off-campus Internet access, how do you connect to the Internet, and what are the monthly fees? Have each team member explore a different question and write their individual answers. Once all of the team members have completed their work, combine your answers into a document that you will deliver to your professor.

2. Researching ISPs

Your team's task is to research various ISPs. Each team member should research one company (such as AOL, MSN, Yahoo!, etc.) Be sure to answer at least the following questions: What is the monthly or annual cost of the service? How many accounts can you create under your name? Why does the company say you should subscribe with them over others? Does it offer online storage? If so, how much? How would you feel about your Internet identity being associated with this provider? Write an informative and collaborative paper that answers these questions and that describes your experience.

3. Revisiting Web Sites

Explain the difference between a browser's history list and Favorites (Internet Explorer) or Bookmarks (Netscape Navigator). Have you used either one? Explain how you have used them. Did you know that you can place frequently visited Web sites in your Links Toolbar (Internet Explorer) or in your Personal Toolbar (Netscape Navigator)? Select one of these two browsers and explain how you can place links to Web sites in the appropriate toolbar. If you have never done this, use the browser's Help feature to learn how. Research the Web and your browser's Help utility to see what you can learn about manipulating the history and Favorites lists. You may to work together on this or assign various tasks to each member. Write a paper that meets your professor's specifications.

4. Using the Internet to Job Hunt

Use the Internet to find two potential jobs in the field of your current or intended major. Give the URLs of the sites that list the positions and describe each job—the organization, location, necessary qualifications, benefits, salary, and so on. Explain why you feel that your major coursework does or does not prepare you to assume either of these two positions. Share your papers with the team. Write a collaborative paper that summarizes your group's work.

5. Is Your E-Mail Really Free?

Several ISPs offer "free" e-mail. But we all know that nothing is truly free. Each team member should research at least one such provider and answer the following questions: Who is the provider? What do they offer? Are you required to allow them to advertise in each and every message you send? What type of advertisements will they use? How do you feel about having advertising included in each of your mail messages? Does the site offer a for-pay option to remove the advertising? Besides advertising, what other reasons do you think the ISP has for offering you free e-mail? Write an informative and collaborative paper that answers these questions and that describes your experience.

On the Web

1. Internet Statistics

The speed at which the Internet is growing is phenomenal, and the total number of users can only be estimated. To compare the growth of the Internet with that of other media, visit the Computer Almanac site at **www-2.cs.cmu.edu/afs/ cs.cmu.edu/user/bam/www/numbers.html**. This site is an online treasury of statistical information about computers. How many years did it take radio to have 50 million listeners? How many years did it take television to achieve 50 million viewers? How many years did it take the Web to reach 50 million U.S. users? (This is a lengthy Web site, so use your browser's find on page feature to search for "50 million.")

2. Internet2 Near You

Internet2, or I2, is a collaborative effort among educational institutions, government agencies, and computer and telecommunications companies to increase Internet bandwidth. Visit the I2 site at **www.internet2.edu**. Presently, how many university members are there? Does your school belong to I2? If not, locate and identify the nearest institution that does. What are the annual membership fees and estimated annual institutional costs to participate in I2? What are the annual membership fees and estimated annual corporate partnership costs to partici- pate in I2? Name two corporate partners and two corporate sponsors. In addition to I2, the U.S. government also sponsors its own advanced Internet initiative. Identify this initiative and list two governmental agencies that participate in it and in I2.

3. Register a Domain Name

Have you ever thought about getting your own domain name? What would you like it to be? Visit the site **register.com** and try different top-level domain names (.com, .net, .org, and so on) to see if they're available. If they are, what is the annual registration cost? If the domain names are already taken, who owns them, when did they acquire them, and when do they expire? What is the minimum bid amount that can be offered to purchase domain names?

4. Online Gaming

Locate a few sites that offer online gaming. You might start out by typing "computer games" or "online games" into your favorite search engine or you could go to the games link at Yahoo! or visit **www.pogo.com**. Write a short paper that answers the following questions about the sites you have visited: Can you play games without registering? Did the registration process require you to give up your e-mail address? If so, what do you think they will do with it? Roughly how many people were on the site with you at the same time? (Hundreds, thousands, more?) Did you play games? Which ones? Can you think of why people might become addicted to playing online games?

5. Term Papers for Sale

Use the search techniques discussed in this chapter to locate two sites that sell research or term papers. Identify the URLs of these sites, describe how to find a paper on a specific topic, and find out how much it costs to purchase a paper. Do these sites post any disclaimers about students using their papers? Do they provide sample papers? If so, what is the quality of the paper? Do you know anyone who has purchased an online paper? Discuss the ethics of using one of these sites to purchase a research or term paper.

Creating an E-mail Filter to Fight Spam

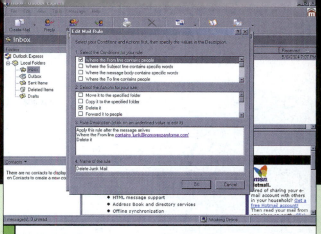

FIGURE 2.32 Outlook enables you to create a custom e-mail filter to help block spam.

Most e-mail clients, including Microsoft's Outlook and Outlook Express, allow you to designate a series of rules that are applied to each and every e-mail message you receive. Outlook Express is installed as a utility to the Windows operating system. Access it from the Start, All Programs menu sequence. If an e-mail message matches any of the rules you have defined, it can be automatically deleted or stored in a folder for you to review at a later date. Building custom e-mail filters can be tedious, but it can also be a great last line of defense against spam if you or your ISP are currently not running automated spam blocking software. In addition to filtering spam, you can also use custom filters to automatically sort and organize your e-mail messages. You can set up a series of rules to automatically put e-mails from friends in one folder, work in another folder, and family in yet another. The following steps will walk you through the process of creating a custom e-mail filter using Microsoft Outlook Express 6 running on Windows XP.

1. Launch Microsoft Outlook Express.

2. From the "Tools" menu, choose "Message Rules" and then select "Mail . . ." If you have never defined any filtering rules, a window titled "New Mail Rule" (similar to the window "Edit Mail Rule" in Figure 2.32) will appear. This window contains four distinct areas that allow you to set the criteria for your e-mail filter. If you have defined mail rules in the past, a window titled "Message Rules" will appear and display your existing rules. You can choose to modify or create a new rule by clicking the appropriate button on the right-hand side of the window.

3. The first section is titled "Select the Conditions for your rule." Here you can identify what part of the e-mail message Outlook should search to find your filtering pattern. You can choose to search areas such as the sender's e-mail address (the "From" line), the subject line, the body of the message, or the recipient's e-mail address (the "To" line). Take some time to look through this list and be sure you are selecting items that are appropriate for your filter. You can select more than one item from this list.

The example in Figure 2.32 shows that Outlook will search only the "From" line of all incoming e-mails. Checking the "From" line option allows you to filter your mail based upon the sender's e-mail address.

4. The next item to select is the action to take once a match is found. The second section, titled "Select the Actions for your rule," provides a long list of possibilities. Probably the most commonly used option, demonstrated in Figure 2.32, is to immediately delete any messages that match your filtering pattern. If you are setting up a filter to help automatically sort and organize your mail, at this point you could select the option "Move it to the specified folder."

5. Once you've identified where to look for a pattern and what to do once a pattern is successfully matched, you now must proceed to the next section, which is where you actually define the pattern used to filter your e-mail messages. If you followed the previous steps, you should see a hyperlink (blue underlined text) in the area just below the title "Rule Description." Click on that link to open up a new window where you can identify the pattern or patterns that you would like to use to filter your mail. In the example provided in Figure 2.32, the filter is only looking for one e-mail address. Outlook will automatically delete any mail received from the address **junk@nomorespamforme.com**.

6. The final step is to name your filter in the "Name of the rule" section. Be sure to use a descriptive title such as "Delete Junk Mail" or "File E-mail From Friends," because you will probably build many filters over time.

7. Once you are happy with how you have configured your filter, press OK. Any future e-mails received from the address **junk@nomorespamforme.com** will now be automatically deleted.

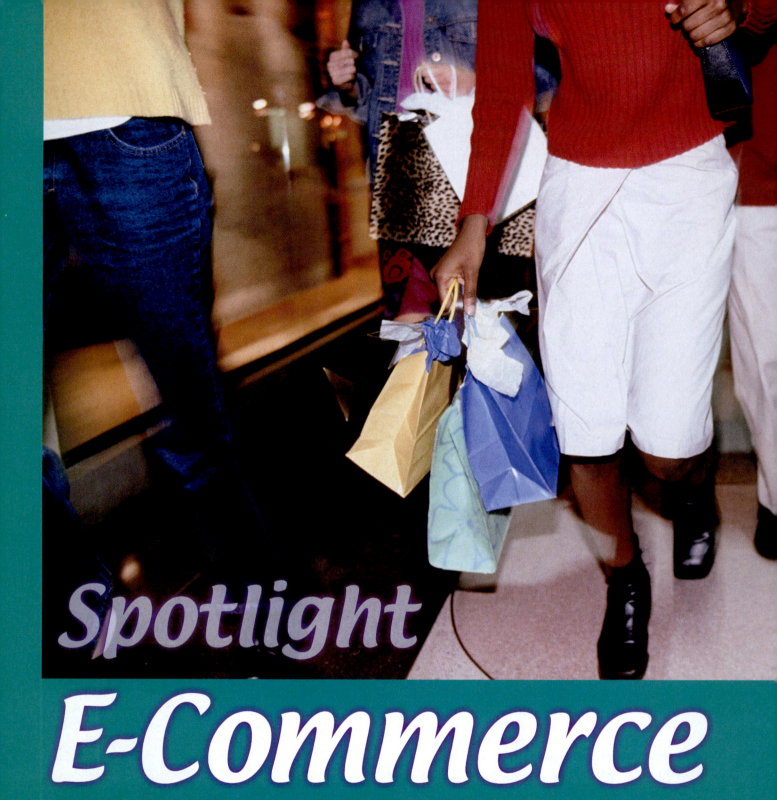

Spotlight

E-Commerce

What do you want to buy online today? Many e-tailers (Web-based retailers) hope you're asking yourself this question. Online merchants sell books, CDs, clothes, and just about anything else you might want to buy. If you buy online, you're one of millions engaging in e-commerce.

Figure 2A

E-commerce has become accessible to anyone with an Internet connection and a Web browser.

Commerce is the selling of goods and/or services with the expectation of making a reasonable profit. **Electronic commerce**, or **e-commerce**, is the use of networks or the Internet to carry out business of any type. E-commerce supports many types of traditional business transactions, including buying, selling, renting, borrowing, and lending.

E-commerce isn't new; companies have used networks to do business with suppliers for years. What is new is that, thanks to the Internet and inexpensive PCs, e-commerce has become accessible to anyone with an Internet connection and a Web browser (Figure 2A).

Increasingly, Internet users are shopping, banking and paying bills, trading stocks, and utilizing other services online. In total dollars, e-commerce is still in its infancy—currently, 99 percent of retail sales occur in traditional brick-and-mortar stores—but it's growing. Between 2002 and 2003, U.S. retail e-commerce sales grew by 25 percent. By 2009, online retail sales are expected to reach 7 percent of total U.S. sales. According to one Microsoft Corporation executive, within a generation—25 to 30 years—approximately one-third of all consumer transactions will occur over the Internet.

In this Spotlight, you will explore three types of e-commerce: business-to-business (B2B), consumer-to-consumer (C2C), and business-to-consumer (B2C).

83

BUSINESS-TO-BUSINESS E-COMMERCE

Although most people think of online shopping when they hear the term *e-commerce*, much of the growth of e-commerce involves business-to-business transactions. **Business-to-business (B2B) e-commerce** occurs when a business uses the Internet to provide another business with the materials, services, and/or supplies it needs to conduct its operations. According to International Data Corporation (IDC), global B2B e-commerce amounted to about $1.4 trillion in 2003, a 75 percent increase from 2002.

Even though as a consumer you might not engage in B2B, you'll probably recognize many of the industries and companies that do. Some of the different industries engaged in B2B include agriculture, health care, aerospace and defense, real estate, automotive, and construction, as well as familiar computer and software companies such as Dell, IBM, and Microsoft.

In addition, many traditional and online retailers have special B2B units. For example, the popular office supplies chain Staples has a B2B division that operates the Web site StaplesLink.com, which services over 14,000 companies and 3.3 million individual users (Figure 2B). The B2B unit has been experiencing steady growth for the last 3 years, with annual sales of $1 billion. The Staples B2B division works with business customers to help them control costs.

Unlike B2B, you may have engaged in the next type of e-commerce: consumer-to-consumer.

CONSUMER-TO-CONSUMER E-COMMERCE

Consumer-to-consumer (C2C) e-commerce is the online exchange or trade of goods, services, or information between individual consumers. C2C often involves the use of an intermediary such as eBay—the most popular online auction destination. eBay puts buyers in contact with nearly 1 million sellers worldwide. The site holds more than 10 million electronic auctions per month (Figure 2C). Other C2C sites include Yahoo! Auctions and Amazon.com Auctions.

Perhaps one of the most difficult parts of C2C e-commerce is the awkwardness in the timing of the exchange. Do you send the goods and then wait for the other person to send the money? Or, do you send the money and then trust that the other person will send the goods? As online auctions have grown in popularity, fraud has also increased. Many auction participants get ripped off each day.

So, what can you do to protect yourself? Perhaps the most important thing you can do is to arm yourself with as much information and understanding of the auction process as possible. This includes knowing what you are bidding on, knowing the maximum value that you are willing to pay (you can do pricing research on the auction site or through a general search of the Web), and knowing what the terms and conditions of the sale are. You should also try to find out as much as you can about the seller and his or her feedback rating and pay with a credit card whenever possible.

Figure 2B
StaplesLink.com provides Staples with a very strong B2B presence.

If you intend to sell something on an auction site, you need to find out what it will cost to register with the site, what it will cost per sales transaction, and any terms or conditions that may exist for using the auction site. You will also need to provide an accurate description of what you are offering for sale and a digital photo of the item (perhaps from different perspectives and including some form of size reference such as a ruler or other object of known size). When you receive e-mail inquiries during the bidding process, you should respond quickly. As soon as the bidding closes, you should contact the highest bidder. Finally, you should take care in packing the item for shipping and you should ship it as soon as possible after the sale.

C2C e-commerce makes up more than one-third of all e-commerce. Total retail e-commerce transactions in the United States amounted to some $45 billion in 2003. Of that, approximately $15 billion in transactions was attributed to the C2C giant eBay. In fact, eBay's listings of auction items grew by 51 percent between 2001 and 2002 to over 632 million items.

Just as you can have fun and enjoy yourself in everyday storefront shopping experiences, online auctions and other C2C shopping venues can be fun as well. Many users of online auctions clearly enjoy the hustle and bustle of bidding and of becoming a part of the online trading community. Most online auction sites have message boards that help collectors and buyers learn from others. These sites include FAQs (Frequently Asked Questions) and often provide an area for threaded discussion groups.

In the next section, you will learn about companies that use the Internet as a part of their business strategy.

BUSINESS-TO-CONSUMER E-COMMERCE

Business-to-consumer (B2C) e-commerce occurs when a business uses the Internet to supply consumers with services, information, and/or products. B2C is essentially the same as shopping at a physical store—you have a need or want, and the marketplace offers products and solutions. The primary difference is that B2C e-commerce is not place or time specific, which means that you don't have to be in any particular place at any particular time in order to participate. This freedom of time and place enables you to shop whenever you wish and to choose from more products and services than could ever be assembled in one place.

ONLINE SHOPPING

In 2003, nearly two-thirds of Web users bought something online; and this percentage is growing each year. In 2000, only 36 percent of Internet users had made such purchases. What's more, nearly three-quarters of Internet users researched potential purchases using the Internet, even if they subsequently bought the items from a bricks-and-mortar store.

Getting Good Deals Online
Have you ever tried to comparison shop on the Web? After surfing at 10 different sites (or more!), it can be daunting to keep track of where you saw the best price on that new digital camera you want. You

Figure 2C
eBay is the most well-known C2C trading site.

might want to turn to shopping portals such as Shopping.com, BizRate.com, Froogle.com, and others. These sites help you conduct price and product comparisons. They also offer reviews on just about any product you can imagine (Figure 2D). You can search and sort by brand, price range, or product rating. To save even more, you can also check sites that offer coupons and rebates, such as dealcatcher.com and FatWallet.com.

What kinds of shopping can you do online? Just about any kind you can imagine—even your groceries.

Online Grocery Shopping

Companies such as Peapod.com and Netgrocer.com provide online grocery and sundries shopping. Initially, that may sound crazy. Why would anyone want to buy groceries over the Internet? Well, if you've got lots of money and can afford to pay for the savings in the time and inconvenience of traditional shopping trips, online grocery shopping may be for you. In fact, online grocery shopping accounted for over $1.3 billion in revenues in 2002.

Once you start looking at the concept more closely, it doesn't sound so crazy. For the price of a good bottle of wine, you can select your groceries from an online grocery store and have them delivered to your home. What's more, the online supermarket "remembers" your last grocery list, so you can see what you bought the last time—and will probably need to buy again. You can even set up recurrent transactions so that you receive needed perishables, such as milk and eggs, on a fixed schedule. Some online supermarkets even offer budgeting, automatically tracking your expenditures so that you can stay within the limits you've set.

Peapod.com, for example, offers grocery delivery in several U.S. metropolitan areas (Figure 2E). Peapod works with local grocery store retailers to select and pack grocery orders in temperature-controlled bins. The bins are delivered to customer's homes in trucks that Peapod leases. Peapod allows customers to choose the time and date of delivery—an important matter for people with busy schedules. Some consumers have found one very important advantage to online grocery shopping: It cuts down on impulse buying.

Online grocery stores can be broken down into two groups: pure play (there is not a physical store that you can visit) and partnerships (there is a bricks-and-mortar store as well as an online presence). Most of the pure-play start-ups have gone out of business due to the large overhead required to warehouse large

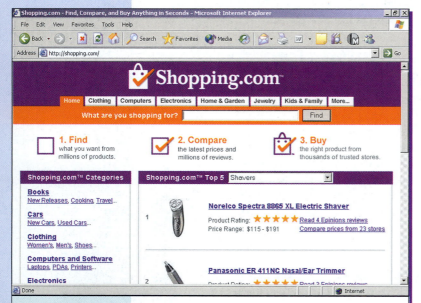

Figure 2D
Shopping portals such as Shopping.com help you conduct price and product comparisons. They also offer reviews on just about any product you can imagine.

Figure 2E
Peapod.com offers grocery delivery in several U.S. metropolitan areas.

numbers of items that may or may not sell. Some of the pure-play companies that tried and failed include Webvan, Streamline, Homegrocer, and Shoplink. Peapod was able to transform itself from a pure play to a partnership by buying out a bricks-and-mortar grocery chain and then layering its Internet presence over the chain's distribution area.

Conversely, traditional grocery stores are now developing a Web presence. In this case, instead of layering the Internet over a traditional store, the traditional store is layering itself with the Internet. For instance, Albertsons.com and Safeway.com provide online shopping and delivery in select areas. Online grocery shopping isn't for everyone, but it may become an integral part of the mix of shopping options. Many other businesses are concluding that they must have an Internet presence or they'll soon be out of business.

THE DOT-COM PHENOMENON

Much e-commerce occurs in the *dot-com world,* the universe of Web sites with the suffix *.com* appended to their names. This unique world has only been in existence since 1995. Before 1995, companies were not able to sell over the Internet. But in 1995, the government eliminated all taxpayer funding of the Internet and opened it up to commercial development. The period between 1995 and 2000 is referred to as the *dot-com boom.*

As the dot-com crash of 2000 made painfully clear, not every online business is able to succeed. The dot-com bubble blew up so quickly because existing businesses and start-ups found that it was fairly easy and relatively inexpensive to establish a Web presence. Many companies grew to hundreds of employees and millions of dollars in revenues as customers decided to give online buying a try. The problem was that many of their business plans failed to materialize because their customer base was not sustainable. For example, Pets.com, with its sock-puppet dog mascot, couldn't seem to find the niche of customers who would buy pet food and supplies online. The company claimed losses of $147 million by September of 2000 and couldn't raise additional funds to stay in business. Even though the company had more than 570,000 customers and ran high-profile and expensive TV ads during the Super Bowl, Pets.com was just one of hundreds—if not thousands—of dot-com companies that went out of business during the big bust.

A dot-com company that has held its ground and become profitable is Amazon.com (Figure 2F). Books, it seems, are a commodity that is well-suited for online trade. Amazon.com has built into the book-buying process a plethora of added benefits to entice buyers to access, shop, and complete their sales online. It offers professional book reviews, peer reviews, author matching, subject matching, and, in some cases, sample chapters. To top it all off, Amazon.com has offered free shipping for the past couple of years, and will most likely continue to do so.

It seems that B2C e-commerce ventures fail when they attempt to bring traditional retailing concepts— face-to-face immediate customer service; the ability to examine the look, feel, and functionality of a product in person; and immediate possession after purchase—to the Internet. Business experts believe that part of the problem lies in the fear of poor customer service: Would-be customers are afraid something will go wrong with their order and they won't be able to talk to anyone about it.

Figure 2F
Amazon.com provides both breadth and depth of products and services.

For this reason, **click-and-brick** stores—retailers that have both an online and a traditional retail store presence, such as Circuit City, Best Buy, and Wal-Mart—are winning consumer confidence. Why? Shoppers can return products locally if there's something wrong with an online order. In addition, customers like to use the Internet to research products before they make a purchase. Although fewer than 3 percent of new car sales are made online, more than 40 percent of new car buyers research their purchase on the Internet.

Some Web sites also rely on advertising to generate revenue. You've probably seen digital billboards, called banner ads, peppered on the Web pages you visit (Figure 2G). In fact, if you spend any time on the Web at all, it is nearly impossible to avoid them. How do these ads work? When you click a banner ad, you're taken to another page or site. When the page loads onto your screen, it electronically records how you arrived there. The advertising company then gives the site from which you clicked anywhere from a penny to as much as $50 if a sale occurs as a result of your click.

Another common way for a site to earn money is to become a "sponsored" site. Sponsors often are large companies that agree to provide financial assistance to small companies or organizations in exchange for advertising space on their

site. So, although they can be annoying, banner ads do serve a purpose on the Web.

The Web won't come close to taking over traditional stores for other reasons as well. Most people enjoy the instant gratification of obtaining their purchased item at a store. In addition, shipping costs often make Web purchases more expensive than items purchased offline. Also, the cost of shipping large items—big-screen televisions, refrigerators, and most furniture—can negate any price discount offered on the Web.

If one word could sum up what B2C and C2C sites share, it would be **disintermediation**, the process of removing an intermediary—for example, a bookseller, car salesperson, or auctioneer—and providing a customer with direct access to information and products. B2C and C2C sites put customers in direct contact with incredibly rich sources of information. They enable customers to make their own choices without being bothered with a salesperson's interference.

Building Your Own Online Business

One of the tremendous advantages of B2C e-commerce is the low capital investment needed to start an online business. For less than $1,000, a person can open a Web storefront and start selling products online. In contrast, a bricks-and-mortar business requires land, a building, utility costs, display shelving, and salespeople. A Web-based storefront only requires an ISP, a Web site, a Web site administrator, and the ability to ship goods or services to customers.

The first thing you need to do when starting any business is to develop a business plan (Figure 2H). You must decide what product(s) to offer, who your target market is, and how many items you plan to sell and at what price. Who will pay for shipping? Will there be service provided after the sale? Who are your competitors? What profit margin do you expect to achieve?

All businesses need to have a name, and an online business is no different, except that the online business's name is almost always the same as its Web site or domain name. So, once you've completed your business plan you will need to shop for a domain name. Perhaps the easiest way to accomplish this is to go to **register.com**. You will most likely want a name with a .com extension. Try to pick a name that will be easy for your customers to remember.

Figure 2G
Banner ads help Web sites generate revenue.

In a traditional business, the owner needs to select a building site, develop the company logo and identity, manage the inventory, and provide customer service. For your online business, someone will need to create the Web pages that will make up your Web site, which is a potentially time-consuming and complex process (Figure 2I). In many cases, a professional Web designer can be a great help in developing and maintaining a site. When developing a Web site, you will need to consider the design of the site, budgeting adequate time and money for site development, advertising the site, and ongoing site maintenance. At a minimum, the Web site will need a home page, product pages, and a page for taking orders.

You may also wish to employ an electronic shopping cart. This feature is much like the physical shopping cart you'd use at a grocery store. It remembers your customer's order items and provides the results to the summary order page. Your Web page should be designed and managed in such a way that it projects professionalism so that your customers will have confidence in your product or service. Go to **goodpractices.com** for some Web site development guidelines.

Now that you've gotten your name and developed the Web pages for your Web site, you will need to make arrangements for Web hosting. Web hosting services provide server space, make your site available to the public, and offer site management utilities such as preprogrammed shopping cart services. There are thousands of Web hosting companies. Register.com is a good place to start your search for a Web host, or you may wish to type "Web hosting" into your favorite search engine. Expect to pay a start-up fee as well as a monthly amount that is usually based on a one-year contract.

You can ensure that your site gets listed with search engines by visiting each engine's Web site (**google.com**, **yahoo.com**, **dogpile.com**, **msn.com**, and so on) and searching for "submitting my site." Provide the information requested, and when someone searches for keywords that match your site, it will be one of the sites that is provided in the search results answer screen.

Figure 2H
Sites such as Entrepreneur.com can help get your small business plan off to a good start.

Figure 2I
For your online business, someone will need to create the Web pages for your Web site. Do-it-yourselfers can find design tips and guidelines for developing a Web storefront.

To operate a business, you need a way to receive payments. Just like in a traditional retail business, perhaps the best option may be to take credit cards. You should be aware that there are many costs involved with setting up and maintaining a credit card acceptance account—but the benefits may well outweigh the costs. Customers are comfortable using their credit cards online and many feel more secure knowing that the credit card company is there in case of a dispute or fraudulent use.

Using an online payment transaction company such as PayPal may also be a good solution (Figure 2J). PayPal manages over 40 million accounts worldwide. Transaction fees range from 2 to 3 percent and there is a per-transaction fee of about 30 cents per transaction. The benefits to such a solution include the relatively easy setup on their site (no local installation is needed), the instant recording of transactions, a resource center with tools and links to help you grow your business, and a fraud protection policy that protects you from those who would attempt to take advantage of the transaction process.

All businesses need monthly and annual reports to know where they stand and where they are headed, so one of the utilities you should look for in a Web host is the ability to obtain back-end reports. These reports will tell you how many "hits" your site has had, when the site has the most traffic, what your total sales volume is, and a variety of other important information.

Here's a bonus. Go to **Smallbusiness .yahoo.com**. Yahoo! will help you set up and then host a trial business site for 30 days—for free (Figure 2K)! You might try setting up a pseudo-business just to see how all the pieces fit together.

Figure 2J
You can accept credit card payments on your site using services such as PayPal.

ONLINE TRAVEL RESERVATIONS

Another area of e-commerce experiencing rapid growth is online travel reservations. Sites such as CheapTickets.com and Expedia.com enable leisure travelers to book flights, hotels, and car rentals online, as well as find the cheapest fares based on their trip parameters (Figure 2L). Most travel sites provide e-tickets so that you can quickly check in at airport terminals by using small self-service kiosks. In fact, e-tickets cost $10 to $15 less than standard paper tickets.

In addition, nearly every hotel and car rental agency is now online, which means you can check room or car availability and book a reservation without making a single call. And if you're looking for backpacking trails at a national park, you're sure to find plenty of free information using any search engine. Travel and travel-related sites not only simplify your trip planning and booking, but also save you money.

Expedia.com, for example, provides a very rich booking experience. You can use features that compare fares and then keep a running total price summary as you add hotels, cars, and entertainment packages to your trip. You can set options for Expedia.com to remember who you are by taking advantage of the My Travel and Express Purchase features. You can also make use of vacation and cruise wizards that will walk you through the process of developing the best options for your excursion. All of these

Figure 2K
Smallbusiness.yahoo.com *can help you get started with your business Web presence.*

technologies make a sometimes complex and expensive process work to your advantage.

Expedia.com has recently branched out into corporate travel services. Online booking of corporate travel accounted for only 9 percent of all corporate travel reservations in 2002. Expedia's CEO estimates that online corporate travel bookings will reach 40 to 60 percent by 2010. In addition to online travel booking, Expedia.com also offers corporations 24-hour access to travel agents with whom they can book reservations over the phone, a feature not offered to leisure travelers who use the site. Expedia.com hopes to compete well against traditional corporate travel agencies by offering lower fees and better service. However, 80 percent of business travelers book their own travel, with half of them doing it online. If this trend continues, it does not bode well for Expedia.com's new corporate travel division.

Personal online travel booking does have some drawbacks. Online travel sites get revenues from advertising on their Web pages as well as kickbacks and fees that are charged to the airlines, car rental agencies, hotel chains, and entertainment venues. While this is almost always advantageous to the consumer, other businesses have been greatly affected. As more and more consumers use the Web to do their own travel booking, the offline travel agency business continues to decline. It seems that the use of the electronic middleman is making the traditional travel agent obsolete.

ONLINE BANKING

Online banking enables you to use a Web browser to access your accounts, balance your checkbook, transfer funds, and even pay bills online (Figure 2M). In fact, nearly 7 percent of Americans used online banking services by the end of 2002. The use of online banking is expected to grow 14 percent per year by the end of 2007. By that time, some 30 percent of Americans (67 million individuals) will be using online banking services. Currently, banks that offer online banking gain a competitive advantage over those that do not, because most customers now consider it a necessary and expected service, like ATMs. What else is in it for banks? Plenty. Online banking helps banks cut down on the expenses of maintaining bank

Figure 2L
Sites such as Expedia.com are popular because they help travelers find the cheapest fares and reservations available.

branches and paying tellers and also allows them to provide advanced levels of electronic customer service.

Banks implement online banking in different ways. One method makes use of personal finance programs such as Microsoft Money or Intuit's Quicken, enabling customers to balance their checkbooks automatically. An advantage of this to customers is that Microsoft Money and Quicken offer powerful features for budgeting and analyzing spending habits. The drawback of this method, however, is that you can only access your online bank account from the computer that holds all the Money or Quicken data.

Easier online banking tools are Web-based systems that require only one program: a Web browser. All the data are stored on the bank's computer, not your own, which means that you can access your account from any computer connected to the Internet. Although Web-based online banking doesn't offer the advanced budgeting and analysis features that Money and Quicken do, it's much easier to use because you are directly manipulating your accounts online instead of recording copies of your work in offline programs.

Figure 2M
Online banking enables customers to access their accounts, balance checkbooks, and even pay bills online.

Figure 2N
Some sites, such as Bankrate.com, provide helpful overviews of online banking.

Besides the convenience of doing your banking from home, online banking relieves you from hand-writing checks (and buying stamps!). Online banking is also cheap—many banks offer online banking for free. Some banks, such as Chase, even offer customers cash incentives to try online bill paying. However, online banking is not trouble-free. If you switch banks, it can be a time-consuming hassle to switch from one bank's online system to another. You also have to be aware that when you pay a bill online, the money is deducted from your account much more quickly than with offline bill paying. You can research online banking on sites such as Bankrate.com (Figure 2N).

However, the biggest concern for most people is security. Many people who would like to use online banking are concerned about losing their money. As long as you follow certain precautions, you have little need for concern. In fact, you are 10 percent less likely to have your personal information stolen using online versus offline bill paying. When you access a bank account online, be sure you're doing so in your browser's secure mode. In **secure mode**, the browser scrambles and encodes the data when it communicates with the bank's server. Check your browser's documentation to find out where the secure mode icon appears and what it looks like. Above all else, keep your password safe.

Another concern is the security of the bank's **electronic vault**, the server that stores account holders' information. Because no computer system is totally secure, it's reasonable to be concerned that an intruder could gain access to the vault and steal your money. Still, the threat is minor. Online banks use state-of-the-art security systems, including measures such as **active monitoring**, in which a security team constantly monitors the vault for signs of unauthorized access.

ONLINE STOCK TRADING

Online stock trading (also referred to as e-trading) is the purchase or sale of stock through the Internet. In use only since 1996, online stock trading now accounts for one out of every six stock trades, easily making it the fastest-growing application in B2C e-commerce. Offering secure connections through the customer's Web browser, online stock trading sites enable investors to buy and sell stocks online without the aid of a broker (Figure 2O).

The attraction of online stock trading can be summed up in one word: cost. Traditional, full-service brokerages charge up to $100 per trade; discount brokerages charge about $50. But the most aggressive e-traders have cut the charges to $10 per trade or less. E-traders, such as E*TRADE and Ameritrade, can offer such low prices because the trading is automatic—no human broker is involved.

However, many potential online investors are concerned with security and timeliness. The issue of making secure online trades isn't really any different from the general issue of online security. All financial institutions use secure connections. This doesn't mean that transactions can't be intercepted or redirected, but millions of dollars are transacted online every day without incident. Online trading of stocks is regulated by the Securities and Exchange Commission (SEC) in the same way other methods of trading are. Most brokerages use trade confirmation methods that help to ensure that all trades are transacted properly.

Timeliness is an issue only if there is a delay in completing a transaction that causes you to miss an opportunity. Delays can be caused by power outages, dropped connections, computer overloads, and batch processing. Despite these occasional delays, however, most online transactions take place in a timely manner.

According to investment professionals, online trading does have a disadvantage. Online trading appeals to an amateur investor's worst instincts—namely, buying when the market is at its peak of enthusiasm (and prices are also at their peak) and then selling when prices start to drop. This translates to buying high and selling low. You don't make money that way; you lose money. That's true even when, overall, the market is going up. Most investment counselors believe that amateurs are well advised to avoid frequent trading (sometimes called day trading). Also, when the market plunges, electronic investors often receive a rude shock: due to overloaded Internet servers, they can't unload their stocks until the market hits bottom.

NONRETAIL ONLINE SERVICES

Many nonretail sites provide dating services; credit reports; health and medical advice; news, weather, and sports information; real estate listings (for homes and apartments); and insurance products (for car or home) (Figure 2P). These sites offer various levels of access and services for members and nonmembers. Some services, such as insurance quotes, up-to-the-minute news reports, and severe weather alerts are free. You can also post dating profiles or receive diet

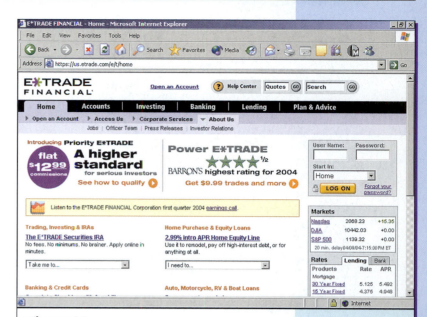

Figure 20
E-trading sites enable investors to buy and sell stocks online without going through a traditional broker.

and other health-related profiles, as well as trial passes for sports subscriptions. Many news and newspaper sites give you free access to some online content, but you must pay for additional content, such as archived articles. You can also subscribe to e-mailed newsletters on health, sports, and other related topics.

AVOIDING E-COMMERCE HAZARDS

Although there are many benefits to engaging in e-commerce, it also entails risks. These risks include identity theft, personal information exposure, money loss, and being ripped-off by unscrupulous charlatans. To protect yourself you should carefully create user names and passwords, particularly at sites where you must pay for goods or services. You should avoid e-commerce with little-known companies, at least until you've taken the opportunity to check their legitimacy. You can check on shopping portals how other shoppers rate a new retailer before buying from one. Even though you are most likely protected from monetary losses by your credit card company, you should always be careful when giving out your credit card information, and you should only do so on secure sites. Never share credit card or account numbers or user name and password information with others; even if you receive an e-mail requesting that information from what seems to be a legitimate source. Some of the things you should look for on a secure site (one that is protected from intrusion of your personal business by others) are the *https://* protocol in the address of the site instead of the usual *http://*. The added "s" stands for "secure site." Other things you can look for are the VeriSign logo, the golden lock symbol, or a logo from other site-security entities such as Verified by Visa. Another security alert is a message box that indicates "You are entering (or leaving) a secure Website."

Sometimes you will find that the seller is a person just like you—that they don't have the ability to take credit cards

and they have set up an account with an online transaction processing system such as PayPal. It is the seller who decides which vendor to use for the goods/payment transaction. For instance, if you see the PayPal logo on an eBay auction item site, it means that you can use PayPal as a payment option. In fact, sometimes this is the only option available. The PayPal Web site even offers a tool to help you manage your buying experience. The PayPal AuctionFinder searches eBay for items you've recently won and prefills your payment form with details taken straight from the item listing. With AuctionFinder, you can eliminate errors and pay for your items instantly. Always use extra care and caution whenever you conduct financial transactions on the Internet.

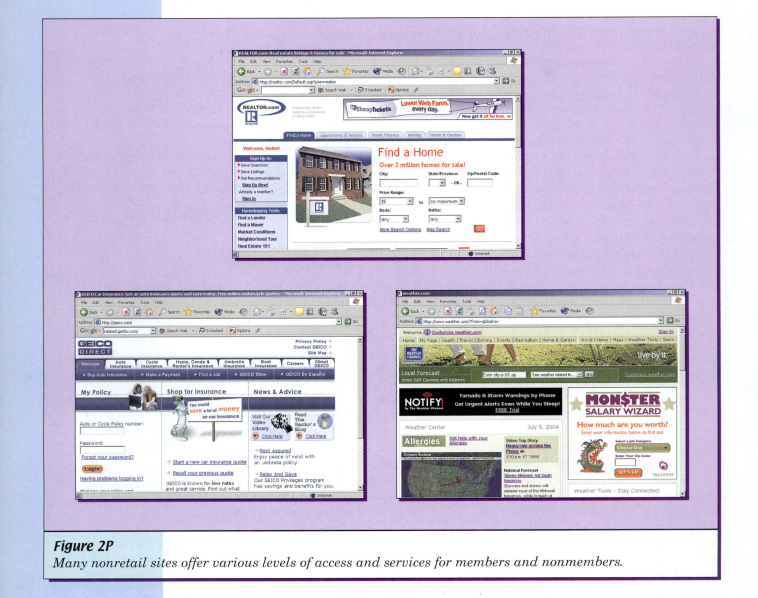

Figure 2P
Many nonretail sites offer various levels of access and services for members and nonmembers.

SPOTLIGHT EXERCISES

1. Use your browser to go to **peapod.com**. Choose the link for *New to Peapod* and then select the link to *Groceries for your Home*. Type in your zipcode to see if Peapod is available in your area. If it is not, then type in zipcode 20010 which is the Washington D.C. shopping area. Browse through the online store and write down the name and price of at least 5 products. Now use local newspaper ads or a trip to the local grocery store to compare the pricing of the online goods. Factoring in delivery costs, which shopping method is the most economical (include the cost of fuel and time to go to the local store). Would you shop for groceries online? Why or why not?

2. Have you purchased an item from a merchant over the Internet? Describe the item, the merchant, and the method of payment. Would you use the Internet to make another purchase? Explain why or why not.

3. Type the word *travel* into your favorite search engine's search window. Choose a travel link that will allow you to book a flight. Work through the site's dialog boxes in order to book a mock trip to a tropical destination. Write down the cost, connections, and total travel time. Now go back to the search engine and choose a competing travel site and repeat the process. How much difference in cost, connections, and travel time do you find? Try booking one of the trips on different days of the week to see if there is a difference. Finally, list the cheapest itinerary you can find. Would you travel for the cheapest rate or would you choose another option. Why?

4. Are you in the mood to do a little shopping? Visit eBay at **ebay.com** and track the sale of an item. Select and describe an item that you wish to purchase. There are two methods for finding your item.

   - You can select a general category and then refine your search by selecting successive subcategories.
   - You can enter a description of the item in the search textbox and then click the Search button.

   Try both methods. Which method do you prefer? How many items met your criteria? If the number is too large, refine your criteria. View the list of items and sellers, and select a specific item. Identify the item, the seller, the first bid, the current bid, the bid increment, the number of bids, and the amount of time left in the auction. Click the bid history link, and identify the bidders and how many bids they have submitted. Click the "Read feedback reviews" link to see the seller's rating. What is the seller's overall number of positive, neutral, and negative ratings? Based on buyer activity and the seller's profile, determine the amount of money that you would initially bid for this item. Track the bidding of this item until the auction closes, increasing your imagined bid as necessary. When the auction ends, determine whether you would have been the successful bidder. If not, what was your maximum bid? What was the final bid? Would you consider actually bidding for items in an online auction? Explain why you would or would not use an Internet auction to sell or purchase an item.

5. Online stock trading is one of the fastest-growing applications in consumer-based e-commerce. To see why, visit E*TRADE, one of the most popular online trading sites, at **www.etrade.com**. What were the last levels of the NASDAQ, DJIA, S&P 500, and 30-year bonds? Although you will not formally open an account online, look at the steps that are needed to open one. (Enter the requested information, but don't accept the agreement!) What personal information is needed? What information is needed to create your investment profile? How do you feel about this? How much does it charge per transaction? What is its annual fee? Would you trust it? Why or why not?

6. For this exercise, you will create your own business Web site. Use whichever tools you wish (a word processor's Web page design wizard, Yahoo!'s free Web site development section, and so on) to create a home page and at least two other linked pages. Your site does not need to have a registered name, but your home page should clearly identify your business. Post your completed site to the Web and then provide your instructor with the address.

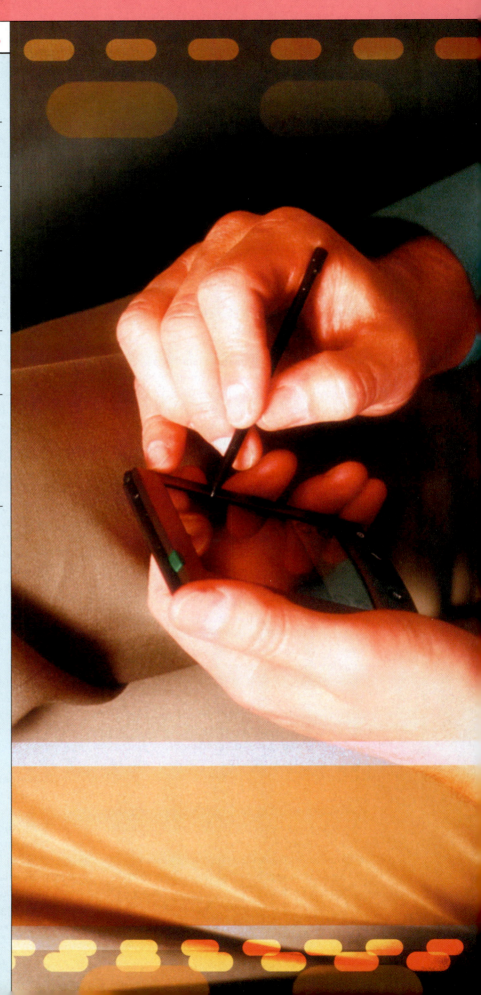

What You'll Learn . . .

- Define *bandwidth* and discuss the bandwidth needs of typical users.

- Discuss how modems transform digital computer signals into analog signals.

- List transmission media and explain several transmission methods.

- Explain the limitations of the public switched telephone network (PSTN) for sending and receiving computer data.

- Describe multiplexing and digital telephony, including their impact on line usage.

- Provide examples of how digitization and convergence are blurring the boundaries that distinguish popular communications devices, including phones and computers.

- Discuss various wired and wireless applications.

Wired & Wireless Communication

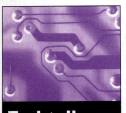

Techtalk

baud rate
You may encounter the term *baud rate* when a modem's data transfer rate is discussed. The baud rate is the maximum number of changes that can occur per second in the communications channel. Note that the technical definitions of baud rate and bps rate differ. The correct measurement of a modem's data transfer rate is the bps rate.

Suppose you're on a trip but left your laptop at home and need to access your e-mail. No problem; you just use your Web-enabled cell phone to retrieve your messages. As for sending e-mail messages back, again, no problem; you can do this with most messaging devices. Back at home, you hop on your ultra-fast DSL connection to download and upload files. The whole time, you're experiencing the realities of **connectivity**. Defined broadly, this term refers to the ability to link various media and devices. Connectivity enhances communications and improves access to information. In this chapter, we'll examine the various technologies involved in communications, whether they're **wired** (connected by a physical medium) or **wireless** (connected through the air or space).

Moving Data: Bandwidth and Modems

Communications (data communications or telecommunications) is the process of electronically sending and receiving messages between two points. Communications occurs over communications channels. **Communications channels** (also referred to as links) are the path through which messages are passed from one location to the next. In communications, a source encodes messages and sends them over the communications channel to a destination that decodes messages (Figure 3.1). When you send a message from your computer, the message is converted into an electrical signal.

In communications, both analog and digital signals move data over communications channels. Phones and phone lines send and receive analog signals. **Analog signals** take data (most often audio of the human voice) and translate it into continuous waveforms that travel over communications channels. An analog signal can carry only so much data, limiting its usefulness.

In contrast, computers send and receive digital signals. **Digital signals** convert data into discontinuous pulses in which the presence or absence of electronic pulses represents 1s and 0s (Figure 3.2). Because 0s and 1s are discrete, the data arrives in a much clearer format, because the receiving end knows exactly how to reconstruct the data back into its original form. Digital signals also transfer much more data than analog and at much greater speeds. For instance, digital TV systems can now deliver over 200 stations across digital cable, which not only allows for more stations than analog cable, but also more features as well.

So how are the digital signals from your computer prepared to travel over analog telephone lines? Let's look at two additional considerations for sending data over communications channels: bandwidth and modems.

BANDWIDTH: HOW MUCH DO YOU NEED?

Bandwidth refers to the amount of data that can be transmitted through a given communications channel. The physical characteristics of the transmission medium and the method used to represent and transmit data via the transmission medium determine bandwidth. For analog signals, bandwidth is expressed in cycles per second, or hertz (Hz). For digital signals, bandwidth is expressed in bits per second (bps).

Broadband refers to any transmission medium that transports high volumes of data at high speeds, typically greater than

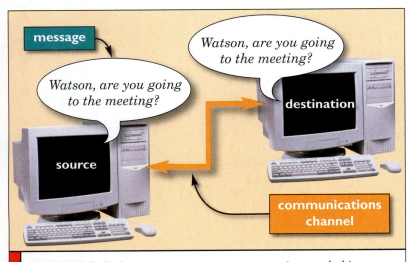

FIGURE 3.1 In communications, a message is encoded into electrical signals at the sending end and then decoded at the receiving end.

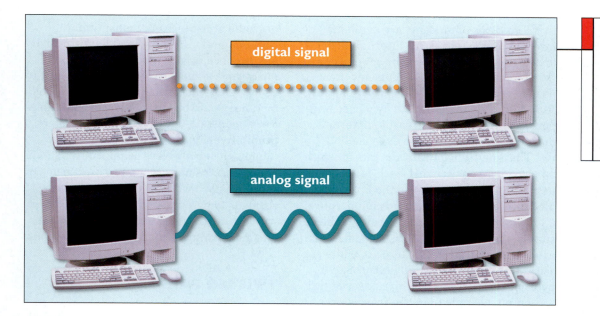

FIGURE 3.2
Digital signals are composed of on/off pulses, whereas analog signals use continuous waveforms.

1 Mbps. So how much bandwidth do you need? For sending and receiving textual data only, a transmission medium with a low bandwidth of 56 Kbps is sufficient. That rate, however, is often painfully slow for the highly graphical Web (unless you're *really* patient). Exploring the Web is a more pleasant proposition if you use a transmission medium with high bandwidth or a data transfer rate of 128 Kbps or faster.

Broadband digital connections aren't widely available yet. According to one estimate, by 2005 only about 5 percent of households in the United States had digital connections operating at speeds of 1.5 Mbps or greater.

MODEMS: FROM DIGITAL TO ANALOG AND BACK

Modems are communications devices used to transmit data over telephone lines. On the sending end, the modem uses a process called *modulation* to transform the computer's digital signals into analog tones that can be conveyed through the telephone system. On the receiving end, the process used is *demodulation,* whereby the other modem transforms the signal from analog back to digital. Modems can perform both modulation and demodulation—the name *modem* is short for modulator/demodulator (Figure 3.3).

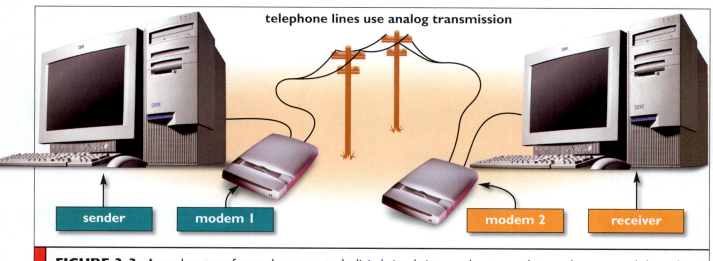

FIGURE 3.3   A modem transforms the computer's digital signals into analog tones that can be conveyed through the telephone system.

Two types of modems are available: internal and external. An internal modem is designed to fit inside your computer's system unit. Internal modems get their power from the system unit's power supply. An external modem has its own case and power supply. For this reason, external modems are slightly more expensive.

The data transfer rate, the rate at which two modems can exchange data, is measured in bps and is referred to as the bps rate. Modems communicate at a maximum rate of 56 Kbps. (In practice, modems rarely achieve speeds higher than 42 Kbps.) A modem that can transfer 56 Kbps (about 56,000 bits per second) is transferring only about 8,000 bytes per second, or about five pages of text.

Often, a single message travels over several different wired and wireless transmission media, including telephone lines, coaxial cable, fiber-optic cable, radio waves, microwaves, and satellite, before arriving at its destination. For now, we'll look at each of these types of wired and wireless transmission media in more detail.

Wired and Wireless Transmission Media

Unlike communications using wired transmission media such as twisted-pair, coaxial, and fiber-optic cables, wireless media don't use solid substances to transmit data. Rather, wireless media send data through air or space using infrared, radio, or microwave signals. Why would you want to use wireless media instead of cables? One instance would be in situations where cables can't be installed or the costs to do so are prohibitive. More and more colleges are implementing wireless computing capabilities on their campuses because users demand connectivity but the cost of wiring classrooms is too great. We'll discuss wired and wireless media along with their advantages and disadvantages in the following sections.

TWISTED PAIR

The same type of wire used for telephones, **twisted pair** uses two insulated wires twisted around each other to provide a shield against electromagnetic interference, which is generated by electric motors, power lines, and powerful radio signals (Figure 3.4). Although twisted pair is an inexpensive medium, the bandwidth of traditional twisted-pair telephone lines is too small to carry video, voice, and data simultaneously. Twisted pair carries data at transfer rates of 1 Kbps.

COAXIAL CABLE

Familiar to cable TV users, **coaxial cable** consists of a center copper wire surrounded by insulation, which is then surrounded by a layer of braided wire. Data travels through the center wire, while the braided

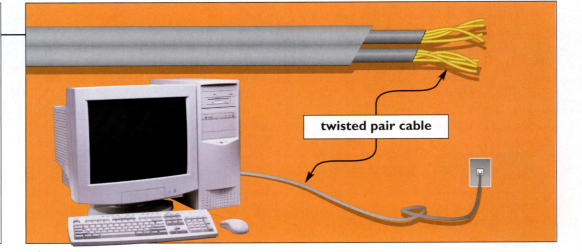

FIGURE 3.4
Twisted pair refers to inexpensive copper cable that's used for telephone and data communications. The cable is twisted to prevent interference from electrical circuits.

twisted pair cable

FIGURE 3.5 With coaxial cable, data travels through the center copper wire and is shielded from interference by the braided wire.

FIGURE 3.6 Fiber-optic cable consists of thin strands of glass that transmit data by means of pulses of light.

Techtalk

cat-5

Cat-5 wire is similar to telephone wire but consists of four twisted pairs instead of just two. Cat-5 wire uses an RJ-45 connector that looks very similar to a telephone jack connector but is a little wider and thicker.

wire provides a shield against electrical interference (Figure 3.5). Coaxial cable carries data at transfer rates of 10 Mbps. In contrast to twisted pair, coaxial cable makes it easy to achieve very-high-bandwidth data communications. Your home is probably already wired with coaxial cable if you subscribe to a cable TV service.

FIBER-OPTIC CABLE

Fiber-optic cable consists of thin strands of glass that carry data by means of pulses of light (Figure 3.6). Broadband uses fiber-optic or coaxial cable to transmit data. Fiber-optic cable can carry more data without loss of signal strength for longer distances than twisted pair or coaxial cable. Fiber-optic cable carries data at transfer rates of 1 Gbps.

INFRARED

If you use a remote control to change television channels, you're already familiar with infrared signaling. **Infrared** is a wireless transmission medium that carries data via beams of light through the air. No wires are required, but the transmitting and receiving devices must be in line of sight or the signal is lost. When the path between the transmitting and the receiving devices is not obstructed by trees, hills, mountains, buildings, or other structures, infrared signals can work within a maximum of about 100 feet.

To utilize infrared technology with your computer system, you need an IrDA port (Figure 3.7). You may encounter an IrDA port on a mobile computing device or peripheral such as a PDA, digital camera, laptop, mouse, printer, or keyboard. The most common use of the IrDA port is to transfer data from your PDA to your desktop or laptop computer or another PDA. To enable data transfer, the IrDA port on the

FIGURE 3.7 An IrDA port allows for more flexibility in managing external devices such as a mouse, keyboard, phone, or PDA.

transmitting device must be in line of sight (usually a few feet) of the port on the receiving device. IrDA ports offer data transfer rates of 4 Mbps. With all of these restrictions, why would you want to use infrared? If you had a situation where hooking devices together with cables wasn't an option, such as with a wireless keyboard or mouse, infrared would be a good choice. Plus, it's more convenient to simply point and transfer than it is to connect wires or cables!

RADIO

Radio transmissions offer an alternative to infrared transmissions. You probably have experienced one type of radio transmission by listening to your favorite radio station. But you may not realize the impact that radio waves have on your daily life or on society in general. All kinds of gadgets—from cell and cordless phones to baby monitors—communicate via radio waves. Although humans cannot see or otherwise detect them, radio waves are everywhere.

With **radio** transmission, data in a variety of forms (music, voice conversations, and photos) travels through the air as radio frequency (RF) signals or radio waves via a transmitting device and a receiving device. Instead of separate

transmitting and receiving devices, radio transmissions can also use a wireless transceiver, a combination transmitting and receiving device equipped with an antenna. Data transfer rates via radio transmission are variable but generally fall in the low-bandwidth range of 64 Kbps to 720 Kbps.

A major disadvantage of radio transmission is noise susceptibility and interference. One of radio's advantages is that radio signals are long range (between cities, regions, and countries) and short range (within a home or office).

Bluetooth

Bluetooth is a short-range radio transmission technology that has become very popular in recent years. Named after the infamous tenth-century Danish Viking and King Harald Blatand (translated as Bluetooth in English) who united Denmark and Norway, Bluetooth was first conceived by Swedish cell phone giant Ericsson (Figure 3.8). Bluetooth technology relies on a network called a piconet or a PAN (personal area network) that enables all kinds of devices—desktop computers, mobile phones, printers, pagers, PDAs, and more—within 30 feet of each other to communicate automatically and wirelessly.

How exactly does Bluetooth work? Bluetooth-enabled devices identify each other using identification numbers that are unique to each device. When these devices are within 30 feet of each other, they automatically "find" and link to one another. You don't have to worry about being connected to Bluetooth devices that you don't want to connect to: the device requires that you confirm a connection before making it final. Up to eight Bluetooth-enabled devices can be connected to each other in a piconet at any one time.

Unlike infrared technologies, Bluetooth doesn't require a direct line of sight to be connected. Because the frequency used by Bluetooth devices changes often, Bluetooth devices never use the same frequency at the same time and don't interfere with each other. Bluetooth can accommodate data transfer rates of up to 1 Mbps. At Bluetooth's maximum transfer capacity, you would be able to easily move a document within just a few seconds.

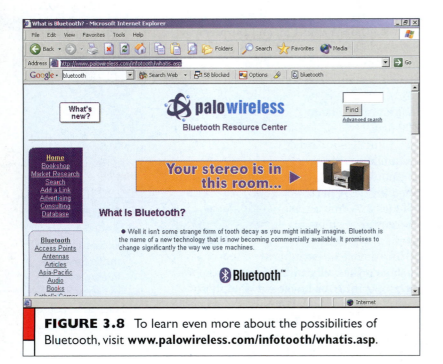

FIGURE 3.8 To learn even more about the possibilities of Bluetooth, visit **www.palowireless.com/infotooth/whatis.asp**.

MICROWAVES

Microwaves are high-frequency, electro-magnetic radio waves with very short frequencies that are used to transmit data. Using relay stations similar to satellite dishes (including an antenna, transceiver, and so on), microwave signals are sent from one relay station to the next. Because microwaves must travel in a straight line with no obstructions such as buildings, hills, mountains, and so on, relay stations are built at a distance of approximately every 30 miles (the line-of-sight distance to the horizon) or closer if the terrain blocks transmission. Microwave relay stations are also often situated on the tops of buildings or mountains.

Microwave transmission eliminates the need for a wired infrastructure. It is useful in areas where the use of physical wires is impractical or impossible. Microwaves are also useful for communities of users who are within the line-of-sight horizon, such as universities, hospitals, and private and government organizations. Disadvantages include the 30 mile line-of-sight restriction, sensitivity to electrical and/or magnetic interference, and the costs of maintaining the multitude of relay stations it takes to transfer messages across long distances.

SATELLITES

Essentially microwave relay stations suspended in space, communications **satellites** are positioned in geosynchronous orbit, which matches the speed of the Earth's rotation, and therefore are permanently positioned with respect to the ground (Figure 3.9). Satellites transmit data by sending and receiving microwave signals to and from Earth-based stations. Devices such as handheld computers and Global Positioning System (GPS) receivers can also function as Earth-based stations.

Direct Broadcast Satellite (DBS) is a consumer satellite technology that uses an 18- or 21-inch reception dish to receive digital TV signals broadcast at a bandwidth of 12 Mbps. Increasingly, DBS operators offer Internet access as well as digital TV service, but at much lower bandwidth. Currently, Hughes Network

FIGURE 3.9 Communications satellites are often permanently positioned with respect to the Earth to provide specific areas of coverage.

Systems offers satellite Internet access at 400 Kbps, but there are a couple of drawbacks. To access the Internet using satellite technology, you need a satellite dish, a satellite modem card, and a relatively clear view of the southern sky (in the United States). Additionally, current subscription rates are about double that of land-based services.

Broadband cable is not readily available in many rural or other low-population areas, thus many of these areas are prime candidates for DBS. Unfortunately, the major weakness of DBS systems is their inability to upload data. This means that you can browse the Internet and read e-mail, but you cannot send replies or upload data to an FTP site. You will also probably need to install new hardware onto your computer and pay installation charges and a monthly service fee.

To utilize these various wireless transmission media, a computer system must also use a special communications device called a **network access point**, which sends and receives data between computers that contain wireless adapters. Access points enable you to move a laptop with a wireless adapter to different locations.

Destinations

A good overview of a DBS can be found at **www .starband.com**. There you will learn why DBS systems require a clear view of the southern sky and other interesting facts.

So, what is it about wireless connectivity that is so interesting? Well, one answer is that wireless technology removes "place-specific" restrictions; that is, the need to be in a certain place to receive a service. Some forms of wireless technology allow you to be wherever you choose to be and still have the ability to be connected.

Now that you know more about wired and wireless media, the next section will explore the most common wired communication system: the public switched telephone network.

Wired Communication via the Public Switched Telephone Network

Although 80 percent of Internet users in the United States log on using dial-up access via the telephone system, it's important to understand the phone system's limitations.

The **public switched telephone network** (**PSTN**) is the global telephone

system, a massive network used for data as well as voice communications, comprising various transmission media ranging from twisted-pair wire to fiber-optic cable. Some computer users derisively (and somewhat unfairly) refer to the PSTN as the Plain Old Telephone Service (POTS). The derision comes from the fact that most analog telephone lines are based on standards that date back more than a century (Figure 3.10). The analog service the PSTN offers isn't ideal for data communications. As you'll see, though, it's not true that the PSTN is an entirely analog network. It's on the verge of becoming all digital, which will mean positive changes for data communications.

Most home and business telephones in use today are analog devices. These telephones are linked to subscriber loop carriers by means of twisted-pair wires. A **subscriber loop carrier** (**SLC**) is a small, waist-high curbside installation that connects as many as 96 subscribers; you've probably seen one in your neighborhood. The area served by an SLC is called the **local loop**.

From the SLC on though, the PSTN is increasingly a digital network. The SLC transforms local analog calls into digital signals, routing them through high-capacity fiber-optic cables to the **local exchange switch**, which is also based on digital technology capable of handling thousands of calls. The local exchange switch is located in the local telephone company's central office (CO). From the local phone company's central office, the call can go anywhere in the world. It continues on the digital portion of the PSTN's fiber-optic cables and can even be converted to radio waves and sent out over cellular networks (Figure 3.11).

Although analog connections are still common, this situation is changing as new digital telephony services become available. **Digital telephony** is the use of all-digital telephone systems: The telephones are digital and the transmission is handled digitally. Compared with analog devices, which are prone to noise and interference, digital phones offer noise-free transmission and high-quality audio. You've probably already used a digital phone: Large organizations, such as corporations and universities, typically install their own internal digital telephone systems, called private branch exchanges

FIGURE 3.10 Most telephone lines provide an analog connection that is based on standards that date back more than a century.

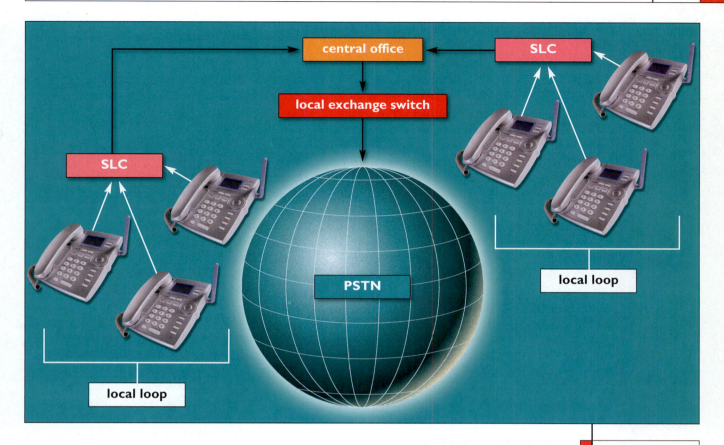

central office

SLC

local exchange switch

SLC

PSTN

local loop

local loop

FIGURE 3.11
Pathways on
the PSTN

(PBXs). By using a PBX, an organization avoids the high cost of paying for a line to the local telephone company's exchange switch for each employee. Calls to the outside must be translated into analog signals to connect to the PSTN.

Because long-distance lines must handle thousands of calls simultaneously (32 calls per second, 24 hours a day, 7 days a week in the United States), a technique called **multiplexing** is used to send more than one call over a single line. The electrical and physical characteristics of copper wire impose a limit of 24 multiplexed calls per wire, but fiber-optic cables can carry as many as 48,384 digital voice channels simultaneously. In contrast to the analog local loop, most long-distance carriers use digital signals so that they can pack the greatest number of calls into a single circuit.

The inability of homes or businesses to access the PSTN's high-speed fiber-optic cables, along with the bottleneck of data on the last mile of twisted-pair phone lines connecting homes and businesses, is often referred to as the **last-mile problem**. Here's why. In most areas of the United States, only the local loop is still using analog technology, because nearly all existing

buildings were originally constructed with built-in twisted-pair wiring. These analog lines are vulnerable to noise and can't surpass a theoretical limit of 56 Kbps. For the local loop to change over to digital lines, all of this wiring would have to be redone—an expense that is simply too great. The cost to replace all the twisted pair that currently delivers phone service to homes and offices worldwide would be upwards of $325 billion, and that is not likely to happen anytime soon. So in the meantime, computer users desiring high-speed data communications can consider a number of "last mile" technologies as well as wireless options.

LAST-MILE TECHNOLOGIES

Because the local loop's last mile of twisted-pair wiring will be with us for many years, phone companies and other providers offer a number of interim digital telephony technologies that make use of twisted-pair wiring. Sometimes called **last-mile technologies**, these solutions include digital telephone standards (such as ISDN and DSL) that use twisted-pair

Destinations

To learn more about the PSTN and new wired and wireless technologies, a great place to start is HelloDirect.com's "Get Informed" tutorials at **telecom.hellodirect .com/docs/Tutorials /default.asp**

IMPACTS

Debates

Sharing Bandwidth

As more and more of the world enters cyberspace, the ethical issues become more complex. Do we need new rules for today's wireless world? For example, many people argue that compensation for use rather than access is ethical— that is, you should have to pay for each user on a DSL line, not for the DSL line itself. Others think that if you've subscribed to a DSL line, you should be able to share it with anyone or everyone.

Imagine the following scenario: You just signed up for fast Internet access with an expensive DSL provider and started sharing your bandwidth with your roommate. You're even thinking of sharing it with your entire apartment building. After all, you're paying for access, and you're not profiting by offering it to others for free. What could be wrong with that?

Plenty. First, most DSL providers don't allow this kind of sharing, so you'd be breaking the contract you signed with your provider. Second, you'd be breaking the law even if you didn't earn any money by letting others use your DSL line.

So can bandwidth ever be shared legally? Some businesses are already giving away a little of their unused bandwidth so that "community members" can access the Internet using laptops and other wireless devices for free. Users must be within a certain distance of the server to take advantage of the free bandwidth, but that range can be about as far as a city block. Proponents suggest that businesses should pay a higher flat fee for their bandwidth so they can offer access to the public. In Austin, Texas, the Schlotzsky's delicatessen chain has no problem with people using the "hot spots" of Internet access surrounding its stores during nonbusiness hours, because when the stores are open, free access attracts users who buy food to snack on while they surf.

The idea of creating free wireless communities is already taking off. In New York City, for example, NYCWireless operates hot spots in parks, coffee shops, and building lobbies (Figure 3.12). A few hundred miles away, a consulting firm operates one public-access hot spot in Bethesda, Maryland, and a second in downtown Washington, D.C. Across the country, a growing number of hotels offer free high-speed access so that customers can check their e-mail and surf the Web from rooms or restaurants.

The trick now is to make free wireless network communities safe and secure from malicious users and people slowing the system with hefty downloads. If you're planning to log on from a public hot spot, be sure your security software is up-to-date and turned on so that others using the same access point can't snoop into your files. Yes, this takes a few extra keystrokes, but it will keep your data— personal or corporate—safe from prying eyes and let you feel part of the network community without fear.

FIGURE 3.12   Wireless hot spots allow users to send and receive messages, documents, and data and to browse the Web as well.

wiring as well as "always on" high-speed wired services (such as coaxial cable and cable modems).

ISDN (Integrated Services Digital Network)

ISDN (Integrated Services Digital Network) is a standard that provides digital telephone and data service. ISDN offers connections ranging from 56 to 128 Kbps (Basic Rate ISDN) or 1.5 Mbps (Primary Rate ISDN) using ordinary twisted-pair telephone lines. The cost of an ISDN line is often two to three times that of an analog phone line, but there's a payoff. With a 128-Kbps ISDN service, you

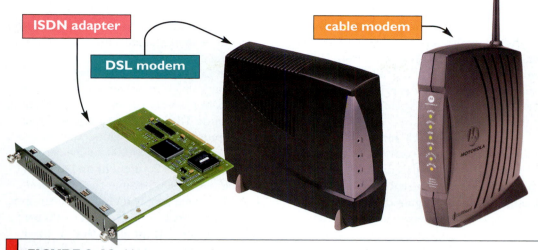

FIGURE 3.13 Various types of modems facilitate the connection between your computer and last-mile technologies.

get two telephone numbers with one ISDN account; you can use one for computer data and the other for voice or fax. When you're using the connection for computer data only, the system automatically uses both data channels to give you the maximum data transfer rate; if a phone call comes in, the connection automatically drops back to 64 Kbps to accommodate the incoming call. What's more, connection is nearly instantaneous. Unlike analog connections with a modem, there's no lengthy dial-in procedure and connection delay.

To connect computers to ISDN lines, you need an **ISDN adapter** (also called a **digital modem**, although it isn't actually a modem) (Figure 3.13). ISDN adapters are 100 percent digital and can cost as little as $50 and as much as $350 for in-home use. Commercial use can run in the thousands of dollars. Monthly service rates range from $29 to $60 for home use. Note that you must have the correct wiring to your house; this may require having new wire installed from the SLC to your home.

DSL (Digital Subscriber Line)

DSL (**Digital Subscriber Line**), also called **xDSL**, is a blanket term for a group of related technologies, including ADSL (Asymmetric Digital Subscriber Line), that offer high-speed Internet access. ADSL and related DSL technologies are expected to provide 1 Mbps access. Already available in major metropolitan markets, ADSL is akin to ISDN in that it uses existing

twisted-pair wiring. But ADSL is much faster: typically, up to 1.5 Mbps when you're downloading data and up to 256 Kbps when you're uploading data. (Note that downloading speeds are much faster than uploading speeds; the discrepancy explains why the service is called asymmetric. ADSL isn't the best choice if you need to upload huge amounts of data.)

To use DSL, you need a DSL phone line and a DSL service subscription. Unlike conventional telephone service, which is available to almost any home, DSL service is limited by the distance from the central office (CO) or switching station to your home. You also need a **DSL modem**, which is similar to a traditional telephone modem in that it modulates and demodulates analog and digital signals for transmission over communications channels. However, DSL modems use signaling methods based on broadband technology for much higher transfer speeds (Figure 3.13). One problem is that DSL service isn't standardized, so you'll need to select a modem that's compatible with your telephone company's particular type of DSL service. Standardization efforts are under way, however; and these efforts will reduce the cost and complexity of DSL installations. DSL modems cost between $29 and $300 depending on the number of ports and the transfer capacity. DSL service will run between $40 and $600 per month depending upon the number of connected computers.

Destinations

To help you decide on which last-mile technology might be right for you, check out the "Cable or DSL" tutorial at **telecom.hellodirect .com/docs/Tutorials /CableVsDSL .1.030801.asp**

Coaxial Cable and Cable Modems

Currently, the leading contender in the high-bandwidth sweepstakes is your local cable TV company. Approximately 100 million homes in the United States now subscribe to cable TV service, and an additional 50 million are within easy reach of cable systems.

Does the cable TV industry's huge installed base of coaxial cable hold the key to high-bandwidth digital service delivery? Not yet. The cable TV system was designed to run signals in one direction only: toward the house, not away from it. But data communications requires two-way communication. Only about one-quarter of the homes in the United States have cable service that's capable of two-way data communications; the cable industry is busily upgrading the rest of its infrastructure to provide this capability.

For computer users, these services offer data transfer rates that leave ISDN in the dust. **Cable modems**, devices that enable computers to access the Internet by means of a cable TV connection, now deliver data at bandwidths of 500 Kbps to 1.5 Mbps or more, depending on how many subscribers are connected to a local cable segment (Figure 3.13). You'll hear figures stating that cable modems are capable of bandwidths of 30 Mbps or more, but this bandwidth must be divided among the 2,000 or more subscribers in the cable company's service area. Cable service costs $29 to $69 per month. The cable modem may be free if you sign up for a contract period or you may spend as much as $250 to purchase a cable modem.

Leased Lines

A **leased line** is a specially conditioned telephone line that enables continuous, end-to-end communication between two points. The earliest type of permanent digital connection, the 56-Kbps leased line, has declined in popularity as services such as ISDN and DSL have become more widely available. Larger organizations, such as ISPs, corporations, and universities, connect using leased **T1 lines**, which are specially conditioned copper wires that can handle up to 1.544 Mbps of computer data. This is a costly service that individuals and most small businesses can't afford. Leased lines may use modems, cable modems, or other communications devices to manage the transfer of data into and out of the organization.

Other Last-Mile Technologies

There are also interim technologies that make better use of existing fiber-optic cables. Fiber-optic **T3 lines** can handle 43 Mbps of computer data. A T3 connection will cost between $3,000 and $7,000 for the necessary communications equipment and another $2,000 to $15,000 per month for the line itself. Some extremely high-speed fiber-optic connections cost as much as $50,000 per month! Another technology that utilizes fiber-optic cable, **SONET (Synchronous Optical Network)** is a standard for high-performance networks. The slowest SONET standard calls for data transfer rates of 52 Mbps; some enable rates of 1 Gbps or faster. SONET is expected to provide fiber-optic cable services for Broadband ISDN (BISDN), but this service isn't expected to benefit homes and small businesses.

In addition to adapting twisted-pair wiring, broadband coaxial cable, and fiber-optic cable, wireless technologies are helping to solve the last-mile problem as well. Here's a look at two wireless solutions.

MMDS (Multichannel Multipoint Distribution Service, sometimes called Multipoint Microwave Distribution System) can be thought of as wireless cable. MMDS was originally slated as a wireless alternative to cable television, but now its main application is Internet access. Service providers offer MMDS Internet access within a 35-mile radius of the nearest transmission point at projected speeds of 1 Gbps, about 1,000 times faster than DSL, cable, or satellite.

In rural areas where installing new coaxial or fiber-optic cable may be inconvenient or expensive, LMDS (Local Multipoint Distribution Service) is a possible solution. This fixed wireless technology delivers high-bandwidth services on the "last mile" connecting homes and businesses. One LMDS node can supply phone and data services for up to 80,000 customers in a radius of 3 to 5 miles. LMDS can transfer data at rates of 1.5 to 2 Gbps, but data transfer rates typically average around 38 Mbps.

In mountainous areas or other places where there are obstructions, MMDS and LMDS don't work well because they are line-of-sight technologies. Line-of-sight means the transmitting and receiving devices have a clear path between them.

In the next section, we will explore the phenomenon of the coming together of these communications technologies.

Convergence: Is It a Phone or a Computer?

We've been examining various technologies that carry computer data over voice lines as well as through the air. At the core of this process is **digitization**, the transformation of data such as voice, text, graphics, audio, and video into digital form. Digitization enables convergence. **Convergence** refers to the merging of disparate objects or ideas (and even people) into new combinations. Within the IT industry, convergence means two things: (1) the combination of various industries (computers, consumer electronics, and telecommunications) and (2) the coming together of products such as PCs and telephones.

Wireless devices are proliferating at a tremendous pace. Today, it is not unusual for your phone to talk to your PDA or computer or for your computer to be controlled by a wireless mouse or keyboard. Some futurists think that convergence may mark the end of the digital revolution, at which point all forms of digital information (voice, video, and data) will travel over the same network (Figure 3.14).

Digitization also enables media convergence. Media convergence is the unification of all forms of media (including newspapers, TV, and radio). The Internet is already a major source of breaking news, rivaling such traditional sources as newspapers and television. And, according to a recent estimate, more than 5 percent of all long-distance voice telephone calls will someday travel over the Internet, creating a $9 billion industry that would pose a genuine threat to the traditional public switched telephone network.

Another threat to the PSTN is the December 2001 legislation on telephone number portability. Under this rule, anyone with traditional telephone service can cancel it and switch their home phone number over to their cellular phone service. Although this might seem like a great idea to begin with—who would not want to save $30 to $100 per month or more on their home and long-distance bills—there are some drawbacks. For instance, cell phone batteries can run low, the phone might be in a no-man's-land with poor or no reception, service might drop in the middle of an important call, or weather could interfere with signal strength, causing the transmission and reception quality

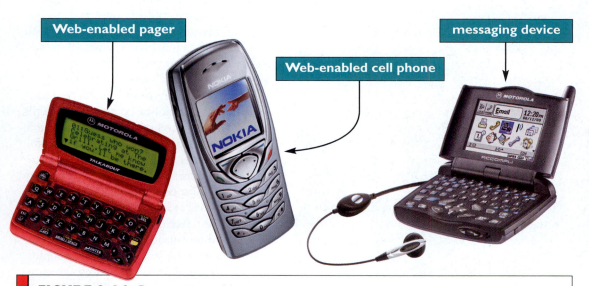

Web-enabled pager

Web-enabled cell phone

messaging device

FIGURE 3.14 Digitization enables convergence, a process of technological morphing in which previously distinct devices lose their sharply defined boundaries and blend together.

to suffer. Still, traditional phone companies worry that even though only a small percentage of Americans claim their cellular phones are their only phones, surveys indicate they could lose as many as 6 million customers to this phenomenon by 2008.

Why should you care about convergence? Because understanding convergence will help you make more informed decisions about current and future technology purchases. This section explores some of the dimensions of computer–telephony convergence, a process of technological morphing in which previously distinct devices lose their sharply defined boundaries and blend together. As you'll see, it's creating some interesting hybrids.

CELLULAR TELEPHONES

The PSTN isn't the only analog phone technology around. Analog **cellular telephones** (known as the first-generation, or 1G, of cellular technology) enable subscribers to place calls through a wireless communications system (Figure 3.15). A wireless communications system uses radio or infrared signals to transmit voice or text data.

In 1971, AT&T built a network of transmitters that automatically repeat signals. This network of transmitters,

which are called **cell sites**, broadcasts signals throughout specific, but limited, geographic areas called **cells**. When callers move from cell to cell, each new cell site automatically takes over the signal to maintain signal strength. But who or what monitors your cell phone's signal strength so that you have the best reception? That's the job of the **mobile telephone switching office** (**MTSO**), which connects cell towers to the telephone company's central office and the PSTN. MTSOs are located in cities that serve the local cell region. Each MTSO is owned and maintained by a cellular service provider (Figure 3.16). Each cell tower reports signal strength to the MTSO, which then switches your signal to whatever cell tower will provide the clearest connection for your conversation.

Analog cellular telephone service was introduced to the market in 1983. Even though it is still a predominantly analog system, more than 167 million people use cell phones in the United States today.

Terrain, interference, weather, antenna position, and battery strength can all affect signal strength. However, there may be times when you've extended your antenna, recharged your battery, have clear weather, and are standing at the top of a hill—and still cannot achieve a good signal. In this case, you may be able to help your cellular service provider by calling in or sending them a report. They may not know that there is a hole in their service or they may offer to service your phone to see if it has any defects.

Cell phone providers are dealing with another customer service issue: allowing users to keep their cell phone numbers when they change service providers. Although this may sound attractive to cell phone subscribers, be aware of pitfalls such as interrupted service or being double-billed for service by two providers. This phenomenon is heating up competition among providers like Cingular, Sprint, and Verizon to offer better calling plans and other benefits to their existing customers to keep them from switching.

Cell phone etiquette and safety are other issues to be aware of. Many people may be irritated or concerned by the careless use of cell phones in public places and by people driving motor vehicles. Some states have banned drivers from using

FIGURE 3.15 Cellular telephones enable subscribers to place calls through a wireless communications system.

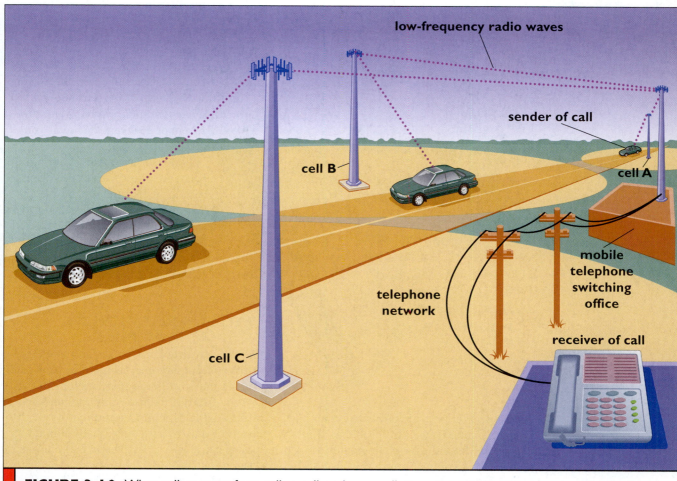

low-frequency radio waves

sender of call

cell B

cell A

mobile
telephone
switching
office

telephone
network

receiver of call

cell C

FIGURE 3.16 When callers move from cell to cell, each new cell site automatically takes over to maintain the strength of the signal. The mobile telephone switching office (MTSO) is the switching office that connects cell towers to the telephone company's central office and the PSTN.

handheld cell phones while operating a motor vehicle. Other agencies have policies on cellular phone use in aircraft, trains, and hospitals. Businesses may limit the use of cell phones in movie theaters and restaurants. In addition, your college or university may restrict the use of cell phones in classrooms on your campus.

Besides cell phone etiquette and safety, burgeoning cell phone use has another societal impact. Just as with old computer equipment, you need to think about the proper disposal of your cell phone when you upgrade or damage it beyond repair. The average life of a cell phone is 18 months; about 100 million phones are disposed of each year in the United States alone. Discarded cell phones are toxic waste. When they end up in landfills, they threaten the environment through the release of arsenic, lead, cadmium, and

other heavy metals that can creep into the water supply and cause cancer or birth defects. Verizon, AT&T Wireless, and many other providers, as well as indirect retailers, will accept old phones. The bottom line: Recycling your old cell phone is good for the environment.

PCS (Personal Communication Service)

Digitization is bringing the same rapid change to cellular phone service that you're seeing in other media. A group of related digital cellular technologies called **PCS (Personal Communication Service)** is quickly replacing most analog cellular services. PCS is also referred to as 2G, for second-generation cellular technology, or dual-band service. Digital PCS phones offer noise-free sound and improved coverage, but that's just the beginning. PCS

Destinations

For tips on responsible cell phone use while driving, check out the tutorial at **telecom .hellodirect.com /docs/Tutorials/ DrivingResponsibly .1.061101.asp**

So what's better for you, should you get an analog or digital cell phone? Analog cellular service does offer better voice quality, but digital PCS is closing the gap. Because they use a lower frequency than digital PCS (800 versus 1900 MHz), analog systems provide a broader range of coverage. What if you don't know whether your cell phone service is analog or digital? A couple of indicators might give you a hint. If you have analog cell service and go out of range, you will hear static before the call is lost. With digital cell service, the voice transmission becomes garbled before you completely lose the connection.

FIGURE 3.17
Nokia's latest smart phone.

offers protection from eavesdropping and cellular phone fraud, two problems that plague analog cellular technologies. It also offers a spate of new computer-based telephony services such as voice-recognition technology that enables users to screen incoming calls or to place calls without dialing a phone number. In short, PCS enables computers and cellular phones to be combined into devices referred to as "smart phones," and the result is a profusion of technologies that are transforming the way we communicate (Figure 3.17).

PCS is making mobile computing a reality for millions of people. Because PCS technology is digital, it's much more amenable to data communications than analog cellular services. It's possible to access the Internet by means of a modem connected to an analog cellular phone, but data transfer rates are as low as 4 Kbps due to line noise and poor connections. Emerging PCS standards will enable speeds of up to 384 Kbps for downloads.

The International Telecommunication Union (ITU) has released a specification for the third generation (3G), or triband, mobile communications technology. 3G offers speeds that vary depending on the application—384 Kbps while walking, 128 Kbps in a moving vehicle, and 2 Mbps in fixed locations.

WEB-ENABLED DEVICES

A **Web-enabled device** is any device that can display and respond to the codes in the markup languages, such as HTML (HyperText Markup Language) or XML (eXtensible Markup Language), typically used to build Web pages. Web-enabled devices include PDAs, some cell phones, and tablet PCs.

Web-enabled PDAs include the Palm line, which uses the Palm Operating System; Handspring (purchased by Palm in 2003), which features a design that accepts modules such as a camera, software applications, and a phone; the Casio Pocket PC, which uses the Microsoft CE operating system and is often used for barcode scanning and other business-focused applications; and the Sharp Zaurus, which is the leading PDA in Japan. Most popular with mobile professionals is the BlackBerry®, a wireless e-mail device as well as an integrated phone that features AOL Instant Messenger Service, built-in paging, call forwarding, caller ID, conference calling, enhanced voicemail, and hot-spot awareness. The device has coverage in over 9,000 cities in the United States and over 100 countries worldwide and is supported by many wireless service providers, including Nextel and T-Mobile (Figure 3.18).

To work over wireless networks, Web-enabled devices require WAP (short for Wireless Application Protocol). WAP is a standard that specifies how users can access the Web securely using pagers,

FIGURE 3.18 PDAs are the most prevalent Web-enabled devices in use today.

cell phones, PDAs, and other wireless handheld devices.

It doesn't matter which operating system your device uses because WAP is supported by all of them. However, WAP-enabled devices do require a microbrowser, a special Web browser that works with small file sizes. Smaller file sizes are necessary due to the low memory capacities of WAP-enabled devices and wireless networks with low bandwidth.

Now that you understand how convergence is blurring the boundaries between phone and computer devices, let's take a look at some wired and wireless applications used with these devices.

Wired and Wireless Applications

The world of wired and wireless applications is receiving more attention every day. You can't open a magazine, surf the Web, or watch TV without seeing ads for the latest wireless solutions. More and more businesses and home users are implementing these various applications to help them communicate, collaborate, and share text, graphics, audio, and video. You can sit in a classroom today and receive instant messages, e-mail, and stock quotes and even browse the Web—all from your cell phone! And it is happening at increasingly faster speeds, higher data transfer rates, and lower costs.

INTERNET TELEPHONY: REAL-TIME VOICE AND VIDEO

Internet telephony is the use of the Internet for real-time voice communication. Although the Internet isn't ideal for real-time voice, you can place calls via the Internet in a variety of ways. To place free long-distance calls, you'll need a computer equipped with a microphone, speakers, an Internet connection, and a telephony-enabled program such as Microsoft's NetMeeting. Your calls are limited to people using similarly equipped computers—and they need to be online.

What about placing a call to an ordinary telephone? You can't do it for free.

To learn more about Internet telephony, view the video clip on phoning a friend online at **www.prenhall.com/cayf2006**

Electronic Voting: What's Your Vote?

CURRENTS

Computers and Society

Electronic voting is in your future, if it isn't already in your neighborhood polling place. What could be simpler? Touch a computer screen or click a mouse and you've had your say about the candidates and the issues on the ballot.

Voting wasn't always this easy for citizens or for the officials who tally election results. In the nineteenth century, paper ballots were state-of-the-art voting technology. They kept personal choices secret, but counting all those pieces of paper took time—and opened the door to mistakes or outright fraud. By the twentieth century, depending on the preferences of the local government, voters were pressing levers on machines, poking holes in punch-card ballots, or inking ovals on optically scannable ballots.

Fast-forward to the twenty-first century. In the search for a quick, easy, private, yet secure voting method, more than half the states have installed touch-screen electronic voting machines. In fact, Georgia and Maryland won't let you mark your ballot in any other way. Meanwhile, Michigan and other states are testing systems in which you vote from your home or office PC using an ordinary Internet connection. Your vote is encoded for secure transmission, just as retailers encode credit-card numbers for security (Figure 3.19).

But is electronic voting a boon to society? Proponents argue that the technology is more reliable and more convenient, eliminating many of the problems that plagued elections in the past.

Sometimes mechanical voting equipment broke down; sometimes punch-card ballots had to be checked by hand if the holes indicating choices didn't go all the way through. What's more, advocates believe that more people would participate if they could vote from home or by a couple of taps on a computer at the polling place. And with electronic voting, officials could tally the results immediately, instead of counting for hours, or even days.

Critics of electronic voting have four main concerns. First, they worry about security. Can such systems withstand hacker attacks? Can the software or hardware be manipulated to add, change, hide, or prevent votes? Second, critics raise concerns about malfunctions. What if the software doesn't work correctly or the screen blanks out for a time on election day? What if the Internet or wireless connection goes down?

Third, critics worry about verifying votes. How can voters and officials confirm that votes are recorded properly? How can votes be recounted without a paper trail or other proof? Finally, critics are concerned that electronic voting could widen the digital divide. Will people avoid voting if they are wary of computers, can't afford a PC, or don't have Internet access? Will the outcome of an election be affected if people can vote from their homes or offices instead of going to a central polling place?

Experts are already working on solutions. Some rely on paper—for example, you might get a printout after casting your vote electronically at a polling place. If the printout is correct, you would give it to officials for safekeeping so it would be available for a recount. Other solutions rely on technology. You might receive a special card or device to prove your eligibility and to record your choices, either at your own PC or at the local polling place. Once you submit your card, election officials would verify it and hold it in case a recount is needed. Is electronic voting on its way to a polling place near you?

FIGURE 3.19 Electronic voting machines have many advantages and disadvantages—but they are the wave of our voting future.

techtv

To learn more about electronic voting, view the video clip online at **www.prenhall.com/cayf2006**

However, **Internet telephony service providers** (**ITSPs**) such as Net2Phone are stepping into the act by offering computer-to-phone and phone-to-phone services that use the Internet for long-distance transmission (Figure 3.20). Rates are cheap, but the quality isn't always what subscribers expect.

Still, the basic idea of Internet telephony has an enormous advantage: Because the Internet doesn't rely on switches to route messages, like the PSTN does, it's cheaper to operate. Providers can route dozens, hundreds, or even thousands of calls over the same circuit. According to one estimate, routing data over a switched network like the PSTN costs more than three times as much as sending the same data over a switch-free computer network such as the Internet. You can try Internet telephony by using NetMeeting or Netscape Conference, which are supplied with the two most popular browsers, Microsoft's Internet Explorer and Netscape Navigator.

If you and the person you're calling have a digital video camera, you can converse through real-time videoconferencing as well. **Videoconferencing** is the use of digital video technology to transmit sound and video images so that two or more people can have a face-to-face meeting

FIGURE 3.20 Net2Phone is an Internet telephony service provider that offers computer-to-phone and phone-to-phone services using the Internet for long-distance transmission.

even though they're geographically separated (see Figure 3.21). Today, many PCs are sold with Intel Videophone or Microsoft's NetMeeting already installed, as well as cameras such as Bigpicture. However, don't expect spectacular quality; you'll hear echoes and delays in the audio,

FIGURE 3.21
In a videoconference, two or more people can see and communicate with each other, even though they are not physically present in the same room.

and the picture will be small, grainy, jerky, and liable to delays. But there are no long-distance charges!

In addition to Internet voice and video calls, Internet telephony products support real-time conferencing with such features as a shared whiteboard, file exchange capabilities, and text chatting. A **whiteboard**, generally shown as a separate area of the videoconferencing screen, enables participants to create a shared workspace. Participants can write or draw in this space as if they were using a physical whiteboard in a meeting. Current technology doesn't enable you to videoconference with more than one caller at a time, but you can create an audio conference with as many users as you want (Figure 3.22).

A **Web cam** is an inexpensive, low-resolution analog or digital video camera that is designed to sit on top of the computer monitor. Sometimes an individual, company, or organization places a Web cam in a public location, such as a street corner, a railway station, or a museum (see Figure 3.23). Often, the camera is set up to take a "snapshot" of the scene every 15 minutes or so. The image is then displayed on a Web page. Some sites offer streaming cams, also called live cams, that provide more frequently updated images.

If you only want to transmit voice over the Internet, and not video, you can use a dial-up modem and connection with transfer speeds of 56 Kbps. But for any high-bandwidth Internet application, such as

FIGURE 3.22 Microsoft NetMeeting's data conferencing features let you collaborate with a group of people. Conference participants can draw on a shared whiteboard, send text messages, and transfer data.

FIGURE 3.23 EarthCam (**www.earthcam.com**) provides a large number of links to Web cams that are positioned throughout the world.

FIGURE 3.24 Network-based delivery of high-quality videoconferencing requires a bandwidth of at least 10 Mbps.

Destinations

To learn more about videoconferencing, go to **www.motion-media .com/html/products /carestation/cs110 /index.htm**

streaming video, you will need a broadband connection with transfer speeds of at least 128 Kbps. Network-based delivery of high-quality videoconferencing requires a bandwidth of at least 10 Mbps (Figure 3.24). Videoconferencing will be a much smoother experience for all participants with broadband's faster upload speeds.

Streaming video or any other new set of Internet applications that require speeds at least 20 times faster than traditional dial-up phone lines and modems are theoretically possible with broadband. Fiber-optic transmission lines will help to expand this growing communications segment of the market.

Until home users can obtain faster Internet connections, Internet telephony and videoconferencing will prove most useful on corporate networks, which have ample supplies of bandwidth. Still, thousands of Internet users employ Web cams and programs such as NetMeeting to stay in touch with friends and family.

FAXING: DOCUMENT EXCHANGE

Facsimile transmission—or **fax** as it's popularly known—enables you to send an image of a document over a telephone line (Figure 3.25). The sending fax machine makes a digital image of the document. Using a built-in modem, the sending fax machine converts the image into an analog representation so that it can be transmitted through the analog telephone system. The receiving fax machine converts the analog signals to digital signals, converts the digital signals to an image of the document, and then prints the image.

Some computer users use fax modems instead of fax machines. A **fax modem** is a computerized version of a stand-alone fax machine. This device and software allow your computer to do everything a fax machine can: send and receive documents, print documents, and store documents. The big difference between using a regular fax

FIGURE 3.25 Facsimile transmission enables you to send an image of a document over a telephone line to anyone who has a fax machine. If your computer has a fax modem, you can send and receive faxes from your computer instead of a fax machine.

machine and using your computer as a fax machine is that the fax modem does everything in a digitized way. So, you may need a scanner to put a document into a digital format if you want to fax something that's printed or sketched on paper.

If the Internet isn't perfect for voice calls, it has none of those shortcomings for faxes. Faxes don't have to be delivered in real time, like voice does, so slight service delays don't cause any problems.

How does Internet faxing work? You need an Internet connection and an account with an Internet fax service provider. From a fax machine or computer, you send the fax through the Internet to the fax service provider, which then automatically routes the fax through the Internet to a local telephone near your fax's destination.

The service isn't free, but it's 25 to 50 percent cheaper than sending the fax through the phone system.

Because computers can send and receive faxes, it is not a far stretch of the imagination to see that sending and receiving documents will soon be accomplished by network-enabled cell phones or Web-enabled devices, thereby making fax machines as we know them today obsolete.

SATELLITE RADIO, GPS, AND MORE

Many applications use satellite technology, including air navigation, TV and radio broadcasting, paging, and videoconferencing. **Satellite radio** broadcasts radio signals to satellites orbiting more than 22,000 miles above the Earth. The satellites then transmit the signals back to a radio receiver. Unlike ground-based radio signal transmitters, satellite radio is not affected by location, distance, or obstructions. Because of their great height, satellites can transmit signals that are available to a radio receiver wherever it might be located.

Satellite radio is a boon for folks living in areas with limited local radio stations or where regular AM/FM reception is hampered by terrain. Companies that offer monthly satellite radio subscriptions include WorldSpace, XM Radio, SIRIUS, and Delphi SKYFi. Satellite radio can mimic your local radio broadcasting station's style, including commercials. It can provide you with over a hundred channels offering different genres, including continuous music, sports, news, and talk programs. In contrast to music programs that are offered by some cable or satellite in-home providers, satellite radio uses portable receivers that plug into your home or car stereo so it is totally mobile and transportable to wherever you happen to want to listen. Some satellite radio companies such as SIRIUS plan to broadcast video channels to subscribers with video screens in their cars.

GPS

Another interesting application of satellite technology is GPS. **GPS (Global Positioning System)** is actually a cluster of 27 Earth-orbiting satellites (24 in operation and three extras in case one fails). Each of these 3,000- to 4,000-pound solar-powered satellites circles the globe at an altitude of 12,000 miles, making two complete rotations every day. The orbits are arranged so that at any time, anywhere on Earth, at least four satellites are "visible" in the sky. A GPS receiver's job is to locate four or more of these satellites, figure out the distance to each, and use this information to deduce its own location.

A GPS receiver can be either handheld or installed in a vehicle. Navigation systems in rental cars are a typical application of GPS. OnStar® is a multifaceted GPS communications system that enables drivers to talk to a live service representative to obtain driving directions and information

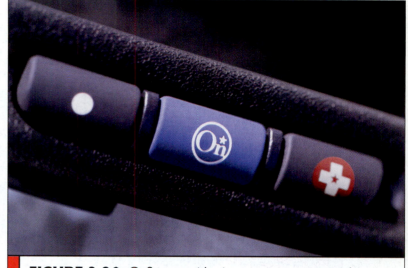

FIGURE 3.26 OnStar provides instant communication between a vehicle and a call center.

on hotels, food venues, and the like. Drivers can also use OnStar to notify the police, fire department, or ambulance service in case of an emergency. Through in-vehicle sensors, it can even detect when a car may have been involved in an accident. Finally, OnStar can unlock car doors should a driver accidentally lock his or her keys inside (Figure 3.26).

GPS applications are becoming even more mobile. Recent GPS products include handheld devices for outdoor activities such as hiking, boating, and golf. These products provide helpful navigation of trails, boat routes, and golf courses. Nextel cell phones come equipped with GPS.

Other Satellite Applications

Echelon is a system used by the United States National Security Agency (NSA) to intercept and process international communications passed via satellites. The system uses ground-based listening devices and up to 120 satellites to intercept messages. It combs through the huge volume of intercepted messages, looking for words and phrases such as "bomb" and "terrorist" and other information of interest to intelligence agencies.

Satellites also bring Internet access to areas that don't have a communication infrastructure. The Navajo Nation, which straddles the borders of Arizona, New Mexico, and Utah and covers a 26,000-square-mile area, faces special challenges

FIGURE 3.27
DirecPC provides a link between satellites and phone lines to offer Internet access to very remote users.

for connecting its residents to the Internet. Approximately half of the households don't even have phone service, and those that do find the quality of that service sometimes lacking. For data communications, the maximum reliable data speed is often limited to 28.8 Kbps. In addition, Internet access through a private service provider is virtually always a long-distance call.

Through the use of satellite technology, Navajo Nation school administrators purchased a system called DirecPC Network Edition, which uses a small 18-inch satellite dish to receive information from the Internet and regular telephone or data lines to send information (Figure 3.27). Because Internet use in an educational environment involves massive amounts of downloaded information, the satellite solution was ideal.

TEXT, PICTURE, AND VIDEO MESSAGING AND MORE

A growing niche in cell phone use is within the K–12 age group. Cell phones give teens (and a growing number of preteens) not only a sense of community, but also a sense of freedom. Cell phone ownership is being compared with the freedom and individuality of having a driver's license. And the cell phone market for teens is growing rapidly. In 1998, 5 percent of teenagers owned cell phones. By 2003, that number had jumped to 17 percent. By 2007, it is expected that 50 percent of teens will have a cell phone—30 to 35 million potential customers.

More so than adults, teens and young adults use their cell phones to do things besides placing and receiving calls. Text, picture, and video messaging are fast becoming the hot applications for mobile devices that e-mail and IM once were for computers. **Text messaging** is similar to using your phone for instant messaging or as a receiver and transmitter for brief e-mail messages (Figure 3.28).

Picture and video messaging are mobile services that will transform the way we electronically interact with each other. People have sent pictures by way of FTP or as e-mail attachments for over 10 years, but the use of the telephone for such services is a fairly recent phenomenon. Today, **picture messaging** allows you to send full-color pictures, backgrounds, and even picture caller IDs on your cell phone. With picture messaging, your phone performs as a camera so that you can send pictures from your vacation or capture spontaneous moments and share them with others (Figure 3.29).

To capture, send, and receive pictures and video you must have a picture- or video-capturing phone as well as the necessary provider accounts to store and send the images. Companies such as Sprint PCS, Verizon Wireless, and AT&T Wireless offer more than 20 different picture phones that range in price (after rebates) from free to $499. Some of the phones will take pictures, and others can shoot up to 15 seconds of video.

Images you capture with your phone can be sent by way of e-mail attachments or as a single picture when calling or talking to someone. Note that the user on the other end needs to have a picture-enabled phone as well and that there is a charge for sending pictures or video.

One cell phone application that is more popular with parents than kids is **location** (or **position**) **awareness**. This new technology uses GPS-enabled chips to pinpoint the location of a cell phone (and its user). Teens may find location awareness to be a downside of owning a cell phone, because their parents will be able to monitor their location. Teens often complain about such surveillance with statements such as "you're intruding on my privacy," "you're treading upon my independence," and "I feel as though I'm always being watched." From the parents' perspective, however, they are simply keeping watch over their children in an effort to help them make better decisions.

Location awareness also has consumer and safety applications. The location-awareness feature enables your cell phone to quickly provide the location of the nearest restaurants and entertainment venues. It also can provide your location to a police station or other emergency service if needed. Law enforcement and government officials with the right credentials can access a Web site and locate a phone within 35 feet of its actual location.

U.S. law mandates that all new cell phones be position aware by 2005. The plus for society is that the 911 system will be able to determine the location of a phone, and thus the user, and then provide whatever assistance is necessary. An estimated 42 million Americans will be using location-awareness technology in 2005—or roughly 14 percent of the U.S. population.

Today's wired and wireless applications provide us with conveniences that were once unimaginable. If your cell phone or PDA is Bluetooth-enabled, you can send files wirelessly from your desktop computer to your printer or to a friend's laptop. You can buy concert tickets online, download the electronic tickets into your Bluetooth-enabled PDA, and then link to the Bluetooth-enabled scanner at the concert house instead of presenting a ticket. One particularly interesting development is the use of a Bluetooth enabled earphone that transmits and receives data from your cell phone, even if it is located in your pocket or backpack. Bluetooth radio chips are small and cheap (approximately $5 each) and growing in popularity. Both Microsoft and Apple came out in support of the technology in 2002. Who knows what tomorrow's wired and wireless applications will enable us to do?

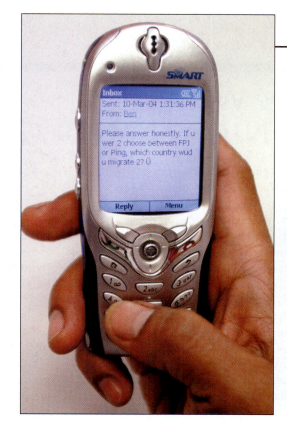

FIGURE 3.28 Text messaging enables users to converse without bothering those nearby.

Destinations

Visit **u-locate.com** to learn more about location-awareness technology.

FIGURE 3.29 Exchanging photos and video using your cell phone adds interest and context to conversations.

What You've Learned

WIRED & WIRELESS COMMUNICATION

- Bandwidth refers to the data transfer capacity of a communications channel and is measured in hertz (Hz) and bits per second (bps). To transmit text, you can get by with low bandwidth (such as a 56-Kbps connection). That rate, however, is often painfully slow for exploring the Web, which is more enjoyable at a high bandwidth of 128 Kbps or faster.

- To send digital data over dial-up phone lines, it's necessary to modulate the signal (transform it into analog form). On the receiving end, the signal must be demodulated (transformed back into digital form). Modems (modulators/demodulators) perform this service.

- Communications require physical and wireless media, including twisted-pair wire, coaxial cable, fiber-optic cable, infrared, radio, microwaves, and satellite. Last-mile technologies, including leased lines, ISDN, DSL, SONET, as well as ISDN adapters, DSL modems, and cable modems, increase the capacity of existing physical media. MMDS and LMDS are technologies that increase wireless media speeds.

- The public switched telephone network (PSTN) is predominantly digital, except for the local loop, which uses low-bandwidth twisted-pair wire connected to analog telephones. Even though most computer users utilize the PSTN for data communications, its limitations—susceptibility to line noise and inability to surpass a data transfer rate of 56 Kbps—make it less than ideal for this purpose.

- Multiplexing is the transmission of more than one telephone call or message on a single line. Digital telephony is the use of all-digital telephone systems: the telephones are digital, and the transmission also is handled digitally. Both technologies enable transmission of more voice data over traditional copper lines as well as fiber-optic cable.

- Digitization is the transformation of data such as voice, text, graphics, audio, and video into digital form. Convergence refers to the coming together of products such as PCs and telephones. Cellular telephones, PCS, and Web-enabled devices enable all types of digital information (voice, video, and data) to travel over wireless communication systems.

- Internet telephony and faxing can now be accomplished through the use of the Internet by traditional wired technology. New wireless technologies allow for text and picture messaging, satellite radio, and GPS services.

Key Terms and Concepts

Go to **www.prenhall.com/cayf2006** to review this chapter, answer the questions, and complete the exercises.

Matching

Match each key term in the left column with the most accurate definition in the right column.

_____ 1. digitization

_____ 2. broadband

_____ 3. SONET

_____ 4. PSTN

_____ 5. wireless

_____ 6. last-mile technologies

_____ 7. convergence

_____ 8. leased line

_____ 9. cell

_____ 10. microwaves

_____ 11. T1 line

_____ 12. videoconferencing

_____ 13. twisted pair

_____ 14. PCS

_____ 15. analog signal

a. the global telephone system, a massive network used for data communications as well as voice communications

b. a communications medium that uses radio or infrared signals

c. interim digital telephony technologies that make use of twisted-pair wire to reach the end user

d. the merging of disparate objects or ideas (and even people) into new combinations

e. the geographic area in which wireless signals are broadcast

f. specially conditioned copper wires that can handle up to 1.544 Mbps of computer data

g. high-frequency radio-wave transmissions which are limited to line-of-sight distances

h. two insulated wires twisted around each other to provide a shield against electromagnetic interference

i. a technology that enables two or more people who are geographically separated to have a face-to-face meeting

j. the transformation of data such as voice, text, graphics, audio, and video into digital form

k. a group of related digital cellular technologies

l. translates data into continuous waveforms

m. a specially conditioned telephone line that enables continuous, end-to-end communication between two points

n. a standard for high-performance optical networks

o. digital transmissions in excess of 1 Mbps

Multiple Choice

Circle the correct choice for each of the following.

1. What type of line uses fiber-optic cables?
   a. T1
   b. T2
   c. T3
   d. 10baseT

2. Which of the following media carries more data for longer distances?
   a. digital coaxial cable
   b. coaxial cable
   c. twisted-pair wire
   d. fiber-optic cable

3. Which of the following is not a transmission medium used to provide regional and long-distance service between local telephone exchanges?
   a. microwaves
   b. fiber-optic cables
   c. common carrier
   d. copper wire

4. Which term describes a cell phone's capability to indicate a user's whereabouts?
   a. location awareness
   b. self-awareness
   c. global awareness
   d. location global positioning

5. What does DBS stand for?
   a. Digital Band Service
   b. Direct Binary Satellite
   c. Digital Broadband Service
   d. Direct Broadcast Satellite

6. When someone makes a cellular phone call, all of the cell sites are connected to which of the following?
   a. public switched telephone network (PSTN)
   b. mobile optical network (MONET)
   c. Mobile Digital Subscriber Line (MDSL)
   d. mobile telephone switching office (MTSO)

7. What is multiplexing?
   a. a multiscreen movie theater
   b. many interconnected networks
   c. the ability to transmit more than one call on a single line
   d. the ability to send data and faxes with a single device

8. Which of the following services requires broadband digital transmission?
   a. digital television
   b. faxing
   c. sending e-mail
   d. none of the above

9. Which of the following terms is a technology that could be used for a wireless keyboard?
   a. InDA
   b. Serial
   c. IrDA
   d. InFRA

10. What videoconferencing technology enables participants to create a shared workspace?
    a. T2 lines
    b. instant messaging
    c. whiteboard
    d. fax modem

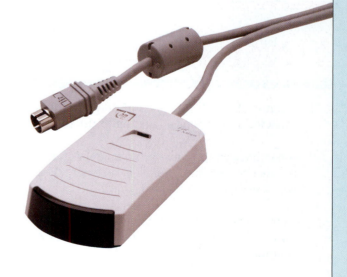

Fill-In

In the blanks provided, write the correct answer for each of the following.

1. A(n) _____ is a small, waist-high curbside installation that connects as many as 96 telephone subscribers.

2. The area served by an SLC is called the _____.

3. A(n) _____ is a device that enables computers to access the Internet by means of a cable TV connection.

4. _____ allows you to send full-color pictures, backgrounds, and even picture caller IDs on your cell phone.

5. _____ is the transformation of data such as voice, text, graphics, audio, and video into digital form.

6. If your computer is equipped with a(n) _____, you can send and receive faxes from your computer.

7. _____ uses the Internet for real-time voice communication.

8. Communications _____ are placed in geosynchronous orbit, which matches the speed of the Earth's rotation.

9. When using _____, no wires are required, but the transmitter and receiver must be in line of sight or the signal is lost.

10. _____ can be described as "low" or "high" as it refers to transmission speeds.

11. _____ refers collectively to a group of related digital cellular technologies.

12. _____ _____ uses two insulated wires twisted around each other to shield against interference.

13. A(n) _____ converts data into discontinuous pulses in which the presence or absence of electronic pulses represents 1s and 0s.

14. Within a range of approximately 30 feet, _____ allows for the transfer of data between itself and other enabled devices.

15. The inability of homes or businesses to access the PSTN's high-speed fiber-optic cables is often referred to as the _____-_____ _____.

Short Answer

1. What is bandwidth? Why is it an important consideration when connecting to the Internet?

2. A computer must have a fax modem and a scanner to fully function as a fax device. Explain why the scanner is needed.

3. In terms of the last-mile problem, explain the limitations of the PSTN for sending and receiving computer data.

4. Define convergence. Provide at least one example of technological convergence.

5. Briefly explain how Bluetooth works.

6. Explain the difference between the terms *modulation* and *demodulation*. Which of these must a modem be able to perform? Explain why.

Teamwork

1. Using Dialpad

Although most people to do not have enough bandwidth to support high-quality videoconferencing, they do have enough for telephone applications. Besides computer-to-computer voice communication, you can also use the Internet to make computer-to-telephone connections. Visit Dialpad at **dialpad.com**. Sign up for free calls and make calls to each other as well as some local and long-distance calls to friends and family. Catalog the quality of the phone conversations. What type of connection—modem, satellite, ISDN, xDSL, cable, or other—did you use? How did the speed of the connection affect the quality of the call?

2. Examining Your Phone Bill

Have each team member examine his or her most recent telephone bill. Answer the following questions and then collaborate on a two-page double-spaced paper that informs your professor of the breadth of your answers. Is your phone a cell phone? What surcharges and taxes are included in the bill? Are you billed separately for local calls, long-distance calls, and surcharges and taxes? Is your long-distance company the same as your local one? Do you manage your account online? Are your telephone bills available online? Can you pay them online? How would you rate the quality of your phone use experience with your current phone and plan?

3. Buying a Cell Phone

Your team is to research various cellular phone plans. Have each team member contact a communications company that provides cellular service in your area. Compare the various rate plans found by each team member. Do any of these plans include long-distance service? Do the companies that you contacted provide Internet access? If they do, describe which Internet services they support and their associated costs. Write a brief paper that summarizes your findings and evaluates each plan.

4. Internet Faxing

Work with your team members to provide the answers to these questions in a one-page summary. Have any team members sent or received a facsimile transmission using a computer? If so, was the fax sent or received from another computer or from an actual fax machine? (Is it even possible to know?) Could you tell the difference? What was the name of the fax software application that was used? Describe the process for sending and receiving the fax. If you sent a fax, describe how you created the document. If you received a fax, did you print it? Why or why not? If not, then find the answers to the preceding questions by either talking with someone who has sent faxes or by doing research on the Web.

5. Internet Cable: One-Way Only?

You may already have cable television in your home. Some cable companies also offer one-way (download-only) Internet service through this cable. However, this service still requires the use of a modem and a telephone connection for uploading. Unfortunately, only a fraction of the cable companies can provide the two-way data communications that is needed for full cable Internet access. Your team is to contact your local cable company to see if you are one of the lucky cable users who can get a two-way Internet cable connection to each of your residences. What additional hardware is needed for Internet cable connections? What is the monthly cost of this service? Do you already have a two-way Internet cable connection? If not, explain why you would or would not consider this high-speed alternative.

On the Web

1. 3G Technology

One of the newest technologies in mobile communications is 3G, which stands for third generation. Type "3G" into your favorite search engine to learn about this new technology. Which organization developed the specifications for 3G? The present speed for using a cellular phone to connect a computer to the Internet is only 14.4 Kbps. What are the expected transmission rates for 3G connections? When are 3G systems expected to be available? Explain why you would or would not consider purchasing or upgrading to a 3G phone.

2. Adventure GPS

Go to the Adventure GPS site at **www.gps4fun.com** to learn more about GPS. Then use your favorite search engine to answer the following questions. Who owns the collection of satellites that make up the GPS system? How many GPS satellites are there, and how high do they orbit? How does a GPS receiver determine its position? How accurate is a GPS reading? List a civilian, a military, and a commercial use of a GPS. Do you know anyone who owns a GPS system? Have you tried one? Find a specific GPS tool. What is its price? How would you use it?

3. Using Bluetooth Technology

Go to the Apple Bluetooth technology site at **www.apple.com/bluetooth** to learn about how Apple is using Bluetooth technology. How does Apple define Bluetooth? What can you do with a Bluetooth-enabled Macintosh? What other devices does Apple suggest for use with Bluetooth technology? Describe the device you will need to enable Bluetooth on a Mac.

4. Camera Sites

Visit EarthCam at **www.earthcam.com**. Follow at least three major category links (e.g., computer cams, science cams, traffic cams, etc.) until you reach a camera site. Be sure that one of the sites you visit is an international site. Which sites did you successfully visit? How many "dead" links did you encounter? What was the subject matter? What was the quality of the image(s) from the cameras? Were you satisfied or disappointed with how current the pictures were?

5. Online Images

On Yahoo!'s home page, just above the Web search dialog box, there is a link to "Images." Click on this link to search for at least three different image types. How many results did you get for each request? Left-click on the picture to visit the Web site where the picture actually resides. Click on the picture again to view it in its full size. Now right-click on the image and choose "Save Picture As" from the pop-up menu. Save at least one picture from each of your searches to a local folder of your choosing. For each picture, describe any concerns you may have concerning copyright. Write a one page summary that uses key terms from the Moving Data section of this chapter to describe how the picture got from where it was to your computer.

How to Find Wireless Hot Spots

Wireless networks are everywhere, but how can you find them if you can't see them? If you have a lot of time on your hands, you can always walk or drive around your town with your wireless-enabled laptop or PDA until you stumble across a wireless access point. A much less cumbersome, and discreet, way to find out if you are currently standing in a wireless hot spot is to use a device such as Kensington's WiFi finder (Figure 3.30). The small device attaches to your keychain, and at the touch of a button it will tell you if a wireless network is nearby and the strength of the wireless signal. Remember, just because a wireless network is nearby doesn't mean that it is configured to allow just anyone to connect to it.

If you're not the adventurous type and would prefer to know in advance if you will be in an area with wireless coverage, a number of Web sites maintain a database of publicly available hot spots. These Web sites, such as the one run by Intel at **intel.jiwire.com** to promote adoption of its Centrino™ mobile technology, enable you to enter an address and see a listing of available wireless access points near that location. These Web site databases do not contain every hot spot in a given area, but they do provide a good starting point for identifying reliable wireless networks and whether a fee or contract with a wireless ISP is required to access them. You can also try to locate hot spots by visiting **www.wifinder.com** or **hotspot-locations.com**.

One initiative that is underway in many large cities is the development of community wireless networks. These networks are built "by the people, for the people." Planned and built by volunteers, these networks are made possible by companies and individuals who host access points throughout a community. These networks

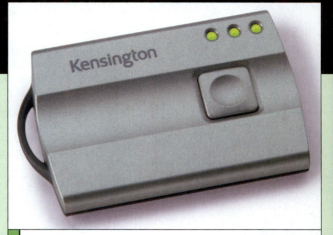

FIGURE 3.30 Kensington's WiFi finder attaches to your keychain. At the touch of a button, it will tell you if a wireless network is nearby and the strength of the wireless signal.

are usually freely accessible, but they may or may not provide access to the Internet, because many of them concentrate on providing information relating directly to the communities they serve. For detailed information about a great working example of a community wireless network, check out the Seattle wireless project at **www.seattlewireless.net**.

Many companies, such as Starbucks and McDonald's, provide wireless Internet access to their customers at many of their locations. If you have a favorite place to hang out, you should check the company's Web site to see if it already offers wireless access. These services, although sometimes free, usually require an hourly fee or a monthly contract with a wireless ISP (such as T-Mobile Hotspot). As with any wireless network, you should do your research to ensure that your wireless equipment is compatible with the network to which you are trying to connect.

SPOTLIGHT HOME

When people hear the word *network*, they often think "Oh, that's too technical for me." Although networks require hardware and software technology, you should simply think of a network as a way to share computing power and resources. An early tongue-in-cheek reference to networks involved the sharing of data between computers by way of a portable storage device, such as a floppy disk, a CD or DVD, or a USB plug-in drive.

NETWORKS

Today a network is a network because there is network operating system software involved and either a wired or wireless infrastructure in place. And don't forget, every time you log on to the Internet, you're using a network!

Approximately two-thirds of all U.S. households own a computer. And more than 20 million of those households own two or more computers. Market research indicates that multicomputer households are becoming more common because people who already own PCs are still buying new ones. It is not unusual for each parent and one or more children in a household to have their own computer or mobile device, such as a PDA (Figure 3A). Why is this important? People in multicomputer households want to share scanners, printers, data, and games among multiple users using different computers. In addition, they want the household to share a single Internet connection. The computers in a single household may be of different makes and models (such as a mix of Macs and PCs). How can these computers share information and resources? The answer is a home network.

FIGURE 3A

It is not unusual for each parent and one or more children in a household to have their own computer.

By the end of 2004, experts estimate that there will be over 16 million home networks in place, and as many as 70 percent of them will be using wireless technology. By 2006, experts expect that figure to almost double to 28 million home networks in U.S. households. A **home network** enables users to quickly and conveniently share files and resources by using network connections between computers and peripheral devices. Home networks, a personal and specific use of network technology, can accommodate both wired and wireless communications. Wired home networks use coaxial cable, telephone wires, Cat-5 wires, or a home's electrical wiring. Wireless home networks rely on radio signals.

This Spotlight examines the various home network options available to you and explains how to set up a home network.

WIRED HOME NETWORKS

There are five basic types of home network configurations, three that use wires and two that use radio waves. Let's first look at the different wired configurations.

HOME ETHERNET NETWORKS

Ethernet is a communications standard that specifies how physically connected computers in a network send data. Ethernet-linked computers send data in small chunks, called *packets*, over wires. You can think of a packet as a letter, addressed for delivery to a different city, that is moving through the mail system. In addition to the actual data, each packet carries your computer's home address and a destination address.

The Ethernet standard also details the types of wires that must be used and how fast data can travel across the network. The most popular type of Ethernet wiring is twisted-pair wire. Twisted-pair wire comes in five categories. Home networks use either Cat-3 or Cat-5 wire. These wires are then connected by RJ-45 connectors, which look like large telephone jacks. Cat-3 wire transfers data at speeds of up to 16 Mbps; Cat-5 transfers data at speeds of up to 100 Mbps.

The simplest form of an Ethernet network is to link different computers together with a connecting hub. See Figure 3B for an example of a simple Ethernet network. In this example, computer 1 sends its message to computer 2 by way of the hub. A **hub** is an external communications device with multiple connectors (ports). A computer attached to one port can communicate with computers attached to any of the other ports. Hubs are available in many configurations. Most have 4 to 12 ports. The majority of home networks use a 10BaseT hub that is capable of a transfer rate of 10 Mbps (10 million bits per second). If you have the money, you can upgrade to a 100BaseT hub with a transfer rate of 100 Mbps. Some dual-speed hubs can transmit at both the 10BaseT and 100BaseT transfer rates.

With an Ethernet network, each networked computer must have an **Ethernet network adapter**, also called a network interface card (NIC). A NIC is an internal communications device that uses electrical signals traveling across cables to enable computers to communicate with each other.

The second type of Ethernet configuration is to dedicate one of the computers on the system as the system's server and then route all network traffic through a hub or a switch. A **switch** is like a hub, but more efficient. Hubs send data received from one port

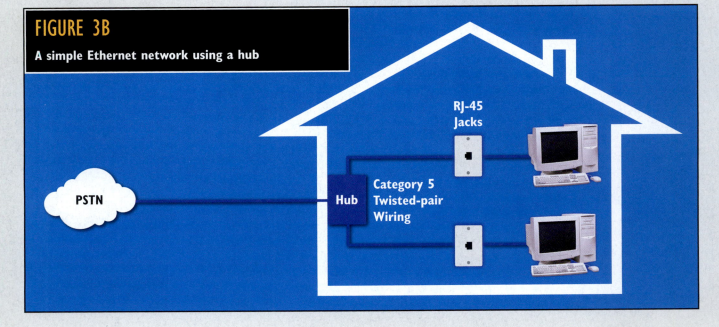

FIGURE 3B

A simple Ethernet network using a hub

RJ-45 Jacks

Hub

Category 5 Twisted-pair Wiring

PSTN

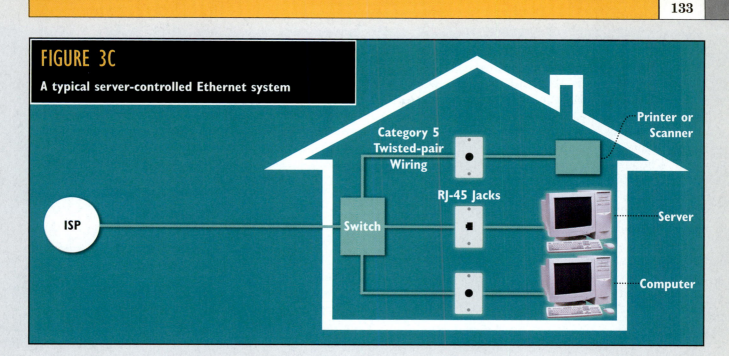

FIGURE 3C

A typical server-controlled Ethernet system

out to all the other ports and then let the computers figure out which computer the data are intended for. In contrast, a switch knows about the computers connected to it and transmits data only to the computer to which the data are addressed. In this case, all peripherals (computers, printers, scanners, and so on) are cabled to the hub or switch, which then coordinates signals to and from the server and peripherals (Figure 3C).

HOME PHONE-LINE NETWORKS

Home phone-line networks use a home's existing telephone wiring. Home phone-line networks work best in situations where computers are in different rooms of the house, because most rooms only have one phone

jack. Home phone-line networks offer many advantages, including simple and inexpensive installation, standardization, reliability, and sufficient speed for multimedia applications. Home phone-line networks are compatible with other home networking technologies and work with all computer makes and models, including Macs and older PCs. Home phone-line networks do not require hubs or switches (Figure 3D).

However, home phone-line networks do have a number of disadvantages. Depending on your ISP and type of service, you may need to install special software or hardware. In addition, you may have to install home phone-line NICs in all of the PCs slated for the network. You may also need to run new phone wiring or additional lengths of phone cord if a phone jack isn't close to a computer.

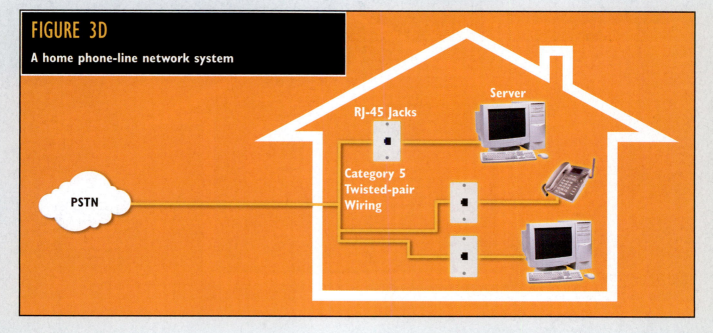

FIGURE 3D

A home phone-line network system

The Home Phone-line Networking Alliance (HomePNA) is a group of networking-technology companies that created the standards for home phone-line networks. HomePNA standards help to ensure that home phone-line technologies are robust enough to handle various house and business phone-line wiring schemes and simultaneously handle telephone traffic. These standards also specify how home phone-line network technology should handle differences in the strength of the signal as it travels throughout the system as well as interference from appliances, cars, radios, cell phones, and other devices in the home.

HPNA 1.0 was the first version of the standard; HPNA 3.0 was released in mid 2004. HPNA 1.0 operated at a somewhat slow 1 Mbps. HPNA 3.0 operates at approximately 128 Mbps—as fast as or faster than Ethernet.

HOME POWER-LINE NETWORKS

Similar to home phone-line networks, **home power-line networks** use a home's existing electrical wiring. Power-line networks use the electrical system to connect computers through power outlets (Figure 3E).

One major advantage of home power-line networks is that most homes have at least one electrical outlet in every room. Inexpensive and easy installation is another advantage. In addition, a peripheral that doesn't have to be directly connected to a computer can be located anywhere. For example, whereas a monitor needs to be physically near a computer in order to be connected and used, a printer could be located in a completely different room or on another floor.

Power-line networks do have some drawbacks. If your home has anything other than 110-volt electrical wiring, you can't install a power-line network. In addition, home power usage and older wiring can affect performance. The devices that power-line networks use to access electrical outlets take up a lot of space inside or outside the walls. Connection speeds are rather slow, ranging from 50 to 350 Kbps. And to ensure network security, all data must be encrypted.

WIRELESS HOME NETWORKS

Although several wireless network standards are currently available, the two you are most probably interested in are HomeRF and Wi-Fi. Wireless network standards have been developed to ensure that companies that build wireless connecting devices do so in compliance with strict definitions and exchange rules. Ultimately, three factors will determine which standard best suits your needs: (1) the cost of the hardware and/or software, (2) the speed at which data can travel over the network, and (3) the range within which you can reliably transmit between devices. Let's start by learning about HomeRF.

HOME RADIO-FREQUENCY NETWORKS

Home radio-frequency (HomeRF) networks are wireless networks in which each computer on the network broadcasts its information to another using radio signals. HomeRF networks use communications devices

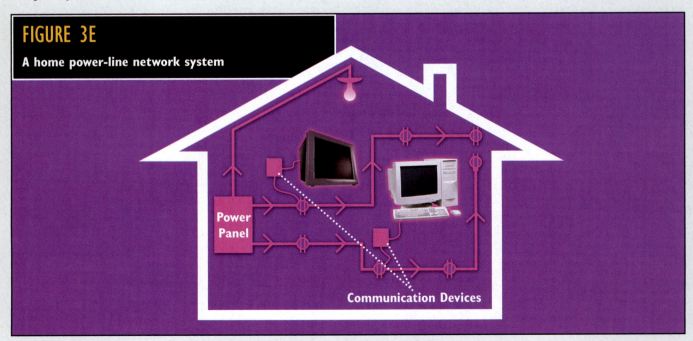

FIGURE 3E

A home power-line network system

Power Panel

Communication Devices

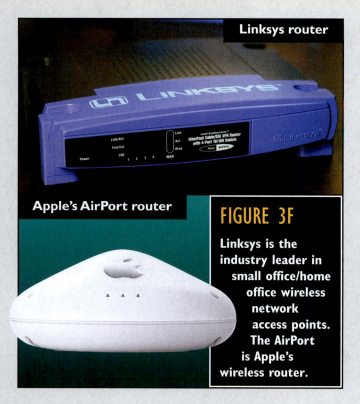

Linksys router

Apple's AirPort router

FIGURE 3F

Linksys is the industry leader in small office/home office wireless network access points. The AirPort is Apple's wireless router.

called **network access points** (also referred to as wireless access points or routers) to send and receive data between computers that have wireless adapters. Network access points enable you to move a laptop with a wireless adapter from room to room or to place computers in different locations throughout a house (Figure 3F).

In a HomeRF network, a peer-to-peer relationship exists among all of the computers in the network. This means that all the computers are equals, or *peers*, with no particular computer acting as the server. However,

some home wireless networks can also be of the client/ server type. In a client/server home network, each computer communicates with the server, and the server then communicates with other computers or peripherals. A client/server network uses a central access point to control all network traffic. All peripherals must be within the range of the central access point, which is usually 100 to 300 feet, depending on the building's construction and thickness of the walls, floors, and ceilings. The central access point routes data between wireless stations or to and from the network server (Figure 3G).

Three dominant HomeRF standards are currently in use. All three are 802.11 standards, a group of wireless transmission specifications. The first standard, developed in 1997, was the 802.11b specification, which operates in the 2.4-GHz radio band. This standard is capable of data transfer rates of up to 11 Mbps. The second standard is the 802.11a specification, which operates in the 5-GHz radio band and can transfer data at up to 54 Mbps. (Why the first standard was "b" and the second standard "a" is not clear.) A third standard is the 802.11g specification, which builds on the 802.11b specification. The 802.11g specification operates in the 2.4-GHz range and has a data transfer rate of at least 54 Mbps. (This standard has not yet been fully developed; its data transfer rate has not been finalized.)

HomeRF is less expensive than other types of wireless home networks. It can transfer data at between 11 and 54 Mbps and has an effective range of up to 150 feet. HomeRF provides adequate performance for most networking tasks but is underpowered when it comes to playing audio across the network or in streaming video content. Recent developments in the HomeRF standard 802.11a turbo allow for transfer rates of up to 108 Mbps.

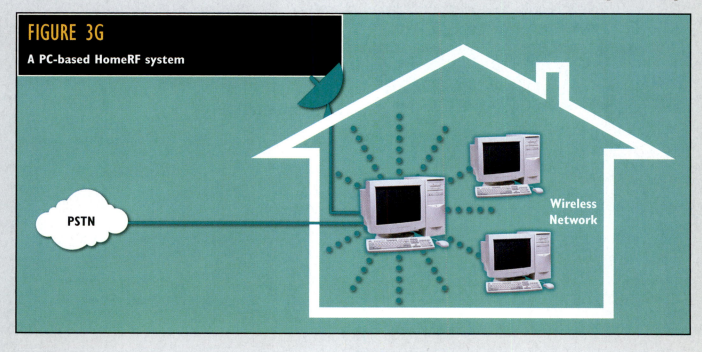

FIGURE 3G

A PC-based HomeRF system

PSTN

Wireless Network

HOME WI-FI NETWORKS

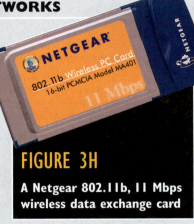

Wi-Fi is a collection of standards for two types of networks: ad hoc and client/server. An ad hoc network is a simple network that doesn't have a central access point or a server in which communications are established between computers and peripherals. All computers and peripherals communicate with each other by way of wireless data exchange cards that are plugged into each peripheral (Figure 3H).

FIGURE 3H

A Netgear 802.11b, 11 Mbps wireless data exchange card

Wi-Fi operates in the 2.4-GHz band. One downside to the use of this frequency is that several other home appliances, such as wireless phones and microwaves, sometimes operate in the 2.4-GHz range as well, resulting in interference. (This is also true of the 802.11b and 802.11g specifications.) Figure 3I shows a simple Wi-Fi system.

Wi-Fi is a good choice for households with Macs, because recent Apple models can be fitted with an inexpensive AirPort card.

Now that we've examined the various types of home networks, let's look at the steps involved in setting one up.

SETTING UP A HOME NETWORK

Setting up any network, including one for your home, goes much more smoothly if you can follow a series of steps. The steps presented in this section correspond roughly to those followed by computer professionals who develop large-scale networks. Don't let that intimidate you though! You don't have to be a computer professional to successfully set up a home network.

PLANNING

As with any type of project, you must first come up with a plan based on your specific home networking needs. Ask yourself realistic questions: What are you trying to accomplish with your network? Is it for a small business or just for personal use? Is it only for your computer and peripherals or will it support multiple family members? Will the hardware be concentrated in one room (such as an office or den) or in many rooms? Based on your answers to these questions and the type of home network you choose, you should develop a needs or requirements checklist. You can determine your specific requirements by visiting your local home electronics store or by reading recommendations you find on the Web.

When planning a home network you will need to do two things. First, you will need to decide which network wiring technology to use. You can choose from the technologies discussed earlier: standard Ethernet, home phone line, home power line, HomeRF, or Wi-Fi. Wired networks may perform faster and more reliably, but wireless networks allow for more flexibility, particularly when using one or more laptops that you might want to move to different locations throughout the house.

Second, you will need to purchase the appropriate hardware and software. Several companies, including Linksys and Belkin, have kits that provide the

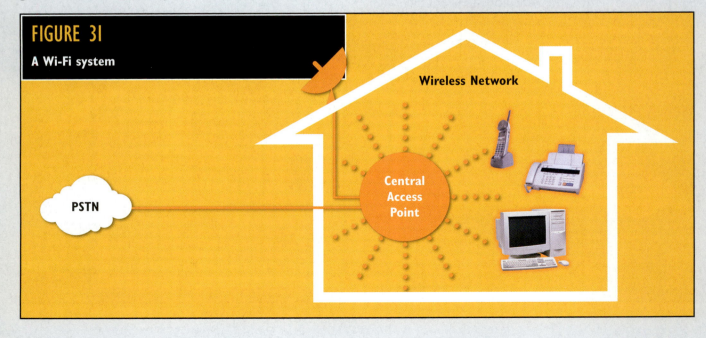

FIGURE 3I

A Wi-Fi system

Wireless Network

PSTN

Central Access Point

essentials for setting up a home network (Figure 3J). For instance, a Linksys fast Ethernet kit includes NICs, hubs, cables, and software. A similar wireless kit includes a router to connect to a server or the Internet, PC data exchange cards, and a software installation disc. Such kits are often referred to as a *network in a box*.

One way to investigate home network components is to visit a computer store or a home electronics store. At the store, you can obtain advice as to which type of network system and configuration might work best for you. You can then buy the routers, hubs, network cards, and other peripherals that you will install in your home.

You should also consider purchasing and installing personal firewall software to keep your home network safe from viruses and hackers (Figure 3K).

Although Ethernet is perhaps the fastest and most robust way to wire a home network, the only practical way to install it is during the construction of a new house. When installing this type of network in an existing home, it is possible to route the cables through the walls by use of either attic or basement access, but it will take a lot of work. If you decide to use Ethernet, you will need to determine if you are going to do the job yourself or whether you are going to hire someone to do it. In either case, the installer must carefully plan the routing of the cables through walls and across floors. You can find tutorials on the Web that will help you layout the appropriate locations to drill into your walls. Search for "home network wiring" in your favorite search engine to find these and other home networking sites.

Once you have purchased the appropriate hardware and software, you must configure the network so that all of the components function together. When your network is properly configured, you will find that a home network improves your home-computing experience.

CONFIGURATION

Depending on which type of network you decide to set up, your configuration options will vary. The main tasks involved with configuration are designating which PCs will be part of the network; installing the proper hardware and software on those PCs; and designating how files, folders, peripherals (printers and scanners), and an Internet connection will be shared.

Every computer on the network needs a network interface that bundles data into chunks to travel across the network as well as a connection point, or port, for the special wiring that connects all the PCs. The port is either built into the computer or provided as an add-in NIC. The NIC sends data to the network and receives data sent from other computers on the network.

FIGURE 3J

Network in a box solutions from Microsoft and Linksys

The next step is to configure the hub. A wire runs from the back of each computer to the hub, which serves as a communications point to connect the signal to the appropriate cable that goes to the intended destination. Printers, scanners, and other peripherals are usually plugged into one of the networked computers and then shared with the others. The hub must be placed in a convenient location so that you can string individual cables from the hub to each port in each room where you want to use the network.

FIGURE 3K

Personal firewall software is a must for home networks.

FIGURE 3L

The Network Setup Wizard in Windows XP

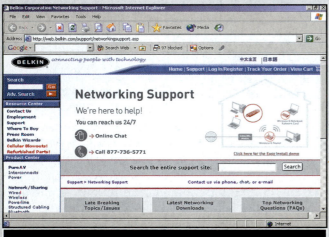

FIGURE 3M

The major router manufacturers maintain Web sites that provide support for their products.

Some home networking kits come with installation CDs that have wizards to walk you through the configuration process. Windows XP even has a Network Setup Wizard. (The Network Setup Wizard can be accessed in several ways. Use the All Programs, Accessories, Communications, Network Setup Wizard menu sequence or Control Panel, Network Connections, Network Tasks, and click on the Set up a home or small office network icon) (Figure 3L). Setup information may also be available from the store where you purchased your networking supplies or from Web searches on home networks.

MAINTENANCE AND SUPPORT

Computer and network problems can be extremely frustrating. You should set up a regular maintenance schedule for both your computer and your network. The good news is that there isn't much to maintain with today's home networking solutions. You may need to blow off dust and lint that accumulates on your router or hub. You also can periodically remove your network cards from your computers and peripherals and clean the contacts with a cotton swab dipped in denatured alcohol (be sure to read the advice and warnings that come with your networking devices). You may also need to use your operating system's network utilities to refresh your network's settings.

When something goes wrong, you should try to think of what might have caused the problem. Sometimes the solution is as simple as restarting your computer and/or unplugging the power source from your router and other peripherals and then plugging them back in. You may also need to restart each computer that is connected to your system. If these actions do not solve the problem, you have several other options. If the problem produces an error message, write down the subject of the error message and then type it into the search box on your favorite search engine site. You can also search manufacturers' Web sites. For instance, if you have a Linksys router and Belkin network cards, you could go to **linksys.com** and **belkin.com** and see if any downloads are available to update your network devices.

THE FUTURE OF HOME NETWORKING

Convergence will be the future of home networking systems. You may be skeptical, but someday you may be able to use home networks to control household appliances to prepare food or to maintain a home's appearance. Networked home security systems already help protect us from intrusion or damage from natural events.

In the near future, new houses will have a central control unit that is capable of managing home network events as well as communication, entertainment, temperature regulation, lighting, and household appliances. It is very possible that someday your refrigerator may send you an e-mail informing you of the state of its cooling coils, including a request that you vacuum out the lint that is blocking good air circulation.

In the future, your home networking system will almost certainly be wireless. It will have capabilities that will help it adapt to new technologies as they develop. Wireless technology will be able to provide the flexibility that is required to seamlessly integrate convenience, simplicity, and, hopefully, long-term cost savings.

SPOTLIGHT EXERCISES

1 The number of households that have more than one computer is increasing. Multicomputer families want to share resources among their respective computers. One of the resources that many want to share is the Internet connection. Although newer versions of Microsoft Windows have software that enables two computers to share an Internet connection, consumers with high-speed connections such as cable or DSL can use a router to share Internet access. Go to a local computer store and investigate cable and DSL routers. How many ports are available? How much do these devices cost? What physical medium is used to connect the computers to the router? Can a router be used to share a printer? What additional hardware is needed to connect computers to the router? If you had a high-speed connection and multiple computers, would you purchase a router? Why or why not?

2 Many homes with cable television service have more than one television set. Connecting multiple televisions to the cable service requires the use of "splitters" to divide the incoming signal and send it to each television set. Some new houses are constructed with coaxial cable running to multiple rooms, but how are multiple television sets connected in older homes? Unfortunately, this usually requires drilling holes in walls, floors, or ceilings or even running cables on the exterior of the residence. Some homeowners and landlords do not want to do this. The same connection problem exists with home computer networks. Fortunately, a wireless access point offers an alternative to running network cables. Go to a local computer store and investigate wireless networking. What are the prices for these wireless access points? How does the wireless connection speed compare with a wired one? What additional hardware is needed to network computers to the wireless access point? If you had a home network, would you consider this networking alternative? Why or why not?

3 Assume that you have both a desktop and a laptop computer and you want them to share a network. To do this, each computer needs a network interface card. Search the Web to find the best price for a NIC for a laptop computer and a desktop computer. How much does each NIC cost? Which type of card is more expensive? Why do you think one card is more expensive than the other? Some desktop computers now include automatic built-in network connectivity. Locate and name two specific desktop and laptop models that have internal networking capability. If you currently have a desktop or laptop computer, does your computer have internal networking capability? How well does it work for you?

4 Some people may need to connect their PDAs to a desktop or laptop computer. What are the benefits of doing this? Search the Web to determine the most popular methods for networking a PDA to a PC. Which of these methods require additional PC hardware? Is the use of the word *networking* correct in this instance? Why or why not?

5 Users can protect their personal computers by using firewalls. A firewall can be implemented through software, hardware, or a combination of both. Two of the leading software applications, McAfee Personal Firewall (**www.mcafee.com**) and Norton Personal Firewall (**www.symantec.com**), are designed for personal computers running various operating systems. According to these and other security utility sites, why should you purchase firewall software? What is the annual subscription fee for McAfee's firewall application? What are the purchase and upgrade prices for Norton's Personal Firewall? After reading descriptions of these products on McAfee and Norton's Web sites, search the Web to find independent evaluations of each product. Identify the URLs of these additional review sites. Explain which firewall application you would purchase and why.

What You'll Learn . . .

- List the two major components of system software.

- Explain why a computer needs an operating system.

- List the five basic functions of an operating system.

- Explain what happens when you turn on a computer.

- List the three major types of user interfaces.

- Discuss the strengths and weaknesses of the most popular operating systems.

- List the seven system utilities that are considered to be essential.

- Discuss data backup procedures.

- Understand troubleshooting techniques and determine probable solutions to any operating system problems you may encounter.

System Software

Without software—the set of instructions that tells the computer what to do—a computer is just an expensive collection of wires and components. Chances are you've already worked with one type of software: application software. Application software helps you to accomplish a task, such as writing a college essay or balancing your checkbook. The other major type of software is system software. **System software** includes all of the programs needed for a computer and its peripheral devices to function smoothly. Although some system software works behind the scenes, some of it requires your guidance and control.

System software has two major components: (1) the operating system and (2) system utilities that provide various maintenance functions. Learning how to use an operating system and system utilities is the first step you can take toward mastering any computer system. Mastering a computer system is not unlike understanding the fundamentals of any system. The more you know about managing the water, filters, plants, and water temperature in your aquarium, the healthier and happier your fish will be. It's the same with computers; the more you know about and understand the operating system, the better your computer will serve you. In this chapter, you'll learn what operating systems do, look at the most popular operating systems, and learn which utilities you should use to ensure that your computing experience is safe and enjoyable.

The Operating System

The **operating system** (**OS**) is essentially a set of programs designed to work with a specific type of computer, such as a PC or a Macintosh. Its most important role lies in coordinating the various functions of the computer's hardware. The operating system also supports the application software you run. An operating system performs five basic functions: It starts the computer,

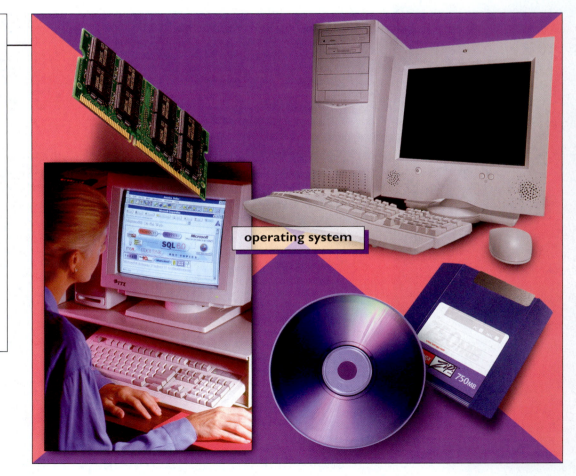

FIGURE 4.1
An operating system works at the intersection of application software, the user, and the computer's hardware. It starts the computer, manages applications and memory, handles messages from input and output devices, and provides a means of communicating with the user.

operating system

manages applications, manages memory, handles messages from input and output devices, and provides the user interface (a means of communicating with the user) (Figure 4.1). The operating system is most often found on a hard disk, although on some small handheld computers it is on the memory chip.

Imagine the traffic in a downtown New York City intersection at rush hour and you'll have a good idea of what it's like inside a computer. Electrons are whizzing around at incredible speeds, transported this way and that by the operating system, the electronic equivalent of a harried traffic officer. Impatient peripherals and programs are honking electronic "horns," trying to get the officer's attention. As if the scene weren't chaotic enough, the "mayor" (the user) wants to come through right now. Just like a traffic officer, the computer's operating system, standing at the intersection of the computer's hardware, application programs, and the user, keeps traffic running smoothly.

Let's examine the five functions of an operating system more closely.

STARTING THE COMPUTER

Starting the computer is the first operating system function. When you start a computer, it loads the operating system into the computer's RAM. (To **load** means to transfer something from a storage device, such as the hard disk, to memory.) RAM is a form of temporary storage that is very fast, but that is erased when the power goes off. The process of loading the operating system to memory is called **booting**. This term has been used in computing circles since the very early days. It comes from an old saying that someone can pull themselves up by their boot straps, or, in other words, get started on his or her own. With a **cold boot**, you start a computer that is not already on. With a **warm boot** (also called a **warm start**), you restart a computer that is already on. Warm boots are often necessary after installing new software or after an application crashes or stops working. On PCs, you can initiate a warm boot by pressing Ctrl + Alt + Del (hold down the Ctrl and Alt keys and then press Del) or

by pressing the Reset button, which is usually located on the front of the system unit. (On the Macintosh, the system will reset when you press Apple, Control, and the Power button at the same time.)

With both types of booting, the computer copies the kernel along with other essential portions of the operating system from the hard disk into the computer's memory, where it remains while your computer is powered on and functioning. The **kernel** is the central part of the operating system that starts applications, manages devices and memory, and performs other essential functions. The kernel resides in memory at all times, so it must be kept as small as possible. Less frequently used portions of the operating system are stored on the hard disk and retrieved as needed. Such portions are called nonresident because they do not reside in memory.

A cold or warm boot is a step-by-step process. The following sections discuss the steps followed by the computer after you initiate a cold or a warm boot (Figure 4.2).

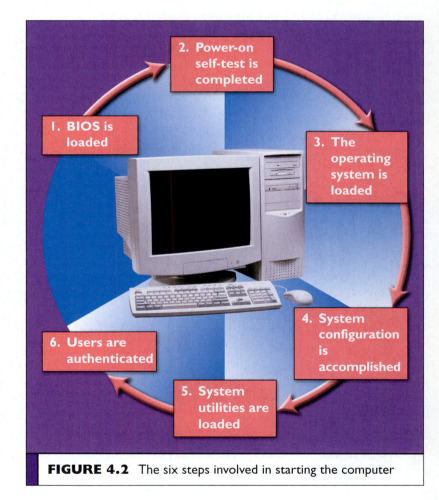

FIGURE 4.2 The six steps involved in starting the computer

1. BIOS is loaded
2. Power-on self-test is completed
3. The operating system is loaded
4. System configuration is accomplished
5. System utilities are loaded
6. Users are authenticated

Techtalk

CMOS

CMOS (complementary metal-oxide semiconductor) is a special type of memory used to store essential startup configuration options, such as the amount of memory that has been installed in the computer. CMOS also keeps track of the day and time on your computer.

Step 1: The BIOS (Basic Input/Output System) and Setup Program

When you first turn on or reset a PC, electricity flows from the power supply through the CPU, which resets and searches for the BIOS. The **BIOS (basic input/output system)** is the part of the system software that equips the computer with the instructions needed to accept keyboard input and display information on the screen. The BIOS is encoded, or permanently written, in the computer's ROM. ROM, or read-only memory, is a kind of memory that is permanent and unchanging. Programs such as the BIOS that are encoded in ROM are meant to be reliably used over and over again. Once the BIOS is located, you may briefly see the BIOS screen, a text-only screen that provides information about the BIOS (Figure 4.3).

While the BIOS information is visible, you can access the computer's setup program by pressing a special key, such as Del or F8. (You'll see an on-screen message indicating which key to press to access the setup program.) The **setup program** includes settings that control the computer's hardware. You should *not* alter or change *any* of these settings unless you are instructed to do so by technical support personnel. We'll look more closely at the setup program in "Step 3: Loading the Operating System."

Step 2: The Power-On Self-Test (POST)

After the BIOS instructions are loaded into memory, a series of tests are conducted to make sure that the computer and associated peripherals are operating correctly. Collectively, these tests are known as the **power-on self-test** (**POST**). Among the components tested are the computer's main memory (RAM), the keyboard and mouse, disk drives, and the hard disk. If any of the power-on self-tests fail, you'll hear a beep, see an on-screen error message, and the computer will stop. You often can correct such problems by making sure that components, such as keyboards, are plugged in securely.

However, some failures are so serious that the computer cannot display an error message; instead, it sounds a certain number of beeps. If this happens, it's time to call for technical support. To help the technician repair the computer, write down any error messages you see and try to remember how many beeps you heard.

Step 3: Loading the Operating System

Once the power-on self-test is successfully completed, the BIOS initiates a search for the operating system. Options (or settings) in the setup program determine where the BIOS looks for the operating system. (These settings are set by default but can be modified by the user.)

On most PCs, the BIOS first looks for the operating system on the computer's hard disk. When the BIOS finds the operating system, it loads the operating system's kernel into memory. At that point, the operating system takes control of the computer and begins loading system configuration information.

Step 4: System Configuration

In Microsoft Windows, configuration information about installed peripherals and software is stored in a database called the **registry**. The registry also contains information about your system configuration choices, such as background graphics and mouse settings.

Once the operating system's kernel has been loaded, it checks the system's configuration to determine which drivers and other utility programs are needed. A

FIGURE 4.3 The BIOS screen provides information about your computer's default input and output settings.

driver is a utility program that makes a peripheral device function correctly. If a peripheral device that is already installed on the system requires a driver to operate, that peripheral's driver will be installed and loaded automatically. If the driver is missing, you may be prompted to insert a disk containing the needed driver.

Operating systems are equipped with Plug-and-Play (PnP) capabilities, which automatically detect new PnP-compatible peripherals that you may have installed while the power was switched off, load the necessary drivers, and check for conflicts with other devices. Peripheral devices equipped with PnP features identify themselves to the operating system.

Step 5: Loading System Utilities

Once the operating system has detected and configured all of the system's hardware, it loads system utilities such as speaker volume control, antivirus software, and a PC card unplugging utility. In Microsoft Windows, you can view available custom configuration choices by right-clicking one of the small icons located on the right side of the Windows taskbar. You can access additional system configuration choices in the Control Panel (Figure 4.4).

Step 6: Authenticating Users

When the operating system finishes loading, you may see a dialog box asking you to type a user name and password. Through this process, called **authentication** (or **login**), you verify that you are indeed the person who is authorized to use the computer.

Consumer-oriented operating systems such as Microsoft Windows and Mac OS do not demand that you supply a user name and password to use the computer. However, you can set up profiles on these systems. Associated with a user name and, optionally, a password, a **profile** is a record of a specific user's preferences for the desktop theme, icons, and menu styles. If you set up a profile for yourself, your preferences will appear on the screen after you log in. You can also enable other users to create and log on to their profiles, and they'll see their preferences without disturbing yours.

On multiuser computer systems such as in a university lab or a corporate office environment, you must have an account to

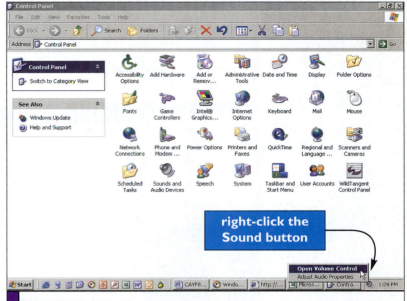

right-click the Sound button

FIGURE 4.4 The Control Panel, which is accessed directly from the Start menu, and the Windows taskbar contain many options for managing and customizing your computer system.

access a computer. Your **account** consists of your user name, your password, and your storage space, which is called a *home directory*. The account is usually created by the computer's system administrator, the person who's responsible for managing the use of the computer in multiuser systems.

Now that the operating system is loaded and running, let's look at another important task that the operating system handles: managing applications.

MANAGING APPLICATIONS

The operating system function that most dramatically affects an operating system's overall quality is running and **managing applications**. When you start an application, the CPU loads the application from storage into RAM. In the early days of personal computing, **single-tasking operating systems** could run only one application at a time, which was often inconvenient. To switch between applications, you had to quit one application before you could start the second.

Today, multitasking operating systems are now the norm. **Multitasking operating systems** enable a user to work with two or more applications at the same time. With multitasking operating systems, the

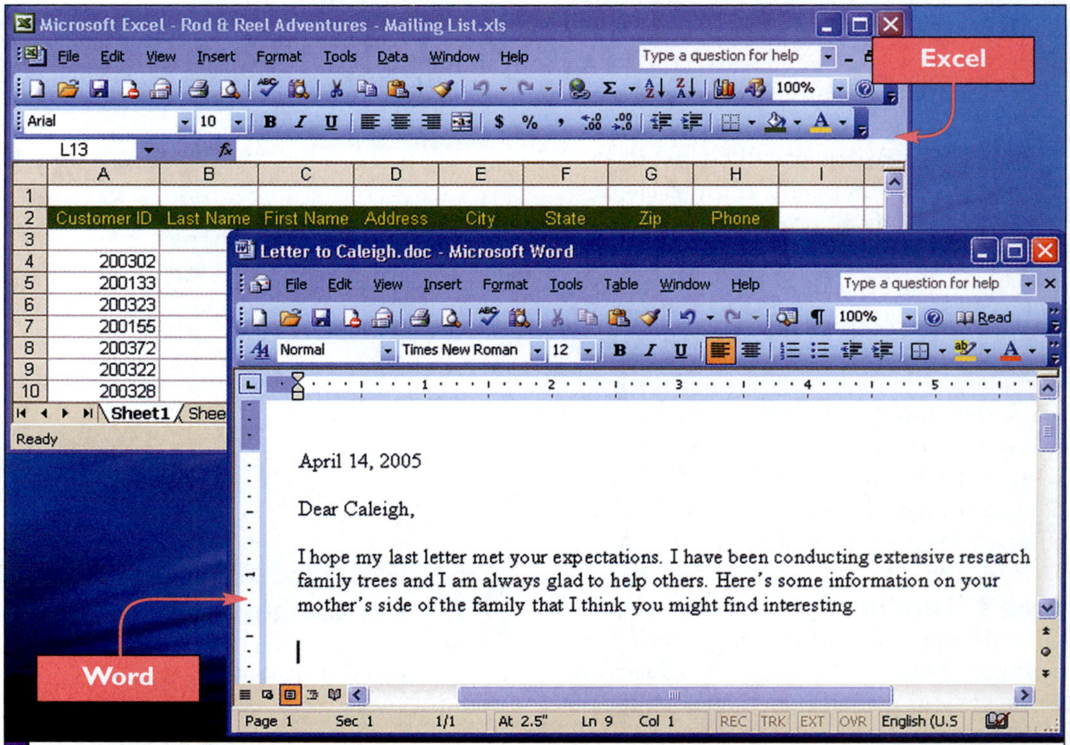

FIGURE 4.5 Multitasking operating systems enable a user to work with two or more applications at once. Here the user is switching between Word and Excel. The Word application is the foreground, or active, application, as indicated by the darkened blue title bar at the top of its window. The Excel application is the background, or inactive, application, as indicated by its grayed-out title bar.

computer doesn't actually run two applications at once; rather, it switches between them as needed. For example, a user might be running two applications, such as Word and Excel, simultaneously. From the user's perspective, one application (the **foreground application**) is active, whereas the other (the **background application**) is inactive, as indicated by how the application appears on the screen (Figure 4.5).

A clear measure of the stability of an operating system is the technique it uses to handle multitasking. If one of the running applications invades another's memory space, one or both of the applications will become unstable or, at the extreme, crash.

A better and more recent type of multitasking called **preemptive multitasking** enables the operating system to regain control if an application stops running. You may lose any unsaved work in the application that has crashed, but the failure of one application does not bring the whole system down. Personal computer operating systems that use preemptive

multitasking include Linux, recent versions of Mac OS, and all current versions of Microsoft Windows.

Now that you understand how the operating system manages applications, let's take a look at how it manages its primary storage function: memory.

MANAGING MEMORY

If the operating system had to constantly access program instructions from their storage location on your computer's hard disk, programs would run very slowly. A buffer is needed to make the processing of instructions more fluid. Computers use a temporary storage medium, called memory, to function as this buffer. The computer's operating system is responsible for **managing memory**. The operating system gives each running program its own portion of memory and attempts to keep the programs from interfering with each other's use of memory (Figure 4.6).

Most of today's operating systems can make the computer's RAM seem larger than it really is. This trick is accomplished by means of **virtual memory**, a method of using the computer's hard disk as an extension of RAM. In virtual memory, program instructions and data are divided into units of fixed size called **pages**. If memory is full, the operating system starts storing copies of pages in a hard disk file called the **swap file**. This file is not an application, but a temporary storage space for bits and bytes that the operating system will access as you do your work. When the pages are needed, they are copied back into memory (Figure 4.7). The transferring of files from storage to memory and back is called **paging**.

Although virtual memory enables users to work with more memory than the amount installed on the computer, paging slows down the computer. Disks are much slower than RAM. For this reason, adding more RAM to your computer is often the best way to improve its performance. With sufficient RAM, the operating system makes minimal use of virtual memory.

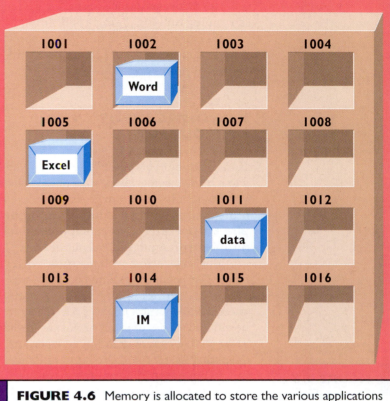

FIGURE 4.6 Memory is allocated to store the various applications you have open at the same time—including the operating system.

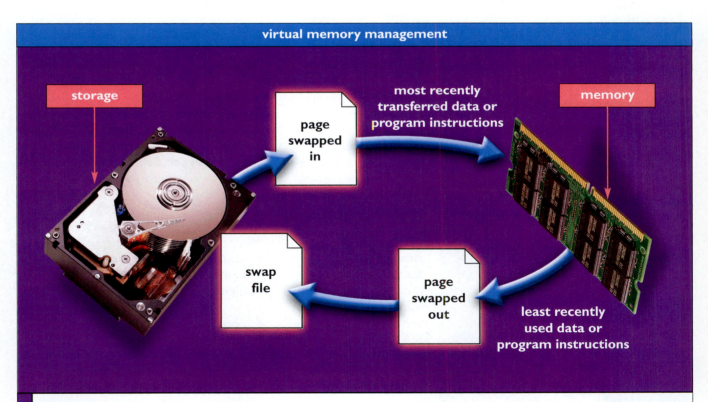

FIGURE 4.7 In virtual memory, program instructions and data are divided into units of fixed size called pages. If virtual memory is full, the operating system starts storing copies of pages in a hard disk file called the swap file. When the pages are needed, they're copied back into memory.

Once the computer's operating system is running and managing applications and memory, it needs to be able to accept data and commands and to represent the results of processing operations.

HANDLING INPUT AND OUTPUT

How does your computer "know" that you want it to do something? How does it show you the results of its work? Another operating system function is **handling input and output**, as well as enabling communication with input and output devices.

Most operating systems come with drivers for popular input and output devices. Device drivers are programs that contain specific information about a particular brand and model of input or output device. They enable communication between the operating system and the input and output components of a computer system. Printers, scanners, monitors, speakers, and the mouse all have drivers (Figure 4.8). Drivers that are not included with the operating system software are supplied by the device manufacturers themselves and are often available on the manufacturers' Web sites. You might need to obtain drivers for any device that was manufactured after your operating system was released. For example, the operating system can't contain the appropriate driver for a printer that wasn't on the market when the operating system was created.

Input and output devices generate **interrupts**, signals that inform the operating system that something has happened (for example, the user has pressed a key, the mouse has moved to a new position, or a document has finished printing). The operating system provides **interrupt handlers**, which are mini-programs that kick in immediately when an interrupt occurs.

Communication between input or output devices and the computer's CPU is handled by **interrupt request** (**IRQ**) lines. Most PCs have 16 IRQs numbered 0 through 16. If two devices are configured to use the same IRQ but aren't designed to share an IRQ line, the result is a serious system failure called an **IRQ conflict**. In most cases, an IRQ conflict makes the system so unstable that it cannot function. To remedy an IRQ conflict, you may need to shut down the computer and remove peripheral devices, one by one, until you determine which one is causing the conflict. Happily, PnP-compatible operating systems and peripherals have made IRQ conflicts much less common. Still, this phenomenon is worth mentioning because it may help you solve a problem with your computer.

Now we will explore the different interfaces that are used to provide interaction with you, the user.

PROVIDING THE USER INTERFACE

From the user's perspective, the most important function of an operating system is **providing the user interface**. The part of the operating system that you see and interact with and by which users and programs communicate with each other is called the **user interface**.

User Interface Functions
User interfaces typically enable you to do the following:

- Start (launch) application programs.

- Manage disks and files. You can format new disks, copy files from one disk to another, rename files, and delete files.

- Shut down the computer safely by following an orderly shutdown procedure.

Types of User Interfaces
The three types of user interfaces are graphical, menu driven, and command line (Figure 4.9).

By far the most popular user interface, a **graphical user interface** (**GUI**;

FIGURE 4.8
Drivers allow the operating system to control internal and external devices such as this headset and mouse.

pronounced "goo-ee") takes advantage of the computer's graphics capabilities to make the operating system and programs easier to use. On today's PCs and Macintoshes, GUIs are used to create the **desktop** that appears after the operating system finishes loading into memory. If someone were to ask you about your desktop, you can say that you are running Linux, or Mac OS, or Windows XP. On the desktop, you can initiate many actions by clicking small images called **icons** that represent computer resources (such as programs, data files, and network connections). Programs run within resizeable on-screen windows, making it easy to switch from one program to another (Figure 4.10). Within programs, you can give commands by choosing items from pull-down menus, some of which display dialog boxes. In a **dialog box**, you

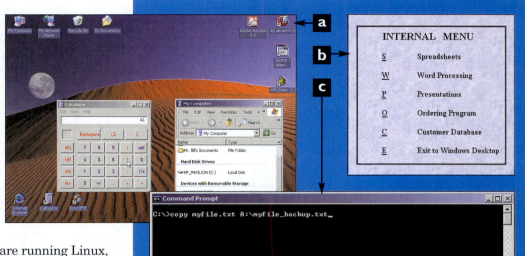

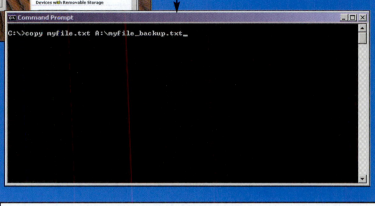

FIGURE 4.9 Examples of (**a**) graphical, (**b**) menu-driven, and (**c**) command-line user interfaces

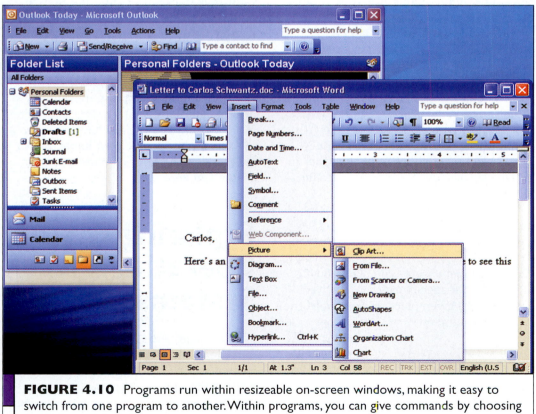

FIGURE 4.10 Programs run within resizeable on-screen windows, making it easy to switch from one program to another. Within programs, you can give commands by choosing items from pull-down menus.

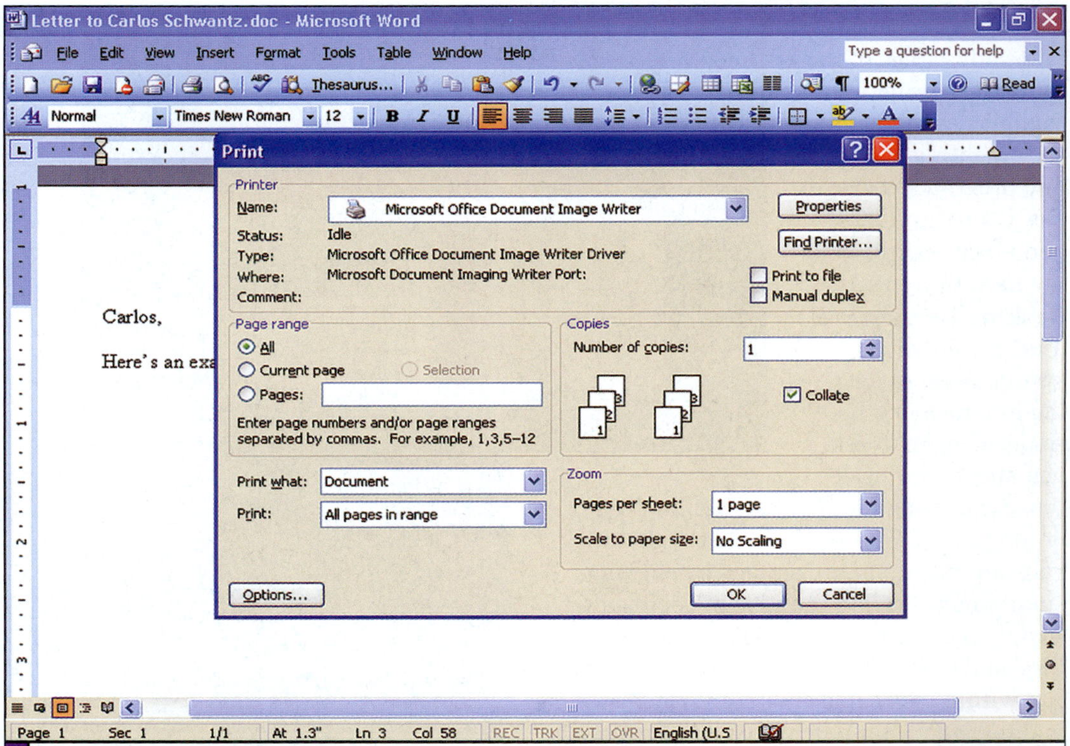

FIGURE 4.11 A dialog box enables you to provide additional information that a program needs. This is the print dialog box.

can supply additional information that the program needs (Figure 4.11).

Menu-driven user interfaces enable you to avoid memorizing keywords (such as copy and paste) and syntax (a set of rules for entering commands). On-screen, text-based menus show all the options available at a given point. With most systems, you select an option with the arrow keys and then press Enter. Some systems enable you to click the desired option with the mouse or to choose a letter with the keyboard.

Command-line user interfaces require you to type commands using keywords that tell the operating system what to do (such as *format* or *copy*) one line at a time. You must observe complicated rules of syntax that specify exactly what you can type in a given place. For example, the following command:

```
copy A:\myfile.txt C:\myfile.txt
```

copies a file from the disk in drive A to the disk in drive C.

Command-line user interfaces aren't popular with most users because they require memorization, and it's easy to make a typing mistake. Although the commands are usually very simple, such as *copy* and *paste*, others are more cryptic. However, some experienced users actually prefer command-line interfaces because they can operate the computer quickly after memorizing the keywords and syntax.

Now that you've seen how the operating system makes itself available to you, let's explore the most popular operating systems in depth.

Exploring Popular Operating Systems

We will begin with Microsoft Windows and then look at the Macintosh operating system, Linux, DOS, and UNIX. Although your choice of operating system is very limited, you should know how the various systems have evolved over time and what their strengths and weaknesses are.

MICROSOFT WINDOWS

Microsoft Windows is by far the most popular operating system. Over the years, it has gone through many iterations (Figure 4.12), and it is now considered *the* operating system of PCs worldwide. When you purchase a computer, it comes with an operating system already installed. Microsoft makes agreements with the major computer manufacturers to provide Windows on almost all of the personal computers that are made today. Some manufacturers offer a choice of operating system, but Windows is and will remain the standard for years to come.

Let's start by looking at the most recent version, Windows XP, and then we'll look at the other operating systems you might encounter on today's personal and corporate computers.

Microsoft Windows XP

Released in the fall of 2001, **Microsoft Windows XP** (Figure 4.13) is the first Microsoft operating system family that uses the same underlying code for all three versions (consumer, corporate desktop, and server). XP is short for "eXPerience," reflecting Microsoft's view that users want

FIGURE 4.12
Windows Time Line

Year Released	Version
2001	Windows XP
2000	Windows 2000/ME
1998	Windows 98
1995	Windows 95
1993	Windows NT
1992	Windows 3.1
1990	Windows 3.0
1987	Windows 2.0
1985	Windows 1.0

computers with rich audio and visual features. Microsoft Windows XP Home Edition, an improved version of Windows 2000 Professional that is designed for home users,

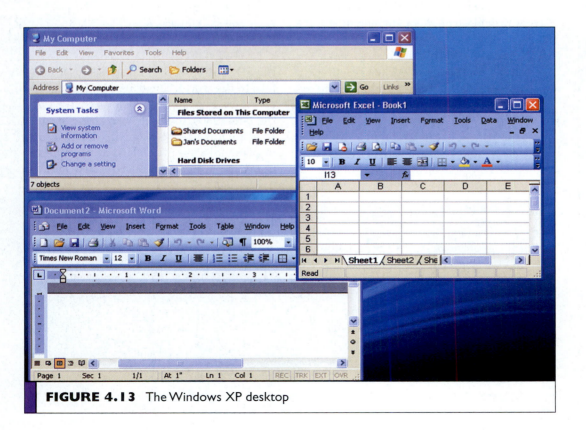

FIGURE 4.13 The Windows XP desktop

Destinations

Explore the features of Microsoft's latest Windows offerings at the Windows home page at www.microsoft .com/windows/ default.mspx

Techtalk

blue screen of death
A feared error message with a blue background that appears when Microsoft Windows NT has encountered an error condition, which is, unfortunately, resolvable in most cases only by rebooting the system – and losing everything that is in memory.

replaces all previous versions of Windows designed for home users. Microsoft Windows XP Professional and Microsoft Windows XP Server are updated versions of the Windows 2000 Professional and Server products, respectively. XP Professional is designed for desktop computer users in networked corporate settings. XP Server is designed to make information and services available on corporate computer networks. XP Tablet PC Edition is designed to run on tablet PCs.

Microsoft Windows NT

Microsoft Windows NT is a sophisticated operating system oriented toward business needs and is specifically designed to support client/server computing systems. Microsoft developed Windows NT to go head-to-head with the powerful UNIX client/server systems that once dominated corporate computing. Windows NT is made up of two components: Windows NT Workstation and Windows NT Server.

The Windows NT Workstation module is designed for individual desktop computers. The real benefits of Windows NT Workstation emerge in a networked corporate environment in which NT desktops link to servers running Windows NT Server.

In a corporate network, Windows NT Server provides the following benefits:

- **Security**. Controls individual workstation access to networked resources, such as a database containing sensitive financial information.

- **Remote administration**. Enables a network administrator to set options remotely for each user's computer,

such as specifying which applications the user can start.

- **Directory services**. Provides a "map" to all the files and applications available on the network.

- **Web server**. Makes Web pages available to the external World Wide Web.

Microsoft Windows CE

Designed for hot-selling PDAs, **Microsoft Windows CE** is a "light" version of Windows designed to run simplified versions of Windows programs, such as Microsoft's own Office applications, which are available in "pocket" versions for Windows CE. This enables users to create documents on a PDA and then transfer them to a desktop computer for further processing and printing.

For mobile computing, Windows CE includes an interactive scheduling calendar, an address book for contacts, an e-mail client, and a Web browser. Users can quickly synchronize these with the corresponding programs on their desktop computers. CE includes handwriting recognition and support for voice recording as well (Figure 4.14).

MAC OS

Mac OS introduced the graphical user interface to the world. The original Macintosh operating system was released in 1984. By the late 1980s, the Mac's operating system was the most technologically advanced in personal computing. However, Apple Computer was unable to capitalize on its

FIGURE 4.14 Windows CE brings Windows and Office functionality to the PDA.

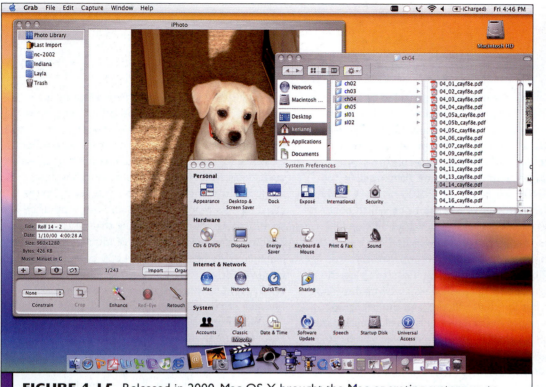

FIGURE 4.15 Released in 2000, Mac OS X brought the Mac operating system up to speed with Microsoft Windows.

lead, and Mac OS (as it came to be called after System 7.5) lost market share to Microsoft Windows. Still, Mac OS is widely considered to be the easiest operating system for beginning computer users. In 1998, Apple was reinvigorated by the return of founder Steve Jobs. A new version of the operating system, called Mac OS X, was released in 2000 and brought Mac OS up to speed with Microsoft Windows (Figure 4.15).

LINUX

In 1991, Finnish university student Linus Torvalds introduced **Linux**, his new freeware operating system for personal computers (Figure 4.16). He hoped Linux would offer users a free alternative to UNIX. Linux has since been further developed by thousands of the world's best programmers, who have willingly donated their

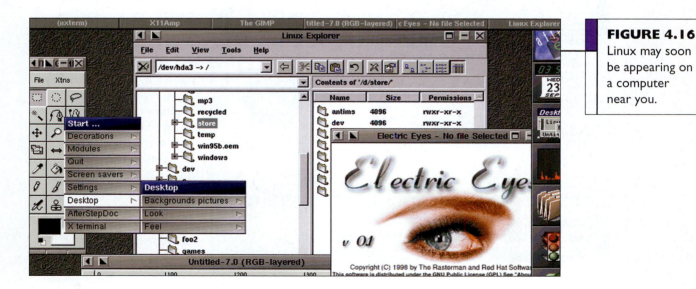

FIGURE 4.16 Linux may soon be appearing on a computer near you.

The Future of Open-Source Software

Fee or free? Corporation-controlled or user-controlled? These two questions are shaping the future of open-source software. Originally, Linus Torvalds wrote the Linux operating system because he couldn't afford to run the UNIX operating system on his home computer. At the time, UNIX was priced at $5,000 or more, and it ran only on powerful workstations, which cost $10,000 each. So Torvalds developed Linux and posted it on an Internet newsgroup for free, inviting people to download and improve the software. Thousands of programmers took up the challenge, adding different bells and whistles—not for pay, but for the challenge and the recognition.

The open-source model is revolutionizing the software world (Figure 4.17). Because the basic code is free, you can find pieces of it running PDAs, supercomputers, cell phones, and many other computer systems. Need Linux in Hungarian, Thai, or Zulu? Not to worry: Volunteers have translated versions of Linux into dozens of languages, giving computer users of all types—individuals, government organizations, and research groups—a free alternative to buying traditional operating systems. You can even download free open-source programs for applications such as word processing and database management.

Although Linux remains free, adapting it to the needs of corporations and other large-scale users has become big business; in fact, Linux claims 30 percent of the Web server market. For example, IBM will customize Linux for corporate customers; Red Hat offers consulting, development, and training services to Linux users. With assistance so readily available and the total price so affordable, it's not surprising that Linux has become so popular. The city of Munich, for instance, switched all of its 14,000 computers from Windows to Linux; DaimlerChrysler, NASA, and others are using Linux to run a number of computers.

However, a legal cloud is on the horizon. SCO Group, a Utah company, says it owns the rights to UNIX's underlying technology and charges that Linux contains some UNIX code. SCO wants users to pay it a licensing fee, and it has filed suit against IBM and several other high-profile Linux users. While the issue moves through the courts, the open-source movement rolls on.

Linux fans are facing another brewing controversy. Reports indicate that some worldwide purchasers are ordering thousands of new PCs with the Linux operating system installed (because it is free), and are then installing illegal copies of Microsoft's Windows operating system. They do this to lower the cost of the PC package. The effect is that the statistics for PCs shipping with Linux are overstating the adoption of Linux as an operating system and reporting an equal decline in the reported use of Windows, when in fact illegal copies of Windows are being installed on those very machines. This does not detract from the attractiveness of Linux to its adopters, but it does show that reports of its adoption may be inflated.

FIGURE 4.17 To learn about the thousands of open-source programs currently in development, visit the SourceForge Web site at www.sourceforge.net.

time to make sure that Linux is a very good version of UNIX. In fact, more than 257 million systems are running Linux. The community approach to Linux has made it a marvel of the computer world and has made Torvalds a folk legend.

Linux is **open-source software**, meaning that its source code (the code of the program itself) is available for all to see and use. Unlike most other commercial software, which hide the program's code and prohibit users from analyzing the code to see how the program was written, users of open-source software are invited to scrutinize the source code for errors and to share their discoveries with the software's publisher. Experience shows that this approach is often a very effective measure against software defects.

What makes Linux so attractive? Two things: it's powerful and it's free. Linux brings all the maturity and sophistication of UNIX to the PC. (Versions of Linux have also been created for Macintoshes.) Linux includes all the respected features of UNIX, including multitasking, virtual memory, Internet support, and a graphical user interface.

Although Linux is powerful and free, many corporate chief information officers (CIOs) shy away from adopting Linux precisely because it isn't a commercial product with a stable company behind it. When someone needs technical support, they have to find a Web site such as **www.redhat.com** or someone who knows more about Linux than they do—this is not the same as calling technical support when your Mac OS X is on the fritz. Also, Linux can't run the popular Microsoft Office applications, which most corporate users prefer. But Linux is gaining acceptance.

The beauty of Linux, and its development model, is that it doesn't run on any particular type of computer: It runs on them all. Linux has been translated to run on systems as small as PDAs and as large as homegrown supercomputers.

MS-DOS

MS-DOS (or **DOS**, which is short for Disk Operating System) is an operating system for PCs that uses a command-line user interface. Developed by Bill Gates and Paul

Allen's fledgling Microsoft Corporation for the original IBM PC in 1981, MS-DOS was marketed by IBM in a virtually identical version, called PC-DOS. The command-line interface is difficult to learn, and the syntax and commands are not easy for the casual user to remember. It is unlikely that you will ever encounter a command-line interface on a modern personal computer.

UNIX

Developed at AT&T's Bell Laboratories, UNIX is a pioneering operating system that continues to define what an operating system should do and how it should work. **UNIX** (pronounced "you-nix") was the first operating system with preemptive multitasking, and it was designed to work efficiently in a secure computer network.

If UNIX is so great, why didn't it take over the computer world? One reason is the lack of compatibility among the many different versions of UNIX. Another reason is that it's difficult to use. UNIX, like DOS, defaults to a command-line user interface, which is challenging for new computer users. In the past few years, a number of GUI interfaces have been developed for UNIX, improving its usability (Figure 4.18).

To learn more about the powerful but virtually unheard of alternative operating system FreeBSD, see the video clip at **www.prenhall.com/ cayf2006**

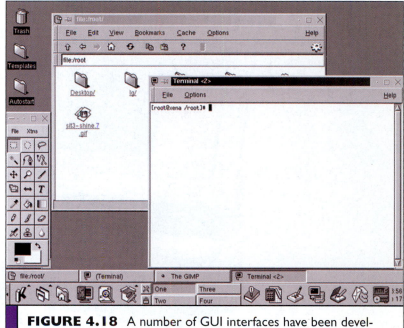

FIGURE 4.18 A number of GUI interfaces have been developed for UNIX in the past few years, improving the usability of this operating system.

PLATFORMS: MAC VERSUS PC

As a computer user, you have two major platforms to choose from. A **platform** is a distinct type of computer that uses a certain type of operating system, such as Apple's Macintosh or Microsoft's Windows. Depending on which operating system is loaded on a computer, it is simply referred to as a Mac or a PC.

The debate over which platform is best has raged on for years, and if market power is anything, PCs are winning by a landslide. But Apple hangs in there with its slew of adherents who choose to "think different." What's the difference between the platforms? Although you'd never know from listening to people who love or hate Macs, there's really not much difference, at least not in terms of power. Still, the debate goes on.

On the one side, Mac lovers say their machines are easier to set up and use. Macs come with everything you need built right in—simply plug them in and you're on your way. Mac lovers also point out that Apple has developed some incredibly advanced technology. (Even PC users will agree to that.)

It's not just the system and the software Mac users love. Most Macophiles love their one-button mice as well as their many shortcut keys. Not to mention the Apple design; many Mac adherents love the look of the Mac above all else (Figure 4.19). Today, you'll find Macs being used in most elementary schools in the United States. (OS X is virtually crash proof!) In addition, certain professions, such as publishing, advertising, and design, rely almost exclusively on Macs.

On the other hand, PCs still dominate, and the race isn't even close. PCs claim the largest chunk of the marketplace and are the choice of corporate America. And thanks to economies of scale, they also tend to be cheaper both in terms of their hardware and software. Indeed, software is a big plus for PC users, who have far more titles to choose from than their Mac counterparts. Because so many more people buy the software, it tends to be better, and it is often developed and published more quickly than similar software for Macs. And as much as Mac lovers claim the one-button mouse is the way to go, PC users love their two-button mouse, which offers more choices in hand.

In recent years, Apple has tried to woo PC users by playing on the idea that Macs are easier to use. Meanwhile, Mac's OS X could improve the number of software products developed for Macs, and that includes games, one reason PCs lead in the marketplace. However, as Apple moves into the PC market with its recent UNIX innovations, it may make itself more vulnerable to the viruses that have been

FIGURE 4.19 PC manufacturers and Apple have produced all-in-one computers for both Windows and Mac platforms.

mostly a PC headache. In any case, Macs have a long way to go to catch PCs—and few users from either camp see that happening any time soon.

All of the operating systems just discussed work in tandem with helper programs called utilities.

System Utilities: Housekeeping Tools

Providing a necessary addition to an operating system, **system utilities** (also called **utility programs**) are used to keep the computer system running smoothly. Sometimes these programs are included in the operating system; sometimes you must purchase them from other software vendors. System utility programs are considered essential to the effective management of a computer system by backing up system and application files, providing antivirus protection, searching for and managing files, scanning and defragmenting disks and files, and compressing files so that they take up less space.

BACKUP SOFTWARE

An essential part of safe, efficient computer usage, **backup software** copies data from the computer's hard disk to backup devices, such as a floppy disks, CDs or DVDs, or Zip disks. Should the hard disk fail, you can recover the data from the backup disk (Figure 4.20).

Backup software can run a **full backup**, in which a "mirror image" is made of the entire hard disk's contents. In an **incremental backup**, the backup software copies only those files that have been created or changed since the last backup occurred. In this way, the backup disk always contains an up-to-date copy of all programs and data. In the event of a hard disk or computer system failure, the backup disk can be used to restore the data by copying the data from the backup disk to a new hard disk. Full backups should be made at least once each month. Incremental backups

should be made regularly, too—in a business environment, once or more per day.

Even if you don't have backup software, you can still make backup copies of your important files: just copy them to a disk. When you finish working on an assignment, always copy the data to a disk and then put the disk away for safekeeping. Don't ever rely on a hard disk to keep the only copies of your work. Backups should be stored away from the computer system so that, in the event of a fire or flood, they don't suffer the system's fate.

Windows XP does not come with a preloaded backup utility, but one easy way to back up your personal files is to create a new folder on your C: drive and name it "Data" or "My Stuff." Then, every time you save a new file, save it to this folder and within the subfolders you will create to organize the type of data that are stored there. Whenever you want to back up your work, simply use the My Computer or other file management software to copy the contents of the Data folder to an external device such as a CD or a DVD. Backup utility programs are also available at your local software store or from sites on the Web such as **free-backup-software.net/ backup-software.htm** and **www.dantz.com/ en/products/personal.dtml**. These programs allow you to create a complete backup of your disk or a partial backup of only the files that have changed since the last backup.

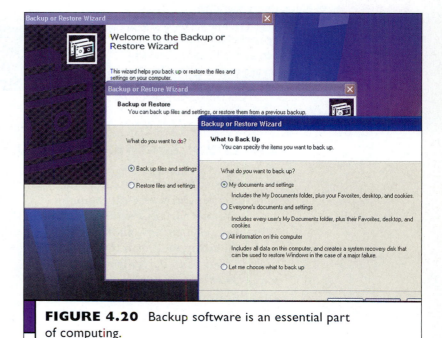

FIGURE 4.20 Backup software is an essential part of computing.

The Making of Malware

Malware, software specifically designed to reproduce itself and infect computer after computer, is the Internet's latest security nightmare. Both malicious and mischievous versions of malware are on the rise—causing billions of dollars' worth of damage by destroying or corrupting data and clogging networks. Some malware writers create self-replicating programs for practice or to show off their expertise and then post them on the Web for the world to see and use. Others actually set the programs in motion, igniting a chain reaction that can affect thousands or even millions of computers within a day or two.

In the past, malware writers tried to erase data on hard drives or disable PCs in other ways. Although today's malware writers may want to leave souvenirs behind, they mainly use hard drives as springboards for multiplying and spreading software to as many PCs as possible rather than erasing files. Despite intense attention from cybersecurity experts and law enforcement officials, the pace of malware attacks is increasing, as are their severity and sophistication. In fact, malware writers are now targeting a wider variety of vulnerabilities in system and application software. And new malware variations are evolving to trick antivirus software by taking on the appearance of innocuous programs.

Meanwhile, malware's enemies are fighting back. Nonprofit organizations such as the Internet Security Foundation are teaching "ethical hacking," helping programmers learn

to test corporate networks and identify potential vulnerabilities. Also, companies such as eEye Digital Security are training programmers to examine corporate customers' network software and plug any holes before malware sneaks in.

How can you guard against malware? If you ever log onto the Internet, your computer can be infected—even if you've installed antivirus software. For security, set your antivirus software for automatic updating, because even daily updates may not provide enough protection against the constant onslaught of malware. Don't download files or open attachments with suspicious names or unknown origins. Finally, strengthen your defenses by downloading the latest security patches for your operating system and other software (Figure 4.21).

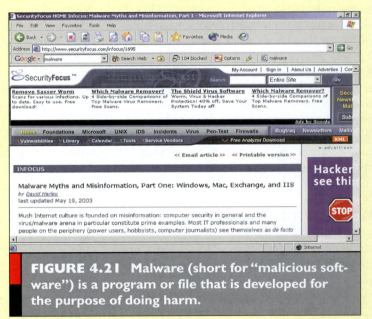

FIGURE 4.21 Malware (short for "malicious software") is a program or file that is developed for the purpose of doing harm.

ANTIVIRUS SOFTWARE

Antivirus software (also called vaccines or virus checkers) protects a computer from computer viruses (Figure 4.22). Such software uses a pattern-matching technique that examines all of the files on a disk, looking for telltale virus code "signatures." One limitation of such programs is that they can detect only those viruses whose "signatures" are in their databases. Most antivirus programs enable you to download the signatures of new viruses

from a Web site. However, new viruses appear every day. If your system becomes infected by a virus that's not in the system's database, it may not be detected. Due to this shortcoming, many antivirus programs also include programs that monitor system functions to detect and stop the destructive activities of unknown viruses.

Norton AntiVirus and McAfee VirusScan are the two most popular antivirus applications in use today. Many higher education institutions make one of these applications available for free to their students. Check with your campus computing center to see which one your institution provides. Both programs provide users with frequent updates for the term of a license. Licenses are typically issued for a year.

Some viruses do their damage immediately, whereas others hide on your hard disk and then wait for a trigger before doing their work. Regardless of when they do their damage, viruses spread quickly and can affect thousands, even millions, of users in a short period of time. This is why it is important to install and use antivirus software. It only takes one nasty virus to cause you a lot of grief.

SEARCHING FOR AND MANAGING FILES

Another important system utility is the **file manager** (My Computer in Windows, File Manager in Mac OS X, and various file management utilities in Linux), a utility program that enables you to organize and manage the data stored on your disk (Figure 4.23). In Windows, the My Computer icon is usually available on your desktop as well as

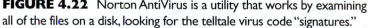

FIGURE 4.22 Norton AntiVirus is a utility that works by examining all of the files on a disk, looking for the telltale virus code "signatures."

on the upper-right panel on the Start menu. The file manager enables you to perform various operations on the files and folders created on your computer's storage devices. You can use file managers to make copies of

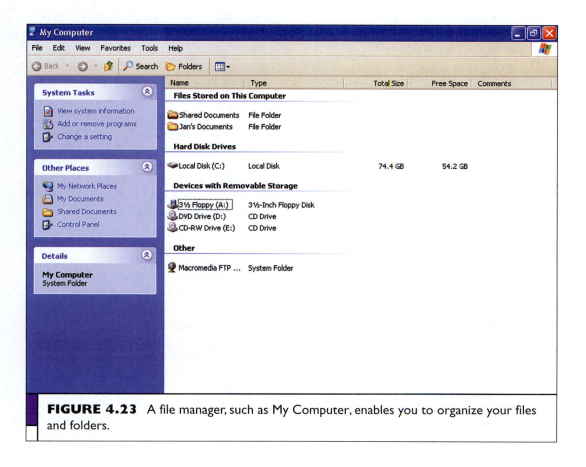

FIGURE 4.23 A file manager, such as My Computer, enables you to organize your files and folders.

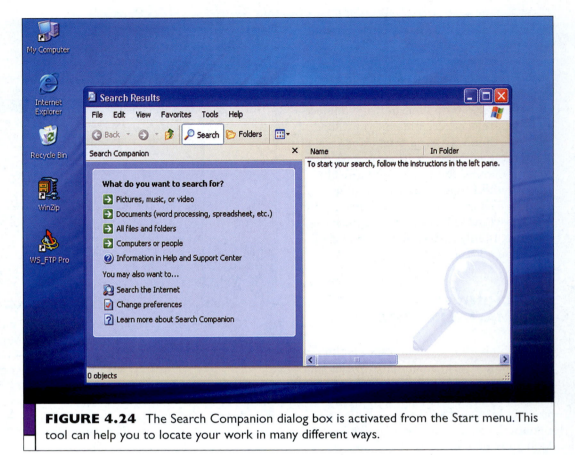

FIGURE 4.24 The Search Companion dialog box is activated from the Start menu. This tool can help you to locate your work in many different ways.

your files, to manage how and where they are stored, and to delete unwanted files. File management is covered in depth in the Spotlight that follows Chapter 4.

On a large hard disk with thousands of files, the task of finding a needed file can be time-consuming and frustrating if you try to do so manually. For this reason, most operating systems include a **search utility**, which enables you to search an entire hard disk for a file. In Microsoft Windows, the Search Companion utility enables you to search for files in a number of ways, including by name, date, and size (Figure 4.24). A similar Mac OS utility, called Find File, offers these same features.

SCANNING AND DEFRAGMENTING DISKS

A **disk scanning program**, or disk scanner, can detect and resolve a number of physical and logical problems that may occur when your computer stores files on a disk. The disk scanning and defragmenting utility in Windows is located in Start, All Programs,

Accessories, System Tools. The Mac OS X scanning utility is called DiskTracker. You can find commercial products that perform this function, but the one that comes with your operating system is usually adequate and best suited for managing your hard disk.

Scanning programs look for a physical problem involving an irregularity on the disk's surface that results in a **bad sector**, which is a portion of the disk that is unable to store data reliably. The scanner can fix the problem by locking out the bad sector so that it's no longer used. Logical problems are usually caused by a power outage that occurs before the computer is able to finish writing data to the disk. **Disk cleanup utilities** can save disk space by removing files that you no longer need.

As you use a computer, it creates and erases files on the hard disk. The result is that the disk soon becomes a patchwork of files, with portions of files scattered here and there. This slows disk access because the system must look in several locations to find all of a file's segments. A disk with data scattered around in this way is referred to as being **fragmented**. A fragmented disk isn't dangerous—the locations of all the data are known, thanks to the operating system's tracking mechanisms—but periodic maintenance is required to restore the disk's performance. **Disk defragmentation programs** are used to reorganize the data on the disk so that the data are stored in adjoining sectors (Figure 4.25). Scanning and defragmentation utilities should be run anywhere from once every 3 or 4 months for the light computer user to as much as once every 3 to 4 weeks for the power user.

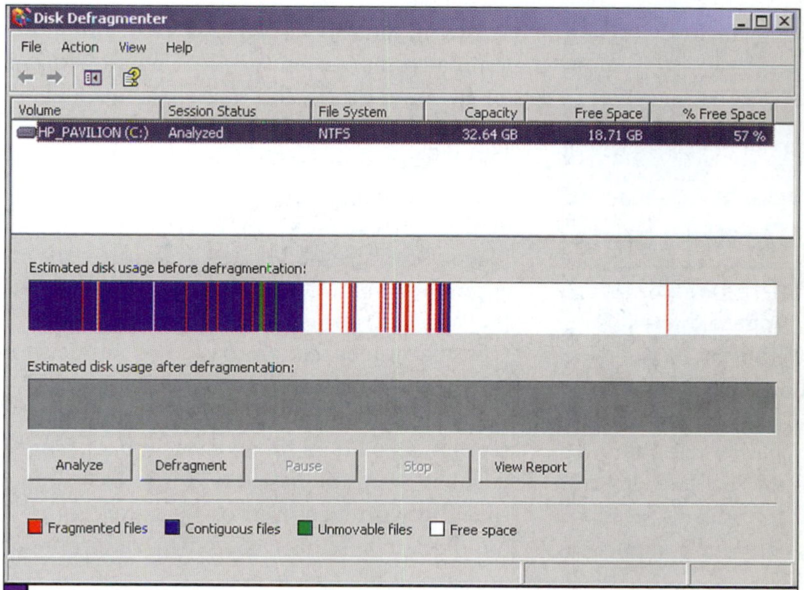

FILE COMPRESSION UTILITIES

Most downloadable software is compressed. To exchange programs and data efficiently, particularly over the Internet, **file compression utilities** (Figure 4.26) can reduce the size of a file by as much as 80 percent without harming the data. Most file compression utilities work by searching the file for frequently repeated but lengthy data patterns and then substituting short codes for these patterns. Compression enables faster downloads, but you must decompress a file after downloading it. When the file is

FIGURE 4.25 Periodically, you should defragment your hard disk to ensure top performance. In Windows XP, the defragmentation utility is found under Start, All Programs, Accessories, System Tools, Disk Defragmenter.

decompressed, the utility restores the lengthier pattern where each code is encountered. After decompressing the downloaded

To learn how to use Windows to compress your files, see the video clip at **www.prenhall.com/ cayf2006**

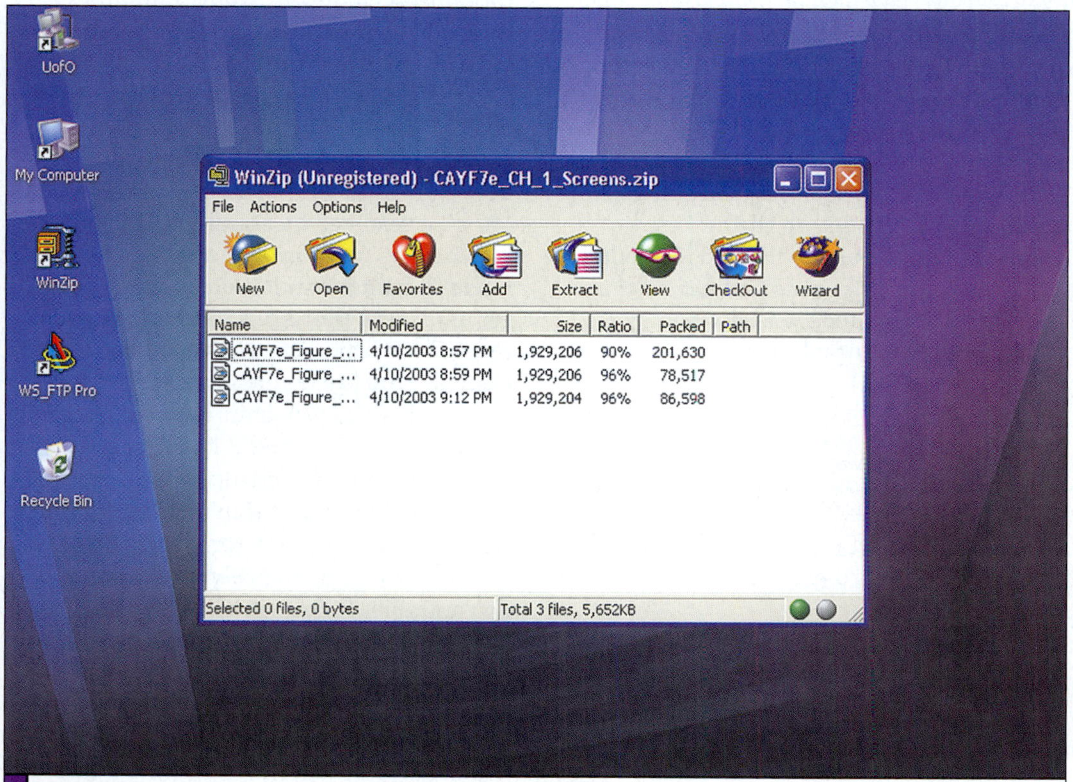

FIGURE 4.26 A file compression utility enables you to create archives and compressed files.

Destinations

Go to **windows update.microsoft .com** or **www.version tracker.com** to learn more about the available system software updates for your computer.

software, you can install it on your computer. Popular compression utilities include WinZip for PCs and StuffIt for Macintosh systems.

Some compressed files are designed to decompress automatically when you launch them; others require you to run compression utility software. You can determine how a file was compressed by looking at the file's extension (Figure 4.27).

Most compression utilities also can create archives. An **archive** is a single file that contains two or more files stored in a special format. Archives are handy for storage as well as file exchange purposes because as many as several hundred separate files can be stored in a single, easily handled unit. WinZip combines compression and archiving functions.

SYSTEM UPDATE

Because the world of computers is rapidly changing, and because Microsoft tends to bring its products to market before they are fully functional, Microsoft provides an operating system update service called **Windows Update** that is meant to keep your operating system up-to-date with any fixes (service patches) or protections against external environment changes. You can help to ensure that your operating system is current in two ways. You can visit **windowsupdate.microsoft.com** and check to see if there are any updates available for your system. Or, better yet, you can go to the same site and set up the automatic update feature, which will send an update notice to your computer's taskbar so that you can click the update icon whenever you are ready to install updates.

The updates will fix problems with the original version of the operating system and will oftentimes provide protection against viruses and worms. Macintosh provides a similar service to its subscribers.

Besides system utilities, there are additional ways to safeguard your data or take care of operating problems.

TROUBLESHOOTING

Almost every user of a computer system experiences trouble from time to time. Whether the trouble stems from starting the computer, running programs, or adding hardware or software, users need troubleshooting tips to get them through a crisis.

If your computer fails to start normally, you may be able to get it running by inserting a **boot disk** (also called an **emergency disk**) into the floppy disk drive. The emergency disk loads a reduced version of the operating system that can be used for troubleshooting purposes. An emergency disk sometimes comes with a new computer, but oftentimes you need to create it yourself. Consult the documentation that came with your computer or choose Help from the My Computer program to learn about this process.

In Microsoft Windows, configuration problems can occur after adding a new peripheral device such as a Zip drive or new printer to your system. Conflicts can often be resolved by starting the computer in Windows' **safe mode**, an operating mode in which Windows loads a minimal set of drivers that are known to function correctly. Within safe mode, you can use the Control Panel to determine which devices are causing the problem. You access safe mode by pressing the F8 key repeatedly during the initial start-up process. Or you can start the computer in safe mode, which will reset or report any conflicting programs or device drivers, and then simply shut it down and let it boot up normally.

System slowdown can sometimes occur because something has changed gradually over time to cause performance to degrade or there has been a hardware or software change. A number of different situations can be responsible for changes in system performance:

FIGURE 4.27	Compression Software	
Extension	**Compression Software Needed**
.exe	None, this file is designed to decompress itself automatically
.zip	WinZip (**www.winzip.com**) or ZipIt (**www.maczipit.com**)
.sit	StuffIt Expander (**www.stuffit.com**)
.hqx	StuffIt Expander

- Viruses can slow the system down. Run your antivirus software to scan for viruses on your system.

- If you've recently added memory to your system, you may need to double-check that it is configured properly. You should have received documentation with your purchase or you might return to the place of purchase to ask for help.

- Check the processor to make sure that it is not overheating and make sure that the CPU fan is still running. Some systems will intentionally slow the CPU down if they detect a failed fan. You can turn off your computer, unplug it, remove the cover from the system unit, and then use a can of air to blow out any lint, dust, or other debris that has accumulated on the fan blades, the fan unit, and/or the cover and case vents.

File fragmentation can lead to reduced performance. Try defragmenting the hard disk. The best way to ensure that your system runs optimally is to never change more than one thing at a time. That way, if the system has problems, you can undo your last action or installation and see if the problem goes away.

Help and Support

Sometimes the best place to look for troubleshooting guidance is right on your own computer. Microsoft Windows includes a Help and Support utility. You can explore its contents by clicking the Start button and then clicking Help and Support. The Windows Help and Support Center includes a variety of ways to manage and maintain your computer (Figure 4.28). For example, you could choose Performance and Maintenance from the Pick a Help Topic list. The left task pane displays categories of tasks, such as perform maintenance, manage performance, free up disk space, keep your system safe, use system restore, and access advanced performance and maintenance tools. The right task pane displays the specific tasks within each category.

When you click a link in the right task pane, the window's contents are replaced with text and links that explain the steps you will take to perform the chosen task. Some tasks involve using a step-by-step

wizard, which asks you questions and then responds with suggestions based on your answers. Take the time to explore some of these topics; you may be surprised at the confidence you will gain by interacting with your operating system.

Shutting Down Your System

When you've finished using the computer, be sure to shut it down properly. Don't just switch off the power without going through the full shutdown procedure. In Microsoft Windows XP, click Start and then select Turn Off Computer. In Mac OS, click Special and then select Shut Down. If you switch the power off without shutting down, the operating system may fail to write certain system files to the hard disk. The next time you start the computer, the operating system will need to run the disk scanning utility to check for file fragments. File fragments that result from improper shutdown could result in permanent damage to the operating system or to personal files.

An alternative to completely shutting down your system is to put it on Standby. In Microsoft Windows XP, **Standby** is a low-power state that enables you to restore your system to full power quickly without going through the lengthy boot process. Standby is accessed in the same way as Turn Off Computer from the Start, Turn Off Computer menu sequence. In Mac OS, this option is called **Sleep**.

Destinations

You can find all sorts of troubleshooting sites for both PCs and Macs on the Web. Some offer free advice and user forums, whereas others, such as Ask Dr. Tech, offer support packages for a price. Type "troubleshooting" into your favorite search engine or visit sites such as **www.macfixit.com** or **www.askdrtech.com** to find out more.

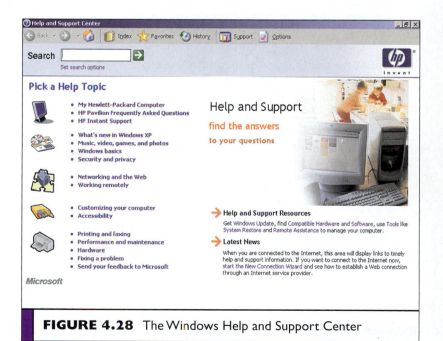

FIGURE 4.28 The Windows Help and Support Center

What You've Learned

SYSTEM SOFTWARE

- System software has two major components: (1) the operating system and (2) system utilities that provide various maintenance functions.

- Without software—the set of instructions that tells the computer what to do—a computer is just an expensive collection of wires and components. The operating system (OS) coordinates the various functions of the computer's hardware and provides support for running application software.

- An operating system works at the intersection of application software, the user, and the computer's hardware. Its five basic functions are starting the computer, managing applications, managing memory, handling internal messages from input and output devices, and providing a means of communicating with the user.

- When you start or restart a computer, it reloads the operating system into the computer's memory. A computer goes through six steps at startup: loading the BIOS, the power-on self-test, loading the operating system, configuring the system, loading system utilities, and authenticating users.

- The three major types of user interfaces are graphical user interfaces (GUIs), menu-driven user interfaces, and command-line user interfaces.

- The two major operating systems for the personal computer are Microsoft Windows and Macintosh OS X. The major strength of Windows is that it has dominated the market for more than 15 years and is installed and maintained on over 90 percent of the personal computers in the world. The major strength of OS X is that it has been modified and upgraded for more than 20 years and is the most stable graphic OS. The biggest weakness of Windows is that Microsoft continues to bring new versions to market before all of the bugs and security holes have been resolved. The main disadvantage of OS X is that it is only used on approximately 5 percent of the computers in the world and thus does not support as many applications as Windows does.

- Essential system utilities include backup software, antivirus software, file managers, search tools, file compression utilities, disk scanning programs, and disk defragmentation programs.

- A sound backup procedure begins with a full backup of an entire hard disk and continues with periodic incremental backups of just those files that have been created or altered since the last backup occurred.

- Troubleshooting your system can be as simple as restarting and as complex as tracking down a virus or a bad memory chip. A good rule of thumb is to only do what you feel comfortable doing and then consult a professional technician at your local computer shop.

Go to **www.prenhall.com/cayf2006** to review this chapter, answer the questions, and complete the exercises.

Key Terms and Concepts

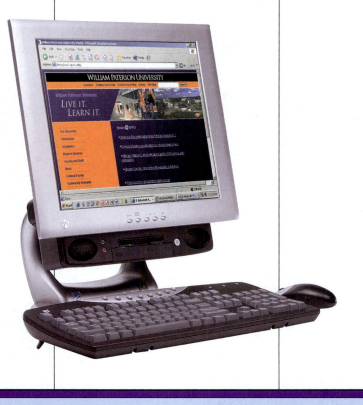

Go to **www.prenhall.com/cayf2006** to review this chapter, answer the questions, and complete the exercises.

Matching

Match each key term in the left column with the most accurate definition in the right column.

_____ 1. operating system

_____ 2. multitasking operating system

_____ 3. Linux

_____ 4. dialog box

_____ 5. GUI

_____ 6. disk scanning program

_____ 7. emergency disk

_____ 8. interrupts

_____ 9. kernel

_____ 10. foreground application

_____ 11. file manager

_____ 12. driver

_____ 13. icon

_____ 14. backup software

_____ 15. disk defragmentation program

a. an essential part of safe, efficient computer usage

b. a utility that can detect and resolve physical and logical problems on a disk

c. a file that helps the operating system manage input and output devices

d. enables a single user to work with two or more applications

e. essential portions of an operating system

f. signals that inform the operating system that something has happened

g. an open-source operating system

h. the program that is active when one or more programs are running at the same time

i. manages programs, parcels out memory, deals with input and output devices, and provides a means of communicating with the user

j. is used to organize a disk or file whose data is scattered

k. allows users to supply additional information to a program

l. contains a reduced version of the operating system that can be used for troubleshooting purposes

m. a utility program that enables you to organize and manage the data stored on your disk

n. a program interface that takes advantage of the computer's graphics capabilities to make the program easier to use

o. graphical representation of a computer resource

Multiple Choice

Circle the correct choice for each of the following.

1. Which kind of software enables a computer and its peripheral devices to function smoothly?
   a. application
   b. system
   c. defragmentation
   d. file management

2. Which of the following is not typically handled by the operating system?
   a. managing applications
   b. managing input and output devices
   c. publishing Web pages
   d. interacting with the user

3. What type of memory is created if RAM is full?
   a. read-only memory
   b. on-the-fly memory
   c. add-on memory
   d. virtual memory

4. Which version of Windows is designed for PDAs?
   a. Windows CE
   b. Windows NT
   c. Windows ME
   d. Windows PDA

5. Which of the following is a key component of a graphical user interface?
   a. command words
   b. icons
   c. keyboard
   d. virtual memory

6. Which operating system is considered to be the easiest for beginners?
   a. Mac OS X
   b. Linux
   c. Windows XP
   d. UNIX

7. What term describes the central part of the operating system that starts applications, manages devices and memory, and performs other essential functions?
   a. master
   b. kernel
   c. general
   d. boss

8. Which of the following operating systems is ideally suited for a networked corporate environment?
   a. Windows XP
   b. Linux
   c. Windows NT
   d. Windows CE

9. If your computer fails to start normally, you may need to use which of the following?
   a. emergency disk
   b. system utility
   c. file utility
   d. nonemergency disk

10. Which acronym is used to describe the part of the system software that equips the computer with the instructions needed to accept keyboard input and display information on the screen?
    a. POST
    b. LINUX
    c. BIOS
    d. CMOS

Fill-In

In the blanks provided, write the correct answer for each of the following.

1. _____ user interfaces are the most popular interfaces.

2. When multiple programs are running on a computer, the one currently in use is the _____ application.

3. If an operating system uses virtual memory when memory is full, the operating system starts storing parts of memory in a(n) _____ on the hard drive.

4. Files can be located by using the _____ utility.

5. Unlike Windows 95 and Windows 98, _____ is specifically designed for client/server systems.

6. _____ is a free and powerful operating system that brings all the maturity and sophistication of UNIX to the PC.

7. If a file's data is not stored in contiguous locations on a disk, then the user should run a _____ to increase the computer's efficiency.

8. _____ software protects a computer from viruses.

9. A(n) _____ is used to copy and delete files.

10. _____ are programs that can reduce the size of a file by as much as 80 percent without harming the data.

11. A(n) _____ is a single file that contains two or more files.

12. A(n) _____ is a portion of a disk that is unable to store data reliably.

13. _____ is a special type of memory that is used to store essential startup configuration options.

14. _____ is an operating system for Intel-based PCs that uses a command-line user interface.

15. _____ enable a single user to work with two or more applications at the same time.

Short Answer

1. Explain the purpose of the power-on self-test (POST). In addition to a computer system, do you know of any other systems that perform a POST?

2. Visit **www.microsoft.com** and locate your operating system. Now use the search box to search for the term "legitimate." Read one or more articles on operating system software legitimacy.

3. What are the advantages of multitasking? Describe the multitasking that happens during one of your typical computer sessions.

4. What is the purpose of a device driver? Have you ever had to install a device driver when connecting a new peripheral device to a computer? If you did, what was the device? Was the driver supplied by the operating system or by the device's manufacturer?

5. Explain the differences between a full backup and an incremental backup. Have you ever lost important files because you did not back them up? If you have done a backup, did you copy the entire disk or just selected files? When was the last time you performed a backup?

Go to **www.prenhall.com/cayf2006** to review this chapter, answer the questions, and complete the exercises.

Teamwork

1. Operating Systems

Your team is to research three of the operating systems presented in this chapter. What are the basic functions that need to be performed by an operating system? What future improvements in each operating system can you envision? If you have used several versions of the same operating system, what improvements have been incorporated into new versions? Go to **www.microsoft.com** and choose a link or search for "operating systems." Scroll around or search for Microsoft's operating system comparison section. Did you learn anything? How does the operating system you use stack up? Collaborate on a one to two page paper that summarizes your findings. Be sure to include information on Linux, Mac OS, and Windows.

2. Mac OS vs. PC OS

Your team is to locate one or more labs on campus that have PCs and Macs. Experiment with both a Macintosh computer and a PC in determining the answers to the following questions. What version of each operating system did you use? Is it the latest release of the operating system? How are the two operating systems similar? Can you determine the strengths of each system? Which operating system do you prefer? Why? Write a paper that meets your professor's specifications.

3. Exploring UNIX

Despite its cryptic commands, UNIX has remained a popular operating system for about 30 years. Many educational institutions have computers running this operating system, and most Internet servers run UNIX. Use the strengths of each member of your team to split the workload in answering the following questions. If you have used a UNIX computer, explain how and why you used it. Does your school have computers that use UNIX? If so, do you have an account? Can you get an account, or are the accounts restricted on these computers? Do you have an ISP? If you do, identify your provider and determine whether it uses UNIX to support customer Web sites. Write a one page paper with your answers to these questions.

4. Using System Tools

Work as a team to determine the answers to the following questions. Use a different computer for each of your team members. To see how much you can learn about the Windows operating system, have each group member use a Windows based PC to do the following. Choose Start, All Programs, Accessories, and System Tools. Now choose the System Information. How much memory is installed on the computer? How much virtual memory is defined? Now choose Start, Help and Support. Browse the left and right panes of the Help and Support screen and have each member of your team write about two of the help features that are there.

5. Buying a PDA

You and your teammates are to consider the purchase of a PDA. Split the following questions up among the team members. What companies manufacture PDAs? Some of these devices require special operating systems and application software. Go to a local computer store and take a PDA out for a test drive. Specifically, try out the operating system. Do these computers use a special version of Windows? If they use Windows, what version and release is it? How does this operating system compare with those on desktop and laptop computers? How does the PDA operating system differ? Now that you have "kicked the keyboard" and taken a PDA out for a spin, explain why you would or would not purchase one.

On the Web

I. File Compression

In this exercise, you'll examine the file compression tool. Write a one page paper that summarizes your answers to these questions.

- Have you used a file compression program?
- If you have, identify the brand name and version of this software application. Which operating system were you using? Was the file compression program simple or complicated to use? Would you recommend this product to someone else? Why or why not?
- If you have not, visit the sites of two popular file compression programs, WinZip at **winzip.com** and StuffIt at **stuffit.com**. Which operating system(s) does each work with? What are the current versions and suggested retail prices for each? Are free or evaluation versions available? Would you purchase one of these products? Explain why or why not.

2. Antivirus Programs

In this exercise, you'll examine antivirus software. Have you ever had to disinfect a file that was infected by a virus? Write a one page paper that summarizes your answers to these questions.

- If you have, identify the brand name and version of the antivirus application you used and which operating system you were using. Were you able to disinfect the file successfully? Was the antivirus program simple or complicated to use? Would you recommend this product to someone else? Why or why not?
- If you have not, visit the sites of the two most popular antivirus applications, Norton AntiVirus at **www.symantec.com/nav** and McAfee VirusScan at **www.mcafee.com/anti-virus**. Which operating system(s) does each work with? What are the current versions and suggested retail prices of each? Are free or evaluation versions available? Would you purchase one of these products? Explain why or why not.

3. Windows XP

Visit **microsoft.com/windowsxp/default.asp** for information on the latest version of Windows.

Write a brief paper that summarizes your answers to the following questions.

- Why would users of Windows NT/2000 upgrade to XP?
- Why would users of Windows 95/98 upgrade to XP?
- What other types of users will benefit from XP?
- What are the minimum hardware requirements for XP?
- What are the purchase and upgrade prices for XP?
- Would you consider purchasing XP? Why or why not?

4. Using CNET

Go to **www.cnet.com**. Type "operating systems" into the search window. Review at least two articles about an operating system of your choice. Which operating system did you choose? What are three advantages and disadvantages to using this operating system? Would you consider using this operating system? Explain why or why not. Write a one page paper that summarizes your findings.

5. Exploring Linux

Visit the Linux home page at **www.linux.com/howtos/HOWTO-INDEX/os.shtml** to learn more about this operating system. Write a one page paper that summarizes your answers to these questions.

- What is the primary objective of this tutorial?
- What is a dual-boot system? What are the advantages and disadvantages of creating one?
- What is another name for the "root" user, and what is the purpose of having one?
- What is the command to change your password?
- What is the command to go to the home directory? What is the command to see what is located in it?
- What type of files are located in the /bin, /etc, and /usr directories?
- Spend some time exploring the remainder of the tutorial. Do you feel that the tutorial met its primary objective? Explain why you would or would not install a Linux system.

Viruses: How to Tell If Your System Is Infected

Does your computer seem to have a mind of its own? Does it go to Web pages all by itself? Does it run really, really slowly at times? Do error messages fill your screen when your computer starts up? Is your computer doing something today that it wasn't doing yesterday? If so, you can be pretty sure that your computer has a virus. Computers infected by a virus oftentimes display symptoms in the same way that you do when you get sick. The following are some tips to help you keep your computer virus-free as well as some general guidelines for what to do in the event that your computer does get infected.

The best way to cure your computer of a virus is to not get one in the first place! Programs such as Symantec's Norton AntiVirus and McAfee's VirusScan will help protect your computer from nearly all known viruses and should be the first program installed on any computer that will ever be connected to the Internet. Once installed, these programs should be updated on a regular basis so they can protect you from the newest online threats. If you have a high-speed Internet connection, such as cable or DSL, then you can usually configure your antivirus software to perform these updates automatically. Most antivirus software comes with a year of free updates. After the year is up, you will have to pay a small service fee or upgrade to the newest version of the software to continue receiving essential updates. Anyone who has ever lost a lot of data due to a virus will tell you that this is definitely money and time well spent. Do not let your antivirus update subscription lapse. New threats are released onto the Internet every day, and old virus software is as good as no virus software at all.

In addition to keeping your antivirus software up-to-date, you should also keep your operating system up-to-date with the latest security patches. Most viruses take advantage of systems that do not have the latest security enhancements installed. Windows users should regularly run the program "Windows Update" by launching Microsoft Internet Explorer and going to **windowsupdate.microsoft.com** and following the directions on the screen. Any items identified by Windows Update as "Critical Updates and Service Packs" should be installed as soon as possible to avoid compromising your computer.

In the event that your computer does become infected with a virus, the manufacturer of your antivirus software should provide you with a solution for cleansing your computer. You should check the manufacturer's Web site and the antivirus software user manual ahead of time so that you know where to find this information as well as the proper procedures to follow in the case of an emergency. Any damage from a virus infection can be further minimized by keeping backups of important files on removable media such as CDs or floppy disks. You do backup your important files, right?

For a detailed list of ways to protect your computer from all types of threats, go to the Home Computer Security section of the CERT® Coordination Center's Web site at **www.cert.org/homeusers/HomeComputer Security**. Microsoft also provides a great security resource at **www.microsoft.com/security/** (Figure 4.29).

FIGURE 4.29 Microsoft's Web site provides information on how to protect your computer from threats, such as the latest viruses.

FILE MANAGEMENT

You've just finished your term paper—where should you save it? You never know when you may need a writing sample for a graduate school or job application, so you'll want to keep it someplace safe. The secret to finding what you're looking for in the future is good file management now. Managing computer files is an essential skill for any computer user.

For most people, managing files is intuitive; it's simple once they learn the basics. You can think of managing computer files as being similar to the way you organize and store paper files and folders in a file cabinet (Figure 4A). You start with a storage device (the filing cabinet), divide it into definable sections (folders), and then fill the sections with specific items (documents) that fit the defined sections. Most people tend to organize the things in their lives, and the organizational principles used are the same when managing computer files.

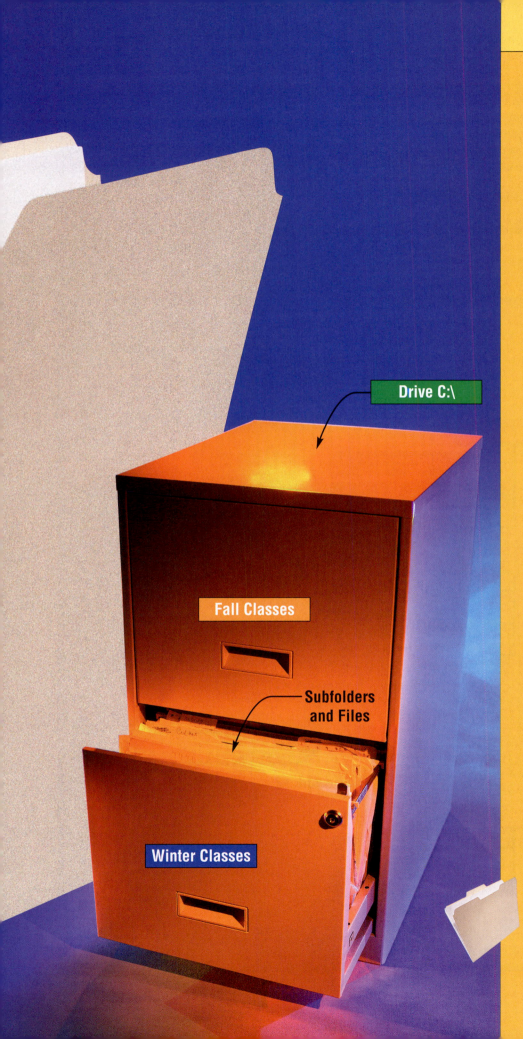

Drive C:

Fall Classes

Subfolders and Files

Winter Classes

The Big Picture: Files, Folders, and Paths

A **file** is a named unit of related data stored in a computer system. Your data (as well as the programs installed on your computer) are stored in files. Files store Word documents, music, photo images, Excel spreadsheets, applications, and a variety of other digital compilations. Every file that is stored has certain attributes. An **attribute** is a setting that provides information such as the file's date of creation, its size, and the date it was last modified.

You use **folders** (also called **directories**) to organize groups of files that have something in common. Many folders have **subfolders**—folders within folders—that enable you to organize your files even further. For example, you might create a folder called "Classes," and then create subfolders for each school term, and then subfolders within each school term for your individual classes (Figure 4B).

All of the files and folders you create must reside on a storage device called a **drive**. The primary storage devices on desktop computers are the **hard drive**, the **floppy disk drive**, the **Zip drive**, and **CD** and **DVD drives**. On PCs, these storage devices are designated by drive letters. A **drive letter** is simply a letter of the alphabet followed by a colon and the backslash character. For instance, the floppy disk drive is almost always referred to

Figure 4A
You can organize files on your computer the same way you would organize documents in a filing cabinet.

as A:\. The hard drive is generally referred to as C:\. Other drives, such as an external Zip drive, might be labeled drive E (E:\). (On the Mac, drives are not labeled with letters. You'll see them as icons appearing on your screen.)

For the computer to access a particular file, it needs to know the path it should take to get to the file. A **path** is the sequence of directories that the computer must follow to locate a file. A typical path might look like this:

C:\Classes\ Expository Writing 201\Homework#1_draft1.doc

In this case, the C:\ in the path indicates that the file is located on the C:\ drive. The **top-level folder**, "Classes," contains, as the name indicates, things that have to do with classes. The subfolder named "Expository Writing 201" is the subfolder for your writing class. The file at the end of the path, "Homework#1_draft1.doc," is the first draft of your first homework assignment. The .doc extension indicates that the file is a Microsoft Word document. We'll discuss filenames in greater depth shortly. Figure 4B illustrates what a hierarchical drive, folder, and file structure might look like.

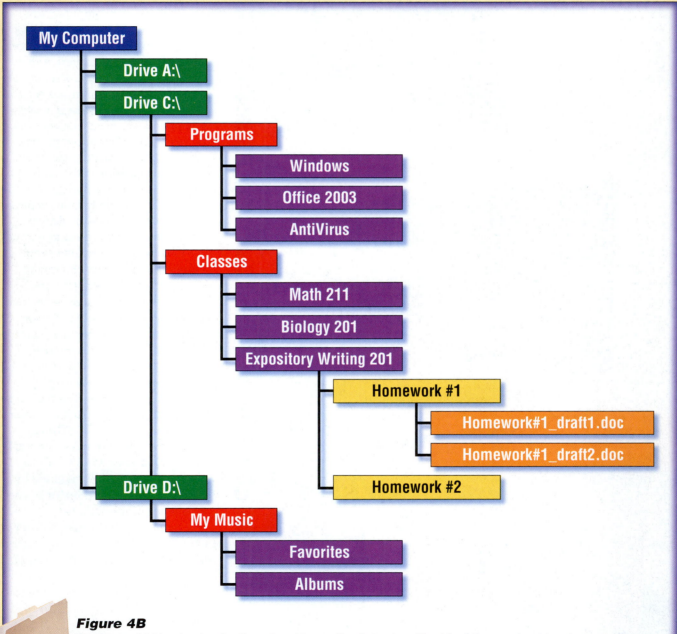

Figure 4B
The drive and folder structure is often referred to as a "tree" structure. The drive letters can be pictured as roots, the folders as branches, and the files as leaves.

FILE-NAMING CONVENTIONS

To save a file, you need to know where you're going to store it—in other words, on which storage device and in which folder. In addition, each file needs a specific filename. The **filename** is the name that the storage device uses to identify each unique file, so the name must differ from all other filenames used within the same folder or directory. You may use the same name for different files, but they must exist on different drives or in different folders. Be careful to include enough detail in naming a file so that you will be able to recognize the filename when you need the file later. The name you use when you create a file is usually very obvious to you at the time—but the name may elude you when you try to remember it in the future.

Every filename on a PC has two parts that are separated by a period (read as "dot"). The first part, the part you're probably most familiar with, is called the **name**. The second part is called the **extension**, an addition to the filename typically three characters in length. In a file called Homework#1_draft1.doc, Homework#1_draft1 is the name and .doc is the extension; together they make up the filename.

Typically, an extension is used to identify the type of data that the file contains (or the format it is stored in). Sometimes it indicates the application used to create the file. In Microsoft Windows, each application automatically assigns an extension to a file when you save it for the first time. For example, Microsoft Word automatically assigns the .doc extension. Workbooks created in Microsoft Excel use the .xls extension. When naming files, you never need to be concerned about typing in an extension, because all programs attach their extension to the filename by default.

Program files, also called application files, usually use the .exe extension, which stands for

Commonly Used Filename Extensions

Extension	File Type
.exe	Program or application
.doc	Microsoft Word
.xls	Microsoft Excel
.ppt	Microsoft PowerPoint
.mdb	Microsoft Access
.pdf	Adobe Acrobat
.txt	ASCII text
.htm or .html	Web pages
.rtf	Files in Rich Text Format
.jpeg or .jpg	Picture or image format

Figure 4C

executable. The term *executable* is used because when you use an application, you execute, or run, the file. Figure 4C lists the most commonly used extensions and their file types. Note that when using Mac OS, extensions are not needed because Macintosh files contain a code representing the name of the application that created the file. However, it is generally recommended that Mac users add the appropriate extension to their filenames so that they can more easily exchange them with PC users and avoid conversion problems. Extensions can now include up to five characters, but most still use three.

In Microsoft Windows, you can use up to 250 characters in a filename, including spaces. Windows filenames cannot include any of the following characters: forward slash (/), backslash (\), greater than sign (>), less than sign (<), asterisk (*), question mark (?), quotation mark ("), pipe symbol (|), colon (:), or semicolon (;). In Mac OS, you can use up to 31 characters in a filename, including spaces, and all characters except the colon.

Now that you understand the basics of paths, folders, and file-naming conventions, let's turn our attention to the business of managing files.

Managing Files

Files can be managed in two ways: (1) with a file management utility such as My Computer or (2) from within the programs that create them. In the following sections, we'll explore both methods.

FILE MANAGEMENT UTILITIES

Windows comes with two file management programs. The Start, All Programs, Accessories menu sequence contains an icon for a program named Windows Explorer. The Start menu and an icon on the Windows desktop can be used to launch a program called My Computer. The Windows Explorer program works just like the My Computer program, which is described in the following paragraphs.

The My Computer window contains the familiar Windows title bar, a menu bar, and a toolbar (Figure 4D). The window is split into two panes.

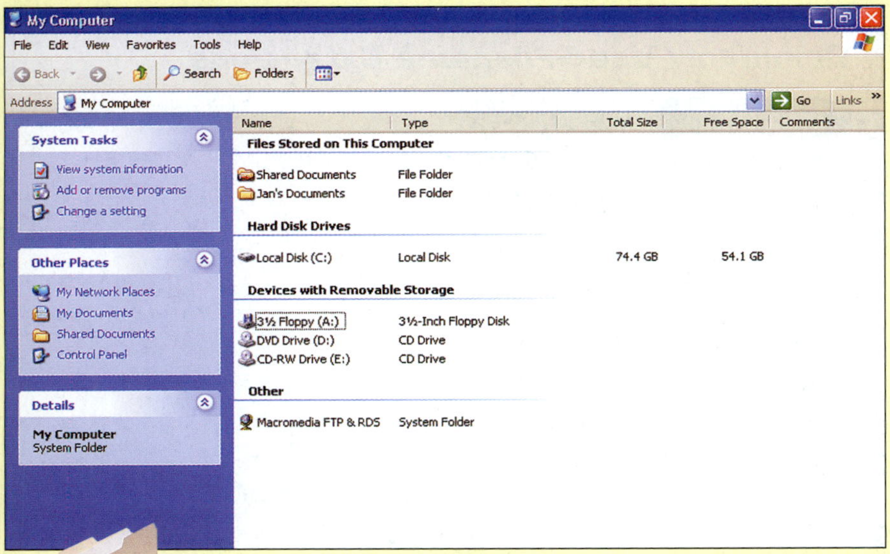

Figure 4D
The My Computer window is divided into two panes: the left pane shows system tasks and links to other places on your computer; the right pane shows the various files and drives you can currently choose from.

The *left* pane displays links to system tasks, such as viewing system information, adding and removing programs, and changing settings. The left pane also displays links to "Other" places besides the available drives, such as My Network Places, My Documents, Shared Documents, and the Control Panel.

The left pane is dynamic; that is, if you click items in the right pane, the left pane gives you choices that are specific to the particular folder or drive you've clicked. The *right pane* contains a listing of available drives and folders. You may sort within the right pane by filename, file type, or file size. You can do this by clicking the Name, Type, or Total Size bars at the top of the window. You can also use this view to manage folders

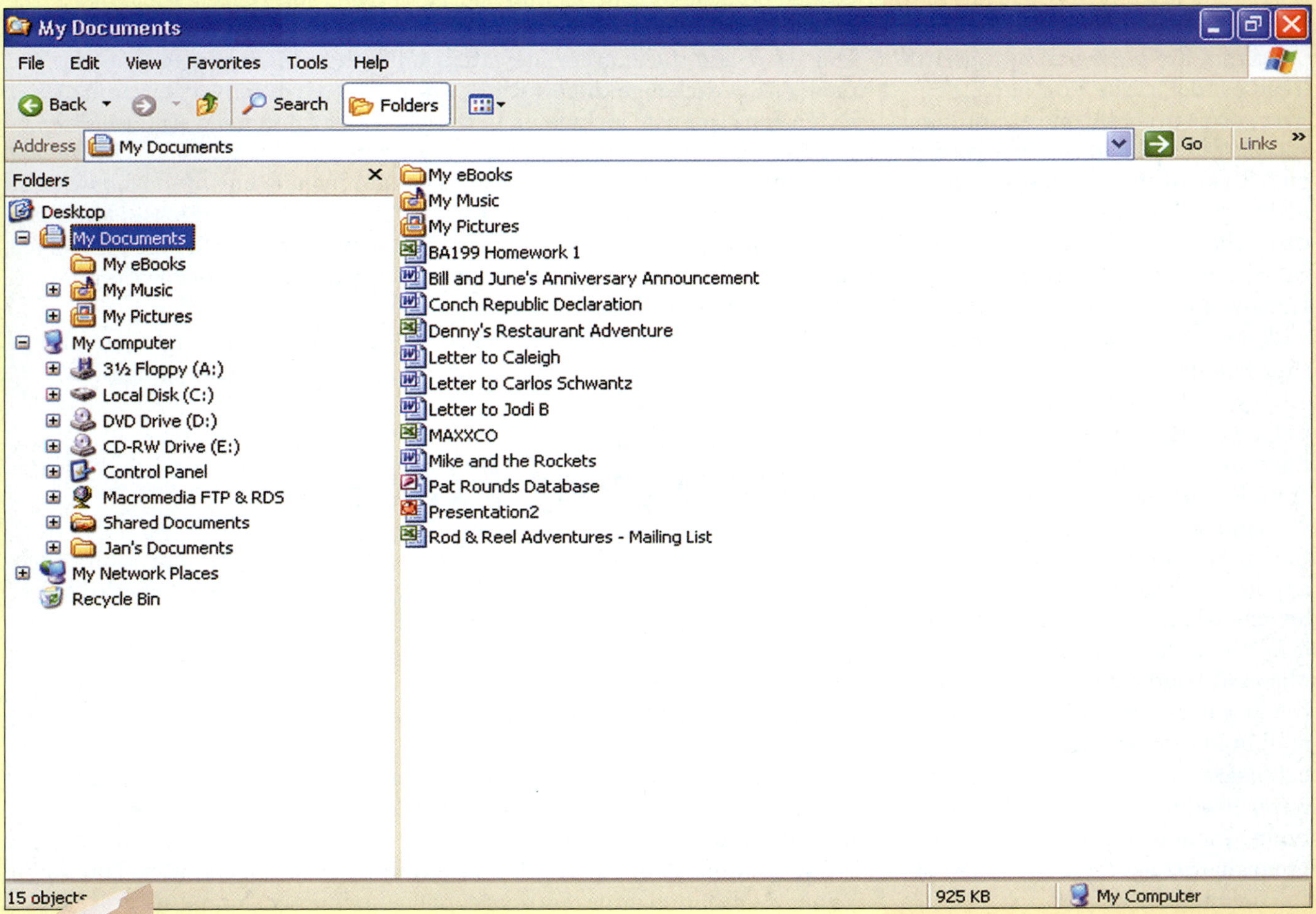

Figure 4E
When you click the Folders button on the Standard toolbar in My Computer, you'll see the Folders view.

and files. Simply double-click the drive name in the right pane, and the left pane changes to show you the tasks you can accomplish, such as creating, managing, and deleting folders and files.

To use My Computer strictly in file management mode—without a dynamic left pane—click the Folders button on the Standard toolbar. In Folders view, the left pane shows the names of the drives and folders, and the right pane shows the subfolders and files within the folders (Figure 4E).

To view more detail about the drives or folders in the left pane, simply click the icons in the left pane and the detail appears in the right pane. To open folders and files, double-click the icons in the right pane. (You may also use the menu sequence View, Explorer Bar, Folders to toggle between the default view and the Folders view.)

You can view the contents of the right pane in several ways. The different views are accessible from the View menu or from the Views button on the Standard toolbar. The thumbnail view is particularly helpful if you're searching through pictures and photographs, because it enables you to preview a thumbnail-sized copy of the images you have in the folder—before you open them (Figure 4F). The list view simply lists the names of the files, whereas the details view offers you information regarding file size, file type, and the date a file was last modified (Figure 4G).

Formatting

Formatting makes a disk functional with your operating system. This process is necessary because different types of computers store data in different ways. For this reason, a PC cannot read Macintosh disks unless the PC is running special software. However, most Macintoshes are equipped with software that enables them to read PC disks.

Almost all of the floppy disks that you buy today are preformatted.

Figure 4F
The thumbnail view is especially handy for previewing images.

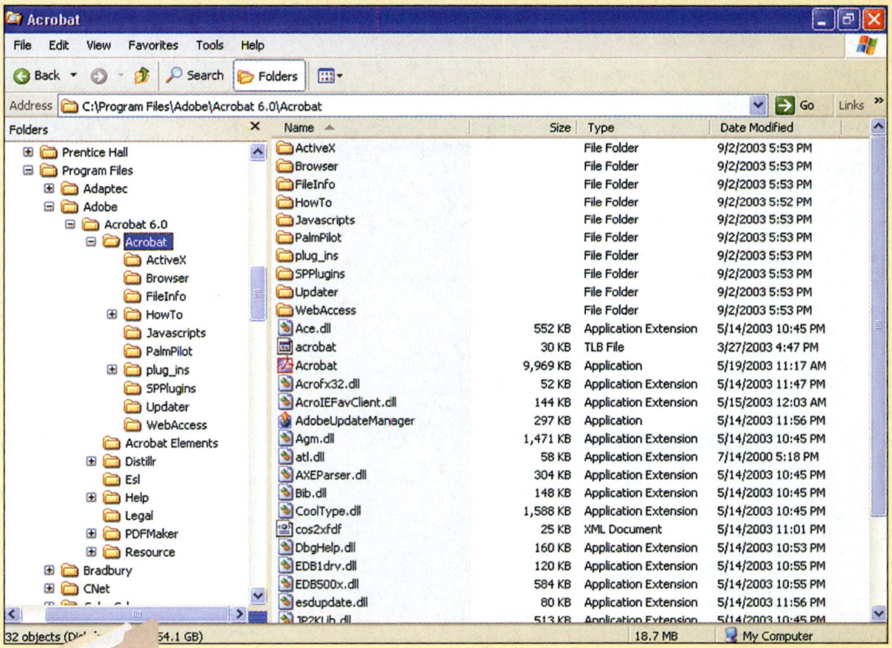

Figure 4G
The details view enables you to see the file size, file type, and the date a file was last modified.

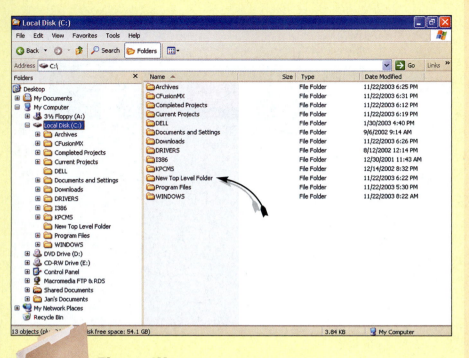

Figure 4H

This top-level folder has been created at the root of the C:\ drive on the hard disk.

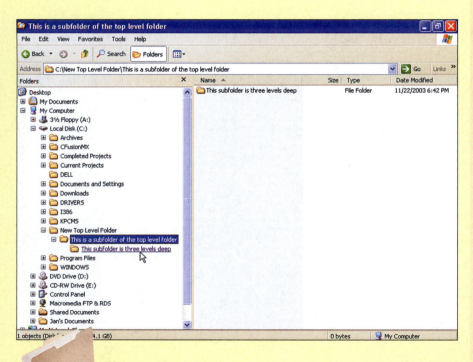

Figure 4I

This new subfolder is located three levels deep on the hard disk.

Most CDs and DVDs need to be initialized before they can be written to as well. You may someday need to format a floppy disk so that it is in reusable and pristine condition. Let's explore the My Computer formatting capability.

When you place a floppy disk in your floppy disk drive (be sure that the disk does not contain anything you wish to keep) and launch the My Computer program, you can right-click on "3 ? floppy (A:)" and then choose Format from the context-specific menu. You should type in a Volume Label—something that identifies the disk's potential content—and then decide whether to use the Quick Format option. If you choose Quick Format, the My Computer formatting utility will overwrite any content on the disk with formatting code. If you choose not to use Quick Format, the My Computer formatting utility will overwrite every bit on the disk with formatting code. If you are sure you know what you are doing, click "yes" when warned that formatting will erase all of the content on the disk and then click "OK" after the formatting is complete. Should you encounter a message that says there are bad sectors on the disk, throw the disk away and try a different one—it's not worth 20 cents to store data on a floppy disk with bad sectors.

Be aware that formatting destroys all the data that's been recorded on a disk. You should never format a disk that contains valuable data. In addition, you should never format the computer's hard disk unless you've just purchased a new hard disk and are following the installation instructions.

Creating Folders

Another way to manage your files effectively is to create a **folder** or **directory structure** (the terms *folder* and *directory* are synonymous)—an organized set of folders to save your files to. The process of creating a folder structure is accomplished in two steps:

STEP 1

Decide which drive, such as a floppy drive, hard drive, or CD drive, you will create your folder on. Then click the drive letter or designator in the left pane of your file management utility.

STEP 2

Establish the primary, or top-level, folder. Choose the File, New, Folder menu sequence to place a new folder at the root of the storage device or in a selected preexisting folder. In other words, if you have selected the C:\ drive, the new folder will be placed at the top level. See Figure 4H for an example of a new folder that has been created at the root of the C:\ drive.

If, however, you selected a top-level folder or subfolder as your starting point, then the new folder will be placed within it (Figure 4I).

You can repeat this process as many times as is necessary to create your desired folder structure. For example, if you're taking three classes, you might want to create three separate subfolders with the appropriate class names under a top-level folder called "Classes." That way, you'll know exactly where to save a file each time you create one, and you'll avoid having a cluttered and disorganized storage space.

Of course, creating a well-organized folder structure requires that you add, rename, and move folders as your needs change. For example, if you add a class to your schedule, you'll want to create a new subfolder in your top-level "Classes" folder. Next term, you'll create new subfolders for each of your classes.

One Windows method that is effective for managing, modifying, and creating folders, subfolders, and files is the use of the right-click mouse action. Right-clicking within either pane of My Computer will cause a pop-up context-sensitive menu to appear. Here's an example: with drive C:\ open, right-click in the right pane and choose "New, Folder" from the menu. You could name the folder "Classes" and then left-double-click on the folder to open it. You could then right-click in the empty right pane of My Computer and choose "New, Folder" to create a folder that you would name for one of your classes, or you could create a folder for each term of each school year and then make folders for each of your classes. Your finished structure might look something like this: C:\Classes\Fall_06\Psych_221.

Transferring Files

Once you've created a useful folder structure, you're ready to transfer files and folders that already exist. Whether you're working with files or folders, the same rules apply. Files and folders can be transferred in two ways: you can copy them or you can move them. The easiest way to accomplish these tasks is to simply *right-drag* the files you want to transfer to the new location. When you release the right mouse button, a context-sensitive menu appears, allowing you to choose the result of your right-drag (Figure 4J). The choices on this menu are Copy, Move, Create a shortcut, or Cancel the action.

- **Copying** creates a duplicate file at the new location and leaves the existing file as is.

- **Moving** is similar to cutting and pasting; the file is moved from its original location to the new location.

- **Creating a shortcut** leaves the original file in place and creates a pointer that will take you to the file you've created the shortcut to. This action is handy for files that you access often.

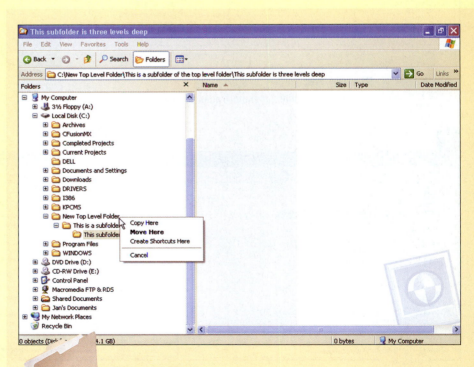

Figure 4J
The right-drag context-sensitive menu enables you to copy or move files, create a shortcut, or cancel an action.

If you *left-drag* a file *within the same drive*, the file is automatically moved to the new location on the drive. Left-dragging *between drives* creates a copy of the file in the new location.

Right-clicking a file invokes a context-sensitive menu that enables you to choose among many common tasks, such as copying, deleting, and renaming files and creating shortcuts (Figure 4K). You may also use the File menu or toolbars to accomplish these and other file management tasks.

Backing Up

You can create a backup copy of your files in several ways. The first, and easiest, way is to create intermediate copies as you work. You can do this by using the File, Save As menu sequence every 15 or 20 minutes. Name your intermediate copies by appending a number or letter to the filename. For example, Writing121_homework.doc would become Writing121_homework1.doc, then Writing121_homework2.doc, and so forth.

Additionally, you can use the My Computer program to drag a copy of your file to a floppy disk or CD/DVD drive. Backing up files to the same drive that the original copy is on introduces the risk of losing both copies in the case of disk failure or other disaster, so you should always use a remote or portable medium for your backups.

A third way to be sure that you don't lose your work is to use backup software that is specifically designed to backup files.

Getting Help

If you need help when working within the My Computer program, choose the Help menu selection, click Help and Support, and then type "managing files" into the Search dialog box, which is located in the top left corner of the window. This will bring up Tasks, Overviews, Articles, and Tutorials that will help you to further understand file management practices.

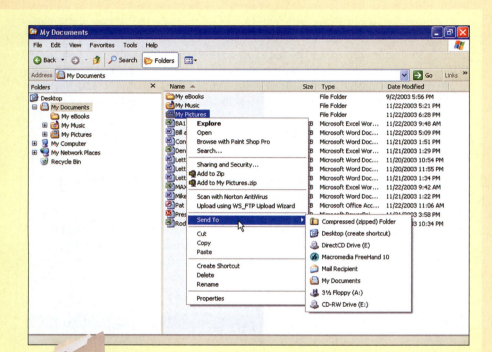

Figure 4K
The right-click context menu provides you with a shortcut to common tasks.

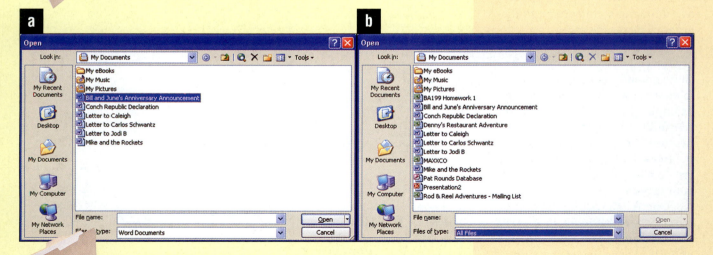

Figure 4L
Word's Open dialog box in (**a**) All Word Documents view and (**b**) All Files view.

MANAGING FILES FROM WITHIN PROGRAMS

As mentioned earlier, all software applications use program-specific filename extensions. The advantage of using a default file extension is that both you and your computer will be able to easily associate the file with the program with which it was created. By using appropriate extensions, you can double-click a file in a file management utility such as My Computer and the program will launch the appropriate application.

You can use an application to open a file or use a file to launch the application that created it. Let's say you create a document in Microsoft Word. You give the file the name "Letter Home," and Word assigns the extension ".doc" by default. Later, you use the My Computer file management utility to locate the file and then use the mouse to double-click the filename. The file will open in Word. Alternately, you could launch Word and then use the File, Open menu sequence to locate the file and open it. The Open dialog box defaults to showing only those files that have the .doc extension. This way, you only see files that were created in Word and are not distracted by the names of files that are not Word files. Figure 4L shows the Open dialog box in its default All Word Documents view and in the All Files view.

The File, Open menu sequence in many programs, including Microsoft Office applications, also enables you to manage files. There are icons for creating new folders and for deleting files, and there is a menu choice called Tools that enables you to copy, rename, and create shortcuts to files. Pointing to a file and pressing the right mouse button within the Open menu also invokes a file management menu with various tasks (Figure 4M).

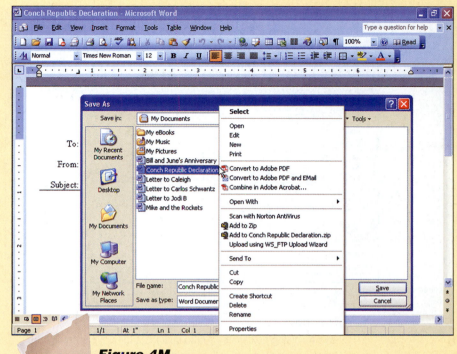

Figure 4M
Right-clicking a file in either the Save As or Open dialog box invokes file management commands.

SAVING FILES

Saving refers to the process of transferring a file from the computer's temporary memory, or RAM, to a permanent storage device, such as a hard disk. In Microsoft Windows, documents are saved by default to a folder called My Documents unless you specify another folder from within the Tools, Options menu. A critical decision you'll make when managing files is whether to use the Save or Save As command to save files.

Save or Save As?

Many computer users never figure out the difference between Save and Save As. It is actually quite simple. When you choose the Save command under the File menu, the program takes what you've created or modified in memory and writes over or replaces it to the same storage device and folder, with the same filename that it had when it was opened in the application. When you first save a file, the initial File, Save menu sequence always invokes the Save As dialog box, because the drive, path, and filename must be designated the first time a file is saved. But when you're working with a previously saved file, you need to be more careful. The Save command doesn't allow you to designate a different drive, folder, or filename; it simply replaces what is stored with the contents of memory.

The Save As command, however, brings up a dialog box that offers all of the choices you had when you first saved a file (Figure 4N). You may choose a different drive or a different folder or simply modify the filename. Modifying the filename is a good way to save various versions of your work, just in case something happens to what is in memory and you need to go back to a previous version.

Once you've successfully saved a file, you can always save another copy elsewhere by using the Save As command, which enables you to save the file using a new location, a new filename, or both. You might also use

Figure 4N
The Save As dialog box allows you to designate the drive or folder you want to save your file in as well as assign an appropriate filename.

the Save As command to save a copy of your finished work on a floppy disk or in an alternate folder as backup, just in case something happens to your original work.

Intermediate Files

Follow these steps to help prevent the loss of your work:

- Begin work and save your file.

- Continue working for an additional 10 to 20 minutes.

- Use Save As to save the intermediate work in the same place, but with a modified filename. (Use the original filename, but add an incremental number.)

So, say your original file is named "resume.doc." You would then name the intermediate copies "resume1.doc," "resume2.doc," "resume3.doc," and so on. Then, when your iterations result in a final document that you are happy with, you perform a final Save As and name the file "resume" or "resume-June-05." You can then delete the intermediate copies.

Managing E-mail

Many e-mail users quickly become overwhelmed by the number of messages they receive. It's not unusual, even for college students, to get dozens, or even hundreds, of messages every day. You can handle the deluge by organizing your messages into folders.

Most e-mail programs enable you to create your own mail folders. For example, you could create folders for each of the classes you're taking. In each folder, you can store mail from the teacher as well as from other students

in the same class. You could create another folder to store mail from your family.

If you're trying to find a message in a lengthy message list, remember that you can sort the mail in different ways. By default, your e-mail program probably sorts mail in the order the messages were received. You can also sort by sender or recipient; some programs give you more ways to sort. With Microsoft Outlook—and Outlook Express— you can quickly sort messages by clicking one of the buttons at the top of the message list. For example, to sort messages by date, click the Received button. Click it again to sort the list in the opposite order.

Still can't find a message? Most e-mail programs provide Find commands, which enable you to search for information in the message header. The best programs enable you to search for text in the message body as well. To search for a message within Outlook or Outlook Express, click the Find button and choose the search options you want in the Find Messages dialog box.

A Few Last Reminders

Good file management is the hallmark of a competent computer user. File management should not be an intimidating or frustrating task. Computers are tremendously complex and powerful devices, but the principles of managing your work are simple. Plan and construct folder structures that make sense to you. Name your files in such a way that you can easily find them. Always begin at the beginning. If something doesn't work, go back to when it did. Read the manual. Follow directions carefully. Make backup copies of your work. And, if all else fails, don't be afraid to ask for help.

Spotlight Exercises

1. Launch either My Computer or Windows Explorer. Right-click anywhere on the toolbar (the buttons under the pull-down menu titles) and choose Customize from the bottom of the menu. Practice adding and removing icons from the toolbar. You may place separators anywhere you wish. When you are finished, you can either keep your changes or click the Reset button from within the Customize Toolbar window. Write a paragraph that describes this little-known feature.

2. In this exercise, you will use the My Computer program to build a folder structure on an empty floppy disk. Create a top-level folder named Junk that contains three subfolders and then right-drag two or more files from some other source into one of the three subfolders. Choose the Folders button at the top of the My Computer window. Click the Junk folder in the left pane and then click on the subfolder that contains the files. Now press the Print Screen key that is at the top of the right side of your keyboard. Open a word processor, choose Edit, Paste. Type you name below the picture on your screen. Choose Print from the File menu. Turn in this sheet to your professor.

3. Create a new folder at the root of your hard disk and name it "Junk." Launch your favorite Web browser and go to your favorite search engine's home page. Choose the link that is just above the search topic window that says "Images." Type in anything you'd like to see a picture of. After finding the picture, click on the image to go to the page on the Web where it resides. Write down the URL (address) of the Web site and note the day and time. Right-click on the image and save it to your Junk folder. Write a few paragraphs that describe what you've accomplished.

4. In this exercise, you will practice changing the default folder icon image. From within My Computer, right-click on any folder name or icon. Choose Properties from the bottom of the menu. Choose the Customize tab at the top right of the window. At the bottom of the window there are two choices for changing the appearance of the icon. The first choice is to change how the icon looks in Thumbnail view. To experiment with the different views, choose the View menu and then from the second section of the View menu click on Thumbnails, Tiles, Icons, List, and Details. If you change the image of the first choice, you will only see the image when My Computer is in Thumbnail view. The second choice on the menu changes the default icon that you see in all five of the views. Create a folder and name it "Junk." Create a subfolder within Junk and give it a name of your choosing. Now use the right-click, Properties sequence to change the image of each of these folders. When you are finished, double-click on Junk in the left pane to reveal your subfolder(s) in the right pane and then press the Print Screen key that is at the top of the right side of your keyboard. Open a word processor, choose Edit, Paste. Type your name below the picture on your screen. Choose Print from the File menu. Turn in this sheet to your instructor.

5. Open your e-mail program. Create a new folder using the File, New, Folder menu sequence (in Outlook and Outlook Express—other mail readers will have a similar method). For the folder name, use the name and year of the term you are in now, such as Fall2005. Open your new folder and create a folder for each of your classes. Now practice dragging messages back and forth between your deleted files folder and your new folders. Feel free to delete these folders when you are through. Write a paragraph describing your experience.

6. Use your favorite Web browser to go to **www.worldstart.com/tips/windows-explorer/**. Browse the links to locate at least three that you find interesting. Use the Start, All Programs, Accessories menu sequence to find and launch Windows Explorer. Try the tips and tricks you learned at the Web site. Write a short paper describing where you went and what you learned.

- Understand how system software supports application software.

- List the most popular types of general-purpose applications.

- Discuss the advantages and disadvantages of standalone programs, integrated programs, and software suites.

- Discuss the advantages of Web technology and file compatibility.

- Explain the concept of software versions and software upgrades.

- Understand how commercial software, shareware, freeware, and public domain software differ.

- Describe the essential concepts of application software and the skills needed to use it.

CHAPTER 5

Application Software: Tools for Productivity

Application software generally refers to all of the programs that enable you to use the computer for your work. In this sense, application software differs from system software, the programs that enable the computer to function properly. You use application software to work efficiently with the documents that are created in almost any line of work, such as invoices, letters, reports, proposals, presentations, customer lists, newsletters, tables, and flyers. Referring back to our aquarium analogy, applications are the fish that swim in the water (the operating system). The operating system provides the environment in which the applications run. It supports the functions of input, processing, output, and storage, whereas the applications enable users to accomplish specific tasks. People use applications to create products, to communicate with others, and to store and find information. They also derive entertainment from certain types of applications.

In this chapter, you'll learn how to make sense of the world of application software. You'll read about the various types of application software and learn how to install, maintain, and upgrade the programs that you use each day.

General-Purpose Applications

General-purpose applications are applications used by many people to accomplish frequently performed tasks. These tasks include writing (word processing), working with numbers (spreadsheets), and keeping track of information (databases). General-purpose applications include productivity, multimedia and graphics, Internet, and home and educational programs. These applications are likely to be found on home and business users' personal computers. Figure 5.1 lists the various types of general-purpose application software.

PERSONAL PRODUCTIVITY PROGRAMS

The most popular general-purpose applications are **personal productivity programs**, which, as the name implies, help individuals do their work more effectively and efficiently. Productivity

---

FIGURE 5.1   General-purpose Application Software

Personal Productivity Programs	Multimedia and Graphics Software	Internet Programs	Home and Educational Programs
Word processing	Desktop publishing and multimedia authoring programs	E-mail programs	Personal finance software
Spreadsheet		Web browsers	
	Paint, drawing, and animation programs		Tax preparation software
Database		Instant messaging software	
Presentation graphics	Image-editing programs		Home design and landscaping software
		Videoconferencing software	
Personal information management	3-D rendering programs		Computer-assisted tutorials
	Audio software		Computerized reference information (e.g., encyclopedias, street maps)
	Video-editing software		
			Games

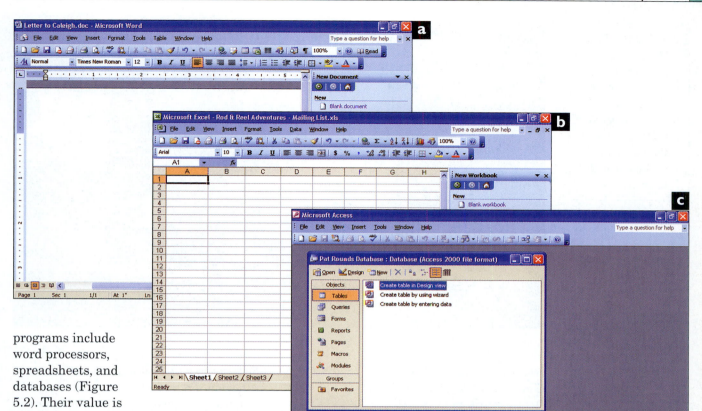

FIGURE 5.2 Personal productivity programs include (**a**) Microsoft Word (word processing), (**b**) Microsoft Excel (spreadsheet), and (**c**) Microsoft Access (database).

programs include word processors, spreadsheets, and databases (Figure 5.2). Their value is that they perform their functions regardless of the subject matter. For instance, a word processor is equally valuable for typing a term paper for your writing class as it is for typing one for your marketing class.

You should use the appropriate application for the appropriate purpose. Excel can be used for a presentation, but it is much better to use PowerPoint and embed Excel spreadsheets and charts in it. You can use tables to add numbers together in Word, but Excel is much better suited to this task. One maxim you may have heard is that "You can drive a screw with a hammer—but a hammer is best used for driving nails and a screw should be set with a screwdriver." The same rule applies to using the right productivity program for the right job. You can increase your productivity by choosing an application such as Excel to manage numbers and an application such as Word to manage text.

Personal information managers, which offer electronic address books and scheduling tools, and presentation graphics programs, which enable you to develop slides and transparencies for presentations, are also considered personal productivity software. PowerPoint is an example of a popular presentation graphics program (Figure 5.3).

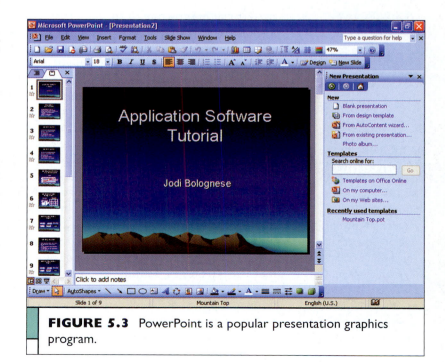

FIGURE 5.3 PowerPoint is a popular presentation graphics program.

FIGURE 5.4
Multimedia presentations involve two or more media. Such presentations are now the norm in professional settings.

Destinations

A great site to learn more about multimedia and graphics software is About's Web page on "Graphic Software" at **graphicssoft.about .com**

Techtalk

pixel
Short for picture element. A pixel is a dot or point that represents color in a graphic image. Pixels are the smallest elements that a device, such as a monitor, can display.

MULTIMEDIA AND GRAPHICS SOFTWARE

What exactly is **multimedia**? The standard definition is that it is any application that involves two or more media, such as audio, graphics, or video (Figure 5.4). By this definition, any TV show or movie is a multimedia experience, because it uses both audio and video. Some multimedia applications offer another exciting characteristic: interactivity. For example, in an interactive multimedia presentation, users can choose their own path through the presentation. The interactive dimension makes computer-based multimedia a non-couch-potato technology; instead of sitting back and letting someone else determine the presentation's flow, you're in control.

One of the reasons the Web is so popular is because of its interactivity. In fact, the Web could be viewed as a gigantic multimedia presentation. Most Web pages include graphics along with the text, and many also offer animations, videos, and sounds. On some Web pages, you can click parts of a graphic to access a different page.

Computer applications use multimedia features where text alone would not be effective. Graphics, sounds, animations, and video can often do a more effective job of involving the user (and conveying information) than text alone.

Multimedia and graphics software includes professional desktop publishing (such as QuarkXPress) and multimedia authoring programs; paint, drawing, and animation programs; image-editing programs (such as Photoshop); 3-D rendering programs (such as computer-aided design [CAD] programs); audio software; and video-editing programs.

A multimedia presentation typically involves some or all of the following: bit-mapped graphics, vector graphics, edited photographs, rendered 3-D images, edited videos, and synthesized sound. In the following sections, we'll discuss each of these and look briefly at some of the software used to create multimedia productions.

Compression and Decompression

Computers can only work with art, photographs, videos, and sounds when these multimedia resources are stored in digitized files, which require huge amounts of storage space. For example, an average-sized hard disk might store only 30 or 40 audio CDs, and there wouldn't be much room left for system software or applications. To reduce the size of multimedia files, most software uses compression/decompression algorithms called **codecs**.

Codecs use two different approaches to compression: lossless compression and lossy compression. With **lossless compression**, the original file is compressed so that it can be completely restored, without flaw, when it is decompressed. With **lossy compression**, the original file is processed so that some information is permanently removed from the file. Lossy compression techniques eliminate information that isn't perceived when people see pictures or hear sounds, such as frames from a video that are above the number needed to eliminate the flicker effect and very high musical notes.

Paint Programs

Paint programs are used to create **bit-mapped graphics** (also called **raster graphics**), which are composed of tiny dots, each corresponding to one pixel on the computer's display (Figure 5.5). You can use a professional paint program such as Fractal Design Painter to create beautiful effects. Although paint programs enable artists to create pictures easily, the resulting bit-mapped image is difficult to edit. To do so, you must zoom the picture so that you can edit the individual pixels, and enlargement may produce an unattractive distortion called the *jaggies*.

Paint programs can save your work to the following standard formats:

- **Graphics Interchange Format (GIF)** (pronounced "jiff" or "giff"). GIF is a 256-color file format that uses lossless compression to reduce file size. It's best for simple images with large areas of solid color. Because this file format is a Web standard, it's often used for Web pages.

- **Joint Photographic Experts Group (JPEG)** (pronounced "jay-peg"). JPEG files can store up to 16.7 million colors and are best for complex images, such as photographs. This image format is also a Web standard. The JPEG file format uses lossy compression to reduce file size.

- **Portable Network Graphics (PNG)** (pronounced "ping"). This is a new alternative to GIF that doesn't require companies to pay royalties for the use of the lossless compression technique.

- **Windows Bitmap (BMP)**. This is a standard bit-mapped graphics format developed for Microsoft Windows. Compression is optional, so BMP files tend to be very large.

FIGURE 5.5 Paint programs are used to create bit-mapped graphics, which are composed of tiny dots, each corresponding to one pixel on the computer's display.

Drawing Programs

Drawing programs are used to create **vector graphics** in which each on-screen object is stored as a complex mathematical description. What this means, in practice, is that every object in a vector graphic can be independently edited and resized without introducing edge distortion, the bane of bit-mapped graphics. To compose an image with a drawing program, you create independent lines and shapes; you can then add colors and textures to these shapes. Because the resulting image has no inherent resolution, it can be any size you want. The picture will be printed using the output device's highest resolution.

Professional drawing programs, such as Macromedia Freehand and Adobe Illustrator, save files by outputting instructions in PostScript, which is an automated page-description language. PostScript graphic files are saved to the Encapsulated PostScript (EPS) format, which encapsulates the PostScript in a file that also contains a bit-mapped thumbnail image of the enclosed graphic. (The thumbnail image enables you to see the graphic on the screen.)

One drawback of drawing programs is the lack of Web support for vector graphics. Several proposals have been made for adopting a standard, and one should be in place in the next few years.

Techtalk

page-description language (PDL)

A programming language capable of precisely describing the appearance of a printed page, including fonts and graphics. PostScript is an established PDL standard widely used in desktop publishing.

3-D Rendering Programs

A 3-D rendering program adds three-dimensional effects to graphic objects. The results are strikingly realistic. Objects can be rotated in any direction to achieve just the result the artist is looking for.

In the past, rendering software required a high-powered engineering workstation, but today's top desktop computers are up to the task. One rendering technique, **ray tracing**, adds amazing realism to a simulated three-dimensional object by manipulating variations in color intensity that would be produced by light falling on the object from multiple directions (which is the norm in the real world).

Image Editors

Image editors are sophisticated versions of paint programs that are used to edit and transform—but not create—complex bit-mapped images, such as photographs. These programs make use of automated image-processing algorithms to add a variety of special effects to photographic images. They also enable skilled users to doctor photographs in ways that leave few traces behind. After using imaging editors to improve your photos, you can share them with friends and family at Web sites such as PhotoWorks (**www.photoworks.com**; Figure 5.6).

Professional design studios have used image editors such as Adobe Photoshop for years (Figure 5.7), but image editors may soon capture a wider market due to the booming market for digital cameras. Programs such as Adobe's PhotoDeluxe are designed for beginners who want to perform the most common image-enhancement tasks quickly and easily and then print their pictures on a color printer. PhotoDeluxe can be used to remove red-eye from flash snapshots and adjust a picture's overall color cast.

FIGURE 5.6 You can use Web-based photo communities such as PhotoWorks (**www.photoworks.com**) to upload photos and make them available to your friends and family at no charge.

Animation Programs

When you see a movie at a theater, you're actually looking at still images shown at a frame rate (images per second) that is sufficiently high to trick the eye into seeing continuous motion. Like a movie, an animation consists of the same thing: images that appear to move. Animators create each of the still images separately. In computer animation, the computer provides tools for creating the animation as well as for running it.

It's easy to create a simple animation using the GIF file format, which enables programs to store more than one image in a GIF file. The file also stores a brief script that tells the application to play the images in a certain sequence and to display each image for a set period of time.

FIGURE 5.7 Adobe Photoshop is an image editor that has been used by professional design studios for years.

FIGURE 5.8 Ulead.com's GIF animator is a popular Web animation product.

Because Web browsers can read GIF files and play the animations, GIF animations are common on the Web (Figure 5.8).

Professional animation programs provide more sophisticated tools for creating and controlling animations, but they create proprietary files. To view these files on the Web, you need a special plug-in program such as Macromedia's Flash Player or Shockwave Player (Figure 5.9).

Audio Software

A variety of programs are available for capturing and processing sound for multimedia presentations, including sound mixers, compression software, bass enhancers, synthesized stereo, and even on-screen music composition programs. You won't see any tape recorders in today's recording studios—just computers!

Sound files contain digitized data in the form of digital audio waveforms (recorded live sounds or music), which are saved in one of several standardized sound formats. These formats specify how sounds should be digitally represented and generally include some type of data compression that reduces the size of the file:

FIGURE 5.9 To view animations on the Web, you need a special plug-in program such as Macromedia's Flash Player or Shockwave Player.

- **MP3** (or **MPEG-3**). A sound file format with almost unbelievable characteristics; you can compress CD-quality digital audio by a factor of 12:1 with

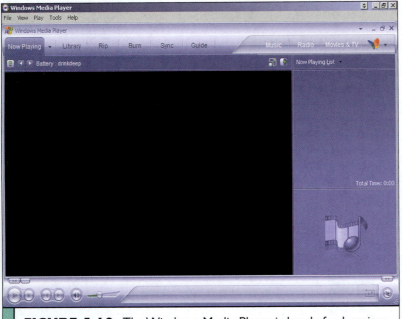

FIGURE 5.10 The Windows Media Player is handy for burning CDs and for creating MP3 files.

Streaming audio formats are available that enable Internet-accessed sounds to play almost immediately after the user clicks an audio link. The most popular streaming audio format, RealAudio, can deliver voice-quality audio over dial-up connections.

Video Editors

Video editors are programs that enable you to modify digitized videos. With a video editor, you can cut segments, resequence frames, add transitions, compress a file, and determine a video's frame rate (the number of still images displayed per second).

Video editors also enable you to save video files to some or all of the following video file formats:

- **Moving Picture Experts Group** (**MPEG**). A family of video file formats and lossy compression standards for full-motion video. The most recent version, MPEG-2, is the video format used by DVD-ROM discs. MPEG-2 videos offer CD/DVD-quality audio.

- **QuickTime**. A video file format developed by Apple Computer. The latest version, QuickTime-6 Pro, plays full-screen, broadcast-quality video as well as CD/DVD-quality audio. It is widely used in multimedia CD-ROM productions.

- **Video for Windows**. The native (or original format a program uses internally) video file format for Microsoft Windows. Often called AVI because these files use the .avi file extension, this format is inadequate for full-screen, broadcast-quality video.

Because a huge amount of data must be stored to create realistic-looking video on a computer, all video file formats use codec techniques. For the best playback, special video adapters are required. These adapters have hardware that decodes videos at high speed.

To make video available on the Internet, streaming video formats have been developed. These formats enable the video picture to start playing almost immediately after the user clicks the video

no perceptible loss in sound quality (Figure 5.10).

- **Sun/NeXT (AU)**. A low-fidelity monaural (single channel) format developed for Sun and NeXT workstations that is now widely used due to the small size of AU files. It's often used to distribute short audio clips over the Internet.

- **WAV**. The default Microsoft Windows sound file format (called WAV due to the .wav extension used to store these sounds) can be saved with a variety of quality levels, from low-fi mono to CD-quality stereo. WAV sounds usually aren't compressed, so they tend to take up a lot of disk space.

- **Ogg Vorbis**. A new digital format that is an even faster format than MP3. Ogg files are also about 20 percent smaller than MP3 files, so you can fit more of them on your hard disk or MP3 player.

- **Musical Instrument Digital Interface** (**MIDI**). MIDI files don't contain waveforms. They are text files that contain a text-based description that tells a synthesizer when and how to play individual musical notes.

Destinations

The following site has lots of links to video editors: **dmoz.org/Arts/ Video/Video _Editing/Equipment _and_Software/ Professional/**

FIGURE 5.11
Tucows provides links to audio, images, and video for use in creating multimedia on a Macintosh.

link. (With nonstreaming video, the user has to wait for the entire file to be transferred to his or her computer before it begins to play.) Streaming video formats rely on compression, low frame rates, and small image size to deliver video over the Internet, which does not have sufficient bandwidth (signal-carrying capacity) to disseminate broadcast-quality video. A variety of competing streaming video formats are available; the most popular is RealNetworks' RealVideo format.

Multimedia Authoring Systems

Authoring tools are used to create multimedia presentations. These tools enable you to specify which multimedia objects to use (such as text, pictures, videos, or animations), how to display them in relation to each other, how long to display them, and how to enable the user to interact with the presentation. To take full advantage of an authoring tool's capabilities, it's often necessary to learn a scripting language (a simple programming language). A leading authoring package is Macromedia Director.

Commercial authoring tools such as Macromedia Director save output in proprietary file formats. To view Macromedia presentations on a Web site, it's necessary to download and install a plug-in program (software that extends a browser's capabilities). Some users do not like to download viewers, so the Web's standards-setting body, the World Wide Web Consortium (W3C), recently approved the Synchronized Multimedia Integration Language (SMIL), a simple multimedia scripting language designed for Web pages. Once SMIL is supported by Web browsers, Internet users will be able to enjoy enhanced multimedia without having to download plug-in programs.

Macromedia's Studio MX media development kit, released in late 2002, is a powerful tool for developing multimedia Internet applications. If you are a Macintosh user, you will most likely be interested in visiting **www.apple.com/ilife** to learn about Apple's multimedia iLife suite. With the iLife package, you can create music with GarageBand; integrate and organize your music, photos, and home videos with iTunes, iPhoto, and iMovie; and pull it all together on your own DVD with iDVD (Figure 5.11).

One thing to keep in mind is that multimedia authoring programs tend to use lots of disk space and often require extra memory to run efficiently. Be sure to read the program's minimum system requirements, which are usually listed on the packaging or in the documentation, and realize that the numbers truly are minimums.

INTERNET PROGRAMS

Internet programs, such as e-mail clients, instant messaging programs, Web browsers, and videoconferencing software were discussed in detail in Chapters 2 and 3. For now, simply note that they are general-purpose applications because they help us to communicate, learn, and interact.

HOME AND EDUCATIONAL PROGRAMS

General-purpose software also includes **home and educational programs**, such as personal finance and tax preparation software, home design and landscaping software, computerized reference information (such as encyclopedias, street maps, and computer-assisted tutorials), and games.

Hot sellers in the reference CD/DVD-ROM market include multimedia versions of dictionaries (which include recordings that tell you how to pronounce difficult words), encyclopedias (replete with sound and video clips from famous moments in history), and how-to guides (which use multimedia to show you how to do just about anything around the home) (Figure 5.12).

Computer Games: MUDs and Graphical MUDs

By any standard, computer games are big business. In the United States, they bring in sales at a clip of $6 billion per year, and the market shows no signs of shrinking. This highly profitable industry got its start in the 1970s, when the earliest computer video games (such as Pong) appeared in bars and gaming arcades. Video games then entered the living room with the advent of Atari, Nintendo, and Sega console game players, which are special-purpose computers designed to display their output on a TV screen. Games soon migrated to personal computers—and from there, to the Internet.

Multiplayer online gaming, an Internet-based gaming service, enables players to interact with characters who are controlled by other players rather than by the computer. Combining a rich graphical virtual environment with multiplayer thrills, these services are attracting increasing numbers of users. Role-playing games are a natural for Internet-connected computers, which enable players to participate even if they're not physically present in the same room. Although several types of Internet-mediated role-playing games exist, they're generally called **MUDs**, an acronym for **multiuser dungeons** (or **dimensions**). The name MUD is based on the noncomputerized Dungeons and Dragons role-playing game in which players assume the personalities and powers of fantasy characters as they interact with other players.

MUDs and their various offshoots offer users a text-only environment consisting (generally) of a number of rooms—sometimes thousands of them—inhabited by various online characters. You can ask for a description of the room, a list of players present in the room, and additional facts. You interact with other players by means of text chatting, very much like

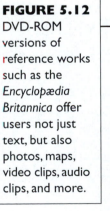

FIGURE 5.12
DVD-ROM versions of reference works such as the *Encyclopædia Britannica* offer users not just text, but also photos, maps, video clips, audio clips, and more.

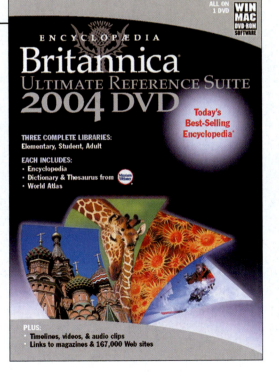

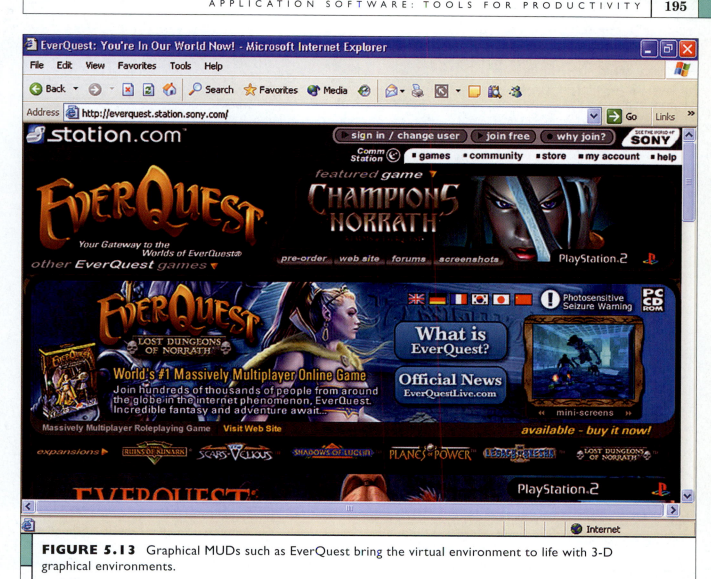

FIGURE 5.13 Graphical MUDs such as EverQuest bring the virtual environment to life with 3-D graphical environments.

the chat rooms on America Online or IRC channels.

If MUDs are text only, what's so engrossing about them? It's a matter of using your imagination. Within a MUD, you can construct a persona, build a fantasy environment, and share the experience with other players.

The latest MUD development, **gMUDs** (**graphical MUDs**), brings the virtual environment to life in 3-D graphical environments (Figure 5.13). Many are directly accessible online and do not require any special equipment other than a Web browser. A new trend is a commercial gMUD that relies on a locally installed game package to speed up processing. Examples of such commercial gMUDs include Ultima Online and EverQuest. Players fork over up to $40 for the locally

installed software and $10 or more per month for online usage.

If you can't find general-purpose applications to meet your computing needs, you might consider tailor-made applications.

Tailor-Made Applications

Tailor-made applications are designed for specialized fields or the consumer market. For example, programs are available to handle the billing needs of medical offices, to manage restaurants, and to track occupational injuries (Figure 5.14).

Tailor-made applications designed for professional and business use often cost

FIGURE 5.14
Medical offices often use tailor-made applications to manage their scheduling and billing.

much more than general-purpose applications. In fact, some of these programs cost $10,000 or more. The high price is due to the costs of developing the programs and the small size of most markets.

If the right application isn't available, programmers can create custom software to meet your specific needs.

CUSTOM VERSUS PACKAGED SOFTWARE

In the world of application software, a distinction can be made between custom software and packaged software. **Custom software** is developed by programmers and software engineers to meet the specific needs of an organization. Custom software can be quite expensive, but sometimes an organization's needs are so specialized that no alternative exists. An example of a custom software package might be the grade-tracking software that has been programmed to meet the needs of your college registrar's office. Custom software is almost always a tailor-made application.

Packaged software, in contrast, is aimed at a mass market that includes both home and business users. Although packaged software can be customized, it is designed to be immediately useful in a wide variety of contexts. An example of packaged software is the presentation software program your instructor may use to create class presentations. The payoff comes with the price: Packaged software is much cheaper than custom software.

In addition to the choices of custom or packaged software, users have three other options when purchasing software: standalone programs, integrated programs, and software suites.

Standalone Programs, Integrated Programs, and Software Suites

A **standalone program** is a program that is fully self-contained. Microsoft Word and Excel are examples of standalone programs. You can purchase and install them separately, and they function perfectly well all by themselves. However, standalone programs require a lot of storage space. For example, if you purchase Word and install it and then purchase Excel and install it, neither program would know about the other, nor would they share any resources, such as menus, drivers, graphics libraries, or tools. Obviously, this is a very inefficient way to install and use software when the programs have so many resources they could share.

Integrated programs offer all of the functions of the leading productivity programs in a single easy-to-use program. Integrated programs such as Microsoft Works are generally aimed at beginning users. They offer easy-to-learn and easy-to-use versions of basic productivity software. All of the functions, called **modules**, share the same interface, and you can switch between them quickly. The individual modules, however, may be short on features compared with standalone programs or office suites. The lack of features may make these easy programs seem more difficult when you start exploring the program's more advanced capabilities.

Microsoft Works contains a word processor that is very similar to Word, a spreadsheet program that is very similar to Excel, a database program, a calendar, and other productivity tools. The modules of an integrated program are not available as standalone programs—you cannot purchase the spreadsheet program in Works as a standalone product.

A **software suite** (sometimes called an **office suite**) is an interconnected bundle of programs that share resources with each other and are designed to help workers accomplish the tasks they perform in a typical office environment. If Microsoft Windows is your desktop, then Microsoft Office is the set of tools that you typically use at work. A suite may include as many as five or more productivity applications. Today, most personal productivity software is sold in office suites, such as Corel WordPerfect Office 12, Lotus SmartSuite, and the market leader, Microsoft Office (Figure 5.15). Sun's StarOffice is another personal productivity software suite that has a small but loyal following.

The advantage of a software suite is that the individual applications share

FIGURE 5.15
Microsoft Office is the most popular office suite in the world.

FIGURE 5.16 Office Suites Available for Microsoft Windows

	Microsoft Office	WordPerfect Office 12	Lotus SmartSuite
Word processing	Microsoft Word	WordPerfect	Word Pro
Spreadsheet	Microsoft Excel	Quattro Pro	Lotus 1-2-3
Database	Microsoft Access	Paradox	Lotus Approach
Presentation graphics	Microsoft PowerPoint	Corel Presentations	Freelance Graphics
Personal information managers	Microsoft Outlook	Corel Central	Lotus Organizer

common program code, interface tools, drivers, and graphics libraries. For instance, if you purchased Word and Excel as standalone applications, each would require you to install a printer. Each would have its own dictionary, thesaurus, toolbars, and graphics library. When you use Word and Excel as a part of Microsoft Office, all of these features are shared.

Office suites typically include a full-featured version of leading word processing, spreadsheet, presentation graphics, database, and personal information manager programs (Figure 5.16):

- **Word processing programs** enable you to create, edit, and print your written work. They also offer commands that enable you to format your documents so that they have an attractive appearance. Although some people still prefer to use other writing tools, word processing programs are the most often used office suite software.

- **Spreadsheet programs** present users with a grid of rows and columns, the computer equivalent of an accountant's worksheet. By embedding formulas within the cells, you can create "live" worksheets in which changing one of the values forces the entire spreadsheet to be recalculated. Spreadsheets are indispensable tools for anyone who works with numbers.

- **Presentation graphics programs** enable you to create transparencies, slides, and handouts for presentations.

- **Database programs** give you the tools to store data in an organized form and retrieve the data in such a way that it can be meaningfully summarized and displayed.

- **Personal information managers** (**PIMs**) provide calendars, contact managers, task reminders, and e-mail capabilities.

WEB TECHNOLOGY: A NEW WAY TO SHARE FILES

The new wave in office suites is **Web technology**, which, for application software, means the capability to save your files in a form that contains the HTML code that underlies Web documents. Why save files in HTML format? The answer boils down to one costly process: file conversion.

Many large organizations have spent millions of dollars dealing with file incompatibility problems caused by the use of proprietary file formats. *Proprietary* means that the file formats are limited to a specific vendor's software or computer model. For instance, if you don't have Microsoft Word installed on your system, you can't view a Word file unless you have a conversion program. The use of proprietary file

Destinations

To learn more about other office suites that offer Web integration, visit **www.wordperfect .com** and **wwws.sun.com/ software/star/ staroffice/**

formats imposes severe burdens unless everyone in the company is using the same product. Even then, file incompatibility problems may emerge because software publishers introduce new file formats in new versions to support new features. Programs that can save data to HTML can eliminate file conversion costs, because the file can be read by anyone with a Web browser.

File conversion costs come into play, too, when companies want to publish documents on the Web for use on the Internet. To put any document on the Web generally requires saving the document in plaintext format and then reformatting it from scratch for Web publishing. The capability to save documents in HTML format eliminates these costs. Microsoft Word, Excel, and PowerPoint include a Save as Web Page feature.

On February 14, 2002, Microsoft formally unveiled its new long-term vision of the PC as a globally connected device (Figure 5.17). The strategy, called .NET (pronounced "dot NET"), seeks to enable any computer using any operating system and software to share documents and data in their native format across cyberspace. Microsoft hopes that .NET will increase software compatibility through the use of XML Web services, which are applications that connect to each other as well as to other applications via the Internet. Within the next few years, the way we share communications and information with each other across the Internet will change significantly.

Now that you are familiar with the many types of application software and how the software can be packaged, let's look at some other considerations to keep in mind when choosing application software.

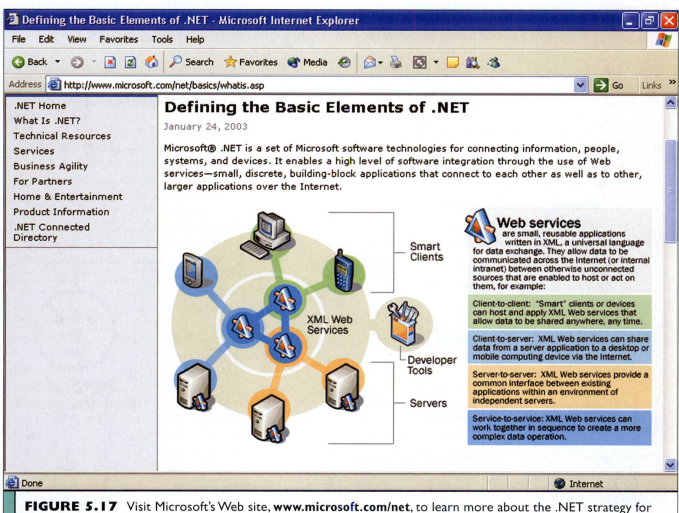

FIGURE 5.17 Visit Microsoft's Web site, **www.microsoft.com/net**, to learn more about the .NET strategy for Web technology.

IMPACTS

Safety and Security

What's Hiding on Your Computer?
Spyware, Adware, and Pop-Ups

Right now, your hard drive probably holds some programs that you don't know about, didn't mean to install, and don't really want—and they're not viruses. Do you know what is hiding on your computer?

Spyware is Internet software that a company, a government agency, or an individual places on your computer without your knowledge, let alone your consent. It monitors your computer or online activity and relays information about you to the spyware's source. Spyware usually enters your system through the Internet, sometimes when you open seemingly innocent e-mails and sometimes when you download software—especially shareware and freeware. Without knowing it, you may have agreed to install the spyware if you clicked "yes" to accept the license agreement of the software you wanted to download. That's when the trouble begins.

Some spyware can record every keystroke you type and every Internet address you visit. It snoops on your login name and password, your credit card numbers, and anything else you input while the spyware is active. Other spyware programs look only at your Web browsing habits so they can arrange for ads keyed to your interests.

If you've ever downloaded software and then seen a banner or pop-up advertisement, you've downloaded a form of adware. Adware is like spyware, only it's created specifically by an advertising agency to collect information about your Internet habits. Although ethically questionable, shareware and freeware creators sometimes allow advertisers to tag along invisibly by bundling adware with their software. Once you accept the license agreement and download the software, the adware is installed on your computer.

No matter how they get into your system, spyware and adware invade your privacy and present a serious security threat. How can you get rid of them? First, find out whether your ISP can help. For example, Earthlink and AOL have built-in clean-up utilities that find and remove spyware and adware. Second, look into utilities from antivirus companies such as McAfee (**www.mcafee.com**) and spyware specialists such as Computer Associates (**www.ca.com**), and SpyBot (**www.safernetworking.org**). These utilities scan your computer's memory, registry, and hard drive for known spyware and then safely eliminate these sneaky programs. Because new spyware is created all the time, remember to scan your system frequently (maybe once a week if you're a heavy Internet user) so you can root out hidden programs.

And if you hate pop-ups, consider the Pop-Up Stopper software offered by Panicware (**www.panicware.com**). (Be warned, however: If you need to use pop-ups for online quizzes or other purposes, Panicware's utility can prevent such pop-ups from functioning properly.) Often you can download free or trial versions of spyware, adware, and pop-up blocking software and then, for a small fee, upgrade to advanced versions with more options. In just a few minutes, you can turn the tables and protect yourself by spying on any intrusive software that may be hiding on your computer. Finally, before you download any software, read the fine print in the licensing agreement to find out whether you're saying "yes" to invisible extras you really don't want.

FIGURE 5.18 Sites such as CA's eTrust PestPatrol Anti-Spyware can help you protect your system from spyware.

To learn more about how to combat spyware, see the video clip at **www.prenhall.com/cayf2006**

System Requirements and Software Versions

When you buy software, your computer system will need to meet the program's **system requirements**, the minimum level of equipment that a program needs in order to run. For example, a given program may be designed to run on a PC with a Pentium-class microprocessor, a CD-ROM drive, at least 16 MB of RAM, and 125 MB of free hard disk space. If you're shopping for software, you'll find the system requirements printed somewhere on the outside of the box or online through a link that is usually called "system requirements." Although a program will run on a system that meets the minimum requirements, it's better if your system exceeds them, especially when it comes to memory and disk space.

You've no doubt noticed that most program names include a number, such as 6.0, or a year, such as 2004. Software publishers often bring out new versions of their programs, and these numbers help you determine whether you have the latest version. In a version number, the whole number (such as 6 in 6.0) indicates a major program revision. A decimal number indicates a **maintenance release** (a minor revision that corrects bugs or adds minor features). The year 2004 would indicate the year that the software was published; however, it does not indicate how many versions of the software there were previously. For example, Office XP is technically Office 10, whereas Office 2003 is Office 11.

Software publishers sometimes offer **time-limited trial versions** of commercial programs on the Internet, which expire or stop working when a set trial period (such as 60 or 90 days) ends. You can download, install, and use these programs for free, but after the time limit is up, you can no longer use them.

Beta versions of forthcoming programs are sometimes available for free. A **beta version** is a preliminary version of a program in the final phases of testing. Beta software is known to contain bugs (errors); it should be installed and used with caution.

SOFTWARE UPGRADES

Software upgrading describes the process of keeping your version of an application current with the marketplace. Some upgrades are small changes called *patches*; sometimes they are major fixes called *service releases* or *service packs*. Service releases keep the current version up-to-date. The ultimate upgrade is when you purchase and install the next version or release of a program. For instance, you might have recently upgraded from Microsoft Office XP to Microsoft Office 2003.

So, how do you know if you should purchase the next version of a software application or if there is a patch or fix available that will make your current version perform better? Well, when it comes to upgrading you should look at two things: Is your current version so out-of-date that you are having compatibility problems? Are there features in the newer version that you find attractive? As for patches, you should occasionally visit the software manufacturer's Web site to see if there are any service releases or patches. Microsoft software has a built-in capability to automatically check with Microsoft's Web site to determine if any updates are available.

DISTRIBUTION AND DOCUMENTATION

Before the Internet came along, most software was available only in shrink-wrapped packages that included floppy disks or CD-ROMs containing the program installation files. Now, many software publishers use the Internet to distribute programs and program updates. Doing so is much cheaper for the company and often more convenient for the consumer than physically delivering a program in a box.

If you buy software in a shrink-wrapped package, you typically get at least some printed **documentation** in the form of tutorials and reference manuals

FIGURE 5.19
Instead of looking up information in a printed user's manual, the Help task pane allows you to access a program's documentation right on the computer.

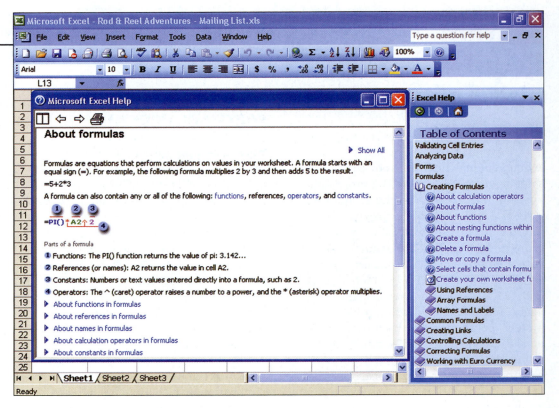

FIGURE 5.19 Instead of looking up information in a printed user's manual, the Help task pane allows you to access a program's documentation right on the computer.

that explain how to use the program. Downloaded software contains "read me" files and help files. A "read me" file is a plaintext document that is readable by any text-reading program. It contains information the software manufacturer thinks you'll find helpful. Many programs also have help screens that enable you to consult all or part of the documentation on-screen (Figure 5.19). You may also find additional information at the software publisher's Web site.

Now that you've chosen the right application software version, considered upgrades, and looked over the documentation, let's look at some other considerations you might have when using application software.

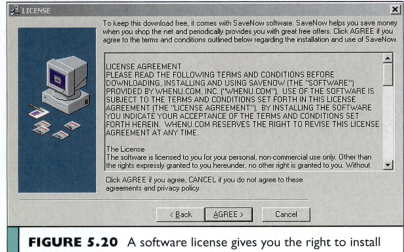

FIGURE 5.20 A software license gives you the right to install and use a program on only one computer. If you want to install the program on more than one computer, you must purchase additional licenses.

Software Licenses and Registration

A **software license** is a contract distributed with a program that gives you the right to install and use the program on only one computer (Figure 5.20). If you want to install the program on more than one computer, you must purchase additional licenses.

Organizations such as colleges and universities often purchase **site licenses**, which are contracts with a software publisher that enable an organization to install copies of a program on a specified number of computers. Site licenses offer large organizations multiple software licenses at a slightly reduced cost.

In addition, when you own an original and legitimate copy of a program, you're entitled to certain warranties and guarantees. With regards to warranties, most software publishers will be happy to replace a defective program disk, but that's it. The software license expressly denies any liability on the publisher's part for any damages or losses suffered through the use of the software. If you buy a program that has bugs, and if these bugs wipe out your data, it's your tough luck. At least that's what software companies would like you to believe. In the past, these licenses haven't stood up in court; judges and juries have agreed that the products were sold with an implied warranty of fitness for a particular use. Many U.S. state legislatures are considering a controversial model act, the Uniform Computer Information Transactions Act (UCITA). This act would give these licenses the force of law, thus requiring manufacturers to stand behind their products.

When you purchase a program, you'll also be asked to register your software by filling out a registration form. If your computer is connected to the Internet, you can often do this online; otherwise, you need to mail the registration form to the software publisher.

Generally, registration is worth the trouble. After you're registered, you'll automatically receive notification of software upgrades. Sometimes you'll have a chance to upgrade to new versions at a price lower than the one offered to the general public. You'll often qualify for technical assistance or other forms of support.

COMMERCIAL SOFTWARE, SHAREWARE, FREEWARE, AND PUBLIC DOMAIN SOFTWARE

The three types of copyrighted software are commercial software, shareware, and freeware. **Commercial software** is software you must pay for before using—such as Microsoft Office, Adobe Acrobat, and Mac OS X. **Shareware** refers to software that you can use on a "try before you buy" basis (Figure 5.21). If you like the program after using it for a specified trial period, you must pay a registration fee or you violate the copyright. **Freeware** refers to software

Destinations

How will UCITA affect you? You can learn more about the UCITA controversy at **archive.infoworld .com/ucita/**

FIGURE 5.21
Shareware is copyrighted software that you can use on a "try before you buy" basis. Tucows, launched in 1993, is renowned for its large library of shareware.

CURRENTS

Debates

Why Be a Beta Tester?

Should you be a beta tester? You may have noticed that a growing number of applications are being offered in beta versions. Users try out these preliminary versions and tell the publisher about any major bugs so they can be fixed before the applications are officially released. But there's more to it than just finding and fixing bugs. As users talk up the program to friends and colleagues, the publisher hopes more people will like what they hear and buy the program themselves.

Microsoft put Office 2003 through two rounds of beta testing, including a "technical refresh" version for testers checking the second beta version's technical features. In all, more than 600,000 testers participated, including customers, partners, developers, and integrators. Sometimes Microsoft invites certain customers or partners to test a "private beta" version before it tests a "public beta" version. Like many software firms, Microsoft asks people to register and submit information about their computer systems so it can select beta testers for specific applications.

Beta testers like trying out new applications for four main reasons. First, many are power users who are extremely involved with a certain program and interested in seeing (and influencing) how it evolves. Second, testers want their voices to be heard when they give the publisher feedback about bugs, features, and functionality. Third, they really enjoy being on the cutting edge, being among the first people to try new versions. And finally, they may get the software for free or at a discount.

However, there's no guarantee that the beta version of any software will work as it should or that it will be compatible with your other software. Even though you know you'll find some bugs—after all, that's the reason for testing beta versions—you may encounter a lot of bugs or have other unexpected problems. You'll have to spend time learning the new software, which reduces your immediate productivity, and you could face security problems in the course of beta testing. To find out about upcoming beta tests, visit the BetaNews site (**www.betanews.com**), check individual software Web sites, or plug "beta test" into your favorite search engine. Yes, beta testing is an important and exciting step in the development of sophisticated applications, but think carefully before you decide to participate.

FIGURE 5.22 Check out the BetaNews site at www.betanews.com to learn more about beta testing.

given away for free, with the understanding that you can't turn around and sell it for profit. Included in the freeware category are programs distributed under the Free Software Foundation's General Public License (GPL), such as the Linux operating system discussed in Chapter 2. There is one type of software that is not copyrighted. **Public domain software** is expressly free from copyright, and you can do anything you want with it, including modify it or sell it to others. Public domain software typically includes games, loan analyzers, and small utility programs such as FreeCAD, Ad-aware, and SpyBot.

When a program includes some mechanism to ensure that you don't make unauthorized copies of it, it is called **copy-protected software**. Examples of such software include the Microsoft Windows operating system and some CDs and DVDs. Copy-protected software isn't popular with users because it often requires extra steps to install and usually requires a call to technical support if any program files become corrupted. Perhaps the loudest objection to copy-protected software, though, is that the copy-protection schemes are beginning to work. It is becoming difficult to "share" a copy of major software programs with friends and family.

Copyright or not, you're always better off owning a legitimate copy of the software you're using. It's the right thing to do, and it offers you the greatest opportunity to derive benefits from the software. You're entitled to full customer support services should anything go wrong as well as any add-ons or enhancements the company offers. You should also be sure that any shareware or freeware is from a reliable source.

Now that you know what to look for when you are purchasing application software, let's look at what to do with that software once you have it.

Installing and Managing Application Software

To use your computer successfully, you'll find it useful to understand the essential concepts and acquire the skills of using application software, including installing applications, launching and exiting applications, and choosing options. The following sections briefly outline these concepts and skills.

INSTALLING APPLICATIONS

Before you can use an application, you must install it on your computer. Once you've purchased software, read the directions both before and during installation. When you purchase the right to use a software program, you are usually provided with CDs or floppy disks that contain the program and an installation or setup utility. **Installing** an application involves more than transferring the software to your computer's hard disk. The program must

also be configured properly to run on your system. Installation software makes sure that this configuration is performed properly.

To install an application on a computer running the Windows operating system, you insert the disk into the appropriate drive and the operating system automatically senses the insertion and attempts to locate and run an install or startup file. You are then prompted for any necessary input as the program installs.

Should inserting the disk not invoke the install program, you will need to click the Windows Start button and then choose Run from the bottom of the right pane. The Run menu sequence will invoke a dialog box into which you can type a command or choose a button labeled Browse. The Browse button brings up a dialog box from which you will choose the drive that contains the startup disk. You will then select the install or startup file and click the Open button. The final step is to click the OK button within the Run window.

If the software was obtained from the Internet, you must first decompress it. Many programs from the Internet include decompression software; you simply open the file, and the decompression occurs automatically. After the program has been installed, you will see its name in menus or on the desktop, and you can start using it.

You should know where the program is being installed, how to access it, and whether shortcuts have been created on the desktop. Shortcuts usually carry the name of the program and use the company logo for an icon. If you don't want these shortcuts on your desktop, delete them by right-clicking the icons and choosing Delete. This doesn't affect the program in any way, because a shortcut is just a pointer to a program or file. The program will still be available via the Start, Programs menu sequence.

If you later decide that you don't want to use an application, you shouldn't just delete it from your hard disk. The proper way to remove or uninstall a program from your computer is to use the Windows Add or Remove Programs utility located on the Control Panel, which is listed on the Start menu (Figure 5.23). **Uninstalling** removes the application's files from your hard disk. Choose the program that you wish to

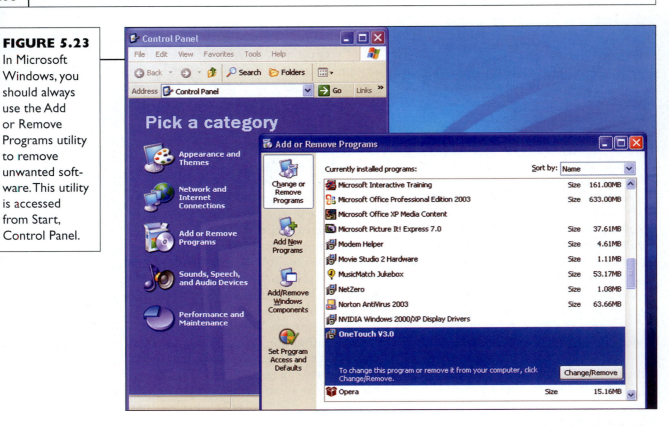

FIGURE 5.23
In Microsoft Windows, you should always use the Add or Remove Programs utility to remove unwanted software. This utility is accessed from Start, Control Panel.

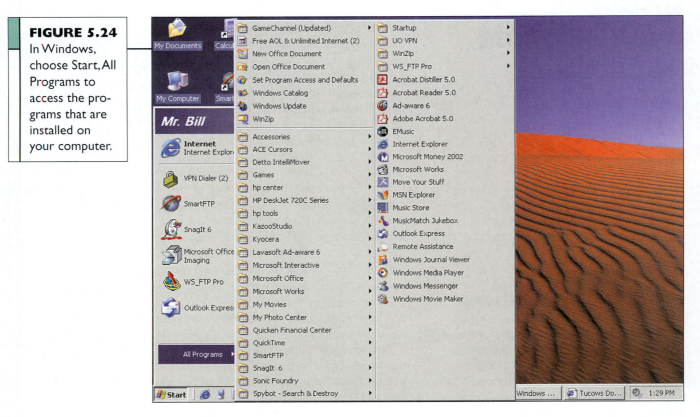

FIGURE 5.24
In Windows, choose Start, All Programs to access the programs that are installed on your computer.

uninstall from the list of installed programs and then provide any input the uninstaller asks you for. Because most programs create library files and ancillary files in various directories, all of the files will not be removed if you simply delete the program icon or delete the program files from within the file management utility. If you don't remove

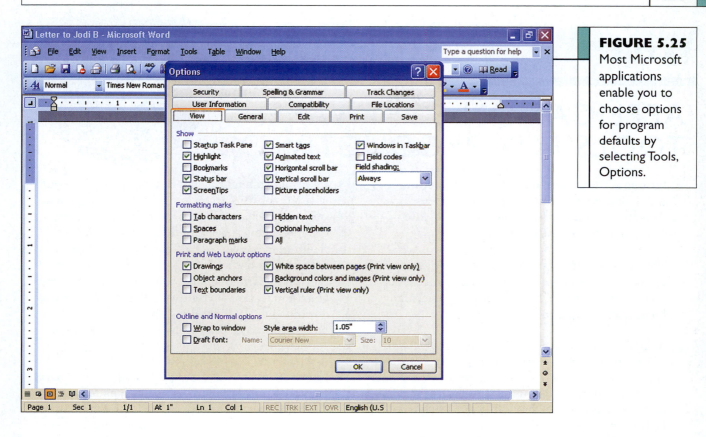

FIGURE 5.25
Most Microsoft applications enable you to choose options for program defaults by selecting Tools, Options.

all of the program files correctly, the operating system may not run efficiently, so you should always use the Add or Remove programs utility to remove unwanted programs.

LAUNCHING APPLICATIONS

Once you have installed an application, you can launch it. **Launching** an application transfers the program code from your computer's hard disk to memory, and the application then appears on the screen. Programs can be launched in a number of ways. The most reliable way in Microsoft Windows is to click the Start menu, point to All Programs, and choose the application you want to launch (Figure 5.24). In Mac OS, you locate the application's folder and double-click the application's icon. Application icons also are often available on the desktop, in the taskbar at the bottom of the desktop, and from toolbars.

CHOOSING OPTIONS

Applications typically enable you to choose **options** that specify how you want the program to operate (Figure 5.25). Your

choices can change the program's **defaults**, which are the settings that are in effect unless you deliberately override them. For example, Microsoft Word enables you to choose an option that allows you to display white text against a blue background, a setting that some writers find to be a bit easier on the eyes.

When you start working with a newly installed application, check the options menu for a setting—usually called **autosave**—that automatically saves your work at a specified interval. With this option enabled, you'll ensure that you won't lose more than a few minutes' worth of work should the program fail for some reason.

EXITING APPLICATIONS

When you've finished using an application, don't just switch off the computer. **Exiting** an application refers to quitting or closing down the program. You exit an application by choosing the Exit command from the File menu. By doing so, you ensure that the application will warn you if you've failed to save some of your work. In addition, you'll save any options you set while using the program.

What You've Learned

APPLICATION SOFTWARE: TOOLS FOR PRODUCTIVITY

- System software provides the environment in which application software performs tasks. Application software enables users to create, communicate, and be entertained.

- The most popular general-purpose applications are personal productivity programs, multimedia and graphics software, Internet programs, and home and educational programs.

- A standalone program provides just the software tool that you need, but it is often nearly as expensive as a complete office suite. Integrated programs are aimed at beginning users and may not include features that some users will want as they become more comfortable with the software. Most people who need personal productivity software purchase an office suite because they can save money by doing so. A potential downside is that suites tend to take up a lot of disk space and may include software that you don't need or want.

- Office suites that incorporate Web technology are becoming popular. These programs can save data to HTML, eliminating file conversion costs, because HTML files can be read by anyone with a Web browser. The HTML format also enables the sharing of files that may otherwise be incompatible.

- Publishers often bring out new or updated versions of their software. In a version number, the whole number (such as 6 in 6.0) indicates a major program revision. A decimal number indicates a maintenance release. These numbers help you determine whether you have the latest version. Software upgrades enable you to keep your version of an application current with the marketplace by downloading and installing small changes called patches or major fixes called service releases or service packs.

- Commercial software is copyrighted software that you must pay for before using, such as Microsoft Office. Shareware is copyrighted but distributed on a "try before you buy" basis. You may use the program for a specified trial period without paying. Freeware is copyrighted but available for free, as long as you don't turn around and sell it. Public domain software is not copyrighted. You can do anything you want with it, including modify it or sell it to others.

- To use your computer successfully, you need to learn the essential concepts and skills of using application software, including installing applications, launching applications, choosing options, and exiting applications.

Key Terms and Concepts

Matching

Match each key term in the left column with the most accurate definition in the right column.

_____ 1. application software

_____ 2. tailor-made application

_____ 3. general-purpose application

_____ 4. standalone program

_____ 5. site license

_____ 6. exiting

_____ 7. lossy compression

_____ 8. copy-protected software

_____ 9. documentation

_____ 10. multimedia

_____ 11. system requirements

_____ 12. autosave

_____ 13. modules

_____ 14. custom software

_____ 15. integrated programs

a. software that is designed for specialized fields as well as the consumer market

b. any application that involves two or more media, such as audio, graphics, or video

c. offer all of the functions of the leading productivity programs in a single easy-to-use program, such as Microsoft Works

d. all of the programs that enable computer users to apply the computer to the work they do

e. quitting or closing down a program

f. printed materials in the form of tutorials and reference manuals that explain how to use a program

g. an option that enables you to save your work automatically at specified intervals

h. the minimum level of equipment that a program needs in order to run

i. a method in which some information is permanently removed from the original file

j. the individual parts in integrated programs that share the same interface and enable you to switch quickly between them

k. self-contained software application that serves one function

l. software that addresses the needs of many people for tasks such as writing, working with numbers, and keeping track of information

m. gives permission to install copies of a program on a specified number of computers

n. created by programmers to meet the specific needs of an organization

o. includes some type of measure to ensure that you don't make unauthorized copies of the software

Multiple Choice

Circle the correct choice for each of the following.

1. Which of the following is a general-purpose application?
   a. computer-aided design software
   b. software to manage a video store
   c. motel management software
   d. word processing program

2. What do you purchase when you buy a software program?
   a. the unlimited rights to the program and its source code
   b. the right to use the software in accordance with the publisher's software license
   c. a box and a distribution medium, such as a CD-ROM
   d. a warranty that guarantees the software will do what you want it to do

3. Which of the following lists the four types of general-purpose applications?
   a. custom programs, sound files, Internet programs, personal productivity programs
   b. integrated programs, home and educational programs, raster graphics, Web technology
   c. home and educational programs, Internet programs, multimedia and graphics software, personal productivity programs
   d. multimedia and graphics software, standalone programs, shareware, packaged software

4. Microsoft Office is an example of what type of program?
   a. standalone
   b. integrated
   c. suite
   d. vertical

5. Which term describes what happens when you activate a program?
   a. launching
   b. activating
   c. exciting
   d. terminating

6. What do you call software that is purchased right off of the shelf?
   a. multipurpose
   b. packaged
   c. prepackaged
   d. single-purpose

7. Which of the following are composed of tiny dots, each corresponding to one pixel on the computer's display?
   a. codecs
   b. modules
   c. bit-mapped graphics
   d. beta versions

8. Which of the following is *not* a sound file format?
   a. FTP
   b. WAV
   c. MP3
   d. MIDI

9. What are maintenance releases?
   a. major revisions to an application
   b. minor revisions to an application
   c. entirely new versions of an application
   d. none of the above

10. The capability to save application files in HTML provides what benefit?
    a. a common format for sharing data with others
    b. the capability to publish on the Web
    c. no need to convert application files
    d. all of the above

Go to **www.prenhall.com/cayf2006** to review this chapter, answer the questions, and complete the exercises.

Fill-In

In the blanks provided, write the correct answer for each of the following.

1. _____ are programs that enable you to modify digitized videos.

2. To reduce the size of multimedia files, most software uses compression/decompression algorithms called _____.

3. _____ is a rendering technique that adds amazing realism to a simulated three-dimensional object by manipulating variations in color intensity.

4. _____ a program is best accomplished by using the Add or Remove utility on the Control Panel.

5. _____ enable you to choose the way you want a program to operate.

6. _____ is copyrighted software that you must pay for before you can use it.

7. Software publishers sometimes offer _____, which expire or stop working when a set trial period (such as 60 or 90 days) ends.

8. Drawing programs are used to create _____, in which each on-screen object is stored as a complex mathematical description.

9. _____ is the process of keeping your version of an application current with the marketplace.

10. In _____, the original file is compressed so that it can be completely restored, without flaw, when decompression occurs.

11. A(n) _____ is a preliminary version of a program in the final phases of testing.

12. _____ an application involves more than transferring the software to your computer's hard disk.

13. The latest MUD development that brings virtual environments to life in three-dimensional graphical environments is called _____.

14. _____ are the settings that are in effect unless you deliberately override them.

Short Answer

1. Select a course that you are taking this semester. List two course activities that may require the use of a computer. Identify two different software applications that could be used to complete these activities.

2. Visit **www.apple.com/support/downloads/** and choose a link to a software or system software update. Write a paragraph that explains what the update accomplishes.

3. How do shareware, freeware, and public domain software differ? If you have ever used any of these types of software, identify the name of the product and the type of application. Describe your experience. If you have not used any of these programs, then use the Web to locate a program and report on what you learn.

4. Identify a software application you needed to uninstall, and explain why it was necessary to remove it. If the application did not uninstall completely, what directories or files still remained?

5. What are the benefits of registering your software? Do you regularly register your software applications? Why or why not?

Teamwork

1. Making Copies of Software

Have each team member answer the following questions on paper and then share your answers with each other. Have you ever made a copy of software that you've bought for yourself? Did you ever give a copy of it away? Although purchasers are permitted to make a backup copy of software that they have purchased, they are not allowed to make additional copies and distribute them to others. What are your feelings about software piracy, that is, making illegal copies of software? Originally, software applications were installed from a series of floppy disks. However, because most software is now supplied on CD-ROMs, copies must be created using a CD burner. Do you own or have access to one of these burners? Write a one-page report that describes your group's findings.

2. Exploring Shareware

A full-function version of a shareware application can be downloaded, installed, and run on your computer for free for a specified period of time. Although your computer will not self-destruct, the application will no longer function after the time interval expires. Each team member should find and download at least one shareware program, try it out, and then uninstall it. As a consumer, what do you think about this method of distributing and selling software? Write a brief essay based on your findings.

3. Career-Specific Applications

For this exercise, each team member will interview a faculty member from his or her major or intended major department to find out what career-specific applications are used by professionals in that discipline. Alternatively, use the Web to find this information. Identify the discipline and the types of applications used. Explain how each application is used. Pull all of the interview material together and give a class presentation based on your findings.

4. The StarOffice Suite

Your team is to visit the StarOffice site at **wwws.sun.com/software/star/staroffice/index.html**. Divide the individual applications of the StarOffice suite among the team members. Each team member should learn as much as possible about his or her assigned application. How much does StarOffice cost? How would you compare the application you studied with an application you may have used? For instance, compare the StarOffice word processor with the word processor you are currently using. Take a vote to determine how many team members would use StarOffice on their own computer. Write a brief report based on your findings.

5. Site Licenses

Businesses and institutions frequently use site licenses to purchase multiple copies of software applications. Your team is to contact your computing services center to find out if your school uses this method to purchase software. If it does, identify the applications for which site licenses have been purchased. Is student home use of software applications included in the license? What is the primary advantage of purchasing site licenses for an application? If your university or college does not subscribe to site-licensed software, do research on the Web to see what you can learn about site licensing. Write a brief report based on your findings.

On the Web

1. Exploring Microsoft Office Features

Visit the Microsoft Office site at **www.office.microsoft.com** and research three links that you find interesting. In a brief essay, explain to your professor what the link is, why you chose it, and what you learned.

2. The Uniform Computer Information Transactions Act

In July 1999, the National Conference of Commissioners on Uniform State Laws proposed the controversial Uniform Computer Information Transactions Act (UCITA) as the standard for state laws on software transactions. To learn more about this potential legislation, visit InfoWorld's UCITA Web page at **www.infoworld.com/ucita**. Identify two consequences that would result from the passage of this act. List the names of two organizations and two companies that support the UCITA, and list the names of two organizations and two companies that oppose it. Read the section about UCITA and national security. What is the problem with UCITA with regard to national security? Do you believe UCITA should be done away with? Explain why or why not in a brief essay or oral presentation.

3. Finding Freeware

Do you want some free or inexpensive software? The Internet is frequently used to distribute shareware and freeware applications. Go to **www.yahoo.com** and type "freeware" (without the quotes) in the Search box at the top of the window. Browse some of the more than 6 million sites returned by your search. Pick one or two to write about. Be sure that your description includes the product name, file size, function, and whatever caution you would exercise in using it.

4. Microsoft Office versus Microsoft Works

Microsoft offers two software packages that are aimed at productivity: Office for business and higher-education markets and Works for home

and K–12 educational customers. Which, if either, of these products does your school use? Did you use either product when attending K–12 schools? Go to Microsoft's Works site at **www.microsoft.com/products/works/** to learn about this product. What is the current version of the Works suite? Name the applications that are included in this version. Which are already available as free downloads from Microsoft's Web site? What components are included with Works Suite 2004? What is the estimated retail price of the Works suite? Explain in a brief essay why you would or would not purchase this product.

5. Competitive Office Suites

The major competitors of Microsoft Office are Corel's WordPerfect Office 12, Lotus' SmartSuite Millennium Edition 9.6, and Sun's StarOffice 7.

- Visit the Corel Web site at **www.corel.com**. Identify the application areas and product names that are included in the professional version of Corel's office suite. What are the suggested full and upgrade prices? Are there different prices for digital and boxed versions? Is a free trial version available?

- Visit the IBM Lotus Software Web site at **www.lotus.com**. Identify the application areas and product names that are included in the professional version of Lotus' office suite. What are the suggested full and upgrade prices? Is a free trial version available?

- Visit the StarOffice site at **wwws.sun.com/software/star/staroffice/**. Identify the application areas and product names that are included in the professional version of Sun's office suite. What are the suggested full and upgrade prices? Are there different prices for digital and boxed versions? Is a free trial version available?

Explain in a brief essay why you would or would not purchase these products.

Capturing a Screenshot and Sending It as an E-mail Attachment

Have you ever tried to explain a weird computer problem to a technical support person or to a friend over the phone? Not only is a picture worth a thousand words, but pictures can also lead to shorter technical support calls. All versions of Microsoft Windows have the built-in capability to capture a *screenshot*. A screenshot is a picture of the screen that's displayed on your monitor. You can save a screenshot to a file that can then be printed, attached to an e-mail message, or published in a book like this one. Here are the steps for taking a screenshot and attaching the file to an e-mail message using the Web-based e-mail service Yahoo! Mail. The process of attaching a file to an e-mail message is similar for most Web-based e-mail services.

FIGURE 5.26 To take a screenshot of the entire desktop, press the Print Screen key one time.

CAPTURING A SCREENSHOT

1. Once you have the screen or screens displayed on your monitor that you would like to capture, determine if you need a screenshot of the entire desktop or just the active window. If you're trying to capture an error message, it is probably best that you take a screenshot of the entire desktop.

2. To take a screenshot of the entire desktop, press the Print Screen key one time (Figure 5.26). To capture just the currently selected window, press and hold down the Alt key and then press the Print Screen key. Nothing will appear to happen, but the screenshot will actually be copied to the Windows clipboard.

3. Launch your favorite word processing or image editing software, such as Microsoft Word, Microsoft Paint, or Corel WordPerfect. Because the screenshot was placed on the Windows clipboard, you will need to paste it into a document. If you're using Microsoft Word, go to the Edit menu and then choose the Paste option.

4. Once the image has been pasted into a document, you can proceed to save or print the file.

ATTACHING A SCREENSHOT

1. Login to your Yahoo! Mail account. Click the Compose button to create a new mail message.

2. Enter an appropriate message and subject along with the e-mail address of the person who will be receiving the e-mail. It is usually considered good netiquette to briefly explain the contents of the attachment in the body of the e-mail message.

3. To attach a file, click the Attach Files hyperlink. You will be taken to a screen where you can attach up to three separate files. To attach a file, click the Browse button next to the first text input box labeled File 1:. A standard Windows file system navigation window will appear. Locate the file you would like to attach and then click Open.

4. If you would like to attach more files, repeat the process in step three and choose the Browse button next to the input boxes for files two and three. When you have completed composing your message and attaching all of your screenshot files, click the Send button.

Many e-mail services limit the number and size of attachments that can be sent and received. Check to ensure that you are within appropriate limits with e-mail attachments of screenshots.

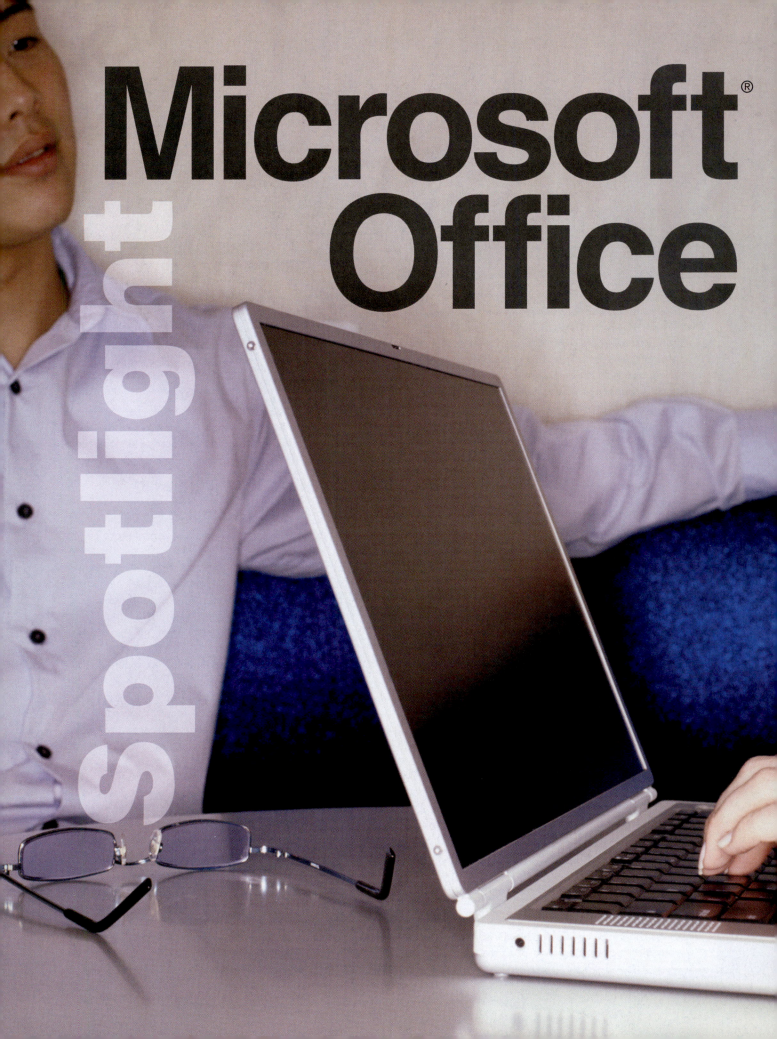

Your boss asks you to create a presentation that she can deliver at the annual stockholders' meeting in two days. Although you know creating a professional presentation is a challenge, this is the opportunity you've been waiting for—you were hired, in part, because of your abilities to use productivity software programs.

You get started right away by using Microsoft Access to generate reports that provide you with important information about your company's activities throughout the year. You then import the data you have extracted from Access into Microsoft Excel so that you can perform some statistical analyses and produce a number of key charts and graphs for the stockholders. Now that you've got the background materials covered, you open Microsoft Word. You paste the Excel charts and a number of the Access reports you have generated into your Word document. You also type and format a meeting agenda that your boss will distribute to the attendees. Now comes the fun part: You open Microsoft PowerPoint and create a professional, visually appealing presentation using the Word, Excel, and Access documents you've already created. As you put the finishing touches on your presentation—embedding an MP3 file into the introduction slide—you realize you've finally been able to use the skills you've worked so hard to acquire.

FIGURE 5A
Knowing how to use software programs, such as those in Microsoft Office, will help you gain a competitive edge in whatever career you choose.

All of the programs you've used to create your presentation are components of a suite of software programs called **Microsoft Office**. *This Spotlight explores the various programs, features, and uses of Microsoft Office (Figure 5A).*

Introducing Office

If Microsoft Windows is your desktop, then you will probably use the tools in the Microsoft Office suite to complete your work. Microsoft Office is retailed in three versions: Standard (also sold as the Student and Teacher edition at reduced price), Small Business, and Professional. The Standard version includes Word, Excel, Outlook (for managing e-mail and contacts), and PowerPoint. (Office for the Macintosh uses a program called Entourage for managing e-mail and contacts.) The Professional version includes the Standard version programs as well as Access and Publisher. Released in 2003, Office 2003 is the most recent version of Office on the market (Figure 5B).

In the following sections, we'll look more closely at how Office components can help you represent your thoughts, ideas, and solutions in a professional way.

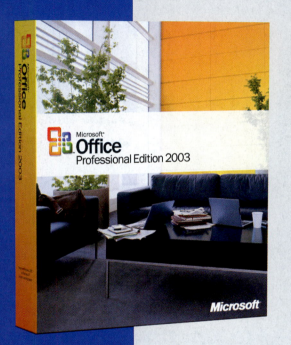

FIGURE 5B
Microsoft Office 2003 is the result of many generations of Office.

THE SHARED OFFICE INTERFACE AND TOOLS

Office applications use many interfaces that are similar to those of Windows. When an application is opened (Figure 5C), you'll see some or all of the following features within the **application window**, the area that encloses and displays the application.

The **application workspace** displays the document you are currently working on. In computing, a **document** is any type of product you create with the computer, including typewritten work, an electronic spreadsheet, or a graphic.

The topmost area of each program interface is called the **title bar**. It includes the program icon, the name of the application, and the name of the file you are working on. If you haven't yet saved the file, you'll see a generic file name, such as Untitled or Document1. Within the title bar, you'll also find **window controls**, which enable you to **maximize**, or enlarge, the window so that it fills the whole screen; **minimize**, or hide, the window so that it's reduced to the size of an icon or button; **restore** the window to the preceding unmaximized size; and close the window once you've finished using it.

In Microsoft applications, you can change the size of a window by dragging a vertical **window border** left or right or a horizontal border up or down. If you click and drag a window corner, you can size the window horizontally and vertically at the same time. (If you are using a Mac, click and drag the Size box, which is positioned in the window's lower-right corner, to resize the window.)

The bottom part of the application interface, called the **status bar**, displays information about the application and the document, such as the current page number and the total number of pages.

If the document with which you are working is larger than can be displayed in a single screen, such as a document that is more than one page long, you'll see one or more scroll bars. You can use scroll bars and scroll arrows to move (scroll) through the document. Typically, you can click the scroll arrows to move line-by-line or drag the scroll bar to move longer distances faster.

The shared interface also includes the menu bar, which is positioned beneath the title bar. (If you are using a Mac, the menu bar is positioned at the top of the screen.) A **menu** is a list of words that signify categories of tasks you can accomplish within an application. When you go to a restaurant, the menu is categorized into sections for appetizers, entrées, beverages, and desserts. Software menus operate with the same idea of categorization in mind. Application menus enable you to manage and modify your documents. The **menu bar** contains the names of **pull-down menus**, which are rectangular lists that include top-level headings such as File, Edit, View, Insert, Format, Tools, and Help. When you click a menu heading, a pull-down list appears, containing the names of the available commands. A **command** performs a specific type of action, such as printing a document or formatting text. A **menu sequence** is the steps you take in selecting a command from a menu or submenu. For instance, in one menu sequence, you might choose the File menu and then the Open command to bring up the Open dialog box.

Although applications organize menus in varying ways, many applications make use of the following standard menu names:

- **File**. On the File menu, you'll find options for creating new documents, opening existing documents, closing documents, saving documents, saving documents with a new file name or new location, printing documents, and exiting the application.

- **Edit**. On the Edit menu, you'll find options for deleting text, cutting text, pasting text, undoing and redoing actions, and finding text within the document. (If you are using a Mac, this menu also contains the Preferences options, which enables you to choose program preferences.)

- **View**. The View menu contains options that enable you to choose how your document is displayed and to manage how toolbars and other features appear on your screen. Typically included are zoom options, expressed as a magnification percentage; various

FIGURE 5C
These features are found in most of the windows in Microsoft Office applications.

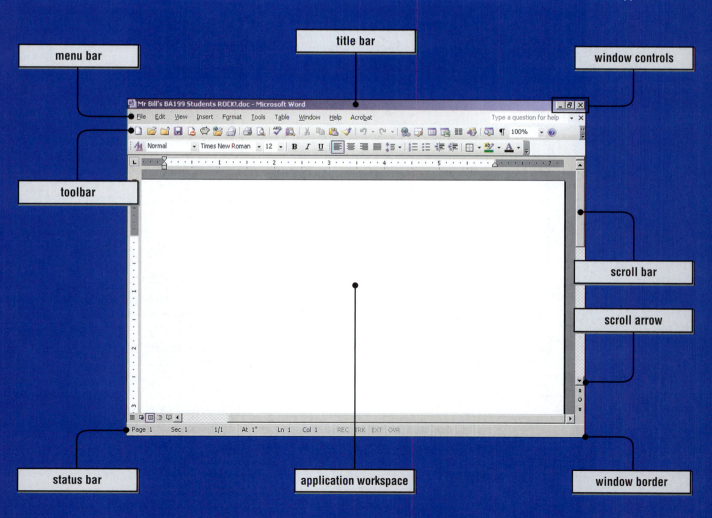

title bar

menu bar

window controls

toolbar

scroll bar

scroll arrow

status bar

application workspace

window border

FIGURE 5D
The Microsoft Office
Assistant can be
an entertaining
way to get help.

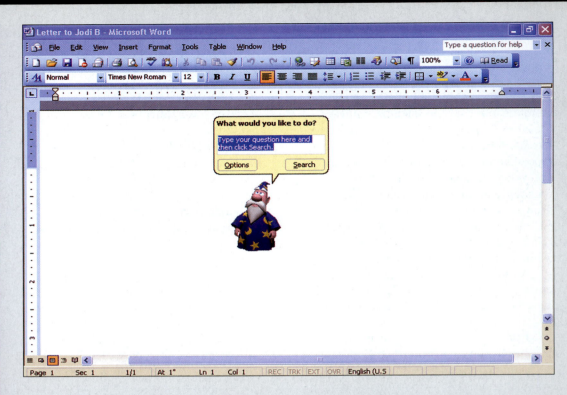

FIGURE 5D
The Microsoft Office Assistant can be an entertaining way to get help.

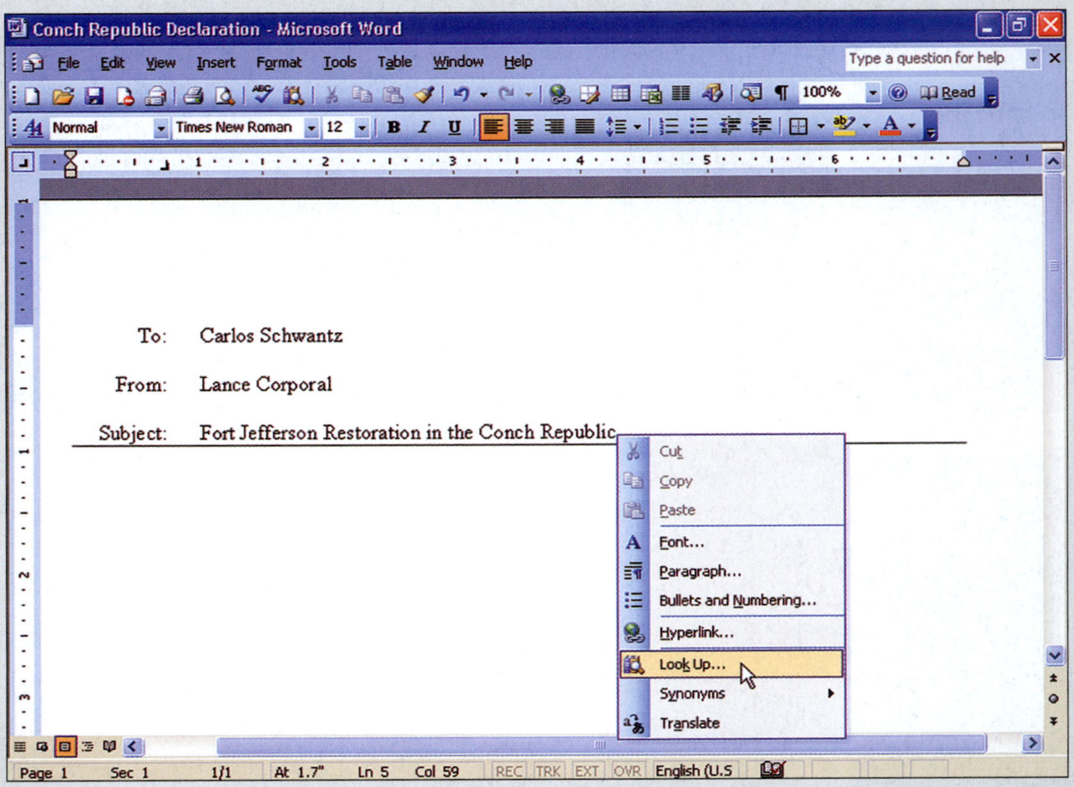

FIGURE 5E
Popup menus display context-specific options.

page views, such as Print layout and Web layout; and options that enable you to hide or display toolbars.

- **Format**. The Format menu enables you to modify such features as the font

style, paragraph settings, borders and shading, bullets and numbering, styles, and themes.

- **Tools**. The Tools menu typically includes useful utilities, such as a spell checker. In Microsoft applications, it also includes Options, a command that enables you to set program preferences.

- **Help**. On the Help menu, you'll find the various options for getting help with the application, which typically include a table of contents of frequently requested items and a searchable index to all available items. Another option for getting help is to activate the Microsoft Office Assistant (Figure 5D). If you find that the Microsoft Office Assistant annoys you, you can turn it back off. If you are connected to the Internet, you may be able to access additional help resources on the Web.

Toolbars, which are located under the menu bar, contain pictures called icons that act as shortcuts to the pull-down menus and the most commonly used commands. Two toolbars, the **Standard toolbar** and the **Formatting toolbar**, are loaded by default in Word, Excel, and PowerPoint. The Standard toolbar includes icons that enable you to open, close, print, spell check, copy, paste, and save, as well as several other options. For instance, if you click the Printer icon on the Standard toolbar, your file is sent directly to the printer. (If you work on a Mac and click the Printer icon, the Print dialog box appears.) The Printer icon takes the place of the File, Print, OK menu sequence that you would use via the menu bar. The Formatting toolbar includes icons that enable you to choose the font type, font size, font style (bold, italic, or underlined), paragraph indentation, bullet style, and more.

Dozens of other toolbars are available within the various Office applications. To activate the various toolbars, select View, Toolbars from the menu bar. You can also customize existing toolbars or create your own toolbars to suit your needs. To do so, choose the View, Toolbars, Customize menu sequence.

In addition to menus and toolbars, most applications also display popup menus (Figure 5E). Typically, a **popup menu**, also called a **context menu**, appears when you click the right mouse button. (On the Macintosh, you can display a popup menu by holding down the mouse button.) Popup menus list the commands that are available for the area where you clicked the mouse button. For example, if you right-click the application workspace within Microsoft Word, you'll see a menu of text-editing and text-formatting commands.

Other Shared Resources and Features

Office applications share a number of other resources, including the Clip Organizer, print drivers, and the Office Clipboard. Recent versions of Office offer such shared features as the task pane and smart tags, as well as templates and wizards.

The **Clip Organizer** is a repository of clip art and images that you can insert into a document or presentation (Figure 5F). You can access the Clip Organizer by selecting Insert, Picture, Clip Art from the menu bar. Whereas each standalone program accesses its own separate gallery of images, in Office all the applications share the same gallery.

Another shared feature of Office applications is the use of drivers. For instance, when you install a printer, print drivers

FIGURE 5F
The Clip Organizer is an efficient way to insert images into documents and presentations.

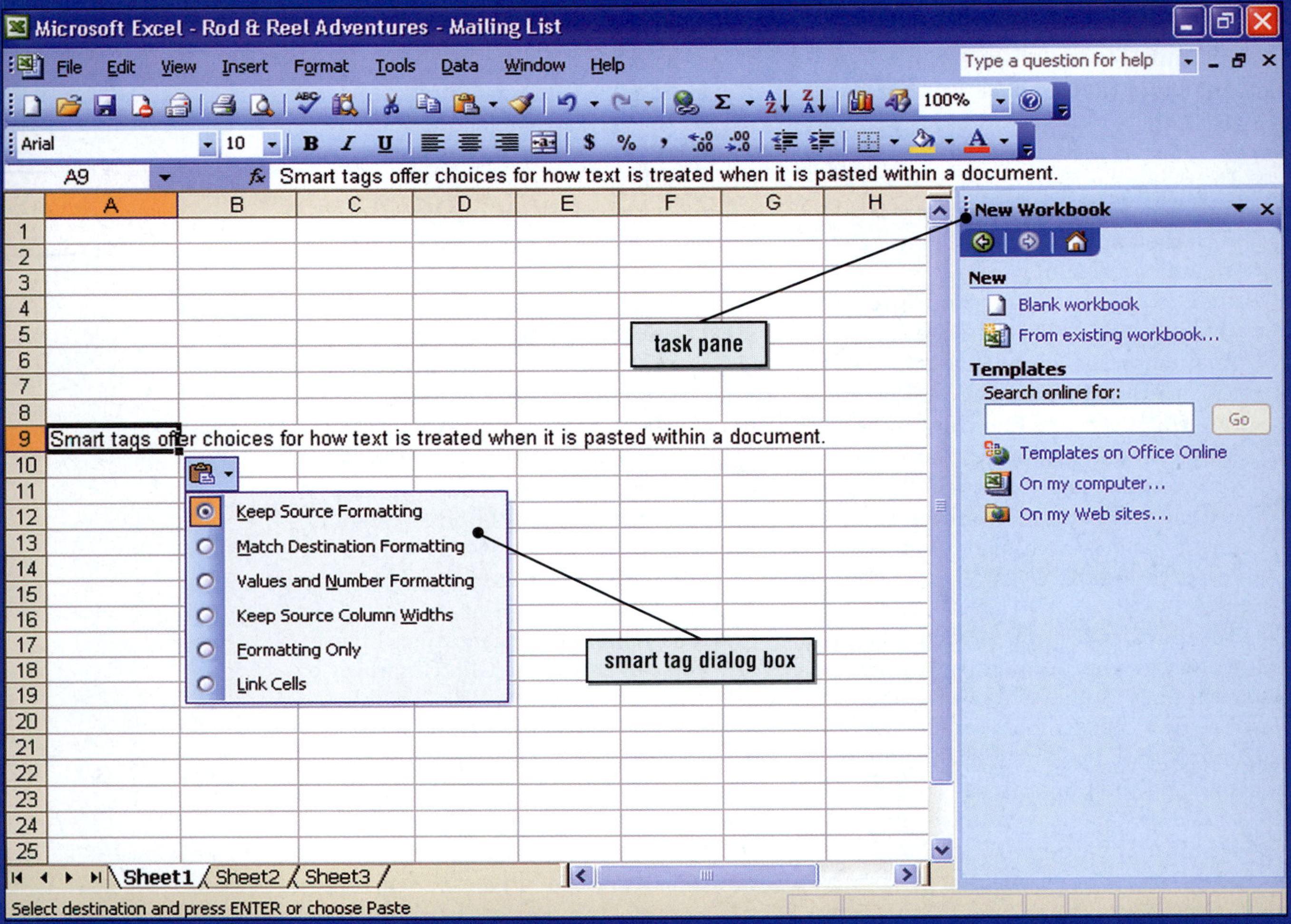

FIGURE 5G
The task pane provides options for creating work. Smart tags offer choices for how text is treated when it's pasted within an application or between applications.

are placed on your hard drive that contain the printer's instructions. Print drivers are installed from the Control Panel and shared by all of the programs installed on your PC.

Office applications also share the Clipboard. The **Office Clipboard** temporarily stores in memory whatever you've cut or copied from a document and makes those cut or copied items available for use within any Office application. For example, you can create a financial summary in Excel, copy it to the Clipboard, and then paste it into Word.

Another shared feature, which first appeared in Office XP, is the task pane (Figure 5G). The **task pane** usually appears on the right side of the window whenever an application is first opened. It contains options for opening work, creating new work, and formatting work, among other things. You can close the task pane by clicking the X in the top right corner and open it by choosing View, Task Pane from the menu bar.

Most Office applications also have smart tags. **Smart tags** are icons that are attached to items that you've pasted or text and data that the program recognizes as a place where you might want to choose different options. When you click a smart tag, a small menu of choices appears. For example, when you copy text from one place in a Word document and paste it to another location or if you switch over into an Excel spreadsheet and paste the text there, a smart tag appears, listing options for how the pasted text should be treated. In this example, the options would be to keep the Word formatting or change the formatting to that of the destination cell in Excel.

You can turn off both the task pane and the smart tags features by selecting Tools, Options, View from the menu bar.

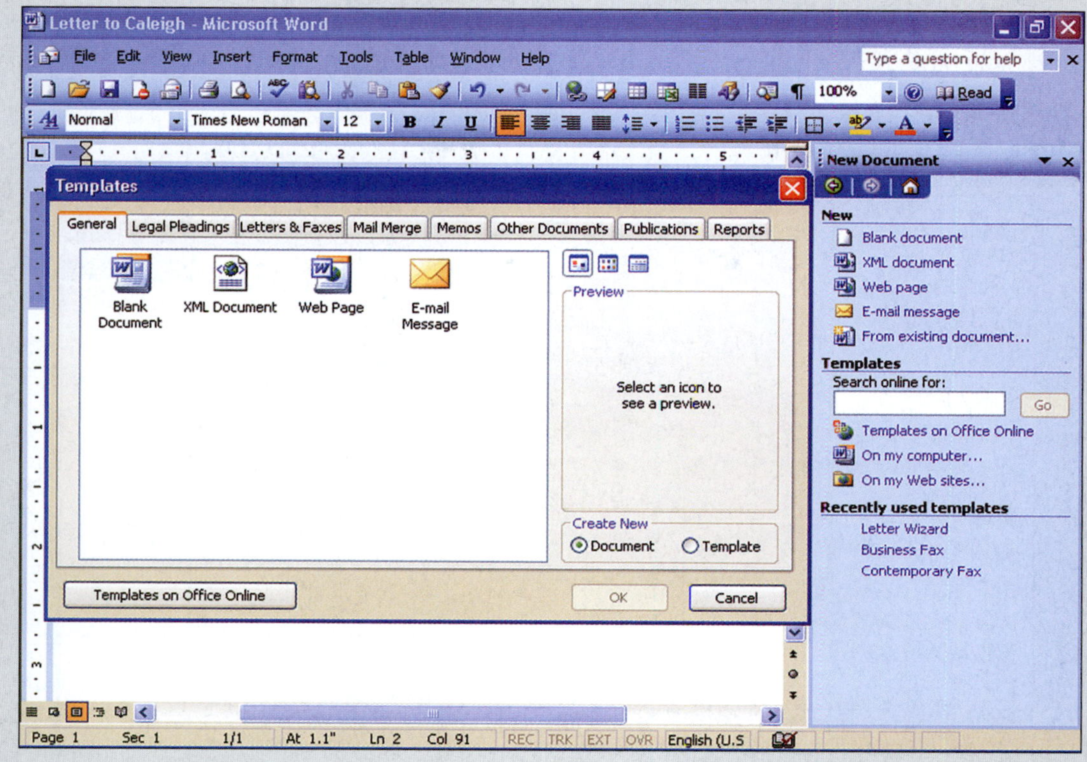

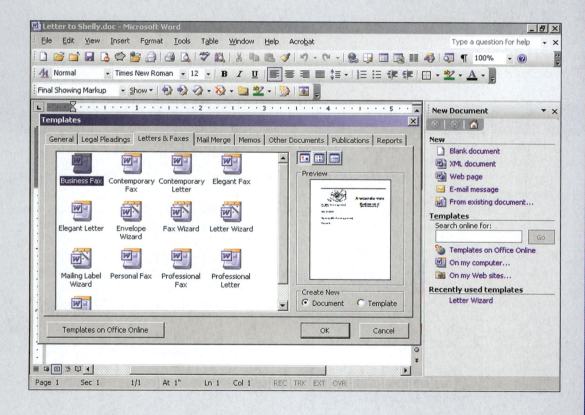

FIGURE 5H
Templates provide consistent back-ground content and formatting for multiple documents.

FIGURE 5I
The Letters & Faxes tab on the File, New, On my computer menu sequence can help you to create better letters.

Other shared features within Office applications include templates and wizards used for creating documents. When you create a new document, you can start with a new blank document or a template (Figure 5H). **Templates** are document

frameworks that are created once and then used many times. For example, word processing programs typically include templates for faxes, letters, memos, reports, manuals, brochures, and many more types of documents. The template

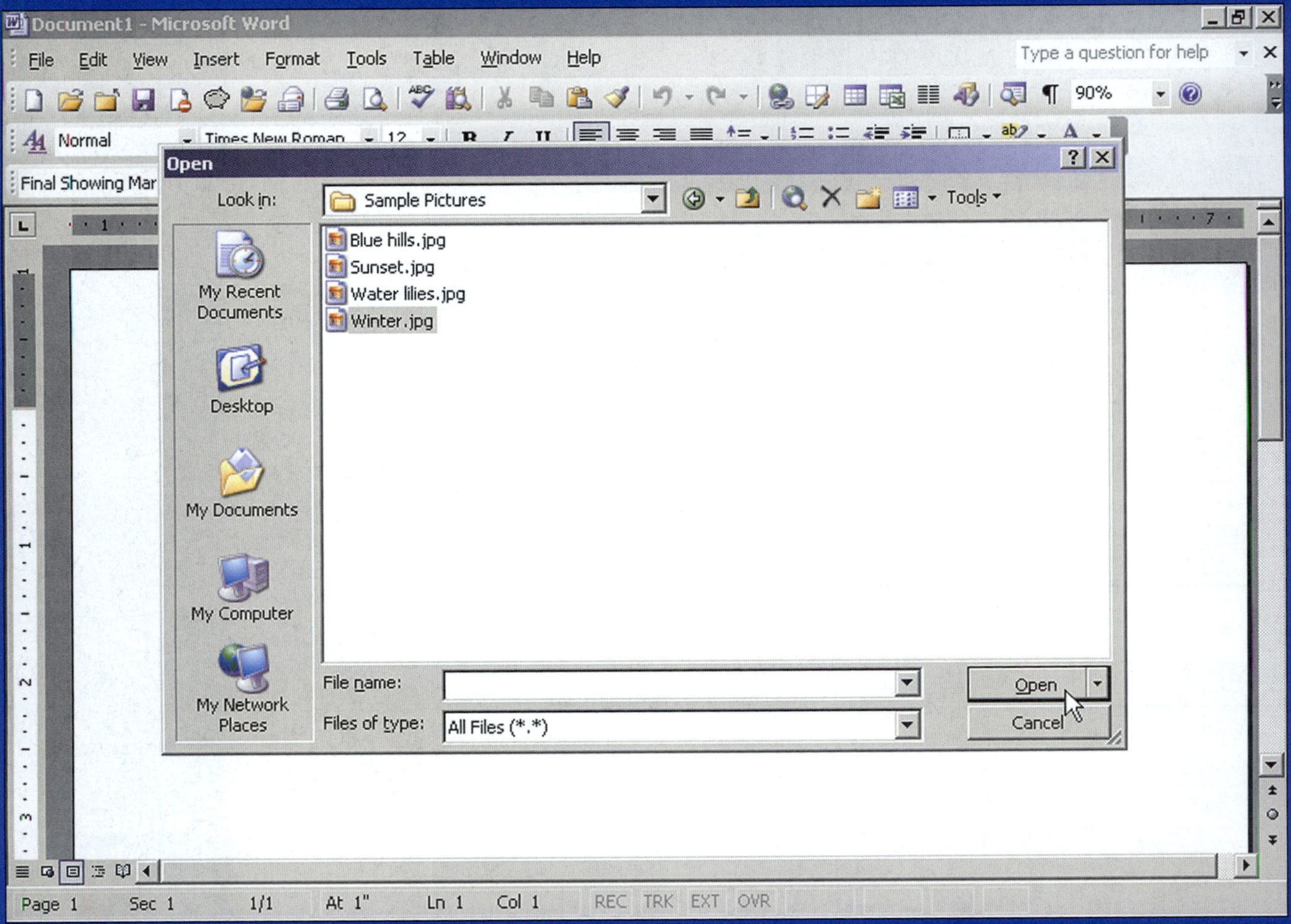

FIGURE 5J
To open a document, select the folder that contains the document, highlight the document's name, and then click Open.

may include text, formatting, graphics, and many other features.

Wizards are not templates, but they are stored in the same location. Applications include wizards to guide users through lengthy or complex operations. **Wizards** provide a series of dialog boxes to guide you through a step-by-step procedure that results in the solution of a task—such as creating a calendar or a meeting agenda. When you finish making choices in each dialog box, click Next to move to the next step (Figure 5I). You can locate wizards by accessing the File, New menu sequence and then select On my computer from the New Document task pane.

To **open** an existing document, you need to locate the document and load it into the application workspace. You can do this through the Open dialog box. Figure 5J shows the typical appearance of an Open dialog box. To open a document, select the folder that contains the document. Next, highlight the document's name. Click Open to transfer the document to the application workspace.

Now that you've gotten an overview of Office, let's explore each of the applications individually.

Microsoft® Word

Microsoft Word is a very powerful word processing program. In fact, it's so powerful that it rivals software made especially for desktop publishing. As with other Office applications, its interface includes the title bar, the Standard toolbar, the Formatting toolbar, and the status bar. The remainder of the screen is basically a blank sheet of paper upon which you can create documents (Figure 5K).

Using Word at its most basic level to create short letters, memos, and faxes is extraordinarily simple; you just type text into the Word document and press the Print button on the Standard toolbar to send your document to the printer. Word features automatic text wrapping, a Find and Replace utility, and the ability to cut, copy, and paste both within the document and between documents or other programs. To improve the presentation of your documents, you can use editing and formatting tools to insert headers and footers, page breaks, page numbers, and dates. Word also includes a number of other features that can enhance your ability to present your thoughts in a formal way. For example, you can create lengthy reports and books that incorporate embedded pictures, graphics, charts, tables, and other objects. You can work with columns and set tabs to align text. You can print your document in portrait (vertical) or landscape (horizontal) orientation. It's almost true that if you can imagine it, you can do it in Word.

If you're using a PC, the files that you create in Word include the .doc extension by default. (If you're using a Mac, no such extension is needed.) Word can also save your documents as plain text (.txt), HTML (.htm), Rich Text Format (.rtf), or formats that can be read by previous versions of Word or by competing products, such as WordPerfect. You will learn about other Office program extensions as you continue reading this Spotlight.

Now that you have a basic understanding of what Word can do for you, you're ready to move on to other Office applications. The following section will introduce you to Excel.

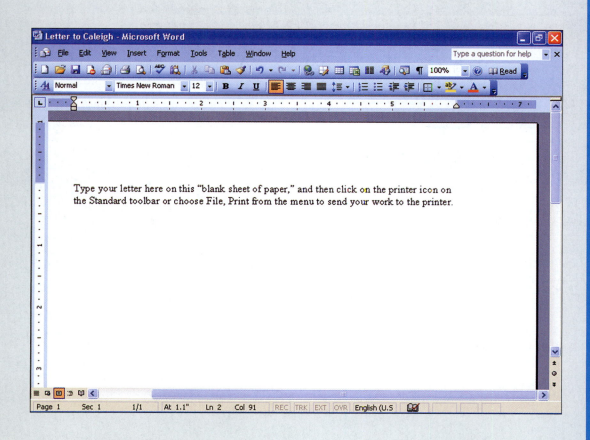

FIGURE 5K
The Word interface is simple and intuitive.

Microsoft® Excel

Microsoft Excel is the most popular spreadsheet program in the world. The primary function of a spreadsheet program is to store and manipulate numbers. You use a spreadsheet either to record things that have actually happened or to predict things that might happen through a method called **modeling**, or what-if analysis. Projected income statements are a good example of spreadsheet modeling. You plug in your assumptive values, and the model provides the prediction. If your assumptions are correct, the model will closely match the actual outcome. If your assumptions are faulty, then you can learn from your experience and perhaps make better assumptions in the future.

Excel's user interface is very similar to that of Word. One major difference is that in Excel, the menu bar has a choice for Data, whereas Word has a choice for Tables. The Standard and Formatting toolbars are almost identical. Like Word, Excel has a status bar at the bottom of the screen and scroll bars that enable you to move your view vertically and horizontally.

In Excel, each file is called a **workbook**. A workbook may contain as many as 255 **sheets**. Each sheet is composed of **columns** and **rows**, the intersections of which are called cells (Figure 5L).

Spreadsheets have a fixed maximum size, which is 256 columns wide (column A through column IV) and 65,536 rows deep. This may not seem important, but it would be limiting if you wanted to have a column for every day of the year or rows with more than 100,000 items. Interestingly, there is

FIGURE 5L
Spreadsheets are composed of cells, on sheets, in workbooks.

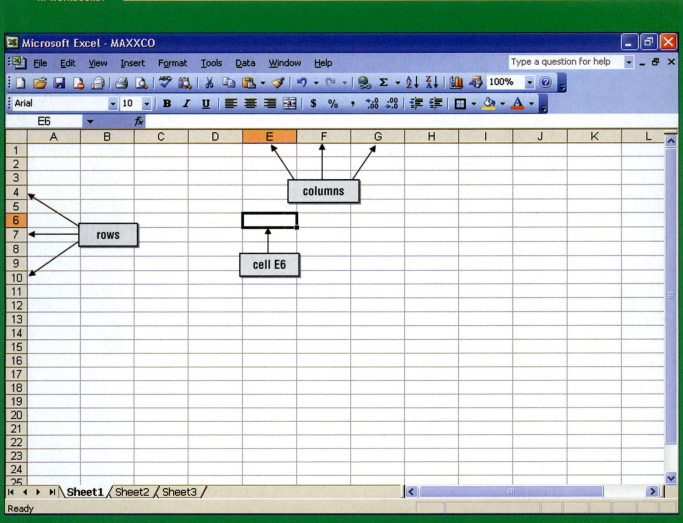

no limit to the number of pages you can create in a Word document, the number of slides you can create in a PowerPoint presentation, or the amount of data you can store in tables in Access. But Excel does have limits. In fact, you can have only as many as 255 sheets in a workbook—a limit that most of us will never encounter, but a limit just the same.

Everything you do in Excel must be contained within a cell. A cell is identified by its column letter and its row number. The columns in a spreadsheet are identified by the letters of the alphabet; rows are represented by numbers. For example, A1, B3, and AC342 each represent an individual cell.

A **range** (two or more cells selected at the same time) of cells is identified by the addresses of the top-left and bottom-right cells separated by a colon. For example, the range from cell A1 to cell D5 would be represented as A1:D5.

Cells store text, numbers, and formulas. Text entries, also referred to as **labels**, are used to identify numeric entries. For example, you might type the label "First month's rent" in cell A5 and then place the value "$650" next to it in cell B5. Labels are also used to identify typed-in numbers and the results of formulas.

A **formula** is a combination of numeric constants, cell references, arithmetic operators, and/or functions that display the result of a calculation. Excel interprets a cell entry as a formula if the entry is preceded by the equals sign (=). Formulas may be mathematic expressions or functions. In a **mathematic formula**, the mathematic order of operations is followed; that is, values in parentheses are acted on first, followed by exponentiation, multiplication, division, addition, and subtraction. (You can remember this order of operations through the mnemonic Please Excuse My Dear Aunt Sallie.) For example, the formula =6*(4−2)/3+2 is equal to 6, because 4 minus 2 is 2, 6 times 2 is 12, 12 divided by 3 is 4, and 4 plus 2 is 6.

The other type of a formula is called a function. A **function** is a very powerful type of formula because it allows you to perform operations on multiple inputs. As an example, the payment function is able

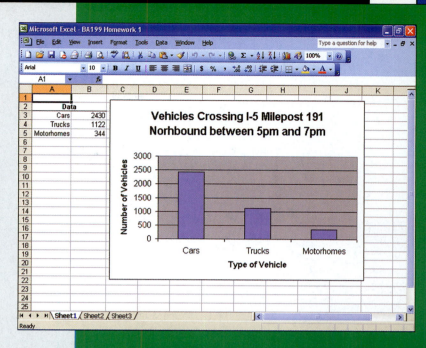

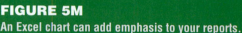

FIGURE 5M
An Excel chart can add emphasis to your reports.

to take the rate of interest, time period, and amount borrowed to produce the payment amount on a loan. Like mathematic formulas, functions begin with the equals sign. However, they then list the name of the function (such as PMT for calculating payments on a loan) and an argument set, which is placed within parentheses. An **argument set** contains the passable parameters or variables in a function. In the loan example, the argument set contains the rate of interest, the time period of the loan, and the amount borrowed. For example, =PMT(.005,48,18000) would return the payment for a loan of $18,000 at an interest rate of 6 percent for 48 months.

Excel also has features for creating **charts**, which are a graphical representation of data (Figure 5M). Charts are based on data sets and the labels that identify the data. The two primary kinds of charts are bar charts and area charts, or pie charts. **Bar charts** show each element in comparison to the other elements in a numeric way (100 cars, 40 trucks, 22 buses). **Area charts**, or **pie charts**, show each element as a percentage of the sum of all the elements. Several other tools are also available for developing, managing, and assessing data. You can create pivot tables and charts (designed so that your data "pivots" about one field of interest) or sorted reports with subtotals, and you can use the database feature to extract information from your data set.

The files that you create in Excel include the .xls extension by default. Excel can also save your documents as plain text (.txt), HTML (.htm), eXtensible Markup Language (.xml), or in formats that can be read by previous versions of Excel or by competing products, such as Lotus.

To learn more about creating charts and reports in Excel, consult the online help at **www.microsoft.com** or the Excel Help wizard.

So, you can use Word to work with words, and you can use Excel to work with numbers. Now we'll take a look at the Office application for managing databases.

Microsoft® Access

Microsoft Access is a database management system (DBMS), which is a software application designed to capture, store, manipulate, and report data and information.

The Access interface is similar to that of Word and Excel; however, it differs from those interfaces in many ways. The opening interface includes the menu bar, the Standard toolbar, and the task pane on the right-hand side of the window (Figure 5N). In Access, you must always work on an existing database or on a new database that you've named and saved to disk. Access does not offer a default blank database

screen like the blank document in Word or the blank worksheet in Excel. Access must always work between storage and memory—you cannot work within the program without first establishing a file on disk.

Access uses objects to manage and present data. In Access, an **object** is a subprogram that manages one aspect of database management. For instance, you use the **Form object** to collect data, the **Table object** to store data, the **Query object** to ask questions of the database, and the **Report object** to present your data (Figures 5O and 5P). The functions of

FIGURE 5N
The Access opening interface is rather stark in comparison to Word and Excel.

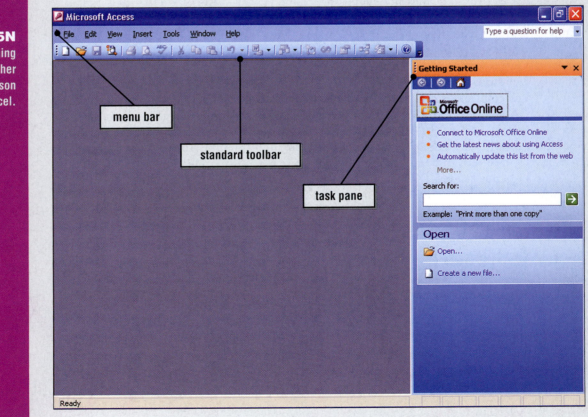

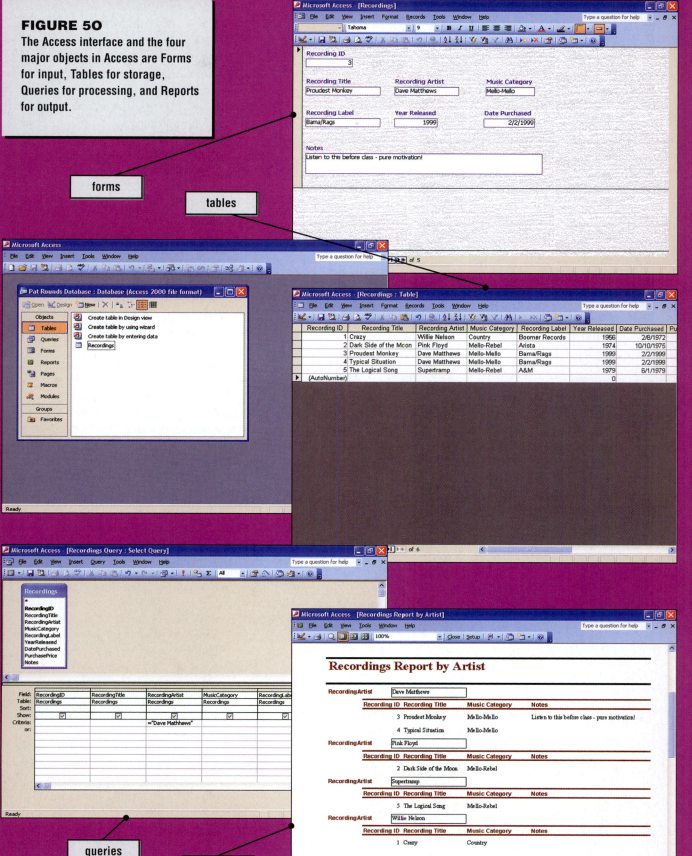

FIGURE 50
The Access interface and the four major objects in Access are Forms for input, Tables for storage, Queries for processing, and Reports for output.

forms

tables

queries

reports

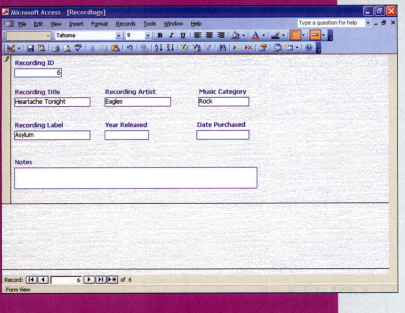

FIGURE 5P

The Form object provides a sophisticated interface to the records that are stored in tables.

these four objects match your computer's input, storage, processing, and output functions. (The order is usually input, processing, output, and storage, but in a database management system, the input has to be stored before it can be processed.) A relatively new feature in Access is the **Data Access Page object**, which is used to post data to the Web so that others can retrieve it.

Access is capable of importing data from many sources, including, of course, Microsoft Excel. If data are not imported from an outside source, then a form is usually used to enter data into the database. A **form** is a template with blank fields in which users input data. You have filled out physical and electronic forms many times in your life. Forms should be organized so that the person who is typing in the data can easily move from one field to the next in a logical order.

To be useful, the data usually must be processed using the Query object. You can use the Query object to ask questions of a data set. A **data set** describes the contents of a table. Let's say you have a data set that includes the names and addresses of family, friends, and business associates. You want to send a mailing to your family to let them know how school has been

going. To find the names and addresses of just your family members, you would run a query on your data set and set the filtering parameter to include only those names that have a field entry under the field name "family."

A **filter** is a condition that a data item must meet. Only data that meet the condition are allowed to pass through the filter. In this case, you are asking Query object to provide you with your family members and no one else. The filtering parameter is that the query will only return records where the field for "family" is checked.

When you use Access, you need to present the results of your query in a manner that is not only useful, but also professional in appearance—in short, you must design a report. The Report object is the only object that most of us see. We receive reports from databases all the time. Junk mail, a utility bill, and credit card solicitations all come from reports that have been generated from massive data sets.

Access is the only Office program that doesn't include the Save As feature to save files. You may use Save As to save an *object* within your database, but you can't save an open database to another location or give it another name. This can be problematic. Access is a complex program, and it's possible that you'll make mistakes that can cost you a lot of lost time and energy if you have to restore your entire database back to the way it was before you made the mistake. Let's look at an example.

When you work in an application such as Word, the work you accomplish is all in memory until you initially save it to disk. Once you've saved your work to disk, the subsequent work you perform is in memory until you either save over the work you've saved before (using the Save command) or choose a new folder and/or filename for your added work (using the Save As command).

Because you can't use the Save or Save As command in Access, if you make a mistake, the work you have in memory is often the same as the work you have on disk. Access doesn't continually save everything you do, but it writes to disk often enough to make it very difficult to predict whether your actions have been recorded over your previously saved work. This means that it's possible for you to lose your entire database if you don't have a backup copy. The solution to this problem is to always make a copy of your work *before* a work session and then work on that copy.

Access uses the .mdb file extension by default. Without the Save As feature, you cannot save Access files in different file formats; however, you can use the File, Export menu sequence to save tables in various formats, including Excel (.xls), plain-text (.txt), eXtensible Markup Language (.xml), and formats for competing products such as DBASE. Access also has a Database object that can be used to publish your database to the Web.

To learn more about how to use Access, visit the online help provided at **www.microsoft.com**. You can also use the Access wizards to create the objects that you'll need to manage whatever projects you may undertake.

Let's now look at a program that's a favorite among many college students: PowerPoint.

Microsoft® PowerPoint®

Microsoft PowerPoint is a popular program used to create and deliver presentations. When you open PowerPoint, you can use the task pane on the right side of the screen to open an existing presentation, a new blank presentation, or a new presentation based on a design template. You can also use a wizard to create a presentation by answering questions or choosing from a list of topics.

FIGURE 5Q

The initial PowerPoint screen features the outline pane on the left, a blank Title slide in the center, and the task pane on the right.

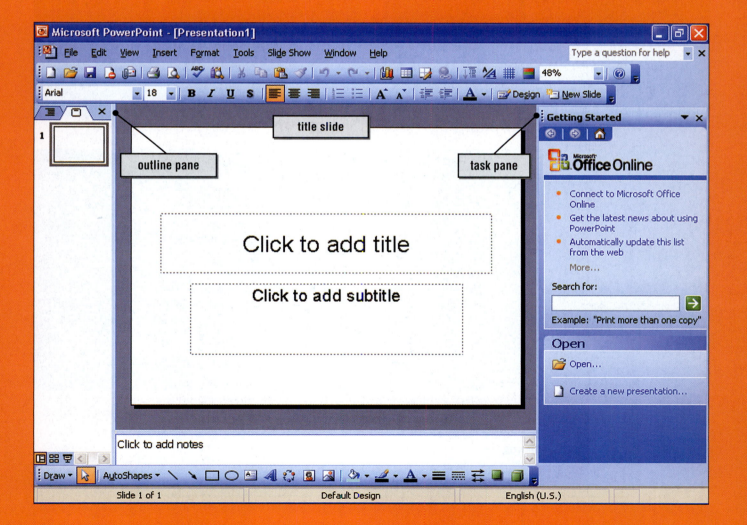

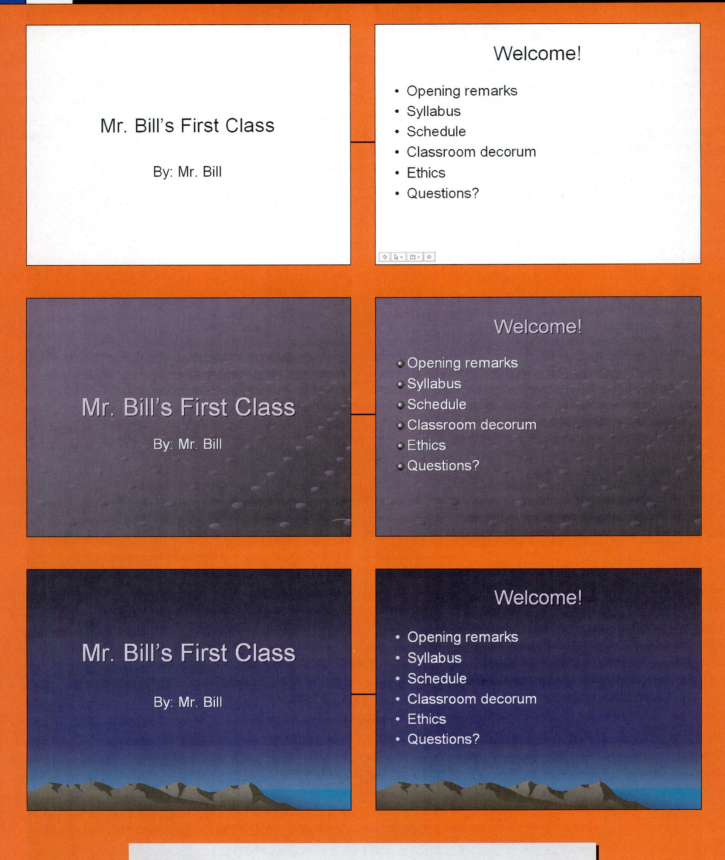

FIGURE 5R
Design templates provide a robust way to present a feeling along with your message.

PowerPoint opens to a blank slide that is in the Title slide format (Figure 5Q). A **slide** is the canvas upon which you organize text boxes and graphics to represent your ideas or points. PowerPoint currently offers 27 slide layouts to choose from. Each layout has text or graphics boxes into which you can type text or embed graphics. The various boxes are in a set position on the slide canvas, but you can modify or move them around on the slide if you wish. Each slide layout has a name. A Title slide has two text boxes. The top box is for the title of your presentation, and the bottom box is for a subtitle or your name. You might choose Title and Text as the layout for your second slide, because it has a text box for the title at the top of the slide and a bulleted list text box for the major presentation points on the lower portion of the slide.

A PowerPoint template contains pre-formatted fonts, locations for text and graphics, and color schemes. **Design templates** are professionally created slide designs that can be applied to a presentation. You might create your slides in the blank presentation (black and white, with no special fonts or effects) and then apply various design templates until you achieve the desired effect (Figure 5R). Some of the templates are quite whimsical, whereas others are appropriate for business purposes. As you create your presentation, keep in mind that the design template used should match the purpose and content of the presentation.

The AutoContent Wizard is an interactive tool that guides you through the process of creating a presentation. It includes presentation categories for home and business projects, as well as the Carnegie Coach. The Carnegie Coach provides presentation outlines on a wide variety of topics—everything from selling your ideas to introducing and thanking a speaker. The coach suggests the content; you simply customize it with the details for your particular presentation.

Once you've written your outline, you are ready to create your presentation. The two easiest ways to do so are to use the wizard or to begin with a blank presentation. Using the wizard will result in slides that have a design template applied and at least the beginnings of your presentation embedded. You would then add and remove

FIGURE 5S
A PowerPoint slideshow should serve as a backdrop to a good presentation.

content to complete your work. If you begin with a blank presentation, you will perform an iterative process of typing in your text, choosing whether to include graphics, inserting a new slide that is based on a slide layout template, and then repeating.

It's very easy to get caught up in all of the bells and whistles available in PowerPoint. Ultimately, though, you are the presenter, and therefore you must command your audience. A good PowerPoint slideshow should serve as a backdrop to your presentation; it shouldn't be the main feature (Figure 5S).

Be forewarned: Presentations almost never look the same on a video projector as they do on your computer screen. With this in mind, it's a good idea to try out your presentation in the room where you'll give it. If you allow yourself plenty of time, you'll be able to change the design template to colors that will work best in the room.

PowerPoint applies the .ppt extension by default. PowerPoint can also save your documents as HTML (.htm); in various graphics formats, such as .jpg and .gif; or in formats that can be read by previous versions of PowerPoint.

Let's now move on to a program that will help you communicate with others and manage your busy schedule: Outlook.

Microsoft® Outlook

Microsoft Outlook is an e-mail and organizational communications tool that you can use to send and receive mail, maintain a personal calendar, schedule meetings with coworkers, and store information about your personal contacts. Figure 5T shows the Outlook interface.

When you use the e-mail function of Outlook, you obviously need to know the recipient's e-mail address. For example, an e-mail address might look like **president @whitehouse.gov**. Outlook has an auto-complete feature that suggests the completion of an address you've previously used as you type on the To: line. For example, if you begin typing the address **myfriend @yahoo.com**, the auto-complete feature suggests the complete address when you type the third letter, f, in myfriend. If the suggestion is correct, press the Enter key to insert the address. If the suggestion is not what you intend, then simply keep typing the correct address.

One feature of Outlook that is very helpful is the ability to create folders, which you can use to organize your saved e-mail messages. For example, you could create a Family folder for family mail, a separate folder for each of your classes, and perhaps a Friends folder for personal messages you've received from friends. Placing mail that you've read into these folders will then help you keep your inbox uncluttered.

You may find the Outlook calendar helpful in managing all of the activities associated with school, work, and socializing. The calendar is very easy to use and even features an alarm to alert you 10 or 15 minutes before a scheduled event.

The best way to learn how to use Outlook is to experiment with it. Also remember that you can use the Help program to learn how to use the various features Outlook includes. You'll be surprised at just how easy it is to manage Outlook.

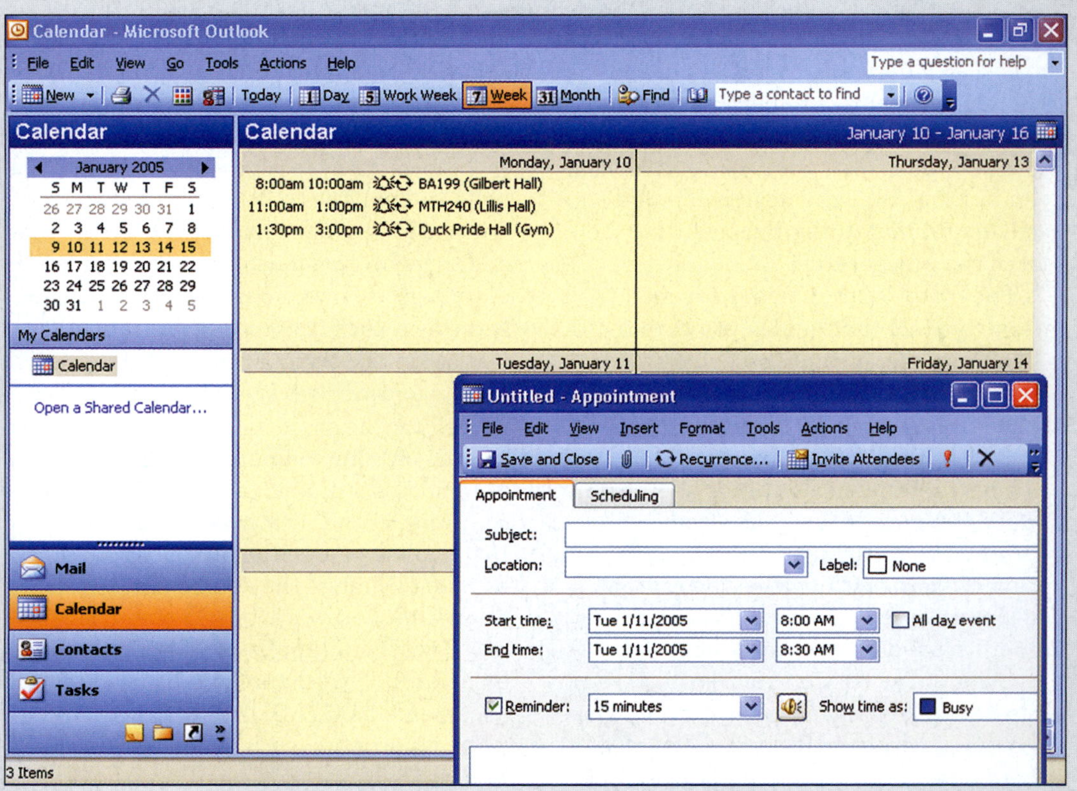

FIGURE 5T
The Outlook calendar is a good way to manage your busy college schedule.

Spotlight Exercises

1. Open any Microsoft Office application from the Start, Microsoft Office menu sequence. Choose the Help, Microsoft Office Online menu sequence. Find the links for Product Information and System Requirements. Prepare a list that compares the minimum system requirements against the specifications of the computer you use most often. Be sure to list the version of Office that you are assessing.

2. Open Microsoft Word from the Start, Microsoft Office menu sequence and choose the Help, About menu sequence. Write down the version of Word, note if it has any service packs installed (you will see text such as SP1), and record the information in the License box. Now choose the File, New menu sequence and then choose Templates on Office Online from the Task Pane menu. Browse the site to learn about at least two templates. Write a short report that describes what you have learned.

3. Open Microsoft Excel from the Start, Microsoft Office menu sequence. Click any cell to select it, type in "Cars," and then press the Enter key. Next, type in "Trucks," press Enter, and then type "Buses." Next, type in a number next to each vehicle type. Select the Cars cell and hold down the left mouse button as you drag down through the vehicles and then over to the bottom number. Choose the Insert, Chart menu sequence and then click the Finish button at the bottom right of the Chart Wizard. Move the chart around and resize it as you see fit. Print the chart so that your professor can see what you've accomplished.

4. Open PowerPoint from the Start, Microsoft Office menu sequence. Choose the File, New menu sequence and then choose the From AutoContent Wizard menu choice. Click Next at the bottom right of the wizard box. Choose Sales/Marketing, Selling a Product or Service, and then Next. Accept the default selection as an On Screen Presentation and click Next. Type in a title for your sales presentation and then select Finish. Scroll through the slides to observe one method of presenting ideas. Have some fun with this—see if you can change the backgrounds or patterns. Use the File, Print menu sequence to choose the Print What feature and then choose Handouts. Now look to the right and choose 6 slides to a page. Staple the pages together and provide them to your professor.

5. You can manipulate the Microsoft Office toolbars to better suit your needs. In this exercise, you will create a new button on the Standard toolbar and reset the way menus are presented across the top of the screen. Open Word from the Start, Microsoft Office menu sequence. Right-click on any toolbar at the top of the window. Choose the Options tab and make sure that both of the top boxes are checked. This will cause your toolbars to appear on two separate bars, and will also cause your Menus to show all commands each time. Now right-click a menu and choose Customize from the bottom of the menu. Click the Commands tab and scroll down the right side of the window until you see the icon for closing files. Drag it up to the top left of the top toolbar and drop it into place next to the icon for opening a file. You can use this method to customize your toolbars with the buttons that you want and need. Write several paragraphs that will inform your professor of what you've learned.

What You'll Learn . . .

- **Understand how computers represent data.**

- **Understand the measurements used to describe data transfer rates and data storage capacity.**

- **List the components found inside the system unit and explain their use.**

- **List the components found on the computer's motherboard and explain their role in the functioning of the computer's systems.**

- **Discuss (in general terms) how a CPU processes data.**

- **Explain the factors that determine a microprocessor's performance.**

- **List the various types of memory found in a computer system and explain the purpose of each.**

- **Describe the various physical connectors on the exterior of the system unit and explain their use.**

Inside the System Unit

As you learned in Chapter 1, computers perform four basic functions: inputting data, processing data, displaying the results using output devices, and storing the results for subsequent use. Computer hardware, especially the system unit, is involved in all of these functions.

The term *performance* refers to how fast a computer can obtain, process, display, and store data. To communicate knowledgeably with others about computer hardware capabilities, you need to know the terminology that's used to describe *how* computers represent data as well as *how much* data computers can transfer or store.

Computer performance is often considered to be the same as the speed of a computer's processor; however, the processor's capabilities are only part of the picture. Imagine that you have an engine that produces 500 horsepower. If you put this engine into your stock sedan and aggressively apply that horsepower, parts of the car will begin to break apart. The stock transmission, drive train, and axles are not designed to handle so much power. Your tires and wheels may not be able to handle the transfer of energy to the pavement. You will have an engine that you cannot fully use. It's the same with computers—all of the components need to be matched with regards to speed and performance.

In this chapter, you'll learn how computers represent data as well as how the components inside and outside the system unit process that data.

How Computers Represent Data

Computers can't do anything without data to work with. For a computer to work with data, the data must be represented by digits inside the computer.

REPRESENTING DATA AS NUMBERS

We're all used to counting with decimal numbers, which consist of 10 digits (0, 1, 2, 3, 4, 5, 6, 7, 8, 9). Computers count with

binary numbers (also called binary digits, or bits for short), which consist of only two digits, 0 and 1. A **bit** is the smallest unit of information that a computer can work with (Figure 6.1).

You can think of a bit as being like a light switch: It has only two possible states, and it is always in one or the other. If you have one light switch, then the switch is either on or off. If you have two light switches, then you have four possibilities: both switches are on, both switches are off, the first switch is on and the second switch is off, or the first switch is off and the second switch is on. Three switches allow for eight possibilities, and so on, up to eight switches, which results in 256 possible combinations.

A **byte** consists of eight bits and represents one unit of storage. Because it takes eight bits (on/off switches) to make a byte, and eight bits results in 256 possible on/off combinations, you'll see the number 256 appearing behind the scenes in many computer functions and applications. A single byte usually represents one character of data, such as the essential numbers (0–9), the basic letters of the alphabet, and the most common punctuation symbols. For this reason, you can use the byte as a baseline for understanding just how much information a computer is storing. For example, a typical college essay contains 250 words per page, and each word contains (on average) 5.5 characters. Therefore, the page contains approximately 1,375 characters. In other words, you need about 1,375 bytes of storage for one page of a college paper.

Bits (1s and 0s) are commonly used for measuring the data transfer rate of computer communications devices such as modems. To describe rapid data transfer

Binary digit	0	I
Bit	○	●
Status	On	Off

FIGURE 6.1 A binary number is composed of binary digits, or bits for short. A bit is the smallest unit of information that a computer can work with.

FIGURE 6.2 Measurements That Describe Units of Data

Measurement	Abbreviation	Amount	Text
Bit	b		none
Kilobits per second	Kbps	1 thousand bits per second	125 characters
Megabits per second	Mbps	1 million bits per second	125 pages
Gigabits per second	Gbps	1 billion bits per second	125,000 pages
Byte	B		one character
Kilobyte	KB or K	1 thousand bytes	one page
Megabyte	MB or M	1 million bytes	1,000 pages
Gigabyte	GB or G	1 billion bytes	1,000 books
Terabyte	TB or T	1 trillion bytes	1 million books

Techtalk

Yottabytes
Because computers use binary numbers to store data, a kilobyte is not exactly 1,000 bytes. The exact measurement is 1,024 bytes (2^{10}). However, the exact amount is close enough that you can think in rounded, approximate terms (1,000, 1 million, or 1 billion) for most purposes. Terms that are becoming more prevalent are terabyte (1 trillion), petabyte (1 quadrillion), exabyte (1 quintillion), zettabyte (1 sextillion), and yottabyte (1 septillion). A yottabyte is 2^{80}—a very large number!

rates, the measurements **kilobits per second (Kbps)**, **megabits per second (Mbps)**, and **gigabits per second (Gbps)** are used. These rates correspond (roughly) to 1,000, 1 million, and 1 billion bits per second. Remember that these terms refer to *bits* per second, not *bytes* per second.

Bytes are commonly used to measure data storage. The measurements **kilobyte (K or KB)**, **megabyte (M or MB)**, **gigabyte (G or GB)**, and **terabyte (T or TB)** are used to describe the amount of data the computer is managing either in memory or in longer-term storage on disk. Figure 6.2 shows these measurements and the approximate equivalent of text data for each.

Binary numbers are difficult to work with because many digits are required to represent even a small number. For example, when you enter the decimal number 14 into your computer, the binary number representation is 1110. In addition, it's time-consuming for computers to translate binary numbers into their decimal equivalents. For these reasons, computers translate binary numbers into **hexadecimal** (**hex** for short) **numbers** using the numbers 0 through 9 and the letters A through F. For example, the letter K is represented as the lengthy binary number 01001011 and then quickly translated into 4B in hex (Figure 6.3).

FIGURE 6.3 Decimal, Binary, and Hexadecimal Numbers

Decimal Number	0	1	2	3	4	5	6	7	8	9	10	11	12	13	14	15
Binary Number	0	1	10	11	100	101	110	111	1000	1001	1010	1011	1100	1101	1110	1111
Hexadecimal Number	0	1	2	3	4	5	6	7	8	9	A	B	C	D	E	F

Representing Very Large and Very Small Numbers

To represent and process numbers that have fractional parts (such as 1.25) or extremely large numbers, computers use **floating-point notation**. The term *floating point* suggests how this notation system works: no fixed number of digits is before or after the decimal point, so the computer can work with very large as well as very small numbers. Floating-point notation requires special processing circuitry, which is generally provided by the floating-point unit (FPU). Almost a standard in the circuitry of today's microprocessors, on older computers the FPU was sometimes a separate chip called the *math coprocessor*.

It would be difficult to use computers if they just spat out numbers at us. Fortunately, thanks to character code, we can understand computer output.

REPRESENTING CHARACTERS: CHARACTER CODE

Character code translates between the computer's numeric world and the letters, numbers, and symbols called **characters** that we're accustomed to using. Computers can recognize several different character codes.

ASCII, EBCDIC, and Unicode

The most widely used character code is the American Standard Code for Information Interchange (ASCII), pronounced "ask-ee," which is used on minicomputers, personal computers, and computers that make information available over the Internet. IBM mainframe computers and some other systems use a different code, Extended Binary Coded Decimal Interchange Code (EBCDIC), pronounced "ebb-see-dic."

Although ASCII and EBCDIC contain some foreign language symbols, both are clearly insufficient for a global computer market. Unicode can represent many, if not most, of the world's languages.

Now that you understand bits, bytes, and how computers represent data, let's take a closer look at the system unit, where these concepts will come into play.

Introducing the System Unit

The **system unit** is a boxlike case that houses the computer's main hardware components (Figure 6.4). The system unit is more than just a case: It provides a sturdy frame for mounting internal components, including storage devices and connectors for input and output devices; it protects those components from physical damage; and it keeps them cool. A good case also provides room for system upgrades, such as additional disk drives.

System units come in a variety of styles. In some desktop computing systems, the system unit is a separate metal or plastic box that's designed to sit on top of a desk. Ideally, the case should have a small **footprint** (the amount of room taken up by the case on the desk). Desktop computer cases are wide and deep, but not very tall. A small case may not have enough room for add-on components. One solution to this problem is the **tower case**, a system unit case that is designed to sit on the floor next to a desk. The tower case is tall and deep; it's a little wider than a desktop case is tall. Smaller versions of tower cases are called **minitower cases**.

In notebook computers and PDAs, the system unit contains all of the computer's components, including input components (such as a keyboard) and the display. Some desktop computers, such as Apple's iMac, contain the display within the system unit (Figure 6.5).

System units also vary in their form factor. A **form factor** is a specification for how internal components, such as the motherboard, are mounted in the system unit.

Now that you know what the system unit is, let's look at what's inside.

Inside the System Unit

Most computer users don't need to open their system unit; they receive their computer in a ready-to-use package. However, if you ever do need to open your system

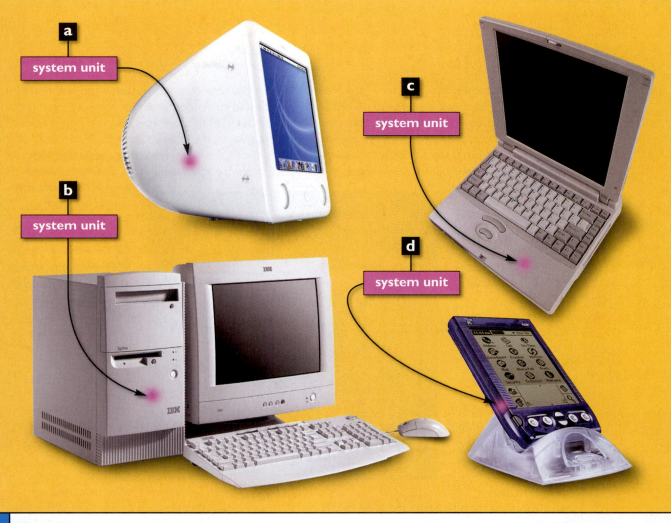

FIGURE 6.4 Every kind of computer has a system unit: (**a**) Apple iMac; (**b**) desktop; (**c**) laptop; (**d**) handheld.

FIGURE 6.5 (**a**) The Apple iMac's system unit sits on the desktop and also contains the computer's display. (**b**) The Macintosh G4 has a tower case that sits on the floor next to the desk.

Safety and Security

Playing It Really Safe

You might accidentally disclose your password or lose your smart card, but you can't easily change your fingerprints or your retina. That's the idea behind biometric authentication, verifying your identity by using hardware to check a unique personal characteristic before allowing access to a computer system. Characteristics may include facial geometry, ear shape, vein patterns, DNA recognition, voice recognition, or odor composition. In the future, you might carry your biometric data with you on a smart card or other chip-equipped token. To use an ATM or to pay for groceries, you would insert the token and look into the retinal scanner or put your finger on a sensor. The system would then check that the biometrics matched before allowing you to continue.

As individualized as biometric authentication may be, it can be fooled. Security experts have been able to lift fingerprints from a computer's previous user and reuse them to gain access. They have also duped face-recognition systems by showing the camera a color photo or a digital video of an authorized user. This is why researchers are working on new authentication methods, such as identifying users by the way they walk or taking fingerprints from three fingers before allowing access.

Even when fraud isn't involved, the environment around the authentication device can

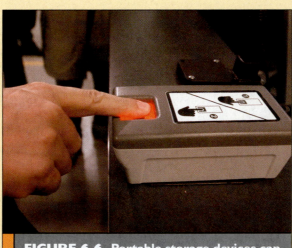

FIGURE 6.6 Portable storage devices can be encoded with fingerprint-identification circuitry to provide data security.

interfere with accuracy. Suppose you were on a crowded street corner trying to withdraw money from an ATM that controls access through voice recognition. If the noise level were too high or a police siren were wailing in the background, chances are you wouldn't be able to get into your account because the security system wouldn't be able to recognize your voice. Or, say you were at an ATM that authenticates identity through facial geometry. If the light were too dim or part of your face was in shadow, the security system probably wouldn't get a clear enough picture to compare with the facial features in your file. Again, no access and no money.

Finally, a fingerprint or retinal scan that enabled you access to a computer system in the United States might not work if you tried to gain remote access when you were outside the country. The reason: No international standards exist for biometric authentication. This means you're either locked out of the system—you wouldn't be able to get money from an ATM in another country—or you would need a different way to verify your identity. Someday you may have to breathe on a special sensing device, insert a small token, and enter a password to gain access to a computer system. Setting up three levels of biometric authentication will not be cheap, but it will add another layer of security to keep sensitive data safe (Figure 6.6).

unit, bear in mind that the computer's components are sensitive to static electricity. If you touch certain components while you're charged with static electricity, you could destroy them. Always disconnect the power cord before opening your computer's case and discharge your personal static

electricity by touching something that's well grounded. If it's one of those dry days when you're getting shocked every time you touch a doorknob, don't work on your computer's internal components.

If you do open your system unit, you'll see the following components (Figure 6.7):

FIGURE 6.7 Inside the system unit, you'll find the motherboard, the power supply, a cooling fan, an internal speaker, internal drive bays, external drive bays, and various expansion cards (such as the sound card and network interface card).

- **Motherboard.** The **motherboard** contains the computer's CPU. You'll learn more about the motherboard and the CPU later in the chapter; for now, remember that the CPU is the computer in the strictest sense of the term; all other components (such as disk drives, monitors, and printers) are peripheral to, or outside of, the CPU.

- **Power supply.** A computer's **power supply** transforms the alternating current (AC) available from standard wall outlets into the direct current (DC) needed for the computer's operation. It also steps the voltage down to the low voltage required by the motherboard. Power supplies are rated according to their peak output in watts. A 250-watt power supply is adequate for most desktop systems, but 300 watts provides a margin of safety if you plan to add many additional components.

- **Cooling fan.** The computer's components can be damaged if heat

accumulates within the system unit. A **cooling fan** keeps the system unit cool. The fan often is part of the power supply, although some high-powered systems include auxiliary fans to provide additional cooling.

- **Internal speaker.** The computer's **internal speaker** is useful only for the beeps you hear when the computer encounters an error. Macintoshes come with built-in stereo sound, but to produce good sound from a PC you need to upgrade the system with sound components (including a sound card and speakers).

- **Drive bays. Drive bays** accommodate the computer's disk drives, such as the hard disk drive, floppy disk drive, and CD-ROM or DVD-ROM drive. Internal drive bays are used for hard disks, in which the disk is permanently contained within the drive's case. Therefore, they do not enable outside access. External drive bays

FIGURE 6.8 Expansion cards enable you to add enhancements to your system.

mount drives to be accessible from the outside (a necessity if you need to insert and remove disks from the drive). External drive bays vary in size. Some bays accommodate 5.25-inch drives (for CD-ROMs and DVD-ROMs), whereas others are designed for 3.5-inch drives (for floppy and Zip disks).

- **Expansion slots.** The system unit also contains **expansion slots**, which are receptacles that accept additional circuit boards or expansion cards. Examples of expansion cards are memory modules, sound cards, modem cards, NICs, and video cards (Figure 6.8).

Now that you have a good overview of the internal components of the system unit, let's look more closely at the most important component: the computer's motherboard.

What's on the Motherboard?

The motherboard is a large printed circuit board (PCB), a flat piece of plastic or fiber-glass that contains thousands of electrical circuits etched onto the board's surface (Figure 6.9). The circuits connect numerous plug-in receptacles, which accommodate the computer's most important components (such as the microprocessor). The motherboard provides the centralized physical and electrical connection point for the computer's most important components. Most of the components on the motherboard are integrated circuits. An **integrated circuit** (**IC**), also called a **chip**, carries an electrical current and contains millions of transistors. A **transistor** is an electronic switch (or gate) that controls the flow of electrical signals to the circuit. A computer uses such electronic switches to route data in different ways, according to the software's instructions. Encased in black plastic blocks or enclosures, most chips fit specially designed receptacles or slots on the motherboard's surface.

So, what do these chips do? Let's look at some of the most important components

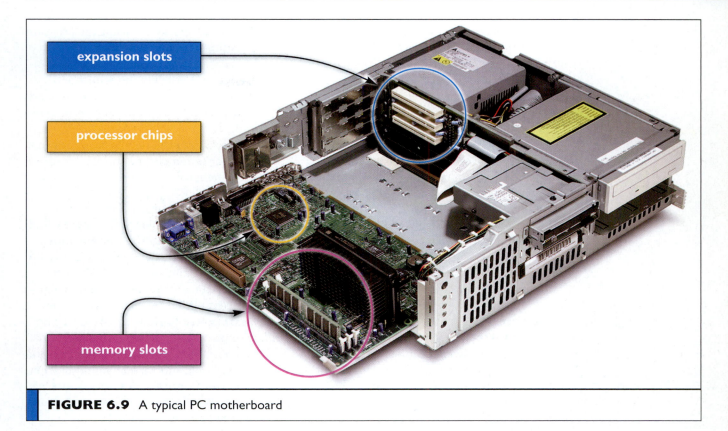

expansion slots

processor chips

memory slots

FIGURE 6.9 A typical PC motherboard

you'll see on the motherboard: the CPU (or microprocessor), the system clock, the chipset, input/output buses, and memory.

THE CPU: THE MICROPROCESSOR

The **central processing unit** (**CPU**) is a **microprocessor** (or **processor** for short), an integrated circuit chip that is capable of processing electronic signals. It interprets instructions given by software and carries out those instructions by processing data and controlling the rest of the computer's components. Carefully inspect your environment and you'll find that processors are found in all kinds of electronic and mechanical devices such as cell phones, calculators, automobile engines, and even industrial and medical equipment. They process information so that humans can enjoy their effective and efficient operation. No other single element of a computer determines its overall performance as much as the CPU.

Although microprocessors are complex devices, the underlying ideas are easy to understand. When you're ready to

buy a computer, you'll need to understand the capabilities and limitations of a given microprocessor.

Processor Slots and Sockets

An integrated circuit of fabulous complexity, a microprocessor plugs into a motherboard in much the same way that other integrated circuits do. However, special slots and sockets accommodate microprocessors. Part of the reason for this is that microprocessors are larger and have more pins than most other chips. In addition, microprocessors generate so much heat that they could destroy themselves or other system components. The microprocessor is generally covered by a **heat sink**, a heat-dissipating component that drains heat away from the chip. To accomplish this, the heat sink may contain a small auxiliary cooling fan. The latest high-end microprocessors include their own built-in refrigeration systems, which are needed to keep these speedy processors cool.

The Instruction Set

Every processor can perform a fixed set of operations, such as retrieving a character

Destinations

The Intel Museum's "How Chips Are Made" feature provides a nicely illustrated overview of the chip-fabrication process. The Intel Museum is located at **www.intel.com/ intel/intelis/ museum/index.htm**

from the computer's memory or comparing two numbers to see which is larger. Each of these operations has its own unique number called an instruction. A processor's list of instructions is called its **instruction set**. Different processors have different instruction sets. Because each processor has a unique instruction set, programs devised for one computer type won't run on another. For example, a program written for the Apple Macintosh will not run on an IBM PC. A program that can run on a given computer is said to be compatible with that computer's processor. Alternatively, if a program is compatible, it's said to be a native application for a given processor design.

The Control Unit and the Arithmetic-Logic Unit

CPUs contain two subcomponents: the control unit and the arithmetic-logic unit. The **control unit** extracts instructions from memory and decodes and executes them. Under the direction of a program, the control unit manages four basic operations (Figure 6.10):

- **Fetch.** Retrieves the next program instruction from the computer's memory.

- **Decode.** Determines what the program is telling the computer to do.

- **Execute.** Performs the requested instruction, such as adding two numbers or deciding which one of them is larger.

- **Store.** Stores the results to an internal register (a temporary storage location) or to memory.

This four-step process is called a **machine cycle**, or **processing cycle**, and consists of two phases: the **instruction cycle** (fetch and decode) and the **execution cycle** (execute and store). Today's microprocessors can go through this entire four-step process billions of times per second. The **arithmetic-logic unit** (**ALU**), as its name implies, can perform arithmetic or logical operations. **Arithmetic operations** include addition, subtraction, multiplication, and division. **Logical operations** involve comparing two data items to see which one is larger or smaller.

Some operations require the control unit to store data temporarily. **Registers** are temporary storage locations in the microprocessor that are designed for this purpose. For example, one type of register

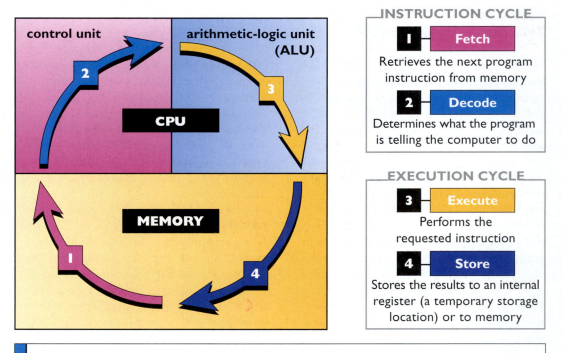

FIGURE 6.10 The control unit manages four basic operations: fetch, decode, execute, and store.

IMPACTS

Computers and Society

Power to the PC

It's not easy to be green when computers, especially laptops, are power hogs. In fact, the higher the clock speed, the more power your microprocessor draws. The cooling fan inside the unit also drains the power supply. Imagine the number of kilowatts consumed if you keep your PC on 24/7 so you can check e-mail or open files at any time. Despite the convenience, this is a little like leaving a car parked with the engine running day and night—it wastes energy and puts stress on the internal components because of the constant heat. How can computers become greener without losing power or convenience?

The Environmental Protection Agency, technology manufacturers, and nonprofit organizations are all working on answers. If your computer bears the EPA's Energy Star logo, it already has the ability to save energy by going to "sleep," that is, powering down when not used for a certain amount of time. This boosts energy efficiency, but it also means that your computer needs a little time to resume normal operation after you press a key to wake it up. However, when you're really in a hurry, you may not want to wait even a fraction of a minute to get into a file or onto the Web, which is why many people disable the sleep function.

Soon you'll have another choice. Experts at Intel, working with the Natural Resources Defense Council and several power-supply manufacturers, have come up with new specifications that may reduce a computer power supply's electrical consumption by 25 percent

or more. Equipping millions of PCs with this type of power supply would save an estimated 16 billion kilowatts per year—perhaps 1 to 2 percent of the country's electricity consumption—and shrink electric bills by a whopping $1.25 billion. You might pay about $10 more for a computer containing this new power supply, but you would save at least that amount on your electric bills every year as well as ease the burden on the nation's power grid.

Several Japanese manufacturers are experimenting with highly efficient fuel-cell power supplies for laptops and other electronic items (Figure 6.11). NEC, for example, is perfecting a fuel-cell power supply that can run a computer for 40 hours on one tank of methanol. Fuel cells last a lot longer than conventional batteries and are more environmentally friendly, but they're much more expensive and not yet ready for prime time. Are fuel cells in your computer's future?

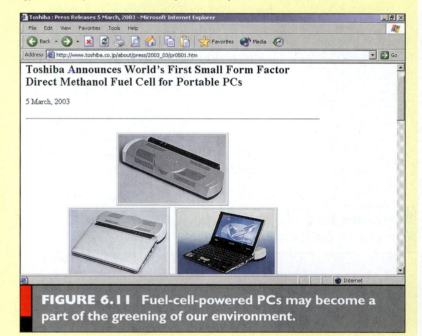

FIGURE 6.11 Fuel-cell-powered PCs may become a part of the greening of our environment.

---

stores the memory location from which data were retrieved. Registers also store the results of intermediate calculations.

Microprocessor Performance

The number of transistors available has a huge effect on the performance of a processor. The greater the number and the closer their proximity to each other, the faster the processing speed. The data bus width and word size, operations per microprocessor cycle, parallel processing, and the type of chip are also factors that contribute to microprocessor performance.

Destinations

To learn more about the 64-bit version of the Microsoft Windows operating system, visit **www.microsoft .com/windowsxp/ 64bit/default.asp**

Data Bus Width and Word Size

The **data bus**, a highway of parallel wires, connects the internal components of the microprocessor. The bus is a pathway for the electronic impulses that form bytes. The more lanes this highway has, the faster data can travel. Data bus width is measured in bits (8, 16, 32, or 64).

The width of a CPU's data bus partly determines the maximum number of bits the CPU can process at once (its **word size**). Data bus width also affects the CPU's overall speed, because a CPU with a 32-bit data bus is capable of shuffling data around twice as fast as a CPU with a 16-bit data bus. The terms *8-bit CPU*, *16-bit CPU*, *32-bit CPU*, and *64-bit CPU* sum up the maximum number of bits a given CPU can handle at a time.

A CPU's word size is important because it determines which operating systems the CPU can use and which software can be run. Figure 6.12 lists the word-size requirements of past and current operating systems.

Today's personal computer market is dominated by 32-bit CPUs and 32-bit operating systems. However, 64-bit CPUs and 64-bit operating systems are beginning to enter the marketplace. Intel's 64-bit Itanium processor, introduced in late 2000, brought 64-bit computing to the PC market for the first time. In 2003, Mac OS X was using a 128-bit word size and 64-bit versions of the popular Linux and Microsoft Windows operating systems were also released.

The System Clock   Within the computer, events happen at a pace controlled by a tiny electronic "drummer" on the motherboard called the system clock. The **system clock** is an electronic circuit that generates pulses at a rapid rate and synchronizes the computer's internal activities. These electrical pulses are measured in billions of cycles per second (gigahertz or GHz) and referred to as a processor's **clock speed**. Any computer you purchase today will have a clock speed of more than 1 GHz. Thus, a 3-GHz processor is capable of processing 3 billion cycles in 1 second. In general, the higher the processor's clock speed, the faster the computer. As a frame of reference, can you figure out how many seconds there are in the average human life span? The answer may surprise you (77 years x 365.25 days x 24 hours x 60 minutes x 60 seconds)!

Operations per Cycle   The number of *operations* per clock tick (one pulse of the system clock) also affects microprocessor performance. You might think that a CPU can't perform more than one instruction per clock tick, but thanks to new technologies, that's no longer the case. **Superscalar architecture** refers to the design of any CPU that can execute more than one instruction per clock cycle. Today's fastest CPUs, such as the Pentium 4, use superscalar architectures. Superscalar architectures depend on **pipelining**, a processing technique that feeds a new instruction into the CPU at every step of the processing cycle so that four or more instructions are worked on simultaneously (Figure 6.13).

Pipelining resembles an auto assembly line in which more than one car is being worked on at once. Before the first instruction is finished, the next one is started. If the CPU needs the results of a completed instruction to process the next one, it is called **data dependency**. It can cause a pipeline stall in which the assembly line is held up until the results are known. To cope with this problem, advanced CPUs use a technique called **speculative execution** in which the processor executes and temporarily stores the next instruction in case it proves useful. CPUs also use a technique called **branch prediction** in which the processor tries to predict what will likely happen (with a surprisingly high degree of accuracy).

FIGURE 6.12 **Word Size Capacity (in bits) of Popular Operating Systems**

Operating System	Word Size	When in Time?
MS-DOS	8	Past
Windows 3.1	16	Past
Windows 95/98/NT/2000/XP	32	Current
Windows XP 64-Bit Edition 2003	64	Current
Linux	64	Current
Mac OS X (with Velocity Engine chip)	128	Current

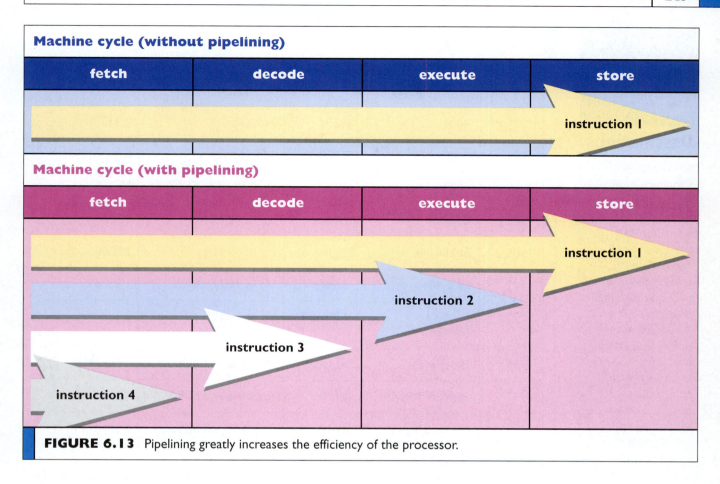

Machine cycle (without pipelining)			
fetch	decode	execute	store

instruction 1

Machine cycle (with pipelining)			
fetch	decode	execute	store

instruction 1

instruction 2

instruction 3

instruction 4

FIGURE 6.13 Pipelining greatly increases the efficiency of the processor.

Parallel Processing Another way to improve CPU performance is with **parallel processing**, a technique that uses more than one processor running simultaneously, in parallel (Figure 6.14). The idea is to speed up the execution of a program by dividing the program into multiple fragments that can execute simultaneously, each on its own processor. A program being executed across more than one processor

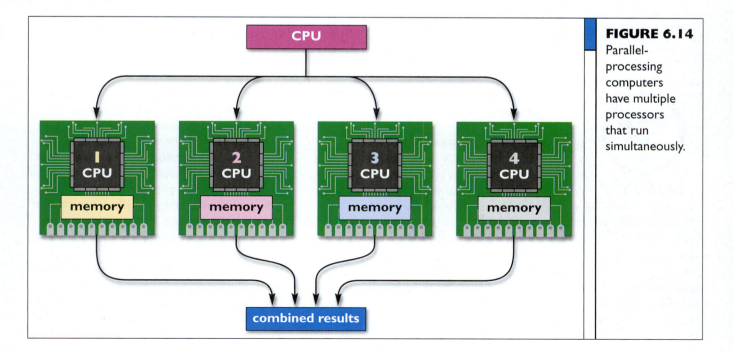

FIGURE 6.14
Parallel-processing computers have multiple processors that run simultaneously.

CPU

1 CPU   memory

2 CPU   memory

3 CPU   memory

4 CPU   memory

combined results

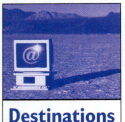

Destinations

For the latest information on the hottest and fastest processors, take a look at the aptly named "Chip Geek" at **www.ugeek.com/ procspec/procmain .htm**. You'll find the latest news on new, superfast processors as well as performance comparisons, reviews, and tips for putting together the ultimate high-speed system.

FIGURE 6.15 The Evolution of Intel Microprocessors

Year	Chip	Bus Width	Clock Speed	Transistors
1971	4004	4 bits	740 KHz	2,300
1974	8080	8 bits	2 MHz	6,000
1979	8088	8 bits	Up to 8 MHz	29,000
1982	80286	16 bits	Up to 12 MHz	134,000
1985	80386	32 bits	Up to 33 MHz	275,000
1989	Intel 486	32 bits	Up to 100 MHz	1.6 million
1993	Pentium (original)	32 bits	Up to 200 MHz	3.3 million
1995	Pentium Pro	32 bits	200 MHz and higher	5.5 million
1997	Pentium MMX	32 bits	233 MHz and higher	4.5 million
1998	Pentium II	32 bits	233 MHz and higher	7.5 million
1998	Xeon	32 bits	400 MHz and higher	7.5 million
1998	Celeron	32 bits	400 MHz and higher	7.5–19 million
1999	Duron	32 bits	600 MHz and higher	18 million
1999	Pentium III	32 bits	450 MHz and higher	9.5–28.1 million
2000	Pentium 4	32 bits	1.4 GHz and higher	34 million
2000	Itanium	64 bits	800 MHz and higher	25 million

techtv

To learn more about Intel's Centrino processor, watch the video clip at **www.prenhall.com/ cayf2006**

will execute faster than it would by using a single processor.

Popular Microprocessors

The most commonly used microprocessors are those found in IBM-compatible computers and Macintoshes. Most PCs are powered by chips produced by Intel; although AMD, Cyrix Corporation, and other firms also make IBM-compatible chips. Figure 6.15 shows how popular microprocessors for PCs have improved since the days of the first PC. In 2001, Intel released a version of the Pentium 4 microprocessor with a clock speed of 2 GHz, the first commercially available chip

to attain that speed (Figure 6.16). Since 2003, Intel has been concentrating on producing processors that are suited to certain computing needs—such as the release of the Centrino processor for mobile computing. Intel now rates their processors not only by cycles per second, but also by features such as architecture, cache, and bus type. The rating, then, is the power and usefulness of the processor—not just the clock speed.

For years, Motorola Corporation has made the chips for Macintosh computers. The chips fall into two processor families: the 68000 series (68000 to 68040) and the PowerPC series. PowerPC microprocessors

FIGURE 6.16 The Pentium 4

FIGURE 6.17 The Evolution of Motorola Microprocessors

Year	Chip	Bus Width	Clock Speed
1979	68000	16 bits	8 MHz
1984	68020	32 bits	Up to 40 MHz
1988	68040	64 bits	Up to 120 MHz
1994	PowerPC 603	64 bits	Up to 160 MHz
1995	PowerPC 603e	64 bits	Up to 300 MHz
1995	PowerPC 604e	64 bits	Up to 300 MHz
1998	PowerPC 750 (G3)	64 bits	200 MHz and higher
2000	PowerPC 7400 (G4)	64 bits	400 MHz and higher
2003	G4 (Velocity Eng)	128 bits	1.4 GHz and higher

run earlier Macintosh software by emulating the earlier processor's characteristics. Figure 6.17 shows how these processors have improved since the first ones appeared in 1979. Note that Apple Computer gives its own name to the PowerPC chips: Motorola's 750 is the same thing as Apple's G3, whereas Motorola's 7400 becomes the G4 in Apple's marketing materials.

THE CHIPSET AND THE INPUT/OUTPUT BUS

Another important motherboard component is the chipset. The **chipset** is a collection of chips that work together to provide the switching circuitry that the microprocessor needs to move data throughout the rest of the computer. One of the jobs handled by the chipset is linking the microprocessor with the computer's input/output buses.

An **input/output (I/O) bus** extends the computer's internal data pathways beyond the boundaries of the microprocessor to communicate with input and output devices. Typically, an I/O bus contains expansion slots to accommodate plug-in expansion cards.

Today's PCs and Macs use the **PCI (Peripheral Component Interconnect) bus**. Many motherboards still contain an Industry Standard Architecture (ISA) bus

and have one or two ISA slots available. The Accelerated Graphics Port (AGP) is a bus designed for video and graphics display. I/O buses extend adapters.

The microprocessor is just one of several chips on the computer's motherboard. Among the other chips are those that provide the computer's memory.

MEMORY

The CPU needs to interact with multiple input/output requests at the same time. That's the job of the computer's memory. **Memory** refers to the chips that enable the computer to retain information. Memory chips store program instructions and data so that the CPU can access them quickly. As you'll see in this section, the computer's motherboard contains several different types of memory, each optimized for its intended use.

RAM

The large memory modules housed on the computer's motherboard contain the computer's RAM. **Random access memory (RAM)** stores information temporarily so that it's directly and speedily available to

Destinations

To learn more about RAM, see Kingston Technology's "Ultimate Memory Guide" at **www.kingston.com/ tools/umg/default .asp**, which explains how memory works, what memory technologies are available, and how to select the best RAM chips for your computer system.

Techtalk

PROM, EPROM, EEPROM

PROM (programmable read-only memory) requires a special device to write instructions on a blank memory chip one time only. EPROM is erasable PROM that can be rewritten many times. EEPROM is electrically erasable PROM that can be overwritten without being removed from the computer.

the microprocessor. This information includes software as well as the data to be processed by the software. The contents of RAM are erased when the computer's power is switched off. RAM is designed for fast operation; the processor acts directly on the information stored in RAM.

Why is it called *random access* memory? *Random access* doesn't imply that the memory stores data randomly. A better term would be *address*, because each memory location has one—just like a post office box. Using this address, called a **memory address**, the processor can store and retrieve data by going directly to a single location in memory (Figure 6.18).

Of the various types of RAM available, today's newest and fastest PCs contain either DDR SDRAM (Double Data Rate Synchronous Dynamic RAM) or RDRAM (Rambus Dynamic RAM). These types of RAM must have a constant power supply or they lose their contents.

How much RAM does a computer need? In general, the more memory the better. Windows XP and Mac OS X theoretically require only 64 MB of RAM, but neither

system functions very well with so little. For today's Microsoft Windows, Linux, and Macintosh operating systems, 128 MB of RAM is a practical working minimum. Oftentimes, these operating systems use virtual memory in addition to RAM. The computer uses virtual memory when RAM gets full (which can easily happen if you run two or more programs at once). Disk drives are much slower than RAM, so when virtual memory kicks in, the computer slows down to a frustratingly slow pace. To avoid using virtual memory, you're better off with 256 MB of RAM, and increasingly, systems are sold with 512 MB of RAM.

ROM

If everything in RAM is erased when the power is turned off, how does the computer start up again? The answer is **read-only memory** (**ROM**), a type of memory on which instructions have been prerecorded. The instructions to start the computer are stored in read-only memory chips. ROM only allows these instructions to be read; they cannot be erased. In contrast with RAM, ROM retains information even when the power is switched off.

Cache Memory

RAM is fast, but it isn't fast enough to support the processing speeds of today's superfast microprocessors, such as the Motorola G4 or the Pentium 4. These microprocessors use cache memory to function at maximum speed. **Cache memory** is a small unit of ultrafast memory built into the processor that stores frequently or recently accessed program instructions and data. (The term *cache* is pronounced "cash.") Cache memory is much faster than RAM, but it's also more expensive. Although generally no larger than 512 KB, cache memory greatly improves the computer system's overall performance.

Two types of cache memory are available. The first type, called **primary cache** or level 1 (L1) cache, is included in the microprocessor chip. The second type, called **secondary cache** or level 2 (L2) cache, is included on a separate printed circuit board. To improve secondary cache performance, the latest microprocessors are housed in plastic modules that provide a special type of secondary cache called *backside cache*. Keeping the secondary

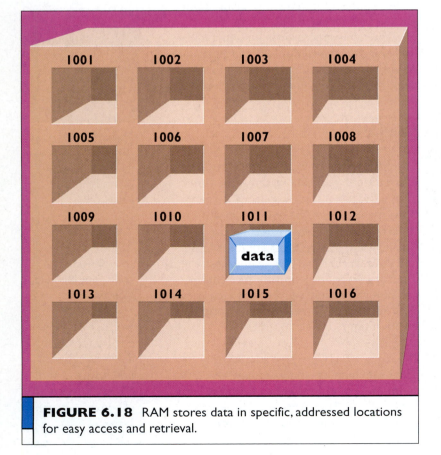

FIGURE 6.18 RAM stores data in specific, addressed locations for easy access and retrieval.

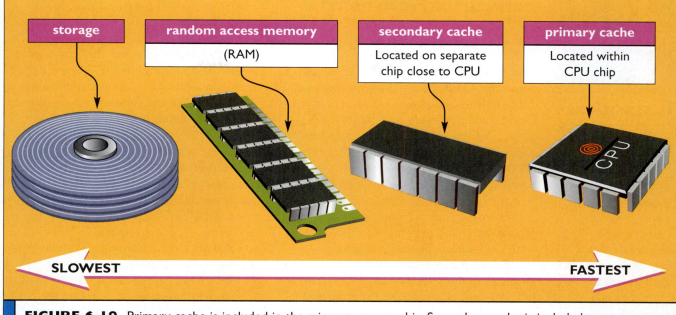

storage	random access memory	secondary cache	primary cache
	(RAM)	Located on separate chip close to CPU	Located within CPU chip

SLOWEST ← → FASTEST

FIGURE 6.19 Primary cache is included in the microprocessor chip. Secondary cache is included on a separate printed circuit board. Keeping the secondary cache as close as possible to the processor improves performance.

cache as close as possible to the processor improves performance (Figure 6.19).

The following sections explore what can be found on the outside of the system unit of a typical desktop computer.

What's on the Outside of the Box?

You'll find the following features on the outside of a typical desktop computer's system unit:

- The front panel with various buttons and lights

- The power switch

- Connectors and ports for plugging in keyboards, mice, monitors, and other peripheral devices

THE FRONT PANEL

On the front panel of most computers, you'll find a **reset switch** (which enables you to restart your computer in the event of a failure), a **drive activity light** (which tells when your hard disk is accessing data), and a **power-on light** (which indicates whether the power is on). You may also find a key lock that you can use to prevent others from operating the machine. Do not press the reset switch unless you are certain that your computer is no longer responding to input. If your computer freezes up, always try pressing the Control, Alt, and Delete keys simultaneously to activate the Windows Task Manager and attempt to shut down your system normally. If you have any unsaved work when you press the reset switch, you will most likely lose it.

The **power switch** is usually located on the front of the computer. In earlier days, it was placed on the back of the system unit because of fears that users would accidentally press it and inadvertently shut down their system. Computers don't handle sudden power losses well. For example, a power outage could scramble the data on your hard drive. Likewise, just turning off your computer instead of shutting it down properly can leave the system unstable and possibly unable to restart. You should always follow the appropriate shutdown procedure to shut off your computer.

Destinations

To learn more about PC interfaces, including serial and parallel ports, see **www.howstuff works.com.** Type "ports" in the search box that is located near the top right corner of the screen.

CONNECTORS AND PORTS

A **connector** is a physical receptacle that is designed for a specific type of plug that fits into the connector. The plug is sometimes secured by thumbscrews. **Expansion cards** (also called expansion boards, adapter cards, or adapters) are plug-in adapters used to connect the computer with various peripherals. Connectors on the outside of the case enable you to connect peripheral devices, such as a printer, keyboard, or mouse (Figure 6.20). Connectors are described as being *male* (those with external pins) or *female* (those with receptacles for external pins).

Figure 6.21 summarizes the connectors you may find on the computer's case. Most of these connectors are on the back of the

case, but sometimes you'll find one or more of them on the front.

It's important to remember that a connector isn't the same thing as a port. A **port** is an electronically defined pathway or interface for getting information into and out of the computer. A connector is the physical device—the plug-in—whereas a port is the interface—the matching of input and output flows. A port almost always uses a connector, but a connector isn't always a port. For example, a telephone jack is just a connector—not a port. To function, a port must be linked to a specific receptacle. This linking is done by the computer system's startup and configuration software.

In the following section, *port* is used as if it were synonymous with *connector*, in line with everyday usage; however, it's important to keep the distinction in mind. Let's now look at the types of ports found on the exterior of a typical computer system's case.

Parallel Ports

A **parallel port** is typically used to connect a PC to a printer and is rarely used for much else. Parallel ports send and receive data eight bits at a time over eight separate wires. This enables data to be transferred very quickly; however, the required cable is bulky because of the number of individual wires it must contain.

On PCs, access to the parallel port is provided by a 25-pin (DB-25) female connector. Macs use a six-pin (mini-DIN) connector.

The newest parallel ports—*enhanced parallel ports* (*EPPs*) and *extended capabilities ports* (*ECPs*)—offer higher speeds than traditional parallel ports. In addition, they enable two-way communication between the printer and computer. If the printer encounters an error, it can send a detailed message to the computer explaining what went wrong and how to fix it.

Serial Ports

A **serial port** sends and receives data one bit at a time (Figure 6.22). This is how data streams are sent and received across communications lines, whether they are telephone lines, coaxial cable lines, fiber-optic lines, or satellite transmissions. Although a serial port takes eight times as long as a parallel port to transfer each byte of data,

FIGURE 6.20 The connectors on the outside of a system unit enable you to connect peripherals such as a printer, a keyboard, or a mouse.

- power cord
- mouse
- keyboard
- printer
- monitor
- network
- telephone line
- speaker

it can achieve two-way communication with only three separate wires—one to send, one to receive, and a common signal ground wire. This feature is a tremendous advantage when transferring data more than a dozen feet or so because it uses a maximum of three wires instead of eight and it meets the criteria of sending streams of bits instead of bytes.

Serial ports weren't considered very important when computers had few capabilities for communicating or working with lots of different peripherals. But today, serial port use is proliferating at an increasing rate because the computer is no longer a standalone device, but rather a connected device that facilitates communications, data transfer, and the use of many types of peripherals.

IBM-compatible PCs typically have at least two serial ports and one parallel port. Even though these two types of ports are used for communicating with external devices, they work in different ways.

IBM-compatible PCs have four serial ports: COM1, COM2, COM3, and COM4. However, a PC may have only one or two physical connectors for serial devices. In addition, some expansion boards contain serial ports that connect directly to the computer's internal wiring.

The difference between a serial port and a parallel port is similar to the difference between a one-lane road and a freeway. You might imagine a serial port's relationship to transferring data as that of a one-lane road with lots of cars moving along it like a procession of ants. Unlike a serial port, which can transfer only one bit of information at a time, parallel ports can transfer eight bits of information (a byte) simultaneously (Figure 6.23).

USB Ports

A **USB** (**universal serial bus**) **port** can connect multiple peripherals, such as a keyboard, a mouse, and a digital camera, at one time. A single USB port can connect up to 127 peripheral devices. USB ports use an external bus standard that supports data transfer rates of 12 Mbps. The external bus supports data transfer between the computer and its peripheral devices—not between devices within the system unit.

Connector	Use
DB-25, 25-pin female	parallel port for printer
DB-25, 25-pin male	serial port for printers, modems, or scanners
DIN, 6-pin female	mouse or keyboard
DB-15, 15-pin female	VGA video (monitor)
RJ-11	phone line
RJ-45	network
stereo miniplug female	microphone, speakers, or headphones
USB	port for many devices on PCs and Macintoshes
FireWire	port for cameras and portable storage

FIGURE 6.21 Most of these connectors are on the back of the computer's case, but some of them may be in front.

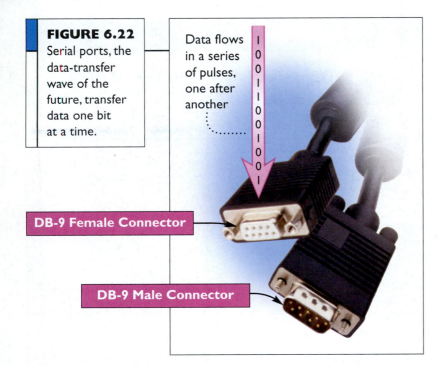

FIGURE 6.22 Serial ports, the data-transfer wave of the future, transfer data one bit at a time.

Data flows in a series of pulses, one after another

DB-9 Female Connector

DB-9 Male Connector

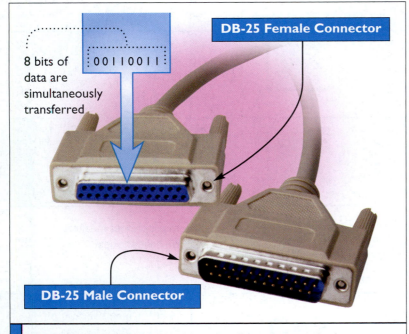

DB-25 Female Connector

8 bits of data are simultaneously transferred

DB-25 Male Connector

FIGURE 6.23 Parallel cables transfer eight bits of information simultaneously and are used to connect printers and computers.

Beginning in 1996, a few computer manufacturers started including USB support in their new machines. It wasn't until the release of the best-selling iMac in 1998, though, that USB became widespread. Now, USB ports are expected to completely replace other serial and parallel ports as technology continues to move forward (Figure 6.24). USB enables **hot**

swapping, or the ability to connect and disconnect devices without shutting down your computer. This is convenient when you're using devices that you want to disconnect often, such as a digital camera.

An additional advantage of USB is its built-in Plug-and-Play support. With **Plug-and-Play** (**PnP**), the computer automatically detects the brand, model, and characteristics of the device when you plug it in and configures the system accordingly.

Also referred to as *Hi-Speed USB*, USB 2.0 is an external bus that supports data rates of up to 480 Mbps (480 million bits per second). USB 2.0 is an extension of USB 1.1. Hewlett-Packard, Intel, Lucent, Microsoft, NEC, and Philips jointly led the initiative to develop a higher data transfer rate than the USB 1.1 specification to meet the bandwidth demands of developing technologies. USB 2.0 is fully compatible with USB 1.1 and uses the same cables and connectors. The USB 2.0 specification was released in April 2000.

SCSI Ports

A **SCSI** (short for **S**mall **C**omputer **S**ystem **I**nterface** and pronounced "scuzzy") **port** is a type of parallel interface increasingly found on PCs. Unlike a standard parallel port, a SCSI port enables users to connect up to eight SCSI-compatible devices, such as printers, scanners, and digital cameras, in a daisy-chain series. The most recent SCSI standard, called SCSI-2, can transfer data at very fast rates.

External connectors for SCSI peripherals vary. Some SCSI adapters have 68-pin connectors with a click-in locking mechanism for the plug, whereas others use a standard 50-pin (D50) connector.

Some high-end systems use a SCSI-2 or SCSI-3 adapter to connect internally with the computer's hard disk. (A high-end system is a computer priced higher than systems with a typical configuration.) Hard disks with such connections often offer the best performance because data can be retrieved and deposited faster.

1394 Ports (FireWire)

You have probably heard the term *FireWire* if you have any interest in digital video. Or perhaps you know it as *Sony i.Link* or as *IEEE 1394*, the official name for the standard. Originally created by Apple and standardized in 1995 as the IEEE 1394 High Performance Serial Bus specification, **FireWire** is very similar to USB in that it offers a high-speed connection for dozens of peripheral devices (up to 63 of them).

On non-Apple systems, this port is called a **1394 port**, after the international standard that defines this port. Like USB, FireWire enables hot swapping and PnP. However, it is more expensive than USB and is used only for certain high-speed peripherals, such as digital video cameras, that need greater throughput (data transfer capacity) than USB provides. With the advent of USB 2.0 and the promise of an even faster USB interface in the future, use of the 1394 FireWire standard will most likely fade away.

FIGURE 6.24 USB ports and connectors will be the standard for years to come.

Video Connectors

Most computers use a video adapter (also called a video card) to generate the output that is displayed on the computer's screen or monitor. On the back of the adapter, you'll find a standard **VGA (Video Graphics Array) connector**, a 15-pin male connector that works with standard monitor cables.

On some computers, the video circuitry is built into the motherboard. This type of video circuitry is called **on-board video**. On such systems, the video connector is found on the back of the case.

Additional Ports and Connectors

You may find the following additional ports and connectors on the exterior of a computer's case or on one of the computer's expansion cards:

- **Telephone connector.** The standard modem interface, this connector (called RJ-11) is a standard modular telephone jack that will work with an ordinary telephone cord.

- **Network connector.** Provided with networking adapters, this connector (called RJ-45) looks like a standard telephone jack, but it's bigger and capable of much faster data transfer.

- **PC card slots.** On notebook computers, one or more PC card slots are provided for plugging in PC cards. Like USB devices, PC cards can be inserted or removed while the computer is running.

- **Sound card connectors.** PCs equipped with a sound card (an adapter that provides stereo sound and sound synthesis) as well as Macs with built-in sound offer two or more sound connectors. These connectors, also called jacks, accept the same stereo miniplug used by portable CD players. Most sound cards provide four connectors: Mic (microphone input), Line In (accepts input from other audio devices), Line Out (sends output to other audio devices), and Speaker (sends output to external speakers).

- **Game card.** Game cards provide a connector for high-speed access to the CPU and RAM for graphics-intensive interaction.

- **TV/sound capture board connectors.** If your computer is equipped with TV and video capabilities, you'll see additional connectors that look like those found on a television monitor. These include a connector for a coaxial cable, which can be connected to a video camera or cable TV system.

Techtalk

PCMCIA
Short for Personal Computer Memory Card International Association, PCMCIA refers to the I/O bus design invented by the International Association. Developed for notebook computers, PCMCIA provides one or more slots for credit card-sized adapters, such as modems and networking cards. Originally, these cards were called PCMCIA cards—but just try pronouncing that phrase! Today, PCMCIA cards are simply called PC cards.

What You've Learned

INSIDE THE SYSTEM UNIT

- For a computer to work with data, the data must be represented by digits inside the computer. The basic unit of information in a computer is the bit, a single-digit binary number (either 1 or 0). An eight-bit sequence of numbers called a byte is sufficient to represent the basic letters, numbers, and punctuation marks in most languages.

- Data transfer rates of communications devices, such as modems, are measured in bits per second (bps), as well as Kbps (approximately 1,000 bits per second), Mbps (approximately 1 million bits per second), and Gbps (approximately 1 billion bits per second). Data storage capacity is measured in bytes, such as kilobyte (K or KB, approximately 1,000 bytes), megabyte (M or MB, approximately 1 million bytes), gigabyte (G or GB, approximately 1 billion bytes), and terabyte (T or TB, approximately 1 trillion bytes).

- The system unit contains the motherboard, which acts as the central connector for the processor, memory, and circuits within the computer. It also contains the power supply, which converts AC power to DC; a cooling fan, which keeps the processor and circuits cool; and an internal speaker, which emits beeps and a few basic tones. Additionally, the system unit holds drive bays for storage devices and expansion cards for additional memory, a modem, sound, video, and games.

- The computer's motherboard contains the microprocessor (the CPU—the "brains" of the computer), the system clock (which generates pulses to synchronize the computer's activities), the chipset (chips that help the processor move data around), and memory modules. Expansion slots give expansion cards access to the computer's input/output (I/O) bus, which provides access to the CPU and other system services to devices such as modems, sound cards, game controllers, and more.

- A computer's central processing unit (CPU) processes data in a four-step cycle called a machine cycle using two components: the control unit and the arithmetic-logic unit (ALU). The control unit follows a program's instructions and manages four basic operations: fetch, decode, execute, and store. The ALU can perform arithmetic operations and logical operations.

- Factors that affect a microprocessor's performance include the data bus width (how many bits it can process at once), clock speed (the number of operations the chip can execute per clock cycle), pipelining (a processing technique that feeds a new instruction into the CPU at every step of the processing cycle), and parallel processing (using multiple processors running in parallel).

- The computer's main memory, random access memory (RAM), holds programs, data, and instructions for quick use by the processor. Read-only memory (ROM) holds prerecorded startup operating instructions. Primary and secondary cache memory operate at very high speeds and keep frequently accessed data available to the processor.

- Almost all computers have serial ports (for mice, external modems, and some printers), parallel ports (mainly for printers), and a video port. Some computers also have a SCSI port (for SCSI devices such as scanners), a USB port (for USB peripherals, including USB digital cameras and USB printers), a 1394 (FireWire) port (for FireWire peripherals such as digital video cameras), input and output jacks for microphones and speakers, a telephone connector, and a network connector.

Go to **www.prenhall.com/cayf2006** to review this chapter, answer the questions, and complete the exercises.

Key Terms and Concepts

Matching

Match each key term in the left column with the most accurate definition in the right column.

_____ 1. parallel port

_____ 2. bit

_____ 3. RAM

_____ 4. character code

_____ 5. byte

_____ 6. parallel processing

_____ 7. kilobyte

_____ 8. USB port

_____ 9. pipelining

_____ 10. register

_____ 11. port

_____ 12. fetch

_____ 13. instruction set

_____ 14. cache memory

_____ 15. serial port

a. describes a technique that uses many processors running at the same time

b. consists of eight bits and represents one unit or character of storage

c. 1,000 bytes

d. additional memory that improves the computer system's overall performance

e. retrieves the next program instruction from memory

f. a processing technique that feeds new instructions to the CPU at every step of the processing cycle

g. a port used for peripherals such as printers

h. temporary storage location in the CPU

i. the smallest unit of information that a computer can work with

j. a processor's list of instructions

k. sends and receives data one bit at a time

l. stores information temporarily so that it's directly and speedily available to the microprocessor

m. a code that translates between the numerical words of the computer and the letters, numbers, and symbols that we are accustomed to using

n. an electronically defined pathway

o. a port that can connect multiple peripherals at one time

Multiple Choice

Circle the correct choice for each of the following.

1. Which of the following is *not* typically located on the outside of the system unit?
   a. port
   b. power switch
   c. drive activity light
   d. motherboard

2. Fetch and decode are associated with the
   a. execution cycle.
   b. instruction cycle.
   c. expansion card.
   d. expansion slot.

3. About how many bytes (rounded) are in a terabyte?
   a. 1,000,000
   b. 1,000,000,000
   c. 1,000,000,000,000
   d. 1,000,000,000,000,000

4. What term describes the specification for how internal components, such as the motherboard, are mounted in the system unit?
   a. form factor
   b. footprint
   c. component spec
   d. form footprint

5. Which of the following is *not* a variation of the Intel Pentium CPU?
   a. PowerPC
   b. Pentium II
   c. Xeon
   d. Celeron

6. Which of the following is not a type of memory?
   a. RAM
   b. ALU
   c. cache
   d. ROM

7. What is the name for the boxlike case that houses the computer's main hardware components?
   a. computer unit
   b. system unit
   c. expansion unit
   d. computer processing unit

8. Which of the following extracts instructions from memory and then decodes and executes them?
   a. control unit
   b. RAM
   c. ROM
   d. data bus

9. This is the name given to an electronic circuit that carries data from one computer component to another.
   a. trace
   b. data lead
   c. bus
   d. chip

10. What do you call the ability of a computer to run more than one processor at a time?
    a. multiple processing
    b. parallel processing
    c. serial processing
    d. dual processing

Fill-In

In the blanks provided, write the correct answer for each of the following.

1. A(n) _____ is a physical receptacle designed for a specific type of plug.

2. _____ is another name for the IEEE 1394 port that is used for high-speed video input.

3. _____ is a type of memory on which instructions have been prerecorded.

4. _____ enables external components to be plugged and unplugged while the computer is running.

5. A(n) _____, also called a chip, carries electrical current and contains millions of transistors.

6. The _____ _____ executes and stores data during the processing cycle.

7. A(n) _____ is an electronic switch (or gate) that controls the flow of electrical signals to the integrated circuit.

8. _____ is the maximum number of bits a CPU can process at once.

9. _____ refers to the chips that enable the computer to retain information.

10. A(n) _____ is an electronically defined pathway for getting information into and out of a computer.

11. The _____ enables a computer to perform mathematical operations more quickly.

12. _____ is the measurement that describes the storage of approximately 1 billion bytes.

13. A(n) _____ extends the computer's internal data pathways beyond the boundaries of the microprocessor so that the microprocessor can communicate with input and output devices.

14. The other type of cache memory is _____ _____, which is included on a separate printed circuit board and not on the microprocessor chip.

15. The _____ is an electronic circuit that generates rapid pulses and synchronizes the computer's activities.

Short Answer

1. Explain the difference between RAM and ROM. Why are both types of memory used in a computer?

2. What is a drive bay and how does it work?

3. What factors affect the performance of a computer?

4. What is the difference between a serial port and a parallel port? Why are keyboards connected to the serial port? (Note: Some keyboards, as well as mice, are connected to USB ports.)

5. How does the control unit work?

Teamwork

1. Exploring Ports

You have read about a variety of ports, so now let's look at some actual computers to see which ones are installed. Divide your team into two groups. Each group should locate at least three different computers. You may use your own computers or campus computers. Determine the number and types of ports that are available and identify the external devices that are connected to each port. Write a one-page report that describes each brand of computer and the configuration of external devices and ports found on each brand.

2. Pipelining and Parallel Processing

As a team, work together to answer the following questions and then write a one-page summary based on your findings. Most of the newer processors use pipelining. Explain how pipelining enhances overall processing speed. Give a non-computer example of pipelining (that is, an activity that you have personally performed that requires multiple steps to complete and in which you can begin the next step before the current one is completed). Explain parallel processing. Compare parallel processing and pipelining.

3. Working with Cache

Your team is to research the purpose of cache memory. Explain the difference between level 1 (L1) and level 2 (L2) cache. Although it was not discussed in the textbook, there is a third level of cache memory called L3. See what information you can find about this additional level of cache. Prepare a group presentation that includes a diagram showing how each level of cache memory relates to the processor.

4. Buses for Data

As processor size and speed have improved, system bus improvements have not been as dramatic as those for processors. The size of data buses in the first generation of personal computers was 8 bits, and they operated at a speed of 2 or 4 MHz. Your team is to work together to find the current size and speed of the Intel Pentium 4 and Motorola PowerPC data buses. How do the bus speeds compare with the processor speeds? Construct a table (or a chart) that shows the processors and speeds. Embed this table within a one-page document that explains why data bus size and speed are important.

5. Biometric Security

As a group, compile a list of different ways that biometrics can be used to enforce security. Have each group member research one of the items on the list. Get back together to discuss your findings. Each team member should then write two to three paragraphs based on his or her research. Combine these paragraphs into a single paper.

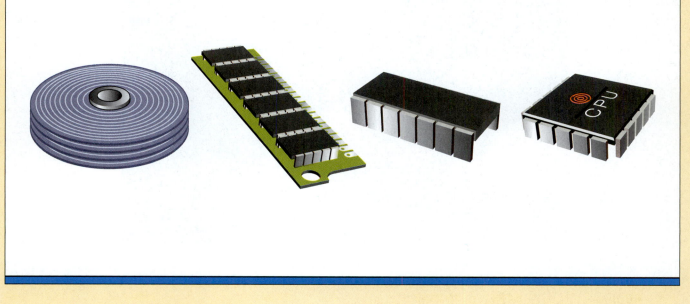

On the Web

1. Speeding Processors

Because technology changes rapidly, some of the information printed in this textbook may no longer be up-to-date. Currently, the fastest Intel processor for a personal computer is the Pentium 4, with a clock speed of more than 3 GHz, and the fastest Motorola processor is the G4, with a clock speed of more than 1.4 GHz. Visit Intel at **www.intel.com** and Apple at **www.apple.com** to find their fastest processors (type the word processor into each home page's search box). Use other sites or research tools to find additional information on these processors. Which computer system would you purchase if you used speed as the deciding factor? (Remember that processor speed alone does not determine the overall speed of the computer.)

2. The Cost of Storage

Unlike today's computers, in which memory chips are located on the motherboard, memory for the first microcomputers (circa 1978) was located on separate expansion cards, and 4 KB (not 4 MB) cost $295! Warm up your calculator and divide the cost by the number of bytes to determine the cost per byte of storage. Visit **www.cnet.com** and find the current price for 256 MB of RAM. Again, divide the cost by the number of bytes to determine the cost per byte. Using 1978 prices, how much would 256 MB of RAM cost today?

3. Discovering Serial Ports

Serial ports enable you to connect a mouse, cameras, external DVD drives, and lots of other devices to your computer. Visit **computer.how stuffworks.com/serial-port.htm** to learn more about how serial ports work and what they can do for you. Write a short paper that describes how USB 1.1 and USB 2.0 differ.

4. Motherboard Functions

Go to **computer.howstuffworks.com/mother-board.htm** to see what else you can learn about motherboards. Look for some of the key terms that you learned in this chapter. Write a short paper that clearly explains what the motherboard does and how it performs at least one function within the system unit. For instance, the motherboard acts as the connection point for electrical circuits within the system unit.

5. Managing Memory

Go to **www.kingston.com/tools/umg/default.asp** to learn how computers use memory. Browse at least three of the links that you find there. Develop three questions that you think someone might have about memory and then provide detailed answers. You cannot copy your information from the Web site; you must paraphrase your answers. Your document should be roughly two pages, double spaced.

CPUs—What's the Difference?

Although many factors affect the overall performance of a computer, the one feature that is most often touted by manufacturers is the speed of the computer's main processor or CPU. Years of advertising have convinced most people that a faster processor is always a better processor. If faster is always better, then why aren't there more people driving around in Ferraris? Because of price!

When purchasing a new PC, it is important that you balance your computing needs with your bank account. This can be a difficult task, because most companies that manufacture CPUs produce several product families that are targeted at various price and performance levels. How can you decide which CPU is right for you? The following are some tips to help you choose.

First, make a list of everything you plan to do with your computer. Will you use your computer for tasks such as composing e-mails, doing your taxes, and surfing the Web? Or will you perform more advanced tasks such as editing video or designing graphics? Be sure to write down everything that you might use your computer for over the next few years.

Once you have identified exactly how you would like to use your computer, you will need to match those needs with the appropriate type of processor. Most computers today come with CPUs manufactured by Intel. You will likely encounter three different families of Intel processors when you look for a new computer (Figure 6.25):

- **Intel Celeron.** The Celeron provides a good mix of performance and value. It is geared more toward those who use their computers for basic tasks such as word processing, Web surfing, and buying and listening to music online.

- **Intel Pentium 4.** The Pentium 4 is the current workhorse of Intel's consumer processor line and is geared toward advanced applications such as gaming, video editing, and advanced digital photography. The increase in performance also comes with an increase in price.

- **Intel Pentium M.** This is a newer processor from Intel that is made specifically for mobile devices such

FIGURE 6.25 The three different families of Intel processors are (**a**) Celeron, (**b**) Pentium 4, and (**c**) Pentium M.

as laptops and tablet PCs. The Pentium M is a good example of a processor that is capable of doing more work at slower speeds in comparison to other types of processors.

Once you have matched your needs with a particular type of processor, you will need to determine what processor speed is appropriate for you. Processor speeds are measured in gigahertz (GHz); the higher the number, the faster the processor. It is really only accurate to compare the speed of processors in the same family. A 2.4-GHz Celeron processor will almost always be slower than a 2.4-GHz Pentium 4 because of how they are designed. It is also important to realize that you will probably not gain much in performance by paying extra for a computer with a 2.6-GHz processor versus a 2.4-GHz processor. When it comes to incremental speed differences, do some research to determine if the increase in processing speed is worth the extra money. A great resource for detailed information on a large variety of processors and other computer hardware is **www.tomshardware.com/cpu**.

HT
Buying and Upgrading Your Computer System

When buying a computer, you need to know a lot to make a good decision. But buying a computer doesn't have to be intimidating! Many students successfully purchase and maintain their own computers. In fact, at a typical state university, 80 percent of students own a computer.

By having your own PC, you can type term papers, create slide presentations, and, in many cases, use a high-speed network connection right in your own dorm room. Many schools encourage students to purchase a computer before they arrive on campus. Even though schools still provide computer labs, with your own computer you can work when you want and, in the case of laptops, where you want.

This Spotlight will guide you step-by-step through the process of buying your own computer. Read on to learn how to choose the equipment you'll need at the best prices on today's market.

Getting Started the Right Way

There's a right way and a wrong way to select a computer system. The right way involves understanding the terminology and the relative value of computer system components. You then determine your software needs and choose the computer that runs this software in the most robust way. What's the wrong way? Buying a computer system based only on price, being influenced by sales hype, or purchasing a system you know nothing about. First we'll discuss how to select the right hardware.

Choosing the Right Hardware

You'll need to understand and evaluate the following hardware components when buying your computer:

- ✗ Processors
- ✗ Memory
- ✗ Hard disks
- ✗ Internal and/or external drives
- ✗ System units
- ✗ Monitors and video cards
- ✗ Printers
- ✗ Network cards
- ✗ Modems
- ✗ Speakers and sound cards
- ✗ Keyboards and mice
- ✗ Uninterruptible power supplies

The following sections examine each of these components (Figure 6A).

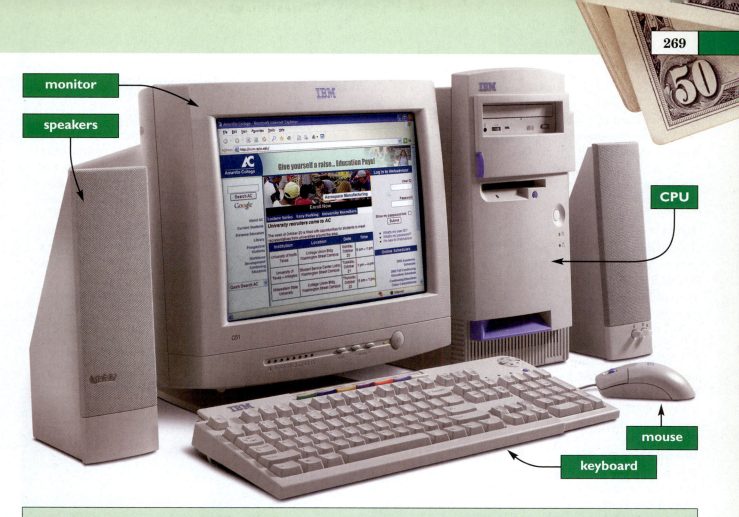

monitor

speakers

CPU

mouse

keyboard

FIGURE 6A Computer systems include the system unit, which houses the CPU and memory; internal and external drives; input devices, such as a keyboard and a mouse; and output devices, such as a monitor and speakers.

PROCESSORS

One of the most important choices you'll make when buying a computer is the type of microprocessor and its speed (Figure 6B). For example, you might compare an HP a550e Pavilion using a 3.4-GHz AMD Athlon 64 processor with an a550y Pavilion using a 3.4-GHz Intel Pentium 4 processor or a Dell Dimension 4600C 2.8-GHz processor. Each system will have its strengths and weaknesses; however, the processor is the heart of the machine and often dictates the robustness of the rest of the components. You should not put the fastest processor available on a low-end machine.

When researching different processors, keep in mind that you'll pay a premium if you buy the newest and fastest processor available. One approach is to buy the second-fastest processor on the market. That way you'll get plenty of speed without paying a penalty for being the first to have the most. In addition, today's processors are so powerful that it's not always necessary to have the fastest one. You only need enough processing power to handle the work or play you intend to accomplish. If you're a heavy game user, you may need a lot of processing power, but if you

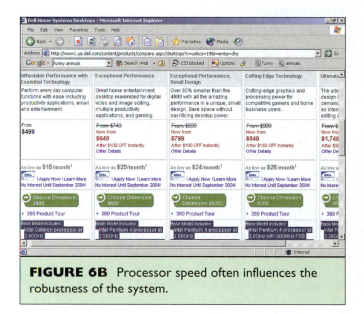

FIGURE 6B Processor speed often influences the robustness of the system.

will only use your computer to surf the Web, play audio files, and communicate using e-mail and instant messaging, a mid-speed processor should suit your needs just fine.

MEMORY

The next item to consider when buying a computer is how much memory you need. Two important issues are the amount of RAM and whether the system has cache memory. You really can't have too much memory; a good rule of thumb is to buy as much as you can afford.

RAM

To maximize your computer's performance, you should seriously consider purchasing at least 256 MB of RAM; 512 MB would be even better. Currently, the fastest type of RAM is SDRAM. For PCs with Pentium 4 processors, you need SDRAM capable of running at a speed of 100 MHz. This type of RAM is often called PC100 SDRAM.

When purchasing a new computer, ask if the memory can be upgraded, because you never know what your future use will demand. You may find that you already own a perfectly good system that just needs more memory to be effective and efficient.

Secondary Cache

When researching cache memory, keep in mind that systems with cache memory tend to be faster than systems without it. (Refer to Chapter 6 for an in-depth discussion of secondary cache memory.)

HARD DISKS

A common mistake made by first-time buyers is underestimating the amount of disk storage they'll need. Today, 10 GB (gigabytes) may sound like a lot, but you won't believe how quickly it will fill up. A good rule of thumb is to use no more than 25 percent of your hard-disk space for the operating system and applications. Because Windows XP and Microsoft Office consume up to 2 GB of disk space, a 10-GB drive should be a minimum. Most entry-level systems on today's market come with a 40-GB hard disk, and it's relatively inexpensive to upgrade to 60 or 80 GB.

When comparing computer systems that have the same type of processor, hard-disk speed makes the biggest contribution to overall system speed. For example, suppose you're looking at two Pentium 4 computers with 3-GHz processors, one of which is less expensive than the other. The less-expensive one uses a slow hard drive, which slows the system down so much that it isn't much faster than a well-designed 2-GHz computer. In particular, pay attention to rotation speed; drives that spin at 5,400 RPM are adequate, but better drives spin at 7,200 or 10,000 RPM.

INTERNAL AND/OR EXTERNAL DRIVES

A **drive** is a connected storage device. Drives can be internal (installed within the system unit) or external (attached to the system unit by a cable connected to a port). For instance, to install new software, most of which is distributed on CD-ROMs, you'll want a CD-ROM drive, which is either internal or purchased as a standalone external device. You can get CD-ROM drives with speeds of up to 70x (70 times the original CD-ROM standard of 150 Kbps). You may consider a DVD-ROM drive instead of a CD-ROM drive. In addition to reading CD-ROMs, a DVD-ROM drive enables you to view movies on DVDs. With DVDs, you can also store up to 5 GB of data, the equivalent of approximately 1,300 MP3 files (Figure 6C). It's also a good idea to buy a system with a CD-RW or DVD-RW drive to write files to CDs or DVDs.

FIGURE 6C DVDs can store more data than CD-ROMs. A DVD-ROM drive can also be used to read ordinary CD-ROMs.

MONITORS AND VIDEO CARDS

Monitors are categorized by the technology used to generate images, the colors they display, their screen size, and additional performance characteristics.

CRT (short for cathode-ray tube) monitors are relatively inexpensive compared with other types of monitors, but they consume more energy and take up more desktop space. In contrast, LCD monitors consume less electricity, weigh less, and take up much less room, because they are both flat panel and flat screen. Flat-panel monitors are very thin, usually no more than 2 inches deep. Flat-screen monitors have just that, a flat screen. Flat screens provide nearly as good resolution as CRTs, but weigh less because they are not made of glass.

The quality and resolution of the display you see on your monitor is determined by the computer's **video**

FIGURE 6D
(a) A 17-inch monitor is considered to be the industry standard. **(b)** Flat-screen monitors are becoming increasingly popular.

card. The current standard display for a Windows PC is a **Super Video Graphics Array** (**SVGA**) **monitor** with a resolution of either 1024 x 768 or 1280 x 1024. High-end video cards can display resolutions of 1600 x 1200. The higher the resolution, the more memory that is required. To display 1600 x 1200 resolution with a color palette of 16.7 million colors, for example, you need to equip your video card with 8 MB of **video RAM** (**VRAM**), which is memory that's set aside for video processing.

Advanced systems offer a special bus design that directly connects the video circuits with the microprocessor, increasing performance speed. In Windows PCs, the best systems currently offer an **Accelerated Graphics Port** (**AGP**), which transfers video data much more quickly than the standard PCI bus.

If you plan to run Microsoft Windows, look for a system that has a graphics accelerator built into the video card. A **graphics accelerator** is a display adapter that contains its own dedicated processing circuitry and VRAM, enabling faster display of complex graphics. This accessory can double or triple the performance of Windows.

Monitors are available in different sizes. You can purchase anything from a 14-inch to a 21-inch monitor, but the larger the monitor, the higher the cost. Increasingly, a 17-inch monitor is considered to be the industry standard (Figure 6D). If you plan to do any desktop publishing or CAD work, you may want to upgrade to a 21-inch monitor. For CRT displays, the quoted size of the monitor is the size of the CRT's front surface measured diagonally. However, because some of this surface is encased and unavailable for display purposes, it's important to distinguish between the monitor's quoted size and its viewable area. Although more expensive than traditional CRTs, flat-screen monitors have gained in popularity because they have less distortion and therefore cause less eye strain.

The monitor's dot pitch is also an important factor. **Dot pitch** (also called aperture grill) is a physical characteristic that determines the smallest dot the screen can display. Don't buy a monitor with a dot pitch larger than .28 mm—the smaller the dot pitch, the better your display.

PRINTERS

Printers fall into four basic categories: color inkjet printers, monochrome laser printers, color laser printers, and multifunction devices that fax and scan as well as print. For college use, cost considerations will probably rule out color laser and multifunction devices, so you'll most likely want to choose between color inkjet and monochrome laser printers.

Although laser printers continue to slightly outperform inkjet printers, the difference in print quality is not enough to justify the price differential. As a result, your budget will likely determine which printer is best. Although monochrome laser printers are more expensive than color inkjet printers, laser printers are cheaper to use in the long run because laser toner cartridges, priced on a cost-per-page basis, are cheaper than inkjet cartridges.

Speed matters, too. The slowest laser printers are faster than the fastest inkjet printers, and the slowest inkjet printers operate at a glacial pace. High-end laser printers can print as many as 60 ppm (pages per minute). Still, the best inkjet printers churn out black-and-white pages at a peppy pace—as many as 18 ppm. If you go the inkjet route, look for a printer that can print at least 8 ppm.

Stay with a major brand name, and you'll be served well. It's always a good idea to purchase an extra print cartridge and stash it away with 30 or 40 sheets of paper. This way, Murphy's Law won't catch you at 2 a.m. trying to finish an assignment without ink or paper.

SPEAKERS AND SOUND CARDS

To take full advantage of the Internet's multimedia capabilities, you will need speakers and a sound card. On Macs, the sound is built in; however, you'll need external speakers to hear stereo sound. Windows PCs require a sound card. Look for a sound card that offers **wavetable synthesis**, which uses stored samples of real musical instrument sounds, as well as a PCI bus, which will reduce demands on your processor. For the richest sound, equip your system with a subwoofer, which realistically reproduces bass notes.

Be aware that many computers, especially the lowest-priced systems, come with cheap speakers. If sound matters a lot to you—and it does to many college students—consider upgrading to a higher-quality, name-brand speaker system.

MODEMS AND NETWORK CARDS

If you plan to log on to the campus network, you'll need a modem and/or a **Network Interface Card** (**NIC**). Many computers now come with a built-in modem, so buying an external modem is unnecessary. Today's standard modem uses the 56 Kbps V.90 protocol. Check with your campus computer center to find out how to connect to your school's system, which modem protocols are supported, and what kind of network card you need. Most colleges run 10-Mbps (10baseT) Ethernet networks, but some require you to get a 100-Mbps (100baseT) network card.

Macintoshes have built-in support for Ethernet networks, but you'll need a **transceiver**—a device that handles the electrical connection between the cable and the Mac's Ethernet port—to actually connect. On Windows PCs, you'll need an Ethernet card, which already includes the transceiver (Figure 6E). Look for a card that plugs into your computer's PCI bus.

KEYBOARDS AND MICE

Most computers come with standard keyboards. If you use your computer keyboard a lot and you're worried about carpal tunnel syndrome, consider upgrading to an ergonomic keyboard, such as the Microsoft Natural Keyboard.

Most systems also come with a basic mouse, but you can ask for an upgrade. With Windows PCs, there's good reason to do so, thanks to the improved mouse support built into Windows XP. Any mouse that supports Microsoft's IntelliMouse standard includes a wheel that enables you to scroll through documents with ease. Wheel mice also include programmable buttons to tailor your mouse usage to the software application you're using (Figure 6F).

FIGURE 6E An Ethernet card is a NIC that works with Ethernet local area networks (LANs).

FIGURE 6F A wheel mouse includes a scrolling wheel and programmable buttons.

To choose a good keyboard and mouse, go to a local store that sells computers and try some out. The button placement and action vary from model to model. You'll be using these input devices a lot, so be sure to make an informed decision.

UNINTERRUPTIBLE POWER SUPPLIES

"I'm sorry I don't have my paper. I finished it, and then a power outage wiped out my work." If this excuse sounds familiar, you may want to purchase an **uninterruptible power supply** (**UPS**), a device that provides power to a computer system for a short period of time if electrical power is lost. With the comparatively low price of today's UPSs—you can get one with surge protection for less than $200—consider buying one for your campus computer, especially if you experience frequent power outages where you live or work. A UPS gives you enough time to save your work and shutdown your computer properly until the power is back on.

Now that you know what to look at when choosing hardware for your computer system, let's examine how to choose between a notebook or desktop model.

Notebook or Desktop?

Deciding whether to buy a notebook or a desktop computer is often one of the hardest decisions you'll have to make when considering which computer to buy (Figure 6G). Today's notebook (or laptop) computers rival the power of desktop machines. The best of them are truly awesome machines, with big (over 14-inch) displays and fast processors.

The main advantages of a notebook are portability and size. Because notebooks are portable, you can take them to class in a specially designed carrying case (Figure 6H). Once in class, you can easily fit a notebook on your desk to type notes. As you're probably well aware, campus housing or shared rental units often limit the amount of desk space, which makes notebooks even more appealing.

On the downside, notebook computers cost more than comparable desktop models. You also should consider that notebooks can be easily lost or stolen. And, if your notebook goes missing, your precious data will go along with it. More than 250,000 notebook computers are stolen each year, mostly from airports and hotels. Recently, however, thieves have been targeting college campuses, making safety another important factor when considering a notebook.

In the end, the decision most often hinges on convenience versus expense. Pay a visit to your professor

FIGURE 6G Notebook computers are convenient but more expensive than comparable desktop models. Deciding whether to buy a notebook or a desktop computer is often one of the hardest decisions college students have to make.

FIGURE 6H Notebook computers enable you to take your work with you wherever you go. Special carrying cases protect your computer from the wear and tear of traveling.

to ask his or her advice. In addition, your family, friends, and coworkers can tell you what they have used and preferred. Notebooks have come a long way, but the desktop computer is still the most popular model on the market.

Besides choosing a notebook or desktop model, another decision you'll need to make is which platform: Mac or PC.

Mac or PC?

There are two main computer system platforms: Windows (PC) and Macintosh (Figure 6I). If you ask around, you'll find that some users prefer the Mac,

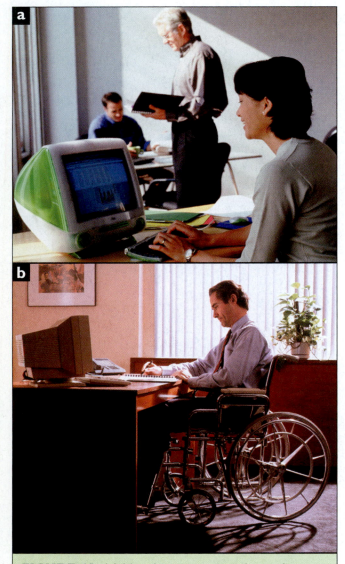

FIGURE 6I **(a)** Macs have a strong niche market in artistic fields, such as publishing, music, graphics, illustration, and Web site design. **(b)** PCs figure prominently on the desktops of engineers and businesspeople.

whereas others prefer Windows. Each thinks their platform is the best, and rarely do they cross platforms. How do you know which platform is best for you?

Today's top-of-the-line Macintoshes and PCs are virtually indistinguishable in terms of features and performance. However, only about one Macintosh is sold for every 20 Windows PCs. So how do you decide? First, you need to know some of the differences between Macs and PCs that can become major issues for some people.

One difference between Macs and PCs is software availability. More than 90 percent of the computers in use today are PCs, and developers are more inclined to develop software for the broadest market. Consequently, far more programs are available for Windows PCs than for Macintoshes. Many software companies that formerly focused on the Macintosh are deemphasizing Mac software and bringing out Windows products. Other publishers are dropping Mac products altogether. For example, Autodesk, publisher of the top-selling CAD program AutoCAD, dropped its sluggish-selling Mac version to focus on its Windows products. Even software publishers that continue to support the Mac typically bring out the Mac versions later and don't include as many features.

Another point in favor of the PC is Linux. Although a version of Linux is available for the Mac, the PC version is where you'll find all the action. You can run Linux on the same hard drive along with Windows or Mac OS, giving you the best of both worlds.

Although Macs can read most PC files and conversion software is available, file compatibility can be a problem. If your professor or place of work uses PCs, you'll probably have fewer file conversion problems if you also have a PC. In some cases, the type of computer doesn't make a difference, but oftentimes, compatibility issues can cause real headaches.

Do software availability and compatibility really make a difference? If you're planning to use your computer only for basic applications, such as word processing, spreadsheets, databases, presentation graphics, e-mail, and Web browsing, the Mac-versus-PC issue really isn't important. Excellent software for all of these important applications is available for both platforms. But look down the road. What if you declare a major a couple of years from now, only to find that your professors want you to use special-purpose programs that run on the platform that you don't have?

Thus, when deciding whether to buy a PC or a Mac, it's important that you anticipate your future software needs. Find out which programs students in your major field of study are using, as well as which programs are used by graduates working in the career you're planning to pursue. To find out what type of computer is preferred by people working in your chosen career, interview appropriate professionals.

In general, Macs have a strong niche market in artistic fields, such as publishing, music, graphics, illustration, and Web site design. PCs figure prominently on the desktops of engineers and businesspeople. The classic stereotype is that the successful artist has a Mac, but her accountant uses a PC. But like all stereotypes, this is not always the case. For example, you might think that scientists would use PCs, but that's not necessarily true. In the "wet" sciences (chemistry and biology), Macs have many adherents, because these sciences involve visual representation, an area in which Macs excel.

If you're on a budget, consider cost, too. Although the price gap is narrowing, Macs and Mac peripherals and software are somewhat more expensive than comparable PC equipment. Macs used to be easier to set up and use, but thanks to improvements in Microsoft Windows, Macs and PCs are now about even.

Now that you understand your choices for a computer system's physical components, let's look at some other decisions you will have to make when shopping for your new system.

Shopping Wisely

As you get ready to buy a computer, it's important to shop wisely. Should you buy a top-of-the-line model or a bargain-bin special? Is it better to buy at a local store or through a mail-order company? What about refurbished or used computers or a name-brand versus a generic PC? Let's take a look at some of these issues.

TOP-OF-THE-LINE MODELS VERSUS BARGAIN-BIN SPECIALS

A good argument for getting the best system you can afford is that you don't want it to become obsolete before you graduate. In your senior year, do you want to spend time upgrading your hard drive when you should be focusing on your studies? In addition, every time you open the computer's cover and change something, you risk damaging one of the internal components.

The most important consideration is the type of software you plan to run. If you'll be using basic applications such as word processing, you don't need the most powerful computer available. In this situation, a bargain-bin special may be okay, as long as you exercise caution when making such a purchase. But what if you decide to declare a major in mechanical engineering? You might want to run a CAD package, which demands a fast system with lots of memory. In that case, you'd be better off paying extra to get the memory you need up front, rather than settling for a bargain-bin special that may end up being inadequate later.

LOCAL STORES VERSUS MAIL-ORDER/ONLINE COMPANIES

Whether you're looking for a Windows PC or a Macintosh, you need to consider whether to purchase your system locally or from a mail-order or online company. If you buy locally, you can resolve problems quickly by going back to the store (Figure 6J). With a

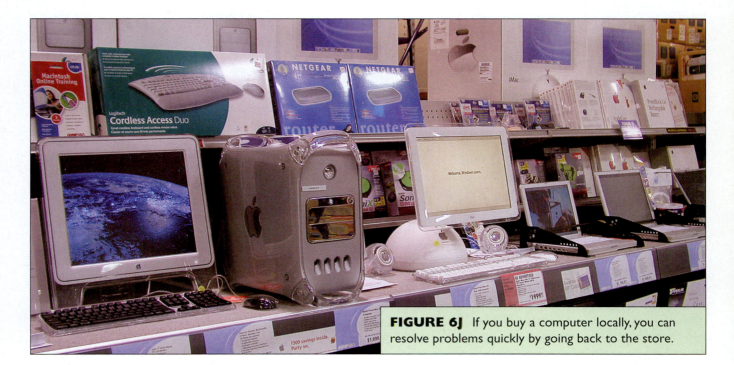

FIGURE 6J If you buy a computer locally, you can resolve problems quickly by going back to the store.

Shopping Comparison Worksheet

VENDOR _____   Date _____

    Brand Name _____

    Model _____

    Real Price _____ (including selected components)

PROCESSOR

    Brand _____

    Model _____

    Speed _____ MHz

RAM

    Type _____

    Amount _____ MB

HARD DRIVE

    Capacity _____ GB   Seek time _____ ns

    Speed _____ rpm   Interface _____

MONITOR

    Size _____ x _____ pixels   Dot pitch _____ mm

VIDEO CARD

    Memory _____ MB   Max. resolution _____ x _____ pixels

    Accelerated? .... ☐ yes ☐ no

FLOPPY/ZIP DRIVE(S)

    Capacity _____ KB   Number _____

REMOVABLE DRIVE

    Type _____

    Location ....☐ internal ☐ external

CD-ROM DRIVE

    Speed _____

CD BURNER

    Included? .... ☐ yes ☐ no

DVD-ROM DRIVE

    Included? .... ☐ yes ☐ no

SPEAKERS

    Included? .... ☐ yes ☐ no

    Upgraded? .... ☐ yes ☐ no

SUBWOOFER

    Included? .... ☐ yes ☐ no

SOUND CARD

    Included? .... ☐ yes ☐ no

NETWORK CARD

    Included? .... ☐ yes ☐ no

    Speed (10/100) _____

MODEM

    Included? .... ☐ yes ☐ no

    Protocol _____

KEYBOARD

    Upgraded? .... ☐ yes ☐ no

    Model _____

MOUSE

    Included? .... ☐ yes ☐ no

    Upgraded? .... ☐ yes ☐ no

UPS

    Included? .... ☐ yes ☐ no

SOFTWARE

_____

_____

WARRANTY _____

    Service location _____

    Typical service turnaround time _____

FIGURE 6K

Shopping Comparison Worksheet

system from a mail-order or online company, you'll have to call the company's technical support line.

If you're considering ordering through the mail or online, look for companies that have been in business a long time—and particularly those that offer a no-questions-asked return policy for the first 30 days. Without such a policy, you could get stuck with a "lemon" system that even the manufacturer won't be able to repair. Be aware that the lowest price isn't always the best deal—particularly if the item isn't in stock and will take weeks to reach you. Also, don't forget about shipping and handling charges, which could add considerably to the price of a system purchased online or through the mail.

In addition, make sure you're not comparing apples and oranges. Some quoted prices include accessories such as modems and monitors; others do not. To establish a level playing field for comparison, use the Shopping Comparison Worksheet in Figure 6K. For the system's actual price, get a quote that includes all of the accessories you want, such as a modem, a monitor, and a UPS.

You should also consider warranties and service agreements. Most computers come with at least a 1-year warranty for parts and service, with an additional 2 years of parts-only coverage. Some companies offer service agreements for varying lengths of time that will cover anything that goes wrong with your system—for a price. In the vast majority of cases, a computer will fail within the first few weeks or months. You should be as fully covered as you feel comfortable with during the first year. Be aware, though, that extra warranty coverage and service contracts can add significantly to the cost of your system.

BUYING USED OR REFURBISHED

What about buying a used system? It's risky. If you're buying from an individual, chances are the system is priced too high. People just can't believe how quickly computers lose their value. They think their systems are worth a lot more than they actually are. Try finding some ads for used computers in your local newspaper and then see how much it would cost to buy the same system new, right now, if it's still on the market. Chances are the new system is cheaper than the used one.

A number of reputable businesses refurbish and upgrade systems for resale. National chains such as MacWarehouse have standards to ensure that their systems are "as good as new" when you make a purchase. As always, check out the storefront and stay away from establishments that don't look or feel right. And most important, your refurbished machine should come with a warranty.

NAME-BRAND VERSUS GENERIC PCS

Name-brand PC manufacturers, such as Hewlett-Packard, Dell, and Gateway, offer high-quality systems at competitive prices. You can buy some of these systems from retail or mail-order stores, but some, such as Dell computers, are available only by contacting the vendor directly.

If you're buying extended warranty protection that includes on-site service, make sure the on-site service really is available where you live; you may find out that the service is available only in major metropolitan areas. Make sure you get 24-hour technical support; sometimes your problems don't occur between 8 a.m. and 5 p.m.

One disadvantage of name-brand systems is their use of proprietary components. If something breaks down, you have only one repair option: go back to the manufacturer. And, after the warranty has expired, you may end up paying a premium price for parts and repairs. Fortunately, this is becoming less and less of an issue. Almost all of today's name-brand computers run well right out of the box, and in-service failure rates are declining.

What about generic PCs? In most cities, you'll find local computer stores that assemble their own systems using off-the-shelf components. These systems are often just as fast (and just as reliable) as name-brand systems. You save because you don't pay for the name-brand company's marketing and distribution costs. Because of their smaller client base, the staff at local computer stores have a better chance of knowing their customers personally, and thus may provide more personalized service. Their phones are not nearly as busy, and should something go wrong with your computer, you won't have to ship it halfway across the country. Ask the technician about his or her training background and experience. Another thing to consider is that the industry's profit margin is razor-thin; if the local company goes bankrupt, your warranty may not mean much.

What if you don't need an entire new computer system, but just want to improve your current system's performance? That's when you should consider upgrading your system.

Upgrading Your System

You may want to upgrade your system for a variety of reasons. You may have purchased new software that requires more memory to run properly. You may decide to add a game controller. You could decide that a new monitor and printer will enhance your computing experience. Many computer owners improve their systems' performance and utility by adding new hardware, such as modems, sound cards, and additional memory. This section discusses the two most common hardware upgrades: adding expansion boards and adding memory.

Before you decide to upgrade your computer on your own, be aware that doing so may violate your computer's warranty. Read the warranty to find out. You may need to take your computer to an authorized service center to get an upgrade. Also, although it can be relatively simple to install new components, it can be risky. If you aren't absolutely certain of what you're doing—don't do it! Also consider whether it may be more cost-effective to purchase a new computer than to upgrade your existing one.

REMOVING THE COVER

To upgrade your system, begin by unplugging the power cord and removing all of the cables attached to the back of the system unit. Make a note of which cable went where so that you can correctly plug the cables back in later. With most systems, you can remove the cover by

removing the screws on the back of the case. If you don't know how to remove the cover, consult your computer manual. Keep the screws in a cup or bowl so they'll be handy when you reassemble the computer.

ADDING EXPANSION BOARDS

To add an expansion board to your system, identify the correct type of expansion slot (ISA, PCI, or AGP) and unscrew the metal insert that blocks the slot's access hole. Save the screw, but discard the insert. Gently, but firmly, press the board into the slot. Don't try to force it, though, and stop pressing if the motherboard flexes. If the motherboard flexes, it is not properly supported, and you should take your computer to the dealer to have it inspected. When you've pressed the new expansion board fully into place, screw it down using the screw you removed from the metal insert. Before replacing the cover, carefully check that the board is fully inserted.

UPGRADING MEMORY

Many users find that their systems run faster when they add more memory. With additional memory, it's less likely that the operating system will need to use virtual memory, which slows the computer down. To successfully upgrade your computer's memory, you'll find it helpful to learn a few terms and concepts.

Older computers use memory chips supplied on 72-pin **single inline memory modules** (**SIMMs**); most newer computers use 168-pin **dual inline memory modules** (**DIMMs**). SIMMs and DIMMs are printed circuit boards (with affixed memory chips) that snap into specially designed sockets on the computer's motherboard. Most motherboards have either four SIMM sockets or two to three DIMM sockets (Figure 6L). SIMMs must be installed in pairs, which limits their flexibility. Because DIMMs do not have to be installed in pairs, they're often easier to work with.

SIMMs and DIMMS are available in various capacities, ranging from 8 to 128 MB. You will need to consult your computer's manual to determine whether your computer uses SIMMs or DIMMs and where you can add them. For example, suppose your computer has two 8-MB SIMMs in the first two sockets, leaving two sockets empty. Because you must install SIMMs in pairs, you can add two 8-MB SIMMs (for a total of 32 MB of memory—the original 16 plus the additional 16), two 16-MB SIMMs (for a total of 48 MB of memory—16 + 32), or two 32-MB SIMMs (for a total of 80 MB of memory—16 + 64).

Consult your computer's manual to determine which type of memory technology your computer uses. Older computers use the slowest of these technologies, **fast-page mode** (**FPM**) **DRAM**, which is available only in SIMMs. Newer computers use the faster **extended data out (EDO) DRAM**, which is available in both SIMMs and DIMMs. Still newer computers use the fastest available memory—**synchronous dynamic RAM (SDRAM)**—which is available only in DIMMs.

You also need to consider the speed of the memory chips. FPM and EDO DRAM chips are rated in nanoseconds (ns)—billionths of a second. The smaller the number, the faster the chip. Pentiums require 60-ns chips, whereas older systems can work with 70- or 80-ns chips. For SDRAM chips, the speed is rated in megahertz (MHz), and this speed must match the speed of the motherboard's data bus (66 MHz, 100 MHz, or 133 MHz).

When you purchase memory modules, a knowledgeable salesperson might help you determine which type of module you need and how much memory you can install. But in most cases the salesperson won't know any more about installing memory than you do.

Before you install memory modules, be aware that memory chips are easily destroyed by static electricity. Do not attempt to install memory chips without wearing a **grounding strap**, a wrist-attached device that grounds your body so that you can't zap the chips. Remember: Don't try to force the memory modules into their receptacles; they're supposed to snap in gently. If they won't go in, you don't have the module aligned correctly or you may have the wrong type of module.

REPLACING THE COVER

When you have checked your work and you're satisfied that the new hardware is correctly installed, replace the cover and screw it down firmly. Replace the cables and then restart your system. If you added PnP devices, you'll see on-screen instructions that will help you configure your computer to use your new hardware.

If you're thinking about upgrading your system or if you want to understand what a particular component does, a great place to start is the "PC Guide" at **www.pcguide.com\intro\over.htm**. Site author Charles Kozierok presents a free, detailed survey of PC system components, including special sections on system care and system enhancement.

Whether your computer system is brand new or merely upgraded, you need to know how to properly maintain your system's components.

FIGURE 6L Memory modules are affixed to slots on the motherboard.

Caring for Your Computer System

After your computer is running smoothly, chances are it will run flawlessly for years if you take a few precautions:

✗ *Equip your system with a surge protector, a device that will protect all system components from power surges caused by lightning or other power irregularities (Figure 6M).*

✗ *Consider purchasing a UPS. These devices protect your system should the computer lose power.*

✗ *Don't plug your dorm refrigerator into the same outlet as your computer. A refrigerator can cause fluctuations in power, and a consistent power supply is critical to the performance and longevity of your computer.*

✗ *There should be sufficient air circulation around the components. Don't block air intake grilles by pushing them flush against walls or other barriers. Heat and humidity can harm your equipment. Your computer should not be in direct sunlight or too close to a source of moisture.*

✗ *Before connecting or disconnecting any cables, make sure your computer is turned off.*

✗ *Cables shouldn't be stretched or mashed by furniture. If your cables become damaged, your peripherals and computer might not communicate effectively.*

✗ *Clean your computer and printer with a damp, soft, lint-free cloth.*

✗ *To clean your monitor, spray some window cleaner on a soft, lint-free cloth—not directly on the monitor— and then wipe the surface clean.*

✗ *Avoid eating or drinking near your computer. Crumbs can gum up your mouse or keyboard, and spilled liquids (even small amounts) can ruin an entire system.*

✗ *If your mouse gets gummed up, twist off the ring on the bottom of the mouse, remove the ball, and clean the ball with warm soapy water. Rinse and dry the ball thoroughly with a clean, lint-free cloth. Clean the rollers with a cotton swab, and remove any lint that may have accumulated.*

✗ *To clean your keyboard, disconnect it from the system unit and gently shake out any dust or crumbs. You can also use cans of compressed air to clear dust or*

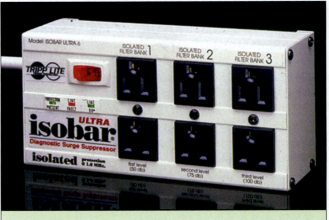

FIGURE 6M Surge protectors prevent costly damage to delicate circuitry and components.

crumbs from underneath the keys. Vacuums specially designed for keyboards also are on the market. Never use a regular vacuum cleaner on your keyboard, because the suction is too strong and may damage the keys.

✗ *To keep your hard disk running smoothly, run a disk defragmentation program regularly. This program ensures that related data are stored as a unit, increasing retrieval speed.*

✗ *Get antivirus software and run it frequently. Don't install and run any software someone gives you on a disk until you run a virus check on the disk and its contents. If someone gives you a document file on a disk, check for macro viruses.*

Some Final Advice

Conducting research before you buy a computer is fairly painless and very powerful. To prepare for buying a computer, peruse newspaper and magazine ads listing computer systems for sale. Another great source is the Web, which makes side-by-side comparison easy. For instance, typing "PC comparison shopping" (including the quotes) into the Google search engine returns more than 15 pages of links. It's also a good idea to visit a comparison site, such as CNET, MySimon, Yahoo!, AOL, or PCWorld. To research particular computer manufacturers (such as Apple, Dell, IBM, Gateway, and so on), simply type the manufacturer's name in the address bar of your Web browser and add the .com extension. Use as many resources as you can, and then remember that no matter how happy or unhappy you are with the result, you'll most likely be doing it all again within 3 years.

Spotlight Exercises

1. Have you considered purchasing a used or refurbished computer? Just as with automobiles, you can purchase a computer from a company or from an individual. What are some of the advantages and disadvantages of purchasing a used or refurbished computer from a company or individual? Visit **buycsn.com**, which offers refurbished systems, and select a specific laptop computer. Identify the computer, its specifications, and its cost. Review this Spotlight and then write a short paper that shows that you understand at least six key terms from the chapter as they apply to purchasing a used computer.

2. Create a table in a word processor or use a spreadsheet program to replicate Figure 6K. Save your file without filling in the blank fields. Research the purchase of a new laptop computer and determine the specifications of at least three different models or manufacturers. Fill in the details in your checklist, creating a new file for each computer. Write a cover sheet that includes a paragraph that explains why you would purchase one system over the others. Use key terms from the chapter to support your argument.

3. Use your favorite browser to go to **www.dealtime.com/xPP-Monitors**. Locate and compare two 17-inch monitors—one CRT monitor and one flat-panel type. Use key terms from the Monitors and Video Cards section of this Spotlight as a basis for comparing the two. Write a paper that includes a table that compares the monitors on at least four points and that explains why you would purchase one monitor type over the other.

4. Research comparable notebook and desktop computers. Your task is to make an argument as to why one would suit your needs better than the other. Consider such things as cost, speed, output quality (monitor size), flexibility, connectivity, and reliability. You may even wish to use the checklist in Figure 6K as a guide. Write a paper that explains why you would be more likely to purchase either a notebook or a desktop.

5. Compare online shopping with in-store shopping. Pick any online computer sales vendor and build a system of your choice. Write down or print out the details and specifications of the computer you've built, including the price with shipping. Visit a store that sells computers, such as Wal-Mart, Best Buy, Circuit City, or a local shop, duplicating what you accomplished online. (If you do not have a computer store in your area, use newspaper or magazine advertisements). Write at least two paragraphs about each experience. Which did you prefer? What are the advantages and disadvantages of each? Would you rather buy online or in person? Why?

6. Use the Start, All Programs, Accessories, System Tools menu sequence to access the System Information utility. Write a short paper that includes a table with the values for the following components: the operating system, processor, total physical memory, available physical memory, total virtual memory, and available virtual memory. Using what you learned in the sections on processing, memory, and RAM, is your system current with today's standards? Should you upgrade your computer? Why or why not?

What You'll Learn . . .

- Explain the purpose of the special keys on the keyboard and list the most frequently used pointing devices.

- List the types of monitors and the characteristics that determine a monitor's quality.

- Identify the two major types of printers and indicate the advantages and disadvantages of each.

- Distinguish between memory and storage.

- Discuss how storage media and devices are categorized.

- List factors that affect hard disk performance.

- Explain how data is stored on hard disks and floppy disks.

- List and compare the various optical storage media and devices available for personal computers.

Input/Output and Storage

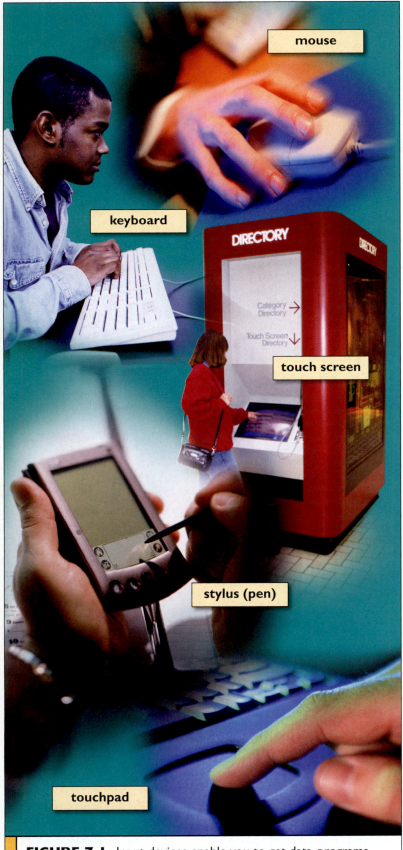

mouse

keyboard

DIRECTORY

touch screen

stylus (pen)

touchpad

FIGURE 7.1 Input devices enable you to get data, programs, commands, and responses into the computer's memory.

Now that you've learned about hardware and software, let's take a look at the practical impact of inputting data and commands, receiving audio and visual output, and storing your work. When using a computer, your attention is focused on the input and output devices, typically a keyboard, a mouse, and a monitor. Input devices enable you to direct the computer's activity. Output devices transform processed digital information into forms that make sense to humans. They put our senses in contact with processed data, engaging our eyes, our ears, and even our sense of touch. Finally, storage devices provide nonvolatile (permanent) storage for the programs and data you work with.

In this chapter, you'll learn about input devices, output devices, the importance of storage, and the types of devices used to store your data.

Input Devices: Giving Commands

As you learned in Chapter 1, **input** refers to any data or instructions that you enter into the computer. This section discusses **input devices**, the hardware components that enable you to get data and instructions into the computer's memory (Figure 7.1).

KEYBOARDS

Despite all of the high-tech input devices on the market, the keyboard is still the best way to get data into the computer. A **keyboard** is an input device that provides a set of alphabetic, numeric, punctuation, symbolic, and control keys.

How do keyboards work? When you press a key, the keyboard sends a digital impulse through a cable (usually a USB cable) to the computer. When the computer receives the impulse, it displays a character, such as a letter, number, punctuation mark, or symbol, on the screen. The character appears at the on-screen location of the

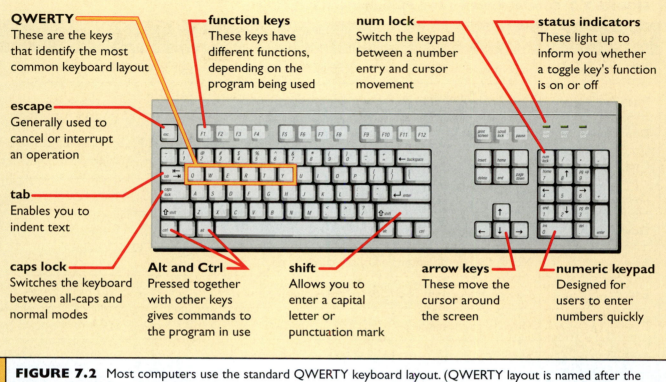

QWERTY
These are the keys that identify the most common keyboard layout

escape
Generally used to cancel or interrupt an operation

tab
Enables you to indent text

caps lock
Switches the keyboard between all-caps and normal modes

function keys
These keys have different functions, depending on the program being used

Alt and Ctrl
Pressed together with other keys gives commands to the program in use

num lock
Switch the keypad between a number entry and cursor movement

shift
Allows you to enter a capital letter or punctuation mark

status indicators
These light up to inform you whether a toggle key's function is on or off

arrow keys
These move the cursor around the screen

numeric keypad
Designed for users to enter numbers quickly

FIGURE 7.2 Most computers use the standard QWERTY keyboard layout. (QWERTY layout is named after the first six letters at the upper left of the letter area.) This enhanced QWERTY keyboard also includes a number of special keys and a numeric keypad.

cursor (also called the **insertion point**), which shows where text will appear when you type. The cursor may be a blinking vertical line, a blinking underscore, or a highlighted box.

Using a Keyboard
All keyboards include keys that enable you to type letters, punctuation marks, and numbers. The keyboard has an assortment of other special keys that enable you to backspace over or delete characters, use a 10-key number pad, navigate software programs, and give commands to the operating system. Desktop PCs typically come equipped with an enhanced keyboard, which has 101 keys (Figures 7.2 and 7.3). The Macintosh equivalent, called the *extended keyboard*, has almost the exact same key layout.

Let's look at some of the special keys on the keyboard. If you don't want to type where the cursor is located, you can use the mouse or **cursor-movement keys** (also called **arrow keys**) to move the cursor around.

A **toggle key** is a key named after a type of electrical switch that has only two positions: on and off. For example, the Caps Lock key functions as a toggle key. It switches the Caps Lock mode on and off. When the Caps Lock mode is engaged, you do not have to press the Shift key to enter capital letters. To turn off the Caps Lock mode, just press the Caps Lock key again.

Above the letters and numbers on the keyboard, you'll find **function keys** (labeled F1 through F10 or F15), which are used to provide different commands, depending on the program in use. Near the function keys, you'll also notice the Esc key, which is short for Escape. The Esc key's function also depends on which program you're using, but it's generally used to interrupt or cancel an operation.

Some keys have no effect unless you hold them down and press a second key. These are called **modifier keys**, because they modify the meaning of the next key you press. You'll use modifier keys for keyboard shortcuts, which provide quick keyboard access to menu commands.

Destinations

For a list of keyboard shortcuts for many Microsoft products, see Microsoft's "Keyboard Assistance" at **www.microsoft .com/enable/ products/ keyboardassist .aspx**. Macintosh shortcuts can be found at **docs.info.apple .com/article.html? artnum=75459**

FIGURE 7.3 **Special Keys on the PC Enhanced Keyboard**

Key Name	Typical Function
Alt	In combination with another key, enters a command (example: Alt + X = cut).
Backspace	Deletes the character to the left of the cursor.
Caps Lock	Toggles Caps Lock mode on or off.
Ctrl	In combination with another key, enters a command (example: Ctrl + C = copy).
Delete	Deletes the character to the right of the cursor.
Down arrow	Moves the cursor down.
End	Moves the cursor to the end of the current line.
Esc	Cancels the current operation or closes a dialog box.
F1	Displays on-screen help.
Home	Moves the cursor to the beginning of the current line.
Insert	Toggles between insert and overwrite mode, if these modes are available in the program you're using.
Left arrow	Moves the cursor to the left.
Num Lock	Toggles the numeric keypad's Num Lock mode so that you can use the keypad to enter numbers.
Page Down	Moves down one full screen or one page.
Page Up	Moves up one full screen or one page.
Pause/Break	Suspends a program. (This key is not used by most applications.)
Popup menu key	Displays the popup menu for the current context (Windows only).
Print Screen	Captures the screen image to a graphics file or prints the current screen on the printer.
Right arrow	Moves the cursor to the right.
Up arrow	Moves the cursor up.
Windows key	Displays the Start menu in Microsoft Windows.

Using Alternative Keyboards

Although most desktop computers come equipped with a keyboard that is connected by a keyboard cable, some computers are equipped with an infrared port that enables them to use a wireless keyboard (also called a cordless keyboard). These keyboards use infrared or radio waves to send signals to the computer.

Popular among handheld computer users are portable keyboards, which are small folding keyboards that can be connected to a handheld computer. Portable keyboards enable you to type just as you

FIGURE 7.4 Portable keyboards are popular among handheld users because they enable users to type information quickly and easily.

would when using a standard keyboard with a desktop computer (Figure 7.4).

Now that we've discussed the basics of using keyboards, let's move on to another piece of equipment commonly used for input: pointing devices.

THE MOUSE AND OTHER POINTING DEVICES

A **pointing device** gives you control over the movements of the on-screen pointer. The **pointer** is an on-screen symbol that signifies the type of command, input, or response you can give. Pointing devices such as a mouse also enable you to initiate actions, such as clicking, double-clicking, selecting, and dragging. By these actions, you can give commands and responses to whatever program the computer is running. Pointing devices can also be used to provide input. For example, pointing devices can be used in graphics programs to draw and paint on the screen, just as if you were using a pencil or brush (Figure 7.5).

The most widely used pointing device is the mouse, which is a standard piece of equipment with today's computer systems. As you probably know, a **mouse** is a palm-sized pointing device that is designed to move about on a clean, flat surface called a **mouse pad**. As you move the mouse, its movements are mirrored by the on-screen pointer. You can initiate actions by using the button (or buttons) on the mouse.

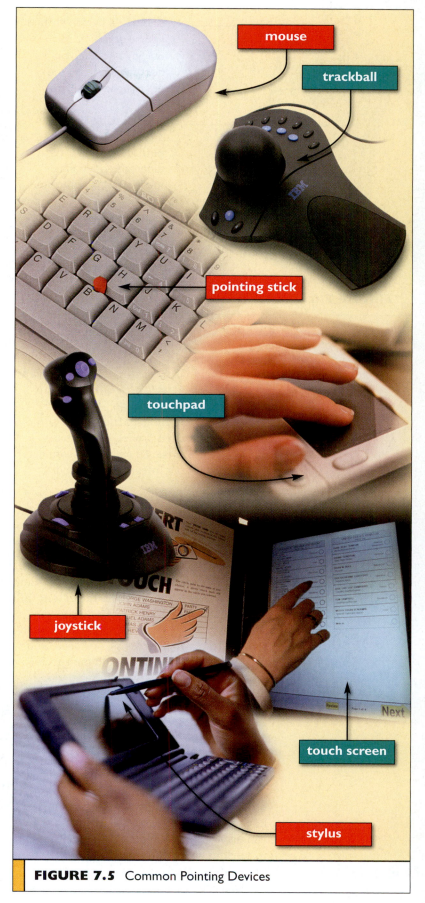

FIGURE 7.5 Common Pointing Devices

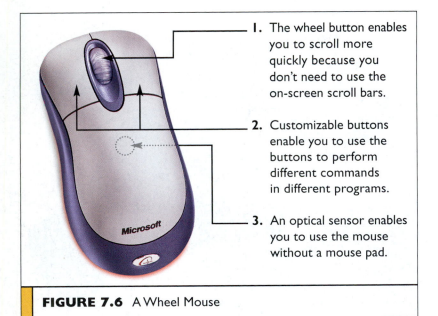

1. The wheel button enables you to scroll more quickly because you don't need to use the on-screen scroll bars.

2. Customizable buttons enable you to use the buttons to perform different commands in different programs.

3. An optical sensor enables you to use the mouse without a mouse pad.

FIGURE 7.6 A Wheel Mouse

Developed by Microsoft, the **wheel mouse** includes a rotating wheel that can be used to scroll text vertically within a document or on Web page (Figure 7.6). Another type of mouse, the cordless mouse (also called a wireless mouse), uses invisible infrared signals to connect to the computer's infrared (IrDA) port.

Mouse Alternatives

Although the mouse is by far the most popular pointing device, some people prefer alternative devices, such as trackballs, pointing sticks, or touch pads. These alternatives are especially attractive when desktop space is limited or nonexistent (as is often the case when using a notebook computer). Additional input devices, such as joysticks, touch screens, styluses, and light pens, are also available for special purposes, such as playing games, using ATMs, and managing PDAs.

A **trackball** is basically a mouse flipped on its back. Instead of moving the mouse, you move the rotating ball. Trackballs usually come with one or more buttons that work in the same way as mouse buttons.

A **pointing stick** is a small, stubby nub that protrudes from the computer's keyboard. Pointing sticks are pressure sensitive; You use the stick by pushing it in various directions with your finger. Separate buttons initiate clicking and dragging motions in conjunction with the pointing stick.

Many notebook computers use a touch pad for a pointing device. A **touch pad** (also called a **trackpad**) is a pressure-sensitive device that responds to your finger's movement over the pad's surface.

A **joystick** is an input device with a large vertical lever that can be moved in any direction. Although you can use joysticks as pointing devices, they're most often used to control the motion of an on-screen object in a computer game or training simulator.

A **touch screen** is a pressure-sensitive panel that detects where a user has tapped the display screen with a fingertip. Because touch screens are reliable, easy to use, and virtually impossible to steal, they are often used in kiosks. A **kiosk** is a booth that provides a computer service of some type, such as an ATM. Though most frequently seen in banks, touch-screen kiosks are also used to provide information to tourists and generate e-tickets at airport terminals.

Because human fingers are much bigger than an on-screen pointer, software designers must provide fewer options and larger on-screen buttons on touch screens. These characteristics of touch screens make them best suited to simple, special-purpose programs. For more detailed work, light pens can be used. **Light pens** contain a light source that triggers the touch screen's detection mechanism (Figure 7.7).

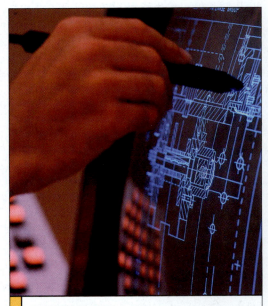

FIGURE 7.7 Light pens provide a way to get input into a touch-screen system.

One example of pen computing is using a light pen to sign your name electronically when making a credit card purchase. This branch of computing involves light pens as well as styluses and PDAs.

A **stylus**, which looks like an ordinary pen except that the tip is dry and semiblunt, is commonly used with PDAs. Styluses also are often used in CAD applications and other graphics applications that have a graphics tablet, a digitizing tablet consisting of a grid on which users design objects such as cars, buildings, medical devices, and robots.

ALTERNATIVE INPUT DEVICES

Though keyboards and pointing devices are most commonly used to input data, a number of specialized input devices also are available. This section introduces some of these alternative input devices and their uses.

Speech recognition, also called **voice recognition**, is a type of input in which the computer recognizes spoken words. To accept speech, a computer must have a microphone. A **microphone** is an input device that converts sound input into electrical signals that the computer can process. Computers must also be equipped with sound cards to accept sound input from a microphone. A sound card is an expansion board designed to record and play back sound files. (Sound is built into Macintosh computers.)

IBM's Via Voice and Dragon's Naturally Speaking are just two of the many computer-dictation software products available. Microsoft's new XP operating system also enables you to use speech recognition with any document. Office XP and 2003 come with two modes of operation: dictation, for dictating letters and e-mail messages, and voice command, for accessing menus and commands by speaking into a microphone.

To use speech-recognition software, you first have to "train" the software to understand how you speak and how to translate this speech into typed words. You do this by dictating a number of prepared passages into the computer through a microphone so that the software can "learn" how you speak—your accent, enunciation, and pronunciation. The more you train the software,

FIGURE 7.8 Speech-recognition technology enables users to issue commands and enter text.

the better it becomes at correctly recognizing your words. If the computer doesn't know which word you have spoken (for example, if it hears "to" but isn't sure if it's "to," "too," or "two"), it will figure out which word is correct based on the context in which it is found.

Early speech-recognition systems used discrete speech recognition—you had to speak each word separately. In contrast, today's continuous speech-recognition software enables users to speak without pausing between words.

Although many people use speech-recognition as a simple dictation device, speech-recognition software not only improves productivity, relieving tired and overused hands, but it also provides an alternative input option for people who are not able to use a keyboard (Figure 7.8).

Scanners copy anything that's printed on a sheet of paper, including artwork, handwriting, printed documents, and typed documents. Most scanners use **optical character recognition** (**OCR**) software that automatically converts the scanned text into a text file. This technology has improved so much that most printed or typed documents can be scanned into text files, eliminating the need to retype such documents to get them into the computer.

Destinations

For the latest on speech recognition technology, including reviews of the latest software, visit "21st Century Eloquence" at **www.voice recognition.com**

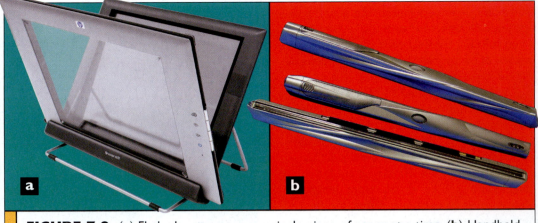

a

b

FIGURE 7.9 (**a**) Flatbed scanners scan a single piece of paper at a time. (**b**) Handheld scanners are more portable and flexible and are often used to scan text and small photos into a microcomputer.

Flatbed scanners work on a single sheet of paper at a time (Figure 7.9a). Sheet-fed scanners draw in the sheets to be copied by a roller mechanism. Handheld scanners can be used to copy text and small photographs (Figure 7.9b).

One of the earliest scanning systems was developed by the banking industry in the 1950s for processing checks. The **magnetic-ink character recognition (MICR) system** encodes the bank, branch, account number, and check number on each check. After the customer has used a check, the bank has to enter manually only the amount of the check.

In many retail and grocery stores, employees use a **bar code reader**, a handheld or desktop-mounted scanning device that reads an item's universal product code (UPC). The UPC is a pattern of bars printed on merchandise that the store's computer system uses to retrieve information about an item and its price. Today, bar codes are used to update inventory and ensure correct pricing. For example, FedEx uses a bar code system to identify and track packages.

In class, every time you take a test on a Scantron form, you're creating input suitable for an optical mark reader. An **optical mark reader (OMR)** is a scanning device that senses the magnetized marks from your #2 pencil to determine which responses are marked. Almost any type of questionnaire can be designed for OMR devices, making it helpful to researchers who need to tabulate responses to large surveys.

Now that we know how to get our data into a computer system, let's look at how those data are presented back to us with output devices.

Output Devices: Engaging Our Senses

Output devices enable people to see, hear, and even feel the results of processing operations. The most widely used output devices are monitors and printers.

MONITORS

Monitors (also called **displays**) display output. The on-screen display enables you to see your processed data. It's important to remember that the screen display isn't a permanent record. To drive home this point, screen output is sometimes called *soft copy*, as opposed to *hard copy* (printed output). To make permanent copies of your work, you should save it to a storage device or print it.

The large monitors that look like television screens connected to desktop computers are **cathode-ray tube (CRT) monitors** (Figure 7.10). In a CRT monitor, three light "guns" (corresponding to the colors red, green, and blue) are combined in varying intensities to produce on-screen colors.

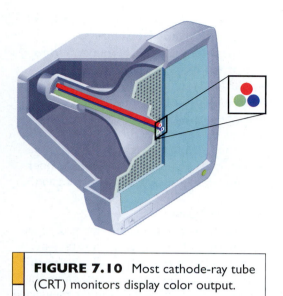

FIGURE 7.10 Most cathode-ray tube (CRT) monitors display color output.

FIGURE 7.11 Samsung Wiseview™ monitors use TFT-LCD technology and are considered to be among the most advanced monitors on the market today.

The thinner monitors used with notebooks and newer desktop computers are known as **liquid crystal displays** (**LCDs**) or **flat-panel displays**. The least expensive LCDs are called passive-matrix LCDs (also called dual scans). These monitors may generate image flaws, such as an unwanted shadow next to a column of color, and they are too slow for full-motion video. Thin Film Transistor (TFT) LCDs, also known as active-matrix LCDs, use transistors to control the color of each on-screen pixel (Figure 7.11).

Other flat-panel display technologies include gas-plasma displays and field-emission displays (FEDs). An intriguing new technology, FEDs look like LCDs, except that a tiny CRT produces each on-screen pixel.

LCD monitors are ideal for portable computers, including notebooks, PDAs, and Web-enabled devices, such as digital cellular telephones (Figure 7.12).

Screen Size

Monitors are also categorized by their size. For CRTs, the **quoted size** is the size of the CRT's front surface measured diagonally.

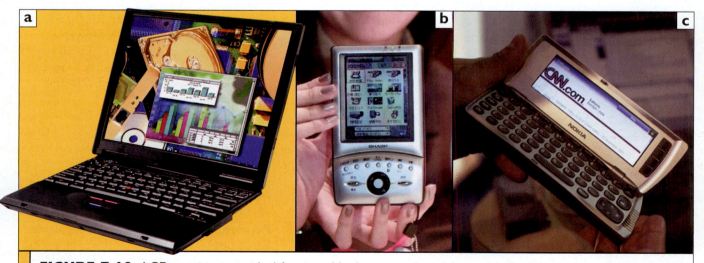

FIGURE 7.12 LCD monitors are ideal for portable devices such as (**a**) notebooks, (**b**) Web-enabled devices, and (**c**) PDAs.

FIGURE 7.13 Quoted Monitor Size and Actual Viewable Area

Monitor Size	Viewable Area
21 inches	20 inches
19 inches	17 inches
17 inches	16 inches
15 inches	14 inches

But some of this surface is hidden by the monitor's casing and unavailable for display purposes. For this reason, it's important to distinguish between the monitor's quoted size and its **viewable area**, the area available for viewing. Figure 7.13 shows typical relationships between quoted size and viewable area. Vendors now disclose both sizes, thanks to a consumer lawsuit.

How big should your monitor be? Increasingly, 17-inch monitors are considered standard. For desktop publishing and other applications that require full-page displays, 21-inch monitors are preferred. An alternative to a 21-inch display is a type of 17-inch display that can rotate to a vertical position and display a full page.

Resolution

The term **resolution** generally refers to the sharpness of an image. Video adapters conform to standard resolutions that are expressed by the number of dots (pixels) that can be displayed horizontally, followed by an "x" and the number of lines that can be displayed vertically (for example, 1024 x 768). Figure 7.14 lists common PC monitor resolutions.

For color graphics displays, **Video Graphics Array** (**VGA**) is the lowest-resolution standard (640 x 480). Most of today's monitors are equipped with at least **Super VGA** (1,024 x 768). The newest models sport Super and Ultra eXtended Graphics Array video adapters—allowing for an amazing 1,600 pixels per line and 1,200 lines of pixels per screen!

Refresh Rate

Another important measurement of video adapter quality is the refresh rate generated at a given resolution. The **refresh rate** refers to the frequency at which the screen image is updated, and it's measured in hertz (Hz) or cycles per second. Below 60 Hz, most people notice an annoying, eye-straining flicker. Very few people notice flicker when the refresh rate exceeds 72 Hz.

Televisions as Monitors

Using TVs for computer output is certain to become more common once High Definition Television comes into widespread use. **High Definition Television** (**HDTV**) is the name given to several standards for digital television displays. Although all HDTV devices support higher resolutions than today's nondigital standards, the technology has been slow to develop because of its high cost and the lack of international agreement regarding standards. It is just beginning to be available in major cities and will someday be the standard for all televisions and broadcast media. HDTV provides extremely high-quality video and audio representation due to its ability to carry so much information (11 Mbps) to the television receiver.

Now that we've discussed monitors and soft copy, let's move on to devices that produce hard-copy output: printers.

PRINTERS

Printers produce a permanent version or *hard copy* of the output on the computer's display screen. Some of the most popular printers are inkjet printers and laser printers (Figure 7.15).

FIGURE 7.14 Common PC Monitor Resolutions

640 x 480	VGA	Video Graphics Array
800 x 600	XGA	eXtended Graphics Array
1,024 x 768	SVGA	Super Video Graphics Array
1,280 x 1,024	SXGA	Super eXtended Graphics Array
1,600 x 1,200	UXGA	Ultra eXtended Graphics Array

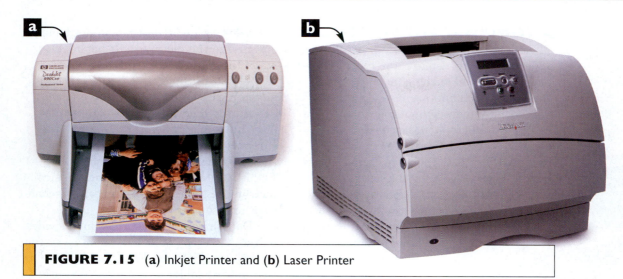

FIGURE 7.15 (a) Inkjet Printer and (b) Laser Printer

Inkjet printers (also called **bubble-jet printers**) are the least expensive and produce excellent color output, which makes them popular choices for home users. Inkjet printers form an image that is composed of tiny dots. The printout is difficult to distinguish from the fully formed characters printed by laser printers. Inkjet printers are relatively slow compared with laser printers, and per-page printing costs can be high due to the high cost of ink cartridges.

A **laser printer** is a high-resolution printer that uses a similar version of the electrostatic reproductive technology as copy machines. Under the printer's computerized control, a laser beam creates electrical charges on a rotating print drum. These charges attract toner, which is transferred to the paper and fused to its surface by a heat process. Laser printers print faster than inkjets; some laser printers can crank out 60 or more pages per minute. Although they are initially more expensive than inkjet printers, laser printers generally have lower per-page printing costs.

Dot-matrix printers, which were once the most popular type of printer, are declining in use. Some line printers can crank out hard copy at a rate of 3,000 lines per minute. Although their print quality is below that of inkjet and laser printers, these printers are mainly used for printing backup copies of large amounts of data.

The best color printers are **thermal-transfer printers**, which use a heat process to transfer colored dyes or inks to the paper's surface. The best thermal-transfer printers are called dye sublimation printers. These printers are slow and expensive, but they produce results that are difficult to distinguish from high-quality color photographs. Less expensive are snapshot printers, which are thermal-transfer printers that print the output of digital cameras.

A **plotter** is a printer that produces high-quality images by physically moving ink pens over the surface of the paper. A continuous-curve plotter draws maps from stored data (Figure 7.16). Computer-generated maps, such as those used by cartographers and weather analysts, can be retrieved and plotted or used to show changes over time.

FIGURE 7.16 Large printing devices such as plotters are indispensable for creating computer-generated maps, charts, and architectural plans.

ALTERNATIVE OUTPUT DEVICES

Speakers are needed to listen to computer-generated sound such as music and synthesized speech and are now standard equipment on new computer systems. Like microphones, speakers also require a sound card to function. Sound cards play the contents of digitized recordings, such as music recorded in WAV and MP3 sound file formats. Some sound cards do this job better than others. Quality enters into the picture most noticeably when the sound card reproduces MIDI files. MIDI files play over **synthesizers**, electronic devices that produce music by generating musical tones. Sound cards have built-in synthesizers. Better sound cards use wavetable synthesis, whereby the sound card generates sounds using ROM-based recordings of actual musical instruments. The latest sound cards include surround-sound effects.

Data projectors take a computer's video output and project this output onto a screen for an audience to see. For example, an **LCD projector** enables a presenter to project the computer's screen display onto a screen similar to the one used with a slide projector, making it ideal for presentations to small audiences. In contrast, the latest technology, **digital light-processing** (**DLP**) **projectors**, employs millions of microscopic mirrors embedded in a microchip to produce a bright, sharp image. This image is visible even in a brightly lit room, and it is sharp enough for very large screens, such as those found at rock concerts and large auditoriums. Because of the complexity of these projectors, they are often very expensive and built directly into an arena or auditorium.

As you learned in Chapter 3, computers equipped with a fax modem and fax software can receive incoming faxes. The incoming document is displayed on the screen, and it can be printed or saved.

Computers can also send faxes as output. To send a fax with the computer, you must save your document using a special format that is compatible with the fax program. The fax program can then send the document through the telephone system to a distant fax machine. This output function is helpful because you don't have to print the document to send it as a fax (Figure 7.17).

Multifunction devices combine inkjet or laser printers with a scanner, a fax machine, and a copier, enabling home office users to obtain all of these devices without spending a great deal of money (Figure 7.18).

Now that you've learned about a variety of output devices, let's look at how you can store data for later use.

FIGURE 7.17 (**a**) The ViewSonic PJ250 is a powerful portable digital light-processing projector. (**b**) A fax machine performs both input and output.

FIGURE 7.18 A multifunction device combines an inkjet or laser printer with a scanner, a fax machine, and a copier.

Wearables:
The Fashion of Technology

After getting dressed in the morning, you head down the street in your "wearables." As you walk to the library, you use your wrist pad to e-mail a friend, asking her to meet you for lunch later. At the library, the network automatically recognizes you by your ring. You search your pocket for your stylus, find it, point at a library computer screen, and the computer acknowledges you. You use your monocle to access your documents. You open one and jot notes by waving your pen in the air. As you leave the library, you call three of your friends and visually chat together through your monocle and earpiece until your next class. Your wearables seamlessly connect you to a network throughout your day.

Sound intriguing but unbelievable? Some of these technologies already exist. Xybernaut makes wearable computers equipped with Optimus software to link firefighters and other emergency workers by voice and video to each other, to their supervisors, and to local hospitals. Users wear a light, portable CPU (on a belt or in a vest) and either tap a wrist-mounted keyboard or give voice commands through the microphone on the head-mounted display screen. Not only can they check for information over the Internet, they can send or receive e-mails and access applications and files on the server.

Most wearable technologies have been incorporated into headsets and glasses, backpacks and fanny packs, rings and wristbands, and multipocketed pants (Figure 7.19). Now wearables with even more possibilities are on the way. "Smart thread" fiber, similar to nylon, conducts electricity and can be woven into clothing with computer-like abilities to connect soldiers or emergency workers with command centers. "Smart skin" material, studded with microsensors, can be made into gloves or suits that send a signal when industrial workers or astronauts are exposed to toxic chemicals.

If you don't need all the functions of wearables, you might get "chipped" by having a microchip implanted in your arm. Already, members of exclusive European beach clubs are getting chipped to enter the VIP lounge or pay for a drink simply by waving to the electronic receiver. Will getting "chipped" catch on as the next high-tech fashion with function?

FIGURE 7.19 Most wearable technologies have been incorporated into headsets and glasses, backpacks and fanny packs, rings and wristbands, and multipocketed pants.

Storage: Holding Data for Future Use

Storage (also called **mass storage** or **auxiliary storage**) refers to the various ways a computer system can store software and data. Computer storage can be divided into two major categories. **Storage media** include hard disks, floppy disks, Zip disks, CDs, and DVDs that run on storage devices. A **storage device** is computer hardware that is capable of retaining data even when electrical power is switched off. In other words, storage devices are the various drives (hard drive, floppy drive, Zip drive, and so on) that enable the disks to operate.

Organizations are increasingly turning to computer storage systems to store all of their computer software, data, and information. The reason? Storing information on paper is expensive and offers no opportunity for electronic manipulation and sharing. As you'll learn in this section, a simple storage device can store the same amount of information for less than $10 per gigabyte that would cost $10,000 to store on paper. In fact, storage devices are increasing in capacity to the point that they can hold an entire library's worth of information. Read on to learn why storage is necessary, what kinds of storage devices and media are out there, and which will best fit your computing needs.

MEMORY VERSUS STORAGE

To understand the distinction between memory and storage, think of the last time you worked at your desk. In your file drawer, you store all of your personal items and papers, such as your checking account statements. The file drawer is good for long-term storage. When you decide to work on one or more of these items, you take it out of storage and put it on your desk. The desktop is a good place to keep the items you're working with; they're close at hand and available for use right away. Your desktop can be thought of as memory—the place where you temporarily store things that you are working on.

Computers work the same way. When you want to work with the contents of a file, the computer transfers the file to a temporary workplace: the computer's memory. Memory is a form of storage, but it is temporary. Why don't computers just use memory to hold all of those files? Here are some reasons:

- **Storage devices retain data when the current is switched off.** The computer's RAM is **volatile**. This means that when you switch off the computer's power, all of the information in RAM is irretrievably lost. In contrast, storage devices are **nonvolatile**. They do not lose data when the power goes off.

- **Storage devices are cheaper than memory.** RAM operates very quickly to keep up with the computer's CPU. For this reason, RAM is expensive—much more expensive than storage. In fact, most computers are equipped with just enough RAM to accommodate all of the programs a user wants to run at once. In contrast, a computer system's storage devices hold much more data and software than the computer's memory does. Today, you can buy a storage device capable of storing 4 GB of software and data for about the same amount you'll pay for 256 MB of RAM (Figure 7.20).

- **Storage devices play an essential role in system startup operations.** When you start your computer, the BIOS reads essential programs into the computer's RAM, including one that begins loading essential system software from the computer's hard disk.

- **Storage devices are needed for output.** When you've finished working, you use the computer's storage system as an output device to save a file. When you save a file, the computer transfers your work from the computer's memory to a storage device. If you forget to save your work, it will be lost when you switch

FIGURE 7.20 Memory Versus Storage

		Access Speed	Cost per MB	Storage Capacity
Memory	Cache memory	Fastest	Highest	1 MB
	RAM	Fast	High	1 GB
Storage	Hard disk	Medium	Medium	400 GB
	CD-ROM disc	Slow	Low	650 MB

off the computer's power. Remember, the computer's RAM is volatile!

For all of these reasons, demand for storage capacity is soaring. Storage capacity is measured in bytes (KB, MB, GB, and TB). Capacities range from the floppy disk's 1.44 MB to huge room-filling arrays of storage devices capable of storing a dozen or more terabytes of data. To provide this much storage with print-based media, you'd need to cut down several million trees. According to one estimate, the need for digital storage is increasing 60 percent each year, and the pace shows no signs of slowing down.

Now that you understand the importance of storage, let's look at the devices and media used to hold data.

HARD DISK DRIVES

On almost all computers, the hard disk drive is by far the most important storage device. A **hard disk drive** (or simply **hard disk**) is a high-capacity, high-speed storage device that usually consists of several fixed, rapidly rotating disks called **platters**.

The computer's hard disk is also referred to as online storage. **Online storage** (also called **primary storage**) consists of the storage devices that are actively available to the computer system and that do not require any action on the part of the user. Hard disks can also be categorized as random access or magnetic storage devices. A **random access storage device** can go directly to the requested data without having to go

through a linear search sequence. **Magnetic storage devices** use disks that are coated with magnetically sensitive material.

With magnetic storage devices, an electromagnet called a **read/write head** moves across the surface of a disk and records information by transforming electrical impulses into a varying magnetic field. As the magnetic materials pass beneath the read/write head, this varying field forces the particles to rearrange themselves in a meaningful pattern of positive and negative magnetic indicators. This operation is called *writing*. When *reading*, the read/write head senses the recorded pattern and transforms this pattern into electrical impulses.

A hard disk contains two or more vertically stacked platters, each with two read/write heads (one for each side of the disk). The platters spin so rapidly that the read/write head floats on a thin cushion of air, at a distance 300 times smaller than the width of a human hair. To protect the platter's surface, hard disks are enclosed in a sealed container.

How does the read/write head know where to look for data? To answer this question, you need to know a little about how stored data are organized on a disk. Like a vinyl record, disks contain circular bands called **tracks**. Each track is divided into pie-shaped wedges called **sectors**. Two or more sectors combine to form a **cluster** (Figure 7.21).

To keep track of where specific files are located, the computer's operating system records a table of information on the disk. This table contains the name of each file and the file's exact location on the disk.

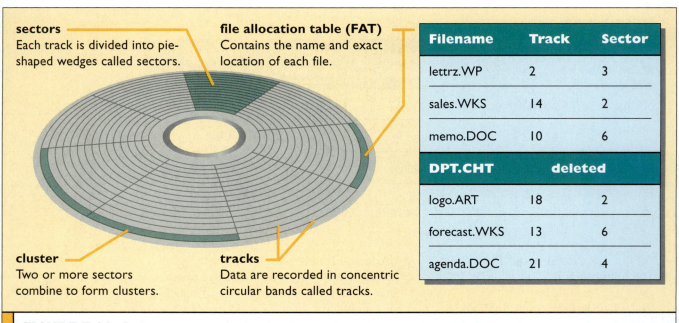

sectors
Each track is divided into pie-shaped wedges called sectors.

file allocation table (FAT)
Contains the name and exact location of each file.

Filename	Track	Sector
lettrz.WP	2	3
sales.WKS	14	2
memo.DOC	10	6
DPT.CHT	**deleted**	
logo.ART	18	2
forecast.WKS	13	6
agenda.DOC	21	4

cluster
Two or more sectors combine to form clusters.

tracks
Data are recorded in concentric circular bands called tracks.

FIGURE 7.21 Disks contain circular bands called tracks, which are divided into sectors. Two or more sectors combine to form a cluster.

On Microsoft Windows systems, this table is called the **file allocation table**, or **FAT**.

Hard disks can be divided into partitions. A **partition** is a section of a disk set aside as if it were a physically separate disk. Partitions are often used to enable computers to work with more than one operating system. For example, Linux users often create one partition for Linux and another for Microsoft Windows. In this way, they can work with programs developed for either operating system.

To communicate with the CPU, hard disks require a hard disk controller. A **hard disk controller** is an electronic circuit board that provides an interface between the CPU and the hard disk's electronics. The controller may be located on the computer's motherboard, on an expansion card, or within the hard disk.

Removable Hard Disks

Most hard disks are fixed; that is, they cannot be removed. However, **removable hard disks** enclose the platters within a cartridge that can be inserted into or removed from a drive bay. Removable hard disks are referred to as near-online storage. **Near-online storage**, also called **secondary storage**, consists of storage that isn't directly available but that can be easily made available by some simple action on the user's part, such as inserting a disk. The popularity and survival of near-online storage devices will depend on their cost and versatility.

Internet Hard Drives

An **Internet hard drive** is storage space on a server that is accessible from the Internet. In most cases, a computer user subscribes to the storage service and agrees to rent a block of storage space for a specific period of time. Instead of sending e-mail attachments to share with family and friends, you might simply post the files to your Internet hard drive and then allow them to be viewed or retrieved by others. You might save backup copies of critical files or all the data on your hard disk to your Internet hard drive.

The key advantage of this type of remote storage is the ability to access data from multiple locations. You can access your files from any device that can connect with the Internet, so everything you store on the site is available to you at any time. Some disadvantages are that your data may not be secure; the storage device might become corrupt, causing you to lose your data; and the company offering the Internet storage may go out of business.

Factors Affecting
Hard Disk Performance

If a hard disk develops a defect or a read/write head encounters an obstacle, such as a dust or smoke particle, the head bounces on the disk surface, preventing the computer from reading or writing data to one or more sectors of the disk. Hard disks can absorb minor jostling without suffering damage, but a major jolt—such as one caused by dropping the computer while the drive is running—could cause a head crash to occur. Head crashes are one of the causes of **bad sectors**—areas of the disk that have become damaged and that can no longer reliably hold data. If you see an on-screen message indicating that a disk has a bad sector, try to copy the data off the disk and don't use it to store new data.

A storage device's most important performance characteristic is the speed at which it retrieves desired data. The amount of time it takes for the device to begin reading data is its **access time**. For disk drives, the access time includes the **seek time**, the time it takes the read/write head to locate the data before reading begins. **Positioning performance** refers to how quickly the drive positions the read/write head to begin transferring data and is measured by seek time.

Transfer performance refers to how quickly the disk transfers data from the disk to memory. One way disk manufacturers improve transfer performance is to increase the speed at which the disk spins, which makes data available more quickly to the read/write heads. Another way is to improve the spacing of data on the disk so that the heads can retrieve several blocks of data on each revolution.

Another way to improve hard disk performance is with a type of cache memory called disk cache (Figure 7.22). A **disk cache** is a type of RAM that stores the program instructions and data you are working with. When the CPU needs to get information, it looks in the disk cache first. If it doesn't find the information it needs, it retrieves the information from the hard disk.

Although hard disks are currently the most important storage media, the disks explored in the next section are examples of portable storage, which means that you can remove a disk from one computer and insert it into another.

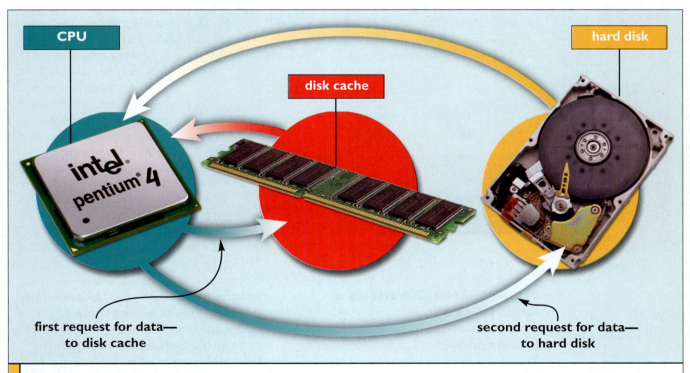

FIGURE 7.22 Disk cache, a type of RAM, dramatically improves hard disk performance. When the CPU needs to get information, it looks in the disk cache first.

IMPACTS

Milestones

The Drive Toward Smarter Cars

Cars are getting smarter all the time, thanks to computer technology. And the auto industry is just beginning its drive toward smarter cars. The OnStar system, installed in some General Motors cars, can give you verbal directions and display maps using GPS navigation software. In an emergency, you can reach an OnStar representative by pressing a cell phone button on the dashboard. If you accidentally lock yourself out, OnStar can remotely unlock the car doors. Can't find your car in a vast parking lot? OnStar can flash the headlights or sound the horn to show you the way. And if your car is stolen, OnStar can track its location for police.

Smarter cars are on the way that will alert you about a possible front or rear collision, monitor your health, offer real-time weather and traffic updates, and keep your car at a safe distance from others. Ford is testing a voice-activated computer system that will announce instructions to bypass traffic jams and flash safety alerts on the dashboard display. Also in testing are night-vision displays projected on the windshield to help you see ahead on dark roads and digital adaptive headlights that aim the beams into a turn when you steer around a corner.

Not too far in the future, you may insert a smart card into your car's dashboard to automatically move the driver's seat to your preferred position, set the interior temperature, or download digital music files for your listening pleasure. Your car's computer will read the car's maintenance history on the smart card and let you know when repairs are needed. The smart card will store your address book and transfer numbers to your cell phone to place calls quickly via voice activation. The goal is to make your driving experience safer and easier, but will you need another driver's education class to master all this new technology? Steer your Web browser to **www.delphi.com/products/auto/safety/** to find out more about advanced safety systems (Figure 7.23).

FIGURE 7.23 With the industry's most extensive portfolio of safety products and an in-depth understanding of vehicle systems integration, Delphi is revolutionizing onboard vehicle safety.

FLOPPY AND ZIP DISKS AND DRIVES

Like removable hard disks, floppy and Zip disks are forms of near-online, or secondary, storage. A **floppy disk** (also called a **diskette**) is a portable storage medium that contains a circular plastic disk coated with a magnetically sensitive film, the same material that's on a cassette tape. A **floppy disk drive** is a device that enables a computer to read and write data to floppy disks. In desktop computer systems, a floppy disk drive is internal or mounted in one of the system unit's drive bays. In laptops, the floppy drive is sometimes external, plugging into the system's case (Figure 7.24).

FIGURE 7.24 (**a**) A Floppy Disk Drive and (**b**) an External Floppy Disk Drive

Almost all floppy disks used today are of the high-density (HD) type, giving them more storage capacity than their predecessors—up to 1.2 MB for Macintosh disks and up to 1.44 MB for PC disks. However, as computer programs (and users' data files) have grown significantly in size, floppies are becoming less and less useful. For this reason, several companies no longer include a floppy drive with their new systems, but offer alternatives that have much higher storage capacities.

A **Zip disk drive** is almost identical to a floppy disk drive except that it holds the slightly thicker and larger Zip disks. A **Zip disk** is a magnetic portable storage medium capable of storing up to 750 MB of data (Figure 7.25) by data compression. This technique arranges data to take up less disk space when it is stored and then converts the data back to its original arrangement when it is read from the disk. Another disk storage option is Sony's HiFD, a removable storage drive that uses cartridges capable of holding more than 200 MB. HiFD drives have an advantage over Zip drives: They are downwardly compatible with 3.5-inch floppy disks.

Protecting the Data on Your Disks

Because disks are portable media, they are designed to keep your data safe. A sliding metal shutter protects the disk from fingerprints, dust, and dirt. Still, the metal shutter can't protect your disk entirely. The following are a few tips for handling disks:

FIGURE 7.25 Zip disks offer a storage solution that makes it easy for consumers to move, protect, share, and backup information on their computers.

- Don't touch the surface of the disk. Fingerprints can contaminate the disk and cause errors.

- Don't expose disks to magnetic fields (such as those from transformers, desktop telephones, and magnets). Because data are magnetically encoded on the disks, direct exposure to magnetic fields may cause loss of data.

- To avoid contamination, don't eat or drink around disks as crumbs and spillage may damage or destroy the disk.

- To avoid condensation, keep disks in a dry place.

- Don't expose disks to excessive temperatures.

Techtalk

Floppy Disks
Introduced by IBM in the 1970s, floppy disks were originally packaged in 8-inch flexible, or "floppy," enclosures. Even though most of today's floppy disks are packaged in 3.5-inch hard plastic cases, the term *floppy* is still commonly used.

Magneto-Optical (MO) Drives
These storage devices combine two basic technologies: magnetic and optical. In the future, MO discs no larger than today's CD-ROMs will contain up to 100 GB of storage.

FIGURE 7.26 CD-ROM and/or DVD-ROM drives, which run the most popular and least expensive optical discs, come standard on today's personal computers.

CD AND DVD TECHNOLOGIES

Because most software, music, and movies are distributed on CDs and DVDs, CD-ROM and DVD-ROM drives are standard and necessary equipment on today's personal computers. **CD-ROM** (short for **compact disc–read-only memory**) and **DVD-ROM** (**digital video** or **versatile**

disc–read-only memory) are the most popular and least expensive types of optical disc standards. These discs are read-only discs (Figure 7.26), which means that the data recorded upon them are meant to be read many times, but it cannot be changed.

CD-ROM and **DVD-ROM drives** are read-only disk drives that read data encoded on CDs and DVDs and transfer these data to a computer. These drives are referred to as optical storage devices. **Optical storage devices** use tightly focused laser beams to read microscopic patterns of data encoded on the surface of plastic discs (Figure 7.27). Microscopic indentations called **pits** absorb the laser's light in certain areas. The drive's light-sensing device receives no light from these areas, so it sends a signal to the computer that corresponds to a 0 in the computer's binary numbering system. Flat reflective areas called **lands** bounce the light back to a light-sensing device, which sends a signal equivalent to a binary 1.

CD-ROM discs are capable of storing up to 650 MB of data, the equivalent of more than 400 floppy disks. DVD-ROM discs can store up to 17 GB of data— enough for an entire digitized movie. Whereas CD-ROM drives can transfer data at speeds of up to 150 Kbps, DVD-ROM drives can transfer data at even higher speeds (up to 12 Mbps; comparable to the data transfer rates of hard drives). DVD-ROM drives read CD-ROM discs as well as DVD-ROM discs.

CD-R, CD-RW, DVD-R, and DVD+RW Discs and Recorders
Several types of optical read/write media and devices are available. Declining prices have placed read/write CD and DVD technologies within the budget of many computer owners. For this reason, these read/write discs are a popular, cost-effective alternative medium for archival and storage purposes.

CD-R (short for **compact disc-recordable**) is a "write-once" technology. After you've saved data to the disc, you can't erase or write over it. An advantage of CD-Rs is that they aren't expensive; in quantities of 20 or more, they're often available for less than $1.00 per disc. **CD-RW** (short

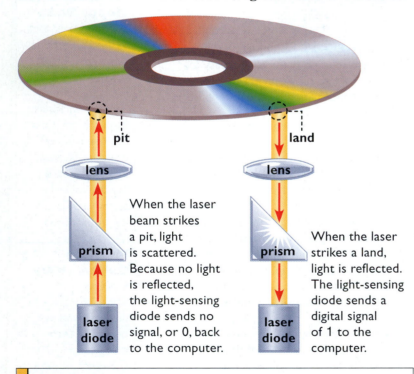

pit   land

lens   lens

prism   When the laser beam strikes a pit, light is scattered. Because no light is reflected, the light-sensing diode sends no signal, or 0, back to the computer.   prism   When the laser strikes a land, light is reflected. The light-sensing diode sends a digital signal of 1 to the computer.

laser diode   laser diode

FIGURE 7.27 In optical storage devices such as CD-ROM and DVD-ROM drives, a tightly focused laser beam reads data encoded on the disc's surface. Some optical devices can write data as well as read it.

for **compact disc-rewritable**), which is more expensive than CD-R, allows data that have been saved to be erased and rewritten. **CD-RW drives**, also known as **burners** or **CD burners**, provide full read/write capabilities.

DVDs come in two standards. The first is the DVD+ (DVD plus) standard. This standard employs two types of discs, DVD+R and the DVD+RW. **DVD+R** is a recordable format that enables the disc to be written to one time and read many times. The **DVD+RW** is a recordable format that can be rewritten many times. This scheme is supported by manufacturers such as Philips, Sony, Hewlett-Packard, Dell, Ricoh, and Yamaha.

The second format is the DVD- (DVD dash) standard. **DVD-R** operates the same way as CD-R; you can write to the disc once and read from it many times. With **DVD-RW**, you can write, erase, and read from the disc many times. This format is supported by manufacturers such as Panasonic, Toshiba, Apple, Hitachi, NEC, Pioneer, Samsung, and Sharp.

A relatively new read/write drive, called **DVD-RAM**, enables computer users to burn DVDs containing up to nearly 5 GB of data. Like most new technologies, a profusion of incompatible formats has made consumers reluctant to embrace DVD-RAM, but it is expected to take off once clear standards emerge.

The future of CD-ROM drives and discs is already marked. In the home entertainment market, the DVD player has decimated the market for CD players. As the technology develops and DVD drives become less and less expensive, the use of CD-ROM drives will decline. In fact, the day will come in the not so distant future when we'll use DVD-read/write drives in the same manner that we once used the ubiquitous floppy disk drive.

Protecting the Data on Your Discs

As with disks, it's important that you handle CDs and DVDs carefully. The following are a few things to remember when caring for discs:

- Do not expose discs to excessive heat or sunlight.

- Do not touch the underside of discs. Hold them by their edges.

- Do not write on the label side of discs with a hard instrument, such as a ballpoint pen.

- To avoid scratches, do not stack discs.

- Store discs in jewel boxes (plastic protective cases) when they are not being used.

STORAGE HORIZONS

In response to the explosive demand for more storage capacity, designers are creating storage media and devices that store larger amounts of data and retrieve it more quickly. Exemplifying these trends are FMD-ROM and solid-state storage devices.

FMD-ROM

Scientists believe that the physics of light limits optical media to a maximum of five gigabits of storage per square inch. However, new optical technologies break this barrier by using discs with more than one layer.

Here's the idea: Each layer on the disc contains data, but the layer is transparent enough to allow a laser beam to shine through. The laser beam focuses on only one layer at a time. If this sounds futuristic, take a look at a DVD-ROM. It contains two layers—which is why DVD-ROMs store so much more data than their single-layer predecessor, the CD-ROM.

On an **FMD-ROM** (short for **fluorescent multilayer disc–read-only memory**) each storage layer is coated with a fluorescent substance. When the laser beam strikes each layer, the light that is bounced back is also fluorescent. This type of light can pass undisturbed through the disc's many layers. Research indicates that FMD-ROMs of up to 100 layers are possible. Although no larger than today's CD-ROM, such discs could each contain up to a terabyte of data.

Initial efforts to bring this technology to market stalled in 2002, but the idea is sound and surely others will try to develop and market this medium. A trillion bytes on a single disc—imagine the possibilities!

Techtalk

Disk or Disc?
If the subject is magnetic media, the correct spelling is *disk*. *Disc* is used to describe optical media.

To learn more about unique USB devices, see the video clip at **www.prenhall.com/cayf2006**

Solid-State Storage Devices

A **solid-state storage device** consists of nonvolatile memory chips, which retain the data stored in them even if the chips are disconnected from a computer or other device. The term *solid state* indicates that these devices have no moving parts; they consist only of semiconductors. Solid-state storage devices have a number of important advantages over mechanical storage devices such as disk drives: They are small, lightweight, highly reliable, and portable. Among the solid-state storage devices in common use are PC cards, flash memory cards, and smart cards.

A **PC card** (also called a **PCMCIA card**) is a credit-card-sized accessory typically used with notebook computers (Figure 7.28). PC cards can serve a variety of functions. For example, some PC cards are modems, others are network adapters, and still others provide additional memory or storage capacity.

When used as storage devices, PC cards are most commonly used to transfer data from one computer to another. (However, each computer must have a PC card slot.) For example, a notebook computer user can store documents created on a business trip on a solid-state memory card and then transfer the documents to a desktop computer.

PC cards follow standards set by the Personal Computer Memory Card

FIGURE 7.28 PC cards are about the size of a credit card and fit into PC card slots, which are standard in most notebooks.

International Association (PCMCIA), a consortium of industry vendors. As a result, a notebook computer equipped with a PC card slot can use PC cards from any PC card vendor.

Increasingly popular are flash memory cards, which use nonvolatile flash memory chips (Figure 7.29). **Flash memory cards** are wafer-thin, highly portable solid-state storage systems that are capable of storing as much as 1 GB of data. Flash memory cards are also used with digital cellular phones, MP3 players, digital video cameras, and other portable digital devices. To use a flash memory card, the device must have a compatible **flash memory reader**—a slot or compartment into which the flash memory card is inserted.

SmartMedia flash memory cards are among the smallest solid-state storage systems available, but their small size and relative simplicity limit their storage capacity (up to 128 MB). Increasingly popular are CompactFlash cards. CompactFlash cards are thicker than SmartMedia cards and they can store up to 1 GB of data.

The Sony Memory Stick is a chewing-gum-sized flash memory card that is currently available in capacities of up to 1 GB. Memory Stick readers are found mainly in Sony-made devices, although a few other manufacturers are beginning to use Sony's technology.

USB key drives or flash memory sticks, also called JumpDrives, pen drives, or flash drives, are up-and-coming players in the portable storage market. They work with both the PC and the Mac, and no device driver is required—just plug the device into a USB port and its ready to read and write. These drive sticks are made of plastic and are shock-proof, moisture-proof, and magnetization-proof (Figure 7.30). Capacities range to more than 2 GB, with a cost of approximately 20 cents per megabyte. They read and write at 1 Mbps. Watch for capacities to go up and prices to come down. Due to their small size and universal ease of use, they may be *the* portable storage device of the future!

A **smart card** is a credit-card-sized device that combines flash memory with a tiny microprocessor, enabling the card to

FIGURE 7.29 Flash memory cards are thin, portable solid-state storage systems.

FIGURE 7.30 USB key drives come in a variety of colors and sizes.

process as well as store information. Smart cards have many applications. For example, tomorrow's credit cards will use smart card technology to provide far more convenience, functionality, and safety than today's credit cards. One smart card will replace the collection of credit cards, club cards, store cards, and travel mileage cards that the average consumer carries around today. By inserting the card into a compatible reader, users will be able to access their account information by a secure Internet connection (Figure 7.31).

Many applications for smart cards already exist, and more are on the way.

Digital cash systems, which are widespread in Europe and Asia, enable users to purchase a prepaid amount of electronically stored money to pay the small amounts required for parking, bridge tolls, transport fares, museum entrance fees, and similar charges.

FIGURE 7.31 Smart card readers enable users to access accounts.

What You've Learned

INPUT/OUTPUT AND STORAGE

- The computer keyboard's special keys include cursor-movement keys (arrow keys and additional keys such as Home and End), the numeric keypad (for entering numerical data), toggle keys (for switching keyboard modes on and off, such as Num Lock and Caps Lock), function keys (defined for different purposes by different applications), modifier keys (such as Ctrl and Alt for use with keyboard shortcuts), and special keys for use with Microsoft Windows. The most frequently used pointing device is the mouse. Other pointing devices include trackballs, pointing sticks, touch pads, joysticks, touch screens, styluses, and light pens.

- The large monitors that look like television screens are cathode-ray tube (CRT) monitors. The thinner monitors used on notebook and newer desktop computers are known as liquid crystal displays (LCDs) or flat-panel displays. Among factors determining a monitor's quality are the quoted size and viewable area (the larger, the better), resolution, and refresh rate (72 Hz or higher).

- Printers use either inkjet or laser technology. Inkjet printers produce excellent quality text and images for a reasonable price. However, they are slow, and ink cartridges may be expensive. Laser printers are faster and produce excellent quality text and graphics, but color models are expensive.

- Memory uses costly, high-speed components to make software and data available to the CPU. Memory must have enough capacity to hold the software and data that are currently in use. RAM is volatile and doesn't retain information when the computer is switched off. In contrast, storage is slower and less costly, but it offers far greater capacity. Storage devices are nonvolatile; they retain information even when the power is switched off. Storage devices play important input and output roles by transferring information into memory and saving and storing your work.

- Storage media and devices can be categorized as read-only or read/write, random access, magnetic or optical, and online (primary) or near online (secondary).

- Factors that affect a hard disk's performance include head crashes, positioning and transfer performance, and disk cache. A head crash can cause bad sectors, areas of the disk that have become damaged and can no longer hold data reliably. Positioning performance refers to how quickly the drive positions the read/write head to begin transferring data. Transfer performance is how quickly the drive sends the information once the head has reached the correct position. Disk cache stores the program instructions and data you are working with, so the CPU doesn't need to access the hard disk itself.

- Disks store data in circular bands called tracks. Each track is divided into pie-shaped wedges called sectors. The sectors are combined into clusters, which provide the basic unit of data storage. To access data on the drive, the read/write head moves to the track that contains the desired data. Hard disks store data in much the same way floppies do, except that the hard disk contains multiple platters.

- CD-ROM and DVD-ROM discs and drives are standard equipment in today's computer systems, largely because most software, music, and movies are now distributed on discs. CD-R, DVD-R, and DVD+R are read-only technologies. CD-R drives can record once; CD-RW, DVD-RW, and DVD+RW drives can be rewritten multiple times. Another read/write medium, DVD-RAM, has been slow to catch on due to standardization squabbles.

Go to **www.prenhall.com/cayf2006** to review this chapter, answer the questions, and complete the exercises.

Key Terms and Concepts

Matching

Match each key term in the left column with the most accurate definition in the right column.

_____ 1. near-online storage

_____ 2. DVD-ROM

_____ 3. Zip disk

_____ 4. touch pad

_____ 5. speech recognition

_____ 6. plotter

_____ 7. flash memory card

_____ 8. seek time

_____ 9. partition

_____ 10. pointing stick

_____ 11. function keys

_____ 12. laser printer

_____ 13. DLP projector

_____ 14. sector

_____ 15. track

a. a wafer-thin, highly portable solid-state storage system that is capable of storing as much as 1 GB of data

b. a pressure-sensitive device that responds to a finger's movement over the pad's surface

c. a small, stubby pointing nub that protrudes from the computer's keyboard

d. storage that is not directly available

e. located above the letters and numbers on the keyboard, these keys are labeled F1 through F10 or F15

f. a circular band on a disk

g. an area on a disk that is a pie-shaped wedge

h. the time it takes the read/write head to locate data before reading or writing begins

i. a nonimpact high-resolution printer that uses a version of the electrostatic reproductive technology of copy machines

j. a section of a disk set aside as if it were a physically separate disk

k. an output device that draws images on paper using pens

l. a type of input in which the computer recognizes spoken words

m. digital video disk–read-only memory

n. projectors that use millions of microscopic mirrors to project an image

o. magnetic portable storage medium capable of storing up to 750 MB of data by data compression

Multiple Choice

Circle the correct choice for each of the following.

1. Which of the following is a popular input device?
   a. synthesizer
   b. monitor
   c. plotter
   d. mouse

2. Which term best describes computer hardware equipment that is capable of retaining data even when the electrical power is switched off?
   a. storage media
   b. storage devices
   c. input devices
   d. output devices

3. Which of the following printers is considered to be the best color printer?
   a. dot-matrix printer
   b. thermal transfer printer
   c. line printer
   d. color laser printer

4. These are microscopic indentations that absorb the laser's light in certain areas of a disc.
   a. lands
   b. clusters
   c. pits
   d. sectors

5. This storage device does *not* use magnetic media for recording information.
   a. CD-ROM drive
   b. Zip drive
   c. hard disk drive
   d. floppy disk drive

6. Which of the following is not included among the computer keyboard's special keys?
   a. toggle keys
   b. cursor-movement keys
   c. optical storage keys
   d. modifier keys

7. This technology allows CDs to be rewritten.
   a. CD-RAM
   b. CD-ROM
   c. CD-RW
   d. CD-R

8. What does FAT stand for?
   a. floppy advanced transfer
   b. fixed all-purpose tape
   c. fast access time
   d. file allocation table

9. This type of storage device retains its information, even when the power is switched off.
   a. secondary storage
   b. nonvolatile storage
   c. solid-state storage
   d. volatile storage

10. Why is FMD-ROM a promising technology?
    a. It provides fast access to data.
    b. It has multiple layers on which data can be stored.
    c. It creates network connections to CD-ROM jukeboxes.
    d. It stores redundant data on different DVD-ROMs.

Fill-In

In the blanks provided, write the correct answer for each of the following.

1. A(n) _____ is a mouse flipped on its back.

2. A(n) _____ is a device that enables a computer to read and write data to floppy disks.

3. A(n) _____ is a pointing device that is commonly used to control the motion of on-screen objects in computer games.

4. _____ devices combine an inkjet or laser printer with a scanner, a fax machine, and a copier.

5. The amount of time it takes for a storage device to begin reading data is its _____ .

6. RAM is said to be _____ , because when you switch off the computer's power, all of the information in RAM is irretrievably lost.

7. The _____ is the size of the CRT's front surface measured diagonally.

8. A(n) _____ uses a transparent pressure-sensitive panel to detect where users have tapped the display screen with their fingers.

9. A(n) _____ is made up of several fixed, rapidly rotating disks.

10. A(n) _____ copies anything that's printed on a sheet of paper, including artwork, handwriting, printed documents, and typed documents and converts what's copied into a text file.

11. _____ is memory that is used to improve hard disk performance.

12. Damaged areas on a disk are called _____ .

13. A(n) _____ is a credit-card-sized device that combines flash memory with a tiny microprocessor.

14. A(n) _____ is storage space on a server that is accessible from the Internet.

15. The hardware components that enable you to get data and instructions into the computer's memory are called _____ .

Short Answer

1. If you have used a laptop computer, which of the various pointing devices—trackball, touchpad, or pointing stick—have you used? Which input device do you prefer? Explain why. Would you consider using an auxiliary mouse (a regular mouse that you plug in to a laptop)? Why or why not?

2. What is the difference between memory and storage?

3. Many instructors use blackboards, white-boards, or overhead projectors to display course materials. Do any of your instructors use data projectors to complement the presentation of their lectures or labs? If so, are they LCD or DLP projectors? What types of software do they use? What are your feelings about using this technology to deliver classroom instruction?

4. What is the difference between a magnetic storage device and an optical storage device? Give an example of each.

5. Explain the difference between inkjet and laser printers. What are the pros and cons of each?

Teamwork

1. Long-Term Storage

The ability to store data for long periods of time is extremely important. For example, how long does your school need to store student transcripts? Your team is to discuss the inability of computers to store data permanently. Use material in this chapter and other resources to describe the two major hindrances of using computers to store and access data "forever." Give a thoughtful and detailed example of each barrier. Is paper a good storage medium? Why or why not? Write a short paper summarizing your findings.

2. Understanding Disk Capacity

When hard disks first became available, their storage capacities were around 5 MB. At the time, this seemed like an enormous amount of storage. Because many applications and some data files now use tens of megabytes of storage, current personal computers come with hard disks that are measured in gigabytes. Your team is to split up the following tasks and then collaborate in writing a one- or two-page paper that clearly describes the answers in detail.

Select any brand of personal computer and determine the hard disk capacity for both the least and the most expensive computer models. Do you think that you would ever fill the hard disk on even the least expensive model? Why or why not?

Use the Internet to find the storage requirements for the following popular applications:

- Any version of Microsoft Office
- Adobe Photoshop
- Netscape Navigator

Certain data files also require large amounts of storage. What types of files do you think would require several megabytes of storage?

3. Cordless Input Devices

Until the release of the first Macintosh computer in 1984, a mouse was just a rodent that ate cheese. With the advent of cordless technology, users of mice (and keyboards) are no longer tethered to their computers. Explain how cordless mice and keyboards work. Check newspaper advertisements or call or visit a local vendor and compare the purchase prices of conventional mice and keyboards with the prices of cordless ones. Based on cost and convenience, explain why you would or would not upgrade to a cordless mouse or keyboard or purchase one with a new computer. Write a short paper that describes your findings.

4. Portable Memory

As a team, research portable memory devices. Be sure to research memory sticks, memory cards (used in digital cameras), and USB key drives. What is the storage capacity of each type of device and how much does it cost? Construct tables to show the different amounts of memory the cards hold, their total cost, and the cost per megabyte. Write a paragraph or two that describes your prediction of the future of portable memory devices. Also discuss how you think such devices will be used in the future.

5. Comparing Printers

Work together or split up the tasks in this exercise and then write a one-page paper that provides the answers to the following questions. Visit your school or department computer facilities to determine what types of printers are available for student use. Do students have access to dot-matrix, inkjet, or laser printers? Which, if any, of the printers are capable of color output? Are printing services free? If not, what are the printing costs? If you have a personal computer, which type of printer do you have? Explain why you prefer to use your own or your school's printers.

On the Web

1. Portable Storage

Although Iomega was not the first company to market removable high-capacity disks, it has been the most successful. Visit Iomega's Web site at **iomega.com/na/landing.jsp** to learn more about its products. What is the storage capacity of its Zip disks? What are two ways to connect a Zip drive to a computer? Write a short paragraph that describes your findings. Include your thoughts on how using a removable storage device might, or might not, fit into your computing practices.

2. The DVD Revolution

Because a DVD-ROM can store up to 14 times the amount of information that a CD-ROM can, DVD-ROM drives have replaced CD-ROM drives on some new computers. Visit CNET's DVD site at **www.cnet.com** (type "DVD" into the search box) and find the best price on the fastest DVD-ROM drive available. (Hint: Click "re-sort by price.") In addition to video, what other types of information can be stored on a DVD-ROM? Explain why you would or would not purchase a new computer with a DVD-ROM drive or upgrade your present CD-ROM drive to a DVD-ROM one. Write a short paper that describes your findings.

3. Internet Storage

One method for increasing your storage capacity is to use an Internet hard drive. Have you ever considered using an Internet hard drive? Visit the Xdrive site at **www.xdrive.com to** learn more about an Internet storage site. Perform a Web search to determine which two major ISPs also offer Internet storage. List at least one advantage and one disadvantage of using Internet storage. In addition to storage, what other services do ISPs provide? Some sites provide free storage, whereas others charge a fee. Select a site that offers free storage and describe the following:

- The registration process
- The amount of free storage space
- Additional services provided

Would you consider using this site? Explain why or why not. Write a one- to two-page paper that discusses your findings.

4. Computer Voice Commands

Tired of entering input with a keyboard? One of the new features of Microsoft Office XP is speech recognition. Go to Microsoft's speech recognition site at **www.microsoft.com/office/evaluation/indepth/speech.asp** to learn about this novel method of entering input. What three actions can speech recognition help users perform? According to this Web page, what types of users will benefit from this technology? Why did Microsoft design a bimodal approach to its speech recognition? That is, why can't users enter dictation and commands simultaneously? How do users switch between dictation and command modes? In addition to voice-recognition training, what are two of Microsoft's suggestions for minimizing speech-recognition errors?

Although most computer systems include a sound card and speakers, a microphone may not be supplied. If you have a computer, was a microphone included in the purchase price? What are the names and costs of the microphone and headset combinations that Microsoft suggests to use with Office XP? In a short paper, answer these questions and explain why you would or would not consider using speech-recognition technology.

5. Surround Sound

Use your favorite browser and search engine to find information on surround-sound systems for PCs. What is the range of costs for such systems? What components are required? Is it acceptable to buy at the low end, or is there a mid-range point that will ensure a good result? Is there much to install? Can a nontechnical person install a surround-sound system? Based on your research, which system would you recommend? (Include a list of the components and the cost.) Why? Construct a one-page summary of these questions aimed at the novice user. The paper should help the reader understand surround-sound systems.

Backing Up Your Data

When it comes to the data stored on your computer, it is not a matter of if it will be lost but rather a matter of when. A comprehensive backup strategy is not just a good idea, it's a necessity. Consider the following when preparing a backup plan for your data.

1. **The amount and type of data that you want to backup.** Do you only want to backup a few files or directories? Or do you want to backup your entire hard disk, including the operating system and your important data files? If your hard disk crashes, it may be easier to restore your computer's operating system and applications manually, as long as you have your original system restore disks. However, this can be time-consuming, depending on the number of applications you had installed and need to restore. You also should ask yourself if you really want to backup all of your data. If you have a large music collection stored on your hard drive, it might not be worth backing it up, because the original CDs are your backup.

2. **Backup frequency.** Should you backup your data every day? Every week? To determine the backup schedule that is appropriate for you, ask yourself one question: If my computer goes down, how much data am I willing to lose or re-create? If your answer is none, then everyday backups are probably best. On the other hand, if you don't use your computer every day, then maybe your data files don't change often enough to warrant such an aggressive backup schedule. The right backup schedule is the one that makes you feel secure in knowing that your data are safe.

3. **The capacity of your storage device or medium.** The capacity of your storage device or medium obviously determines the amount of data you can back up. Does your computer system have a CD burner, a DVD burner, an external hard disk, a Zip drive, or other high-capacity storage device? DVD burners are great for backing up data, and they are getting cheaper every day. You can use DVD burners to read from and write to DVDs and CDs. And DVDs can hold upwards of 4 GB of data.

FIGURE 7.32 Products such as Retrospect Backup can help you to schedule, manage, catalog, and execute your backups.

However, if you're backing up only a few small selected files, then floppy or Zip disks are definitely the way to go.

If you only have a small number of files or directories to back up infrequently, then manually backing up files is probably OK. *Manual backup* means copying or dragging and dropping your files to the storage medium. If you need to back up large amounts of data (such as the operating system) on a regular basis, you should consider purchasing backup software to automate and manage the backup process. You can use products such as Norton's Drive Image (**www.symantec.com**) and Dantz's Retrospect (**www.dantz.com**) to help you schedule, manage, catalog, and execute your backups. You can use these tools to compress your backed-up files to require less storage space and to split large amounts of data into chunks to be spread over several types of smaller-capacity storage media. For example, a total of 1.7 GB of compressed data could be split up and burned to three separate CD-Rs.

If you really want your data to be 100 percent secure, you should consider keeping your important backup files somewhere safe, such as a bank safety deposit box, a friend's house, or any trusted location that is physically separated from your home. Nobody wants to think about a disaster occurring, but the reality is that your backups are useless if they are destroyed in the same fire as your computer. Your computer can be replaced; the data stored on it cannot.

SPOTLIGHT

MULTIMEDIA DEVICES

Multimedia has been around for a long time, but now

because of computer and Internet technologies it's much easier to implement. Multimedia is one of the reasons that the Web is so popular. Simply put, **multimedia** can be defined as *multisensory stimulators*, or things that stimulate our senses of sight, sound, touch, smell, or taste. For our purposes, we'll consider multimedia that stimulates the senses of sight, sound, and touch.

Just a few years ago, most personal computers needed additional equipment to run multimedia applications. Today, such equipment—sound cards, a CD-ROM or DVD-ROM drives, and speakers—is standard issue. However, for advanced multimedia applications, you may still need additional equipment, such as a pen-based graphics tablet, a stereo microphone, a digital camera, or a video adapter. If you enjoy playing games, you'll want a 3D video accelerator, which is an add-on video adapter that works with your current video card. For surround sound, you'll need a sound card capable of producing the surround effect. And, you'll probably want to pick up a few extra speakers and a subwoofer.

Multimedia is part of computer games of all kinds, but it is also being used more and more in computer-based education (CBE), distance learning, and computer-based training (CBT). Businesses use it in multimedia presentations using PowerPoint and other software. It's also finding its way into **information kiosks**, which are automated presentation systems used to provide information to the public or employee training (Figure 7A).

What if you want your multimedia files to travel with you? Today, a number of portable multimedia devices are available, from MP3 players and digital cameras to Web-enabled devices such as smart phones, PDAs, and portable televisions. In this Spotlight, you'll learn about a variety of multimedia devices, both mobile ones and those used with desktop computers.

FIGURE 7A Multimedia is finding its way into information kiosks and training systems. This woman is using an information kiosk at an airport.

AUDIO: MP3 PLAYERS AND VOICE RECORDERS

Unlike previous forms of push technology (products marketed by industries to consumers), such as cassette tapes and CDs, the MP3 movement has been largely fueled by music lovers' use of the Internet to compile and share libraries of digitized music files. Files are created and shared by the users—without industry involvement. An MP3 file is a compressed audio format that is usually used for music files. The term MP3 is derived from the acronym MPEG, which stands for the Motion Picture Experts Group; the "3" refers to audio layer 3.

Without losing any noticeable sound quality, the MP3 format reduces the size of sound files by eliminating those frequencies and sounds that the human ear cannot hear. A song on a typical music CD takes up approximately 32 MB. The same song in MP3 format takes up 3 MB.

MP3 works like this: A CD has a sample rate of 44,100 times per second. Each sample is two bytes in size, and separate samples are taken for the left and right speakers. Thus, the sample rate in bits per second is 44,100 x 8 bits per byte x 2 bytes x 2 channels, which is 1,411,200 bits per second. This equals a sample rate of 176,000 bytes per second times 180 seconds in an average song, or roughly 32 MB per song. As a result, an MP3 file is 10 times smaller than an uncompressed sound file.

You can record, store, and play MP3 files on your computer. You can legally copy music from CDs that you own or you can purchase files from Web sites such as **www.apple.com/itunes**. Windows-based PCs come with the Windows Media Player already installed (Figure 7B). Other systems may have a different default player or you may need to download one, such as Winamp, from the Internet. You can find a list of more than 80 players at **www.mpeg.org/MPEG-audio-player.html**.

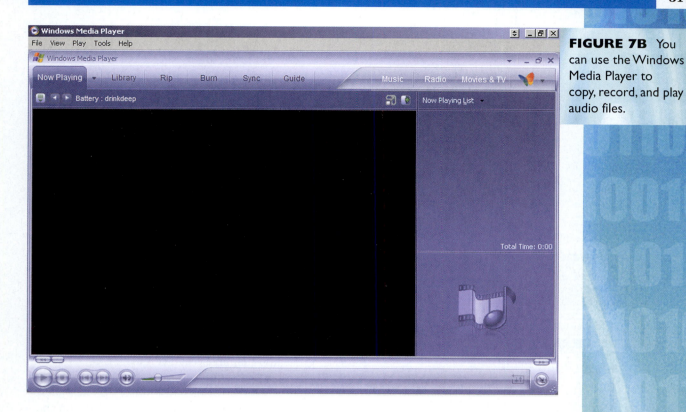

FIGURE 7B You can use the Windows Media Player to copy, record, and play audio files.

MP3 files also can be stored on portable players. Portable players come in many shapes and sizes (Figure 7C). When purchasing an MP3 player, make sure to consider the battery life and storage capacity of the device. Over 3.5 million MP3 players were shipped in 2003, and sales are expected to grow almost 50 percent per year for the next several years.

MP3 players have several components: a data port that is used to upload files, memory, a processor, a display screen, playback controls, an audio port for output, an amplifier, and a power supply. When you select a file to listen to on your MP3 player, the device's processor pulls the file from storage and decompresses the MP3 encoding. The decompressed bytes are converted from digital to analog, amplified, and then sent to the audio port for your enjoyment. MP3 players plug into your computer by way of a USB or FireWire port. Most players have solid-state memory, but some use a microdrive (a tiny hard drive) to store files. MP3 players are usually very small, portable, and battery-powered. They range in price from less

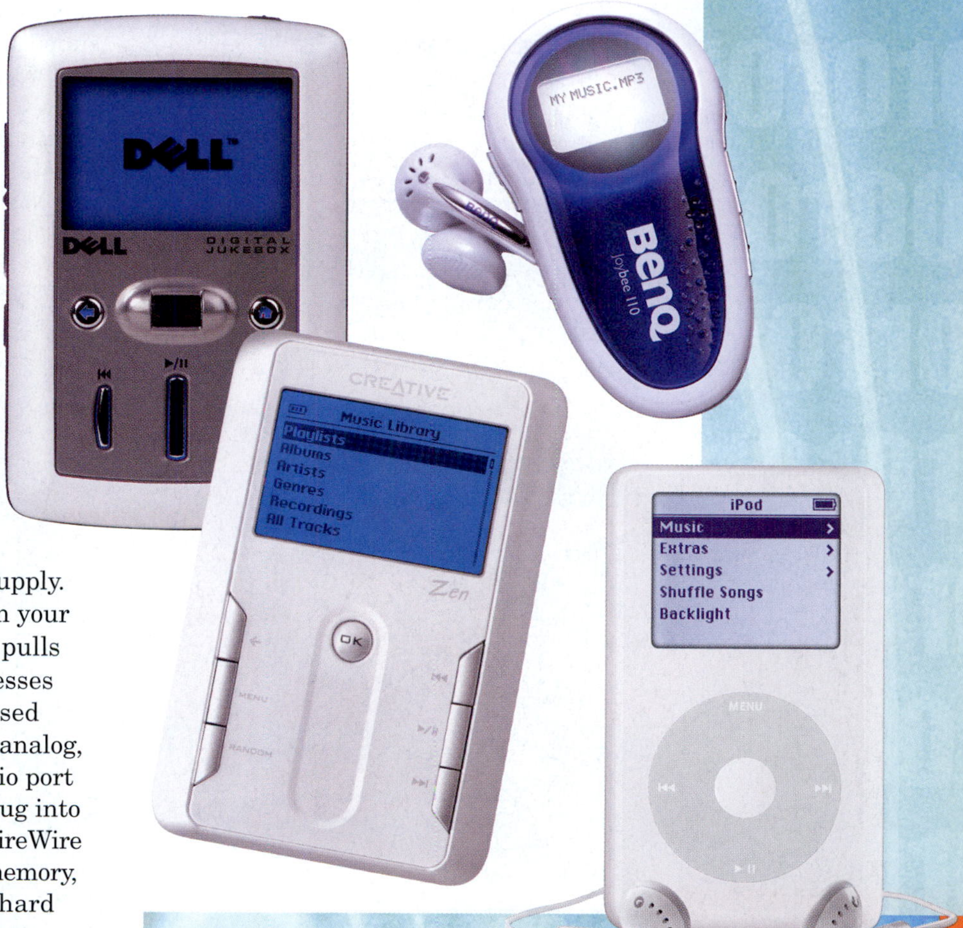

FIGURE 7C You can use a portable MP3 player to take your music with you.

than $100 to more than $450 for the Apple iPod with 40 GB of storage.

You can use a digital voice recorder to record voice and sounds that can later be retrieved from the device or downloaded to your computer. The device captures sound through a built-in microphone and then stores it on a memory chip. Several companies make these devices (Figure 7D). Two things to consider when purchasing a digital voice recorder are the amount of storage offered and the price.

FIGURE 7D Digital voice recorders such as the Olympus DM-1 provide advanced recording and playback features.

VISUAL: E-BOOKS, DIGITAL CAMERAS, AND CAMCORDERS

E-books have the potential to provide a richness that is not possible in a printed book. An **e-book** is a book that has been digitized and distributed by means of a digital storage medium (such as flash memory or a CD-ROM disc). An **e-book reader** is a book-sized device that displays e-books. E-book readers may be devices that are built solely for reading e-books or they may be PDAs, Palmtops, or other computing devices that have a processor and display screen (Figure 7E).

Someday you may read an e-book that provides background music for each page or scenario. You may find hot links on the page that will take you to pictures that support the scene. Or, better yet, you may find a link to a video of the scene. All of this extra material can be easily stored on a flash memory card along with the text of the story. It may not be long before you can use your cell phone as an e-book reader!

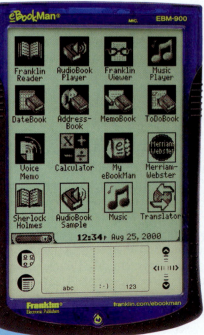

FIGURE 7E E-book readers share the market with PDAs and other computing devices.

DIGITAL CAMERAS

It seems as though it was just yesterday that computer technology was so difficult to use that only computer scientists were able to use it. But today's digital technology is so easy to use that you can even digitize your family photo album!

One of the hottest products on today's consumer market is the digital camera (Figure 7F). Approximately 40 percent of U.S. households owned at least one digital camera at the end of 2004. A **digital camera** is a camera that uses digital technology to store and display images instead of recording them on film. When you take a photo with a digital camera, the shot is stored in the camera until it is transferred to a computer for long-term storage or printing.

Like traditional cameras, digital cameras have a lens, a shutter, and an optical viewfinder. What sets digital cameras apart from traditional cameras is their inner workings—specifically, how an image is saved. With digital cameras, the captured image's light falls on a charge-coupled device (CCD), a photosensitive computer chip that transforms light patterns into pixels (individual dots). A CCD consists of a grid made up of light-sensitive elements. Each element converts the incoming light into a voltage that is proportional to the light's brightness. The digital camera's picture quality is determined by how many elements the CCD has. Each CCD element corresponds to one pixel, or dot, on a computer display or printout; the more elements, the sharper the picture.

A 1-megapixel digital camera has a CCD consisting of at least 1 million elements; such a camera can produce a reasonably sharp snapshot-sized image. With at least 2 million elements, 2-megapixel cameras can take higher-resolution pictures; you can expect to get near-photographic quality prints at sizes of up to 5 x 7 inches with such a camera. Three- and 4-megapixel cameras can produce images that can print at sizes of 8 x 10 inches or even 11 x 14 inches. Today's 5- to 10-megapixel cameras produce high-quality photographs that can be greatly enlarged without loss of quality.

Because digital cameras do not have film, any photos you take are stored in the

FIGURE 7F Digital cameras are among today's hottest products.

camera until you transfer them to a computer for long-term storage or printing. The two most popular methods of storing images in the camera are **CompactFlash** and **SmartMedia** (Figure 7G). Both use flash memory technologies to store anywhere from 64 MB to 4 GB of image data. About 12 MB of flash memory is the equivalent of a standard 12-exposure film roll. However, most cameras enable you to select from a variety of resolutions, so the number of shots you get will vary depending on the resolution you choose. If you need more "film," you need only carry more flash memory cards. Many digital cameras enable you to preview the shots you've taken on a small LCD screen, so you can create more room on the flash memory cards by erasing pictures that you don't like.

In most cases, you'll need to download the image data to a computer for safekeeping and printing. Some cameras are designed to connect to a computer by means of a serial or USB cable. Others can transfer data into your computer by means of an infrared port. If you're using a digital camera that stores images on flash memory cards, you can obtain a PC card that contains a flash memory card reader. This type of PC card enables the computer to read the images from the flash memory card as if it were a disk drive. Also available are standalone flash memory readers,

FIGURE 7G Flash memory can store hundreds of high-quality photos.

which serve the same purpose. Once you've transferred the images to the computer for safekeeping and printing, you can erase the flash memory card and reuse it, just as if you had purchased a fresh roll of film.

Once the images are transferred to the computer, you can use a **photo-editing program** to enhance, edit, crop, or resize them. Photo-editing programs also can be used to print the images to a color printer. Some specially designed printers called **photo printers** have flash memory card readers that enable you to bypass the computer completely (Figure 7H).

How good are digital cameras? With the exception of a few expensive high-end digital cameras, most digital cameras are the equivalent of the point-and-shoot 35mm cameras that dominate the traditional (film-based) camera market. They take pictures that are good enough for family photo albums, Web publishing, and business use (such as a real estate agent's snapshots of homes for sale); however, they are not good enough for professional photography. A color printer or a

FIGURE 7I
Point-and-shoot cameras are designed for portability and for grabbing quick shots.

photo printer can make prints from digital camera images that closely resemble the snapshots you used to get from the drugstore, but only if you choose the highest print resolution and use glossy photo paper. Getting good printout results takes time—most consumer-oriented printers will require several minutes to print an image at the printer's highest possible resolution—and it costs money, too. The best photo printing papers cost as much as $1 per sheet.

But printing is only one of the distribution options that are open to you when you use a digital camera—and that's exactly why so many people love digital photography. In addition to printing snapshots for the family album, you can copy the images onto CDs or DVDs, send them to friends and family via e-mail, and even display them on the Internet.

Point-and-shoot digital cameras are designed so that anyone can take good pictures (Figure 7I). Their features typically include automatic focus, automatic exposure, built-in automatic electronic flash with red-eye reduction, and optical zoom lenses with digital enhancement. Some point-and-shoot cameras come with a built-in LCD viewfinder, so you can preview the shot to make sure it comes out right.

FIGURE 7H The Kodak Easyshare printer dock makes the process of printing your pictures as easy as a plug and a click.

Single-lens reflex (SLR) digital cameras are much more expensive than point-and-shoot cameras, but they offer the features that professional photographers demand, such as interchangeable lenses, through-the-lens image previewing, and the ability to override the automatic focus and exposure settings (Figure 7J).

DIGITAL CAMCORDERS

Just as digital cameras are revolutionizing still photography, there are indications that **digital video** is poised to do the same for full-motion images—animations, videos, and movies.

In the past, most full-motion images were captured and stored by means of analog techniques. A video-capture board is a device that inputs analog video into a computer. A video-capture board (also called a video-capture card) transforms an analog video into its digital counterpart. Because a digital video file for even a short video requires a great deal of storage space, most video-capture boards are equipped to perform on-the-fly data compression to reduce file size using one of several **codecs** (compression/decompression standards), such as MPEG, Apple's QuickTime, or Microsoft's AVI. Three-dimensional games have driven computer video card manufacturers to new feats of technical innovation; today's 3D video cards offer sophisticated, ultrafast graphics processing that only a few years ago would have required a supercomputer.

Video-capture boards enable computers to display and process full-motion video—a "movie" that gives the illusion of smooth, continuous action. Like actual movies, digitized video consists of a series of still photographs called **frames** that are flashed on the screen at a rapid rate. The frame-flashing speed—the **frame rate**—indicates how successfully a given video can create the illusion of smooth, unbroken movement. A rate of at least 24 frames per second (fps) is needed to produce an illusion of smooth, continuous action. What can you "capture" with a video-capture board? You can use just about any video source, including TV broadcasts, taped video, or live video from video cameras.

FIGURE 7J The Sony Cybershot DSC-T1 digital camera is billed as "the high-end camera that fits in your back pocket."

Increasingly popular are **digital video cameras**, which use digital rather than analog technologies to store recorded video images. Like digital cameras, digital video cameras can connect to a computer, often by means of a USB port. Because the signal produced by a digital video camera conforms to the computer's digital method of representing data, a video-capture board is not necessary. Most digital video cameras can take still images as well as movies (Figure 7K).

For reviews, comparisons, and price information for digital cameras, see the "Digital Camera Buyer's Guide" at **www.digital-camerastore.com**

FIGURE 7K Panasonic's SV-AV100 is a compact yet powerful digital video recorder.

TELEVISION AND COMPUTER APPLIANCES

You're sitting in front of your television, and your eyes never leave the screen. The show you're watching is boring, so you spend some time checking your e-mail and surfing the Web. While you're on the Web, you check an interactive channel guide featuring your local cable television listings, jump to some television-related Web sites, and finally find something worth watching. You can do all of this via your television thanks to MSN® TV. **MSN® TV** is an Internet service that can be accessed through an inexpensive **set-top appliance** (also referred to as an Internet appliance), using your television as a display (Figure 7L). To navigate the Web, you use a wireless keyboard or a remote control unit. Others offering such services are Akimbo.com, launched in May 2004, and AOLTV, which launched in July 2004.

PORTABLE TELEVISIONS AND JUKEBOXES

You can use portable televisions and digital jukeboxes to carry your multimedia with you wherever you go. Portable televisions have come a long way. Sony released its LocationFree™ television in January 2004. The system uses the industry's first dual-band (more than one frequency) wireless connection and high-speed Ethernet port to receive and transmit data. It features a 12.1-inch wireless touch-screen LCD monitor that enables users to enjoy television, video, Internet browsing/streaming video, e-mail, and digital photos—all without a PC. It employs the IEEE 802.11a/11b/11g standards for a wide selection of transmission channels

FIGURE 7L MSN® TV enables you to access the Internet using your television as a display.

FIGURE 7M The Sony LocationFree™ portable television

and switches the channel for minimized interference when used up to 100 feet from the base station (Figure 7M). The portable 12-inch TV (800 x 600 SVGA LCD panel) delivers improved video and audio quality from various content sources using high-performance circuitries found in high-end televisions.

Another player in the in-home portable television market is Sharp. The wireless AQUOS™ LC-15L1U-S features a built-in rechargeable battery and wireless audio visual center that is less than 3 inches deep and has a screen that measures 15 inches diagonally (Figure 7N). You can carry the television from room to room and watch it as long as it is within 50 feet of the base unit without worrying about power cords.

The Thompson Lyra Audio/Video Jukebox 2860 is a digital all-in-one device: It is a video player–recorder, music player, portable hard drive, and digital photo album (Figure 7O). This device has audio–video inputs and outputs and a USB 2.0 port so that it can be connected to a PC, a stereo system, or a television. The 20 GB of hard disk space translates into 100,000 pictures, as many as 80 hours of recorded or downloaded video, or 5,000 songs. It has a built-in reader for CompactFlash memory cards and a slide-show mode so that you can present pictures accompanied by an audio track. It features a 3.5-inch color LDC display and costs less than $400.

FIGURE 7N The Sharp AQUOS™ can be viewed throughout the house as long as it is within 50 feet of the base unit.

FIGURE 7O You can use digital juke-boxes to carry your multimedia with you wherever you go.

DIGITAL VIDEO RECORDERS

Digital video recorders (DVRs) are similar to VCRs, but instead of using tape to store video they use a hard disk. Hard disk storage is digital, thus the user can quickly move through video data, fast-forwarding through commercials. You can use a DVR just like a VCR or you can subscribe to a DVR-management service. One service provider, TiVo®, can record up to 140 hours of a viewer's favorite shows automatically to a DVR every time they're on (Figure 7P). This way, all of your entertainment is ready-and-waiting for you to watch, whenever you are. Just buy a DVR, activate the TiVo service, and you can enjoy television viewing your way. TiVo's competitors include ReplayTV, UltimateTV, DirecTV, and others.

FIGURE 7P You can use a DVR and a service such as TiVo® to capture your favorite shows and watch them when it is convenient for you.

COMPUTER GAMING DEVICES

Computer game consoles such as PlayStation and Microsoft's Xbox are popular multimedia devices. You can use these devices to load and play interactive games using a television or computer screen as the display device. You also can go online and play games against a diverse population of players. Gaming accessories also are available, such as game consoles, specialized backpacks, wireless support, and cable accessory packs.

Game consoles are similar to computers. A game console has a processor, a graphics driver, an audio driver, memory, and an operating system. It reads input from a storage device, such as a CD or memory card, processes that input into sounds and animation, and then stores user input for further processing as the game progresses.

Gamers can use portable handheld game consoles such as Nintendo's popular Game Boy to take their games with them. Sony released its newest version of its popular PlayStation console in July 2004. Called PSone, the device is much smaller than the bulky PlayStation console.

Headsets

Perhaps the ultimate multimedia device is the headset. A **headset** (also called **head-mounted display**) is a wearable device that includes twin LCD panels. When used with special applications that generate stereo output, headsets can create the illusion that an individual is walking through a 3D environment (Figure 7Q).

Gaming enthusiasts can use the **Cave Automated Virtual Environment** (**CAVE**) to dispense with the headsets in favor of 3D glasses. In the CAVE environment, the walls, ceiling, and floor display projected 3D images. More than 50 CAVEs exist. Researchers use such CAVEs to study topics as diverse as the human heart and the next generation of sports cars.

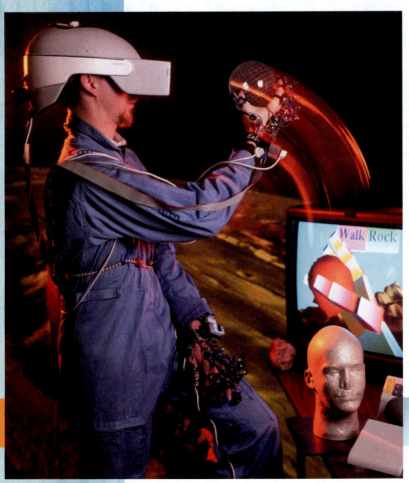

FIGURE 7Q Headsets are essential to many computer gaming experiences.

SPOTLIGHT EXERCISES

1. To learn about MP3 files, software, and portable players, visit the MP3 site at **www.mp3.com**. Explore the software link, determine which application you might purchase, and explain why. Explore the hardware link, choose which MP3 player you might purchase, and explain why. Although illegal MP3 copies of copyrighted music are available, why would an artist choose to place free copies of his or her work on the Internet? Write a short paper that includes the answers to these questions and that includes a summary paragraph of what you've learned.

2. Have you tried MSN® TV? Visit the MSN® TV site at **www.webtv.net/pc/** to explore this communications medium. Write your answers to the following questions:

   - What is needed to connect an MSN® TV?
   - What are the manufacturer's suggested retail prices for the two receivers? Explain which, if either, you would purchase and why.
   - What are the six service plans? Explain which, if any, you would purchase and why.

3. Use your favorite search engine and the World Wide Web to research digital cameras. How many pixels will suffice for your picture-taking needs? What is the price range for such cameras? What is the difference between optical zoom and digital zoom? How much optical zoom would be acceptable for your personal use? What is the storage medium of your chosen camera? How many pictures can you store on a 16-MB disk? How much storage capacity will you buy? What will it cost? Write a brief paper describing what you've learned.

4. Do some research on multifunction camcorder devices. Compare the features of an entry-level product with those of a top-of-the-line model. Pick one that you might purchase for yourself and describe it in a one-page paper that clearly explains why you would choose this camera for your video recording needs.

5. You can use portable televisions and digital jukeboxes to carry your multimedia with you wherever you go. Choose one or the other and research your choice as if you were going to purchase one for yourself. Write a one-page paper that describes the portable television or jukebox you've researched. List three of its features and explain why you would purchase it.

6. Use your favorite browser and the World Wide Web to learn more about Sony's PSone. In addition to visiting the Sony Web site, visit other sites, such as CNET or PCWorld, to see what else you can learn. Write a one-page summary based on your findings.

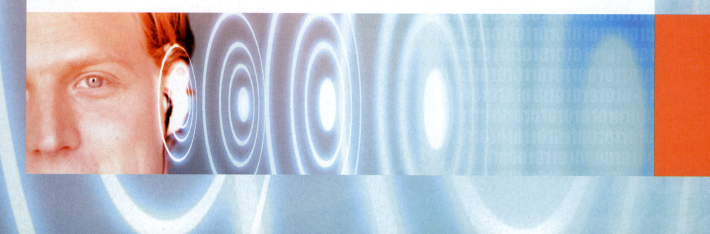

Networks: Communicating and Sharing Resources

Fast forward a few years and imagine that you are building a house. Everyone in your five-person family wants a computer, a printer, and an Internet connection. You could pay for five computers, five printers, and five Internet accounts. Or you could pay for five computers, one really good printer, one Internet account, and inexpensive network hardware so that everyone can share the printer and the Internet connection. If you think the second option makes sense, you've just joined the huge and growing number of people who've discovered the benefits of networking.

Businesses of all sizes are already convinced that networking is a great idea. They're spending billions of dollars annually on networking equipment. The benefits of networking go far beyond saving money on shared peripherals. Networks enable organizations to create massive, centralized pools of information, which are vital to performing their mission. In addition, networks enable people to communicate and collaborate in ways that were not possible before computers could be connected to each other (Figure 8.1).

As an informed and literate computer user, you need to know enough about networking to understand the benefits and possibilities of connecting computers. In addition, learning about networking is a good idea for anyone looking for a job these days; employers like to hire workers who understand basic networking concepts. This chapter presents essential networking concepts and explains the basic networking terms you'll need to know to discuss the subject intelligently.

Network Fundamentals

Although computer networking is increasingly important, many people consider the topic to be too technical for the average person to understand. However, the concepts behind computer networking are easy to understand: Computer networking is all about getting connected.

A **network** is a group of two or more computer systems linked together to exchange data and share resources, including expensive peripherals such as high-performance laser printers (Figure 8.2).

Computer networks fall into two categories: local area networks and wide area networks. A **local area network** (**LAN**) uses cables, radio waves, or infrared signals

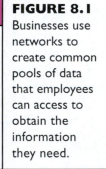

FIGURE 8.1
Businesses use networks to create common pools of data that employees can access to obtain the information they need.

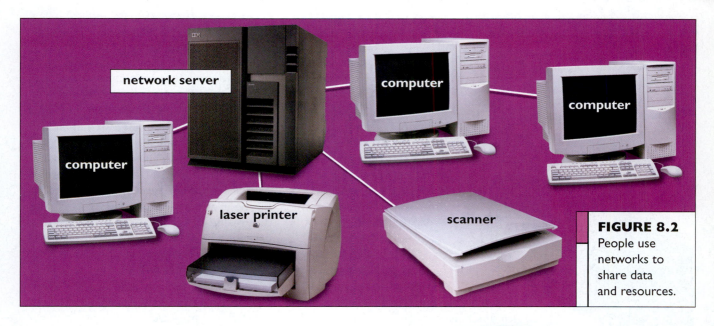

network server

computer

computer

computer

laser printer

scanner

FIGURE 8.2
People use networks to share data and resources.

to link computers or peripherals, such as printers, within a small geographic area, such as a building or a group of buildings. A **wide area network** (**WAN**) uses long-distance transmission media to link computers separated by a few miles or even thousands of miles. The Internet is the largest WAN—it connects millions of LANs all over the globe.

A network needs communications devices to convert data into signals that can travel over a physical (wired) or wireless medium. **Communications devices** include computers (workstations), modems, routers, switches, wireless access points, and network interface cards (NICs). These devices transform data from analog to digital signals and back again, determine efficient data-transfer pathways, boost signal strength, and facilitate digital communication (Figure 8.3).

When a computer is connected to a network, the computer is called a **workstation**. Networked workstations also can be called **clients**. The term **node** describes any workstation or peripheral (such as a printer) that's connected to the network. Every node on the network has a unique name that is visible to users as well as a unique numeric network address.

A computer needs a network interface card to connect to a network. **Network interface cards** (**NICs**) are expansion boards that fit into a computer's expansion slots. They provide the electronic connection between a computer and the network

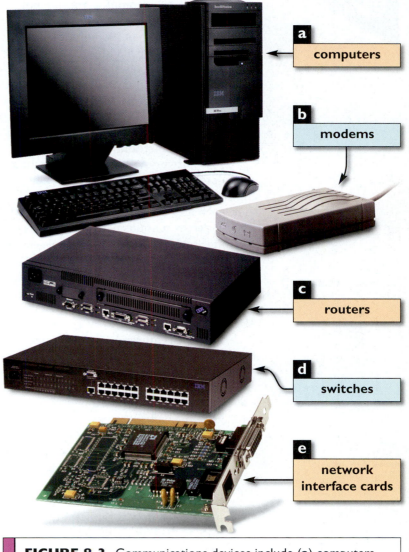

a computers

b modems

c routers

d switches

e network interface cards

FIGURE 8.3 Communications devices include (**a**) computers, (**b**) modems, (**c**) routers, (**d**) switches, and (**e**) network interface cards.

FIGURE 8.4
A network interface card (NIC) provides the electronic connection between a computer and a network.

(Figure 8.4). Some NICs are designed to work with a specific type of cabling, but others can work with more than one type.

Routers, switches, and wireless access points provide similar functions in a network. **Routers** are complex devices that are used to connect two or more LANs or WANs. Routers have the capability to determine the best path to route data and locate alternative pathways so that the data reaches its destination. Wireless access points don't possess this capability. Switches are very similar to routers but are typically used only to connect LANs.

Each computer on the network must also be equipped with additional system software that enables the computer to connect to the network and exchange data with other computers. Most operating systems, including UNIX, Linux, Windows, and Mac OS, now include such software in their standard installations.

Most networks also typically include a **file server**, which is a high-capacity, high-speed computer with a large hard disk, such as a mainframe or minicomputer. The file server contains network versions of programs and large data files. The file server also contains the **network operating system** (**NOS**), the software required to run the network. A network operating system, such as Novell's NetWare or Microsoft's Windows NT Server, is a complex program that requires skilled technicians to install and manage it. A network operating system provides:

- File directories that make it easy to locate files and resources on the LAN

- Automated distribution of software updates to the desktop computers on the LAN

- Support for Internet services such as access to the World Wide Web and e-mail

In addition to a network's special hardware and software, people are also

necessary for the proper functioning of a network. **Network administrators** (sometimes called *network engineers*) install, maintain, and support computer networks (Figure 8.5). They interact with users, handle security, and troubleshoot problems.

A network administrator's most important task is granting access to the network. In most cases, a network user provides a user name and a password to gain access to the network. Once logged in, the user has access to his or her folders that reside on the server. In some cases, the user may be able to access other people's folders that the user has permission to see or use. The user also gains access to peripheral devices on the network, such as printers, and to the Internet, if the network is connected.

As you read through this chapter, note that some of the concepts discussed apply to local networking, in which all of the computers and peripherals are locally connected, whereas others apply to networks that are made up of computers and

FIGURE 8.5 Network administrators are essential to the efficient management of networks.

peripherals that may be tens or hundreds of miles apart.

What's the point of having a computer network instead of many standalone computers and peripherals? Let's look at some of the benefits as well as the risks of networking.

Advantages and Disadvantages of Networking

When you connect two or more computers, you see gains in every aspect of computing, especially with regards to efficiency and costs:

- **Reduced hardware costs.** Networks reduce costs because users can share expensive equipment. For example, dozens of users on a network can share a high-capacity printer, storage devices, and a common connection to the Internet.

- **Application sharing.** Networks enable users to share software. Network versions of applications installed on a file server can be used by more than one user at a time. For example, at Platt Electric Supply, an Oregon-based industrial electric supply firm, sales representatives upload orders from notebook computers to an order-tracking program that resides on the company's file server. After the company installed the network, employees found that they had up to 20 percent more time to focus on their customers' needs.

- **Sharing information resources.** Organizations can use networks to create common pools of data that employees can access. At publisher Prentice Hall, for example, book designers can use the network to access a vast archive of illustrations, greatly reducing the amount of time spent tracking down appropriate photographs for textbooks and other publishing projects.

- **Centralized data management.** Data stored on a network can be accessed by multiple users. Organizations can ensure the security and integrity of the data on the network with security software and password protection. Centralized storage also makes it easier to maintain consistent backup procedures.

- **Connecting people.** Networks create powerful new ways for people to work together. For example, workers can use groupware applications to create a shared calendar for scheduling purposes. Team members can instantly see who's available at a given day and time. What's more, these people don't have to work together in the same building. They can be located at various places around the world and still function effectively as a team.

The advantages of networks are balanced out by some disadvantages as well:

- **Loss of autonomy.** When you become a part of a network, you become a part of a community of users. Sometimes this means that you have to give up personal freedoms for the good of the group. For example, a network administrator may impose restrictions on what software you can load onto network computers.

- **Lack of privacy.** Network membership can threaten your privacy. Network administrators can access your files and may monitor your network and Internet activities.

- **Security threats.** Because some personal information is inevitably stored on network servers, it is possible that others may gain unauthorized access to your files, user names, and even your passwords.

- **Loss of productivity.** As powerful as networks are, they still fail. Access to resources is sometimes restricted or unavailable due to viruses, hacking, sabotage, or a simple breakdown. Data loss can be minimized by good backup practices, but waiting for your data to

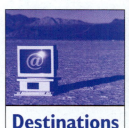

Destinations

To learn more about the advantages and disadvantages of networks, visit **www.cedar.u-net .com/two/online/ art2007.htm**

be restored is an inconvenience, or worse yet, a direct threat to your ability to produce work on time.

Now that you know the benefits and risks of using networks, let's look at the specific types of networks.

Local Area Networks (LANS)

Have you ever walked into your dorm, your school's computer lab, or your office at work and wondered how all of the separate computers in each room, seat, or office are able to work at the same time?

The answer is through a local area network. A home network is also an example of a LAN. It comprises two or more computers that communicate with each other and with peripheral devices such as a printer or cable modem.

LANs transform hardware into what appears to be one gigantic computer system. From any computer on the LAN, you can access any data, software, or peripherals (such as fax machines, printers, or scanners) that are on the network (Figure 8.6).

With a **wireless LAN**, users access the network through radio waves instead of wires. Wireless LANs come in handy when users need to move around a building. In Veterans Administration hospitals, for example, wireless LANs help hospital personnel track the distribution

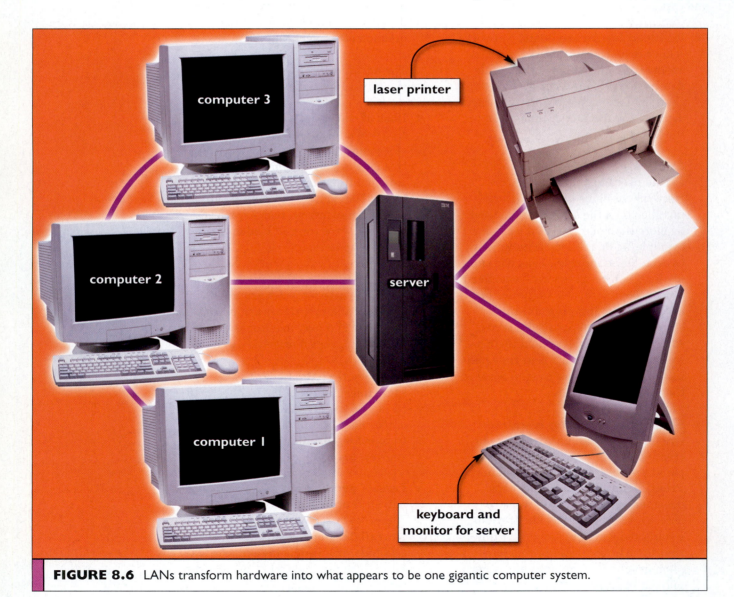

FIGURE 8.6 LANs transform hardware into what appears to be one gigantic computer system.

of controlled substances, a job that's both time-consuming and prone to error without the computer's help. Nurses use bedside computers that are connected to the network through wireless signals to track the use of these controlled substances. Many campuses also are installing wireless LANs to serve students seamlessly as they move around the campus.

Most wireless LANs ensure security with a radio transmission technique that spreads signals over a seemingly random series of frequencies. Only the receiving device knows the series, so it isn't easy to eavesdrop on the signals. Radio-based wireless LAN signals can travel about 1,000 feet.

Whether wired or wireless, LANs can be differentiated by the networking model they use: peer-to-peer or client/server.

PEER-TO-PEER NETWORKS

In a **peer-to-peer network** (**P2PN**), all of the computers on the network are equals, or peers—that's where the term *peer-to-peer* comes from—and there's no file server.

But there is file sharing, in which each computer user decides which, if any, files will be accessible to other users on the network. Users also may choose to share entire directories or even entire disks. They also can choose to share peripherals, such as printers and scanners.

Peer-to-peer networks are easy to set up; people who aren't networking experts do it all the time, generally to share an expensive laser printer or to provide Internet access to all of the workstations on the LAN (Figure 8.7). Peer-to-peer networks tend to slow down as the number of users increases, and keeping track of all of the shared files and peripherals can quickly become confusing. For this reason, peer-to-peer LANs aren't suitable for networks that connect more than one or two dozen computers.

CLIENT/SERVER NETWORKS

The typical corporate or university LAN is a **client/server network**, which includes one or more file servers as well as clients (Figure 8.8). Clients can be any type of computer: PCs, Macs, desktops, laptops, or

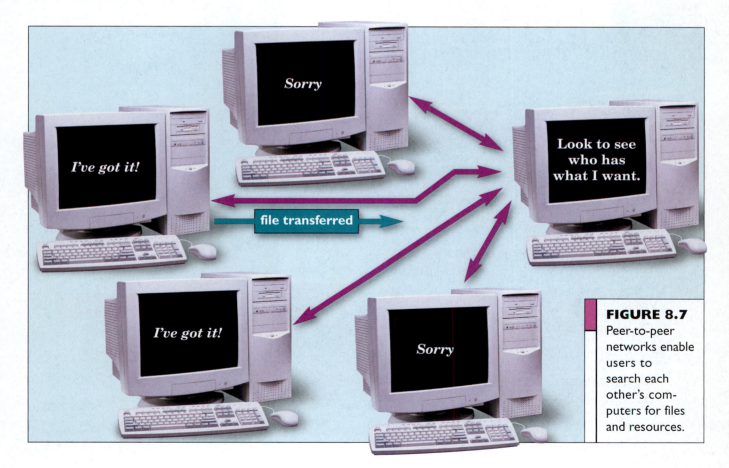

FIGURE 8.7
Peer-to-peer networks enable users to search each other's computers for files and resources.

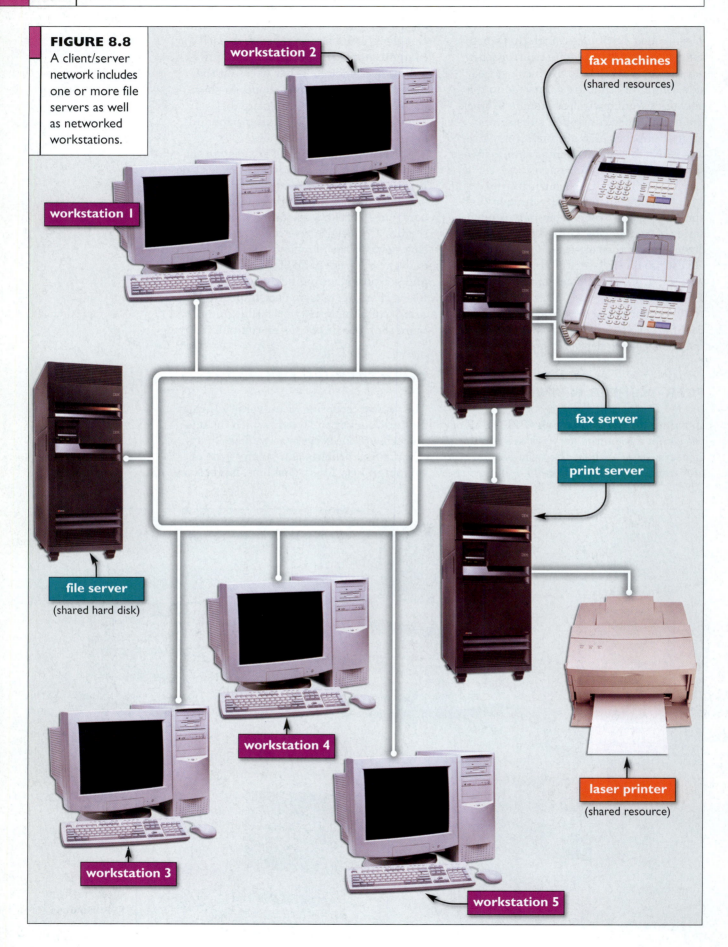

FIGURE 8.8
A client/server network includes one or more file servers as well as networked workstations.

workstation 2

fax machines
(shared resources)

workstation 1

fax server

print server

file server
(shared hard disk)

workstation 4

laser printer
(shared resource)

workstation 3

workstation 5

even PDAs. Clients send requests to the server. They can connect via modem, dedicated physical connection, or wireless connection. The client/server model works with any size or physical layout of LAN and doesn't tend to slow down with heavy use.

Now that you've learned about the different types of LANs, let's look at their various physical layouts.

LAN TOPOLOGIES

Consider the typical college dorm or corporate office. Each separate room, office, or cubicle contains a computer. How does data travel across the network when you are in your dorm room working on your computer at the same time as your neighbor across the hall and your neighbor next door? How can you all use the same Internet connection and the printer in the common area down the hall at the same time? It all depends on the type of network topology in place. The physical layout of a LAN is called its **network topology**. A topology isn't just the arrangement of computers in a particular space; a topology provides a solution to the problem of **contention**, which occurs when two workstations try to access the LAN at the same time. Contention sometimes results in **collisions**, the corruption of network data caused when two workstations transmit simultaneously.

With a **bus topology**, also called a daisy chain, the network cable forms a single bus; every workstation is attached to that bus (Figure 8.9a). At the ends of the bus, special connectors called *terminators* signify the end of the circuit. With a bus topology, only one workstation can transmit at a time. Other limitations of a bus topology include length restrictions due to the loss of signal strength and practical limits as to the number of workstations attached due to increases in contention caused by each added workstation. On the plus side, bus networks are simple, reliable, and easy to expand. The bus topology is practical in a relatively small environment such as a home or small office.

To resolve the contention problem, bus networks use some type of **contention management**, a technique that specifies what happens when a collision occurs. A

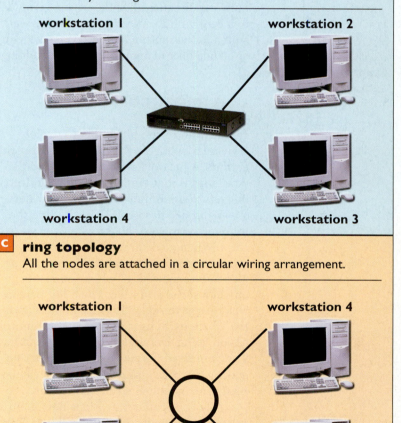

a **bus topology**
The network cable forms a single bus to which every workstation is attached.

workstation 1   workstation 3
workstation 2   workstation 4

b **star topology**
A central wiring concentrator called a hub makes it easy to connect new users by running a cable to the hub.

workstation 1   workstation 2
workstation 4   workstation 3

c **ring topology**
All the nodes are attached in a circular wiring arrangement.

workstation 1   workstation 4
workstation 2   workstation 3

FIGURE 8.9 Most networks use (a) bus, (b) star, or (c) ring topology.

Techtalk

Negotiation

When you use your computer's modem to connect to a network, the funny screeching noises and static you hear are called *negotiation.* Your modem is communicating with the modem on the other end of the line to determine how fast each modem can transfer data and how the bits to be exchanged are going to be handled.

common contention-management technique is to abandon any data that could have been corrupted by a collision.

A **star topology** solves the expansion problems of the bus topology with a central wiring device called a **hub** (Figure 8.9b). Adding users is simple; you just run a cable to the hub and plug the new user into a vacant connector. Star networks also generally use contention management to deal with collisions. The star topology is ideal for office buildings, computer labs, and WANs.

With a **ring topology**, all of the nodes are attached in a circular wiring arrangement. This topology provides a unique way to prevent collisions (Figure 8.9c). A special unit of data called a **token** travels around the ring. A workstation can transmit only when it possesses the token. Although ring networks are circular in that the token travels a circular path, they look more like star networks because all of the wiring is routed to a central hub. The ring topology is well suited for use within a division of a company or on one floor of a multifloor office building.

LAN PROTOCOLS

In addition to the physical or wireless transmission media that carry the network's signals, a network also uses **protocols** (standards) that enable network-connected devices to communicate with each other.

What are protocols? They're like the manners you were taught when you were a child. When you were growing up, you were taught to say certain fixed things, such as "It's nice to meet you," when you met someone in a social situation. The other person was taught to reply, "It's nice to meet you, too." Such exchanges serve to get communication going. Network protocols are similar. They are fixed, formalized exchanges that specify how two dissimilar network components can establish a communication.

All of the communications devices in a network conform to different protocols. Take modems, for example. To establish communications, modems must conform to standards called **modulation protocols**, which ensure that your modem can communicate with another modem, even if the second modem was made by a different manufacturer.

Several modulation protocols are in common use. Each protocol specifies all of the necessary details of communication, including the data transfer rate, the rate at which two modems can exchange data. The protocol also includes standards for data compression and error checking.

Two modems can communicate only if both follow the same modulation protocol. When a modem attempts to establish a connection, it automatically negotiates with the modem on the other end. The two modems try to establish which protocols they share and the fastest data transfer rate that each is capable of. If a computer with a 9,600 bps modem is connected to a computer with a 14,400 bps modem, the data are transferred between the two computers at 9,600 bps.

A single network may use dozens of protocols. The complete package of protocols that specify how a specific network functions is called the network's **protocol suite**. Collectively, a protocol suite specifies how the network functions, or its **network architecture**. The term *architecture* may sound daunting, but in the next section you'll learn that the basic idea isn't much more complicated than a layer cake.

Network Layers

Because they're complex systems, networks use a network architecture that is divided into separate **network layers**. Each network layer has a function that can be isolated and treated separately from other layers. Because each layer's protocols precisely define how each layer passes data to another layer, it's possible to make changes within a layer without having to rebuild the entire network.

The Protocol Stack How do layers work? To understand the layer concept, it's helpful to remember that protocols are like manners, which enable people to get communication going. Let's look at an example.

Suppose you're sending an e-mail message. Now imagine that each protocol is a person, and each person has an office on a separate floor of a multistory office building. You're on the top floor, and the network connection is in the basement. When you send your message, your e-mail client software calls the person on the next floor down, "Excuse me, but would you please translate this message into a form the server can process?" The person on the floor below replies, "Sure, no problem." That person then calls the person on the

IMPACTS

Debates

Peer-to-Peer Networks: The Controversy Continues

Remember Napster? Once known for offering free peer-to-peer music file sharing and then attacked in court for copyright infringement, the company has a new owner and now sells unlimited music downloads for one monthly subscription fee. Even though Napster has gone mainstream, the controversy over P2PN is far from over. Maybe you've heard of Kazaa, a very popular program that's currently fighting a legal battle over copyright infringement as the recording industry tries to stop illegal file sharing and put digital music on a paying basis.

However, not everybody wants to stop P2PN music swapping. Some artists offer free downloads in hopes that fans will share the files with friends and buy more songs. Yoo-hoo (the beverage company, **www.drinkyoo-hoo.com**) and a few other firms are even sponsoring music downloads that link their products with promising new groups and build goodwill as the groups' music files move from computer to computer. And P2PNs are good for sharing more than music. Through ShareALot (**sharealot.com**) and similar sites, you can download software to quickly exchange digital photos (Figure 8.10).

If you decide to join a P2PN, give some thought to privacy and security. Unless you read all the fine print before you download free versions of programs such as Kazaa, you may not realize that you're also getting adware, spyware, and other files. And keep your antivirus software up-to-date to avoid getting a nasty surprise in the form of infected files from another computer on the P2PN.

Some of the biggest P2PN security threats come from Backdoor.Sinit and other malware designed to hijack infected PCs so that hackers can conduct illegal acts. Scammers might pay to have ads pop up on the networked PCs or direct the PCs to make expensive pay-per-minute phone calls. Here, P2PN's strengths—not having a central file server and not needing technical expertise to set up the network—can actually make you vulnerable, because the rogue programs spread quickly and automatically from one PC to another. Clearly, the controversy over P2PN will continue for some time. What do you think the future of P2PN should be?

FIGURE 8.10 Yoo-hoo offers free music downloads as a way to spice up its advertising. But peer-to-peer networking isn't only for sound files. ShareALot uses the technology for sharing pictures across the Internet.

next floor down, "If it isn't too much trouble, would you please put this translated message in an envelope and address it to such-and-such computer?" And so it goes, until the message finally reaches the physical transmission medium that connects the computers in the network.

At the receiving computer, precisely the opposite happens. The message is received in the basement and is sent up. It's taken out of its envelope, translated, and handed up to the top floor, where it's acted on.

To summarize, a network message starts at the top of a stack of layers and

Destinations

To learn more about Ethernet, check out Charles Spurgeon's Ethernet Web site at **www.ethermanage .com/ethernet/ ethernet.html**. The site covers all of the Ethernet technologies in use today and includes a practical guide for do-it-yourselfers.

moves down through the various layers until it reaches the bottom (the physical medium). Because the various layers are arranged vertically like the floors in an office building, and because each is governed by its own protocols, the layers are called a **protocol stack**. On the receiving end, the process is reversed: the received message goes up the protocol stack. First, the network's data envelope is opened, and the data are translated until they can be used by the receiving application. Figure 8.11 illustrates this concept.

LAN Technologies

By far the most popular LAN standard for large and small businesses is **Ethernet**. The various versions of Ethernet are used by approximately 80 percent of all LANs.

Ethernet uses a protocol called Carrier Sense Multiple Access/Collision Detection, or CSMA/CD. Using the CSMA/CD protocol, a computer looks for an opportunity to place a data unit of a fixed size called a **packet** onto the network and then sends it on its way. Every time a packet reaches its destination, the sender gets confirmation, and the computer waits for a gap to open to shoot off another packet. Devices along the way read the address and pass the packet along to the next device, routing it toward its destination. Occasionally, two devices send a packet into the same gap at the same time, resulting in a collision and the loss of both packets, but only for the moment. When packets collide, the computers that sent them are instantly notified, and each chooses a random interval to wait before it resends the packet. This approach helps prevent network gridlock.

Although early versions of Ethernet (called 10Base2 and 10Base5) used coaxial

cable in bus networks, the most popular versions today are Ethernet star networks that use hubs and twisted-pair wire. Currently, three versions of Ethernet are in use: 10BaseT (10 Mbps), Fast Ethernet (100 Mbps, also called 100BaseT), and Gigabit Ethernet. The hardware needed to create a 10BaseT Ethernet for five PCs can cost as little as $200. The newest version, Gigabit Ethernet is not as widely implemented as the other two versions. Gigabit Ethernet sends data at 1 Gbps; a 10-Gbps version is on the horizon. These superfast connections are often used to create large networks because they prevent data bottlenecks.

Perhaps the simplest LAN technology is **LocalTalk**, the networking system built into every Macintosh computer. You can quickly create a LocalTalk network by buying some LocalTalk connectors and ordinary telephone cables. Although LocalTalk is easy to implement, data transfer rates are slow, and LocalTalk can only be used with Macs. Other popular LAN protocols are listed in Figure 8.12.

Wi-Fi Wi-Fi (short for "wireless fidelity," like *hi-fi* for "high fidelity" audio equipment) is a wireless LAN standard that offers Ethernet speeds without the wires. Wi-Fi networking may remove the wires, but such networks still need a central server or access point. In other words, with Wi-Fi technology computers can communicate with each other, but to access the Internet or to communicate across distances a central access point is required. Most access points have an integrated Ethernet controller that connects to an existing wired-Ethernet network. The controller also has an omnidirectional antenna to receive the data transmitted by

FIGURE 8.11

A message starts at the top of a stack of layers and moves down through the various layers (protocol stack) until it reaches the bottom, or physical medium. On the receiving end, the process is reversed.

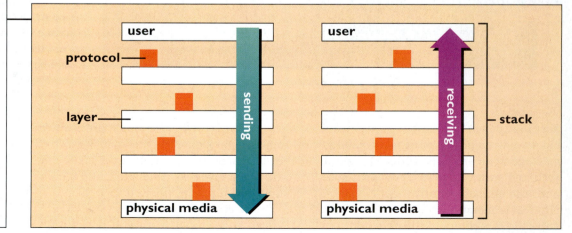

FIGURE 8.12 **Popular LAN Protocols**

Protocol Name	Data Transfer Rate	Physical Media	Topology
LocalTalk	230.4 Kbps	Shielded twisted-pair cable (phone connector cords)	Bus
Ethernet (10Base5 and 10Base2)	10 Mbps	Coaxial cable	Bus
Ethernet (10BaseT)	10 Mbps	Twisted-pair cable	Star
Fast Ethernet (100BaseT)	100 Mbps	Twisted-pair or fiber-optic cable	Star
Gigabit Ethernet	1,000 Mbps	Fiber-optic cable	Star
IBM Token Ring Network	4–16 Mbps	Twisted-pair cable	Star

Destinations

To learn more about how a home network works, go to **computer.how stuffworks.com/ home-network.htm**

To learn how to set up a home network, see the video clip at **www.prenhall.com/ cayf2006**

wireless transceivers. The majority of Wi-Fi wireless transceivers available are in PCMCIA card form.

The Wi-Fi Alliance is an organization made up of leading wireless equipment and software providers (Figure 8.13). Its mission is to certify all 802.11-based products (802.11 refers to the 802.11b, 802.11a, and 802.11g wireless transmission specifications) for interoperability and to promote the term Wi-Fi as the global brand name across all markets for any 802.11-based wireless LAN product. Although all 802.11-based products are called Wi-Fi, not all products are "Wi-Fi Certified" (a registered trademark), which indicates the radio-frequency band used (2.5 GHz for 802.11b or 802.11g, 5 GHz for 802.11a).

Wi-Fi devices communicate at a speed of 11 Mbps whenever possible. If signal strength or interference disrupts the data, the devices will drop back to 5.5 Mbps, then 2 Mbps, and finally down to 1 Mbps. Though it may occasionally slow down, this keeps the network stable and very reliable.

The following are some of the advantages of Wi-Fi:

- It's fast (11 Mbps).

- It's reliable.

- It has a long range (1,000 feet in open areas, 250 to 400 feet in closed areas).

- It's easily integrated into existing wired Ethernet networks.

Some of its disadvantages are:

- It can be expensive.

- It can be difficult to set up.

- Speed can fluctuate significantly.

FIGURE 8.13 The Wi-Fi Alliance coordinates wireless transmission specifications and promotes the term *Wi-Fi* as the brand name for any 802.11-based wireless LAN product.

CURRENTS

Computers and Society

Make a Difference: Lend Your Computer to Science

You can help save the planet, save lives, or find new life in space by offering your computer's idle time to science. Distributed computing, in which networked computers work on small pieces of large complex tasks, is revolutionizing research in a number of areas. Nearly 5 million Windows PC and Macintosh users are already lending their computing power to such projects as Climateprediction.net (to simulate climate changes), Folding@Home (to study the behavior of human proteins), and SETI@home, (to analyze radio signals in the search for extraterrestrial life), among others (Figure 8.14). The combined power of these networked computers is equivalent to years of supercomputer time—an enormous help to nonprofits with limited resources but ambitious goals.

To volunteer your computer, you will need to download and install a special screensaver program. If this software detects that your computer is on and not busy with something else, it uses your Internet connection to reach the research center's server, downloads numbers to crunch or data to sift, and then submits the results to the server. At the other end, the research center's computer assembles all of these bite-sized answers to complete one task and then parcels out pieces of the next task. Your computer's spare computing power may be used dozen of times daily or just a few days a

week depending on what the scientists are working on at that time. To see how much computing time your computer has contributed, you can check the screensaver or the project's Web site.

Until recently, you needed a different screensaver to participate in different research projects. However, the Berkeley Open Infrastructure for Network Computing (Boinc) is now becoming the standard, which means that your computer can work on multiple projects by using just a single screen saver. If you decide to get involved, you will need to update your security program regularly to protect against hackers. Is distributed computing in your future?

FIGURE 8.14 Volunteer your computer's spare time to find out if we are not alone with SETI@home, which analyzes radio signals in the search for extraterrestrial life.

Whether wired or wireless, LANs enable an organization to share computing resources in a single building or across a group of buildings. However, a LAN's geographic limitations pose a problem. Today, many organizations need to share computing resources with distant branch offices, employees who are traveling, and even people outside the organization, including suppliers and customers. This is what wide area networks (WANs) are used for—to link computers separated by even thousands of miles.

Wide Area Networks (WANs)

Like LANs, WANs have all of the basic network components—cabling, protocols, and devices—for routing information to the correct destination. WANs are like long-distance telephone systems. In fact, much WAN traffic is carried by long-distance voice communication providers, such as AT&T, MCI, and Sprint. So, you can picture a WAN as a LAN that has long-distance communications needs among its servers, computers, and peripherals. Let's look at the special components of WANs that differentiate them from LANs: a point of presence and backbones.

POINT OF PRESENCE

To carry computer data over the long haul, a WAN must be locally accessible. Like long-distance phone carriers or ISPs, WANs have what amounts to a local access number, called a point of presence. A **point of presence** (**POP**) is a WAN network connection point that enables users to access the WAN by a local analog telephone call (using a modem) or a direct digital hookup that enables a continuous, direct connection. For this reason, WANs have a POP in as many towns and cities as needed.

BACKBONES

The LANs and WANs that make up the Internet are connected to the Internet backbone. **Backbones** are the high-capacity transmission lines that carry WAN traffic. Some backbones are regional, connecting towns and cities in a region such as southern California or New England. Others are continental, or even transcontinental, in scope (Figure 8.15).

Whatever their scope, backbones are designed to carry huge amounts of data traffic. Cross-country Internet backbones, for example, can handle nearly 2.5 Gbps, and much higher speeds are on the way. A current federally funded research project is constructing a backbone network that will operate at speeds of 9.6 Gbps.

To understand how data travel over a WAN, it helps to understand how data travel over the Internet. This journey can be compared with an interstate car trip. When you connect to the Internet and request access to a Web page, your request travels by local connections—the city streets—to your ISP's local POP. From there, your ISP relays your request to the regional backbone—a highway. Your request then goes to a network access point—a highway on-ramp—where regional backbones connect with national backbone networks. And from there, the

message gets on the national backbone network—the interstate. When your request nears its destination, your message gets off the national backbone network and travels regional and local networks until it reaches its destination.

WAN PROTOCOLS

Like any computer network, WANs use protocols. For example, the Internet uses well over 100 protocols that specify every aspect of Internet usage, such as how to retrieve documents through the Web or send e-mail to a distant computer. Internet data can travel over any type of WAN because of Internet protocols.

The Internet Protocols

The Internet protocols, collectively called **TCP/IP**, are open protocols that define how the Internet works. TCP/IP is an abbreviation for Transmission Control Protocol (TCP)/Internet Protocol (IP). However, more than 100 protocols make up the entire Internet protocol suite.

Of all of the Internet protocols, the most fundamental one is the **Internet Protocol** (**IP**) because it defines the Internet's addressing scheme, which enables any Internet-connected computer to be uniquely identified. IP is a connectionless protocol. This means that with IP, two computers don't have to be online at the same time to exchange data. The sending

Techtalk

GigaPoP (gigabits per second points of presence) A gigaPoP is a POP that provides access to a backbone service capable of data transfer rates in excess of 1 Gbps (1 billion bits per second). These network connection points link to various high-speed networks that have been developed by federal agencies.

FIGURE 8.15 Some backbones are regional, connecting towns and cities in a region such as southern California or New England. Others are continental, or even transcontinental, in scope.

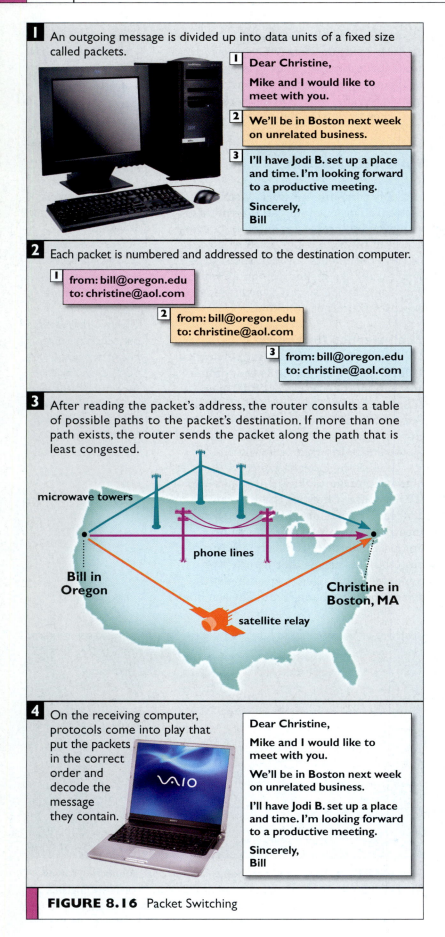

1 An outgoing message is divided up into data units of a fixed size called packets.

> **1** Dear Christine,
>
> Mike and I would like to meet with you.

> **2** We'll be in Boston next week on unrelated business.

> **3** I'll have Jodi B. set up a place and time. I'm looking forward to a productive meeting.
>
> Sincerely,
> Bill

2 Each packet is numbered and addressed to the destination computer.

> **1** from: bill@oregon.edu
> to: christine@aol.com

> **2** from: bill@oregon.edu
> to: christine@aol.com

> **3** from: bill@oregon.edu
> to: christine@aol.com

3 After reading the packet's address, the router consults a table of possible paths to the packet's destination. If more than one path exists, the router sends the packet along the path that is least congested.

microwave towers

phone lines

Bill in Oregon

Christine in Boston, MA

satellite relay

4 On the receiving computer, protocols come into play that put the packets in the correct order and decode the message they contain.

> Dear Christine,
>
> Mike and I would like to meet with you.
>
> We'll be in Boston next week on unrelated business.
>
> I'll have Jodi B. set up a place and time. I'm looking forward to a productive meeting.
>
> Sincerely,
> Bill

FIGURE 8.16 Packet Switching

computer just keeps trying until the message gets through.

Because IP enables direct and immediate contact with any other computer on the network, the Internet bears some similarity to the telephone system (although the Internet works on different principles). Every computer on the Internet has an **Internet address**, or **IP address** (similar to a phone number). A computer can exchange data with any other Internet-connected computer by "dialing" the other computer's address. An IP address has four parts, which are separated by periods (such as 128.254.108.7).

The **Transmission Control Protocol** (**TCP**) defines how one Internet-connected computer can contact another to exchange control and confirmation messages. You can see TCP in action when you use the Web; just watch your browser's status line. You'll see messages such as "Contacting server," "Receiving data," and "Closing connection."

Circuit and Packet Switching

WAN protocols are based on either circuit- or packet-switching network technology, but most use packet switching. The Internet uses packet switching, whereas the PSTN uses circuit switching. Still, the Internet does for computers what the telephone system does for phones: It enables any Internet-connected computer to connect almost instantly and effortlessly with any other Internet-connected computer anywhere in the world.

With **circuit switching**, data are sent over a physical end-to-end circuit between the sending and receiving computers. Circuit switching works best when it is essential to avoid delivery delays. In a circuit-switching network, high-speed electronic switches handle the job of establishing and maintaining the connection.

With **packet switching**, the sending computer's outgoing message is divided into packets (Figure 8.16). Each packet is numbered and addressed to the destination computer. The packets then travel to a router, which examines each packet it detects. After reading the packet's address, the router consults a table of possible pathways that the packet can take to get to its destination. If more than one path exists, the router sends the packet along the path that is most free of congestion. The packets may not arrive in the order in

which they were sent, but that's not a problem. On the receiving computer, protocols put the packets in the correct order and decode the message they contain. If any packets are missing, the receiving computer sends a message requesting retransmission of the missing packet.

Which Is Best?

Compared with circuit switching, packet switching has many advantages. It's more efficient and less expensive than circuit switching. What's more, packet-switching networks are more reliable. A packet-switching network can function even if portions of the network aren't working.

However, packet switching does have some drawbacks. When a router examines a packet, it delays the packet's progress by a tiny fraction of a second. In a huge packet-switching network—such as the Internet—a given packet may be examined by many routers, which introduces a noticeable delay called **latency**. If the network experiences **congestion** (overloading), some of the packets may be further delayed, and the message can't be decoded until all of its packets are received.

The oldest packet-switching protocol for WAN usage, **X.25**, is optimized for dial-up connections over noisy telephone lines and is still in widespread use. Local connections generally offer speeds of 9.6 to 64 Kbps. X.25 is best used to create a point-to-point connection with a single computer. A point-to-point connection is a single line that connects one communications device to one computer. It is widely used with ATMs and credit card authorization devices. New protocols designed for 100 percent digital lines, such as Switched Multimegabit Data Service (SMDS) and Asynchronous Transfer Mode (ATM), enable much faster data transfer rates (up to 155 Mbps).

Now that you understand how WANs work, let's explore how they are used.

WAN APPLICATIONS

WANs enable companies to use many of the same applications that you use, such as e-mail, conferencing, document exchange, and remote database access. Some WANs are created to serve the public, such as those maintained by online service providers such as AOL and MSN. Other WANs are created and maintained for the sole purpose of meeting an organization's internal needs. For instance, The Condon Group, Ltd. maintains a WAN for offices in five states.

LAN-to-LAN Connections

In corporations and universities, WANs are often used to connect LANs at two or more geographically separate locations. This use of WANs overcomes the major limitation of a LAN—its inability to link computers separated by more than a few thousand feet. Companies can now use new services from AT&T, Sprint, and MCI to connect their LANs at 100 Mbps, the same data transfer rate used by most companies' internal systems. With these connections, users get the impression that they're using one huge LAN that connects the entire company and all of its branch offices.

Transaction Acquisition

When you make a purchase at a retail store such as Sears or Starbucks Coffee, information about your transaction is instantly relayed to the company's central computers through its WAN. That's because the "cash register" the clerk uses is actually a computer, a point-of-sale (POS) terminal, that's linked to a data communications network (Figure 8.17). The acquired data are collected for accounting purposes and analyzed to see if a store's sales patterns have changed.

Destinations

To learn more about WAN protocols, visit Cisco's WAN documentation site at **www.cisco.com/ univercd/cc/td/doc/ cisintwk/ito_doc/ introwan.htm**

FIGURE 8.17 POS terminals instantly relay information about transactions to the company's central computers through its WAN.

What You've Learned

NETWORKS: COMMUNICATING AND SHARING RESOURCES

- Computer networks link two or more computers so that they can exchange data and share resources, such as printers, scanners, and an Internet connection. Networks are of two primary types: local area networks (LANs), which serve a building or a small geographic area, and wide area networks (WANs), which can span buildings, cities, states, and nations. Networks consist of special hardware, software, and people. For example, most networks have nodes (which can be workstations, communications devices, or file servers), NICs, network operating systems, and network administrators.

- Computer networks can reduce hardware costs, enable application sharing, create a means of pooling an organization's mission-critical data, and foster teamwork and collaboration. Disadvantages of computer networks include loss of autonomy, threats to security and/or privacy, and potential productivity losses due to network outages.

- A peer-to-peer LAN doesn't use a file server. It is most appropriate for small networks of one or two dozen computers. Client/server networks include one or more file servers as well as clients such as desktops, laptops, and even PDAs. The client/server model works with any size or physical layout of LAN and doesn't slow down with heavy use.

- The physical layout of a LAN is called its network topology. A topology isn't just the arrangement of computers in a particular space; a topology provides a solution to the problem of contention, which occurs when two workstations try to access the LAN at the same time. The three different LAN topologies are bus (single connections to a central line), star (all connections to a central hub), and ring (tokens carry messages around a ring).

- Protocols define how network devices can communicate with each other. A network requires many protocols to function smoothly. When a computer sends a message over the network, the application hands the message down the protocol stack, where a series of protocols prepares the message for transmission through the network. At the other end, the message goes up a similar stack.

- The most widely used LAN protocol is Ethernet, which is available in two versions that use hubs and twisted pair wiring: 10BaseT (10 Mbps) or 100BaseT or Fast Ethernet (100 Mbps). The newest version, Gigabit Ethernet, can transfer data at the rate of 1,000 Mbps or 1 Gbps.

- The special components that distinguish a WAN from a LAN are a point of presence and backbones. A point of presence (POP) is a WAN network connection point that enables users to access the WAN by a local analog telephone call (using a modem) or a direct digital hookup that enables a continuous, direct connection. Backbones are the high-capacity transmission lines that carry WAN traffic.

- Circuit switching creates a permanent end-to-end circuit that is optimal for voice and real-time data. Circuit switching is not as efficient or reliable as packet switching; it is also more expensive. Packet switching does not require a permanent switched circuit. A packet-switched network can funnel more data through a medium with a given data transfer capacity. However, packet switching introduces slight delays that make the technology less than optimal for voice or real-time data.

Key Terms and Concepts

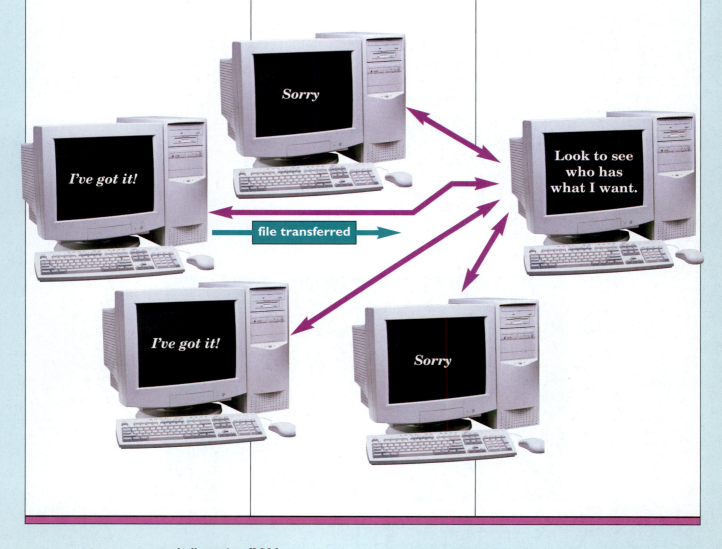

Matching

Match each key term in the left column with the most accurate definition in the right column.

_____ 1. network operating system (NOS)

_____ 2. network architecture

_____ 3. protocols

_____ 4. Ethernet

_____ 5. Internet protocol

_____ 6. peer-to-peer network

_____ 7. routers

_____ 8. clients

_____ 9. token

_____ 10. packets

_____ 11. latency

_____ 12. bus topology

_____ 13. network topology

_____ 14. collision

_____ 15. node

a. all of the computers that access the server

b. defines the Internet's addressing scheme

c. a computer or peripheral that is connected to the network

d. a network in which all of the computers are equal

e. a special unit of data that travels around a ring in a ring topology

f. communications devices that examine each packet they detect

g. delay in packet transmission due to router examination

h. data units of fixed size that are used with packet-switching networks

i. the most popular lower-level protocol stack standard

j. standards that specify how a network functions

k. the overall design of a network

l. also known as a daisy chain

m. the physical layout of a LAN

n. software required to run the network

o. the corruption of network data caused by two workstations transmitting data simultaneously

Multiple Choice

Circle the correct choice for each of the following.

1. Which of the following is *not* a computer network?
   a. local area network (LAN)
   b. leased-line area network (L2AN)
   c. wide area network (WAN)
   d. peer-to-peer network (P2PN)

2. Which technology enables networks to funnel messages to their correct destination?
   a. circuit switching
   b. packet switching
   c. both a and b
   d. none of the above

3. Which term describes a computer that is connected to a network?
   a. unit
   b. mode
   c. workstation
   d. terminal unit

4. To connect to a LAN, a computer must be equipped with which of the following?
   a. network interface card (NIC)
   b. backbone
   c. both a and b
   d. none of the above

5. Which type of network topology is centered on a hub?
   a. star
   b. ring
   c. bus
   d. LAN

6. Which of the following is *not* a LAN topology?
   a. ring
   b. star
   c. hub
   d. bus

7. Which term describes the phenomenon of more than one computer trying to use the network at the same time?
   a. contention
   b. competition
   c. communication
   d. congestion

8. Which of the following is a WAN network connection point that enables users to access the WAN through a local phone call?
   a. point of presence (POP)
   b. leased line
   c. permanent virtual circuit (PVC)
   d. frame relay

9. Which of the following is the most popular LAN standard?
   a. ISDN
   b. LocalTalk
   c. Ethernet
   d. Synchronous Optical Network (SONET)

10. Which of the following is the oldest and most widely used packet-switching protocol for WAN usage?
    a. 10BaseT
    b. category 5 (cat-5)
    c. X.25
    d. T1

Fill-In

In the blanks provided, write the correct answer for each of the following.

1. A(n) _____ links two or more computers together to enable data and resource exchange.

2. A(n) _____ uses direct cables, radio waves, or infrared signals to link computers within a small geographic area.

3. When a PC is connected to a LAN, the PC is called a(n) _____.

4. A(n) _____ is a PC expansion board needed to connect a computer to a LAN.

5. With _____, an outgoing message is divided into data units of a fixed size called packets.

6. _____ is a set of standards that offers Ethernet speed without wires.

7. _____ install, maintain, and support computer networks, interact with users, handle security, and troubleshoot problems.

8. In a(n) _____, the network cable forms a single bus to which every workstation is attached.

9. A network uses _____ (standards) that enable network-connected devices to communicate with each other.

10. The high-capacity transmission lines that carry WAN traffic are called _____.

11. _____ defines how one Internet-connected computer can contact another to exchange control and confirmation messages.

12. With a(n) _____, file sharing allows users to decide which computer files, if any, are accessible to other users on the network.

13. _____ is the networking system built into every Macintosh computer.

14. A(n) _____ uses long-distance transmission media to link computers separated by a few miles or even thousands of miles.

15. With _____, the network creates a physical end-to-end circuit between the sending and receiving computers.

Short Answer

1. Describe a protocol stack and then draw a diagram that shows what you have described.

2. Explain the difference between peer-to-peer and client/server networks.

3. How do LANs and WANs differ?

4. Name three types of LAN topologies and describe how each works.

5. What is the difference between contention and congestion?

6. How do circuit switching and packet switching differ? What are the advantages of each method?

Teamwork

1. Finding IP Addresses

Frequently, the IP addresses of an organization's Internet-connected computers begin with the same several digits. For example, all of the computers at Buffalo State College have an IP address of the form 136.183.xxx.xxx. The last two sets of numbers usually denote the campus building and the individual computer. Have one of your team members stop by your school's computing services center and find out if your institution has a common set of IP addresses for its computers. If it does, what are the common digits? Have each team member access your school's Windows-based networked computers to determine their IP addresses. Go to Start, select Run, in the Open box type "winipcfg," and click the OK button. What is the IP address of each computer? Do they begin with a common set of digits? Write a short paper that describes your findings.

2. Computer Lab Topologies

Have each team member visit campus computer labs and determine the network topology used. In addition to workstations, what other devices are connected to each network? What types of physical media are used to connect the computers and the peripherals in each lab? How does your school connect to the Internet? Write a short paper that describes your findings.

3. Designing a Network

If you were responsible for setting up a network for a company that had offices in five different states, how would you do it? What part would the Internet play in your plans? Assume that each office is on one floor of a building and has three divisions, each having six employees. Each division needs access to a printer and an Internet connection. All divisions at all five locations need to have 24/7 access to each other. As a team, collaborate on a paper that describes the network (including a schematic of the network and one division). Be sure to use several of the key terms from this chapter.

4. Researching Routers

The number of households that have more than one computer is increasing, and families want to share resources among them. One of these resources is the Internet connection. Although newer versions of Microsoft Windows offer software that enables two computers to share an Internet connection, consumers with high-speed connections such as cable or DSL also can use a router to share Internet access. Your team is to go to a local computer store and investigate cable/DSL routers. How many ports do these devices have? How much do they cost? What physical medium is used to connect the devices to the router? Can a printer be shared using a router? What type of network topology is used? What additional hardware is needed to network the computers to the router? If you had a high-speed connection and multiple computers, would you purchase a router? Why or why not?

5. Wireless Networks

Your team is to go to a local computer store and investigate wireless access points. What are the prices for these devices? How do wireless connection speeds compare with wired ones? What type of network topology is used? What additional hardware is needed to network computers to the wireless access point? If you had a home network, would you consider this networking alternative? Why or why not? Write a paper that answers these questions and that describes your experience at the computer store.

On the Web

1. Establishing a Wired Home Network

Visit CNET at **www.cnet.com** to learn more about establishing a home network. Although you may find information on wireless networking, restrict your research to wired networks. Assume that you have two computers, a printer, and a scanner that you wish to network. What hardware and software will you need to purchase? How much will your network cost? Will you connect to the Internet? If so, how and at what cost? If not, why not?

2. Researching Fast Ethernet

The text discussed Gigabit Ethernet technology that enables LAN connection speeds of up to 1 Gbps. Go to the "10 GEA" site at **www.10gea.org/ Tech-whitepapers.htm** to learn more about this promising technology. What does 10 GEA stand for? When was it formed? Name three of the founding organizations. What is the name of the new standard that is being developed? When is ratification of the new standard expected? What types of companies, organizations, or institutions do you think will use this technology?

3. Exploring NICs

Assume that you have both a desktop and a laptop and you want to network them together. To do this, each computer needs a NIC. Go to **www.pricegrabber.com** to find the best price for a NIC for a desktop and a laptop computer. What are the prices for each? Why do you think laptop cards are more expensive? Many desktops and laptops now have automatic built-in network connectivity. Locate and name specific desktop and laptop models that have internal networking capabilities. If you currently have a desktop or laptop, does your computer have internal networking capabilities?

4. A PDA for You

Because of their small size, PDAs are popular mobile computing devices. Do you own or have you considered buying a PDA? Go to **www.dartek.com/ Browse/index.cfm** to find information on PDAs. What are the most popular methods for networking a PDA to a desktop computer? Which of these methods require additional PC hardware? Is the use of the word *networking* correct? Explain why or why not.

5. Novell Network Operating Systems

One of the oldest and most widely used network operating systems is Novell's NetWare. Visit the Novell site at **www.novell.com**. What is the latest version of NetWare? In addition to LAN software, what Internet features does NetWare support? What are the initial purchase and upgrade costs for a small system that supports a server and five workstations? What products qualify for competitive upgrades? In addition to English, name three other languages in which NetWare is available. Does NetWare support Macintosh and UNIX-based computers? Does your school use any Novell networking software?

Choosing an ISP

Your ISP is your lifeline to the online world. Every month you spend your hard-earned money to maintain that connection. Depending on the speed and type of Internet connection, you can spend anywhere from $10 to $50 each month to read your e-mail, surf the Web, and trade files with your friends (legally of course). That monthly fee can quickly add up to more than $600 a year just to get online! Before you pay your next ISP bill, you should ask yourself exactly what you get in return for your monthly service fee. Speed is important, but it shouldn't be the only determining factor when choosing an ISP. Here are some tips to help you determine if you and your ISP are a good match as well as some ideas on how to get the most bang for your buck each month.

CHOOSING AN ISP

How much time do you spend online each month? Do you need unlimited access, or do you only occasionally check your e-mail and visit Web sites? Many ISPs provide a discounted service for users who don't go over a specific number of hours per month. Why pay for unlimited access if you don't need it? (Figure 8.18)

Do you really need a high-speed connection? The difference in price between dial-up and cable or DSL access can be significant. You'll need to determine if the price is worth the extra money. If you rarely download large files and you spend a limited amount of time online each month, then you may want to consider using a dial-up service at home and using computers at school or your local library for those few times when speed really does matter. (Be sure to check in advance if this is an acceptable use of computing resources wherever you choose to download files.)

What else do you get for your money? Services such as AOL charge a premium for access to their custom content and features. (AOL also is a great choice if you are new to the Internet and all it has to offer.) Some other questions you should ask yourself include: Do you need an e-mail address for each member of your family? Would you like to host a Web site? Do you need parental controls? It is important to create a list and prioritize everything you would like from your ISP before you start to shop around.

FIGURE 8.18 Visit NetZero at **www.netzero.net/** to learn about free or low-fee Internet service.

Web sites such as **www.freedomlist.com/info.php?mid=2** can be helpful when shopping for an ISP. Alternatively, type the letters ISP into your favorite search engine.

GETTING THE MOST FOR YOUR MONEY

Find out how many e-mail accounts are available to you and use them all. Have separate e-mail accounts for activities such as online purchases, correspondence with friends and family, work, Web site memberships, and so on.

If your ISP provides you with storage space to host a Web site, then what are you waiting for? A variety of Web resources are available to help you learn HTML, and it isn't very difficult to create a basic Web site. Many ISPs will even provide you with an automated tool to help you create and manage your Web pages. Who knows, you and your Web site may even be famous someday!

If you pay for a broadband connection, you should download, download, download! Many sites sell downloadable music, books, and movies. Instead of taking a trip in your car to rent a movie, the next time you're bored why not try downloading and playing a movie from the Web? If your computer has the appropriate connections, you can even watch the movies using your TV. If you're paying for a lot of bandwidth, use it!

What You'll Learn . . .

- Understand how technological developments are eroding privacy and anonymity.

- List the types of computer crime and cybercrime.

- List the various types of computer criminals.

- Understand computer system security risks.

- Describe how to protect your computer system and yourself.

- Define *encryption* and explain how it makes online information secure.

- Describe the U.S. government's proposed key recovery plan and explain why it threatens the growth of Internet commerce.

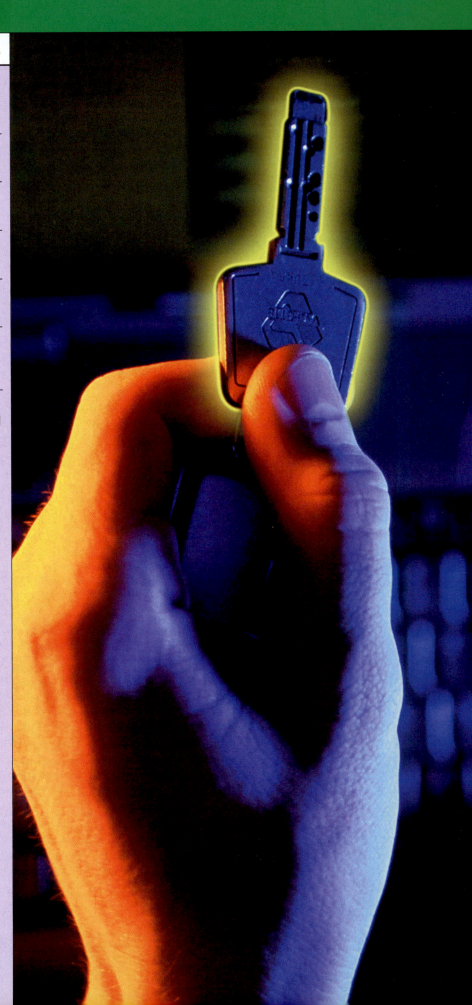

Privacy, Crime, and Security

The public nature of the Internet raises privacy issues as more and more corporations and private citizens conduct business online. Just as stores in your neighborhood lock their doors at night to protect merchandise and equipment, electronic businesses employ a variety of security measures to protect their interests and your privacy from cybercriminals. In this chapter, you will explore how being online can threaten your privacy, personal safety, and computer system and learn how to protect yourself from online threats.

Privacy in Cyberspace

Of all the social and ethical issues raised by the spread of widely available Internet-linked computers, threats to privacy and anonymity are among the most contentious (Figure 9.1).

Defined by U.S. Supreme Court Justice Louis Brandeis in 1928 as "the right to be left alone," **privacy** refers to an individual's ability to restrict or eliminate the collection, use, and sale of confidential personal information. Some people say that privacy isn't a concern unless you have something to hide. However, this view ignores the fact that individuals, governments, and corporations sometimes collect and use information in ways that may harm people unnecessarily.

THE PROBLEM: COLLECTION OF INFORMATION WITHOUT CONSENT

Many people are willing to divulge information when asked for their consent and when they see a need for doing so. When you apply for a loan, for example, the bank can reasonably ask you to list your other creditors to determine whether you'll be able to repay your loan.

Much information is collected from public agencies, many of which are under a legal obligation to make their records available to the public upon request (public institutions of higher education, departments of motor vehicles, county clerks, tax assessors, and so on). This information finds its way into computerized databases—thousands of them—that track virtually every conceivable type of information about

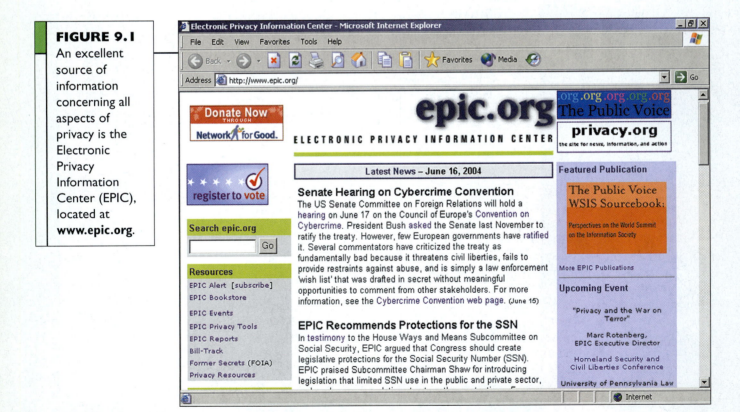

FIGURE 9.1
An excellent source of information concerning all aspects of privacy is the Electronic Privacy Information Center (EPIC), located at **www.epic.org**.

individuals. You are probably aware of credit reporting databases that track your credit history (Figure 9.2). Other databases include information such as your current and former addresses and employers, other names you've used (and your previous name, if you're married and use a different name now), current and former spouses, bankruptcies, lawsuits, property ownership, driver's license information, criminal records, purchasing habits, and medical prescriptions.

Most of the companies that maintain these databases claim that they sell information only to bona fide customers such as lending institutions, prospective employers, marketing firms, and licensed private investigators. They maintain that their databases don't pose a threat to the privacy of individuals because they are highly ethical firms that would not release this information to the general public.

According to privacy activists, the problem is what happens to information after it's sold. The Internet has made it much easier and much cheaper for ordinary individuals to gain access to sensitive personal information. If you search the Web for "Social Security numbers," you'll find dozens of Web sites run by private investigators who offer to find someone's Social Security number for a small fee, which can easily be charged to your credit card (Figure 9.3). Sites such as InfoUSA (**www.infousa.com**) offer information such as estimated income, marital status, buying habits, and hobbies for more than 120 million U.S. households.

TECHNOLOGY AND ANONYMITY

Marketing firms, snoops, and government officials can use computers and the Internet to collect information in ways that are hidden from users. The same technology also makes it increasingly difficult for citizens to engage in anonymous speech. **Anonymity** refers to the ability to convey a message without disclosing your name or identity.

Anonymity can be abused because it frees people from accountability. As a result, people may abuse the privilege of anonymous speech. Still, the U.S. Supreme Court recently held that anonymity—

FIGURE 9.2 Credit reporting agencies such as Equifax, Experian (formerly TRW), and TransUnion collect and store data about your credit history.

FIGURE 9.3 Web sites can sell your Social Security number or other personal information to anyone they please. In the United States, you have no legal recourse against those who collect and sell sensitive personal information.

despite its unpalatable aspects—must be preserved. In a democracy, it is essential that citizens have access to the full range of possible ideas to make decisions for themselves. Freeing authors from accountability for anonymous works, the Court argued, raises the potential that false or misleading ideas will be brought before the public, but that this risk is necessary to maintain a free society.

Two technologies that threaten online anonymity are being used more and more—cookies and global unique identifiers.

Cookies

Cookies are small files that are written to your computer's hard disk by many of the Web sites you visit (Figure 9.4). In many cases, cookies are used for legitimate purposes. For example, online retail sites use cookies to implement "shopping carts," which enable you to make selections that will stay in your cart so that you can return later to the online store for more

browsing and shopping. What troubles privacy advocates is using cookies to gather data on Web users' browsing and shopping habits without their consent.

Several Internet ad networks, such as DoubleClick, use cookies to track users' browsing actions across thousands of the most popular Internet sites. When you visit a Web site that has contracted with one of these ad networks, a cookie containing a unique identification number is deposited on your computer's hard drive. This cookie tracks your browsing habits and preferences as you move among the hundreds of sites that contract with the ad network. When you visit another site, the cookie is detected, read, and matched with a profile of your previous browsing activity. On this basis, the ad network selects and displays a **banner ad**, a rectangular advertisement that is not actually part of the Web page you are viewing, but an ad supplied separately by the ad network (Figure 9.5).

In response to concerns that their tracking violates Internet users' privacy, ad network companies claim that they do not link the collected information with users' names and addresses. However, current technology would enable these firms to do so—and privacy advocates fear that some of them already have. Internet ad networks such as DoubleClick can collect the following:

FIGURE 9.4
Online businesses record information about your browsing habits with cookies, small files written to your computer's hard disk by Web sites.

Personal information concerning Web site visit.

- Your e-mail address

- Your full name

- Your mailing address (street, city, state, and zip code)

- Your phone number

- Transactional data (names of products purchased online, details of plane ticket reservations, and search phrases used with search engines)

Internet marketing firms explain that by collecting such information, they can provide a "richer" marketing experience, one that's more closely tailored to an individual's interests. Privacy advocates reply that once collected, this information could become valuable to others. These kinds of debates ensure that cookies and

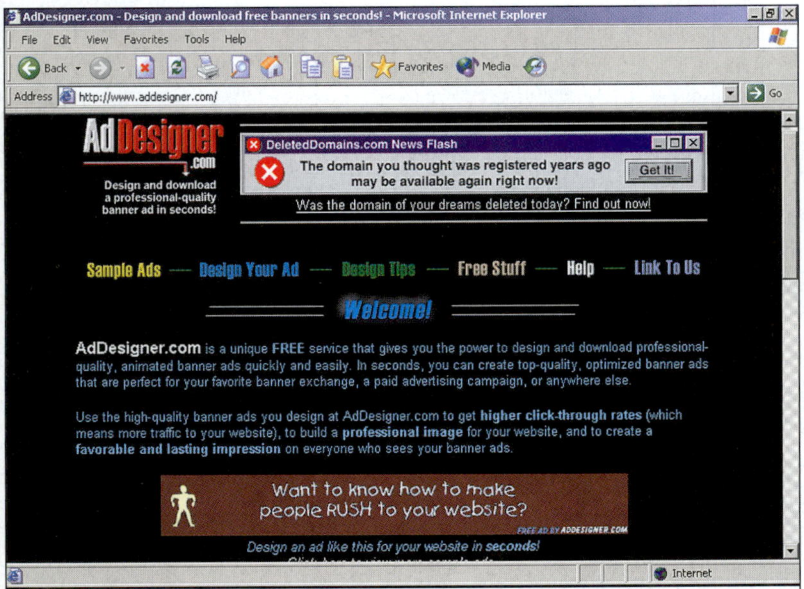

FIGURE 9.5   Banner ads can be tailored to match your customer profile.

the information they collect will remain on the forefront of the privacy controversy for years to come.

Global Unique Identifiers

A **global unique identifier** (**GUID**) is an identification number that is generated by a hardware component or a program. Privacy advocates have discovered several instances in which popular computer components or programs made GUIDs available in such a way that anonymous usage of the Internet would become more difficult, if not impossible:

- Intel Corporation placed a GUID in its Pentium III processors. According to Intel, the GUID could be used to positively identify shoppers—an important step in the fight against online fraud. However, analysts discovered that the Pentium III GUID can be accessed by Web servers, which increases the risk that any site you visit on the Web could learn your identity. In response to public outcry, Intel redesigned the Pentium III processor with the GUID turned off by default.

- RealNetworks' RealJukeBox player sent information back to the company when users accessed online streaming audio or video content. The information included the user's name, e-mail address, and a description of the content being viewed.

- Microsoft Word 97 and Excel 97 embedded GUID information in every document created with these applications. This information could have been used to trace an anonymous document back to a particular computer used on a university or corporate network.

Companies that introduce GUIDs into their products generally conceal this information from the public. When forced to admit to using GUIDs, the firms typically remove the GUID-implanting code or enable users to opt out of their data collection systems. Advocates of online anonymity insist that these companies are missing the basic point: Users, not corporations, should determine when and how personal information is divulged to third parties.

In 2001, Microsoft introduced a free service called **.NET Passport** as part of its new .NET strategy (Figure 9.6). A .NET Passport profile stores your e-mail address and a password. If you choose, your profile information will automatically be shared

Destinations

To see an online demonstration of how banner ad tracking can be paired with user names through site registrations, visit Privacy.net's demonstration page at **www.privacy .net/track**

FIGURE 9.6
With .NET Passport, you can manage a single user profile that identifies you to partner Web sites.

Techtalk

Web Bug

A Web bug is a tiny, all-but-invisible graphic, typically only one pixel in size, that is included on a Web page so that a third-party can monitor "hits" on that page. Combined with HTML code, the graphic can send a third party—such as an Internet ad network—the contents of an identification cookie. Web bugs also can be included in HTML-formatted e-mail messages to reveal the recipient's address and whether a recipient has received a message.

with participating Web sites to provide you with personalized services. One advantage of .NET Passport is that you can manage your profile. In addition, Microsoft has a privacy policy agreement with .NET Passport–affiliated vendors to protect your privacy. However, it is often very difficult to manage the integrity of a personal identification system that has many partners with many different interests.

Now that you've read about some of the privacy threats posed by the Internet, let's discuss how you can protect your privacy.

PROTECTING YOUR PRIVACY

How should governments protect the privacy of their citizens? Privacy advocates agree that the key lies in giving citizens the right to be informed when personal information is being collected as well as the right to refuse to provide this information.

In the European Union (EU), a basic human rights declaration gives all citizens the following privacy rights:

● Consumers must be informed exactly what information is being collected and how it will be used.

● Consumers must be allowed to choose whether they want to divulge the requested information and how collected information will be used.

● Consumers must be allowed to request that information about themselves be removed from marketing and other databases.

Apart from the Fair Credit Reporting Act, which provides limited privacy protection for credit information, no comprehensive federal law governs the privacy rights of U.S. citizens. Instead, privacy is protected by a patchwork of limited federal and state laws and regulations. Most of these laws regulate what government agencies can do. Except in limited areas covered by these laws, little exists to stop people and companies from acquiring and selling your personal information (Figure 9.7).

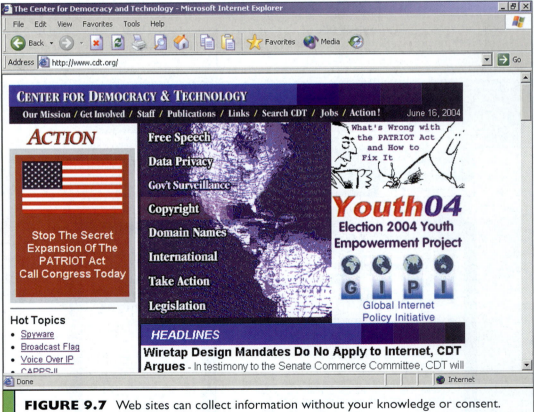

FIGURE 9.7 Web sites can collect information without your knowledge or consent. To learn more about this and other privacy issues, visit the Center for Democracy and Technology's home page at **www.cdt.org**.

Marketing industry spokespeople and lobbyists argue that the U.S. government should not impose laws or regulations to protect consumers' privacy. They argue that the industry should regulate itself. Privacy advocates counter that technology has outpaced the industry's capability to regulate itself, as evidenced by the widespread availability of highly personal information on the Internet.

The Direct Marketing Association (DMA) claims to enforce a basic code of ethics among its member organizations. However, many of the most aggressive Internet-based marketing firms have no ties to or previous experience with the DMA. The DMA takes steps to ensure that confidential information doesn't fall into the wrong hands and that consumers can opt out of marketing campaigns if they wish (Figure 9.8). However, opt-out systems on the Internet are already used for fraudulent purposes. For example, e-mail spammers typically claim that recipients can "opt out" of mass e-mail marketing campaigns. But recipients who respond to such messages succeed only in validating their e-mail addresses, and the result is often a major increase in the volume of unsolicited e-mail.

So far there isn't much that can be done. In June 2004, the U.S. Congress decided against creating a No Spam list (similar to the National Do Not Call list to combat telemarketers), citing the potential for misuse and the inability to provide effective enforcement. Private lawsuits have not been effective yet, but they may be a bright spot on the horizon. The threat of monetary penalties may be the only thing that can thwart the growth of the spam industry.

Consumer fears regarding the use of information collected by Web sites may be impeding the growth of e-commerce. According to a recent survey by *Business-Week* magazine, consumers cite privacy concerns as their primary reason for not going online. However, online businesses don't seem to be getting the message. According to a recent study, more than two-thirds of the most popular commercial Web sites displayed "privacy policy" pages that explained how they intended to collect and use personal information about site visitors, but only 10 percent of these sites gave visitors any meaningful control over the use of this information (Figure 9.9). In

FIGURE 9.8 The Direct Marketing Association takes steps to ensure that consumers can opt out of marketing campaigns if they wish.

FIGURE 9.9 Yahoo!'s Privacy Center can be found at privacy.yahoo.com/privacy/us/.

yet another survey, 82 percent of Internet users strongly object to the sale of their personal information, so it's hardly surprising that the Internet retail sector is growing more slowly than anticipated.

Privacy Online
Internet users overwhelmingly agree—by a ratio of three to one—that the U.S.

government needs to adopt laws that will safeguard basic privacy rights. Until then, it's up to you to safeguard your privacy on the Internet. To do so, follow these suggestions:

- Browse anonymously by surfing from sites such as the Anonymizer (**www.anonymizer.com**) (Figure 9.10) or The Cloak (**www.the-cloak.com**).

- Disable cookies on your Web browser or use cookie management software such as Junkbuster (**www.junkbusters.com**).

- Use a "throwaway" e-mail address from a free Web-based service such as Hotmail (**www.hotmail.com**) for the e-mail address you place on Web pages, mailing lists, chat rooms, or other public Internet spaces that are scanned by e-mail spammers.

- Tell children not to divulge any personal information online without first asking a parent or teacher for permission.

- Don't fill out site registration forms unless you see a privacy policy statement indicating that the information you supply won't be sold to third parties.

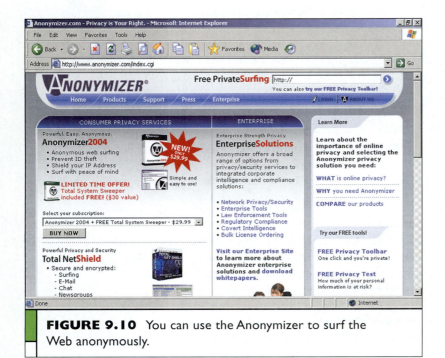

FIGURE 9.10 You can use the Anonymizer to surf the Web anonymously.

Privacy at Home

Do you own a cell phone? Are you aware that all new cell phones in the United States must have GPS awareness? This means that your phone can be located, usually within 30 feet, by law enforcement and emergency services personnel when you dial 911. Some services, such as uLocate and Wherify, provide the exact location of a cell phone. This can come in handy when a parent is trying to keep track of a child, but it can be intrusive when an employer uses it to track an employee using a company cell phone.

Some software is so powerful that it will send a notification to the home unit whenever the cell phone leaves a designated geographic area. In theory, someone could map you to a certain classroom and be notified when you and your cell phone left the room. This location-aware tracking software is already in use by the criminal justice system to keep track of offenders who are sentenced to home detention. The subject is fitted with an ankle or wrist bracelet and then the software is set to trigger an alarm if the bracelet strays from the designated area. These bracelets also are being used to keep track of Alzheimer's patients.

Privacy at Work

In the United States, more than three-quarters of large employers routinely engage in **employee monitoring**, observing employees' phone calls, e-mails, Web browsing habits, and computer files. One program, Spector, provides employers with a report of everything employees do online by taking hundreds of screen snapshots per hour (Figure 9.11). About one company in four has fired an employee based on what it has found.

Such monitoring is direct and invasive, but it will continue until laws are passed against it. Why do companies monitor their employees? Companies are concerned about employees who may offer trade secrets to competitors in hopes of landing an attractive job offer. Another concern is sexual harassment lawsuits. Employees who access pornographic Web sites or circulate offensive jokes via e-mail may be creating a hostile environment for other employees—and that could result in a huge lawsuit against the company.

FIGURE 9.11 Employers can use Spector, an employee-monitoring program from SpectorSoft, to track everything employees do online.

To protect your privacy at work, remember the following rules:

- Unless you have specific permission, don't use your employer's telephone system for personal calls. Make all such calls from a pay phone or from your personal cell phone.

- Never use your e-mail account at work for personal purposes. Get your own account with an ISP and be sure to send and receive all personal mail from your home computer.

- Assume that everything you do while you're at work—whether it's talking on the phone, using your computer, taking a break, or chatting with coworkers—may be monitored and recorded.

Now that you've learned about some important privacy issues, let's take a look at some intentional invasions of your privacy—computer crime.

Computer Crime and Cybercrime

Privacy issues, such as collecting personal information and employee monitoring, should be distinguished from **computer crimes**, which are actions that violate state or federal laws. **Cybercrime** describes crimes carried out by means of the Internet. A new legal field—**cyberlaw**—is emerging to track and combat computer-related crime.

To combat these new types of crime, President Clinton established the President's Working Group on Unlawful Conduct on the Internet in 2000. This group was charged with informing the president of ways that the federal government can "ensure the safety and security of those who use the Internet." At another level, the National White Collar Crime Center maintains an informative site at

FIGURE 9.12
Sites, such as Victim Assistance Online's white collar cybercrime page, provide links to organizations and institutions that deal with cybercrime.

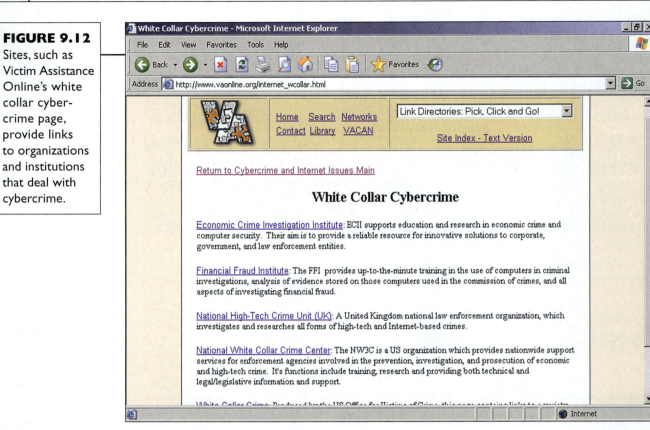

www.cybercrime.org and offers training on how to fight cybercrime (Figure 9.12). This section explores the various types of cybercrime and the kinds of computer criminals that may be putting you at risk.

TYPES OF COMPUTER CRIME

Anyone who wants to invade or harm a computer system can use a variety of tools and tricks. Pay close attention; you'll learn several facts that could help you avoid becoming a victim.

Identity Theft

The phone rings and it's a collection agency demanding immediate payment for a $5,000 stereo system bill that's past due. You can't believe what you're hearing— you always pay your bills on time, and you haven't purchased any stereo equipment lately. What's going on?

It's identity theft, one of the fastest-growing crimes in the United States and Canada. With **identity theft**, a criminal obtains enough information about you to open a credit account in your name and then maxes it out, leaving you with the bill. Although laws limit liability for fraudulent charges to $50, victims of identity theft have found themselves saddled with years of agony. The bad marks on their credit reports can prevent them from buying homes, obtaining telephone service, and even getting jobs.

What do criminals need to pull off identity theft? They need only your address, Social Security number, and a little more information, such as the addresses you've lived at for the past few years. How does somebody get this information? Dozens of Web sites sell individuals' Social Security numbers for as little as $6 each.

In a new twist on identity theft, a "phisher" poses as a legitimate company in an e-mail or on a Web site in an attempt to learn personal information such as your Social Security number, user name, password, and account numbers. For example, you might receive an e-mail that appears to come from XYZ Company asking you to confirm your e-identity (user name and password). Because the communication looks legitimate, you comply. The phisher can now gain access to your accounts.

CURRENTS

Ethical Debates

Software Piracy: Warez Can Get You into Big Trouble

It's called warez, and there's one important thing to know about it: It's illegal. The term *warez* (pronounced "wares") is widely used in the computer underground to describe illegal copies of commercial programs, such as Adobe Photoshop or Microsoft Office. Thanks to the Internet, trafficking in illegally duplicated software is rampant and rapidly increasing. According to the Business Software Alliance (BSA), an industry group that fights piracy, unauthorized duplication robs software firms of an estimated $13 billion every year. At this clip, the cost to the U.S. economy amounts to more than 100,000 jobs and $1 billion in lost tax revenues.

Much of the online warez trafficking takes place on Internet Relay Chat (IRC), which makes it difficult to trace the actions of individuals—but not impossible. The BSA recently filed suit against 25 people after the FBI raided their homes and confiscated computer equipment and software. If convicted, each of the accused could face civil fines of up to $100,000 for *each* case of copyright infringement, criminal penalties of up to $250,000, and a jail term of up to 5 years.

What about sharing programs without money changing hands? That's illegal, too—and equally dangerous for participants: Under the No Electronic Theft (NET) Act, prosecutors need not prove a profit motive in cases of criminal copyright infringement. Still, software piracy remains rampant in the United States, where perhaps 25 percent of all business software programs in use may have been obtained

illegally. The situation is worse overseas, where some pirates use CD duplication factories and high-speed Internet connections to sell warez on a massive scale.

Law-enforcement officials are fighting warez through cross-border cooperation. Take Operation Fastlink, an initiative that resulted in the seizure of 200 computers, 30 servers, and more than 65,000 pirated works in 27 states and 10 countries.

The BSA is hot on the trail of such pirates (Figure 9.13). When BSA investigators work online, they cover their tracks using software that switches their computers to different ISPs every minute. Although the battle never lets up, new laws and new technology are improving the odds that people who sell or trade warez will be caught.

FIGURE 9.13   The purpose of the Business Software Alliance is to promote a safe and legal digital world.

Computer Viruses

A **computer virus** is hidden code within a program that may damage or destroy the infected files. Like living viruses, computer viruses require a host (such as a program file), and they're designed to make copies of themselves.

Typically, virus infections spread when somebody inserts a disk containing an infected program into a computer and then starts the infected program. You might also get a virus by downloading an infected program from the Internet. Most viruses are called **file infectors** because they attach themselves to a program file. When the program is executed, the virus spreads to other programs on the user's hard disk. Should you copy a file on your computer to

Destinations

To find out what the "z" in warez stands for, go to **brasslantern.org/community/companies/warez-b.html**

a disk and give it to someone, the infection spreads even further (Figure 9.14).

Most computer viruses are spread by e-mail attachments. When you open an e-mail, you may see a dialog box asking whether you want to open an attachment. Don't open it unless you're sure the attachment is safe.

Consider the following scenario. A professor with a large lecture section of 100 students receives an e-mail from a former student with an attachment named "Spring Break" that apparently contains a picture of the student's spring break and so opens it. The attachment appears to do nothing, and the professor goes about his or her business. The attachment, however, is doing something. It is sending a copy of itself to everyone in the professor's e-mail address box—including each of the 100 students in the class. Now the attachment is propagating to the e-mail address lists of each of the students. The attachment is received by parents, friends, other professors, and fellow students. Many open the attachment, and the process accelerates very rapidly.

Executable file attachments pose the most serious risk. You can tell an executable file by its extension. In Microsoft Windows, the extension is .exe, but executable files also can be named .com, .bin, or .bat. However, you can't be sure that a file is executable by its extension alone. You should also be wary of opening Microsoft Office documents, such as Microsoft Word (.doc) and Microsoft Excel (.xls) files. The best policy is to always check attachment files with an antivirus program before you open them.

Although many viruses are best categorized as nuisances or pranks, all consume system memory and slow the computer's processing speed, and some even damage data. In the prank category is the Wazzu virus, which randomly relocates a word in a Microsoft Word document and sometimes inserts "wazzu" into the text. Still others, such as Disk Killer, are far more malicious: Disk Killer wipes out all of the data on your hard drive.

A far more serious type of virus is a boot sector virus. A **boot sector virus** also propagates by an infected program, but it installs itself on the beginning tracks of a hard drive, where code is stored that automatically executes every time

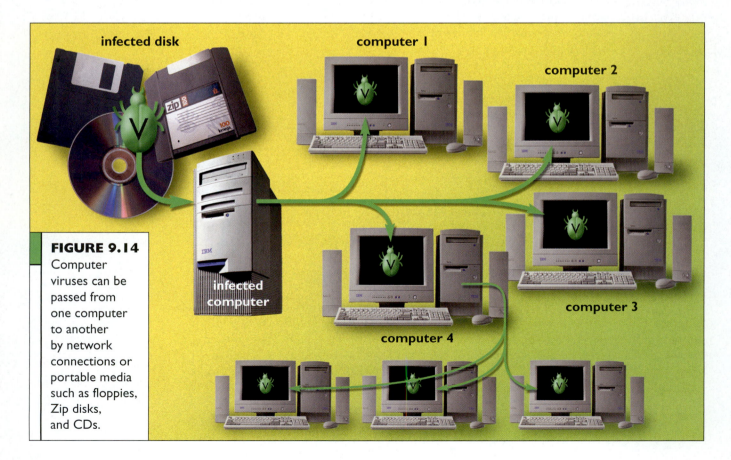

FIGURE 9.14
Computer viruses can be passed from one computer to another by network connections or portable media such as floppies, Zip disks, and CDs.

you start the computer. Unlike file infectors, boot sector viruses don't require you to start a specific program to infect your computer; starting your system is sufficient. Boot sector viruses also may lead to the destruction of all the data stored on your hard drive.

A **macro virus** takes advantage of the automatic command execution capabilities (called **macros**) of productivity software, such as word processing and spreadsheet programs. Macro viruses infect data files, which contain the data created with an application such as Microsoft Word. When these files are shared with others, the virus infects their computer. The only way to be certain of preventing the spread of viruses is to use antivirus software to check these kinds of files.

More than 20,000 computer viruses are in existence, and more are being written each day. Two of the most famous and devastating viruses, the Melissa virus of 1999 and the Love Bug virus of 2000, are estimated to have cost businesses and individuals worldwide more than $10 billion in lost data, computer repairs, lost work time, and lost sales. A particularly nasty virus, SirCam, appeared in the fall of 2001 and spread so rapidly that the Internet and many corporate networks were all but brought to a standstill.

Computer virus authors are trying to "improve" their programs. Some new viruses are self-modifying; each new copy is slightly different from the previous one, making it difficult to protect your computer (Figure 9.15).

More Rogue Programs

Viruses aren't the only type of rogue program. Other destructive programs include time bombs, worms, zombies, and Trojan horses.

A **time bomb**, also called a **logic bomb**, is a virus that sits harmlessly on a system until a certain event or set of circumstances causes the program to become active. For example, before leaving a Texas firm, a fired programmer planted a time bomb program that wiped out 168,000 critical financial records.

A **worm** is a program that resembles a computer virus in that it can spread from one computer to another. Unlike a virus, however, a worm can propagate over

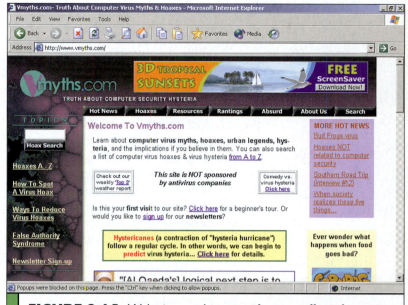

FIGURE 9.15 Web sites such as **vmyths.com** offer information on computer viruses and debunk the myths surrounding them.

a computer network, and it doesn't require an unsuspecting user to execute a program or macro file. It takes control of affected computers and uses their resources to attack other network-connected systems. First reported on April 13, 2004, the Sasser worm, which exploits a weakness in Microsoft Windows, took the Internet by storm. Microsoft quickly responded with a fix, but months later the Sasser worm was still infecting vulnerable computers. Other recent threats include the Netsky and Sober worms.

Another type of threat is a denial of service attack. With a **denial of service (DoS) attack** (also called **syn flooding** due to technical details of the attack method), an attacker bombards an Internet server with a huge number of requests so that the server becomes overloaded and unable to function. Because network administrators can easily block data from specific IP addresses, hackers must commandeer as many computers as possible to launch their attack. These commandeered computers are called **zombies** because they simply do what the hacker's DoS program tells them to do.

A **Trojan horse** is a rogue program disguised as a useful program, but it contains hidden instructions to perform a malicious task instead. Sometimes a Trojan horse is disguised as a game or a utility program that users will find appealing. Then, when users begin running the game, they discover that they have loaded another program entirely. A Trojan horse may erase the data on your hard disk or cause other irreparable damage.

Fraud and Theft

When computer intruders make off with sensitive personal information, the potential for fraud multiplies. For example, employees of the U.S. Social Security Administration used their computer-access privileges to gather Social Security numbers and other information on 11,000 U.S. citizens and sold this information to criminals specializing in credit card fraud.

Physical theft of computer equipment is a growing problem as well (Figure 9.16). An estimated 85 percent of computer thefts are inside jobs, leaving no signs of forced physical entry. In addition, it's difficult to trace components after they've been taken out of a computer and reassembled. Particularly valuable are the microprocessor chips that drive computers. **Memory shaving**, in which knowledgeable thieves remove some of a computer's RAM chips but leave enough to start the computers, is harder to detect. Such a crime might go unnoticed for weeks.

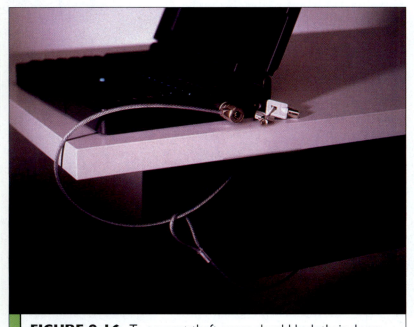

FIGURE 9.16 To prevent theft, users should lock their doors and turn off their computers. In some cases, it may be wise to secure hardware to desks.

Tricks for Obtaining Passwords

The most publicized computer crimes involve unauthorized access, in which an intruder gains entry to a supposedly secure computer system. Typically, computer systems use some type of authentication technique—usually plaintext passwords—to protect the system from uninvited guests. Many techniques are used to guess or obtain a password Figure 9.17. Another widely used technique involves exploiting well-known holes in obsolete e-mail programs, which can be manipulated to disclose a user's password.

Salami Shaving and Data Diddling

With *salami shaving*, a programmer alters a program to subtract a very small amount of money from an account—say, two cents—and diverts the funds to the embezzler's account. Ideally, the sum is so small that it's never noticed. In a business that handles thousands of accounts, an insider could skim tens of thousands of dollars per year using this method.

With *data diddling*, insiders modify data by altering accounts or database records so that it's difficult or impossible to tell that they've stolen funds or equipment. A Colorado supermarket chain recently became the victim of data diddling when it discovered nearly $2 million in unaccounted losses.

Forgery

Knowledgeable users can make Internet data appear to come from one place when it's really coming from another. "Anonymizer" sites and programs strip the sender's tracking data from a message and then resend the message.

Forged messages and Web pages can cause embarrassment and worse. A university professor in Texas was recently attacked with thousands of e-mail messages and Usenet postings after someone forged a racist Usenet article in his name. In Beijing, a student almost lost an $18,000 scholarship when a jealous rival forged an e-mail message to the University of Michigan turning down the scholarship. Fortunately, the forgery was discovered and the scholarship was reinstated, but only after a lengthy delay. And, reportedly, there exists a Microsoft Word macro virus that sends copies of a victim's Word documents

FIGURE 9.17 Techniques Used to Obtain Passwords

Password guessing	Computer users too often choose a password that's easily guessed, such as "password." Other popular passwords are "qwerty" (the first six letters of the keyboard), obscene words, personal names, birthdays, celebrity names, movie characters such as Frodo or Gandalf, and cartoon characters such as Garfield.
Shoulder surfing	In a crowded computer lab, it's easy to peek over someone's shoulder, look at their keyboard, and obtain their password. Watch out for shoulder surfing when using an ATM machine, too.
Packet sniffing	A program called a packet sniffer examines all of the traffic on a section of a network and looks for passwords, credit card numbers, and other valuable information.
Dumpster diving	Intruders go through an organization's trash hoping to find documents that contain lists of user IDs and even passwords. It's wise to use a shredder!
Social engineering	This is a form of deception to get people to divulge sensitive information. You might get a call or an e-mail from a person who claims, "We have a problem and need your password right now to save your e-mail." If you comply, you might give an intruder entry to a secure system.
Superuser status	Enables system administrators to access and modify virtually any file on a network. If intruders gain superuser status, they can obtain the passwords of everyone using the system.

to 23 different Usenet newsgroups under subject lines such as "New Virus Alert!" and "How to find child pornography."

Blackmail

According to one estimate, more than 40 percent of all computer crimes go unreported. Why? Suppose you're running a bank. You've lost $1 million due to computer theft. What's going to cost you more, covering the loss or telling the world that depositors' money isn't safe?

According to news reports, adverse publicity fears have been used to blackmail financial institutions. In London, computer attackers have reportedly extorted nearly $650 million from banks in the past few years after demonstrating to senior executives that they could completely wipe out the banks' computer systems.

Now that you've learned about the types of computer crime and cybercrime, let's discuss the kinds of computer criminals you may run into on the Web.

MEET THE ATTACKERS

A surprising variety of people can cause security problems, ranging from pranksters to hardened criminals, such as the Russian intruders who recently made off with $10 million from Citibank. Motives vary, too. Some attackers are out for ego gratification and don't intend any harm (Figure 9.18). Others are out for money or on a misguided crusade; some are just plain malicious.

FIGURE 9.18 Some attackers are out for ego gratification and don't intend any harm.

Techtalk

IP Spoofing
With IP spoofing, hackers send a message with an IP address disguised as an incoming message from a trusted source to a computer. The hacker must first locate and modify the message packet headers of a trusted source (called a port) and then manipulate the hacker's own communication so that it appears to come from the trusted port.

To learn more about the ethics of hacking, see the video clip at **www.prenhall.com/cayf2006**

Destinations

To learn more about ethical hackers, visit **eeye.com** and **www.atstake.com**

Hackers, Crackers, Cybergangs, and Virus Authors

The most celebrated intruders are computer hobbyists and computer experts for whom unauthorized access is something of an irresistible intellectual game. **Hackers** are computer hobbyists who enjoy pushing computer systems (and themselves) to their limits. They experiment with programs to try to discover capabilities that aren't mentioned in the software manuals. They modify systems to obtain the maximum possible performance. And sometimes they try to track down all of the weaknesses and loopholes in a system's security. When hackers attempt unauthorized access, they rarely damage data or steal assets. Hackers generally subscribe to an unwritten code of conduct, called the **hacker ethic**, which forbids the destruction of data. Hackers form communities. Such communities have a pecking order that is defined in terms of an individual's reputation for hacking prowess (Figure 9.19). **Cybergangs** are groups of hackers or crackers working together to coordinate attacks or post online graffiti, as well as other malicious conduct.

Crackers (also called **black hats**) are hackers who become obsessed (often uncontrollably) with gaining entry to highly secure computer systems. Like

hackers, they generally don't intend to harm or steal data, but the frequency and sophistication of their attacks can cause major headaches for system administrators. A Pentagon official recently disclosed that the U.S. Department of Defense computer systems experience more than 1,000 unauthorized access attempts per day, and that as many as 96 percent of such attempts evade detection.

Like hackers, crackers are often obsessed with their reputation in the hacking and cracking communities. To document their feats, they often leave calling cards, such as a prank message, on the systems they penetrate. One especially famous case occurred in 1996 when the CIA Web site was penetrated by a group of Swedish crackers who altered the home page to say "Welcome to the Central Stupidity Agency." Sometimes these traces enable law enforcement personnel to track them down.

Hackers and crackers should be distinguished from criminals who seek to use unauthorized access to steal money or valuable data. Keep in mind, however, that anyone who tries to gain unauthorized access to a computer system is probably breaking one or more laws. However, more than a few hackers and crackers have turned pro, offering their services to companies hoping to use hacker expertise to shore up their computer systems' defenses. Those who undertake this type of hacking are called **ethical hackers** or **white hats**.

Computer virus authors create viruses to vandalize computer systems. Virus authors are typically teenage males who want to see how far they can push the boundaries of antivirus software. They usually see no harm in what they're doing. They claim that all technological progress is inevitable, and that somebody else would eventually create the programs they write. Most eventually stop writing viruses after they've matured a bit and found something more worthwhile to do with their time.

Swindlers

Swindlers typically perpetuate bogus work-at-home opportunities, illegal pyramid schemes, chain letters, risky business opportunities, bogus franchises, phony goods that won't be delivered, overpriced

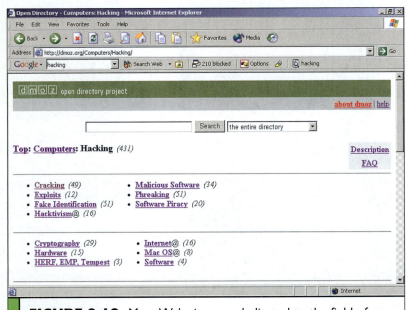

FIGURE 9.19 Many Web sites are dedicated to the field of hacking. This is a sample listing of the links available on the DMOZ Open Directory Project's page on hacking.

scholarship searches, and get-rich-quick scams. Today, the distribution media of choice include e-mail, Internet chat rooms, and Web sites.

Estimates of the scope of the problem vary, but the U.S. National Consumers League believes that consumers are losing millions of dollars on a variety of Internet scams—and the figure is growing by leaps and bounds (Figure 9.20).

Shills

Internet auction sites such as eBay attract online versions of the same scams long perpetrated at live auctions. A *shill* is a secret operative who bids on another seller's item to drive up the price. The practice made headlines recently when an abstract painting's price shot from 25 cents to $135,805 after speculation that the work was a long-lost canvas by the renowned artist Richard Diekenborn. In this case, the shill was the seller, who used a different e-mail address to bid up his own offering. In response, the auction site cancelled the sale and suspended the seller's account.

Cyberstalkers and Sexual Predators

One of the newest and fastest growing of all crimes is **cyberstalking**, using the Internet, e-mail, or other electronic communications to harass or threaten a person repeatedly. For example, one San Diego university student terrorized five female classmates for more than a year, sending them hundreds of violent and threatening e-mail messages. In an Internet chat room, a 16-year-old boy was contacted by a woman who asked him to make a videotape of himself being tied up and tickled. When the boy refused, the woman bombarded him with more than 30,000 e-mail messages demanding the videotape and threatening to tell the boy's parents. A former security guard used the Internet to terrorize a woman who refused his sexual advances. He impersonated his 28-year-old victim in Internet chat rooms, posting messages that she fantasized about being raped. On at least six occasions, the woman received visitors—sometimes at night—who said they were there to rape her.

Cyberstalking has one thing in common with traditional stalking: Most perpetrators are men, and most victims are women, particularly women in college. One in every eight women attending college has been followed, watched, phoned, written, or e-mailed in ways that they found obsessive and frightening.

Children are at risk from online sexual predators who are much more numerous than most parents realize. According to a study conducted by the National Center for Missing and Exploited Children, about one in every five kids has received invitations to engage in sexual activities while participating in Internet discussions. Online predators may encourage children to run away from home or meet them while their parents are away.

Online predators also look for new victims on cyberdating sites. Most cyberdating

Techtalk

Phreaking
When a computer or other device is used to trick a telephone system, it's called *phreaking*. When successful, a phone phreak is able to make free telephone calls or have calls charged to a different account.

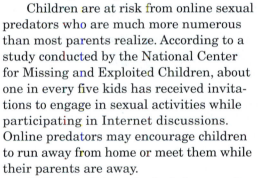

FIGURE 9.20 Internet Scams

Rip and tear	A Seattle man posted ads for Barbie dolls and other goods on eBay, collected more than $32,000 in orders, and never delivered any goods. Swindlers move to a new state once their activities are uncovered. The perpetrators believe that law enforcement won't be concerned with the relatively small amounts involved in each transaction.
Pumping and dumping	Crooks use Internet stock trading sites, chat rooms, Usenet discussions, and e-mail to sing the praises of worthless companies in which they hold stock. Then, after the share prices go up, they dump the stocks and make a hefty profit.
Bogus goods	Two Miami residents were recently indicted on charges of mail and wire fraud after selling hundreds of "Go-boxes," which purported to turn red traffic lights to green. The boxes, which were actually nothing more than strobe lights, sold for between $69 and $150.

FIGURE 9.21 To protect site users from unscrupulous predators, True.com actively conducts criminal and marital status checks on its communicating members and requires all site users to agree to a member code of ethics.

sites use profiling to match potential mates. The downside is that it is difficult to check someone's cyberidentity against his or her actual identity. Many of these sites are now engaging in background checks—verifying everything from gender and county to marital status and checking criminal records (Figure 9.21).

Now that you understand the types of perpetrators who pose a risk to your online privacy and safety, let's look closer at the growing risks to equipment and data security.

Security

As our entire economy and infrastructure move to networked computer systems, breaches of computer security can be costly. Even when no actual harm has occurred, fixing the breach and checking to ensure that no damage has occurred require time, resources, and money. It's no wonder that security currently accounts for an estimated 3 to 5 percent of all corporate expenditures on computer systems.

SECURITY RISKS

Not all of the dangers posed to computer systems are caused by malicious, conscious intent. A **computer security risk** is any event, action, or situation—intentional or not—that could lead to the loss or destruction of computer systems or the data they contain. Some research indicates that security breaches may cost individuals and industry as much as $9 billion per year because of their impact on customer service, worker productivity, and so on.

Wireless Networks

Wireless LANs are inherently insecure, but they are beginning to benefit from emerging security standards. Unlike wired networks, which send traffic over private dedicated lines, wireless LANs send their traffic across shared space—airwaves. Because no one owns the space that airwaves travel across, the opportunity for interference from other traffic is great and the need for additional security is paramount.

To break into a wireless network, you must be within the proximity limits of the wireless signal. In a process called *war driving*, an individual drives around with a wireless device, such as a laptop or PDA, to look for wireless networks. Some people do this as a hobby and map out different wireless networks, whereas hackers look for wireless networks to break into. It is fairly easy to break into an unsecured wireless network and obtain confidential information. War-driving applications carry names such as Aerosol, Airfart, and AirJack and are readily available for download from the Internet.

The 802.11b standard includes a provision called WEP (Wired Equivalent Privacy). As with all security technologies, WEP has its vulnerabilities. In September 2004, AirSnort, which runs on Linux, appeared on the Internet. AirSnort infiltrates the WEP coding system and defeats the security it provides. The need for wireless security is great, thus the development of new and more powerful security systems is inevitable. Wireless network owners should implement the security that is currently available so that the system is at least protected from the casual browser.

Corporate Espionage

Corporate computer systems contain a great deal of information that could be valuable to competitors, including product development plans and specifications, customer contact lists, manufacturing process knowledge, cost data, and strategic plans. According to computer security experts, **corporate espionage**, the unauthorized access of corporate information, usually to the benefit of a competitor, is on the rise—so sharply that it may soon eclipse all other sources of unauthorized access (Figure 9.22). The perpetrators are often ex-employees who have been hired by a competing firm precisely because of their knowledge of the computer system at their previous place of employment.

According to one estimate, 80 percent of all data loss is caused by company insiders. Unlike intruders, employees have many opportunities to sabotage a company's computer system, often in ways that are difficult to trace. They may discover or deliberately create security holes called **trap doors** that they can exploit after leaving the firm to get even with the company. They can then divulge the former employer's trade secrets to a competitor or destroy crucial data.

The espionage threat goes beyond national borders. Nations bent on acquiring trade secrets and new technologies also are trying to break into corporate computer systems. According to a recent estimate, the governments of more than 125 countries are actively involved in industrial espionage.

Information Warfare

Information warfare is the use of information technologies to corrupt or destroy an enemy's information and industrial infrastructure. A concerted enemy attack would include electronic warfare (using electronic devices to destroy or damage computer systems), network warfare (hackerlike attacks on a nation's network infrastructure, including the electronic banking system), and structural sabotage (attacks on computer systems that support transportation, finance, energy, and telecommunications). However, we shouldn't overlook old-fashioned explosives directed at computer centers. According to one expert, a well-coordinated bombing of only 100 key computer installations could bring the U.S. economy to a grinding halt.

According to experts, defenses against such attacks are sorely lacking. A recent U.S. Department of Defense study disclosed

FIGURE 9.22 Corporate espionage may soon eclipse all other sources of unauthorized access to computer systems.

that military systems were attacked a quarter of a million times in 1995, and that number has surely grown since then. In 1995, as a test a U.S. Department of Defense team conducted 38,000 attacks of their own. They were successful 65 percent of the time, and 63 percent of those attacks escaped detection. Former U.S. Deputy Attorney General Jaime Gorelick warns of a "cyber equivalent of Pearl Harbor" if the United States does not take steps to prepare for electronic attack.

Even if no enemy nation mounts an all-out information war on the United States, information terrorism is increasingly likely. Thanks to the worldwide distribution of powerful but inexpensive microprocessors, virtually anyone can construct electronic warfare weapons from widely available materials. These weapons include high-energy radio frequency (HERF) guns and electromagnetic pulse transformer (EMPT) bombs, which can damage or

FIGURE 9.23   A working model of a homemade HERF device.

destroy computer systems up to a quarter of a mile away (Figure 9.23).

If this scenario sounds frightening, remember that information technology is a double-edged sword. Information technology gives despots a potent weapon of war, but it also undermines their power by giving citizens a way to organize democratic resistance. In Russia, for example, e-mail and fax machines played a major role in the failure of the 1989 military coup. In the United States, we have learned more about the importance of redundant data backup systems and the resiliency of the U.S. monetary system since the September 11 attacks, but we're still vulnerable and must develop ways to protect our computer systems and infrastructure.

Security Loophole Detection Programs
Intruders can use a variety of programs that automatically search for unprotected or poorly protected computer systems and notify them when a target is found. They can also use SATAN, a security loophole detection program used by system administrators. In the wrong hands, the program can help an intruder figure out how to get into a poorly secured system.

Public Safety
Perhaps the greatest threat posed by security breaches is the threat to human life;

computers are increasingly part of safety-critical systems, such as air-traffic control. By paralyzing transportation and power infrastructures, attackers could completely disrupt the distribution of electricity, food, water, and medical supplies.

This threat nearly became a reality when a 14-year-old hacker knocked out phone and radio service to a regional airport's communications tower. Although the hacker didn't realize he had accessed an airport computer and meant no harm, his actions paralyzed the airport's computer system and forced air-traffic controllers to rely on cellular phones and battery-powered radios to direct airplanes until the system was back up and running.

Terrorism
Perhaps the brightest spot in the war on terror is the identification of persons of interest using special security software programs. One program that attempts to find such people is called NORA, which stands for Non-Obvious Relationship Awareness. It takes this software just seconds to analyze data to figure out if individuals are connected with unsavory characters. NORA uses actual data to discover similarities and links between individuals. Other security programs try to figure out what hypothetical terrorists might do and then identify terrorists by comparing their behavior with that of the general population. The downside of these methods is the potential for violating individual privacy rights and mistakenly targeting innocent people.

PROTECTING YOUR COMPUTER SYSTEM

Several measures can safeguard computer systems, but none of them can make a computer system 100-percent secure. A trade-off exists between security and usability: The more restrictions imposed by security tools, the less useful the system becomes.

Power-Related Problems
Often caused by lightning storms, power surges can destroy sensitive electronic components, and power outages carry the threat of data loss. To safeguard against data loss caused by surges and outages, some applications offer an autosave feature,

which backs up your work at a specified interval (such as every 10 minutes). You can also equip your system with an **uninterruptible power supply** (**UPS**), a battery-powered device that provides power to your computer for a limited time when it detects an outage or critical voltage drop (Figure 9.24). Many companies have electric generators to run large-scale computer systems when the power fails.

Controlling Access

Because many security problems originate with purloined passwords, password authentication is crucial to controlling authorized access to computer systems. Typically, users select their own passwords—and that is the source of a serious computer security risk. If an intruder can guess your password, the intruder can gain access to the computer system. Any damage that results will appear to have been perpetrated by you, not the intruder. What's a good password? The best passwords are at least eight characters in length, combine upper- and lowercase letters, and include one or more numbers. Xa98MsoZ is an example of a good password.

In addition to password authentication, **know-and-have authentication** requires using tokens, which are handheld electronic devices that generate a logon code. Increasingly popular are smart cards, devices the size of a credit card with their own internal memories (Figure 9.25). In tandem with a supplied personal identification number (PIN), a smart card can reliably establish that the person trying to gain access has the authorization to do so.

However, when used with digital cash systems, smart cards pose a significant threat to personal privacy. Because every smart-card transaction, no matter how minute, is recorded, a person's purchases can be assembled and scrutinized. An investigator could put together a list of the magazines and newspapers you purchase and read, where and when you paid bridge tolls and subway fares, and what you had for lunch.

The most secure authentication approach is **biometric authentication**, which uses a variety of techniques, including voice recognition, retinal scans, fingerprint scans, and face and hand recognition (Figure 9.26). For example, Gateway now offers a built-in biometric fingerprint sensor on its latest laptop that locks access to the computer unless the correct fingerprint is matched. In an experiment in

FIGURE 9.24
A UPS is a battery-powered device that provides power to your computer for a limited time during a power outage.

FIGURE 9.25
Smart cards are devices the size of a credit card with their own internal memories.

FIGURE 9.26 Biometric authentication devices such as (**a**) retinal scanners, (**b**) fingerprint scanners, and (**c**) hand-geometry readers are already in widespread use.

Destinations

Personal firewalls are an excellent way to protect your computer from unauthorized access. For more information about firewalls, go to **computer.how stuffworks.com/ firewall.htm** or **www.zonelabs.com/ store/content/ home.jsp**

Barcelona, Spain, a soccer club verified the tickets of over 100,000 ticket holders as they entered the stadium using a database of ticket barcodes matched with fans' photographs. If the ticket holder's face did not match the face in the database, they were not admitted to the contest.

Firewalls

A **firewall** is a computer program or device that permits an organization's internal computer users to access the external Internet but severely limits the ability of outsiders to access internal data (Figure 9.27). A firewall can be implemented through software, hardware, or a combination of both. Firewalls are a necessity, but they provide no protection against insider pilferage.

Home users opting for "always on" broadband connections, such as those offered by cable modems or DSL, face a number of computer security risks. **Personal firewalls** are programs or devices that protect home computers from unauthorized access.

Avoiding Scams

To avoid being scammed on the Internet, follow these tips:

- Do business with established companies that you know and trust.

- Read the fine print. If you're ordering something, make sure it's in stock and that the company promises to deliver within 30 days.

- Don't provide financial or other personal information or passwords to anyone, even if the request sounds legitimate.

- Be skeptical when somebody in an Internet chat room tells you about a great new company or stock.

Preventing Cyberstalking

To protect yourself against cyberstalking, follow these tips:

- Don't share any personal information, such as your real name, in chat rooms. Use a name that is gender- and age-neutral. Do not post a user profile.

- Be extremely cautious about meeting anyone you've contacted online. If you do, meet in a public place and bring friends along.

- If a situation you've encountered online makes you uncomfortable or afraid, contact the police immediately. Save all the communications you've received.

FIGURE 9.27
A firewall permits an organization's internal computer users to access the Internet but limits the ability of outsiders to access internal data.

your organization's PCs

corporate network

firewall

Internet

IMPACTS

Safety and Security

Tracking an Intruder

If you've ever visited the National Aeronautics and Space Administration (NASA), you know that unless you have top security clearance, getting closer than a binocular view of a space shuttle is impossible. A few years ago, however, a hacker known as "RaFa" was able to get a much closer view of NASA space shuttles—without even leaving his computer. The 23-year-old hacker downloaded about 43 MB of data from a top-security NASA server, including a 15-slide PowerPoint presentation of a future shuttle design.

RaFa supposedly used an anonymous FTP vulnerability in the NASA computer system to hack the design plans. He then sent the plans to a *ComputerWorld* reporter as proof that the NASA system was not secure. Although NASA didn't experience any direct financial loss from RaFa's activities, many companies do lose money because of hacker attacks—as much as $1 million can be lost from a single security incident.

However, a lot more is at stake than just money. What if terrorists or foreign agents could hack the U.S. government's computers and read, change, or steal sensitive documents? What if hackers could disrupt the networks that support vital national infrastructures such as finance, energy, and transportation?

Recognizing the danger, the federal government's National Infrastructure Protection Center has emergency response teams ready to fend off attacks on critical systems. Internationally, a group of security specialists is using "honeypots"—computers baited with fake data and purposely left vulnerable—to study how intruders operate and prepare stronger defenses (Figure 9.28).

FIGURE 9.28 Want to know more about honeypots and cybersecurity? Visit the Honeynet Project at project.honeynet.org.

Now that you've learned some ways to protect your security, let's discuss one of the major security measures used to keep information safe on the Internet: encryption.

The Encryption Debate

Cryptography is the study of transforming information into an encoded or scrambled format. Individuals who practice in this field are known as *cryptographers*. **Encryption** refers to a coding or scrambling process that renders a message unreadable by anyone except the intended recipient. Until recently, encryption was used only by intelligence services, militaries, and banks.

E-commerce requires strong, unbreakable encryption; otherwise, money could not be safely exchanged over the Internet. But now, powerful encryption software is available to the public, and U.S. law enforcement officials and defense agencies aren't happy about it. Criminals, including drug dealers and terrorists, can use encryption to hide their activities. In the aftermath of the September 11 terrorist attacks, U.S.

A	**1**
B	**2**
C	**3**
D	**4**
E	**5**
F	**6**
G	**7**
H	**8**
I	**9**
J	**10**
K	**11**
L	**12**
M	**13**
N	**14**
O	**15**
P	**16**
Q	**17**
R	**18**
S	**19**
T	**20**
U	**21**
V	**22**
W	**23**
X	**24**
Y	**25**
Z	**26**

FIGURE 9.29
This is the decoding key for "I love you."

officials revealed that the terrorist network had used encrypted e-mail to keep their plans and activities secret.

ENCRYPTION BASICS

To understand encryption, try this simple exercise: Consider a short message such as "I love you." Before it is encrypted, a readable message such as this one is in **plaintext**. To encrypt the message, for each character substitute the letter exactly 13 positions to the right in the 26-letter alphabet. (When you reach the end of the alphabet, start counting from the beginning.) This is an example of an **encryption key**, a formula that makes a plaintext message unreadable. After applying the key, you get the coded message, which is now in **ciphertext**. The ciphertext version of the original message looks like this:

```
V YBIR LBH
```

It looks like gibberish, doesn't it? That's the idea. No one who intercepts this message will know what it means. Your intended recipient, however, can tell what the message means if you give him or her the decoding key: in this case, counting 13 characters to the left (Figure 9.29). When your recipient gets the message and decrypts it, your message reappears:

```
I LOVE YOU
```

With **symmetric key encryption**, the recipient must possess the key to decrypt the message. Some of the keys used by banks and military agencies are so complex that the world's most powerful computer would have to analyze the ciphertext for several hundred years to discover the key. However, there is one way to defeat symmetric key encryption: steal the key, or **key interception**. Banks deliver decryption keys using trusted courier services; militaries use trusted personnel or agents, thus providing opportunities for key theft.

PUBLIC KEY ENCRYPTION

Public key encryption is considered one of the greatest (and most troubling) scientific achievements of the twentieth century. In brief, **public key encryption** uses two different keys: an encryption key (the **public key**) and a decryption key (the **private key**). People who want to receive secret messages publish their public key, for example, by placing it on a Web page or including it with a Usenet posting. When the public key is used to encrypt a message, the message becomes unreadable. The message becomes readable only when the recipient applies his or her private key, which nobody else knows (Figure 9.30).

Public key encryption is essential for e-commerce. When you visit a secure site on the Web, for example, your Web browser provides your public key to the Web server; in turn, the Web server provides the site's public key to your Web browser. Once a secure communication channel has been created, your browser displays a distinctive icon, such as a lock, on the status bar. You can now supply confidential information, such as your credit card number, with a reasonable degree of confidence that this information will not be intercepted while it is traveling across the Internet.

Digital Signatures and Certificates

Public key encryption can be used to implement **digital signatures**, a technique that guarantees a message has not been tampered with. Digital signatures are important to e-commerce because they enable computers to determine whether a received message or document is authentic and in its original form. For instance, a digital signature would provide an assurance that an order was authentic and not the result of a hacker who was trying to disrupt a business transaction.

Public key encryption also enables **digital certificates**, a technique for validating one's identity that is like showing your driver's license when you cash a check. For example, to protect both merchants and customers from online credit card fraud, Visa, MasterCard, and American Express collaborated to create an online shopping security standard for merchants and customers called **Secure Electronic Transaction** (**SET**) that uses digital certificates. Although not yet in widespread use, digital certificates are vital to the future of e-commerce. They enable parties engaged in Internet-mediated transactions to confirm each other's identity.

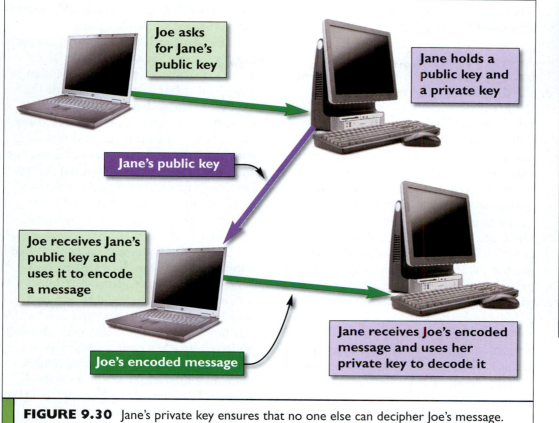

FIGURE 9.30 Jane's private key ensures that no one else can decipher Joe's message.

Toward a Public Key Infrastructure

A **public key infrastructure** (**PKI**) is a uniform set of encryption standards that specify how public key encryption, digital signatures, and digital certificates should be implemented in computer systems and on the Internet. Although there are numerous contenders, no dominant PKI has emerged (Figure 9.31).

One reason for the slow development of a PKI involves the fear, shared by many private citizens and businesses alike, that a single, dominant firm will monopolize the PKI and impose unreasonable fees on the public. Because so many people use Microsoft operating systems, Microsoft is in perhaps the best position to implement a PKI. In fact, Microsoft's .NET Passport system implements a Microsoft-developed PKI. But consumers and businesses fear that Microsoft will use its operating system monopoly and .NET Passport for unfair purposes, such as driving Microsoft's competitors out of business and imposing artificially high costs on the emerging electronic economy. Another reason for the slow development of a PKI

is that governments may step in to regulate public key encryption—or at the extreme, outlaw its use entirely.

FIGURE 9.31 The Federal Public Key Infrastructure Steering Committee establishes guidelines for implementing encrypted messages and signatures.

Destinations

For more information concerning public key encryption, visit the RSA Laboratories' "Frequently Asked Questions on Cryptography" page at **www.rsasecurity.com/rsalabs/node.asp?id=2152**

ENCRYPTION AND PUBLIC SECURITY ISSUES

Just one year before the September 11th terrorist attack on the World Trade Center, FBI Director Louis Freeh told the U.S. Congress that "the widespread use of robust unbreakable encryption ultimately will devastate our ability to fight crime and prevent terrorism. Unbreakable encryption will allow drug lords, spies, terrorists, and even violent gangs to communicate about their crimes and their conspiracies with impunity." In light of the terrorists' use of public key encryption—specifically, Pretty Good Privacy (PGP) (Figure 9.32)—Freeh's warning now seems prophetic. Soon after the attacks, there were calls in the U.S. Congress to outlaw public key encryption.

However, recognizing that public key encryption is vital to the emerging electronic economy, U.S. law enforcement and security agencies have not recommended that public key encryption be outlawed entirely. Instead, they advise that the U.S. Congress pass laws requiring a public key algorithm or a PKI that would enable investigators to eavesdrop on encrypted communications. U.S. government agencies have proposed some possibilities.

The **Clipper Chip** is a microprocessor that could encrypt voice or data communications in such a way that investigators could still intercept and decode the messages (Figure 9.33). The chip would encrypt the messages with a **back door**, a secret decoding mechanism that would enable investigators to decrypt messages without having to first obtain the private key. The Clipper Chip proposal collapsed after an expert cryptographer discovered, relatively easily, how to open the back door.

The Clinton administration proposed a **key escrow plan**, in which an independent key escrow agency would hold a user's private key. It would be divulged to investigators only when a valid court order was produced. However, this plan also was criticized. The key escrow agency would have to store the keys on its computer systems, which might not be adequately secured. The agency's employees would be vulnerable to bribes from criminals, as well as pressure from government investigators, who might try to obtain private keys without going through the lengthy

FIGURE 9.32

MIT manages a Web site for the distribution of Pretty Good Privacy software. This free encryption program is widely recognized as a viable alternative to commercial products.

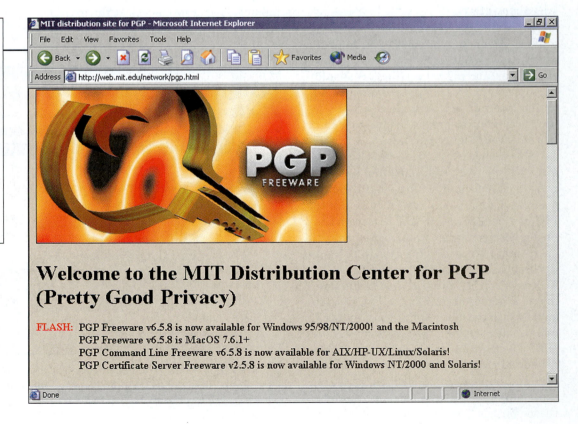

Welcome to the MIT Distribution Center for PGP (Pretty Good Privacy)

FLASH: PGP Freeware v6.5.8 is now available for Windows 95/98/NT/2000! and the Macintosh
PGP Freeware v6.5.8 is MacOS 7.6.1+
PGP Command Line Freeware v6.5.8 is now available for AIX/HP-UX/Linux/Solaris!
PGP Certificate Server Freeware v2.5.8 is now available for Windows NT/2000 and Solaris!

FIGURE 9.33 The Center for Democracy and Technology maintains information on Clipper Chip–type technology.

court-order process. Even if the key escrow system worked perfectly, it would still function too slowly to aid investigators dealing with fast-breaking situations, such as a terrorist attack.

In 1998, FBI director Freeh called for a new back-door-based encryption system. Called **key recovery**, the back door would be built into encryption software, rather than implemented by a microprocessor chip. This would enable encryption-product vendors to fix vulnerabilities, such as the one discovered in the Clipper Chip. By eliminating the cumbersome key escrow bureaucracy, the key recovery system would function much faster and, for this reason, would be more attractive to investigators.

According to law enforcement officials, some type of key escrow system is needed to fight illegal drug trade and terrorism. After the September 11th attack, bills were introduced in the U.S. Congress that mandated stiff penalties for the use of encryption that lacked key-recovery features. However, critics of the key escrow

system reply that the social and economic costs of such a system will be very high. Criminals and terrorists already use strong, unbreakable encryption technology that would be virtually impossible to detect or eliminate. According to critics of key escrow systems, law-abiding citizens would be the ones most likely to suffer if the use of key-recovery software were mandated by law. Such a system would leave citizens open to illegal monitoring for political reasons.

A key recovery system may also impede the further development of e-commerce, which some see as a major factor in continued U.S. economic growth. Corporations and banks will not wholeheartedly embrace e-commerce without strong, secure encryption, and cryptography experts are wary of key recovery systems. Until cryptographers are reasonably certain that an encryption algorithm is safe to use, businesses will not use it to transfer anything other than trivial amounts of money, thus slowing the growth of e-commerce.

What You've Learned

PRIVACY, CRIME, AND SECURITY

- Because no comprehensive federal regulations exist that protect an individual's privacy, many Web sites collect and store highly sensitive personal information, such as Social Security numbers, without informing their visitors. Public agencies and online merchants use computerized databases to track information about individuals. Other personal information, such as browsing habits, is often captured in cookies and by global unique identifiers (GUIDs) in hardware components and programs.

- Computer crime and cybercrime include identity theft; computer viruses; and other rogue programs such as time bombs, worms, zombies, and Trojan horses; fraud and theft; password theft; salami shaving and data diddling; forgery; and blackmail.

- Computer criminals include crackers, cybergangs, virus authors, swindlers, shills, cyberstalkers, and sexual predators.

- A computer security risk is any event, action, or situation—intentional or not—that could lead to the loss or destruction of computer systems or the data they contain. Threats include corporate espionage, information warfare, security loophole detection programs, and attacks on safety-critical systems, such as air-traffic control.

- No computer system is totally secure, but you can do several things to cut down on security risks. Use an uninterruptible power supply (UPS) to combat power-related problems. Use good passwords, know-and-have authentication, biometric authentication, and firewalls to control access to computer systems. Avoid scams and prevent cyberstalking by doing business with well-known companies and by guarding your identity online.

- Encryption refers to a coding or scrambling process by which a message is rendered unreadable by anyone except the intended recipient. Encryption can be used to guard privacy online through public key encryption schemes.

- The U.S. government's key recovery plan involves a new encryption system in which a secret decoding mechanism would enable investigators to decrypt messages without having first obtained a private key. Cryptography experts are wary that key recovery systems are not secure. Therefore, businesses will not use them to transfer anything other than trivial amounts of money, thus slowing the growth of e-commerce.

Key Terms and Concepts

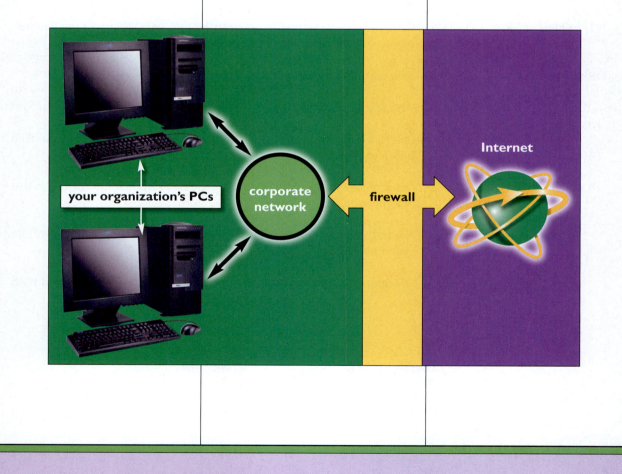

Matching

Match each key term in the left column with the most accurate definition in the right column.

_____ 1. Secure Electronic Transaction (SET)

_____ 2. biometric authentication

_____ 3. Clipper Chip

_____ 4. time bomb

_____ 5. cracker

_____ 6. firewall

_____ 7. macro virus

_____ 8. cyberstalking

_____ 9. privacy

_____ 10. cookies

_____ 11. global unique identifier (GUID)

_____ 12. public key encryption

_____ 13. digital signature

_____ 14. anonymity

_____ 15. encryption

a. an online shopping security standard

b. a computer program that places severe limits on the ability of outsiders to access internal data

c. using the Internet, e-mail, or other electronic communication media to repeatedly harass or threaten a person

d. a microprocessor that encrypts communications so investigators can intercept and decode messages

e. a hacker obsessed with gaining entry to highly secure computer systems

f. a virus that sits on a system until a certain event or set of circumstances causes the program to activate

g. identity verification through a variety of techniques, including voice recognition, retinal scans, fingerprint scans, and face and hand recognition

h. a virus that takes advantage of automatic command execution capabilities in certain software

i. a step-by-step method for encrypting and decrypting a message that uses both public and private keys

j. the encoding or scrambling of messages

k. the ability to convey a message without disclosing one's name or identity

l. small files written to your computer's hard disk by many of the Web sites you visit

m. an identification number that is generated by a computer hardware component or a program

n. an individual's ability to stop the collection, sale, and use of confidential personal information

o. a technique that guarantees a message has not been tampered with

Multiple Choice

Circle the correct choice for each of the following.

1. Which of the following is a rogue program disguised as a useful program that contains hidden instructions to perform a malicious task?
   a. Trojan horse
   b. worm
   c. trap door
   d. macro

2. What is the result of applying an encryption key to a message?
   a. cybertext
   b. decryption
   c. ciphertext
   d. plaintext

3. Of what type are most viruses?
   a. file infectors
   b. boot sector viruses
   c. worms
   d. time bombs

4. These are computer hobbyists who enjoy pushing computer systems to their limits.
   a. crackers
   b. Trojan horses
   c. hackers
   d. cybergang members

5. Which method requires an encryption key to be transmitted to a recipient before a message can be decrypted?
   a. key interception
   b. key recovery
   c. symmetric key encryption
   d. digital certificates

6. A firewall usually protects a network from which of the following?
   a. smoke damage
   b. unauthorized access through the Internet
   c. electronic funds transfer
   d. buggy programs

7. Which of the following is *not* used to limit access to computer systems?
   a. know-and-have authentication
   b. password
   c. UPS (uninterruptible power supply)
   d. firewall

8. A recipient uses which of the following to read an encrypted message?
   a. private key
   b. public key
   c. digital certificate
   d. digital signature

9. What do you call using information technologies to corrupt or destroy an enemy's information and industrial infrastructure?
   a. data warfare
   b. technology bombs
   c. information warfare
   d. data infiltration

10. This item is a rectangular advertisement that is not part of the Web page you are viewing, but is rather a page separately supplied by an ad network.
   a. spam
   b. Adnet ad
   c. Spamnet ad
   d. banner ad

Fill-In

In the blanks provided, write the correct answer for each of the following.

1. A(n) _____ is any event, action, or situation—intentional or not—that could lead to the loss or destruction of computer systems or the data they contain.

2. A(n) _____ is hidden code within a program that may be destructive to infected files.

3. Hackers generally subscribe to an unwritten code of conduct, called the _____, which forbids the destruction of data.

4. Crimes carried out over the Internet are known as _____.

5. A(n) _____ installs itself at the beginning of a hard drive where code is stored and then automatically executes every time you start the computer.

6. In a computer network, a(n) _____ resembles a computer virus but doesn't need an unsuspecting user to execute a program or macro file.

7. A(n) _____ takes advantage of the automatic command execution capabilities of productivity software.

8. _____ is the unauthorized access of corporate information to benefit a competitor.

9. Disgruntled employees may discover or create security holes called _____ that they can exploit after leaving the firm to get even with their former employer.

10. _____ refers to one's ability to convey a message without disclosing a name or identity.

11. _____ are programs or devices that protect home computers from unauthorized access.

12. _____ refers to a coding or scrambling process that renders a message unreadable by anyone except the intended recipient.

13. _____ is emerging to track developments in crime on the Internet.

14. _____ is a uniform set of encryption standards that specify how public key encryption, digital signatures, and digital certificates should be implemented in computer systems and on the Internet.

15. A(n) _____ is a technique for validating one's identity, like showing your driver's license when you cash a check.

Short Answer

1. What are the different cookie settings on the browser that you use most often? (Hint: If you're not sure, click the browser's Help button and enter "cookies.") Describe how to switch the cookie settings. What cookie setting do you prefer? Explain why.

2. What is a digital signature? What is a digital certificate? How do they differ?

3. How do time bombs, worms, and Trojan horses differ?

4. Name some of the common types of passwords that users choose. Why are these poor choices?

5. Do you believe that the online marketing industry can adequately and effectively regulate itself? If not, who should regulate it?

Teamwork

1. Computer Security

Your group is to investigate how individuals and institutions protect their computers. Interview fellow students or a professor, asking the following questions. If you own a computer, especially a laptop, what measures do you take to protect it from theft while on campus or when traveling? Is your computer covered by homeowner's or renter's insurance? If it is covered, what is the deductible? Compile your answers. Split the following questions among the various team members. How does your school secure public computers and computer components against theft? Do the computer labs have any special security provisions in place? How are faculty and staff office computers protected? Check with campus security and find out if any computers have been stolen in the past month. Do you feel that the laboratory and office computers and components are adequately protected from theft? Collaborate on a paper that answers these questions.

2. Password Requirements

Have each team member find the answers to the following questions and then collaborate on a paper that provides an overview of password security at your institution. How do students at your school obtain computer accounts? How are passwords initially assigned? How do users change them? Does your computer system prohibit using common words as passwords? What is the minimum number of characters required in a password? What are some of the tricks intruders can use to obtain passwords? Have any unauthorized persons gained access to your computer account? If they did, do you know how they obtained your password? Did they alter or destroy any of your files? Were you able to find the identity of the intruder(s)?

3. Encryption Standards

Strong encryption is required to prevent certain types of attacks. Both Internet Explorer and Netscape Navigator provide 128-bit encryption versions for domestic use. However, under the International Traffic in Arms Regulations (ITAR) Act, U.S. encryption technologies are considered munitions. Consequently, only 56-bit versions of software browsers are generally available for international users. Currently, the U.S. Department of Commerce grants export permits for programs that contain 56-bit encryption tools, but only if the company promises to develop key recovery tools for domestic surveillance. Have each member of your group identify which browser and version of that browser they use most often. Explain how your browser indicates that you have connected to a secure site. This is especially important when making an online purchase with a credit card. Have you ever made purchases online? Were they always at secure sites? Collaborate on a paper that summarizes your findings and that discusses the necessity of using secure sites for online purchases.

4. Fighting Spam

Have each group member compile a short list of the individuals and companies from which he or she has received unsolicited e-mail or spam and then answer the following questions. Have you received any messages that provide an option to cancel all further mailings? Did you reply that you wished to be removed from future mailings? If you did reply, did you notice an increase in unsolicited e-mail? What do you think can be done about spam? Should the government be involved? Why or why not? Collaborate on writing a paper that discusses your findings and your views on how to stop unsolicited e-mail.

5. Big Brother Is Watching

A recent newspaper article reported that a customer was fined by a car rental company for speeding. Although he was not cited for a speeding violation by any police agencies, his credit card was charged a penalty. His rental car was equipped with a GPS system that reports the location of the vehicle. This feature allowed the company to determine the speed at which the driver was traveling. This type of system is also used by some long-distance trucking companies to monitor the movements of their trucks. Divide your group into two and then have each subgroup take the position of company viewpoint or consumer viewpoint. Debate the following: Should this type of monitoring be allowed? From a privacy standpoint, what are your feelings about these systems? What are the advantages of using these systems? Disadvantages? Write two papers: one that affirms the use of such systems and one that argues against their use.

On the Web

1. Personal Firewalls

Two of the leading personal firewall software applications, McAfee Personal Firewall and Norton Personal Firewall, are designed for personal computers running various Windows operating systems. Visit the McAfee Web site at **www.mcafee.com/myapps/firewall/default.asp** and the Symantec Web site at **www.symantec.com/sabu/nis/npf**. According to these sites, why should you purchase firewall software? What is the annual subscription for McAfee's firewall application? What are the purchase and upgrade prices for Norton's firewall application? Write a short paper that describes your findings.

2. The Enigma Machine

During World War II, the German military used Enigma encoding machines. It appeared that the Allies were unable to break the code generated by these machines. Visit PBS's *NOVA* Web site at **www.pbs.org/wgbh/nova** to learn the truth about these cipher machines (type "cipher machine" in the search window). Write a short paper that answers the following questions. For how many years did the breaking of the Enigma machine code remain a classified secret? Enigma machines were mechanical devices that used wheels and rings that could easily be changed. What made code breaking so difficult was the sheer number of combinations of wheel orders and ring settings. What were the number of wheel orders and ring settings? How many pairings did these produce?

3. Monitoring Software

SpectorSoft produces software that monitors and records all of the activities that take place on a personal computer. Visit the company's Web site at **spectorsoft.com** and answer the following questions. In addition to employees, this software monitors the activities of what two other groups? Identify the three products that SpectorSoft distributes, explain how they differ, and identify their prices. Some people are easily offended by the use of this software, so explain why someone would purchase and use it.

4. Web Bugs

What is a Web bug? Help stamp out bugs by visiting the Bugnosis Web site at **www.bugnosis.org**. From which foundation does Bugnosis get its support? What browser and versions is the anti-Web-bug software limited to? What is the cost of this software? Select the Documentation/FAQ link to learn more about Web bugs. Write a short paper that answers the preceding questions and explains why Web bugs are a potential privacy threat.

5. Electronic Privacy

Visit the Electronic Privacy Information Center at **www.epic.org**. Choose an article from the Latest News list and write a summary of the article for your instructor.

How to Hide from Pop-up Ads

To avoid those annoying pop-up ads while surfing the Web, you just need to think a little bit outside of the box ... or should I say browser! Although Microsoft Internet Explorer gives you the ability to disable all interactive Web site content, it currently does not include any built-in features to help you avoid pop-up ads. To get around this limitation, many users resort to buying third-party software or downloading free extensions to Internet Explorer, such as the Google toolbar (**toolbar.google.com**). If you are the adventurous type, you may find that the best solution to this problem is an increasingly popular Web browser named Mozilla.

Mozilla is an open-source version of the Netscape Web browser. It is available as a free download from **www.mozilla.org**. It is compatible with most major operating systems, including Microsoft Windows. Mozilla includes many features not currently supported by Internet Explorer, including pop-up ad blocking and "tabbed" Web browsing (Figure 9.34a). Tabbed Web browsing enables you to open multiple Web sites in a single window instead of using separate windows to display different Web sites. Notice that the titles of the tabs in Figure 9.34a indicate the Web sites being viewed. Another nice feature is that you can bookmark groups of tabs. When you click the Home button, several sites load at one time. Although many Web sites are designed to work specifically with Microsoft Internet Explorer, you will find little difference when surfing the Web with Mozilla.

The steps below will guide you through the process of configuring pop-up ad blocking using the Mozilla Web browser once it is installed:

1. **Select Edit >> Preferences from the menu bar at the top of the browser window.**

2. **In the Preferences window, click the "+" sign next to the Privacy & Security heading to view available configuration options.**

3. **Select Popup Windows from the list of available options.**

4. **Select the checkbox next to Block unrequested popup windows (Figure 9.34b).**

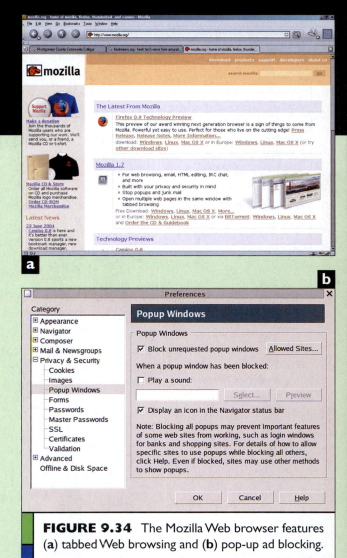

FIGURE 9.34 The Mozilla Web browser features (a) tabbed Web browsing and (b) pop-up ad blocking.

5. **Click OK and you will never be bothered by pop-up ads again!**

Rumors abound that Microsoft will add pop-up blocking capabilities and tabbed browsing to future versions of Internet Explorer (most likely with the release of Windows XP Service Pack 2). But why wait when Mozilla offers you these features today? It is important to read the documentation that accompanies the Mozilla Web browser to learn how to take full advantage of all this unique and powerful Web browser has to offer. If you would like to explore other alternative Web browsers, a good place to start is the Opera Web browser at **www.opera.com**. Those of you who are Macintosh users are probably already familiar with the Mac OS X Safari browser, available at at **www.apple.com/safari**.

What You'll Learn . . .

- Describe traditional information technology (IT) career paths and how these paths are changing.

- Compare and contrast computer science (CS) and computer information system (CIS) curricula in colleges and universities.

- Describe two settings in which most IT workers find employment and list at least three typical job titles.

- Identify the business skills information system (IS) managers want in new IT workers.

- List the technical skills currently in high demand.

- Discuss both the positive and negative aspects of certification.

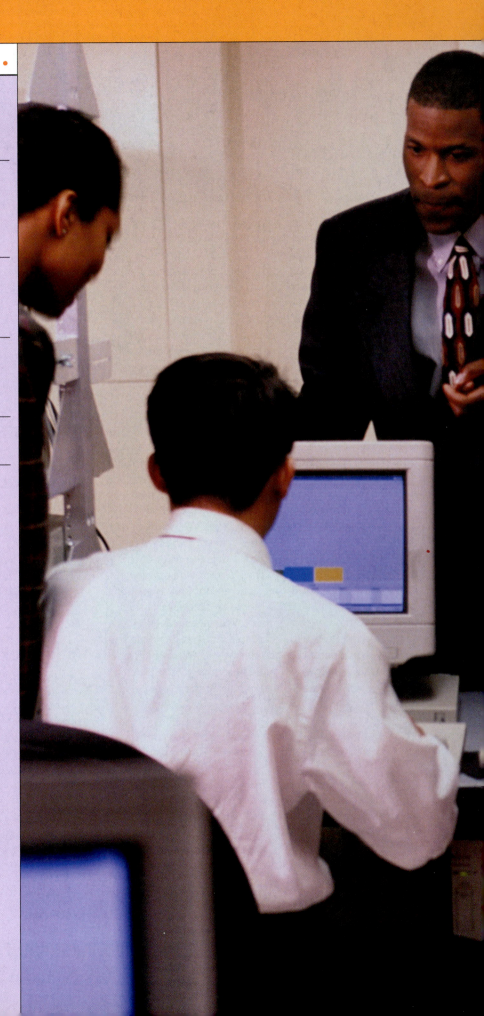

Careers and Certification

FIGURE 10.1 The Web is an indispensable resource for researching a career in the IT industry.

Today, almost all companies, regardless of their size, use computers and information technology (IT). But just because they use IT doesn't make them part of the IT industry. The **IT industry** is made up of organizations that are focused on the development and implementation of technology and applications. This includes companies you're likely familiar with, such as Microsoft, Dell, and Intel, as well as companies from the telecommunications sector, resellers, and suppliers of parts.

Even employers that are not part of the IT industry are demanding higher levels of computer literacy than ever before. It does not matter whether your future career is in health care, retail, finance, or any other industry. Such fields use computers to access medical records and perform procedures, to ring up sales using POS terminals, to research stock or other financial information, and so on. According to a recent study, employers described computer literacy as "important" or "very important" in their hiring decisions. Particularly attractive to employers were the following skills: word processing, e-mail, spreadsheet analysis, database entry and editing, use of presentation software, and Web searching. While you're still in school, you'd be wise to learn as many computer skills as possible.

Is a career in IT for you? How can you investigate the careers or jobs available to you? With regards to job searches, how would you like to send your resume to more than 52 million potential readers? You can accomplish this very easily by using any number of online services that post your resume on the World Wide Web for potential employers to view. Perhaps the most widely known of these sites is Monster.com (**www.monster.com**). The Monster.com database is searchable by keyword, industry, company, or geographic location. The site lists more than 1 million jobs as well as company information and profiles with hyperlinks to corporate Web sites. Companies that have joined Monster.com can place recruitment ads, post company profiles, and gain access to a database of over 10 million current resumes (Figure 10.1).

In the next section, you'll take a closer look at the traditional path to the best IT careers, which require (at a minimum) a four-year college degree. Later in this chapter, you'll learn about new IT career paths that have been created by the strong demand for skilled IT workers as well as rapid technological change. As you'll see, more ways are available than ever before to pursue an IT career.

Traditional Information Technology (IT) Career Paths

In the world of technology, nobody knows what the future will bring. That can be a little troubling for future job seekers attempting to acquire today the skills they'll apply tomorrow. Will the job of your dreams be around when you're ready for employment? Does it even exist yet? How do you prepare for an uncertain career landscape?

Learning about computers and getting a bachelor's degree is a step in the right direction, as is keeping up with emerging technologies. Nobody wants to head down a path toward an occupation that won't exist

in five years. Staying abreast of job trends is an excellent way to ensure you're heading in the right direction. Where do you find such information? The U.S. Bureau of Labor Statistics (BLS) Web site, located at **stats .bls.gov**, is a good place to start (Figure 10.2).

As we look to the year 2010, research indicates that jobs for information technology (IT) professionals will continue to be in high demand. **Information technology (IT) professionals** work with information technology in all its various forms (hardware, software, networks) and functions (management, development, maintenance). Both small and large companies will need computer specialists and administrators who can keep up with the fast-changing technologies needed to keep them growing and competitive. This is especially important when integrating new and increasingly sophisticated technologies.

In the coming years, companies will need many more skilled IT professionals than they're likely to find. U.S. colleges and universities are turning out only about 50,000 graduates with computer science, systems engineering, or computer information systems degrees each year, which will fall short of the numbers needed.

FIGURE 10.2
The Bureau of Labor Statistics Web site is full of links to informative IT-career-related Web sites.

What this means for you is opportunity. If you have the right background and skills, you can find a job as an IT professional. Students straight out of college-level computer science, systems engineering, and computer information systems programs are getting job offers in the $40,000 to $50,000 range.

Ten years ago, most people got into IT careers by obtaining a computer-related bachelor's degree and landing a job with a corporate **information systems (IS) department** (Figure 10.3) (the functional area within companies or universities responsible for managing information technology and systems) or a software development firm (Figure 10.4), also called a **vendor**. The four-year college degree was, and still is, a prerequisite for the best jobs. In a recent survey, 83 percent of surveyed U.S. corporations stated that they require a four-year college degree for entry-level programming jobs.

Because new technologies will continue to be incorporated into businesses, computer support specialists will be needed to provide technical support to customers. Systems administrators, systems analysts, computer scientists, consultants, and database administrators also are projected to be among the fastest-growing occupations through 2012. Security specialists will be in high demand to protect data, communications,

---

FIGURE 10.3 Typical Job Titles and Responsibilities in a Corporate IS Department

Job Title	Responsibilities	Salary Range	Education Level
Chief Information Officer (CIO)	*Senior-level management position* Defines the IS department's mission, objectives, and budgets and creates a strategic plan for the company's information systems	$130,000 to $400,000	Master's, Ph.D.
Director of Computer Operations	*Middle management position* Ensures overall system reliability	$90,000 to $125,000	Master's, Ph.D.
Director of Network Services	*Middle management position* Ensures overall network reliability	$100,000 to $150,000	Master's
Network Engineer	Installs, maintains, and supports computer networks; interacts with users; and troubleshoots problems	$40,000 to $90,000	Master's
Systems Administrator	Installs, maintains, and supports the operating system	$50,000 to $90,000	Master's, Ph.D.
Client/Server Manager	Installs, maintains, and supports client/server applications	$50,000 to $90,000	Master's
Systems Analyst	Interacts with users and application developers to design information systems	$50,000 to $90,000	Bachelor's, Master's
Programmer Analyst	Designs, codes, and tests software according to specifications	$40,000 to $75,000	Bachelor's, Master's
Programmer	Writes code according to specifications	$40,000 to $60,000	Bachelor's

FIGURE 10.4 Typical Job Titles and Responsibilities in a Software Development Firm

Job Title	Responsibilities	Salary Range	Education Level
Director of Research and Development	Senior-level management position in charge of all product development activities	$140,000 to $200,000	Master's, Ph.D.
Software Architect	Computer scientist who is challenged to create new, cutting-edge technologies	$95,000 to $150,000	Master's, Ph.D.
Software Engineer	Manages the details of software development projects	$75,000 to $125,000	Master's, Ph.D.
Systems Engineer	Assists the sales staff by working with current and prospective customers; gives technical presentations and supports products on-site	$55,000 to $100,000	Master's, Ph.D.
Software Developer	Develops new programs under the direction of the software architect	$50,000 to $75,000	Master's, Bachelor's
Customer Support Technician	Provides assistance to customers who need help with products	$40,000 to $90,000	Bachelor's

and technological investments. Companies will continue to seek individuals who are able to apply new technologies and strategies efficiently. Those who not only know the technologies but also can communicate with employees, clients, and consumers using that technology will be the most effective job seekers.

According to the U.S. Bureau of Labor Statistics, software publishing, computer systems design, and related computer services are expected to be the fastest-growing industries in the U.S. economy. Jobs with software publishers are projected to increase 68 percent between 2002 and 2012. In addition, more than 600,000 jobs in computer systems design and related fields will be created between 2002 and 2012. IT professionals (versus less-skilled workers) continue to have the best prospects due to demand for higher-level skills needed to keep up with changes in technology.

Of course, as with any career, computer-related jobs aren't for everyone. IT careers are a particularly poor choice for anyone who is not comfortable adapting to change and learning new skills frequently:

Change, not continuity, is the norm. And today's job market offers no such thing as job security. In a computer-related field, you'll probably work at as many as five or six different jobs before you retire. This trend is due in part to today's global environment in which work is often outsourced or offshored.

Offshoring is the transfer of labor from workers in one country to workers in other countries. Two examples of job categories that have seen work transferred from the United States to India are call center work and computer programming. Some companies are learning, though, that the transfer of labor has its costs—particularly in the case of call center workers who don't always meet customer expectations.

Before the era of corporate downsizing and offshoring, IT workers could remain with a firm for many years, perhaps until retirement. Workers with business savvy and good communication skills could move into management (Figure 10.5). If employees needed to acquire additional skills, the employer might arrange and pay for additional training.

Techtalk

Outsourcing

In the past, the term *outsourcing* meant that a firm used outside sources to fulfill specific business needs that the firm did not have staff to cover, such as the use of an accounting firm or a law firm versus having an accounting department or a corporate law staff. These needs were peripheral to the firm's primary business. Today, outsourcing often means the transfer of labor from the firm to outside entities, such as a software manufacturing firm using the services of independent programmers, who are often offshore, instead of hiring their own.

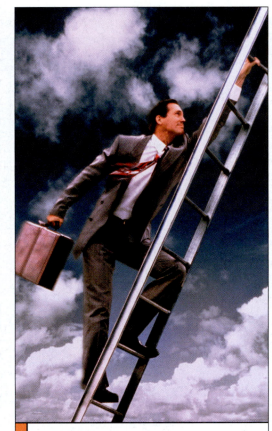

FIGURE 10.5 In traditional career paths, IT professionals could climb the corporate ladder by earning advanced degrees or by moving into management.

The traditional IT career path still exists, but it's changing. Let's look first at the components of a traditional IT career.

EDUCATION FOR TRADITIONAL IT CAREERS

Reflecting the long-standing split in computing between science and business, education for traditional IT careers has been divided between two very different academic departments: computer science and computer information systems. In recent years, systems engineering has emerged to provide a middle-ground approach, offering the rigor of an engineering track combined with a real-world focus on the realities of information systems in contemporary business.

Computer Science
The **computer science** (**CS**) discipline uses scientific and engineering research to improve computing. In general, CS departments emphasize the theoretical rather than the practical aspects of computing, focusing on cutting-edge technologies and fundamental principles rather than teaching marketable skills. At most colleges and universities, CS programs grew out of mathematics programs and are often housed in the engineering school.

CS training is highly technical and usually involves several semesters of higher mathematics, such as calculus, as well as training in several programming languages and theoretical topics, such as programming language structure, advanced computer graphics, artificial intelligence, and relational database design. Qualified CS graduates find that their theoretical and analytical skills make them good candidates for jobs in cutting-edge software development firms. The skills of these graduates may also be needed by IS departments that are working with advanced technologies or developing software in-house.

Computer Information Systems
Generally located in business schools, **computer information systems** (**CIS**) departments are often the mirror image of CS departments; they're focused on the practical rather than the theoretical and emphasize the skills that businesses need right now. Apart from work in programming and systems analysis, CIS departments strongly emphasize topics such as business smarts (including coursework in finance and marketing), communication skills, and the interpersonal skills needed for effective teamwork and leadership. With their business savvy and communication skills, CIS graduates are most likely to find jobs in corporate IS departments. However, software development firms also need IT personnel who have excellent communication skills as well as technical ability (Figure 10.6).

Systems and Software Engineering
The engineering discipline called **systems engineering** applies an interdisciplinary approach to creating and maintaining quality systems. Unlike other engineering disciplines, systems engineering looks at the whole picture, including the people and the organization as well as the technologies. The principles of systems engineering

FIGURE 10.6 With their business savvy and communication skills, CIS graduates are likely to find jobs in corporate IS departments.

are useful for software development, systems analysis, and program development. Systems engineering students learn strong project management skills, and graduates are in high demand.

Computer software engineering is projected to be the fastest-growing occupation over the next five years, especially in the computer and data-processing services industry. **Software engineering** involves upgrading, managing, and modifying computer programs. Software engineers will continue to develop applications for the ever-evolving Internet and a whole new age of Web applications. Software engineers with strong programming, systems analysis, interpersonal, and business skills are those most likely to succeed. Of course, the future will bring with it many new problems for software engineers to solve—problems we can't even think of because they don't exist yet.

Electrical Engineering
The engineering discipline called **electrical engineering (EE)** offers a strong focus on digital circuit design as well as cutting-edge communication technologies. It's the primary choice for those whose interests lean more toward hardware than software.

CONTINUING EDUCATION FOR TRADITIONAL IT CAREERS

In traditional IT careers, professionals keep up with new technologies by going to seminars, subscribing to computer-related periodicals, attending conferences and shows, and actively participating in a professional association.

Training Seminars
Computer-related **training seminars** are typically presented by the developer of a new hardware or software product or by a company specializing in training IT professionals in a new technology (Figure 10.7). These seminars usually last from one day to a week and are often advertised in the local paper's technology or business section as well as in trade magazines such as *PC World* or *Wired*.

Destinations

Most computer industry trade journals are published on the Internet as well as in print. On a journal's Web site, you can read current issues and search the publication's archives. A leading media site is CMP Media (**www.cmpnet .com**). This site offers links to *Byte, EE Times, InformationWeek, Unix Review,* and many other online publications.

In most cases, companies view formal training as a wise investment and pay for training seminars for their employees. According to one study, a single hour of focused, professional instruction is worth six employee hours of ad hoc learning.

Computer Magazines, Newspapers, and Journals

Computer-related trade journals are an indispensable resource for IT professionals. Some, such as *Computerworld,* cover a wide range of computer issues. Others are aimed at a specific part of the IT industry, such as technology management (*Information-Week*), networking (*Network Computing*), or software development (*Byte*). More than 100 of these types of periodicals are in print. If you have a particular area of interest, you can probably find a periodical that reports late-breaking developments in your field. Most of these periodicals also are published on the Web. You can usually find a magazine's site by simply adding ".com" to the name of the magazine.

Conferences and Shows

One way to keep in touch with others in your profession and learn the about the latest trends is to attend conferences and trade shows. **Trade shows** are typically annual meetings at which computer product manufacturers, designers, and dealers showcase their products. Job fairs offering on-the-spot interviews provide incentives for job seekers. Training seminars and product showcases provide

FIGURE 10.7 Typically, training seminars are presented by the developer of a new hardware or software product or by a company specializing in training IT professionals in a new technology.

many opportunities for skill and knowledge development.

One of the largest computer-related trade shows has been the annual COMDEX show (Figure 10.8). With 900 journalists and over 40,000 attendees in 2003, COMDEX provided the perfect opportunity to roll out new products. COMDEX also sponsors well-attended regional events. The COMDEX brand name was purchased by MediaLive

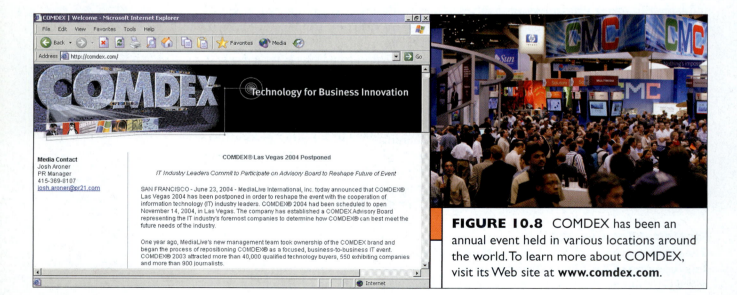

FIGURE 10.8 COMDEX has been an annual event held in various locations around the world. To learn more about COMDEX, visit its Web site at **www.comdex.com**.

International in 2003. In June 2004, MediaLive International announced that the November 2004 Las Vegas event had been postponed until 2005. Other COMDEX events have been scheduled for Scandinavia and Greece during 2005. The future of COMDEX may be uncertain, but other events will surely take its place. Of growing importance is NetWorld+InterOP, a spring trade show in Las Vegas that focuses on Internet and networking technologies.

Professional Organizations

Joining one of the many IT **professional organizations** (also called **associations**) can help you keep up with your area of interest as well as provide valuable career contacts. Some associations have local chapters, and most offer publications, training seminars, and conferences for members. The following are some of the most important IT organizations:

- **Association for Computing Machinery (ACM).** Focusing on computer science, this organization features many special-interest groups in such areas as databases, artificial intelligence, microcomputers, and computer graphics.

- **Association for Women in Computing (AWC).** This professional organization is devoted to promoting women in the field of computing (Figure 10.9).

- **Association of Internet Professionals (AIP).** This is the premier organization for Internet professionals.

- **Data Processing Management Association (DPMA).** This is the premier organization for CIS personnel and managers.

- **Network Professional Association (NPA).** This organization focuses on the professional advancement of networking experts and offers a non-vendor-based skills certification program.

Now that you're familiar with how to prepare for a more traditional IT career path, let's take a look at new career paths in IT.

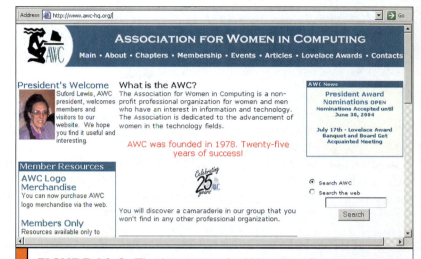

FIGURE 10.9 The Association for Women in Computing is dedicated to the advancement of women in the field of computing.

New IT Career Paths

IT careers are changing, driven both by rapid technological change and by shifts in the nature of today's businesses. Increasingly, a four-year college degree isn't sufficient to convince prospective employers that would-be employees possess needed skills, because many of these skills aren't yet taught in many colleges and universities.

As you'll see in this section, good communication, business savvy, and technical skills are necessary for success in fast-emerging areas such as the Internet and Microsoft Windows NT. For this reason, IT workers must learn how to manage their careers. You may change jobs often or you may forsake the job market altogether, preferring—as do increasing numbers of IT professionals—to work as an independent contractor or consultant. Whichever path you choose, it's increasingly the worker's responsibility to develop the skills needed to keep up with fast-changing technology.

SOUGHT-AFTER BUSINESS SKILLS

Ten years ago, most IT jobs were internally focused: IT professionals worked inside companies. They created and supported

Destinations

Add television to your list of bona fide ways to learn more about computers and technology. Throughout the book, you've been viewing video clips on our Web site. These clips come from TechTV, an entire channel devoted to the IT industry. As you've learned, the channel features shows about the Internet, cybercrime, technology news, and new products. A listing of shows, as well as useful nonbroadcast information, can be found on the channel's Web site at **www.g4techtv.com**

Will Your Dream Job in IT Be There When You Arrive?

Whether you're hunting for your first job or moving into a different job, two simmering controversies may affect your IT career. The first is the offshoring of many IT jobs by U.S. companies to IT workers in other countries. The second is the trend of U.S. companies filling many IT jobs with IT professionals on special visas from other countries. Both controversies could mean the difference between building a long career in the tech world and doing something else to make a living.

Offshoring is controversial but widespread. Many banks, telecommunications firms, software vendors, and other employers have laid off U.S. workers and moved IT work to lower-wage countries. The savings to a company can be substantial; for example, salaries for software programmers in India are about 25 percent of the salaries for comparable U.S. jobs. Companies also see offshoring as a way to extend the work day, because overseas workers can complete projects sent by U.S. offices at the end of their work day. Critics object to offshoring, fearing that good-paying IT jobs will never return. Critics also raise worries about the security of sending sensitive data across time zones and national borders. Will one of your future jobs wind up in another country?

Now consider the second controversy that could affect your career. Many U.S. companies have laid off tech workers and brought in young professionals from India and other countries on H1-B temporary work visas (see Figure 10.10). Congress created the H1-B program more than a decade ago when the software industry was

concerned about severe shortages of IT workers. Critics say that the program facilitates what amounts to age discrimination—and that no shortage would exist if companies were willing to retrain older workers. Industry spokespersons say retraining older programmers is too expensive and time-consuming and that younger employees are more likely to have cutting-edge skills. Statistics don't clearly support one side or the other, but job prospects for U.S. tech workers are a bit rosier now that Congress has limited H1-B visas to 65,000 a year.

What can you do? Start by dedicating yourself to lifelong learning, because today's hot skill set could be tomorrow's prescription for unemployment. Also keep up with industry trends—your career survival may depend on your ability to sense where technology's headed and gain new skills that will make you valuable to any employer.

FIGURE 10.10 H1Base (www.h1base.com) promotes itself as an all-in-one Web portal for information for international workers in the United States.

computer services, such as payroll and inventory systems. But this picture is changing—and it's changing radically.

Today, driven by new network-based information systems, IT jobs increasingly combine both an internal and an external focus. IT professionals are expected to work with a company's external partners

and often with customers. They'll work in teams that include people from different divisions of the enterprise (Figure 10.11). Rather than performing a specific function, IT professionals are much more likely to work on a series of projects on which they'll use different skills. For all of these reasons, today's businesses are

FIGURE 10.11
IT professionals often work in teams with colleagues from finance, marketing, and other corporate divisions.

looking for workers with the following "soft" **business skills** in addition to "hard" technical knowledge:

- **Teamwork.** Increasingly, IT personnel are working in teams with workers from finance, marketing, and other corporate divisions. IT professionals need to appreciate varying intellectual styles, work effectively in a team environment, and understand business perspectives.

- **Project management.** The ability to plan and budget a project, especially with project management software, is a plus for job hunters.

- **Communication.** Today, every employee needs communication skills, even those who formerly worked internally and seldom had contact with people outside their departments. You'll need excellent writing and interpersonal skills, including the ability to give presentations using presentation graphics software.

- **Business acumen.** Information technology is now part of most companies' strategic planning, and IT employees are expected to possess some basic business knowledge. In the past, you could focus on technology and ignore business and communication skills,

but that's no longer true. Older, experienced IT workers who suffer job losses due to downsizing may have difficulty finding employment if they don't possess these skills. As a result, the wise IT student also takes courses in general business subjects, including finance and marketing.

SOUGHT-AFTER TECHNICAL SKILLS

Businesses are also demanding new **technical skills**. Here's what's hot as of this writing:

- **Networking.** Skills related to networking include Ethernet, TCP/IP (Internet protocols), and LAN administration.

- **Microsoft Windows XP.** Expertise in managing Microsoft Office applications and working with Visual Basic continues to pay big rewards within organizations.

- **UNIX.** Despite the success of Windows, UNIX isn't going away. A strong demand exists for IT workers skilled in UNIX operating system configuration and maintenance, UNIX networking, and UNIX systems programming.

To learn more about how to prepare for a high-tech career, view the video clip at **www.prenhall.com/ cayf2006**

- **TCP/IP.** Knowledge of the protocols underlying the Internet is in strong demand, both for external Web servers and for internal intranets.

- **Oracle.** Companies are looking for workers who have experience working with Oracle products, including the Oracle relational database and client/server application tools.

- **C++.** This object-oriented programming language is the language of choice for cutting-edge software development both with vendors (software publishers) and with corporate development shops.

- **Microsoft Visual Basic.** Rapid application development and code reusability make Visual Basic a winner for quick solutions.

Although a four-year degree in CS or CIS may fail to give you some of these desirable skills, the best preparation for a successful IT career still involves the invaluable theoretical background you get from a four-year college degree.

Now that you understand both traditional and new IT career paths, let's examine how IT professionals can adapt to further change.

New Technologies, New Jobs

New technology brings not just more jobs, but new *types* of jobs (Figure 10.12). Many of these new jobs are inherently cross-disciplinary, involving artistic or communication skills as well as top-notch technical capabilities. Existing CS and CIS programs may produce graduates who lack creativity, marketing knowledge, graphic design experience, or communication skills. For this reason, many companies are hiring students who have taken many computer courses but possess degrees in other fields, such as design, marketing, or English.

For example, Web page design involves technical skills and knowledge in areas such as HTTP, HTML, CGI programming, and server configuration. But in many cases, that's not enough to keep a Web site up and running. Increasingly, companies are looking for Webmasters (Web server managers and content developers) who understand marketing, advertising, and graphic design. This new job requires not only technical skills and business smarts, but also artistic sensitivity, including some background in the aesthetics of design and color, coupled with a good deal of creativity (Figure 10.13).

FIGURE 10.12 New Jobs in Information Technology

Job Title	Responsibilities
Interactive Digital Media Specialist	Uses multimedia software to create engaging presentations, including animation and video
Webmaster	Designs and maintains a Web server and related database servers
Web Application Engineer	Designs, develops, tests, and documents new Web-based services for Web sites
Web Specialist	Works with internal and external customers to create high-quality content pages for Web sites
Network/Internet Security Specialist	Installs and maintains firewalls, antivirus software, and other security software; maintains network security

CERTIFICATION

Rapid changes in IT have created a demand for new ways to ensure that job applicants possess the skills they claim. Certification is increasingly seen as a way that employers can assure themselves that newly hired workers can do necessary tasks.

In brief, **certification** is a skills and knowledge assessment process organized by computer industry vendors (and sometimes by professional associations). To obtain a certificate, you choose your preferred method of training. You can take courses at a college or at a private training center or study on your own using vendor-approved books, CD-ROM materials, or the Web. When you're ready, you take a comprehensive examination. If you pass, you receive the certificate (Figure 10.14). But

FIGURE 10.13 Webmasters must understand marketing, advertising, and graphic design.

FIGURE 10.14 Selected Certification Programs

Certification Program	Description
Microsoft Certified Systems Administrator (MCSA)	Microsoft Windows NT Server implementation, management, and maintenance, as well as LAN-based client/server administration (Microsoft Corporation)
Microsoft Certified Systems Engineer (MCSE)	Microsoft Windows NT Server and BackOffice applications; operating system and network planning, design, and implementation, as well as LAN-based client/server development (Microsoft Corporation)
Microsoft Certified Systems Engineer (MCSE) + Internet	Microsoft Windows NT Server configuration and maintenance for Internet and intranet sites (Microsoft Corporation)
Microsoft Certified Solution Developer (MCSD)	Programming and application development with Microsoft development tools, such as Visual Basic (Microsoft Corporation)
Certified NetWare Engineer (CNE)	Novell networking and NetWare network operating systems (Novell Corporation)
Certified Java Programmer	Programming in Java (Sun Microsystems)
Certified Java Developer	Programming and application development in Java (Sun Microsystems)
A+	To validate vendor-neutral skills for entry-level computer technicians (Computing Technology Industry Association—CompTIA)
Net+	To validate vendor-neutral skills for network technicians (Computing Technology Industry Association—CompTIA)
Cisco Certified Network Associate/Professional (CCNA/CCNP)	Installation, configuration, and operation of LAN, WAN, and dial-up access services for small networks (Cisco Systems)

Destinations

The Institute for Certification of Computing Professionals (ICCP) offers credentials for the highest level of computer professionals. The Institute certifies competency for a variety of computer professionals, including systems analysts, computer scientists, and computer programmers, as well as many others. Visit the ICCP Web site at **www.iccp.org**

unlike a college degree, the certificate isn't good for life. To retain certification, you may need to take refresher courses and exams periodically, sometimes as often as every six months.

Benefits of Certification

How does certification pay off for job applicants? A certificate won't guarantee a job or even higher pay, but it does provide a benchmark that enables prospective employers to assess an applicant's skills. In areas of high demand, certification can translate into salary offers that are 10 to 15 percent higher than the norm. For example, applicants who possess the Microsoft Certified Systems Engineer (MCSE) certificate may gain as much as $10,000 in starting salary.

How does certification benefit employers? Although the effects of certification haven't been rigorously studied by independent investigators, vendors and trainers claim that employers who hire certified employees have less downtime and lower IT costs. This makes sense, because certification sets a standard that helps guarantee that new employees will have a certain skill set. When an employee's skill set is matched with the employer's job requirements, everyone wins.

Risks of Certification

Certification entails some risks for employees and employers alike. The reason lies in the nature of the certification process, which emphasizes a form of learning that is both narrow (focused on a specific technology) and deep (rigorous and thorough).

For employees, certification requires that they devote a great deal of time and effort to a specific vendor's technology. But changing technology may make vendor-specific skills less marketable. If you're certified as a Novell NetWare technician, for example, you won't impress a prospective employer who's running a Windows NT network. And Windows NT has gained considerable market share at the expense of Novell's NetWare system. If you make a bad bet on which certificate to pursue, you could wind up with excellent skills in a technology or application that's losing market share (Figure 10.15).

For employers, hiring people with narrow training is a risk. People with narrow training may not be able to adjust to

FIGURE 10.15 To find out which certification will benefit you the most, sites such as *Certification Magazine* (**www.certmag.com**) contain current information about technical certification programs from a variety of vendors.

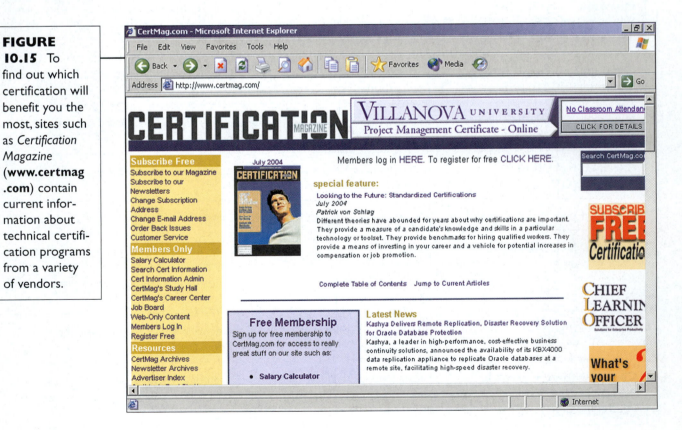

Telemedicine:
How Technology Can Save Lives

Is telemedicine another potential IT career path? *Telemedicine* combines computers and medical expertise to provide "computerized" health care; it is like a long-distance house call—without the doctor being present. Someday your work in hardware, software, telecommunications, or a related field could relieve pain or even save a life.

Consider the following example of telemedicine in action. Imagine that someone living in a rural area visits a local physician for a check-up. The physician detects a problem and recommends that the patient immediately consult a specialist who's located hundreds of miles away. Instead of traveling for hours to visit the specialist, the patient waits while the physician uses an interactive computer and videoconferencing software to send X-rays, CT scans, and other information to the specialist. The specialist downloads the files, examines them, and returns a diagnosis to the local physician, who can then start treatment.

Telemedicine is catching on (Figure 10.16). At one of the world's leading telemedicine centers, the University of North Carolina (UNC) Medical Center, specialists often use network connections and imaging technologies to consult with physicians caring for patients hundreds of miles away. In one case, a young child living in an isolated community suffered a brain hemorrhage and couldn't be moved. The local surgeon used the Internet and videoconferencing software to upload X-rays of the girl's brain and consult with a UNC neurologist. As a result, the subsequent surgery was successful.

One of the latest telemedicine breakthroughs is implanting patients with tiny wireless sensors that measure, record, and transmit data about symptoms such as heart irregularities, brain seizures, or low blood sugar. With real-time data, specialists can watch for abnormalities and quickly adjust treatment as needed. One day soon, healthy people may have sensors implanted so that physicians can track their vital signs and predict heart attacks or strokes before they happen—another way that computers and technology will save lives.

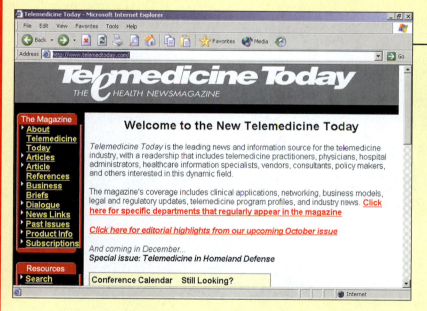

FIGURE 10.16 Telemedicine Today provides news and information for the telemedicine industry.

rapidly changing technologies. In addition, having just one skill isn't enough. Some companies expect employees to possess strong skills in as many as four or five areas. That's why it's a good idea to take as many CS and CIS courses as you can.

With a solid theoretical foundation, you can learn new skills throughout your career. You'll prove most attractive to employers if you combine certification with a good college record, communication skills, and business courses.

What You've Learned

CAREERS AND CERTIFICATION

- Traditional information technology (IT) career paths require a four-year college degree in computer science (CS) or computer information systems (CIS). The traditional career path often led to promotions within the firm and long-term job stability. This path is changing today due to corporate downsizing and the use of offshore labor.

- Training in computer science emphasizes the theoretical and cutting-edge aspects of computing. Training in computer information systems emphasizes more practical aspects of computing in business settings.

- IT workers typically find employment in corporate information systems (IS) departments and at vendor companies. Some typical job titles include network administrator, systems analyst, and Webmaster.

- Today's IS managers are looking for IT workers with business skills such as teamwork, project management skills, communication skills, and business savvy.

- Technical skills that are currently in high demand include knowledge and experience in networking, Microsoft Windows XP, UNIX, C++, and Internet-related technologies.

- Certification provides one way of demonstrating your skills to an employer. Certification also helps to ensure an even playing field and gives an employer some assurance that a prospective hire has the skills necessary to do the job. Negative aspects of certification are that employees may devote too much time to learning vendor-specific skills, which can make them less marketable, and that employers find it risky to hire people with narrow training who may not be able to adjust to rapidly changing technology.

Key Terms and Concepts

Matching

Match each key term in the left column with the most accurate definition in the right column.

_____ 1. computer science (CS)

_____ 2. business skills

_____ 3. vendor

_____ 4. systems engineering

_____ 5. electrical engineering

_____ 6. IT industry

_____ 7. technical skills

_____ 8. certification

_____ 9. offshoring

_____ 10. software engineering

_____ 11. computer information systems (CIS)

_____ 12. trade shows

_____ 13. IT professional

_____ 14. professional organizations

_____ 15. training seminars

a. organizations focused on furthering the design, development, installation, and implementation of technology and applications

b. applies an interdisciplinary approach to creating and maintaining quality systems

c. upgrading, managing, and modifying computer programs

d. includes networking, Microsoft Windows XP, UNIX, TCP/IP, Oracle, C++, and Microsoft Visual Basic

e. a software development firm

f. focuses on the practical rather than the theoretical and emphasizes the skills that businesses need right now

g. teamwork, project management, communication, and business acumen

h. the transfer of labor from workers in one country to workers in other countries

i. a skills and knowledge assessment process organized by computer industry vendors

j. offers a strong focus on digital circuit design as well as cutting-edge communication technologies

k. typically presented by the developer of a new hardware or software product or by a company specializing in training IT professionals in a new technology

l. also called associations, such as Association of Computing Machinery (ACM) and Network Professional Association (NPA)

m. uses scientific and engineering research to improve computing

n. works with information technology in all of its various forms (hardware, software, networks) and functions (management, development, maintenance)

o. periodic meetings in which computer product manufacturers, designers, and dealers showcase their products

Go to **www.prenhall.com/cayf2006** to review this chapter, answer the questions, and complete the exercises.

Multiple Choice

Circle the correct choice for each of the following.

1. Which of the following is *not* characteristic of the traditional career path in information technology (IT)?
   a. A computer-related bachelor's degree is a must.
   b. IT employees with business savvy and good communication skills can move into management.
   c. To have a successful career in IT, it is important not to stay with any one company for very long.
   d. To keep up with trends, IT professionals read professional journals and attend conferences.

2. Which of the following is *not* a typical job title in a corporate IS department?
   a. director of computer operations
   b. software architect
   c. network engineer
   d. programmer/analyst

3. Which of the following is *not* a typical job title in a software development firm?
   a. director of research and development
   b. software engineer
   c. client/server manager
   d. customer support technician

4. Which of the following is *not* true of computer science departments?
   a. They focus on the theoretical rather practical aspects of computing.
   b. They focus on the practical rather than the theoretical aspects of computing.
   c. CS graduates are more likely than CIS graduates to find jobs with cutting-edge software development firms.
   d. CS uses scientific and engineering research to improve computing.

5. Which of the following is a traditional method of continuing education?
   a. conferences
   b. project management
   c. professional organizations
   d. both a and c

6. Which of the following is *not* a professional organization designed to help IT professionals keep up with their areas of interest?
   a. Computers and Machines Association (CMA)
   b. Data Processing Management Association (DPMA)
   c. Association for Women in Computing (AWC)
   d. Association for Computing Machinery (ACM)

7. Which of the following is *not* an association for IT professionals?
   a. Association of Web Professionals (AWP)
   b. Association for Computing Machinery (ACM)
   c. Association of Internet Professionals (AIP)
   d. Network Professional Association (NPA)

8. Which of the following is mentioned in the chapter as being a hot technical skill that businesses are demanding of employees?
   a. UNIX
   b. Windows NT
   c. Visual Oracle
   d. Linux

9. Which of the following is not a new IT job?
   a. Webmaster
   b. Web specialist
   c. systems analyst
   d. interactive digital media specialist

10. Which of the following is a certification program?
    a. Association of Computer Machinery Certificate
    b. Certified NetWare Engineer
    c. Macintosh Certified Solution Developer
    d. Certified BASIC Programmer

Fill-In

In the blanks provided, write the correct answer for each of the following.

1. Many years ago, most people got into IT careers by obtaining a computer-related degree and getting a job with a corporate _____.

2. _____ departments emphasize the theoretical rather than the practical aspects of computing.

3. _____ departments emphasize business coursework, interpersonal skills, and communications skills.

4. The _____ includes companies you're likely familiar with, such as Microsoft, Dell, and Intel, as well as companies from the telecommunications sector, resellers, and parts suppliers.

5. _____ offers a strong focus on digital circuit design as well as cutting-edge communication technologies.

6. The _____ discipline applies an interdisciplinary approach to creating and maintaining quality systems.

7. Today's businesses are looking for workers with "soft" _____ in addition to "hard" technical knowledge.

8. _____ is a skill and knowledge assessment process that is organized by computer industry vendors.

9. The _____ discipline uses scientific and engineering research to improve computing.

10. The _____ is made up of organizations focused on advances in the development and implementation of technology and applications.

11. _____ are periodic meetings in which computer product manufacturers, designers, and dealers showcase their products.

12. In addition to business skills, _____ in areas such as networking, Microsoft Office XP, and Oracle are attractive to employers.

13. The term _____ refers to a software development firm such as Microsoft or Oracle.

14. The Association for Women in Computing (AWC) and the Data Processing Management Association (DPMA) are _____.

15. _____ usually last from one day to one week, are widely available, and are typically presented by the developer of a new hardware or software product or by a company that specializes in training IT professionals in a new technology.

Short Answer

1. What are some of the typical job titles and responsibilities in a corporate IS department?

2. What are some of the basic differences between computer science and computer information systems departments?

3. Describe in detail some of the options for continuing education.

4. Describe some of the typical job titles and responsibilities associated with the newest IT jobs.

5. What is certification? What are its benefits and risks?

Go to **www.prenhall.com/cayf2006** to review this chapter, answer the questions, and complete the exercises.

Teamwork

1. IT Jobs

As a group, check the classified section in the Sunday edition of a local large-city newspaper (use the Internet if you need to) to see how the job salaries provided compare with those given in Figures 10.3 and 10.4. The salary ranges given in the text are based on national averages. Based on the job positions advertised, identify those jobs that pay higher than the averages listed in this chapter and those that are lower. Overall, are the salaries for IT positions in your region above or below the national standards? Prepare a group presentation that compares the salaries in your region with those given in the text.

2. CIS Departments

In this exercise, your team will explore CIS department courses and content. Does your school have a CIS department? If so, look at a school catalog (printed or online) to find information about the program. If you can't find answers to some of the following questions in the catalog, you'll have to contact the department directly. If your school does not have a CIS department, go to another institution's Web site and base your answers on the information provided there.

What are the job titles for which graduates are prepared? If courses in the areas of interpersonal communication, business knowledge, or the Internet are required, identify them by title. Is there an elective or a required course that enables students to intern with an IT company for credit? Write a report based on your findings.

3. IT Professional Training and Education

As a team, use information in this chapter and from any other sources to answer the following

questions. What type of education and training do you think a company would want for a customer support technician? A network engineer? A Webmaster? Explain.

4. Certification Training

Your team is to look in local newspapers and telephone books to see if IT certification training is offered in your area. If it is, contact the training center(s) and answer the following questions. What are the names of the training companies? Do they offer training programs in any of the certifications—such as MCSE, MCSD, and CNE—that are described in the text? What are the duration and cost of these training sessions? Are there prerequisite skills for any of these sessions? After the training program, will the training center help you find a job? Write a short paper that provides answers to these questions and that explains what you've learned.

5. Self-Help for Certification

IT professionals do not have to attend certification training sessions to learn new skills. They can study at home and then take a certification examination. As a team, visit a bookstore and look for books that help professionals study for certification examinations. For each book, list the name of the certification program that is covered, the title, the author, and the price. Select one of these texts and examine the table of contents and selected pages. Does the book appear to provide IT professionals with background knowledge and content depth or does it just focus on passing the examination? Prepare a group presentation based on your findings.

Go to **www.prenhall.com/cayf2006** to review this chapter, answer the questions, and complete the exercises.

On the Web

1. Web-Based Training

Select one of the recognized certification programs identified in the text: MCSE, MCSD, CNE, Certified Java Programmer, or Certified Java Developer. Find a Web site that offers online courses for this certification program. Identify the URL and the cost for a specific course. Can the actual certification examination be taken online? Did you find any references to other providers of computer-related certification training? If so, name two of them.

2. Finding an IT Job

Newspapers are not the only source for finding local or national jobs. Search the Web to find a specific IT position in several different geographic areas. Identify the position, the URLs where you found the job information, and what the salaries are in the different regions. Identify a region where the salaries appear to be exceptionally high and one where they appear to be exceptionally low. Why do you think the salaries between different geographic areas differ?

3. IT Discussion Groups

Besides attending meetings and reading printed materials, members of professional organizations can obtain information online. Discussion groups, also known as listservs, are forums where members can talk about a variety of issues. ISWorld Net at **www.isworld.org/#today** maintains several online discussion groups for IS professionals. Name the current discussion groups that are supported by this organization. In which discussion group would your instructor discuss IS curriculum issues? Which groups discuss IS careers, both from a business and a computer science perspective? These forums are also frequently used to post job openings. In which discussion group would one place an advertisement for a faculty position?

4. Technical Skills Development

The text identifies the following as "sought-after technical skills": networking, Microsoft Windows XP, UNIX, TCP/IP, Oracle, C++, and Microsoft Visual Basic. Go to the Web site of your school's library or to the library Web site of the college of your choice and look at some online magazines and journals that professionals may read to find information on these key skills. Select one of the skills and locate a recent article that may be of interest to IT professionals. Identify the skill as well as the journal that the article is found in and the article's publication date, title, and author(s). Write a one-page review of the article. Submit the URL and your review to your instructor.

5. Training Seminars

In this chapter, you learned that one of the traditional methods for professionals to continue their education is to attend training seminars. Suppose you're a programmer and you wish to learn Visual Basic. Visit the Web site **www.appdev.com** to find a training seminar for beginners. Write a request to your manager justifying your attendance at the seminar. Be sure to include the location, length, and cost of the seminar as well as the benefits to your company.

Ethics: Patents and Copyright Issues

Do you download music and movie files from the Internet using file-sharing software such as Kazaa? Do you plan to write the next big "killer application" for the World Wide Web or start your own technology company? Whether you're planning a career in an IT-related field or just using computers in your everyday life, you should be aware of the computer-related legal and ethical issues that may affect you. Two of the best resources on the Web for familiarizing yourself with the myriad issues and legislation related to technology are the Association for Computing Machinery (ACM; **www.acm.org**) and the Electronic Frontier Foundation (EFF; **www.eff.org).**

One major goal of the ACM is to educate its members about important legal, technical, and ethical issues. If you're unsure where to begin researching issues that may directly affect you as a technology consumer, then the ACM's computing and public policy page at **www.acm.org/ serving** is a great place to start. You'll be able to research everything from the "legal regulation of technology" to copyright policy.

Although not a professional organization like ACM, the EFF shares some similar objectives, such as protecting fundamental rights regardless of technology; educating the media, policymakers, and the public about technology-related civil liberties issues; and defending those liberties. The EFF has done an excellent job of aggregating a large list of important ethical and legislative issues onto a single page, which can be found by clicking on the "Issues" link at the top of their home page and/or by going to **www.eff.org/ sitemap.php** (Figure 10.17). This list includes detailed information on topics such as file sharing, intellectual property law, censorship, and spam. You may agree or disagree with the position the EFF takes on any one specific issue, but the background information and associated links it provides are an excellent starting point for developing or reinforcing your own view on a certain topic.

Once you've identified the issues that affect you and have developed a stance on those issues, you can let the people who enact legislation know how you feel. You can find contact information for your state representatives and senators at **www.house.gov** and **www.senate.gov**, respectively. Although e-mail is convenient, most members of the U.S. Congress are deluged with messages on a daily basis. The power of a handwritten or typed letter sent via "snail mail" can often be a more effective tool in that it may allow your voice to stand out from the rest.

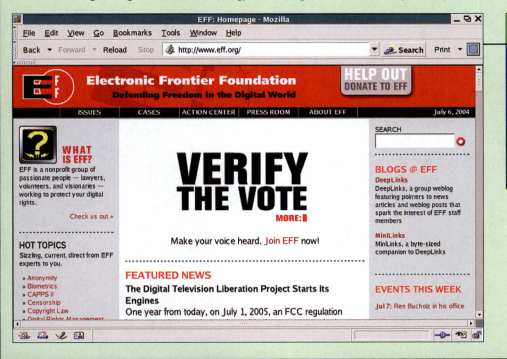

FIGURE 10.17
The Electronic Frontier Foundation (EFF) Web site includes a large list of important ethical and legislative issues. You can find the list by clicking on the "Issues" link at the top of the EFF home page.

What You'll Learn . . .

- Explain what a programming language is.

- Contrast machine language and assembly language.

- Discuss the benefits and drawbacks of high-level programming languages and fourth-generation programming languages.

- Explain how object-oriented languages attempt to remedy the shortcomings of early languages.

- List several popular object-oriented languages and explain their advantage over older languages.

- List the six phases of the program development life cycle (PDLC) and explain why the PDLC is needed.

- Explain why top-down program design makes programs easier to debug and maintain.

- List the three basic types of control structures and the advantages of each.

- Differentiate between syntax errors and logic errors in programs.

Programming Languages and Program Development

Programming is the process used to create the software applications you use every day. These applications are the result of the efforts of programmers, trained experts who work individually or in groups. They create software applications for everything from word processing to virus protection. Knowing the basics of the history and practices of the programming industry will help you to better understand what goes on inside your computer.

Programmers use programming languages to create software (Figure 11.1). Unlike the natural languages that people speak, a **programming language** is an artificial language, one that is deliberately created to tell the computer what to do in a step-by-step manner. Typically, a programming language consists of a vocabulary and a set of rules (called **syntax**) that the programmer must learn. The vocabulary and rules are used to write a program, which in most cases must be translated before a computer can run it. The written computer instructions that programmers create are called **code** (Figure 11.2). The term *code* can be a noun or a verb. For example, a programmer might say, "I wrote most of the code for this project" or "I must code a new program." Code comes in many forms. Program instructions in their original form as written by the programmer are called **source code**, which is the only form of code that humans can read. We'll discuss another form of code called object code in subsequent sections.

Every programming language has its advantages and disadvantages. What's the best programming language? If you ask 10 IT professionals, chances are you'll get 5 different answers. The truth is that there isn't any one language that's best for all programming purposes. The question then becomes, which language is the right one for the job?

In this chapter, you'll learn about programming languages, how these languages have developed, and today's hottest languages. You'll also learn how programs are developed using the program development life cycle (PDLC), an organized method of software development.

Even if you don't plan to learn programming, this chapter will help you understand what all the debate is about. And should you decide to give programming a try, you'll get the background you need to select a good language to learn.

FIGURE 11.1
Programmers use programming languages to create the code that makes up programs.

```
'pounds to kilos ets

Public Function KilogramsToPounds(Kilograms As Single) As Single
KilogramsToPounds = Round(Kilograms / 0.4536, 4)
End Function

Public Function PoundsToKilograms(Pounds As Single) As Single
PoundsToKilograms = Pounds * 0.4536
End Function
```

FIGURE 11.2
This Visual Basic code converts kilograms to pounds and pounds to kilograms.

Development of Programming Languages

Programming languages are classified by levels, or generations. Each generation is a step closer to the languages that humans use. The five generations of programming languages are:

- Machine language

- Assembly language

- Procedural languages

- Nonprocedural languages

- Natural languages

This section will discuss the development of these languages and how they've evolved to keep up with changing technology.

```
FFCF  4C  15  F2  (INPUT one byte)

FFD2  4C  66  F2  (OUTPUT one byte)

FFD5  4C  01  F4  (LOAD something)

FFD8  4C  DD  F6  (SAVE something)
```

FIGURE 11.3
Machine language code is very difficult to understand.

FIRST-GENERATION LANGUAGES: 0S AND 1S

Because the earliest computers predated programming languages, computers had to be programmed in the computer's language, also known as **machine language**. Machine language consists of binary numbers—0s and 1s—that directly correspond to the computer's electrical states. Though tedious for humans to work with, machine language is the only programming language that a computer can understand directly without translation (Figure 11.3). Each type or family of processor requires its own machine language, whose instructions are in accordance with the processor's special characteristics. For this reason, machine language is said to be **machine dependent** (or **hardware dependent**).

During the first generation of computing, programmers had to use machine language because no other option was available. Programmers had to know a great deal about the computer's design and how it functioned. As a result, programs were few in number and lacked complexity.

More recent programming languages make it easier for programmers to write programs, but all of the code they write must still be translated into machine language by special utility programs for the processor to execute the program.

SECOND-GENERATION LANGUAGES: USING MNEMONICS

The first programming language to break programmers' dependence on machine language was assembly language. In **assembly language**, each program statement corresponds to an instruction that the microprocessor can carry out. Assembly language closely resembles machine language in that it's machine dependent and closely tied to what goes on inside the computer. For this reason, it's called a **low-level language**, a programming language that's

FIGURE 11.4
Assembly language code enables programmers to use brief abbreviations such as *adda* to instruct the computer to add a number.

```
8-bit unsigned addition with overflow checking P=N+M on the 6812

N    ds    1    ; first 8-bit number
M    ds    1    ; second 8-bit number
P    ds    1    ; third 8-bit number
add8 ldaa   N    ; first number
     adda   M    ; add second number
; C bit set if unsigned overflow
     bcc    SetP ; skip if no overflow
     ldaa   #255 ; set at maximum (ceiling)
SetP staa   P
     rts
```

one level up from a computer's machine language. Because machine languages are composed of numbers, they are extremely difficult for humans to read and write. Although assembly languages use the same basic structure and commands as machine languages, they enable programmers to use more than just numbers.

To program in assembly language, programmers still need to know exactly how the computer works. However, assembly language doesn't force programmers to program in binary. Instead, it enables programmers to use familiar base-10 (decimal) numbers as well as brief abbreviations for program instructions called **mnemonics** (pronounced "nih-MON-icks") (Figure 11.4). For example, the mnemonic COMPARE A, B tells the processor to compare the data stored in memory locations A and B.

Before an assembly language program can be run on a computer, it must be translated into machine language. The source code is translated into machine language by a utility program called an **assembler**.

Assembly language is still used occasionally, especially when it's important to write a short program that runs very quickly.

THIRD-GENERATION LANGUAGES: PROGRAMMING COMES OF AGE

Due to the difficulties of using machine and assembly languages, third-generation languages were developed. Third-generation languages are still **procedural languages**: They tell the computer what to do and how

to do it in a specific series of steps. However, third-generation languages are high-level languages. Unlike machine and assembly languages, **high-level languages** eliminate the need for programmers to understand the intimate details of how the computer processes data. In other words, high-level languages are more user-friendly. For example, the programmer can write an instruction using familiar English words such as PRINT or DISPLAY. Each such instruction sums up many lines of assembly or machine language code. As a result, third-generation languages are much easier to read, write, and maintain than machine and assembly languages.

Compilers and Interpreters

Just as they do when writing in assembly language, programmers create source code in third-generation languages as well. For the source code to run on a specific type of computer system, it must be translated by a compiler or an interpreter (also referred to as a *language translator*) (Figure 11.5).

A **compiler** is a utility program that translates all of the source code into **object code**, which are instructions in (or close to) a specific computer's machine language. With some compilers, it's necessary to use a program called a linker or an assembler to transform the object code into an executable program (a program that runs on a certain type of computer). When the compiler translates the code, it checks the code for errors. If any errors are found, the program identifies the error's location and prints a program listing (a printout of the source code) that highlights the location and likely cause of the error.

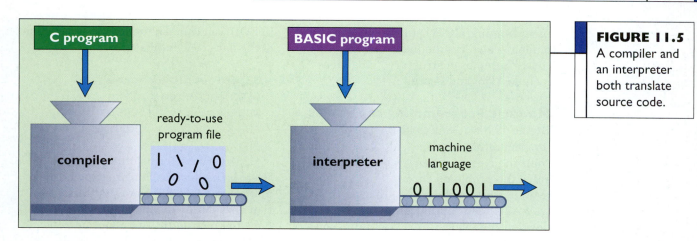

FIGURE 11.5
A compiler and an interpreter both translate source code.

Another translation program, an **interpreter**, doesn't produce object code. Instead, it translates one line of the source code at a time and executes the translated instruction. Although interpreters run programs more slowly than programs compiled into object code, they're helpful tools for learning and ridding a program of errors. As the program executes line by line, the programmer can see exactly what each line does.

For most programming languages, a programmer can use both an interpreter and a compiler. The interpreter comes in handy during program development. When the program is finished, it's compiled for efficient use.

Spaghetti Code and the Great Software Crisis

Early third-generation languages represented a major improvement over assembly and machine languages. However, early third-generation languages used GOTO statements to enable programs to branch to new locations (depending on whether a condition was met). This wasn't a problem for simple, short programs, but for lengthier programs, the use of many GOTO statements resulted in **spaghetti code**. This code was difficult to follow, and, as a consequence, the programs were prone to error (Figure 11.6).

The attempt to create larger and more complex programs led to the software crisis of the 1960s. Programs were not ready on time, exceeded their budgets, contained too many errors, and didn't satisfy customers. A study during the mid-1960s found that COBOL programmers were able, on average, to produce only 10 error-free lines of code per workday.

Structured Programming Languages

One response to spaghetti code problems focused on improving the management of software development. Another response focused on improving the languages themselves. The earliest product of such efforts (in the late 1960s) was the concept of structured programming and languages that reflected structured programming concepts. **Structured programming** is a set of quality standards that make programs more verbose but more readable, reliable, and maintainable. With structured

FIGURE 11.6 In a lengthy program, the use of many GOTO statements resulted in spaghetti code that was difficult to follow and consequently made the programs prone to error.

programming, GOTO statements are forbidden, which results in more readable code. Examples of structured languages include Algol and Pascal.

Modular Programming Languages

By the 1970s, it was clear that structured programming languages, although better than their predecessors, weren't able to solve the problems encountered in the even larger development projects underway. As a result, programmers began to develop the modular programming concept. With **modular programming**, the program is divided into separate modules, each of which takes care of a specific function that the program has to carry out. Each module requires a specified input and produces a specified output, so the programming job can be easily divided among members of the programming team. An important principle of modular programming is **information hiding**, which means that the author of one module doesn't have to be concerned with the details of what's inside another module. This information can remain hidden (and other programmers can ignore it) as long as a given module generates output in the specified form.

FOURTH-GENERATION LANGUAGES: GETTING AWAY FROM PROCEDURE

Although the transition from the second to the third generation of programming languages is reasonably clear, the same can't be said for the transition to fourth-generation languages. Various types of programming languages have claimed to be "fourth-generation," including **report generators** (languages for printing database reports) and **query languages** (languages for getting information out of databases). These languages are nonprocedural languages. **Nonprocedural languages** aren't tied down to step-by-step procedures that force the programmer to consider the procedure that must be followed to obtain the desired result. A specialized query language known as **structured query language**, or **SQL** (pronounced "sequel"), enables users to phrase simple or complex requests for data. For example,

in SQL, you can ask the following question of the data in a database:

```
SELECT employee-name
FROM employee-salary-table
WHERE salary > 50000
AND position = 'Engineer'
```

In everyday terms, this request is to "Get the names of all engineers who make more than $50,000." Note that this question isn't totally nonprocedural; you still have to know quite a bit about how the database is structured. (For example, you have to specify which table the information should come from.)

FIFTH-GENERATION LANGUAGES: NATURAL LANGUAGE

The ultimate nonprocedural language would be **natural language**, the everyday language that people speak. Computers would be much easier to use if they could understand natural language, whether the input was spoken or typed. For example, instead of looking through folder after folder in search of a missing file, imagine asking the computer, "Where's that file I created a couple of days ago? The one I wrote about those two paintings we saw in my art history class?"

Despite years of effort to create natural language interfaces, computers are still not very good at understanding what they hear and acting on this understanding. Much of what passes for a natural language interface amounts to word matching; for example, you can navigate the folders on a Mac by speaking their names and giving a few simple commands, such as "Open" or "Close." Combined with software that can parse (decode) a sentence's grammatical structure, word-matching programs can work well in areas with highly specialized vocabularies of a few thousand words.

Attempts to create natural language systems with more general capabilities have run into profound problems, such as the ambiguity of human language. The term *intelligence*, for instance, has at least four other meanings. In the military, for example, *intelligence* means knowledge

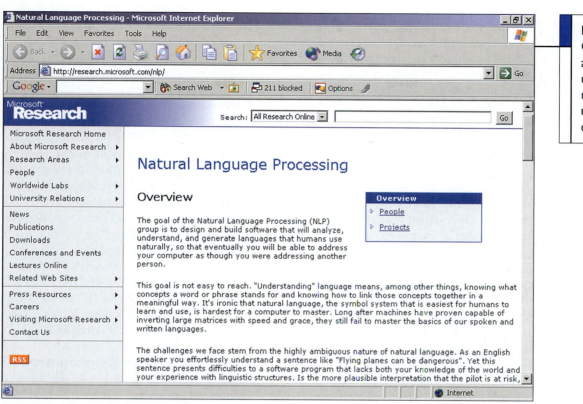

FIGURE 11.7
Companies such as Microsoft are undertaking research into natural language development.

about the enemy. A program capable of understanding the various senses of a word would have to know a great deal about the world. For example, natural language software should be able to understand that "the day before Christmas" is December 24. The underlying problems presented by these ambiguities are exceedingly complex and will require many more years of research to solve (Figure 11.7).

Natural language understanding may lie in computing's future, but major advances have been made in speech recognition, whereby computers translate spoken speech into text. Previously, speech-recognition software worked only if the speaker paused between words. New software is much better at continuous speech recognition. Still, it often takes a long time for speakers to adjust their speech patterns to match the capabilities of the software. It isn't unusual for this process to be misstated; it is often said that the computer "learns" the speaker's speech pattern, but the fact is that the "learning" is on the part of the speaker, not the computer.

Continuous speech recognition is the first step toward a true natural language interface because such an interface would require the computer to recognize anyone's natural speech. With reliable speech-recognition technology developing rapidly, the day is approaching when you'll be able to control a computer solely by talking to it in ordinary speech.

In the next section, you'll learn how expanding a language to work with objects may be a close approximation of a natural language.

OBJECT-ORIENTED PROGRAMMING

Object-oriented programming (**OOP**) is a programming technique based on the use of objects, or generic building blocks, to quickly assemble different sets of objects to solve specific problems.

Objects

An **object** is a unit of computer information that contains data as well as all of the procedures or operations (called **methods**) that can process or manipulate the data. The object also contains information that defines its interface, or its means of exchanging messages with other objects. For example, one object can ask another object, in effect, "What methods do you

Techtalk

Component reusability
The capability to develop well-designed program modules that perform a specific task, such as handling print output. With component reusability, programmers could quickly construct a program by combining ready-to-use modules, which would take a fraction of the time required to develop these modules from scratch.

have available?" and the object will describe them. With object-oriented programming, information hiding, or **encapsulation**, becomes a reality. Users (or other objects) don't have to know the specifics of how the object was implemented internally; the object is simply acted upon by the program and provides whatever information it is asked for.

Suppose you're running a bike shop, and you've created an object called DASHER. This object contains all of the data about Dasher bicycles (including inventory, pricing information, and performance characteristics). It also contains all of the methods that can be used to process the data. You can use a program (which is itself an object) that can query DASHER to find out which methods are available. You'll find out that you can choose from many methods, including totaling the number of Dasher bicycles on hand, updating the inventory, listing available accessories, or computing a sales price that includes specified accessories.

Classes

An important feature of object-oriented programming is the concept of a **class**, a category of objects. In the DASHER example, the DASHER object is part of a broader, more abstract category of objects called BIKES. In other words, it's a subclass of the BIKES class. The BIKES class is a superclass of DASHER because it's more abstract and generic. Other lines of bikes

carried by the same bike shop are SPEEDO and ZOOM-310. Objects exist for these, too, and they, like DASHER, are subclasses of BIKES.

Inheritance

One of the major objectives of object-oriented programming is reusability, the capability to create an object and then reuse it whenever it's needed. With inheritance, possibilities for object reuse are multiplied.

Inheritance refers to an object's capacity to "pass on" its characteristics or properties to its "children," or subclasses. To create objects for the bike shop, a programmer begins by creating the BIKES object. This object is then copied and modified to make the DASHER, SPEEDO, and ZOOM-310 objects, all of which inherit properties from the BIKES object (Figure 11.8).

Rapid Application Development

Because objects can be easily reused, object-oriented programming enables a fast method of program development called **rapid application development** (**RAD**). With RAD, a programmer works with a library of prebuilt objects that have been created for a huge variety of applications. For instance, a text box is an object that contains a label and the contents of a field object. Using RAD, a programmer does not have to write code that describes the object, but instead simply inserts the prebuilt text box and then modifies it to suit the program's needs.

FIGURE 11.8 DASHER, SPEEDO, and ZOOM-310 are subclasses of the BIKES object. They all inherit properties from the BIKES object.

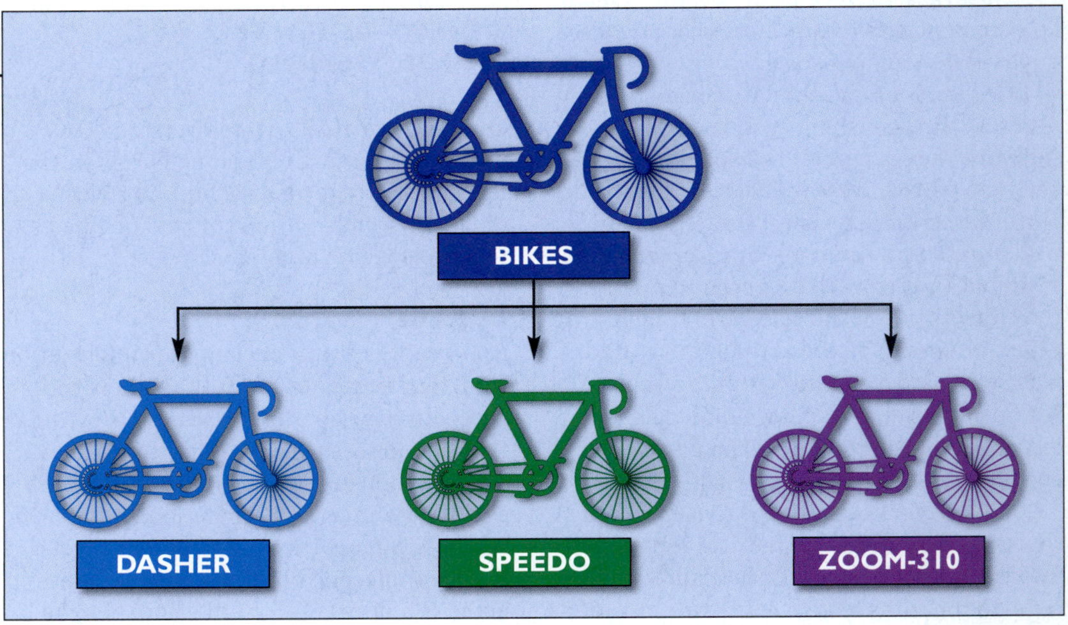

Middleware (Accessing Objects across Networks)

One of the most appealing possibilities of object-oriented programming lies in its suitability for use in computer networks. Suppose you have hundreds, or even thousands, of objects accessible on the network, and each one contains data, as well as the knowledge of how to use that data. To access these objects on the network, middleware is needed. **Middleware** refers to standards that define how programs can find objects and query them about what kinds of data they contain.

Middleware is a fairly new concept, and the standards are still maturing. One leading standard is **CORBA** (**Common Object Request Broker Architecture**), which defines how objects can communicate with each other across a network, even if the objects are written in dissimilar programming languages. For example, oil giant Chevron uses CORBA to give nearly 3,000 employees access to a variety of databases that are written in many different languages. With the Internet Inter-Orb Protocol (IIOP), CORBA capabilities can be built into Web browsers, which transforms them into tools for requesting information from objects (Figure 11.9).

CORBA isn't the only middleware standard. Microsoft Corporation is pushing its own standard, the **Component Object Model** (**COM**), which works best when companies are running nothing but Windows machines.

Other Advantages of Object-Oriented Programming

In traditional programming, the program and data are kept separate. If the data must change—because, for example, a company needs to start tracking the exact time of orders as well as the date—all programs that access that data also must be changed. That's an expensive, time-consuming process.

With object-oriented programming, however, the data are stored along with all of the program procedures needed to access and use the data. If another program accesses the data, it immediately learns which procedures are available, including any new ones. This eliminates the need to change many programs just because of a minor change in the data, which saves both time and money.

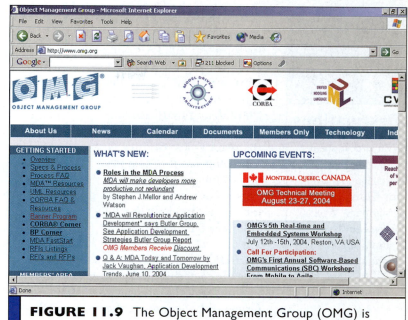

FIGURE 11.9 The Object Management Group (OMG) is a consortium that produces and maintains computer industry specifications such as CORBA.

Object-oriented programming encourages the programmer to start thinking *from the beginning* about the real-world environment in which the program will function, because each object contains the methods for manipulating the object. Proponents of object-oriented programming believe that this focus leads to more usable software.

Now that you understand how programming methods have developed, let's take a look at some of the specific languages that programmers use today.

A Guide to Programming Languages: One Size Doesn't Fit All

This section provides a guide to today's most popular programming languages. As you'll see, each program has its pros and cons. Successful programming involves choosing the right language for the job.

Destinations

Want to find out what kinds of jobs are available for COBOL programmers? Visit www.coboljobs .com/public/ default.asp

COBOL AND FORTRAN

Imagine it's 1959. Cars have big fins. Dwight Eisenhower is president of the United States. Hawaii becomes a state. And computer programmers are using COBOL and FORTRAN.

Now fast-forward. It's the beginning of the twenty-first century. Guess what? More than 50 percent of computer programmers are still using COBOL and FORTRAN. This section explains the origins of these languages and how and why they're still being used today.

COBOL

One of the earliest high-level programming languages, **COBOL** (Common Business-Oriented Language) is the most widely used business programming language in the world. What's more, thousands of jobs are available for COBOL programmers, and businesses are competing to hire COBOL talent.

COBOL's success lies in the simple fact that it's a proven way to tackle a large organization's accounting information, including inventory control, billing, and payroll. In addition, COBOL has some features that more recent programming languages

should imitate. For example, COBOL requires programmers to write in a style that explains what the program is doing at each step. Anyone who knows COBOL can look at someone else's program and quickly figure out how it works (Figure 11.10).

Detractors, whose complaints often include COBOL's verbose, cumbersome, and business-oriented nature, give other reasons for its longevity. Many think that it has more to do with the survival of legacy (obsolete) mainframe computer systems, where COBOL programming dominates. Like other legacy programming languages, COBOL has been updated with structured and even object-oriented versions, so there's a clear path to the future.

FORTRAN

FORTRAN, short for "formula translator," is so well suited to scientific, mathematical, and engineering applications that it's very difficult to pry it out of engineers' hands. In many engineering schools, protracted battles arise over which programming language to teach engineering students; the computer-science-oriented people want to teach C++ (which we'll get to in a bit), and the engineers want to teach FORTRAN.

```
000100 IDENTIFICATION DIVISION.
000200 PROGRAM-ID.      HELLOWORLD.
000300
000400*
000500 ENVIRONMENT DIVISION.
000600 CONFIGURATION SECTION.
000700 SOURCE-COMPUTER. RM-COBOL.
000800 OBJECT-COMPUTER. RM-COBOL.
000900
001000 DATA DIVISION.
001100 FILE SECTION.
001200
100000 PROCEDURE DIVISION.
100100
100200 MAIN-LOGIC SECTION.
100300 BEGIN.
100400     DISPLAY " " LINE 1 POSITION 1 ERASE EOS.
100500     DISPLAY "Hello world!" LINE 15 POSITION 10.
100600     STOP RUN.
100700 MAIN-LOGIC-EXIT.
100800     EXIT.
```

FIGURE 11.10 This COBOL program prints "Hello World!" on the screen.

```
c
c    Hello, world.
c

     Program Hello

     implicit none
     logical DONE

     DO while (.NOT. DONE)
       write(*,10)
     END DO
  10 format('Hello, world.')
     END
```

FIGURE 11.11 This simple FORTRAN program prints "Hello World!" to the screen.

FIGURE 11.12 Augusta Ada Byron helped nineteenth-century inventor Charles Babbage conceptualize what may have been the world's first digital computer.

Destinations

To learn more about the life and times of Augusta Ada Byron and her contributions to computer history, check out **www.cs.yale.edu/ homes/tap/Files/ ada-bio.html**

What's so great about FORTRAN? The answer is in the name: *formula translator*. If you need to solve a complex engineering equation, no other programming language comes close to FORTRAN's simplicity, economy, and ease of use (Figure 11.11). FORTRAN is most likely to be replaced not by another programming language, but by a formula-solving program such as Wolfram Research's Mathematica, which can transform equations into complex (and often beautiful) graphics that reveal underlying mathematical patterns.

STRUCTURED AND MODULAR LANGUAGES

COBOL and FORTRAN still have their places in mainframes and engineering shops, but large-scale program development requires structured and modular languages. The following languages are in widespread use among professional developers and software firms.

Ada

Ada, a programming language that incorporates modular programming principles, is named after Augusta Ada Byron (1815–1852), who helped nineteenth-century inventor Charles Babbage conceptualize what may have been the world's first digital computer (Figure 11.12). Part of Ada's popularity probably lies in the fact that it was the required language for most U.S.

Department of Defense projects until 1996. Major advantages of Ada include its suitability for the reliable control of real-time systems (such as missiles). For example, the U.S. Navy's Seawolf submarine uses more than 5 million lines of Ada code running on more than 100 Motorola processors.

BASIC

BASIC (Beginner's All-Purpose Symbolic Instruction Code) is an easy-to-use, high-level programming language available on many personal computers. Developed at Dartmouth College in the mid-1960s to teach programming basics to beginners, BASIC is used by many hobbyists to create simple programs. It's also widely taught in high schools and some colleges in beginning programming courses. Many educators, however, believe that the original versions of BASIC teach flawed programming skills due to BASIC's reliance on GOTO statements. More recent versions of BASIC incorporate the principles of structured, modular, and object-oriented programming.

BASIC was designed as an interpreted language so that beginners could create a program in an interactive mode, run the program, test it, and fix errors. Interpreted languages are conducive to learning

The Outer Limits of Programming: Fixing Software in Space

Software problems in space are nothing new. Over and over, NASA's experts have diagnosed bugs and mechanical glitches in space probes millions of miles away and then programmed fixes to get things back on track. For example, after the main antenna on one deep-space probe wouldn't unfold to transmit data, NASA programmers transmitted a program ordering on-board recording equipment to store digital photos as they were snapped by the probe's camera. Then they reprogrammed the probe's system to send all data through the secondary antenna to a computer on Earth—ready for access by eager scientists.

When the rovers *Spirit* and *Opportunity* landed on Mars, they sent back riveting color images of the red, rocky landscape—until *Spirit* suddenly stopped responding after three weeks of flawless operation (Figure 11.13). Fearing that they might never regain control of the *Spirit*, NASA's experts methodically tested different problems and solutions on a duplicate rover on Earth. Meanwhile, because programmers had built a "safe mode" into the software, they soon coaxed a single answering "beep" from *Spirit*, followed by brief reports that its heating and power systems were functioning normally. However, the rover's flight system continued to drain the batteries as it endlessly crashed and restarted, crashed and restarted.

Finally, NASA technicians were able to reproduce on Earth the problem that was hobbling *Spirit* on Mars: too much data held in flash memory. At any one time, *Spirit* had the capacity to hold more than 10,000 files in flash memory. As unneeded files and directories piled up, the rover eventually ran out of memory and couldn't switch into sleep mode to recharge its battery. The programmers then ordered *Spirit* to start up without accessing flash memory—and its system stopped crashing. Once the rover shut itself down, recharged its batteries, and rebooted, the programmers transmitted code to remove some files and folders from flash memory. One hundred million miles away, *Spirit* was ready for more Mars adventures.

FIGURE 11.13 NASA programmers can fix bugs in *Spirit* and *Opportunity* as the sister rovers work to discover the secrets of Mars.

programming, but they run much more slowly than compiled programs. As a result, professional programmers avoided using BASIC. Newer versions of BASIC have added compilers to speed up program performance.

Visual Basic

Developed in the early 1990s and based on the BASIC programming language, Microsoft's **Visual Basic** (**VB**) is an event-driven programming language. With an **event-driven programming language**, the program's code is not written to execute in any specific sequence. Instead, the code executes in response to user actions, such as the clicking of a mouse button. Visual Basic enables a programmer to develop an application quickly by designing the graphical

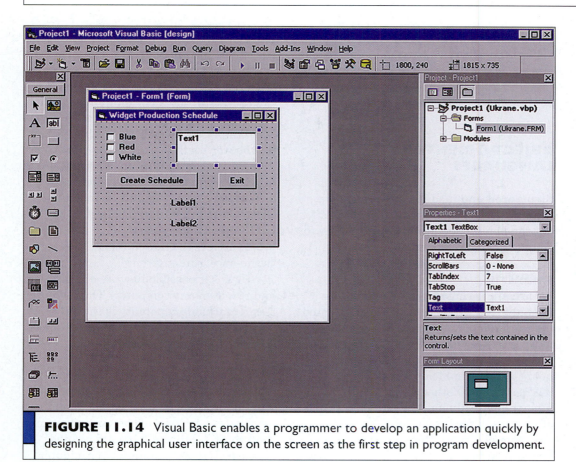

FIGURE 11.14 Visual Basic enables a programmer to develop an application quickly by designing the graphical user interface on the screen as the first step in program development.

user interface on the screen as the *first* step in program development (Figure 11.14).

Each on-screen control, such as a text box or a radio button, can then be linked to a brief BASIC program that performs an action. The programmer doesn't have to worry about any of the code that generates the user interface, because it's all handled automatically by the Visual Basic compiler, which creates an executable program capable of running on its own. Using Visual Basic, even a novice programmer can develop an impressive application in short order.

Visual Basic is one of the world's most widely used program development packages. In the United States, it's part of the programming tool kit of more than 50 percent of the country's 2.4 million professional programmers. Microsoft has sold more than 1 million licenses for Visual Basic 6.0. What's the secret to Visual Basic's success? It's by far the most successful RAD tool in existence for Microsoft Windows applications, and Windows is the operating system used on an estimated 80 percent of the world's computers.

Pascal

Pascal, which is named after seventeenth-century mathematician Blaise Pascal, is a high-level programming language that encourages programmers to write well-structured programs. Pascal has gained wide acceptance as a teaching language and is available in interpreted and compiled versions.

Like many older programming languages, Pascal has been updated to reflect new approaches to programming. An object-oriented version of Pascal provides the foundation for Delphi, a compiler created by Borland International that closely resembles Visual Basic. However, Delphi hasn't been able to match Visual Basic's success because Microsoft controls the market.

C

C is a high-level programming language developed by AT&T's Bell Labs in the 1970s. C combines the virtues of high-level programming languages with the efficiency of an assembly language. Using C, programmers can directly manipulate bits of data inside the processing unit. As a result, well-written C programs run significantly faster than programs written in other high-level programming languages. However, C is difficult to learn, and programming in C is a time-consuming activity.

OBJECT-ORIENTED LANGUAGES

Structured and modular languages are the workhorses of software development, but the honor of being cutting edge goes to object-oriented (OO) languages.

Smalltalk
Smalltalk is considered by many to be the only "100 percent pure" object-oriented programming language. It was developed in the early 1970s at Xerox Corporation's Palo Alto Research Center (PARC), the home of the graphical user interface (GUI) and many other key computing innovations. Although the language is not often chosen for professional software development, more than a few corporations (including American Airlines, FedEx, and Texas Instruments) have chosen Smalltalk for mission-critical applications.

C++
A more recent version of C, C++, was developed at Bell Labs in the 1980s. **C++** incorporates object-oriented features but doesn't force programmers to adhere to the object-oriented model (Figure 11.15). Thanks to this flexibility and the fast execution speed of compiled C++ programs, C++ is in widespread use for professional program development. The software giant Microsoft uses C++ for application development.

Java
Developed by Sun Microsystems for consumer electronic devices, **Java** is an object-oriented, high-level programming language (Figure 11.16). Java is a simplified version of C++, though Java is much easier to learn than C++. According to Java backers, it's the world's first truly **cross-platform programming language**, a programming language capable of running on many different types of computers, including those using the Windows, Mac OS, or UNIX operating systems. Java enables programmers to create programs that "write once, run anywhere."

How is it possible to write one program and run it on any computer? The secret to this remarkable capability is the Java Virtual Machine, which must be installed on any computer that runs Java. The **Java Virtual Machine** (**VM**) is a Java interpreter and runtime environment for Java applets and applications that provides a "home away from home" for Java, no matter what type of computer it's running on. It is called a "virtual machine" because it creates a simulated computer that provides the correct platform for executing Java programs.

Why is the "write once, run anywhere" capability so attractive? The answer is simple: reduced costs. Many companies have acquired computers helter-skelter over the years. They may have UNIX workstations, Windows computers, Macintoshes, and more. At the same time, they need software tools that give all employees the ability to access critical network resources. Java offers the ability to write one program that can run on all of the computers in a firm, without the considerable expense of making several versions of the original program for each type of computer it needs to run on.

Java saves money in another way, too. As opposed to traditional programs, which must be installed and configured on each employee's machine, specially designed Java miniprograms called **applets** are made available through a network. Employees can obtain a program by accessing a Web page, clicking a link, and downloading the Java applet (Figure 11.17). The applet is soon running on the employee's computer, and the distribution costs are next to nothing.

Destinations

For more information on C++, see the C++ Virtual Library at **www.desy.de/user/ projects/C++.html**

```
# include <iostream.h>

void main ()
{
cout <<"Hello World!";
```

FIGURE 11.15 This simple C++ program prints "Hello World!" to the screen.

Java has gained acceptance faster than any programming language in the history of computing. (Note that Microsoft launched its answer to Java on February 14, 2001, with its official kickoff of the .NET initiative. Part of this initiative is XL, a cross-platform markup language, that has Java in its sights. The next few years will be very interesting as the battle heats up!)

Despite Java's considerable advantages, the language has many of the weaknesses of a programming language that's still evolving. For example, downloaded applets pose a security risk, so they're limited to actions that don't involve storage devices. Perhaps worst of all, though, is the fact that Java software is slow. Java programs aren't as slow as interpreted programs, but they're considerably slower than compiled programs.

WEB-BASED LANGUAGES

Whereas programming languages tell the computer what to do and how to do it,

```
class Hello World {
public static void main (String args
{})        {
System. out. println ("Hello World!");
}
```

FIGURE 11.16 Java has gained acceptance faster than any programming language in computing history. Here is an example of Java code.

Web-based languages tell a browser how to interpret text and objects. Web-based languages include markup languages and scripting languages.

Markup Languages

A **markup language** is a set of codes, called **elements**, for marking the format of text that a browser reads, such as a title or a heading. Most elements have two codes, a **start tag** and an **end tag**, that surround the marked-up text. By using start and end tags, markup languages indicate to a browser how text or an object is to be rendered on the

Techtalk

Javabeans
How do Java programmers write programs that will work on multiple computer platforms? Simple! They use javabeans. Javabeans are programming specifications that ensure finished programs can travel across networks and work with larger applications.

Destinations

To learn more about Java, visit Java's home page at Sun Microsystems at **java.sun.com**

FIGURE 11.17 Java Boutique provides more than 120 working Java applets with instructions for downloading and including them in your own Web page.

screen. The following are examples of today's most commonly used markup languages.

HTML   To create a Web page, programmers use a markup language called **HTML (Hypertext Markup Language)**. HTML supports links to other documents as well as graphics, audio, and video files. This means that you can jump from one document to another simply by clicking a link. HTML enables hypertext and describes the structure of Web pages. This markup language sets the attributes of text and objects within a Web page. For example: This text is bold. produces the sentence "**This text is bold.**" when viewed with a Web browser.

The following illustrates HTML for a level 1 (major) heading, a paragraph of text, and an indented quotation:

```
<H1>This is the text of a
major heading.</H1>

<P>This is a paragraph of
text. Most browsers display
paragraph text with a blank
line before the paragraph and
flush left alignment.</P>

<BLOCKQUOTE>This is an indented
quotation. Most browsers display
blockquote material with an
indentation from the left
margin.</BLOCKQUOTE>
```

To see how simple it is to create a marked up document, type a few lines into your word processor and apply bolding or other attributes to different words or phrases. Next, choose File, Save As Web Page or HTML, and then choose View, Source to see the tags that have been added to your text.

A document marked up with HTML contains plaintext (ASCII text). When browsers access the document, they read the markup and position the various portions of the document in accordance with the markup language's format settings.

HTML's simplicity is an important reason for the Web's popularity—nearly anyone can learn how to create a simple Web page using HTML. As a result, it's possible for millions of people to contribute content to the Web. In fact, it may be easier

than you imagine; Microsoft Word, Excel, Access, and PowerPoint allow you to save Web-ready documents in HTML format.

XML   XML (**eXtensible Markup Language**) is a set of rules for creating markup languages that enables programmers to capture specific types of data by creating their own elements. XML is to data what HTML is to text. XML is used for sharing data and complex forms and objects in a Web-based environment. It provides a standardized format that is readable on many different devices, such as PDAs, notebooks, and desktops. XML can be used in HTML documents.

Here's an example of XML that can be used to define part of a bibliographic citation:

```
<citation><last>Smith</last>
<first>Janet</first><pubdate>
2002</pubdate>

<title>Easy Guide to XML</title>
<publisher>Xdirections
</publisher>

<place>Charlottesville, VA
</place></citation>
```

The bibliographic citation tags, such as <last> and <place>, are contained within <citation> tags. An XML-savvy browser doesn't know anything about what these tags mean, but it does know that <last> and <place> (and the other tags) go within the <citation> element. An XML-capable browser, such as Microsoft Internet Explorer versions 5 and later and Netscape Communicator versions 6 and later, can detect the nested structure of XML tags and display the structure in a navigation panel.

What's so great about a browser being able to detect the structure of XML tags? Simple: It means that it's possible for Web authors to invent all the tags they want and still have them displayed in a meaningful fashion. Suddenly, the information presented on a Web page becomes *meaningful*. To understand why this is an advantage, suppose you're running an online art gallery, and you're exhibiting and selling works by Tom Smith—a great artist, but one with a very common name. People searching the Internet for "Tom

Smith" will retrieve over 15,000 pages. On your Web page, the artist's name is coded with XML as follows: <artist>Smith, Tom (1956 –)</artist>. Thanks to XML, people can now search effectively for the very few Tom Smiths who are artists.

Although XML enables anyone to create new tags, efforts are going on in virtually every type of business and profession to develop common XML **vocabularies**, which are sets of elements and tags for a particular field or discipline. For example, architectural associations are developing XML coding schemes for special architectural documents.

XML will be a big part of your computing future as more documents are encoded and placed online. Wireless devices use a specialized form of XML called the Wireless Markup Language (WML). This language enables developers to create pages specifically designed for wireless devices.

Scripting Languages

Scripting languages enable users to quickly create useful **scripts**, simple programs that control any action or feedback on a Web page. A script might control an action that takes place when you roll the mouse over a particular part of a Web page or check what occurs when you enter data into a form. In fact, a script isn't compiled; it's interpreted by the Web browser, line by line. For example, a huge variety of accessory tools enable Visual Basic programmers to accomplish tasks quickly, such as building interfaces to databases and increasing the functionality of Web pages. **VBScript**, a scripting language based on Visual Basic, was created to write scripts that can be embedded in Web pages.

ActiveX controls are miniprograms (mainly written in Visual Basic) that can be downloaded from Web pages and used to add functionality to Web browsers. However, VBScript and ActiveX controls require users to be running Microsoft Windows and Microsoft Internet Explorer.

Like VBScript, **JavaScript** is a simple, easy-to-learn scripting language designed for writing scripts on Web pages. Despite including "Java" in its name, JavaScript isn't based on Java. Rather, JavaScript was created by Netscape Communications. Recently standardized by the European Computer Manufacturers Association

(ECMA), JavaScript is now properly known as **ECMAScript**, and it's in widespread use on the Web.

Visual Studio .NET

Microsoft's answer to Java and JavaScript, **Visual Studio .NET**, is a suite of products that contains Visual Basic .NET, which enables programmers to work with complex objects; Visual C++, which is based upon C++; and Visual C# (pronounced "C sharp"), which is a less complex version of C++ that is used for rapid application development of Web programs. Visual Studio .NET is used for the development of scripts and programs that are accessible from the Web and over the Internet.

Keep in mind that using scripting languages is closer to true programming because scripting languages use complex logic and algorithms, whereas markup languages simply direct browsers to interpret text and objects in a certain way.

You now know enough about programming methods and languages to appreciate the next section, which covers program development.

The Program Development Life Cycle

At the dawn of the modern computer era, no one thought about managing the software development process. Programs were written for specific, well-defined purposes, such as calculating missile trajectories. If a program didn't work, the programmer corrected it. As a result, this approach came to be known as code-and-fix (or "cut-and-run," as detractors put it).

When businesses began using computers for more complex purposes, problems arose. Oftentimes, programmers didn't really understand what managers wanted a program to do, and correcting problems became expensive and time consuming. In addition, programmers didn't document their programs well (if at all), and some developed idiosyncratic programming styles that assured their continued

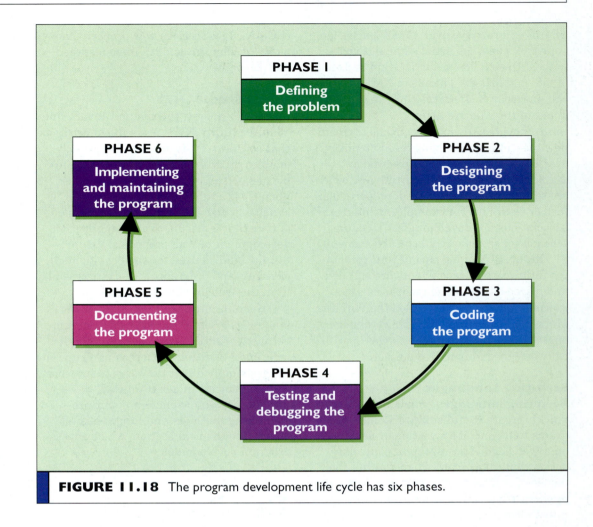

FIGURE 11.18 The program development life cycle has six phases.

employment, because no one else could figure out what their code did! These early programs were almost impossible to maintain (especially if the original programmer had left the company).

To address these problems, the program development life cycle was introduced in the 1970s, and it is still in widespread use today. The **program development life cycle** (**PDLC**) provides an organized plan for breaking down the task of program development into manageable chunks, each of which must be successfully completed before programmers move on to the next phase (Figure 11.18). Let's look at each of these phases in detail.

PHASE 1: DEFINING THE PROBLEM

The first step in developing a program is to define the problem that the program is to solve. This is the job of systems analysts, who provide the results of their work to programmers in the form of a program specification. The **program specification**, or spec, precisely defines the input data, the processing that should occur, what the output should look like, and how the user interface should look. Depending on the size of the job, program development might be handled by an individual or by a team of analysts.

PHASE 2: DESIGNING THE PROGRAM

After an analyst has determined the program's specs, the next step is for programmers to create a program design—a plan drawn on paper that can be reviewed and discussed until everything's right. The program design specifies the components that make the program work.

Top-Down Program Design

Program design begins by focusing on the main goal that the program is trying to achieve and then breaking the program into manageable components. This approach is called **top-down program design**. The first step involves identifying the main routine. A **routine** (also referred to as a procedure, function, or subroutine) is a section of code that executes a specific task in a program. Multiple routines grouped together are called **modules**; modules grouped together make up programs. After identifying the main routine, programmers try to break down the various components of the main routine into smaller subroutines until each subroutine is highly focused and accomplishes only one major task. Experience shows that this is the best way to ensure program quality. For example, if an error appears in a program designed in this way, it's relatively easy to identify the module causing the error.

Structured Design

Within each subroutine, the programmer draws on control structures to envision how the subroutine will do its job. **Control structures** are logical elements grouped in a block with an END statement that specify how the instructions in a program are to be executed. This section discusses the three basic control structures.

In a **sequence control structure**, instructions to the computer are executed, or performed, by the computer in the order, or sequence, in which they appear. Sequence control structures provide the basic building blocks for computer programs. If you can imagine yourself as a computer, here's an example of a sequence of instructions you'd follow to obtain a pizza:

```
Go to the phone.
Dial the pizza place.
Order the pizza.
Hang up.
```

In a **selection control structure** (also called a conditional, or branch, control structure), the program branches to different instructions depending on whether a condition is met. A condition is an expression that compares instructions. Most conditions are based on IF . . . THEN . . . ELSE logic. If a condition is true, one set of instructions is executed. If the condition is not true, a different set of instructions is executed. Here's an example of a selection control structure that includes a *very* important test—making sure you have enough money to order a pizza.

```
Open your wallet.
IF you have enough money,
   THEN  Go to the phone.
         Dial the pizza place.
         Order the pizza.
         Hang up.
   ELSE  Forget the whole thing.
```

A variant of the selection control structure is the case control structure. In a **case control structure**, the condition is fundamental, and each branch leads to its own lengthy series of instructions. For example, the IRS processes tax returns differently depending on five categories of marital status. A coded field indicates whether the taxpayer is married filing a joint return, married filing separately, single, head of household, or widowed. A case control structure can be used so that the computer can determine which of those five categories a taxpayer belongs to and then use the correct set of instructions to process the return.

In a **repetition control structure** (also called a looping, or iteration, control structure), the program repeats the same instructions over and over. The set of instructions that is repeated is called a loop. The two types of repetition structures are DO-WHILE and DO-UNTIL. In a DO-WHILE structure, the program tests a condition at the beginning of the loop and executes the specified instructions only if the condition is true. The following example illustrates a DO-WHILE structure:

```
DO gobble down pizza,
WHILE there is still more
    pizza
```

Note that a DO-WHILE structure doesn't guarantee that the action will be performed even once. If the initial test condition is false, the action doesn't occur.

In a DO-UNTIL structure, the program executes the instructions and then tests to see whether a specified condition is true. If not, the loop repeats. Here's a DO-UNTIL structure:

```
DO gobble down pizza,
UNTIL none remains.
```

Developing an Algorithm

Control structures are combined to create an algorithm. An **algorithm** is a step-by-step description of how to arrive at a solution. You can think of an algorithm as a recipe or as a how-to sheet. But algorithms aren't restricted to computers. In fact, we use them every day. Most people do long division by following an algorithm. Here's another example: Suppose that you want to determine your car's gas mileage. You probably do this by filling the tank and noting your mileage. The next time you get gas, you note the mileage again, determine the number of miles you drove, and then divide the miles driven by the amount of gas you put in. The result tells you your car's gas mileage, which you generated by using a simple algorithm.

In programming, coming up with an algorithm involves figuring out how to get the desired result by nesting control structures. To get programs to do useful things, programmers use **nesting**, a process of embedding control structures within one another. Here's an example that remedies some of the unhealthy implications of the examples in the previous section:

```
DO check to see whether you're
   still hungry,
WHILE there is still more
   pizza.
IF you are still hungry,
THEN gobble down pizza.
ELSE put the rest in the
   fridge.
```

Program Design Tools

A variety of design tools are available to help programmers develop well-structured programs.

Structure charts (also called **hierarchy charts**) show the top-down design of a program. Each box, or module, in the chart indicates a task that the program must accomplish (Figure 11.19). The top module, called the **control module**, oversees the transfer of control to the other modules.

A **flowchart** is a diagram that shows the logic of a program. Programmers create

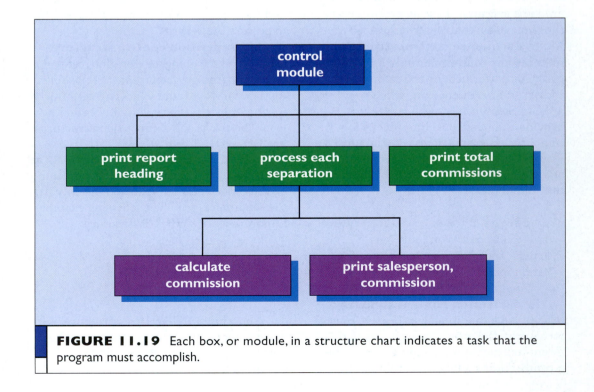

FIGURE 11.19 Each box, or module, in a structure chart indicates a task that the program must accomplish.

flowcharts either by hand using a flow-charting template or on the computer. Each flowchart symbol has a meaning. A diamond, for example, indicates a condition; a rectangle is used for a process; and a parallelogram indicates an input or output procedure (Figure 11.20).

Pseudocode, which was created in the 1970s as an alternative to flowcharts, is a stylized form of writing used to describe the logic of a program. Pseudocode can't be compiled or executed—it doesn't follow any formatting or syntax rules. Instead, pseudocode enables programmers to focus on basic algorithms without having to worry about the details of a programming language. Programmers are even able to write pseudocode without knowing what programming language they're going to use upon implementation.

PHASE 3: CODING THE PROGRAM

Creating the code involves translating the algorithm into specific programming language instructions. The programming team must choose an appropriate programming language and then create the program by writing the code. The programmers must carefully follow the language's rules of syntax, which specify precisely how to express certain operations. For example, different programming languages specify basic arithmetic operations in different ways. Program development tools can check for **syntax errors**, flaws in the structure of commands, while the program is being written. Syntax errors must be eliminated before the program will run.

PHASE 4: TESTING AND DEBUGGING THE PROGRAM

The fourth step in a programming project is to eliminate all errors. After the syntax errors are eliminated, the program will execute. The output may still not be correct, however, because the language translator can't detect logic errors. A **logic error** is a mistake the programmer

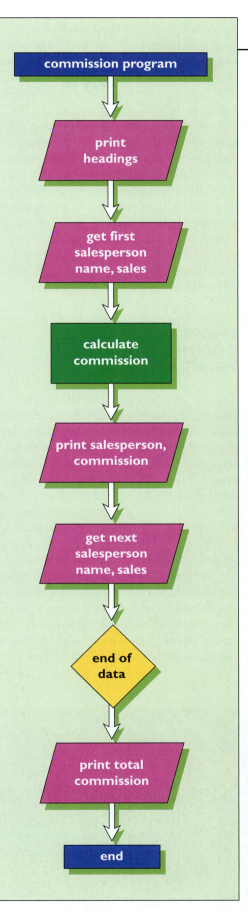

FIGURE 11.20 A flowchart is a diagram that shows the logic of a program. Each flowchart symbol has a meaning.

Destinations

SmartDraw's flow-charting center provides a one-stop resource for everything related to flowcharts and process diagrams. On the SmartDraw Web site you'll find tutorials for drawing flowcharts as well as examples of professional flowcharts and flowcharting templates that can be downloaded for free. Visit SmartDraw at **www.smartdraw .com/resources/ centers/flowcharts/ index.htm**

made in designing the solution to the problem, for example, telling the computer to calculate net pay by adding deductions to gross pay instead of subtracting them. The programmer must find and correct logic errors by carefully examining the program output. Syntax errors and logic errors are collectively known as **bugs**. The process of eliminating these errors is known as **debugging**.

After the visible logic errors have been eliminated, the programming team must test the program to find hidden errors. However, it's not always possible to examine every outcome for each program condition. Inevitably, some errors will surface only when the program is put into use.

PHASE 5: DOCUMENTING THE PROGRAM

The job isn't finished until the program is thoroughly documented. This requires writing a manual that provides an overview of the program's functionality, tutorials for beginning users, in-depth explanations of major program features, reference documentation of all program commands, and a thorough description of the error messages generated by the program. These manuals, along with the program design work, are known as **documentation**.

For example, the structure chart and pseudocode or flowchart developed during the design phase become documentation for others who will modify the program in the future. In addition, other documentation should have been created as the program was coded: lists of variable names and definitions, descriptions of files that the program needs to work with, and layouts of output that the program produces. All of this documentation needs to be gathered together and saved for future reference.

PHASE 6: IMPLEMENTING AND MAINTAINING THE PROGRAM

All that is left is the sixth and final step: implementation and maintenance. Even if the program has been developed by in-house programmers, the program will still need to be tested by the users. Even the best-written program is useless if the user does not understand how to work with it. What's more, no matter how exhaustively the program was tested, users will discover program errors.

As a result, even after a program is complete, it needs to be maintained and evaluated. Maintenance is by far the most expensive part of the software development process, so good design and documentation are crucial to keep costs in check. During **program maintenance**, the programming team fixes program errors discovered by users. The team conducts periodic evaluations asking users whether the program is fulfilling its objectives. The evaluation may lead to modifications to update the program or to add features for the users. It may even lead to a decision to abandon the current program and develop a new one, and so the program development life cycle begins anew.

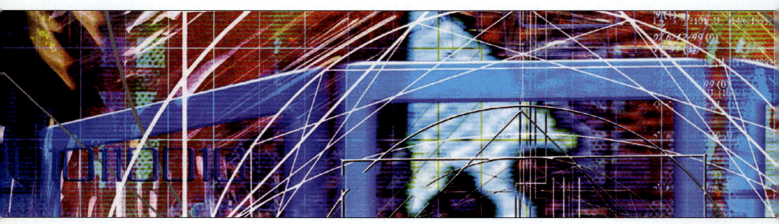

Debugging 5 Million Lines of Code the eBay Way

If you've ever auctioned or purchased anything on eBay, you know that programming is the site's lifeblood. Every day, eBay's sophisticated applications handle 10 million bids, 175 million searches, and $85 million in sales. Now imagine the confusion if the site suddenly stopped functioning: Bidders wouldn't know whether they'd won, and sellers wouldn't know whether their items sold—let alone at what price. And every minute the site is down, eBay loses money. That's why, after suffering through a 22-hour outage in 1999, eBay's IT experts have worked extra hard to maintain near-perfect site availability (Figure 11.21).

Before the outage, when a visitor viewed a page on the site, all data moved from one massive database through a single powerful server. Programmers wrote custom code to keep things moving, but even minor bugs could bring large chunks of the system to a halt. More than once, troubleshooters worked through the night to find and fix problems.

Then eBay switched to a series of 2,500 servers (plus 2,500 back-up servers) linked to 20 databases (plus 6 back-ups). Along with this change, the programmers developed software to identify bugs that slowed system response or served up blank Web pages. When a programmer completes the software for a new feature, eBay now tests it on one server. If the first test is successful, the software is expanded to 25 percent of the servers, tested again, and then expanded to all 5,000 servers. As a result, eBay counts only 325 bugs among its 5 million lines of code—a tremendous improvement over the 3,000 bugs it had in 2003. Because they spot bugs early, programmers need just five hours (not five days or five weeks) to debug code. It all adds up to an impressive record of 99.94 percent site availability and 95 million very happy eBay users.

FIGURE 11.21 After suffering through a 22-hour outage in 1999, eBay's IT experts have worked extra hard to maintain near-perfect site availability.

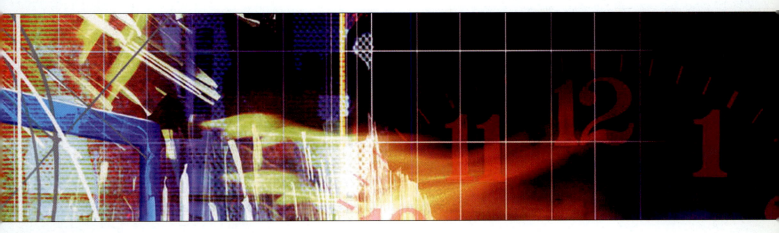

What You've Learned

PROGRAMMING LANGUAGES AND PROGRAM DEVELOPMENT

- A programming language is an artificial language consisting of a vocabulary and a set of rules used to create instructions for a computer to follow.

- The earliest (and lowest-level) programming language is machine language, which consists of instructions using binary numbers—0s and 1s—that directly correspond to the computer's electrical states. Although assembly language uses the same basic structure and commands as machine language, assembly language is easier to use because the programmer can use symbols to sum up program instructions. However, both machine language and assembly language require the programmer to know a great deal about how a particular brand and model of processor works.

- High-level languages (third-generation languages) free the programmer from having to know processor details, but these languages still require the programmer to specify the procedure to be followed to solve the problem. Fourth-generation languages free programmers from having to worry about the problem-solving procedure, but most of these languages are restricted to accessing databases.

- Because third-generation languages failed in their goal of total modularity and information hiding, object-oriented languages emerged. Object-oriented languages achieve these goals by combining procedures and data.

- C++, Java, and ECMAScript are popular object-oriented programming languages. Their advantage over earlier-generation languages is their ability to work with prebuilt objects.

- The six phases of the program development life cycle (PDLC) are (1) defining the problem, (2) designing the program, (3) coding the program, (4) testing and debugging the program, (5) documenting the program, and (6) implementing and maintaining the program. The PDLC is needed because earlier ad hoc programming techniques produced software that was riddled with errors and was virtually impossible to debug or maintain.

- Top-down program design makes programs easier to debug and maintain because program functions are divided into separate modules, each of which has a clear, simple function.

- Using the three basic types of control structures (sequence, selection, and repetition), a programmer can create an algorithm to perform any processing task. Algorithms make programs easy to read and maintain.

- Syntax errors and logic errors are collectively known as bugs. Syntax errors are flaws in the structure of commands while the program is being written that prevent execution. Logic errors are mistakes the programmer made in designing the solution to the problem; they do not prevent execution but do produce incorrect output.

Key Terms and Concepts

Go to **www.prenhall.com/cayf2006** to review this chapter, answer the questions, and complete the exercises.

Matching

Match each key term in the left column with the most accurate definition in the right column.

_____ 1. low-level language

_____ 2. procedural language

_____ 3. code

_____ 4. structured programming

_____ 5. algorithm

_____ 6. class

_____ 7. cross-platform programming language

_____ 8. modules

_____ 9. debugging

_____ 10. syntax

_____ 11. C

_____ 12. top-down program design

_____ 13. scripts

_____ 14. encapsulation

_____ 15. bugs

a. a category of objects

b. simple programs that control action or feedback on a Web page

c. a step-by-step description of how to arrive at a solution

d. rules that specify how to express certain operations

e. a language that tells the computer what to do and how to do it

f. the written computer instructions that programmers create

g. the process of eliminating syntax and logic errors

h. constructing a program so that it uses logical elements; GOTO statements are forbidden

i. a language that is similar to machine language

j. syntax and logic errors

k. a language that enables you to "write once, run anywhere"

l. a programming approach that focuses on the main goal the program is trying to achieve; the program is broken into manageable components, each of which contributes to the program's goal

m. information hiding

n. multiple routines grouped together

o. a programming language developed by AT&T's Bell Labs in the 1970s

Multiple Choice

Circle the correct choice for each of the following.

1. Which programming language can a computer understand directly without the need for translation?
   a. BASIC
   b. assembly language
   c. machine language
   d. C

2. What generation are nonprocedural languages?
   a. first
   b. second
   c. third
   d. fourth

3. Which term is *not* used in object-oriented programming?
   a. encapsulation
   b. data set
   c. class
   d. method

4. What is inheritance?
   a. the capacity of an object to transfer characteristics to an object in a subclass
   b. how an object maintains cohesion from one program to another
   c. the capability of an object to be encapsulated in a class
   d. how concepts are passed from one language generation to the next

5. What is JavaScript now known as?
   a. VBScript
   b. LiveScript
   c. NetScript
   d. ECMAScript

6. This is a set of rules for creating markup languages that enable programmers to capture specific types of data by creating their own elements.
   a. XML
   b. HTML
   c. FORTRAN
   d. COBOL

7. Which of the following is *not* one of the six phases of the PDLC?
   a. developing a prototype
   b. documenting the solution
   c. defining the problem
   d. testing and debugging

8. What is it called when the programming team fixes program errors discovered by users?
   a. program fixing
   b. program maintenance
   c. program error correction
   d. program development

9. Which of the following is *not* a program design tool?
   a. pseudocode
   b. flowchart
   c. structure chart
   d. program specification

10. A repetition control structure is also known as which of the following?
    a. selecting
    b. looping
    c. parsing
    d. verifying

Fill-In

In the blanks provided, write the correct answer for each of the following.

1. The use of many GOTO statements often results in _____.

2. _____ are small Java programs that run over a network.

3. A(n) _____ is a section of code that executes a specific task in a program.

4. To create a Web page, programmers use a markup language called _____.

5. A(n) _____ is a unit of computer information that contains data as well as all the procedures or operations that can process or manipulate the data.

6. In a(n) _____, the program branches off to different instructions depending on whether a condition is met.

7. _____ incorporates object-oriented features but doesn't force programmers to adhere to the object-oriented model.

8. _____ show the top-down design of a program.

9. _____ is a stylized form of writing used to describe the logic of a program.

10. A(n) _____ is a diagram that shows the logic of a program.

11. _____ enables a fast method of object-oriented programming program development.

12. _____ defines how objects can communicate with each other across a network, even if the objects are written in dissimilar programming languages.

13. _____ refers to standards that define how programs can find objects and query them.

14. _____ are miniprograms that can be downloaded from Web pages and used to add functionality to Web browsers.

15. Of the several computer languages discussed in this chapter, only _____ and _____ are named after people.

Short Answer

1. What are the major structured and modular languages in use today?

2. What are the six phases of the PDLC?

3. What are mnemonics? How are they used? Provide at least one example.

4. Identify the basic control structures used in program development and explain the purpose of each.

5. Explain the difference between syntax errors and logic errors. Give an example of each type of error.

6. The translation of a high-level program to a machine language is done by applications known as compilers and interpreters. Distinguish between a compiler and an interpreter. Give an example of a compiled language and an interpreted language.

Teamwork

I. Documentation

Your team is to research the documentation practices followed by computer programmers and then answer the following questions. (Hint: Do a Web search on "documentation practices.") Documentation is created primarily for what two groups? Describe the types of documentation that would be supplied to each group. Differentiate between documentation, which is external to the code, and comments, which are internal. What constitutes good documentation? Write a one-page paper that answers these questions. Be sure to cite your sources.

2. Programming Courses

Does your school have a computer science (CS), computer information systems (CIS), or management information systems (MIS) department? If so, look at a school catalog to see what programming language is covered in the beginning programming courses. If a language is not specified in the course catalog, then contact the department directly to find out. What are the prerequisites, if any, for the programming courses? Are additional computer languages taught in subsequent courses? What additional languages are taught? Prepare a group presentation based on your findings.

3. Program Design Tools

Three program design tools were discussed in this chapter. Name and describe each tool. With which of these tools can a programmer use aids such as a template or special software? Identify which tool each team member would prefer to use and explain why in a group report.

4. Algorithms

Algorithms are not used just for writing programs. They also can be used to describe processes. As a team, design an algorithm that lists the correct steps to safely start and move a motor vehicle. Include at least one selection control structure, either branch or conditional.

5. A BASIC Program

Just as it is easier to read a report than it is to write one, it is easier to read a program than it is to write one. One of the simplest computer languages is BASIC. As a team, write a report that explains the purpose of the three lines of code that follow. Why was it necessary to divide by 100? If the input is 300, 6, 4, what is the resulting output? Are the parentheses necessary in the formula? Explain why they are or are not needed.

```
Input Principal, Rate, Time
Interest =
(Principal * Rate * Time) / 100
Print Interest
```

On the Web

1. FORTRAN, COBOL, and More . . .

In this exercise, you're going to learn more about the more widely used computer languages as well as some other languages by exploring the "Dictionary of Programming Languages" site at **users.erols.com/ziring/dopl.html**. FORTRAN was the first higher-level programming language; what company developed it and during what time period? Although COBOL applications are used for solving business problems, what organization was the major contributor to the development of this language? Why was the Y2K bug a problem, especially for programs written in COBOL? Two other early programming languages are Lisp and Logo. During what time period was Lisp developed? Lisp is described as the "undisputed king" of which research area? When and where was Logo developed? To what group is it designed to teach programming and problem-solving skills?

2. Visual Basic

Let's look at the evolution of Microsoft's Visual Basic by doing some research on the Web. Visit the Microsoft Web site at **msdn.microsoft.com/vbasic**. In what year was Visual Basic first released? Although there were some interim versions, the next major revision allowed programmers to create 16-bit or 32-bit applications. In which year and with which version was this? What was the major emphasis of versions 5 and 6? What name has been given to the next generation of Visual Basic? What are some of the improvements implemented in this version? What is the cost of the new Visual Basic? Is any version of Visual Basic available on your campus? If so, which version?

3. Java

Visit the Sun Microsystems site at **java.sun.com** to answer the following questions. Explain the term *bytecode* and the purpose of the Java Virtual Machine. What terms are used for Java programs that run on a server and for the traditional programs that run on an individual computer? Sun Microsystems offers free versions of Java. What is the title of this software, what is the current version, and for which platforms is it available? Are you interested in downloading a copy? Why or why not?

4. Discovering Mathematica

Mathematica is a relatively new programming language that was briefly mentioned in the text. Visit the Web site **www.wolfram.com/products/mathematica** to answer the following questions. What company produces Mathematica? On which platforms does it run? How much does it cost? Is Mathematica or any other CAS used in any of your school's mathematics classes? If so, identify the CAS and course(s) in which it is used. Have you taken one of these courses and used a CAS?

5. Finding Perl

One language that has been gaining in popularity is Perl. Research the Web site **www.perl.com** to answer the following questions. What do the letters in "Perl" represent? What logo is associated with Perl? What is the current version? Is Perl compiled or interpreted? Name two platforms on which Perl runs. What types of applications are written using Perl? Not only are many Perl applications free, but so is Perl itself. Locate and identify the URL of a site where you can download a free copy of Perl. Are you interested in downloading a copy?

Programming with Alice

Do you want to try computer programming but aren't sure if it's for you? Why not ask Alice?

Alice (**www.alice.org**) is a 3D authoring system currently being developed by the Stage 3 Research Group at Carnegie Mellon University with the goal to "provide the best possible first exposure to programming for students ranging from middle school to college." Unlike most programming languages that require you to learn a bunch of cryptic commands and type them properly into a text editor, Alice is completely visual and allows programs to be built by simply dragging and dropping graphical components and positioning or modifying them according to your desired results. Alice makes programming fun while at the same time teaching fundamental programming concepts.

FIGURE 11.22 A sample virtual world created with Alice.

The programs you create in Alice are really 3D animated movies that aren't too much different from big-budget animated films such as Disney and Pixar's Finding Nemo. You have the capability to create a virtual "world" and then drag different objects into the world and define how those objects interact. Instead of using complex programming syntax to control objects, you can simply use a series of menus to define your object's actions. If, for example, you import an ice skater into your virtual world, you could then choose the appropriate options to make her spin around while jumping through the air. Figure 11.22 shows a sample world that includes a chicken and an airplane sitting in a grassy field. When this program is run, the chicken will hop into the airplane and fly off into the sunset!

You can also make your programs more interesting by adding sound and controlling the movement and position of the camera. When working in Alice, you will feel less like a computer programmer and more like the director of an animated movie. Alice includes a large number of built-in objects to work with, from animals, bugs, and people to trees, instruments, and skateboard ramps. The documentation also states that it is possible to create your own 3D objects using 3D Studio Max and then import them into your Alice world as an ASCII Scene Export file.

Alice can be downloaded for free from the Alice Web site. However, the file download size as of this writing is 63.9MB, so it is recommended that you use a broadband connection to do so. You will also find a large number of resources on the Web site, including instructions for installing and getting started with Alice, minimum system requirements, a FAQ, a community forum, and a few sample chapters from an upcoming Alice textbook. Once installed, Alice includes an extensive tutorial to help get you up and running, but you may find that you can figure many things out by simply diving right into creating your first program.

What You'll Learn . . .

- Recognize the potential uses of database programs.

- Describe the basic components of a database.

- Distinguish between file management programs and relational database management systems and explain the advantages and disadvantages of each.

- Understand advanced database programs and applications, such as data warehouses, data mining, client/server database systems, and Web–database integration.

- Describe the basic qualities of a good database.

- List the components and main functions of an information system.

- Recognize the functional divisions of an organization.

- List the major types of information systems used in today's organizations.

- Describe how the retail sector is taking advantage of computer databases to increase sales and gain a competitive edge.

Databases and Information Systems

Data refers to unorganized text, graphics, sound, or video. Information is data that have been processed and organized in a way that people find meaningful and useful. But information isn't useful if you're buried in it. Computers are used to cut the amount of information down to a more manageable size so that people can cope with it more efficiently. And that's precisely what databases and database programs do.

You can use databases and database management software to input, sort, organize, and store data and turn it into information. Computer users set up personal databases to organize music, names and addresses, research notes, and more. Databases are typically a main component of an information system.

Information systems make information manageable. In businesses, databases and information systems make key information available to employees, managers, executives, and customers. For example, some restaurants use a database program developed by OpenTable.com (**www.opentable.com**). The company's software helps restaurant owners and managers book reservations, manage staff, and track customer orders. Law enforcement, university research centers, government agencies, and even religious groups find databases and their programs invaluable to their missions. Other examples of databases that you have more than likely used include library reference systems, ATMs, and airline reservations systems.

As you'll learn in this chapter, databases are essential in today's fast-paced, wired world. Many of your daily activities—from banking to renewing your driver's license to booking a trip—are supported by databases and database programs. They can even save lives. In London, England, a database of traffic accidents helps authorities sift through accident data to reveal where accidents are most likely to happen, enabling traffic authorities to focus their safety improvements on the most dangerous intersections. Thanks to the database, accidents have been reduced by more than 15 percent.

Learning about database and information systems concepts is a prerequisite for understanding the importance of managing data and information in businesses and society. No matter what line of work you pursue, you will eventually encounter databases and information systems (Figure 12.1).

Before we can understand the true impact of databases on our lives, we need to know how data are organized in a database.

FIGURE 12.1 Understanding database and information systems concepts is a must for many careers and our daily lives in this wired world.

The Levels of Data in a Database

A **database** is any collection of data stored in a way that enables people to add, find, sort, group, summarize, and print the data. In a database, data are constructed from the bottom up, like the layers of a cake (Figure 12.2). At the lowest level, or layer, is the **bit**, a 1 or a 0, which is the smallest unit of data that the computer can store. The next level up, the smallest unit of data that you can work with, is made up of bytes that represent **characters**, including letters, numbers, and special symbols. When you enter characters, the computer translates them into bits. For example, the letter "M" or the number "4" represents the character level of the database. (M in a particular binary code is represented by the bit string 01001101; 4 is represented by 00110100.)

The next layer is a field. In a database, a **field** is a space that accepts and stores a certain type of data. Each field has a name, called a **field name**, which describes what data should be entered into the field. The London traffic accident database, for example, contains a field with the field name "Location," which would store the exact location of an accident. "Piccadilly Circus" is an example of data that would be entered and stored in the field with the field name "Location." Fields contain items that are of the same type. For example, a field named "First_Name" holds only first names. An easy way to remember this is to think of a field of corn or a field of wheat. Neither of these fields would contain anything but a single type of crop. Simply put, fields contain things that are alike.

Fields can be long or short and contain numeric or text data. These qualities are referred to as a field's attributes, or characteristics. Fields accept only a certain type of data, called the **data type**. Common data types include text, numbers, currency, and dates. One data type, a **logical data type**, allows only a "yes" or "no" value. Other data types are used for large units of text (**memos**) and nontext data (**objects**). Examples of objects include pictures, sounds, and videos. The latest databases include a data type for very large objects, such as an entire spreadsheet file or a picture file, called **BLOBs (binary large objects)**. BLOBs may be several megabytes or more in size.

Except for fields containing memo and object data types, each field has a specified field size. For example, a field for U.S. states is two characters in length, such as MN for Minnesota.

Some fields display a **default value**, which is the setting that is automatically selected unless another value is provided. In a field that accepts the date on which data were entered, the default value would be today's date, unless the user specified otherwise.

The next level up from a field is a **record**, which contains a group of related fields. In the London traffic accident database, for example, a record would include all of the related fields about one accident. This record might include fields that contain all known facts about an accident, including the driver's name, the accident

---

FIGURE 12.2 The Levels or Layers of Data in a Database

Database	One or more data files
Data File (or Table)	A collection of records
Record	The combined fields about a person, place, thing, or event
Field	One or more characters
Character	8 bits (the letter M = 01001101)
Bit	0 or 1

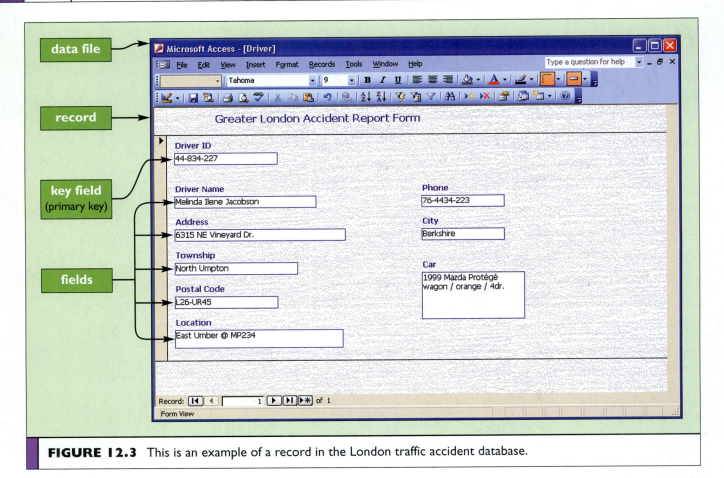

data file
record
key field
(primary key)
fields

Greater London Accident Report Form

Driver ID
44-834-227

Driver Name
Melinda Ilene Jacobson

Address
6315 NE Vineyard Dr.

Township
North Umpton

Postal Code
L26-UR45

Location
East Umber @ MP234

Phone
76-4434-223

City
Berkshire

Car
1999 Mazda Protégé
wagon / orange / 4dr.

FIGURE 12.3 This is an example of a record in the London traffic accident database.

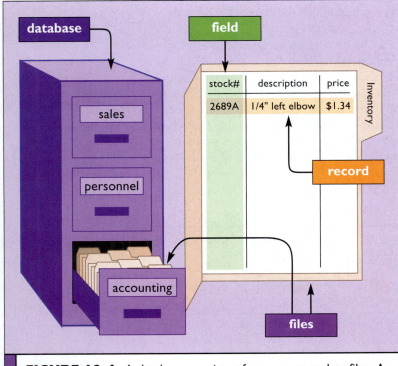

FIGURE 12.4 A database consists of one or more data files. A data file is made up of records, and within a record, information is organized into distinct fields.

location, the investigating officer, weather conditions at the time, and additional information. Another way to think of a record is as a *recording* of a person, place, thing, or event (Figure 12.3).

Within a record, one of the fields is identified as the **key field** (also called the **primary key**). This field contains a code, a number, a name, or some other piece of information that uniquely identifies the record. In your school record, for example, chances are you're identified by your student identification number. When you register for courses or request transcripts, you must supply this number so that the registrar's computer system can find your data. Your student identification number would be the key field, or the primary key, in your school record.

Near the top of the layers in a database is the data file. A **data file**, also called a **table**, is a collection of related records. The London traffic accident database would have data files for investigating officers (badge number, name, rank, division, and so on), drivers (driver's license number, name, address, city, phone, insurance information, and so on), as well as others. A database consists of one or more related data files (Figure 12.4). To summarize, the database (file cabinet) contains data files (file folders) made up of records (inventory items) organized into fields (stock number, description, price, and so on).

Now that you understand the levels that make up a database, let's look at some of the programs you can use to create one.

Types of Database Programs

Database programs are application software tools that are used to create databases or work with the data in existing databases. Two types of database programs enable you to create or work with database files: file management programs and database management systems.

FILE MANAGEMENT PROGRAMS

A **file management program** is a type of database program that creates flat-file databases—databases that contain only one file or table. A **flat file** stores simple lists of information, such as a list of addresses, appointments, or items, such as favorite music CDs or books. Flat-file databases can be accessed randomly to retrieve a specific record or sorted so that the records can be accessed sequentially in a different order. You can create a flat-file database with Microsoft Excel or any other spreadsheet program.

File management programs come in handy when an individual or small business needs to set up a simple computerized information storage and retrieval system. The owner of a baseball card store, for example, could create a flat-file database of available baseball cards for customer reference. This simple database would consist of one file or table containing all of the information related to the available baseball cards. The file would contain a record for each baseball card, including fields for

player name, teams played for, and statistics concerning that player.

Because file management programs are less complex than database management systems, they're also less expensive and easier to use. The ease of use comes at a price, though. The data stored in a flat file database cannot be linked with data in other files. For example, if that same baseball card store owner had another database that contained information on customers, the baseball card file and the customer file could not be linked.

DATABASE MANAGEMENT SYSTEMS

In contrast to file management programs, which manage only a single flat file at a time, a **database management system** (**DBMS**) is a database program that can manage multiple files or tables. A DBMS works in tandem with a database, allowing you to access, store, and edit data. DBMSs come in many types and sizes, from smaller programs for PCs to very large programs for mainframes. DBMSs aren't usually platform specific, but some are. For example, popular DBMSs for PCs include Microsoft Access and Lotus Approach. A popular DBMS for Macs is FileMaker Pro, which also runs on Microsoft Windows (Figure 12.5).

To learn more about how a Canadian bar uses a photo ID system and a database to screen patrons, view the video clip at www.prenhall.com/cayf2006

FIGURE 12.5 *Popular Database Management System Software*

Software	Company
Access 2003	Microsoft
dBASE PLUS	dBASE, Inc.
DB2	IBM
Lotus Approach	IBM/Lotus
Oracle Database 10g	Oracle, Inc.
Paradox	Corel
R:BASE 7.1	R:BASE Technologies, Inc.
Visual FoxPro	Microsoft

FIGURE 12.6
In this Microsoft Access database, four tables are related by common fields.

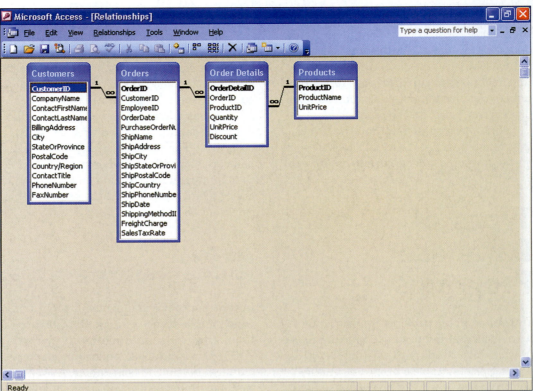

Information from a database can be presented in many different formats, including reports, graphs, or charts. Many DBMSs include built-in components for writing reports, generating graphics, and creating charts.

DBMSs can be further categorized by the way they organize information internally, which impacts how information is extracted. The four major categories of DBMSs are flat, hierarchical, network, and relational. The most widely used type of DBMS is called a *relational database management system* (*RDBMS*). Microsoft Access is the most popular RDBMS for the PC, whereas Oracle commands most of the market for larger computers, such as servers and mainframes.

In a **relational database management system** (**RDBMS**), data in several files are related by a common key field. Each record in the file has the same key field but unique key field contents, so that the field can be used to identify a record. The computer uses this key field as an index to locate records without having to read all the records in the files. As mentioned earlier, your student ID number is often the key field for your records at your school. The common key field "Student ID"

would be used to relate data in several students' records, but the contents of the Student ID field (each student's ID number) would be unique.

A relational DBMS is best envisioned as a collection of two-dimensional tables. In a relational database, each table corresponds to a data file. Each row in the table corresponds to a record, and each column corresponds to a field. A relational database structure can link a Customers table and an Orders table, for example, by a common field, such as customer ID number (Figure 12.6). To keep track of the tables that make up the database, the DBMS uses a data dictionary. The **data dictionary** holds a list of the tables the database contains along with details concerning each table, including field names, field lengths, data types, and validation settings.

An RDBMS is usually more expensive and more difficult to learn than a file management program. What's the advantage of using a relational DBMS instead of a file management program? Before DBMS software came along, it was not unusual for companies to have dozens of database files with incompatible formats. Because some of the same data appeared in different files, data would be typed into the database in

Destinations

For information on object-oriented database vendors, visit **www.service-architecture.com/ products/object-oriented_databases .html**

two or more places, which multiplied the possibility for errors. With relational database programs, it's possible to design the database using two or more tables so that data duplication is eliminated.

Object-oriented databases are the newest type of database and are well suited for multimedia applications in which data are represented as objects. In an object-oriented database, the result of a retrieval operation is an object of some kind, such as a document. Within this object are miniprograms that enable the object to perform tasks, such as display a graphic. Object-oriented databases can incorporate sound, video, text, and graphics into a single database record. A search of a health-related database, for example, could display a record that included pictures of healthy foods, videos of exercise techniques, and recorded lectures from health professionals.

Now that you know about the basic types of database programs, let's look more closely at some advanced database programs and applications.

DATA WAREHOUSES AND DATA MINING

In large corporations, a trend has emerged toward ever-larger databases called **data warehouses**, which are capable of storing all the information that a corporation possesses. These data warehouses are typically the result of combining several smaller databases from different areas within an organization. A data warehouse brings all the data together into a massive database that often contains a trillion bytes of data or more.

The collection of data in data warehouses helps managers make decisions by representing what business conditions look like at a particular point in time. Using a technique called **drill-down**, managers can view performance data for the entire firm and then drill down to lower levels (sales, regions, offices, individual salespeople), viewing summaries at each level. Less ambitious data warehouse projects that support one division rather than the entire organization are called **data marts**.

The payoff from data warehouses can be huge. Lucent Technologies in Murray Hill, New Jersey, for example, saved $10 million

the first day a new data warehouse went into operation—the software found $10 million worth of transactions that had been shipped without follow-up billing. The company previously used smaller, separate databases for billing and shipping, and nobody ever discovered the foul-up.

Using a data exploration and analysis technique called **data mining**, managers also can explore data in an attempt to discover previously unknown patterns (Figure 12.7). Data mining can be used in other sectors besides the business world. The Pentagon is gearing up a massive data mining project that it hopes will protect against terrorist acts. The new surveillance system would tie together a number of different databases housing public and private information. Although groups such as the ACLU believe that this system threatens privacy and civil rights and want its development halted, law enforcement could use the system to find patterns in the data that may help them apprehend potential terrorists.

CLIENT/SERVER DATABASE SYSTEMS

Database server software runs on a LAN and responds to remote users' requests for information. Database server

Destinations

For more information on data warehousing, see the Data Warehousing Institute's home page at **www.dw-institute.com**

For information on data mining in the next millennium, see the online magazine DM Review at **www.dmreview.com/master.cfm?NavID=198&EdID=1637M**

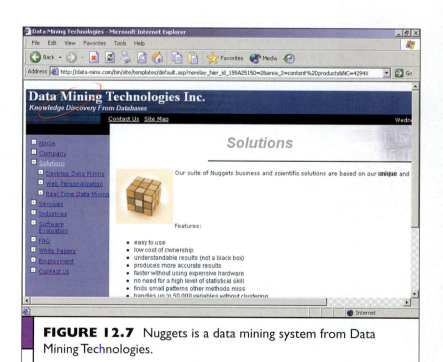

FIGURE 12.7 Nuggets is a data mining system from Data Mining Technologies.

IMPACTS

Success Stories

How Do Companies Use Data Mining?

You've heard of data mining—the process managers use to explore data to discover previously unknown patterns—but what exactly is data mining, how do businesses use it, and which businesses profit most from the information they glean?

Data mining is the discovery of information through statistical analysis and modeling that helps managers to better understand their customers and their market as well as to predict future trends. You would "mine" your company's databases to learn which items are selling best, where and when they're most popular, and who's buying them. Like a prospector panning for gold, you would look for a few precious nuggets of information that revealed purchasing patterns and provided insights that you could use to predict and improve sales in the coming weeks or months.

Retail leader Wal-Mart takes full advantage of data mining. Its 136,000 point-of-sale (POS) terminals worldwide and its Web site send the data warehouse precise records of what each day's 20 million customers have purchased, at what price, where, and when (Figure 12.8). Wal-Mart then slices and dices the data to turn up nuggets of information. For instance, it found that online customers prefer merchandise not carried by the stores, and that before a hurricane shoppers stock up on bottled water and—surprise!—toaster pastries. These patterns help managers make everyday plans and prepare for unusual situations. Wal-Mart's data warehouse was designed with no particular purpose

in mind, but that's the point: Data warehouses are intended to support data mining's exploration and discovery of data patterns that aren't obvious even to experienced managers and executives.

Another company that uses data mining is Delta Airlines. In the past, Delta had difficulty making sense of all the data it had collected. And because Delta's old data were not housed in one central database, it used to take days or weeks for users to get answers to information requests. Now, with the help of National Cash Register (NCR) technologies and solutions, users can get more specific and accurate results in just minutes. Delta also uses the data to determine who its most profitable customers really are—and the results have surprised Delta executives. Data mining has helped Delta decide how best to sell its services to customers, which will hopefully keep the airline running well into the future.

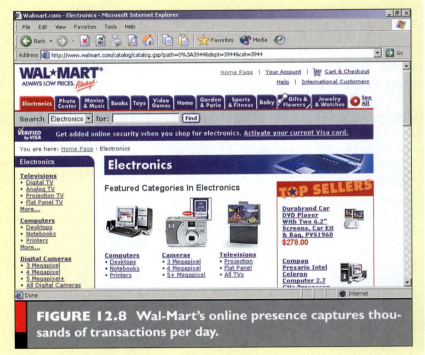

FIGURE 12.8 Wal-Mart's online presence captures thousands of transactions per day.

software is difficult to use because users never interact with the database server software directly. To access the data in the server database, users run a database client program, a user-friendly program that enables them to add data to the database, maintain existing records, perform

queries, and generate reports. Because these database systems draw a distinction between the database server and client, they are often called **client/server database systems**. Many users—hundreds or even thousands—can access the database simultaneously. The *front end* of the database server software consists of the part of the program that the user manipulates. The back end of the software refers to the server and program code. You probably work with the front end of database server software fairly often, for example, whenever you use an ATM or use a computer for online banking. Examples of database server software include the market-leading DB2 from IBM, SQL Server from Microsoft, and Oracle from Oracle Corporation.

To request information from a client/server database, remote users formulate the request as a query. A **query** is a specially phrased question. A college administrator using a client program might query your school's database to provide the names and addresses of students with junior standing who have greater than a 3.5 GPA. A query language uses distinct rules to build a query.

Many DBMSs rely on the query language SQL (Structured Query Language) to request data in a way that the server can understand. SQL isn't difficult to learn. However, most users prefer to use client software that provides more user-friendly tools for constructing SQL queries. One such client is Microsoft Access. With Access, you can build queries that are transformed into SQL queries, which can be sent to a database server. In sum, Access can be used to build local databases. It also can be used as a client to access database servers.

THE INTERNET CONNECTION: GOING PUBLIC WITH DATA

The latest trend in database software is **Web–database integration**, a name for techniques that make information stored in databases available through Internet connections. Web–database integration enables customers of the shipping giant FedEx to access shipping information through the FedEx Web site (Figure 12.9). You don't have to learn SQL or any other query language to use this or similar sites. The Web server accepts your input and translates it into a query that is then sent to the database. The database responds with the

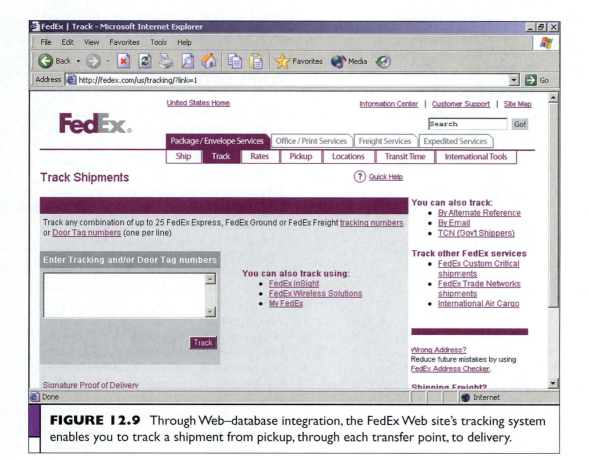

FIGURE 12.9 Through Web–database integration, the FedEx Web site's tracking system enables you to track a shipment from pickup, through each transfer point, to delivery.

requested information, and the server generates a new Web page on the fly that contains the information you've requested.

Many companies are venturing into e-commerce by making enormous internal resources available to the public through the Internet. At AMP, a Pennsylvania-based electronic components manufacturer, an enormous online catalog of nearly 90,000 components is made available to customers through a Web server linked to an Oracle relational database. The payoff for AMP is an annual savings of $2 million in expenses related to catalog production, telephone calls, and customer support.

Employees with knowledge of Web–database integration skills are in high demand. Such skills include knowing how to configure and maintain a Web server, such as Apache (the market leader) or Microsoft's Internet Information Server (IIS); how to write scripts that tell the server how to interact with the database software; and how to design and maintain the database.

You're now familiar with database programs and applications that you might encounter in the real world. Let's take a look at the benefits of using DBMSs and the qualities of a well-built database.

Advantages of Database Management Systems

A DBMS helps people work with all aspects of data in a database. But a database wouldn't be of much use if it contained errors or made confidential data available to people who weren't authorized to access it. For example, a New York Police Department (NYPD) database contained numerous bugs that prevented officers from obtaining up-to-date and accurate reports on domestic violence cases. The database was originally created to help police zero in on and prevent domestic violence in the Manhattan area. Unfortunately, the database was rendered useless and put out of commission. In this section, you'll learn the advantages of DBMSs and five characteristics of quality databases (Figure 12.10).

DATA INTEGRITY

Data integrity refers to the validity of the data contained in a database. Data integrity can be compromised in many ways, including typing errors during input, hardware malfunctions, and data transmission errors. To avoid data integrity errors, database programs use **data validation** procedures, which define acceptable input ranges for each field in a record. If the user tries to input data that are out of this range, an error message is displayed.

Database programs use several different types of data validation (Figure 12.11). An **alphabetic check** ensures that only alphabetic data (the letters of the alphabet) are entered into a field, for instance, state abbreviations. Similarly, a **numeric check** ensures that only numbers are entered. A **range check** verifies that the entered data fall within an acceptable range. For example, a U.S. ZIP code must not exceed 99999 (or 99999-9999). A **consistency check**

FIGURE 12.10 The Five Characteristics of a Good Database

Characteristic	Result
Data integrity	Ensures data are valid.
Data independence	Input data are kept separate from program data.
Avoiding data redundancy	Repetition of input data is avoided.
Data security	Data are not accessible to unauthorized users.
Data maintenance	Set procedures for adding, updating, and deleting records are in place.

FIGURE 12.11 Data Validation Techniques

Technique	Result
Alphabetic check	Ensures that a field contains only letters of the alphabet.
Numeric check	Ensures that a field contains only numbers.
Range check	Verifies that entered data fall within a certain range.
Consistency check	Determines if incorrect data have been entered.
Completeness check	Determines if a required field has been left empty.

examines the data entered into two different fields to determine whether an error has been made. For example, a Web page that asks you to create a user name and a password for yourself typically asks you to type your password twice. If there is a discrepancy between the two typed passwords, you will be asked to type them again. This ensures that you've typed the password correctly. A **completeness check** determines whether a required field has been left empty. If so, the database program prompts the user to fill in the needed data.

DATA INDEPENDENCE

Data independence means that the data in the database are separate (or independent) from the data that control the applications, such as forms, reports, and the actual program itself. Let's look at the database program Microsoft Access as an example. If a user changes data in an Access database, data independence makes further changes to any other applications within the program unnecessary.

In older database programs, the database and the applications that access the database were closely connected, so any changes to data in the database required changing the program's code. DBMSs with data independence are much more flexible, allow other programs to access data, and make it easier to modify data.

AVOIDING DATA REDUNDANCY

Data should be entered once—and only once. **Data redundancy** (repetition of data) is a characteristic of poorly designed systems. For example, in many companies customer names and addresses may appear in two different, unrelated databases. This not only doubles the amount of work needed to update the customer's records should the customer move, but it also increases the chance of an error. Will the data be typed the same way twice? If the data are entered differently, some of the data will be unavailable upon retrieval. Data redundancy can be avoided by proper database design.

DATA SECURITY

Data security means that the data stored in a database shouldn't be accessible to people who might misuse it, particularly when the collected data are sensitive. Sensitive data include personal data such as medical records and data about an organization's finances. Equally important is the protection of data against loss due to equipment failure or power outages. Regular backup procedures are needed so that data can be restored after an equipment failure.

DATA MAINTENANCE

Good database management also involves having a system in place for data maintenance. **Data maintenance** includes procedures for adding, updating, and deleting records for the purpose of keeping the database in optimal shape. Always create a backup copy of the database before performing maintenance and be particularly careful should you ever find it necessary to

Destinations

For information on how to create a database, visit **hotwired.lycos .com/webmonkey/ backend/databases/ tutorials/tutorial3 .html**

Techtalk

Audit trail
An audit trail is a tracking process that records the who and what of computer system access. Audit trails help with maintaining security and recovering lost transactions. Most accounting systems and database management systems include an audit trail component.

delete an entire field. Field referencing, especially fields that have been designated as key fields, is an integral part of a relational database. Do not delete a field unless you are certain that it is not a key field.

Now that you understand databases, let's explore how information systems are used.

Information Systems: Tools for Global Competitiveness

An **information system** is a purposefully designed system that brings data, computers (hardware and software), procedures, and people together to manage information important to an organization's mission (Figure 12.12).

An information system's main functions include accepting input in the form of mission-critical data, processing this data to produce information, storing the data, and disseminating information throughout the organization. Information systems help organizations achieve their goals by providing essential information services, including recording and keeping track of transactions; assisting decision makers by providing them with needed facts and figures; and providing documentation needed by customers and suppliers.

Smart businesses know that information systems aren't merely a cost to the business. Viewed properly, an information system adds more value than its cost and can be considered a wealth-producing asset that enables a firm to compete more effectively on a global scale.

Even with all of these benefits, a company needs to be aware that information systems create a deluge of information, sometimes more than employees and managers can handle. The next section discusses how to combat this problem.

TECHNIQUES FOR REDUCING INFORMATION

It's important that you understand a few things about information in general. For one, not all information is valuable, a fact you'll appreciate after doing some research on the Internet. Figure 12.13 describes the characteristics of valuable information.

Computers are indispensable, but they also pose the threat of producing too much information (information overload) (Figure 12.14). It's important to control information to keep it from overwhelming people in an organization. With an information system, the following control methods are possible:

- Route information only to those people who really need to see it.

- Summarize information so that decision makers do not drown in the details.

- Enable selectivity so that people with specific information needs can get that information (and ignore the rest).

- Eliminate unnecessary information (exclusion) so that it doesn't take up time and resources.

Now that you understand what makes information valuable and why organizations need to control the flow of information, let's examine how information systems fit into existing organizational structures.

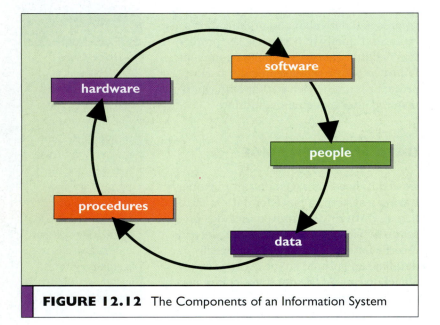

FIGURE 12.12 The Components of an Information System

FIGURE 12.13 The Characteristics of Valuable Information

Characteristic	Result
Accessible	It can be found quickly and easily.
Accurate	It doesn't contain errors.
Complete	It doesn't omit anything important.
Economical	The benefit exceeds the cost of producing the information.
Relevant	It is related to the task you're trying to perform.
Reliable	It is available every time you need it.
Secure	Unauthorized people can't access the information.
Simple	It doesn't overwhelm you.
Timely	It is up-to-date.
Verifiable	It can be confirmed or double-checked.

FIGURE 12.14 Not all information is valuable. All too often, people are overwhelmed with more information than they can use.

FUNCTIONAL DIVISIONS OF AN ORGANIZATION

An organization is composed of functional divisions (also referred to as *functional areas* or *functional units*) that handle each of the organization's core functions (Figure 12.15). No matter which functional unit an information system supports, it still includes hardware, software, data, people, and procedures. Let's look at each of the functional units typically found in an organization and the information systems that support them.

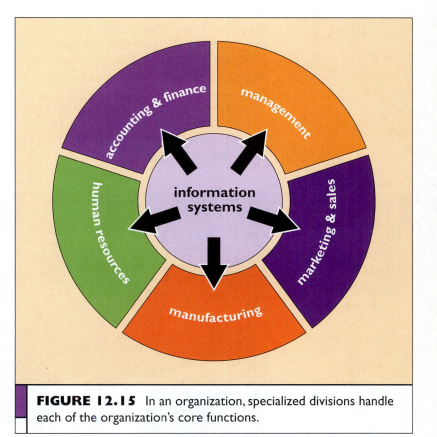

FIGURE 12.15 In an organization, specialized divisions handle each of the organization's core functions.

Accounting and Finance

The accounting function is responsible for accounts payable, accounts receivable, cost accounting, sales information, and

FIGURE 12.16 Peachtree is one of the most popular accounting software packages.

Marketing and Sales

The marketing function is responsible for maintaining the company's image to the public and for generating sales. Marketing professionals use database, spreadsheet, and proprietary software packages to manage sales figures and customers.

Salespeople rely heavily on computers and technology to do their jobs (Figure 12.17). They often use workstations and PCs as well as various mobile computing devices, such as laptops and PDAs, to interact with mainframes and client/server networks.

Human Resources

The human resources function uses technology to keep track of employees and to service employee queries (Figure 12.18). Tracked information includes date of hire, position, rank, salary, and benefits. Employees often have questions about health and retirement benefits. Human resources (HR) managers and staff use workstations to interact with mainframes and PCs to interact with client/server networks. The human resources function often uses spreadsheets, databases, and, in the case of a large organization, an employee relationship management (ERM) system. An ERM system can help an employee gather information regarding his or her retirement account. Most ERM software applications include a Web interface.

accounting reports for management and the government. The finance function is responsible for forecasting, budgeting, cash management, budget analysis, and financial reports. Both accounting and finance use spreadsheet software as well as proprietary software packages such as Peachtree Accounting (Figure 12.16). These functional areas mainly use PCs in a client/server networked environment.

FIGURE 12.17 Salespeople often use mobile technology in support of their work.

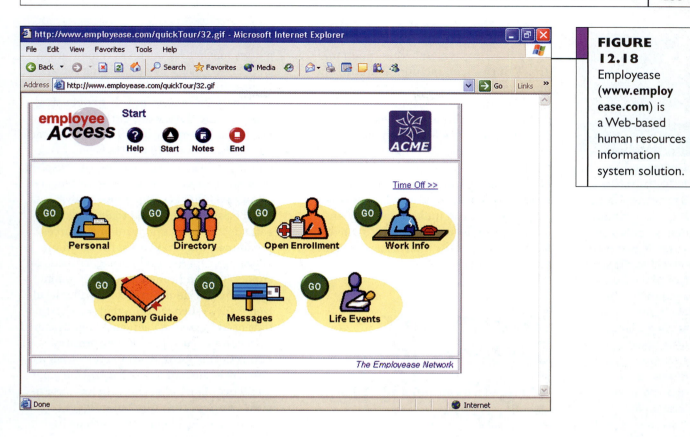

At Charles Schwab & Co., employees utilize a client/server network to access detailed information about benefits, training, technical support, and other company information. Instead of contacting the company's human resources department, employees obtain information about themselves, their responsibilities, and the company itself.

Management
The management function plans, organizes, leads, and controls the organization. Management professionals use workstations and PCs connected to mainframes and client/server networks to make decisions about running the enterprise. They use databases, spreadsheets, and proprietary software packages to keep track of what the company has done and to plan for what the company will do.

Manufacturing
The manufacturing function plans and controls processes that produce goods and services (Figure 12.19). Information systems in this function help monitor and maintain inventories, purchases, and the flow of goods and services. Transportation companies, wholesalers, retailers, banks and brokerage firms, and utility companies

use production/operations information systems to plan and control their operations. Manufacturing systems typically exist on mainframe computers that are accessed by highly specialized control stations.

Information Systems
The information systems function manages all of an organization's computerized

FIGURE 12.19 Computer-aided manufacturing has greatly affected manufacturing efficiency and product quality.

Techtalk

Geographic Information Systems (GIS)

A GIS is a combination of tools that gather information related to the surface of the Earth and produce layers of information to provide a better understanding of a given place. A GIS is often used to find the best location for a new store, to analyze environmental phenomenon, and to help public service agencies provide faster and more efficient service, such as helping a fire department locate landmarks and hazards, plot destinations, and design emergency routes.

information systems. In addition to managing existing systems, this functional area's duties also include planning and purchasing new systems, providing user training and support, and dealing with day-to-day operational problems.

All organizations, including nonprofit organizations and government agencies, tend to develop this functionally differentiated structure, which is sometimes called the **traditional organizational structure**.

Now that you understand how an organization is structured, let's move on to the various ways information systems are used in organizations.

Information Systems in Organizations: A Survey

Many different systems have been developed to meet the information needs of an organization's employees. In a very small business, a single computer might meet all of the business's information needs. Larger organizations supplement single-user systems with minicomputers, mainframe computers, LANs, and WANs. Some of these larger systems are used by teams of two or more people working on the same project; others are available throughout an organization, including all of the organization's branch offices.

TRANSACTION PROCESSING SYSTEMS

A t**ransaction processing system** (**TPS**) (also called an o**perational system** or a **data processing system**) handles an organization's day-to-day accounting needs. It keeps a careful, verifiable record of every transaction involving money, including purchases, sales, and payroll payments. In businesses that sell products, a TPS is often linked with an inventory control system so that sales personnel will know whether an item is in stock. TPSs date to the earliest years of business computing,

and the cost savings they introduced created a huge market for business computers. A TPS saves money by automating routine, labor-intensive recordkeeping.

Early TPSs used **batch processing**, whereby the data were gathered and processed at periodic intervals, such as once per week. In the 1970s, TPSs began to use online processing. With **online processing**, personnel enter transaction data and see totals and other results immediately.

TPSs provide useful tools for employees, such as sales and human resources personnel, but they're useful for managers, too. Operational managers focus on supervision and control, and they make **operational decisions** concerning localized issues (such as an inventory shortage) that need immediate action. A well-designed TPS can produce periodic **summary reports** that provide managers with a quick overview of the organization's performance. They also can provide **exception reports** that alert managers to unexpected developments (such as high demand for a new product).

TPSs are only as good as the integrity of the data they collect and only as useful as the information they provide to the users. Using the example of an inventory control system, you can imagine the problems that would be caused by a TPS that didn't accurately reflect the volume of inventory on hand. Likewise, managers need reports that will help them make good decisions—inaccurate data or unsophisticated reports are not valued.

MANAGEMENT INFORMATION SYSTEMS

TPSs work with management information systems. A **management information system** (**MIS**) is a computer-based system that supports the information needs of different levels of management. This type of system helps management make informed decisions. Middle managers must make **tactical decisions** about how to best organize resources to achieve their division's goals. MISs produce reports that tell middle managers whether they are meeting their goals (Figure 12.20).

Although MISs continue to play an important role in organizations, they do

FIGURE 12.20 A management information system (MIS) produces reports that tell middle managers whether they're meeting their goals.

have drawbacks. They generate predefined reports that may not contain the information a manager wants. The information may not be available when it's needed, and it might be buried within reams of printouts.

DECISION SUPPORT SYSTEMS

A **decision support system** (**DSS**) is a computer-based system that addresses the deficiencies of MISs by enabling managers to retrieve information that cannot be supplied by fixed, predefined MIS reports. For example, a retail chain manager can find information on how an advertising campaign affected sales of advertised versus nonadvertised items. Many DSS applications enable managers to create simulations that begin with real data and ask what-if questions, such as, "What would happen to profits if we used a shipper who could cut our packaging costs by 2 percent, but who would sometimes cause slight delivery delays?"

Some DSSs include **online analytical processing** (**OLAP**) applications that provide decision support by enabling managers to import rich, up-to-the-minute data from transaction databases. For example, managers at Pizzeria Uno, a chain of more than 100 pizza stores, obtain and analyze all of the sales information from each of the firm's stores every morning using OLAP. As a result, they can quickly spot trends that may be emerging in customer preferences and employee performance.

EXECUTIVE INFORMATION SYSTEMS

An **executive information system** (**EIS**), also known as an **executive support system** (**ESS**), supports management's strategic-planning function. Executives in senior management (including the CEO) are concerned with high-level planning and leadership. They make **strategic decisions** concerning the organization's overall goals and direction. Though similar to a DSS, an EIS supports decisions made by top-level management that will affect the entire company.

An EIS filters critical information (including information about the firm's external environment) so that overall trends are apparent and presents this

Destinations

For more information on decision support systems, see **www.howstuffworks.com/ news-item129.htm**

FIGURE 12.21 Types of Decisions and Information Systems for Managers

Managers	Decisions	Type	Information System
Senior managers	Strategic	Determining the organization's goals and direction	Executive information systems (EISs) and expert systems
Middle managers	Tactical	Deciding how to organize resources to achieve their division's goals	Management information systems (MISs) and decision support systems (DSSs)
Operational managers	Operational	Deciding how to handle localized issues requiring immediate action	Knowledge management systems (KMSs) and transaction processing systems (TPSs)

information in an easy-to-use graphical interface. For instance, an executive might create a report that compares the company's inventory levels with the industry average. Little training is required to use these systems. To better understand the various types of decisions that managers must make and the information systems they use to make them, see Figure 12.21.

KNOWLEDGE MANAGEMENT SYSTEMS

Organizations are increasingly aware that information is crucial, but that knowledge also is a valuable asset. As you've already learned, information is data that are organized in a way that has meaning to us. But knowledge is more than just information found in documents, reports, and spreadsheets stored on computers. Knowledge is information in context, including the processes, procedures, best practices, and other information employees create. How can organizations capture the knowledge employees create? A variety of information technologies are being used to create **knowledge management systems** (**KMSs**), which capture knowledge and make it available where it is needed. This process doesn't have to be high tech. For example, at Columbia/HCA, a nationwide hospital chain, a team visits each hospital and writes a report on the most successful

business processes (best practices) found at each site. The knowledge in these reports is then made available on the company's internal Web server.

EXPERT SYSTEMS

An **expert system** (**ES**) is an information system that deals with expert knowledge in a particular area. An expert system formulates a decision in the way that a human expert in the field might. Research in expert systems attempts to formulate the knowledge of human experts (such as doctors) according to if-then rules ("if you have a temperature, then you may have an infection"). These rules formally express the knowledge used by human experts as they reason their way to a conclusion. The process of eliciting these rules from human experts is called *knowledge representation*. Once elicited, the rules are programmed into expert systems. Expert systems use these rules to reach a conclusion the same way that a human expert does.

An expert system relies on a **knowledge base**, a database of represented knowledge. To use an expert system, the user supplies information to the program. Based on the information supplied, the program consults its knowledge base and draws a conclusion, if possible.

Expert systems work best when they are limited to sharply defined subjects,

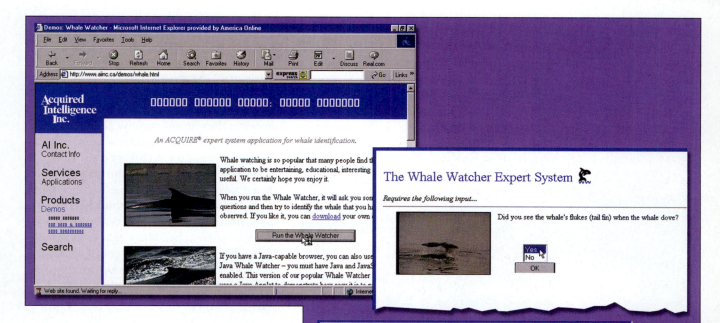

such as jet engine maintenance, planning and scheduling, diagnosis and troubleshooting of a specific device, or financial decision making. However, expert system technology is making its appearance in application software, too. Microsoft Word uses rule-based reasoning to check documents for grammatical errors. MailJail, a junk e-mail detection accessory for Microsoft Outlook, screens out unwanted or unsolicited e-mail, or spam. Created by Omron Advanced Systems, MailJail uses more than 600 rules to decide whether an incoming message is junk e-mail.

Expert systems are improving service in one area in which organizations sometimes perform an unsatisfactory job: providing technical support for customers. Expert systems also can provide expert knowledge in areas outside the business arena, such as with whale watching (Figure 12.22).

COMPUTERS AND DATABASES IN THE RETAIL SECTOR

In the retail sector, computers are indispensable for traditional applications, such as automating the checkout process. But some companies have also figured out how to use computers and databases for strategic purposes, enabling them to get an edge on their competitors. Such companies have grown rapidly and have made fortunes for their shareholders.

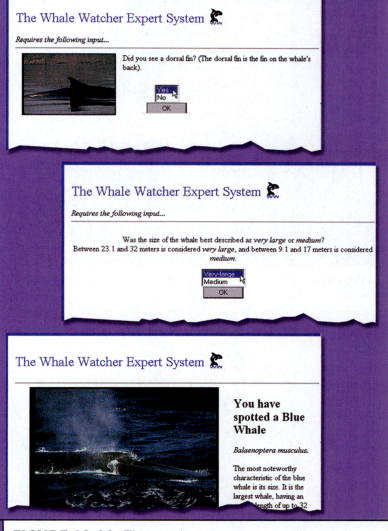

FIGURE 12.22 This sample expert system enables whale watchers to identify observed whales.

At the Checkout Stand

Today's cash registers are really computers—specifically, POS terminals (Figure 12.23). Clerks check out items by passing them over an optical scanner, which reads the item's universal product code (UPC) that is encoded on a label or a tag (Figure 12.24). The use of POS terminals and UPCs has resulted in faster checkout times and fewer price errors.

The latest POS terminals are fully integrated with credit card authorization systems that automatically send calls to call centers. A **call center** is a computer-based telephone routing system that connects to an authorization service and generates an authorization number. Thanks to the volume of credit card authorization calls, firms that make call center equipment have watched their market grow from virtually nothing 25 years ago to a worldwide $200 billion bonanza today.

Because POS terminals produce digitized data, they're useful for more purposes than just determining the customer's bill. POS terminals also are linked to the store's inventory database. When a customer buys an item, the database is automatically updated to reflect the lowered stock level. When the inventory gets too low, the database generates a restocking order.

POS terminals also are used as marketing devices. If a customer buys a particular brand of coffee, the terminal may produce a coupon for a discount on a competing brand. Another POS feature is to list the total of the discounts a customer received on his or her purchase. Marketers believe that creating a sense of well-being at the point of sale will subliminally influence the customer to associate the store with good feelings, causing the customer to come back in the future.

Chain stores such as Wal-Mart link their POS terminals to central computer systems using public data networks (PDNs). Disney, however, is taking POS data to the airwaves. At Walt Disney World, POS terminals at hundreds of retail carts supply data to company computers using wireless communications. As a result, the Lion King cart never runs out of those cute stuffed animals, which means bigger profits for Disney.

POS terminals also can reduce losses due to bad checks and credit card fraud. According to one estimate, banks and retailers lose a staggering $58 billion annually due to bounced checks and check fraud. A **check-screening system** reads a check's account number and

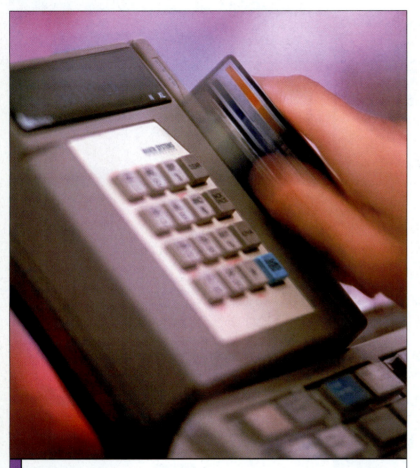

FIGURE 12.23 The latest POS terminals are fully integrated with credit card authorization systems.

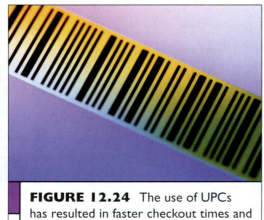

FIGURE 12.24 The use of UPCs has resulted in faster checkout times and fewer price errors.

Scan, Then Buy: The Future of Shopping?

Imagine that you're standing in the supermarket, deciding which type of candy to buy. Would you want to know if one of the sweets had just been recalled or if the parent company of another candy had recently paid a big fine to settle charges of unethical behavior? In the not-so-distant future, you'll be able to research nearly anything and everything about a product before you buy it—without leaving your shopping cart (Figure 12.25).

A researcher at Microsoft has created a prototype that will let you do an on-the-spot product check using a handheld computer, a bar code reader, and a wireless Web connection. Here's how it works. First, you scan the product's bar code. The bar code information is sent over the wireless Web connection to an online database where it will be translated into a text description. You then use keywords in this description as the basis for an Internet search. You might find that a product contains an ingredient you're trying to avoid because of allergy or diet. Or, you might find that a manufacturer has just been honored for its environmentally friendly practices. Digging deeper, you can find out a company's position on social responsibility, trace its global operations, examine its product safety record, learn about its top management, and discover many other details.

With such a system, businesses would be unable to hide anything significant. Most businesses, in order to stay competitive, would be more likely to start disclosing even more information, knowing that customers could check the facts in a matter of clicks. Of course, even in a wireless world, in-depth research takes time, so you probably wouldn't investigate every product on every shopping trip. But if you did a quick scan before buying at least some items, you would be better informed and better prepared to "vote" with your wallet for companies you think are acting properly—and shun those that haven't earned your support.

FIGURE 12.25 IBM has produced one of the first prototypes of a smart shopping cart. Soon you may be able to scan a package of salmon and get a suggestion for a good wine to go with it.

accesses a database containing the delinquent accounts. Check-screening systems reduce bad check losses by as much as 25 percent, translating into big savings for retail firms.

Stores can use **signature capture systems** to capture a customer's signature digitally by having the customer sign the receipt on a pressure-sensitive pad using a special stylus. What's the point? The system cuts down on credit card disputes.

With a receipt signed by the customer, the store can prove that the purchase was made. This system isn't popular with consumers, however, due to fears that a dishonest employee could use the captured signatures for fraudulent purposes. **Photo checkout systems** access a database of customer photos and display the customer's picture when a credit card is used. In a New York test, this system cut credit card fraud by 94 percent.

What You've Learned

DATABASES AND INFORMATION SYSTEMS

- Database programs transform data into information by showing only the information required for a task. You can use database programs to organize and manage your music collection, names and addresses, research notes, and more. In the business world, employees, managers, executives, and customers use database programs to organize and manage key information.

- A database is a collection of data stored in an organized way. A data file is made up of records, which are units of information about a person, place, thing, or event. Each record has one or more fields. Each field stores a certain type of data. Fields are made up of characters (composed of bits) and have a specific field name.

- File management programs work with only one data file, called a flat file, at a time. As a result, they can't eliminate data redundancy. However, they are easy to use and inexpensive to purchase. Relational database management systems (RDBMSs) work with two or more data files, called tables, at a time. The data in the various tables can be related by common fields so that data duplication is eliminated and the chance for errors reduced. RDBMSs are more difficult to use than file management programs; they also are more costly.

- Data warehouses bring data together from many smaller databases in different areas of an organization into a massive database that managers can use to make decisions. Data mining is a data exploration and analysis technique that managers use to explore data in an attempt to discover previously unknown patterns. Client/server database systems enable many users to access the database simultaneously, usually over a LAN. Web–database integration refers to techniques that make information stored in databases available through Internet connections.

- A good database ensures data integrity (validity of the data), promotes data independence (usefulness with more than one application), avoids data redundancy (entry of the same data in two or more places), ensures data security (protection from loss of confidentiality), and provides procedures for data maintenance (adding, updating, and deleting records).

- An information system includes data, hardware, software, people, and procedures. An information system's main functions are accepting input in the form of mission-critical data, processing these data to produce information, storing the data, and disseminating information throughout the organization.

- The functional divisions typically found in an organization include accounting and finance, marketing and sales, human resources, management, manufacturing, and information systems.

- Information systems used in organizations today include transaction processing systems (TPSs), management information systems (MISs), decision support system (DSSs), executive information system (EISs), knowledge management systems (KMSs), and expert systems.

- The retail sector uses inventory databases linked to point-of-sale (POS) terminals, allowing managers to quickly know which products are selling and which are not. POS terminals and databases also can reduce losses due to bad checks and credit card fraud with check-screening systems, signature capture systems, and photo checkout systems.

Go to **www.prenhall.com/cayf2006** to review this chapter, answer the questions, and complete the exercises.

Key Terms and Concepts

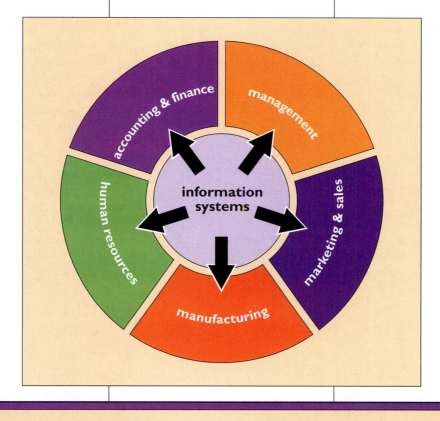

Matching

Match each key term in the left column with the most accurate definition in the right column.

_____ 1. field

a. a field that uniquely identifies each record in a table

_____ 2. flat file

b. processes data to produce information

_____ 3. data dictionary

c. information stored in this cannot be linked to data in other files

_____ 4. information system

d. a technique managers use to view performance data for the entire firm

_____ 5. database management system (DBMS)

e. data are gathered and processed periodically

f. a database of databases

_____ 6. key field

g. supports management's strategic-planning function

_____ 7. executive information system

h. a computer-based system that supports the information needs of different levels of management

i. a database program that can manage multiple files or tables

_____ 8. database

j. an area in a database that stores a certain type of data

_____ 9. check-screening systems

k. defines an acceptable input range for each field in a record

_____ 10. drill-down

l. any collection of data stored in a way that enables the user to add, find, sort, group, summarize, and print the data

_____ 11. data warehouse

m. reads a check's account number and accesses a database containing delinquent accounts

_____ 12. bit

_____ 13. data validation

n. the smallest unit of data that the computer can store

_____ 14. management information system (MIS)

o. holds a list of the tables a database contains, along with details concerning each table

_____ 15. batch processing

Multiple Choice

Circle the correct choice for each of the following.

1. One or more _____ make up a data file.
   a. characters
   b. fields
   c. records
   d. BLOBs

2. Referring to the levels in a database, which group of terms is in the correct order (lowest to highest)?
   a. character, record, field
   b. field, record, character
   c. character, field, record
   d. record, field, character

3. This specifies the type of data stored in a field.
   a. data type
   b. character
   c. record
   d. variable

4. If a ZIP code is entered in a field intended for a phone number, which principle of good database design has been violated?
   a. data independence
   b. data redundancy
   c. data integrity
   d. data security

5. If a database contains the same information more than once, what is this an example of?
   a. data independence
   b. data security
   c. data integrity
   d. data redundancy

6. This system deals with knowledge rather than information.
   a. executive support system (ESS)
   b. decision support system (DSS)
   c. expert system
   d. knowledge management system (KMS)

7. What term describes a technique that is used to discover previously unknown patterns within data?
   a. data mining
   b. data redundancy reduction
   c. relational database
   d. decision support system

8. Which of the following is a data processing system that handles an organization's day-to-day accounting needs?
   a. enterprise processing system (EPS)
   b. transaction processing system (TPS)
   c. batch processing system (BPS)
   d. online analytical processing system (OLAP)

9. An object-oriented database is well suited for which type of application?
   a. general application
   b. horizontal application
   c. financial application
   d. multimedia application

10. What is the latest trend in database software?
   a. data warehousing
   b. Web–database integration
   c. object-oriented design
   d. standalone modules

Fill-In

In the blanks provided, write the correct answer for each of the following.

1. A(n) _____ is any collection of information stored in some organized way.

2. A(n) _____ determines whether a required field has been left empty.

3. A(n) _____ is a type of database program that creates flat-file databases, which contain only one file or table.

4. In a(n) _____, data in several files are related by a common key field.

5. The three data types used for large units of text; nontext data, such as sounds; and very large objects, such as an entire spreadsheet file, are called _____, _____, and _____.

6. Middle managers use an MIS to make _____ about how best to organize resources to achieve their division's goals.

7. Smaller data warehouse projects designed for a single division of an organization are called _____.

8. A(n) _____ is a specially formulated and phrased question.

9. A(n) _____ describes what data should be entered into a field.

10. A TPS produces _____ that provide managers with an overview of the organization's performance and _____ that alert managers to unexpected developments.

11. A(n) _____ enables managers to find answers to questions that can't be answered with fixed, predefined reports.

12. A(n) _____ contains a group of related fields.

13. _____ are the newest type of database and are well suited for multimedia applications in which data are represented as objects.

14. _____ draw a distinction between the database server and client and enable hundreds or even thousands of users to access the database simultaneously.

15. A(n) _____ runs on a LAN and responds to external requests to a database.

Short Answer

1. What are the qualities of a good database?

2. What are the two major types of database programs?

3. What is a key field? How does it work in a relational database?

4. What is the purpose of data warehousing and data mining?

5. What are the levels of management? What are the responsibilities of managers at each level? What information systems are used at each management level?

6. Choose one functional division of an organization and explain how technology is used in that unit.

Go to **www.prenhall.com/cayf2006** to review this chapter, answer the questions, and complete the exercises.

Teamwork

1. Erroneous Data

Preventing erroneous data from being entered into a database is extremely important. As a team, work together to find, identify, and describe the five data validation checks that should be performed when entering data. Which of these have you encountered when entering data on a Web page? Explain the circumstances and any error messages or responses you received. Brainstorm and discuss at least five consequences of entering erroneous data into a database. Write a group report that answers these questions and that summarizes your brainstorming.

2. Valuable Information

In this exercise, your team will identify and briefly describe the 10 characteristics of valuable information. Go to your school's main Web site to determine how many of these characteristics are implemented on the site. Identify those characteristics that you believe have not been implemented and explain why you listed them.

3. Database Tutorials

Each team member should use a search engine to locate information on database management tutorials and then work through part of a tutorial. Team members should then collaborate on writing a group report that describes what you've found. Be sure to cite the URL (Web address), date, and time of access for all of the Web sites mentioned in your report. Your report should include an introductory paragraph, information about each of your experiences, and a summary.

4. Database Templates

Have each team member launch Microsoft Access or a similar database management program and open any of the sample database templates that are located within the General Templates choice in the Task Pane or wherever the program's templates are stored. Have each team member write a brief summary of a different template: How many tables are there? How many forms? Are there any queries or reports? Print one of the tables and draw callouts to a field and to a record. Write a collaborative paper that describes the value of database templates.

5. Management Information System

Many schools have an Office of Instructional Advancement (or some other similar title) that includes areas such as development, finance/accounting, news services, and fundraising. Because this is an important activity, this office is frequently headed by a vice president. What is the formal title of this office at your school? Contact this office and determine whether they use a management information system (MIS) to aid in their efforts. If they do, identify the name of the system and clearly explain how it is used. Be sure to describe the data capture, storage, and retrieval functions. Work together in crafting a paper that describes the information management practices of the office you investigated.

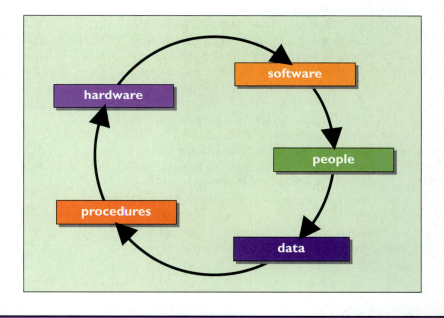

On the Web

1. R:BASE

Visit **www.rbase.com/rbg7** to learn about the features included in R:BASE 7.1. Write a paper that provides an introductory overview of R:BASE 7.1 and at least three of its features. Write a summary paragraph that explains why you would or would not foresee using this product.

2. Expert Systems

Complete the expert system introduction tutorial at eXpertise2Go's Web site, **expertise2go.com**. What is an expert system? What are the three methods for delivering advice without the expert's presence? What are the two parts of a rule? Define forward and backward chaining. What three components does a typical rule-based expert system integrate? What kinds of problems are good candidates for expert systems? In what area were some of the first expert systems developed?

3. Web-Based Queries

At one time, constructing database queries was a difficult task. Users could not simply enter, "Who lives in the South?" Instead, they had to frame their requests using the specific syntax (grammar) of the database they were using. With the development of SQL, users are now able to use a common set of commands for a variety of SQL-based databases. However, this still requires users to learn the SQL syntax. Many Web-based databases ask users a series of questions and display the results without users having to learn how to form queries. Visit Sprint's Web site at **sprint.com** and answer some questions to investigate Sprint's service areas, plans, and mobile phone options.

Do you live in a Sprint PCS service area? If so, look at the various service plans. Overall, which plan is the best one for you? What additional features are included with Sprint's basic service?

Now let's find a phone. Before you decide which phone to purchase, you need to answer a few questions. What is a dual-band phone? Do you need one? What is a "Wireless Internet Ready" phone? Do you need one? Explain which phone best matches your needs.

4. Decision Support Systems

Visit the DSSResources Web site at **dssresources.com** to learn more about decision support applications. What is the definition of a DSS given on this Web site? Is this definition consistent with the one given in the text? Most DSS research centers are located at educational institutions. Which one is nearest to you? Research is not limited to just the United States; name an international DSS site and the country in which it is located. Follow one of the DSS company links and do the following:

- List the company and its URL.
- Name and describe its DSS product.
- Identify whether it is designed for general business use or for a specific application.

5. Online Analytical Processing

Go online to find additional information about online analytical processing (OLAP). When using the Web, you have to be careful that the information you obtain is current. Therefore, when answering the following questions, be sure that the Web pages you access were created or modified no earlier than last year. Find some sites that describe OLAP and provide the following information:

- List their URLs and their creation/modification dates.
- Name a company that produces OLAP applications.
- Name the OLAP product and describe its purpose.
- Identify whether the product is designed for general business use or for a specific application.

Exploring Web Databases

Databases are everywhere and, whether you know it or not, you use them everyday. Search engines such as Google and Yahoo! use large database systems to store all of the information they collect about the Web. When you "search the Web," you are actually searching the huge database of information that has been collected and stored by the company providing the Web-searching service. If a Web page has not been cataloged in a search engine's database, it will not appear in your search results. As of this writing, Google's database contains roughly 4.3 billion Web pages. The total number of Web pages available on the Internet is almost impossible to calculate. Even though Google's database does not contain every page on the Web, the company catalogs more Web pages then any other search engine.

Another database that you may have used is known as CDDB (short for Compact Disc Database). This database contains detailed information on nearly every CD ever produced, including information such as artist, album title, song titles, genre, and year of release. If your computer is connected to the Internet, CDDB is the reason your favorite music player displays detailed information about a CD whenever you play it or rip your favorite tracks (legally of course) to your portable MP3 player. If a CD is new, obscure, or both, and is unavailable in the CDDB, nearly all music players that use the CDDB service will allow you to enter the CD information yourself and submit it to the database for other users to access. Information about CDDB, including details about the database itself, such as the names of tables and data fields, can be found at **www.gracenote.com**.

You can use many online databases to explore topics ranging from obscure computer terminology to pop culture. If you love movies, you may already know about the Internet Movie Database (IMDB) at **www.imdb.com**. Do you want to know all of the movies and television appearances that your favorite star has made? Will there be more *Star Wars* movies? Who did the special effects for *The Matrix*? The IMDB has more information about television shows and movies than you can imagine,

FIGURE 12.26 The Web has many databases, such as Wikipedia, that you can use to explore topics ranging from obscure computer terminology to pop culture.

including cast and crew listings, plot summaries, ratings, dates, interesting tidbits, and user comments.

If movies aren't your thing, take a look at **www.wikipedia.org** (Figure 12.26). Wikipedia claims to be "a free content encyclopedia being written collaboratively by contributors from all around the world." As of this writing, Wikipedia contains approximately 309,000 articles. You can use Wikipedia as you would any traditional encyclopedia, with the exception that you can add new articles as well as correct inaccuracies in articles you find during your research. The site allows any Web user to edit articles by clicking the "Edit this page" link that appears at the top of each page. By using the constantly evolving Wikipedia, you can assure yourself that you won't find an article that discusses how "humans may someday walk on the moon."

If you would like to learn more about databases or possibly even pursue a career as a database administrator (DBA), you may want to download and explore some of the free open-source DBMSs such as MySQL at **www.mysql.com** or PostgreSQL at **www.postgresql.com**. Both Web sites provide you with the necessary information to get started. Books on both of these database management systems are also available at most bookstores. You can also find details about getting certified as a DBA in either Oracle or Microsoft SQL Server by visiting their respective Web sites at **www.oracle.com/ education/certification** and **www.microsoft.com/ learning/mcp**.

What You'll Learn . . .

- **Explain what systems analysts do.**

- **Understand the concept of a system and its life cycle.**

- **Discuss why the systems development life cycle (SDLC) is so widely used.**

- **List the five phases of the SDLC.**

- **Describe the classic mistakes of failed information systems development projects and how systems analysts can avoid them.**

- **Discuss the activities in each of the five phases of the SDLC.**

- **Name the deliverables of each of the five phases of the SDLC.**

Systems Analysis and Design

You may be wondering what systems analysis and design has to do with computers. Well, actually, quite a bit. You see, it's in the analysis and design of information systems that we can create new ways of doing things. This is particularly pertinent today because we're at the very beginning of a new age in human history: the Information Age. Those who understand the fundamentals of this new age will be able to capitalize on its characteristics, the most fundamental of which is the systematic management of information. This chapter explores information systems development, or how to analyze and design systems that help us manage all of the information that comes from living in the Information Age.

As you learned in Chapter 12, an information system processes data to produce information useful to its users. Creating a computerized information system isn't something to take lightly. The benefits are great, but so are the risks. A poorly planned information system can eat up profits, anger customers, and even cause a company to go bankrupt. Unfortunately, poor results are all too common. According to one study, nearly one-third of information system projects are abandoned before completion because it's apparent that the project will fail. The national price tag for these failures may be $80 billion or more.

Is it too much to ask that information systems be finished on time and within budget and that they perform their intended job? Admittedly, information systems development is a difficult challenge, and the unique requirements of many businesses don't make it any easier. Whether it's how they track customers and sales or inventory and expenses, most businesses need something a little different. (For example, a pizza delivery company needs a different information system than does a pharmaceutical firm or an auto maker.) In addition, users and clients may have difficulty clearly communicating their needs, leading to the development of systems that don't satisfy them. And too frequently, time estimates for developing information systems are overly optimistic, typically by as much as 20 to 30 percent. Just like any construction project, such as building a new home, building an information system takes longer than most people care to admit.

In the face of such chaos, it makes good sense to try to get organized. **Systems analysis** is the field concerned with the organized planning, development, and implementation of artificial systems, including information systems. The systems analysis discipline learns from previous development efforts and formulates strategies for improved planning, organization, control, and execution of information systems development projects.

The Information Age is all about managing data to provide information, entertainment, and systems to support society's many activities. With that said, let's now turn our attention to all of the procedures and people involved with information systems development.

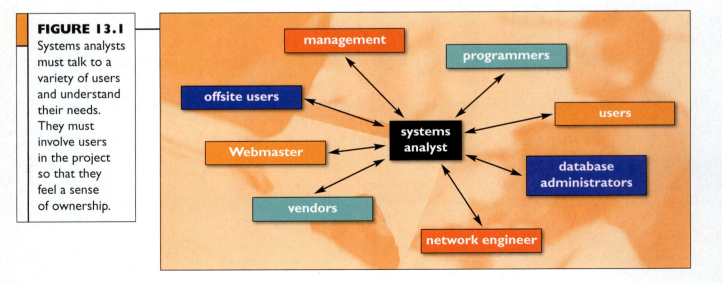

FIGURE 13.1
Systems analysts must talk to a variety of users and understand their needs. They must involve users in the project so that they feel a sense of ownership.

Systems Analysts: Communication Counts

In Chapter 12, you learned that a computerized information system includes data, hardware, software, procedures, and people. The people involved include users as well as trained personnel, such as systems analysts. **Systems analysts** are problem-solving computer professionals who work with users and management to determine an organization's information system needs (Figure 13.1). Systems analysts determine the requirements needed to modify an existing system or to develop a new one. Systems analysts don't ordinarily do the development; the development is reserved for other trained computer professionals called *systems designers* or *developers*. Rather, systems analysts identify and evaluate alternative solutions, make formal presentations to management, and assist in the development of the system after an option has been chosen.

Much of a systems analyst's job involves communication, including listening skills. Systems analysts must understand the organization's mission, including its strategic goals. A strategic goal might be to ensure that each of a company's customers receives accurate, timely, and personalized correspondence at least once a month—thereby building customer loyalty. Analysts also must talk to users and understand their needs. They must involve users in the project so that they feel some ownership of the project. They must keep in close contact with project team members so that they know how the project is progressing. They must write voluminous documentation that explains, at every step, what was performed, why and how it was performed, and who did it. They must know who (the user, the project team, or the vendor) is supposed to do what during the systems development process. To stay organized and keep track of these various tasks, systems analysts follow an organized procedure for planning and building information systems called the systems development life cycle.

The Systems Development Life Cycle: A Problem-Solving Approach

In the early years of business computing, information systems development was a disorganized, ad hoc process that frequently produced discouraging results. Systems typically were delivered late, went over their budgets, and didn't provide the services users expected. The **systems development life cycle** (**SDLC**) is an approach or model used to improve the quality of information systems. By encouraging an organized approach to problem solving, the SDLC can produce better information systems. The SDLC is better understood if it's broken down into digestible pieces. Let's begin with what the "systems" part means.

Systems are collections of components purposefully organized into a functioning whole to accomplish a goal. Systems occur in nature, but what we're talking about here are **artificial systems**, systems deliberately constructed by people to serve some purpose. Systems are all around us. The commercial airline transportation system, for example, is a complex system that does a remarkably good job of safely delivering millions of people to their destinations every day.

Destinations

Visit the following link to see how the State Technology Office for the State of Florida defines its systems development life cycle: **www.myflorida .com/myflorida/ sto/isdm/ step_by_step.html**

Here's a link that defines a six-step life cycle: **www.iwtwireless .com/Methodology .htm**

FIGURE 13.2 The System Life Cycle

Life Cycle Phase	Key Tasks
Preliminary design phase	Identifying systems development goals
Detailed design phase	Designing specific components
Fabrication, assembly, integration, and test phase	Putting it all together
Production and customer support phase	Using the system
Termination and disposal phase	Retiring the system

SYSTEMS DEVELOPMENT LIFE CYCLE

PHASE 1 PLANNING: identify problems and opportunities

▼

PHASE 2 ANALYSIS: analyze and document existing system

▼

PHASE 3 DESIGN: design new system

▼

PHASE 4 IMPLEMEN-TATION: implement new system

▼

PHASE 5 MAINTENANCE: support new system

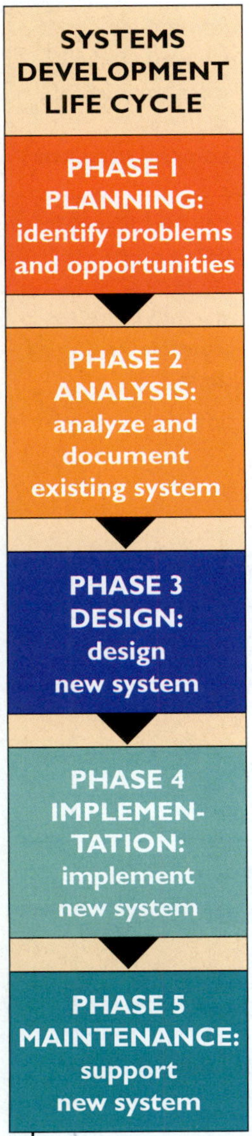

FIGURE 13.3

The five phases of the systems development life cycle

At the core of the systems concept lies the recognition that various parts of a system need to be modified or adapted to function together smoothly. (After all, you wouldn't want to fly on an airplane that had the wrong type of wing installed.) A second important concept about systems is that they have a **life cycle**: They are born, go through a process of maturation, live an adult life, and become obsolete to the point that they have to be modified or abandoned. Figure 13.2 summarizes the phases of a system's life cycle. If you think about yesterday's transportation systems, such as canals or the Pony Express, you'll see it's obvious that systems outlive their usefulness.

At this point, we could be talking about any kind of system, including a manufacturing system such as an assembly line. No organization, not even a small one, can function without an information system of some kind, even if it isn't computer-based. But developing the right information system for the right purpose takes patience, time, and the right plan. That's exactly the function of the SDLC and its five steps or phases.

THE FIVE PHASES OF THE SDLC

At the core of the SDLC model is a simple idea: You shouldn't go on to the next step until you're certain that the current one has been performed properly. Figure 13.3 depicts the five phases (steps or stages) of the SDLC: (1) planning or investigation; (2) analysis; (3) design or development; (4) implementation; (5) maintenance or support. Each phase is intended to address key issues and to produce **deliverables**, which are outcomes or tangible output such as reports or other documents. These deliverables often form the input for the next phase.

Note that different organizations and systems development teams may use modified or slightly different versions of the SDLC; some versions identify more phases than others, and some use different names for the individual phases. The five-part process described here represents what is common practice.

AVOIDING MISTAKES

Systems analysts have learned, often through bitter experience, to avoid the classic mistakes of failed projects. Consequently, the information systems development process looks at an organization's overall goals and objectives and identifies the various systems and subsystems that the organization uses to achieve its goals and objectives. The following essentials of systems development wisdom are built into the SDLC:

- **User involvement is crucial.** Users include any person for whom the system is built, and that may include customers. Users are the ultimate judges of the system's usability, although they may not know how to express their needs coherently. Without user involvement, the system may not meet users' needs, and they may then resist or even sabotage efforts to use the new system.

- **A problem-solving approach works best.** To create an effective system, you must identify the problem, place the problem in context, define the solution, examine alternative solutions, and choose the best one. Without this approach, the new system may not fully address the underlying shortcomings of the existing system.

- **Good project management skills are needed.** Many failed systems development projects are characterized by unrealistic expectations, overly optimistic schedules, lack of solid backing from management, people's inability to make decisions and stick with them, lack of control over insertion of new but unnecessary features, and interference from problem personnel. A poorly managed project may become so chaotic that it must be cancelled.

- **Documentation is required.** The term **documentation** refers to the recording of all information pertinent to the project, for instance, manuals, tutorials, startup procedures, and installation instructions. A **project notebook**, which may or may not be computer based, is often used to store the documentation for a project. The documentation enables everyone connected with the project to understand all the decisions that have been made. Documentation shouldn't be put off until the end of the project, at which time important information or key personnel might not be available. Without documentation, the system can't be properly supported or modified (especially after key development personnel have left).

- **Checkpoints should be used to make sure the project is on track.** At the end of each phase, the project must be critically and independently evaluated to make sure that it's on track. An organization shouldn't be afraid to cancel the project (or repeat a phase) if results aren't satisfactory. Some of the worst development disasters occur when the project team conceals the fact that the system couldn't possibly work.

- **Systems should be designed for growth and change.** A system should be designed so that it won't break down or require a major redesign in the event of change (including unanticipated increases in usage). Failure to anticipate change and growth could make the entire system useless in short order.

Avoiding mistakes doesn't guarantee success. On the other hand, making mistakes may very well guarantee failure!

THE WATERFALL MODEL

Although the SDLC calls for a step-by-step process, it's not always wise to keep going if work in a later stage turns up problems with work performed in an earlier one. For example, in the analysis phase, the team may discover that the problem hasn't been formulated correctly. The **waterfall model** is a systems development method that builds correction pathways into the process so that analysts can return to a previous phase (Figure 13.4). It's the most widely used implementation of the SDLC.

Let's look at phase 1 of the SDLC.

Phase 1: Planning the System

Phase 1 is the planning or investigation phase. In phase 1 of the SDLC, an organization recognizes the need for an information system, defines the problem, examines alternative solutions, develops a plan, and determines the project's feasibility. The result is a project proposal submitted to senior management. If this phase is performed well, it assures that the right information system will be built, and, just as important, it assures that the wrong system won't be built.

RECOGNIZING THE NEED FOR THE SYSTEM

New information systems (or modified ones) result from a recognition of deficiencies in performance, information quality, economics, security, efficiency, or service (Figure 13.5). If the current system demonstrates poor response time, users might experience delays when uploading files to an FTP site. If the existing system lacks information quality, a sales or customer service representative may give a customer an incorrect stock number on an item being ordered or report that an item is out of stock when

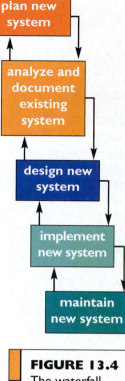

FIGURE 13.4
The waterfall model builds in correction pathways that enable a return to a previous phase. It's the most widely used implementation of the SDLC.

FIGURE 13.5 Recognizing the Need for a New or Modified System

Deficiency in:	Example:
Performance	Slow response time
Information quality	Out-of-date or inaccurate information
Economics	High operating costs
Security	Vulnerability to break-ins
Efficiency	Wasting resources (employee time, printer paper, toner, etc.)
Service	Difficult, awkward to use

Techtalk

Scope
In project management, *scope* refers to the sum total of all project products and their features. *Scope creep* refers to uncontrolled changes in a project's scope.

there are actually plenty in stock. Economic deficiencies need to be addressed if the existing system generates high bills from ISPs or other vendors. If the existing system lacks security, hackers or competitors can steal or destroy valuable company data. An inefficient system might automatically print customer statements even when their account balance is zero, wasting employee time, paper, toner, and other resources. A system demonstrates deficient service when employees must go through unnecessary or repetitive steps to perform a task.

Even if the current system doesn't have obvious deficiencies, it might still be worthwhile to replace it if a redesigned system could generate new business opportunities. For example, a new or redesigned airline reservation system could generate better customer profiles that would identify the need for additional services, such as providing more first class seats, arranging car rentals, making hotel reservations, and so on.

To get the project going, someone makes a formal project request to the organization's **information technology steering committee**, which generally includes representatives from senior management,

information systems personnel, users, and middle managers. The steering committee reviews requests and decides which ones to address. If a project request is approved, the steering committee appoints a project team and phase 1 continues.

DEFINING THE PROBLEM

To solve a problem, you must first understand it. But that's not always as easy as it might seem. Problems are often confused with symptoms. A **symptom** is an unacceptable or undesirable result, whereas a **problem** is the underlying cause of the symptom. Another way to differentiate a symptom from a problem is that a symptom is an indication or a sign of something, whereas a problem is a state of difficulty that needs to be resolved. For example, someone might say that "crime is a symptom of the neighborhood's decay." Although crime may seem like the problem, the neighborhood's decay is actually the problem. In an information system, users might complain about a symptom, such as slow response time when entering a transaction into their computers. Users may think the solution is to demand more powerful computers, because they think the problem is with the computers. But the slow response time is just a symptom. The problem could be any number of different things, such as the slow speed of network transmissions. If this is the case, then it's a waste of money to buy faster computers! In this case, if a symptom is confused with a problem, the wrong solution will be implemented.

Determining the exact problem often is a difficult task. Ideally, the problem definition stage identifies the features that need to be added to or built into the information system to make it acceptable to users. Although users must be involved in defining the problem, they're not accustomed to looking at information systems in a structured, unbiased way. The systems analyst talks to as many users as possible, and slowly a picture emerges of what these people do, when they do it, how they do it, and why they do it (Figure 13.6). From these facts, the analyst then derives recommendations for new system features (if an existing system will be modified) or proposes that a new system be built from scratch.

FIGURE 13.6 To determine the exact problem, the systems analyst must talk to as many users as possible to discover what they do, when they do it, how they do it, and why. The analyst then recommends new system features or an entirely new system.

EXAMINING ALTERNATIVE SOLUTIONS

After the problem has been identified, system requirements need to be specified. A process called **requirements analysis** determines the requirements of the system by analyzing how the system will meet the needs of end users. The requirements analysis is extremely important, because any errors or omissions could lead to expensive missteps or modifications later in the development process because of user dissatisfaction with the new or modified system. It also is important for the project team to focus the requirements analysis primarily on user needs and not get caught up in the technical details.

After system requirements have been determined, the project team then looks at a range of possible solutions. The range of solutions that the project team examines often includes internally developed systems, off-the-shelf software, and outsourcing. The project team should consider the advantages and disadvantages of each potential solution. For example, an internally developed system offers the project team control over each phase of development. However, this control has a price—internally developed systems are usually the most expensive to build and maintain. Purchasing off-the-shelf software would obviously save the project team the hassle of creating their own software or hiring programmers if none exist in-house. However, some companies require specialized software features that aren't available in off-the-shelf software packages. Outsourcing the development of the system offers a range of additional options: a project team may outsource one part of the project for which there is no

in-house expertise (such as programming software) or choose to outsource the entire project. Obviously, the more portions of the project that are outsourced, the more expensive the potential solution becomes. Once the project team agrees on a solution, the project proceeds.

DEVELOPING A PLAN

When an appropriate solution has been identified, the project leader (who may or may not be the systems analyst) formulates a project plan. The project leader also handles project budgets and schedules. The **project plan** identifies the project's goal and specifies all of the activities that must be completed for the project to succeed. For each activity, the plan specifies the estimated time that the project will require as well as the estimated costs. The plan also identifies activities that must be completed before new ones can begin and indicates which activities can occur simultaneously.

Before developing a system, it is imperative that system specifications be created. Think of system specifications in the same vein as blueprints for a building or a house. These specifications act as benchmarks to evaluate as well as implement the system while it is being developed. System specifications also assist in answering tough questions, such as whether the correct system solution is being implemented, if it meets user requirements, and if it matches the project plan.

Project plans are often graphically summarized with a **Gantt chart**, a type of bar chart that shows how different activities are performed over time (Figure 13.7). Project management software, such

Destinations

One business that is adept at solving organizational problems is a company called EDS. Examples of its successes can be found on its Web site at **www.eds.com**

id	task name	duration	jan	feb	mar	apr	may	jun	jul	aug
1	planning	3w	1/26 ▬ 2/13							
2	analysis	10w		2/9 ▬▬▬▬▬ 4/17						
3	design	11w			3/23 ▬▬▬▬▬▬ 6/5					
4	implementation	4w						6/5 ▬▬ 7/3		

FIGURE 13.7 A Gantt chart is a graphical summary of project plans that indicates activities performed over a period of time.

IMPACTS

Computers and Society

Will We Ever Go Paperless?

Since the dawn of the computer age, experts have predicted a paperless world, but will we ever entirely let go of paper? If you've ever pulled out a pen to complete a multipart business form or submitted a government application in duplicate (or triplicate), you know that paper hasn't gone away. E-mailing digitized documents instead of snail-mailing printed copies definitely saves a few trees. However, research shows that nearly three-quarters of all documents composed on computers are still printed out—sometimes once, and often more than once (Figure 13.8).

Online bill paying is making a small dent in the blizzard of checks written every day, but it's been slow to catch on. Fewer paper faxes now whiz from place to place, thanks to PC-to-PC faxing. On the other hand, because digital cameras and color printers are commonplace, people can quickly and easily print more and more copies of their favorite photos. Add it all up, and by the end of 2006, computer users could be printing as many as 2 trillion pages a year.

Why can't we let go of paper? For one thing, many businesspeople prefer to use printed copies when reviewing important documents in progress and when marking comments or changes. As a student, you probably find it easier to flip between chapters and reread key sections when a textbook is in your hands rather than on the screen. Also, if you want to destroy a confidential document, you can quickly shred paper, whereas you might have to go through several steps to delete the electronic version without a trace. So although we can make paper documents look neater and more readable, we're unlikely to give up paper altogether in favor of bits and bytes in the near future.

To learn more about how to go paperless, see the video clip at **www.prenhall.com/cayf2006**

FIGURE 13.8 Digital files lend themselves to multiple printings. We will never be a paperless society, but some savings have been accomplished.

as Microsoft Project, provides an excellent means of developing and modifying project plans.

DETERMINING FEASIBILITY

A feasible project is one that can be successfully completed. To determine whether a project is feasible, three types of feasibility must be examined: technical, operational, and economic.

Technical feasibility means that a project can be accomplished with existing, proven technology. For example, consider a project that requires speech recognition. Although computers are getting much better at recognizing and transcribing human speech, they do make errors. If the error rate is unacceptable, the project isn't technically feasible until speech recognition technology improves.

Operational feasibility refers to a project that can be accomplished with the organization's available resources. If some of the project's goals include changes beyond the organization's control (such as regulations in a foreign country), the project isn't operationally feasible.

When a project demonstrates **economic feasibility**, it can be accomplished with available fiscal resources. Economic feasibility is usually answered by a **cost-benefit analysis**, an examination of the losses and gains related to a project. The costs are the expected costs to develop and run the new system.

A cost-benefit analysis examines both tangible and intangible benefits. You can easily measure **tangible benefits**, such as increased sales, faster response time, and decreased complaints. **Intangible benefits**, such as improved employee morale and customer satisfaction, are often difficult or impossible to measure. Bank managers, for example, may decide to install an ATM because they believe that many people won't deal with a bank that doesn't have one. Improved customer satisfaction that would occur as a result of installing the new system is an intangible benefit.

In many companies, managers will request a study of the proposed system's **return on investment** (**ROI**), its overall financial yield at the end of its lifetime. The money invested in the system should

produce a return that is greater than alternative investments, such as putting the money in the bank.

PREPARING THE PROJECT PROPOSAL

At the conclusion of phase 1, the project leader writes a **project proposal**, a document that introduces the nature of the existing system's problem, explains the proposed solution and its benefits, details the proposed project plan, and concludes with a recommendation. In response, management decides whether to continue the project. The deliverable from phase 1 is the project proposal.

Phase 2: Analyzing and Documenting the Existing Information System

In phase 2 of the SDLC, the systems analyst or the systems development team determines precisely what the new system should accomplish. Here, the emphasis is placed on what the system should do, not how. (That comes next, in phase 3.) This phase includes two steps: analyzing the existing system and determining the needs of the new system. Phase 2 is often referred to as the systems analysis (or just analysis) phase.

ANALYZING THE EXISTING SYSTEM

A study of the existing system (whether computerized or manual) determines which activities currently being performed should be continued in the new system. This step can be simple if the current system is well documented. Unfortunately, most systems are not well documented, and that's especially true of updates to an original system.

Thus, a major part of the analysis of the existing system is to document it. If the existing system is computerized, the current hardware needs to be examined to see whether it's adequate to do the job.

An unexpected but valuable benefit of the systems analysis phase is that it often points out problems that weren't fully identified in phase 1. This analysis may be the first time a group of people has sat down in the same room and talked about the existing system. The discussion can result in new insights, and problems that were not uncovered in the preliminary investigation can be solved.

DETERMINING THE NEW SYSTEM'S REQUIREMENTS

After the existing system has been exhaustively documented, the new system's requirements are precisely stated. This listing of the new system's requirements is the deliverable for phase 2. The requirements state the innovations that need to occur for the system to be acceptable to users. Again, user involvement is crucial, because systems analysts often obtain information about system requirements through interviews, surveys, and observations of how the system is currently used.

Phase 3: Designing the System

Phase 3, the design phase of the SDLC, is concerned with how the new information system will work. This phase isn't concerned

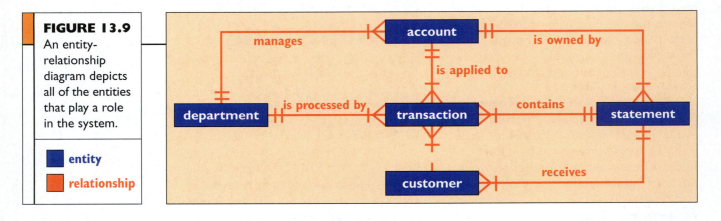

FIGURE 13.9 An entity-relationship diagram depicts all of the entities that play a role in the system.

- ■ entity
- ■ relationship

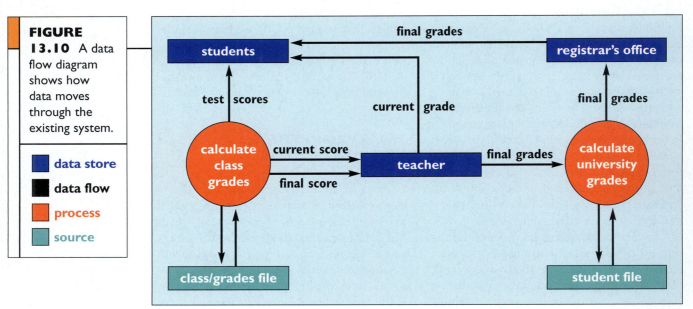

FIGURE 13.10 A data flow diagram shows how data moves through the existing system.

- ■ data store
- ■ data flow
- ■ process
- ■ source

with the nitty-gritty details of how the software will be coded. Instead, this phase's deliverable is a logical design that provides an overall picture of how the new system will work. The goal of this phase of the project is to specify in exact terms the types of data that flow into the system, where the data go, how the data are processed, who uses the data, how the data are stored, what data entry forms are involved, and what procedures people follow. To do this, the project team can use a number of graphical tools, such as entity-relationship diagrams, data flow diagrams, project dictionaries, and data dictionaries.

DESIGN TOOLS

To describe the new information system, analysts use methods of graphical analysis to convey their findings to managers, programmers, and users. An **entity-relationship diagram** (**ERD**) shows all of the entities (organizations, departments, users, programs, and data) that play a role in the system as well as the relationships among those entities (Figure 13.9). A **data flow diagram** (**DFD**) uses a set of graphical symbols to show how data move through the existing system (Figure 13.10). The DFD also specifies the details of how the data are processed.

Team members create a **project dictionary**, which explains all the terminology relevant to the project; they also develop a data dictionary, which defines the types of data that are inputted into the system.

Two recent approaches, prototyping and computer-aided software engineering, are helping to improve the design phase. With **prototyping**, also called **joint application development** (**JAD**), a small-scale mock-up, or prototype, of the system is developed and shown to users (Figure 13.11). The prototype is developed at an early stage and isn't intended to be fully functional. It provides just enough functionality so that users can give feedback. The advantage of prototyping is that users don't have to imagine what the system specifications mean in terms of a working system. They

Destinations

ERD and DFD software is available from several sources. Follow the links provided to learn about just a few:
www.smartdraw .com/specials/ softdesign.asp? id=12079
and
www.ntfaq.com/ Articles/Index.cfm? ArticleID=14036

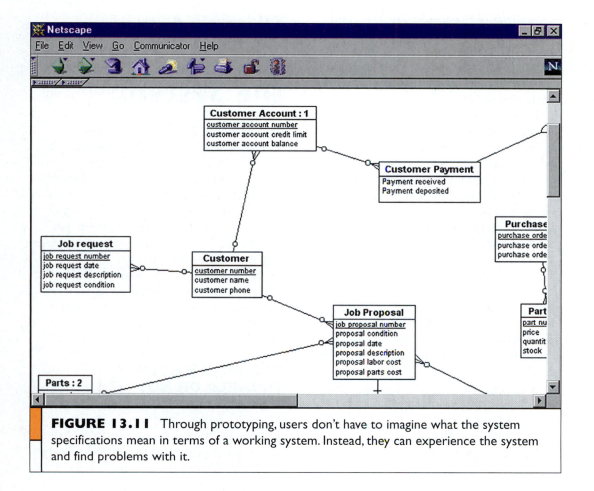

FIGURE 13.11 Through prototyping, users don't have to imagine what the system specifications mean in terms of a working system. Instead, they can experience the system and find problems with it.

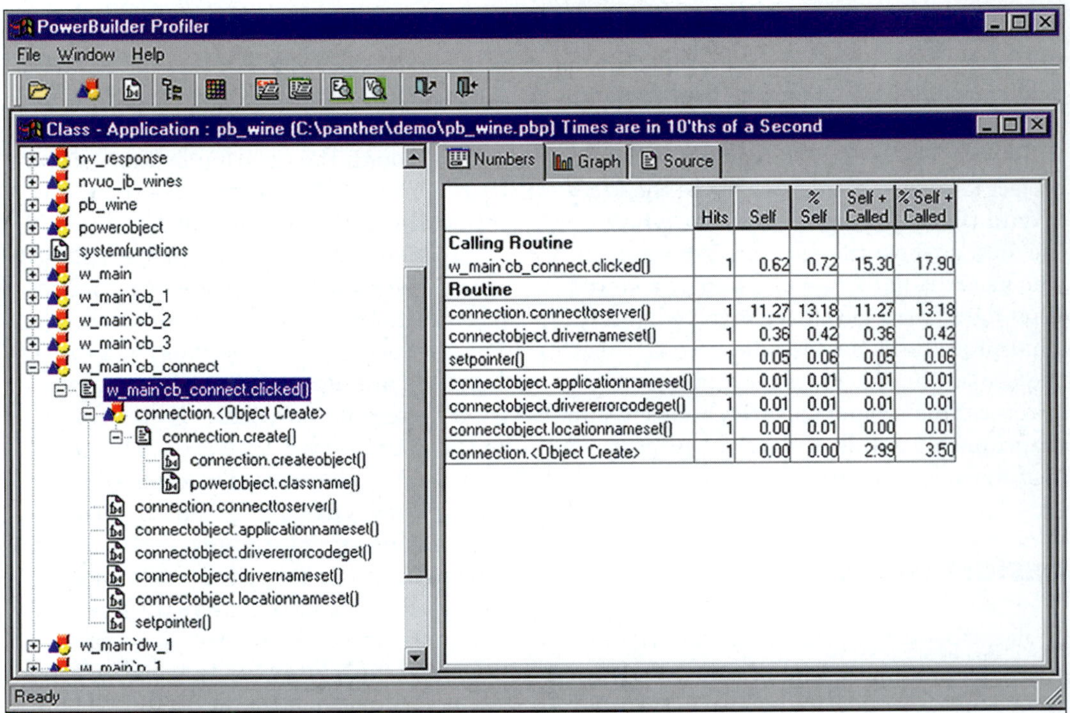

FIGURE 13.12 PowerBuilder is a CASE tool that automates project tasks, including the automatic generation of prototype code.

can experience the system and thus find problems or enhancements that they may not have considered otherwise.

The second approach, **computer-aided software engineering (CASE)**, automates the often tedious task of documenting entity relationships and data flows in a complex new system. Most CASE tools include project management features, data dictionaries, documentation support, and graphical output support; some even automatically generate prototype code (Figure 13.12). CASE software, however, is expensive, requires extensive training, and is difficult to use.

During this phase, it's important that analysts think about the system's logical requirements and not think about what can be accomplished (and what can't) with existing information systems and software. Such thinking might prevent them from realizing that they may need to create an entirely new type of system, one that's never been developed before. This is the reason phase 3 is clearly separated from phase 4, in which attention turns to the system's physical implementation. These two phases must be rigorously kept separate.

Phase 4: Implementing the System

In phase 4 of the SDLC, the system implementation phase, the project team and management decide whether to create the physical system using internal expertise or to purchase it from outside vendors. If the project team decides to build the system in-house, hardware must be purchased and installed, and programs must be written. The system must be exhaustively tested, and users must be trained. When the team is confident that the new system is ready for use, the conversion to the new system takes place.

DECIDING WHETHER TO BUILD OR BUY

After the new system's requirements and logical design have been specified, the project team faces the **build-or-buy decision**: Should the new system be

CURRENTS

Safety and Security

The U.S. Air Traffic Control System: Is It Really Safe to Fly?

Many large-scale organizations are facing crises brought on by legacy systems, information systems based on older-generation computers that can't handle today's demands. Replacing these systems isn't easy. For example, they may rely on programs written in computer languages that are no longer actively used. And all too often, the systems are so complex that the cost of upgrading them is beyond the organization's means.

This is the enormous problem facing the U.S. air traffic control (ATC) system, which is run by the Federal Aviation Administration (FAA). Critics say that in some areas the system still uses 30-year-old computers that break down with alarming frequency. Yet when a failure occurs, public safety is not immediately threatened because backup systems step in to help controllers track aircraft locations. At times, however, the backup systems are a bit slow and cumbersome, which means that controllers must allow more space between flights to ensure safety. The result is flight delays (Figure 13.13).

Updating the ATC won't be easy or cheap. The FAA's 250 computer systems run 23 million lines of code written in 50 different computer languages. Some of the systems are so old that it's increasingly difficult to find qualified technicians and programmers to help in the migration to modernized equipment. Meanwhile, the skies are more crowded than ever with private jets, small planes, and new jumbo jets. Amid calls to vastly expand the ATC's capacity, the FAA has been buying new computers year after year as well as implementing other improvements.

Switching over to a more modern system can lead to a whole new set of problems, as Great Britain recently learned. In a one-region test of a systems upgrade, an unexpected glitch crashed that country's primary air traffic control center and grounded hundreds of flights for hours. So even with billions of dollars to invest in overhauling the ATC, the FAA must plan carefully to avoid air traffic delays, project delays, and cost overruns.

FIGURE 13.13 The FAA concedes that failures due to outdated computer equipment result in air traffic delays that cost airlines $5 billion each year.

Techtalk

Plunge
This is another term for direct conversion. With this type of conversion, the changeover from the old to the new system occurs all at once.

developed in-house or purchased from an outside vendor?

In-house development provides the opportunity for detailed customization, but it often carries with it the high costs of programmers, testing, and time. Most organizations cannot afford to have programmers on staff and don't have the time that is required to properly develop an application. For these reasons an organization will often purchase an off-the-shelf product and then customize it for its specific needs. Another option is to outsource the project to a company that specializes in creating systems applications.

If the decision is made to outsource the project, the project team sends out either a request for quotation or a request for proposal. A **request for quotation** (**RFQ**) is a request for a vendor to quote a price for specific components of the information system. A **request for proposal** (**RFP**) is a request for a vendor to write a proposal for the design, installation, and configuration of the information system. RFQs and RFPs are often sent to vendors called **value-added resellers** (**VARs**), independent companies that combine and install equipment and software from several sources.

DEVELOPING THE SOFTWARE

Developing the software can be considered a separate subset of the information systems development process. However, in most cases, developing the software amounts to less than 15 percent of the time involved in the entire project. To develop the software required for the new system, programmers use the program development life cycle (PDLC).

Software development can impact an organization's cost-benefit analysis based on whether the new software will be used as a replacement for manual processes or simply to automate existing processes.

TESTING

Thorough testing is essential. The two basic types of testing are application testing and acceptance testing. With **application**

testing, programs are tested individually and then tested together. With **acceptance testing**, users evaluate the system to see whether it meets their needs and whether it functions correctly. It's essential that errors or problems be detected before the system is released for use in the organization.

TRAINING

A computerized information system includes not only computer hardware and software, but also knowledgeable users and procedures. A successful conclusion to the project requires training users to use the new system. The best training methods involve sitting users down with the new system in one-on-one training sessions. Users also will need manuals that include tutorials as well as reference information.

CONVERTING SYSTEMS

After the new system has been tested and the users have been trained, conversion to the new system occurs. System conversion can be performed in any of the following ways:

- A **parallel conversion** involves running both the new and the old systems for a while to check that the new system produces answers at least as good as those of the old system. This type of conversion is the safest; the old system can carry the load until any problems with the new system are cleared up. This conversion is also the most expensive, however, because the work is duplicated.

- With a **pilot conversion**, one part of the organization converts to the new system while the rest of the organization continues to run the old system. When the pilot group is satisfied with the new system, the rest of the organization can start using it.

- A **phased conversion** occurs when the new system is implemented over different time periods, one part at a time.

After one part of the new system is running, another piece is implemented.

- A **direct conversion**, sometimes called a **crash conversion**, requires the stopping of the old system and then the starting of the new system. A direct conversion is the most risky type of conversion, but it may be necessary in some situations.

Phase 5: Maintaining the System

In the final phase of the SDLC, the new system is evaluated to ensure that it has met its intended needs and works correctly. A **postimplementation system review** is a process of ongoing evaluation that determines whether the system has met its goals. After conversion, widespread use may reveal errors that were not detected during testing that must be corrected. In addition, changes will be needed as the business environment changes. For example, changes may be needed in data entry forms to deal with an expanded product line.

In addition to the postimplementation review, the system must be maintained. Maintenance includes such tasks as making adjustments to the system as the organization changes; adding, deleting, and adjusting records; making backup copies of files; and providing security for the system. Most organizations spend much more time and money on maintenance than any other component of the SDLC.

In time, the system may be found to be so deficient that a new round of systems development must take place—and the systems development life cycle begins anew.

What You've Learned

SYSTEMS ANALYSIS AND DESIGN

- Systems analysts determine an organization's information system needs by working closely with both users and management. Systems analysts determine the requirements needed to modify an existing system or to develop a new one. They identify and evaluate alternative solutions, make formal presentations to management, and assist in the development of the system after an option has been chosen. To stay organized and keep track of these various tasks, systems analysts follow an organized procedure for planning and building information systems called the systems development life cycle (SDLC).

- A system is a collection of components purposefully organized into a functioning whole to accomplish a goal. Systems occur in nature, but artificial systems are deliberately constructed by people to serve a specific purpose. At the core of the system concept lies the recognition that various parts of the system need to be modified or adapted to function together smoothly. A second important concept about systems is that they have a life cycle: They are born, go through a process of maturation, live an adult life, and become obsolete to the point that they have to be modified or abandoned.

- Before the SDLC came into widespread use, new information systems were often late, over budget, or did not provide what users expected. The SDLC was developed to impose order on earlier, haphazard development processes and to improve the quality of information systems. It breaks information systems development down into discrete stages, or phases, each of which must be successfully completed before the project moves on to the next phase.

- The five phases of the SDLC are (1) planning or investigation, (2) analysis, (3) design, (4) implementation, and (5) maintenance or support.

- The three classic mistakes of failed information systems development projects are lack of user involvement, poor project management, and lack of documentation. Systems analysts can avoid mistakes by involving users, using a problem-solving approach, applying project management skills, keeping thorough documentation, using checkpoints to make sure the project is on track, and designing the system with room for growth and change.

- In phase 1 of the SDLC, the organization recognizes the need for an information system, defines the problem, examines alternative solutions, and determines the project's feasibility. In phase 2 of the SDLC, the systems analyst determines what the new system should accomplish by analyzing the existing system and determining the needs of the new system. In phase 3 of the SDLC, the systems analyst determines how the new system will work. In phase 4 of the SDLC, the management team decides whether to build or buy a new system, develops the software, tests the system, trains users, and converts to the new system. In phase 5 of the SDLC, the new system receives ongoing evaluation and maintenance to ensure that it meets the organization's needs and works properly.

- Each phase of the SDLC provides a deliverable, which serves as the input to the next phase. These deliverables are a project proposal, a graphical analysis of the current information system, a graphical and detailed analysis of the new information system, a finished and tested product, and a postimplementation system review.

Key Terms and Concepts

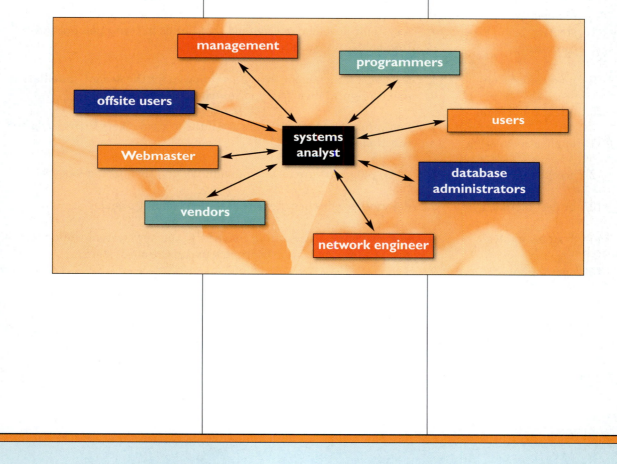

Matching

Match each key term in the left column with the most accurate definition in the right column.

_____ 1. systems analysis

_____ 2. systems development life cycle (SDLC)

_____ 3. waterfall model

_____ 4. postimplementation system review

_____ 5. return on investment (ROI)

_____ 6. data flow diagram (DFD)

_____ 7. request for proposal (RFP)

_____ 8. information technology steering committee

_____ 9. pilot conversion

_____ 10. direct conversion

_____ 11. application testing

_____ 12. acceptance testing

_____ 13. project dictionary

_____ 14. systems analyst

_____ 15. operational feasibility

a. money invested in the system should produce a return greater than alternative investments

b. shows how data moves through an existing system

c. requires stopping the old system and starting the new system

d. a problem-solving computer professional who works with users and management to determine an organization's information system needs

e. the field concerned with information systems development

f. when a project can be accomplished with the organization's available resources

g. reviews project requests and includes representatives from senior management, information systems personnel, users, and middle managers

h. an approach used to improve the quality of information systems

i. explains all terminology relevant to the project

j. a systems development method that builds in correction pathways that enable a return to the previous phase

k. a request for a vendor to write a proposal for the design, installation, and configuration of the information system

l. an evaluation in which users see if the system meets their needs and functions correctly

m. when programs are tested individually and then tested together

n. determines whether the new system has met its goals

o. one part of an organization converts to the new system while the rest of the organization continues to run the old system

Multiple Choice

Circle the correct choice for each of the following.

1. What does the acronym SDLC stand for?
   a. secondary dynamic life cycle
   b. simple data linear compression
   c. systems development life cycle
   d. synchronous data line current

2. Prototyping is also known as which of the following?
   a. phased conversion
   b. outsourcing
   c. joint application development (JAD)
   d. systems design

3. Recognition of which of the following is *not* essential to sound systems development?
   a. hiring value-added resellers
   b. good project management skills
   c. documentation
   d. user involvement

4. Which of the following does not need to be part of a project plan?
   a. resumes of key personnel
   b. goals
   c. scope
   d. necessary activities

5. What is a VAR?
   a. an abbreviation for the variables used in systems analysis
   b. an acronym for value-added resources
   c. a graphical method for showing projected implementation time lines
   d. an independent company that combines and installs equipment and software from several sources

6. Which of the following is *not* a design tool?
   a. entity-relationship diagram
   b. Gantt chart
   c. data flow diagram
   d. project dictionary

7. Which of the following describes a project that can be accomplished with available fiscal resources?
   a. technical feasibility
   b. operational feasibility
   c. economic feasibility
   d. resource feasibility

8. CASE is an acronym for which of the following?
   a. computer-assisted system engineering
   b. community action for system engineering
   c. computer and system enterprises
   d. computer-aided software engineering

9. Training is a part of which development phase?
   a. phase 1
   b. phase 2
   c. phase 3
   d. phase 4

10. Which type of system conversion involves running two systems simultaneously to ensure that the new system produces output similar to or better than the old system?
    a. direct conversion
    b. parallel conversion
    c. pilot conversion
    d. phased conversion

Fill-In

In the blanks provided, write the correct answer for each of the following.

1. A(n) _____ is the deliverable for phase 1 that introduces the nature of the existing system's problem, explains the proposed solution and its benefits, details the proposed project plan, and concludes with a recommendation.

2. A(n) _____ is an unacceptable or undesirable result or an indication or sign that something is wrong.

3. _____ benefits include increased sales, faster response time, and decreased complaints.

4. A(n) _____ is the underlying cause of the symptom or a state of difficulty that needs to be resolved.

5. A(n) _____ is a request for a vendor to quote a price for specific components of the information system.

6. A(n) _____ shows all of the entities that play a role in the system.

7. A(n) _____ may or may not be computer based and is often used to store the documentation for a project.

8. _____ is a process that determines the requirements of the system by analyzing how the system will meet the needs of end users.

9. A(n) _____ determines whether it is economically feasible to undertake a project.

10. A(n) _____ conversion occurs when the new system is implemented over different time periods, one part at a time.

11. A(n) _____ is a collection of components purposefully organized into a functioning whole to accomplish a goal.

12. A project that demonstrates _____ can be accomplished with existing, proven technology.

13. Systems have a(n) _____: They are born, go through a process of maturation, live an adult life, and become obsolete to the point that they have to be modified or abandoned.

14. _____, or outcomes, form the input for the next phase in the SDLC.

15. Whether the new system will be developed in-house or purchased from an outside vendor is called the _____.

Short Answer

1. What are the five phases of the SDLC?

2. Why is it important to document the existing system, regardless of whether it's computerized?

3. What are the advantages of prototyping at an early stage in the development of a system?

4. Name an advantage and a drawback of using a CASE system.

5. Identify the six essentials of systems development. Explain which one you feel is most important.

Teamwork

1. System Conversion

As a team, determine the answers to the following questions and then write a group report based on your findings. What are the four types of system conversions? Which is the most expensive? Which is the most risky? If your school were going to change its student accounts, registration, and financial aid systems, which method of conversion would you want it to use? Explain why. Visit a campus office that uses one of these systems and find out when and how the current system was implemented. Did the office use the implementation method that you preferred? Why did they use the method they did?

2. Systems Analysis

Work together to research and answer the following questions. Does your school have a computer studies department? Typically these departments are identified as computer science (CS), computer information systems (CIS), or management information systems (MIS). If it does, what is the actual title of the department? Look at a school catalog to see if the department offers any systems analysis courses. What, if any, are the prerequisites for the systems analysis courses? Which courses do you think would best prepare you for studies in systems analysis? Find the name of an instructor and contact him or her to find out what software tools are used in the course. If your institution does not have the necessary resources, then use the Web to locate an institution that does and consult their online catalog. Write a one-page summary of your group's findings.

3. Systems Analyst Careers

Each team member should answer the following questions. As a group, write a collaborative paper that describes your collective answers. Individuals who do systems analysis and design are usually called systems analysts. Check the classified section of a Sunday edition of a local large-city newspaper or do a search at an online career site such as **hotjobs.yahoo.com** to see if there are job openings for systems analysts. List the job qualifications, such as the academic degree desired, required skills, work experience, and so on. What is the salary range for systems analysts? Are these positions with local or out-of-town companies? Are you interested in becoming a systems analyst? Why or why not?

4. Library Systems

As a team, take a tour of the school library. Describe the current process used by your school's library for finding, reading, and checking out a book or periodical. Can this system be improved? What improvements would you suggest? What would be the tangible and intangible benefits of implementing your system changes? Be sure to use key terms from this chapter in your answer. Write a one- or two-page paper that describes your group's findings and that provides a recommendation.

5. Build or Buy

Suppose a company is deciding whether to purchase off-the-shelf software or have programmers write new software. Use this chapter and other resources to determine the advantages and disadvantages of each approach. Write a collaborative paper that clearly describes the issues involved in deciding whether to build or buy.

On the Web

1. System Upgrades

In this exercise, you will examine a large-scale system upgrade. Buffalo State College is in the final stages of implementing a comprehensive upgrade to its student information services. This includes enhancements and integration of services such as admissions, registration, financial aid, and student accounts. Visit the college's Web site at **www.buffalostate.edu** and type the words "Sabre project" into the Search dialog box at the top right of the home page to find the answers to the following questions. What does the acronym SABRE mean? What is the time line for implementation of the SABRE project? What company is much of the design and development for SABRE being outsourced to? Which method of conversion is being used to change from the old system to the new one? During the analysis phase of the SDLC, systems analysts obtain information about system requirements through interviews, surveys, and observations of the system's current uses. Several meetings were held with students, and 21 "Wouldn't it be nice if" registration features were voiced. If you were a student at the college, which five features would you consider to be the most important?

2. PowerBuilder

One of the CASE tools illustrated in this textbook is PowerBuilder. Visit the PowerBuilder Web site at **www.sybase.com/home**. What company created this tool? What is the current version of PowerBuilder? PowerBuilder can be used to develop applications in what environments? As with many software applications, a trial version of PowerBuilder is available. After how many days does the trial version expire? Identify a city, a state, a U.S. government organization, and a college or university that has used PowerBuilder. What are the upgrade and purchase prices for this development tool? PowerBuilder training sessions are conducted nationwide. In days, what is the duration of the shortest training sessions and the longest? Name two non–U.S. cities in which PowerBuilder training is offered.

3. The Waterfall Model

One of the SDLC methods described in this chapter was the waterfall model of development. Some computer professionals believe that the waterfall model is inadequate. You can learn about alternatives to the waterfall model in several articles published in the online version of *Software Development Magazine* at **www.sdmagazine.com**. Use the site's search engine to find articles on the waterfall model. Name one or more alternatives to the waterfall model and identify the one that the articles appear to support the most. Describe in your own terms which alternative method you would prefer to use and why.

4. Using Gantt Charts

Search the Web to locate three software applications that create Gantt charts. Identify the manufacturer, the specific product name, and the cost of each application. Identify the products that offer free trial versions and the length of the trial periods. Based on the product descriptions, do you think you could learn how to use one of these applications? Explain why or why not.

5. The Systems Development Life Cycle

What are the five phases of the systems development life cycle that are listed in the text? What questions are asked during each phase? As mentioned in the text, there are several different versions of the SDLC. Some versions identify more phases than others and use different names for individual phases. Search the Web to find three other versions of the SDLC. For each version, identify the URL, the number of phases, and the title of each phase. Explain why you agree or disagree with the author's statement that the five-part SDLC described in the text represents the common practice.

Using the SDLC to Buy a Computer

FIGURE 13.14 You can use Web sites such as **www.tigerdirect.com** to help you shop for a new computer.

Even if you think that being a systems analyst isn't for you, the SDLC can still be an extremely useful process in the right situation. For example, take buying a new computer. You may find that shopping for a new PC is almost as stressful as shopping for a new car. An overwhelming number of options, retailers, manufacturers, numbers, rebates, and salespeople ("What can I do to put you in this computer today?") await unsuspecting consumers who begrudgingly know that anything they buy today will be outdated tomorrow. To successfully navigate this treacherous landscape and get the right computer at the right price, you're going to need a well-constructed plan, and you can use the SDLC to help guide you!

Step 1: Preliminary Investigation

Ask yourself why you need or want a new computer. The type of machine you should buy is directly related to your needs and budget, so you should be extremely honest with yourself. If you need a computer for schoolwork but are also interested in playing a lot of video games, then you won't be happy with a $500 discount machine. Use resources such as the World Wide Web to investigate Web sites that can help you get organized, such as **www.pcworld.com/howto**, which offers "Expert Buying Guides" for desktops and laptops. Make a list of everything you want to be able to do with your new computer as well as the amount of money you have to spend before moving on to the next step.

Step 2: Analysis

Go through the list you made in step 1 line by line. You're most likely going to find out that your needs and wants will be far greater than your available funds. Identify what you must have today, what can wait until tomorrow, and what you can do without until the next time you purchase a new system. It is at this point that you should ask yourself if you really need to buy an entire new system at one time or if you can phase in the necessary new components over a few months to better distribute the drain on your bank account. If you need to start writing papers and doing research today, you could buy a basic system with a fast processor and add a high-end video card and some additional memory at a later date to play games.

Step 3: Design

Would upgrading your computer solve your immediate needs or do you absolutely have to purchase a new computer? A great way to design your perfect system is to visit the Web site of an online retailer such as **www.dell.com** or **www.gateway.com** and spend some time customizing a variety of computers to see how your needs actually translate into dollars. These Web sites enable you to try different configurations with no obligation to buy. You should also take some time to talk to friends, family, colleagues, and anyone else you trust to help better define what your system or upgrade should cost. Figure 13.14 shows a selection of computers offered by TigerDirect at **www.tigerdirect.com**.

Step 4: Implementation

At this point, you need to go ahead and take the plunge. Purchase your new computer or upgrade, bring it home, and set up and configure it. If you have performed the earlier steps properly, you will hopefully find that your new computer does everything you need, and want, it to do. It's important to spend as much time as possible on your computer in the early days to make sure that it adequately suits your needs. Many stores allow computers to be returned, but only within a very short amount of time. It is important to get all of the information about a retailer's return or exchange policies before making your purchase.

Step 5: Maintenance

To get the most out of your computer over time, it is important that you check the manufacturer's Web site for any upgrades to your system or for any additional components you've installed.

- **Contrast enterprise and personal computing.**

- **Define the term *business process* and briefly describe the flow of business processes within an organization.**

- **Differentiate between centralized and distributed technology management.**

- **Name the tools that are commonly used in enterprise computing.**

- **Describe the various enterprise storage systems.**

- **Explain electronic data interchange and the features that make it popular.**

- **Discuss how enterprises use teleconferencing.**

- **Describe telecommuting and workgroup computing.**

Enterprise Computing

Until now, you've been learning primarily about the various technologies involved in personal computing. **Personal computing** refers to any situation or setup where one person controls and uses a PC for personal or business activities. You've learned about what goes on inside a computer with system and application software as well as the various input/output and storage devices. Along with these basic computing concepts, you've also been introduced to how networks, the Internet, wireless applications, and databases work and are used. Now that you have a solid foundation in the concepts of personal computing, let's turn our attention to computing within an enterprise.

An **enterprise** is simply a business organization or any large computer-using organization, which can include universities and government agencies. **Enterprise computing** is defined as the use of technology, information systems, and computers within an organization or a business. Therefore, enterprise computing refers to the use of computers in networks that span the organization—involving different operating systems, protocols, and network architectures. Enterprise computing includes not just the technology, but also the processes and activities involved in operating a business (Figure 14.1).

In this chapter, you will explore various enterprise computing solutions and learn how technology is used to manage the flow of data and information within an enterprise.

FIGURE 14.1
Enterprise
Computing

Business Processes and Activities

As you learned in Chapter 12, companies use information systems to support business processes for internal operations such as manufacturing, order processing, and human resources management. **Business processes** are activities that have an identifiable output and value to the organization's customers. These activities can be viewed as a series of links in a chain along which information flows within the organization. At each link, value is added in the form of the work performed by people associated with that process, and new, useful information is generated. Information begins to accumulate at the point of entry (for example, a customer sends an order to the company) and flows through the various links, or processes, within the organization. New, useful information is added every step of the way (Figure 14.2).

Information systems can be used to support and/or streamline business activities for a competitive advantage. A **competitive advantage** is a condition that gives an organization a superior position over the companies it competes with. For example, an enterprise might use an information system to support a billing process that reduces the use of paper and, more important, the handling of paper, thus reducing material and labor costs. This same system can help managers keep track of the billing process more effectively because they will have more accurate, up-to-date information about it, enabling them to make smart, timely business decisions.

Information systems can support either internally or externally focused business processes. Internally focused systems support functional areas (such as accounting, finance, human resources, and so on) or activities within the organization. For instance, Visa International's accounting system automatically compares outgoing payments with invoices and sends e-mail requests to managers to review any discrepancies.

Externally focused systems coordinate business activities with customers, suppliers, business partners, and others who operate outside the organization's boundaries. Hilton Hotels has implemented an e-business initiative that facilitates interactions among customers, the Hilton Web site, and Hilton's existing reservation systems. Hilton wants profiles on its customers, their history with the company, and their likes and dislikes to be accessible by their hotel staff anywhere in the world. The system enables the company to use the Web to reach more customers in a cost-effective manner and to develop more personal customer relationships than it could through traditional mailings.

Businesses have used information systems to support business processes for decades, beginning with the installation of applications for specific business tasks such as issuing paychecks. Oftentimes,

Techtalk

E-Business

E-business (electronic business) refers to business conducted over the Internet, including buying, selling, providing customer service and support, and collaborating with business partners. IBM was one of the first major users of the term when it launched its now familiar "e-business" campaign in October 1997.

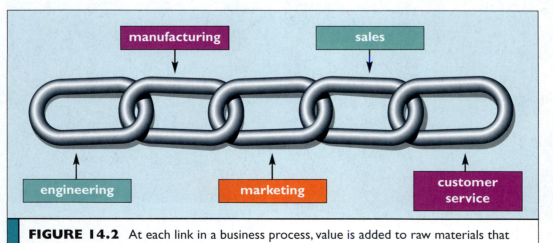

FIGURE 14.2 At each link in a business process, value is added to raw materials that ultimately become finished goods.

Destinations

Want to find
out more? Visit
www.fedex.com/us/
or **www.walmart**
.com for examples
of enterprises
that have estab-
lished a global
electronic presence.

these systems were built on different computing platforms. Each platform often operated in a unique hardware and software environment. Applications running on different computing platforms are difficult to integrate, because custom interfaces are required for one system to communicate with another.

Running different applications on separate computing platforms can create tremendous inefficiencies within organizations if data cannot readily be shared between systems. So how do companies tie together all of these disparate applications and information systems? They do it with enterprise systems.

Enterprise Systems

Enterprise systems are information systems that integrate an organization's information and applications across all of the organization's functional divisions. Rather than storing information in separate places throughout the organization, enterprise systems provide a common central repository and a common user interface to all corporate users. Enterprise systems enable personnel to share information seamlessly no matter where the data are located or who is using the application (Figure 14.3).

To compete in global markets, companies also need to provide quality customer service and develop products faster and more efficiently than their competitors. The emergence of the Internet and the World Wide Web has resulted in the globalization of supplier networks, opening up new opportunities and methods of conducting business. **Globalization** refers to conducting business internationally where the transaction of goods and services is transparent to the consumer (Figure 14.4). This means that a McDonald's in Singapore is almost exactly the same as a McDonald's in Chicago.

Customers have increasing numbers of options available to them, and they are demanding more sophisticated products that are customized to their unique needs. Enterprise systems can help companies find innovative ways to increase accurate and on-time shipments, minimize costs, and ultimately increase customer satisfaction and the overall profitability of the company.

FIGURE 14.3 With enterprise systems, workers share information through a common user interface.

FIGURE 14.4 Globalization creates a near-equal playing field for the enterprise across international borders.

Enterprise systems come in many shapes and sizes, each providing a unique set of features and functionality. Remember that an enterprise system is an information system; therefore, it is composed of data, hardware, software, people, and procedures. It can include network servers, database management systems, workstations, and laptops. When deciding whether to implement enterprise solutions, managers need to consider a number of different issues. One of the most important is selecting and implementing applications that meet the requirements of the business as well as its customers and suppliers. Let's start by examining how enterprise systems are categorized and managed.

CENTRALIZED VERSUS DISTRIBUTED STRUCTURES

The technology infrastructure within an enterprise is managed in one of two ways: It is either centralized or distributed. In a **centralized structure**, technology management is centered in the IT department, and everyone within the organization works with standardized technology solutions in their everyday work. In a **distributed structure**, users are able to customize their technology tools to suit their individual needs and wants (Figure 14.5).

For example, the computer labs at your school are most likely managed in a centralized way. Each time a student begins a work session, the computer operating environment, desktop, and applications are always the same. It doesn't matter which computer in the lab you use—they all look and function the same way. Conversely, your instructor's computer is most likely managed in a distributed way. Some things, such as applications, are the same on all faculty computers, but by and large, your instructor is able to customize the operating environment, desktop, and application configurations to suit his or her individual needs and wants.

Now that you know how information systems can be structured within an enterprise, let's look at how some organizations use business process reengineering to gain a competitive advantage.

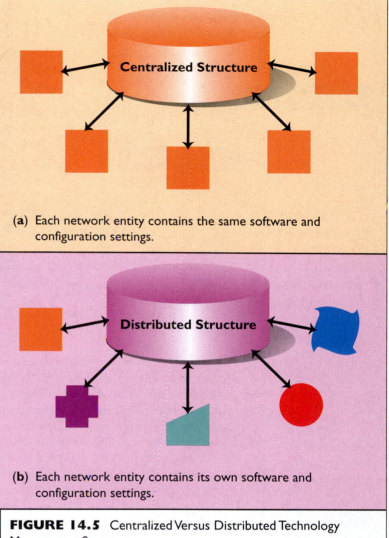

(a) Each network entity contains the same software and configuration settings.

(b) Each network entity contains its own software and configuration settings.

FIGURE 14.5 Centralized Versus Distributed Technology Management Structures

BUSINESS PROCESS REENGINEERING

Business process reengineering (BPR), also known as *reengineering*, refers to the use of information technology to bring about major organizational changes and cost savings. At the core of BPR is the principle that information technology doesn't bring big payoffs if you simply automate existing business processes. The key to big payoffs lies in using information technology to change existing processes.

The structure of a typical organization is shown in Figure 14.6. Each business area has its own information systems and business processes. In BPR, designers ignore an organization's functional divisions and focus instead on business processes.

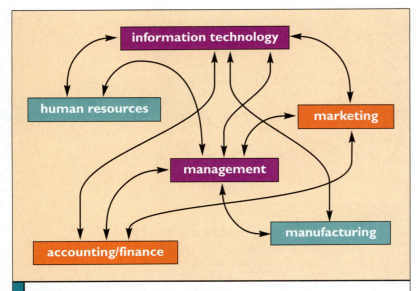

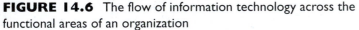

FIGURE 14.6 The flow of information technology across the functional areas of an organization

Destinations

For more information on BPR, visit Prosci's Web site at **www.prosci.com**

For example, product development is a process that often involves many functional divisions, including marketing, engineering, procurement, and finance. In a traditional organization, employees in each functional division would work on the product's development separately, then pass it on to the next division when they've finished with their activities. BPR looks to change this often long, drawn-out, inefficient way of working by restructuring how, where, and when activities are performed.

By using information technology, an organization can be redesigned around business processes rather than functional divisions. After reengineering, cross-functional teams work on a single activity. The members of this cross-functional team complete activities that were formerly separated out among the company's functional units. So in the product development example, marketing, engineering, procurement, and finance would be operating seamlessly as one unit instead of as separate ones.

Reengineering can lead to big payoffs, but a high proportion of early BPR projects failed. Many companies came to see reengineering as a means of downsizing, and employees learned to fear and resist BPR efforts.

Let's now take a look at the practical applications of technology within an enterprise.

APPLYING TECHNOLOGY IN THE ENTERPRISE

In this section, you'll learn about the day-to-day concerns an enterprise encounters as it manages its technology assets. The process is ongoing and active, because technology changes every day. The enterprise must respond by keeping itself current with both its internal and external constituents.

Currency

At any given moment, all of the technology used by an organization is more or less current with the marketplace. One would expect that administrators and end users will have a relatively high level of comfort with the existing technology in the organization because it has been in use for a period of time. However, there is a tension between the current status of the system and the most current technology available. The tradeoff is that implementing the most current technology often means a lower comfort level due to the changes that need to take place.

For instance, let's say that an organization is using Microsoft Office 98, but the current version in the marketplace is Microsoft Office 2003. This would mean that there are five years of tension between the organization's currency and the marketplace's. However, upgrading to Office 2003 will mean that users will have to adapt to the changes that have been made to the software over the five-year time period. Therefore, currency has the benefit of having the latest tools, but it carries the risk of a low comfort level among users.

Upgrading

When an organization decides to upgrade its technology, several things should be considered. First and foremost is the impact on the users. How difficult will it be for the users to adapt to the new application? How much training will they need? What influence will the upgrade have on the organization's business constituents? Is the organization leading with this change or responding to market pressures?

The second consideration is whether hardware upgrades are required. Software applications have minimum hardware requirements, and sometimes hardware must be upgraded when the software is upgraded.

The third consideration is the cost of the upgrade. Not only does the organization need to purchase the requisite number of licenses for the software, but it needs to account for the time necessary to install and customize the software. This is where centralized versus distributed management structures are important. In a centralized structure, upgrading may be relatively easy and less expensive, because all of the computers are managed from one location. In a distributed environment, upgrading might involve sending IT personnel to many different locations to install the upgrade on user-managed machines (Figure 14.7).

Once an upgrade is purchased and installed, users must be trained in how it differs from the preceding version. File compatibility issues also may arise. For example, if external users are not using Office 2003, they may not be able to read files that are generated by software in the Office 2003 suite.

Maintenance

Maintenance is another important consideration in managing technology within an organization. It, too, depends on whether IT structures are centralized or distributed. As with upgrading, maintenance may be easier and less expensive in a centralized environment. With a distributed infrastructure, maintenance and training might require IT personnel to travel to multiple sites for scheduled visits and training sessions.

Scalability

Another important consideration is **scalability**, a hardware or software system's ability to continue functioning effectively as demands and use increase (Figure 14.8). For example, a network is scalable if an organization can easily expand it from a few nodes to hundreds or thousands of nodes. Scalability ensures that an organization's systems won't become obsolete as user needs and demands grow. Scalability does not depend on whether the system is centralized or distributed, although adding nodes to a centralized system is somewhat easier because the software installation is standardized.

Interoperability

As you learned in Chapter 2, **interoperability** is the ability to exchange data with another computer, even if it is a

FIGURE 14.7 When upgrading a distributed system, network personnel may need to visit many locations to install the new software.

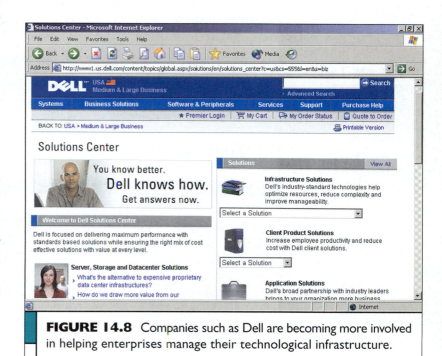

FIGURE 14.8 Companies such as Dell are becoming more involved in helping enterprises manage their technological infrastructure.

different brand or model. Most enterprise systems have computers that run a variety of different platforms. For example, the

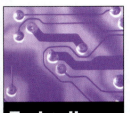

enterprise may use Macs, Windows PCs, UNIX machines, servers, and mainframes. Interoperability enables all of these computers to interact seamlessly on a network. In this case, whether the technology structure is centralized or distributed does not matter, because the network enables any connected computer to operate any remote computer.

Disaster Recovery

Another important application of technology in large enterprises is disaster planning. A **disaster recovery plan** is a written plan with detailed instructions that specifies alternative computing facilities to be used for emergency processing until nonoperational computers can be repaired or replaced.

A distributed technology structure is extremely important in disaster recovery plans. The September 11 attacks forced enterprises not just in New York City, but across the United States, to take a closer look at their backup capabilities—not just *whether* they had a backup system, but also *where* it was located. In fact, many of the companies at the World Trade Center did have backup systems on September 11, but many of these companies relied on

systems in the other tower or at another building in the area affected by the attack.

The idea governing backup systems today is not just to ensure data redundancy, but to ensure that backup data are distributed and stored in geographically dispersed places. Such facilities must be located far from major cities, many of which are seen as potential terrorist targets. Thus, in the aftermath of September 11, many enterprises are moving their backup centers to suburban areas with independent utility and transportation systems. The New York Stock Exchange, for example, is planning to create a backup trading floor in Westchester, New York, to ensure that trading can continue in case of an emergency (Figure 14.9).

Some redundancy centers are used solely in case of an emergency and serve only as storage facilities, complete with their own electrical generators and telecommunications grids. Others are fully functioning business facilities that act as satellite offices while they also duplicate all enterprise data. Because such "mirroring" of data needs to be performed in an organized fashion, professional backup and security companies have experienced increased demands for their services in the wake of September 11.

FIGURE 14.9
Constant, uninterrupted access to critical data is fundamental to an enterprise's viability.

Managing Information Security Across the Enterprise

From natural disasters and threats of terror attacks to computer failures and electronic intrusions, today organizations are concerned not only for the safety of their employees, but also for the security of their mission-critical data and systems. Information security management is a growing field that is increasingly important to even the smallest business, nonprofit organization, or town government.

When planning for possible security problems, some organizations prefer to call in specialists such as Vigilar (Figure 14.10). This company helps management formulate or update comprehensive information security policies and develop detailed procedures for getting or keeping systems up and running if a disaster occurs. Its experts educate managers about potential dangers and help them address issues such as allowing or restricting access to sensitive data, such as customer information; detecting security threats; planning backup systems; defending against viruses and malware; protecting privacy; responding to operational disruptions; and recovering data. Disaster recovery plans often require that data storage and certain systems be housed at an alternate site so that the enterprise can continue to operate even if IT functions are not available.

Technological advances bring many benefits, but they also require organizations to review information security

plans and procedures to avoid potential problems. For example, when The Weather Channel installed a WLAN to cover its eight-story Atlanta headquarters, Vigilar came up with a security design to guard against unauthorized access—from the inside and from the outside. The Weather Channel gives its employees special phones that are able to tap the wireless connection when they are inside the building. The phones are automatically switched to a cellular network when the employees are outside the building. The idea is to allow engineers and other support staff to stay in touch with each other and with management so that they can quickly tackle any information security problems and keep The Weather Channel on the air.

FIGURE 14.10 Vigilar helps management formulate or update comprehensive information security policies.

Adding Workstations and Applications

What do enterprises do when new employees are hired and need a computer to work at? What if they want to implement a new application on a network? Adding a new user's workstation or installing a new application on a network increases the number of locations where problems can occur. One common problem is a single point of failure.

A **single point of failure** (**SPOF**) refers to any system component, such as hardware or software, that causes the entire system to malfunction when it fails.

SPOF problems can be minimized by using a centralized technology management structure because it gives network administrators more control over the software that is installed and managed on the computers throughout the enterprise.

Adding a Network

How can enterprises create networks on the fly, such as connecting devices in a conference or at a meeting? **Zero configuration (Zeroconf)** is a method for networking devices via an Ethernet cable that does not require configuration and administration. Zeroconf is best used in small networking situations where the need for security is low. It also can be used to form a functional network in a home or a small business.

Now that you understand the issues that enterprises must consider when applying technology solutions, let's look at some of the specific software tools that enterprises use.

Tools for Enterprise Computing

Enterprises have many opportunities to apply technology to different situations, whether to improve internal business processes or external interactions with customers and vendors. Software tools help the various areas of the enterprise manage their responsibilities.

FIGURE 14.11 PeopleSoft is a popular provider of enterprise resource planning applications.

ENTERPRISE RESOURCE PLANNING

Enterprise resource planning (ERP) software brings together various enterprise functions, such as manufacturing, sales, marketing, and finance, into a single computer system. Managers implement ERP applications from vendors such as SAP, PeopleSoft, and Baan to support activities in functional areas such as finance and human resources as well as business processes such as order tracking and inventory, accounts payable, accounts receivable, and customer support (Figure 14.11).

Let's take a closer look at the order-tracking process in a typical enterprise. When a customer places an order with the sales division or customer service, the order travels to the various individuals and departments that need to handle it. Errors and delays can be introduced along the way or the order could be misplaced or lost. At any given time, few people in the enterprise can pinpoint the order's status should the customer inquire about it. For example, a salesperson may not have access to the manufacturing department's computer system to see if manufacturing has even begun to fulfill the order.

With ERP software, one software program with separate modules for each functional unit replaces the separate systems that sales and marketing, manufacturing, and other divisions use. The ERP software modules are linked together so that a salesperson can access manufacturing's module to see if an order has been processed. ERP improves the order process, and customers get their orders faster and with fewer errors than before.

Organizations undertake ERP projects to integrate financial, human resources, customer, and order information; to speed up manufacturing processes; and to reduce inventory. So why haven't all organizations implemented ERP systems? Although ERP sounds like an ideal solution, it does have some drawbacks. With ERP, customer service representatives' job duties are no longer confined to merely keying in orders. With ERP, their duties are associated with every department in the organization. They must make decisions and respond to situations that they never had to before, such as whether customers pay on time or if the warehouse can ship orders in a timely manner.

Some ERP projects fail because employees are resistant to change. If an organization simply installs ERP software without requiring employees to change how they do their jobs, it won't experience the benefits of ERP. In fact, it may cause a chain reaction of negative effects. Replacing old software that everyone knows how to use with new software that no one knows how to use can slow business processes, causing delays in production, shipping, and billing. However, when an organization uses ERP to improve its order fulfillment, manufacturing, shipping, and billing processes, it will see value from the software.

Finally, the cost and time involved with ERP implementation sometimes blindsides organizations. A recent Meta Group study looked at the total cost of implementing ERP, including hardware, software, retraining, service, and support costs. The average cost of an ERP project was $15 million. Hidden costs for implementing an ERP system include integration and testing, customization, and data analysis and conversion. ERP vendors often estimate an average implementation time of three to six months. More realistic

time lines usually average between one and three years. According to the Meta Group, companies often don't see any benefits for as long as eight months. However, companies do see as much as $1.6 million in average annual savings from a new ERP system.

Multimillion-dollar ERP projects often fail because the software does not support an organization's most important business processes. When this occurs, organizations can either change business processes to fit the software or change the software to fit the processes. Both of these options have serious disadvantages and the potential to truly cripple an organization.

CUSTOMER RELATIONSHIP MANAGEMENT

Customer relationship management (**CRM**) software keeps track of an organization's interactions with its customers and focuses on retaining those customers. Salespeople can use CRM software to match company resources with customer wants and needs. A recent survey found that it can cost four to seven times more to replace a current customer than it does to keep one (Figure 14.12).

FIGURE 14.12 CRM Daily provides customer relationship management news and information in a magazine-style format.

Due to new advances in technology, companies are changing their approach to customer relationship management. In the twenty-first century, more and more organizations are managing their customer relationships electronically. Today, consumers can access self-service applications and technical support via the Web not only with computers but also with Web-enabled devices such as PDAs and cell phones. Organizations must find ways to personalize customers' online experiences using tools such as help-desk software, e-mail organizers, and Web development applications.

Just as with ERP, an organization must consider its business processes along with its existing IT infrastructure before considering CRM solutions. CRM vendors include FrontRange Solutions, PeopleSoft, SAP, Baan, and eLoyalty (Figure 14.13).

SALES FORCE AUTOMATION

Often used interchangeably with CRM, **sales force automation (SFA)** software automates many of the business processes involved with sales, including processing and tracking orders, managing customers and other contacts, monitoring and controlling inventory, and analyzing sales forecasts (Figure 14.14).

FIGURE 14.13 FrontRange's Goldmine software is a popular customer relationship management solution.

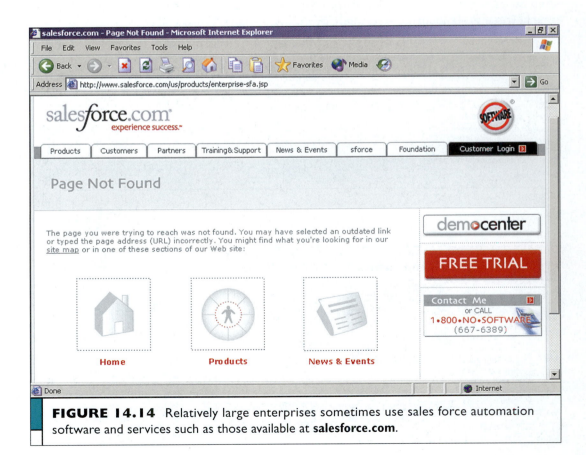

FIGURE 14.14 Relatively large enterprises sometimes use sales force automation software and services such as those available at **salesforce.com**.

EXTENSIBLE BUSINESS REPORTING LANGUAGE

Public and private enterprises use **Extensible Business Reporting Language (XBRL)** to publish and share financial information with each other and industry analysts across all computer platforms and the Internet. XBRL uses standardized formatting to present various types of financial information, including net revenue, annual and quarterly reports, and SEC filings. Current users of XBRL include Morgan Stanley, EDGAR Online, Reuters, and Microsoft. Other early adopters include the UK Inland Revenue and the U.S. Federal Deposit Insurance Corporation (FDIC).

APPLICATION SERVICE PROVIDERS

Whereas an Internet service provider (ISP) provides a point of contact to the Internet, an **application service provider (ASP)** provides software-based services and solutions to companies that want to outsource some or almost all of their information technology needs. ASPs can manage payroll, benefits, business travel and entertainment expenses, Web portals, and a variety of sales- and product-related enterprise applications. ASPs provide their services over a WAN from a centralized data center. An ASP can be a third-party commercial firm that serves many different customers or a nonprofit or government entity that supports its own end users.

Taking ASPs to a slightly higher level, commerce (or e-commerce) service providers (CSPs) help online enterprises buy, sell, and manage their products and services over the Internet. CSPs supply these online businesses with tools and services ranging from online marketing, brand recognition, and building a customer base to Web site development, hosting, and performance monitoring.

OPERATIONAL SUPPORT SYSTEMS

An **operational support system (OSS)** is a suite of programs that supports an enterprise's network operations. OSS originally referred to a system that controlled telephone and computer networks for telecommunications service providers. However, a modern OSS enables any enterprise to monitor, analyze, and manage its network system.

ENTERPRISE APPLICATION INTEGRATION

Enterprise application integration (EAI) is a combination of processes, software, standards, and hardware that results in the integration of two or more enterprise systems. This integration enables multiple systems to operate as one and share data and business processes throughout an organization. In the past, enterprises used custom-built, proprietary software and systems for such functions as inventory control, human resources, sales automation, and database management that ran independently and didn't interact with each other. Enterprises now recognize the need to share information and applications between systems, so many companies are investing in EAI.

Organizations can choose from a range of EAI categories, from database and application linking to data warehousing. When enterprises want all aspects of their computing integrated into one application, it is referred to as a *common virtual system*.

As wonderful as EAI sounds, it is very complex, incorporating every level of the enterprise system: architecture, hardware, software, and processes. EAI vendors include IBM, Microsoft, BEA Systems, and Level 8 Systems. International Data Corporation expects EAI to become the fastest-growing IT sector in the next three to five years.

Now that you are familiar with various enterprise computing software solutions, let's examine storage systems commonly used in an enterprise.

Destinations

For more information on XBRL, visit **www.xbrl.org**

Enterprise Storage Systems

According to a recent estimate, the amount of information an enterprise must store doubles each year. What's more, employees, managers, executives, and customers increasingly expect this information to be

Destinations

For an excellent Web-based tutorial on the different types of RAID, see Advanced Computer & Network Corporation's "RAID Technology" at **www.acnc.com/raid.html**

readily available when and where it's needed—and to be kept safe from prying eyes if it's confidential. At the same time, enterprises are becoming more dependent on computer systems for storing and retrieving vital information. If a storage system fails, it must be possible to bring backup systems online in short order. Not surprisingly, corporate demand for fast, secure, and reliable storage systems is skyrocketing.

New technologies are being developed to meet the unique needs of large organizations. To cope with their information storage needs, many corporations are developing enterprise storage systems. Enterprises invest in enterprise storage systems not necessarily to gain a competitive advantage, but to protect and back up their mission-critical data.

RAID

A group of two or more hard drives that contain the same data is called **RAID** (**redundant array of independent disks**). The key word in this phrase is *redundant*, which means "extra copy." Everything that is recorded on the original drive is instantaneously recorded on the second disk. No matter how many disks a RAID device contains, the computer "thinks" it's dealing with just one disk. All of the disks contain an exact copy of all the data. Should one of the disks fail, service is not interrupted. This helps to ensure against data loss should something happen to the original, or working, drive (Figure 14.15). If the original disk fails, one

of the other disks kicks in and delivers the requested data.

RAID devices offer a high degree of **fault tolerance**; that is, they keep working even if one or more components fail. For this reason, RAID devices are widely used wherever a service interruption could prove costly, hazardous, or inconvenient to customers. Most of the major Web sites use RAID devices to ensure that their Web pages are always available.

RAID is used primarily in medium to large enterprises. Most personal computer users don't need (and couldn't afford) RAID devices. RAID disk drives can be purchased from most computer manufacturers and are installed and maintained by network management personnel. RAID devices run constantly—24 hours a day, 7 days a week, 365 days a year.

CD/DVD JUKEBOXES

Digital content can be one of an enterprise's most valuable assets. But an enterprise loses time and money if employees are constantly searching for, repurchasing, or recreating files. Backup systems should allow for quick and simple access, management, and organization of data. A **CD/DVD jukebox** is an enterprise storage device that offers multiple DVD-ROM and CD-ROM drives to store and give users network access to all of an enterprise's digital content (Figure 14.16).

RAID device

RAID control card

FIGURE 14.15 RAID devices are essential to mission-critical data redundancy and protect against data loss.

FIGURE 14.16 CD/DVD jukeboxes provide centralized backup and storage of files and programs.

What Makes Wal-Mart So Successful?

Try keeping track of 690 million items in 5,000 stores spread across 10 countries. Just think about recording the 20 million daily transactions that over the course of a year add up to $260 billion in sales. Consider that every credit card purchase must be approved—and shoppers won't tolerate waiting more than a second or two. Now you have some idea of the challenge facing Wal-Mart, the largest retailer on the planet. It's not surprising, then, that the secret of Wal-Mart's success is its innovative use of information technology.

Wal-Mart has poured billions of dollars into state-of-the-art systems and, unlike many companies, it does not outsource any of its IT work. As a result, each programmer on the payroll has to be able to write code in at least two (preferably three) computer languages. All of the systems running the company's functional units share the same source code, which is also unusual for such a large enterprise. This uniformity means that an IT change made in one unit can be replicated in every other unit within a few *days*, rather than weeks or months.

Instead of seeing suppliers as adversaries, Wal-Mart views them as partners and allows them access to its database so they can see what's selling and what's not. Wal-Mart trusts suppliers to check merchandise levels and provide re-supply as needed to keep store shelves full. The result? Wal-Mart needs just 36 hours to restock inventory, compared with the industry average of six weeks—and its shoppers usually find what they're looking for. This translates into strong customer loyalty and strong profits.

Wal-Mart's latest IT initiative involves radio frequency identification (RFID) tags. These are tiny electronic markers attached to cartons and pallets that help the retailer track merchandise from the supplier to the warehouse to the storeroom, and finally, to the store shelf (Figure 14.17). Simply knowing exactly how many it has of each item could slash up to $8 billion from Wal-Mart's yearly inventory costs.

However, not everyone is happy with Wal-Mart's success. In some areas, the opening of a new Wal-Mart store spells the end of small, family-run businesses that cannot compete with the chain's pricing. In that respect, Wal-Mart's low prices don't come without costs of their own.

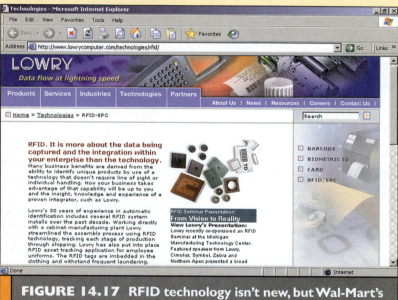

FIGURE 14.17 RFID technology isn't new, but Wal-Mart's mandate that suppliers use RFID tags and the subsequent industry buzz have generated renewed interest in it.

STORAGE AREA NETWORKS

Another type of storage device available to all servers on a LAN or WAN is a **storage area network** (**SAN**). A SAN is a network of high-capacity storage devices that link all of the organization's servers. In this way, any of the storage devices are accessible from any of the servers. In a SAN, servers only provide pathways between end users and stored data, keeping servers available for processing activities. A SAN contains nothing but disks that store data. SANs often make use of network-attached storage.

NETWORK-ATTACHED STORAGE

Network-attached storage (NAS) refers to high-performance devices that offer little more than data and file sharing to clients and other servers on a network. Unlike a file server in a client/server network, which typically handles all processing activities, such as e-mail, authentication, and file management, NAS merely supplies data to users. NAS can be installed anywhere in a LAN, not just within or near a server. When a network uses NAS, more hard disk storage space can be added to the network without shutting down the file servers for upgrading or maintenance. Storage capacities range from 120 GB to as much as 6.7 TB.

We've now examined the software and hardware solutions often employed in enterprise systems. Let's turn our attention to some of the technologies that pull both of these areas together within an enterprise.

Enterprisewide Technologies

Enterprise computing solutions don't exist in a vacuum. If an organization has no overall strategy for implementing CRM, RAID, or any of the other software and hardware solutions previously discussed, there's not much sense in spending hundreds of thousands or millions of dollars to install them. In this section, we will examine many of the enterprisewide technologies being used for competitive advantage.

WEB PORTALS

Web portals (or portals) are Web sites that provide multiple online services. A portal is a jumping off place—a place that provides an organized way to go to other places on the Web. AOL is an example of a Web portal. Even Yahoo! and Google have at least partially turned themselves into Web portals to draw more traffic and dedicated users to their sites (Figure 14.18).

Organizations implement portals for different reasons. Merrill Lynch created an enterprisewide portal to cut expenses and consolidate all of the Web sites and portal sites that had been built throughout the company. To avoid the expense of training its retail associates and partners on how to use many of its standard applications, Guess installed a portal that provides access to Web-based training materials. When Chevron acquired Texaco, merging the various Web applications from both companies would have been time consuming and expensive. Instead, the newly merged Chevron Texaco implemented a portal. Business portals offer centralized knowledge and content management, helping to ensure consistent business processes across different functional units.

ELECTRONIC DATA INTERCHANGE

Electronic data interchange (EDI) is a set of standards that specifies how to transfer data and documents between enterprises using the Internet and other networks. EDI is emerging as a popular way for companies to exchange information and to conduct business transactions (Figure 14.19). For instance, if two companies have compatible systems, they can establish a connection through which purchase orders, shipping notices, and

FIGURE 14.18 Buzzle.com purports to be an "intelligent" jumping off place for adventures on the World Wide Web.

invoices can be sent by EDI—computer to computer. The entire operation occurs without any paper changing hands. EDI can make many business processes more efficient. For example, buyers can use EDI to order parts from suppliers that will be delivered just in time to be used. This capability reduces inventory costs and the time between the buying of the parts and the sale of the finished product.

Telefonica Servicios Avanzados de Informacion (TSAI), a subsidiary of Spain's major supplier of telecommunications services, handles 60 percent of Spain's EDI business. Merchants, suppliers, and others utilize TSAI's services. Whether enterprises link up using traditional dial-up modems and Web browsers or the latest high-speed connections, TSAI's EDI services enable small and large enterprises to send and track orders, invoices, and other business data.

Business-to-business e-commerce enterprises sometimes lease network capacity from a value-added network. A **value-added network** (**VAN**) is a public data network offered by a service provider that an enterprise uses for EDI or other services. Such a network offers end-to-end dedicated lines with guaranteed security. Enterprises can electronically exchange documents and data over a VAN, including shipping orders, tracking requests, and invoices as well as e-mail, management reports, and payments.

But those services come with a hefty per-byte fee for handling an enterprise's data and transactions. What's more, VANs aren't flexible; if a local dial-in doesn't exist, the business can't connect without incurring long-distance charges. Because it is more cost-effective to exchange data over the Internet, VAN providers have had to change their focus, offering additional services such as EDI translation, encryption, and other security measures.

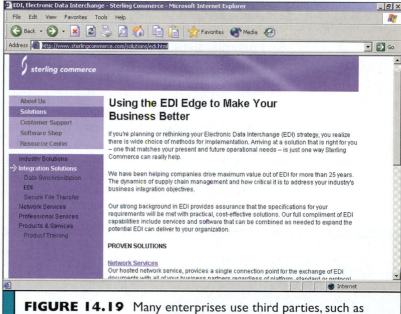

FIGURE 14.19 Many enterprises use third parties, such as Sterling Commerce, to handle their EDI needs.

FIGURE 14.20 Intranets.com offers a customizable intranet solution designed to help businesses collaborate and share information more efficiently.

INTRANETS AND EXTRANETS

Many companies are building internal networks based on TCP/IP protocols called intranets. An **intranet** is a network that belongs to an enterprise and is only accessible by that enterprise's employees or authorized users. Intranets enable users to use the same familiar tools, such as browsers, that they use on the Internet. However, intranets are intended only for internal use and aren't accessible from the external Internet unless the user has a registered user name and password (Figure 14.20).

Intranets are transforming the way organizations produce and share information with employees, vendors, and other select outside partners. Web sites on an intranet are similar to Internet Web sites, except that firewalls protect the enterprise content from unauthorized access. Because it's so easy to create a Web page, companies can distribute Web publishing duties throughout the enterprise. Every department can maintain its own internal Web page, making its resources available to everyone. By moving expensive print-based publications, such as employee manuals and telephone directories, to the intranet, companies can realize enormous

savings and significantly reduce the amount of trash that goes to local landfills.

Some companies allow authorized outsiders, such as research labs, suppliers, or key customers, to access their intranets. Called **extranets**, these networks are connected over the Internet, and data traverse the Internet in encrypted form, safe from prying eyes. Access to an extranet is limited to those provided with valid user names and passwords. These security measures determine the extranet content that outsiders are allowed to view. Extranets have become a viable conduit for sharing information between business partners.

Intranets continue to be one of the fastest-growing enterprise applications in IT. They cost much less to build and maintain than public and private data networks such as VANs and virtual private networks.

VIRTUAL PRIVATE NETWORKS

Enterprises use virtual private networks to connect distributed LANs over the Internet. **Virtual private networks** (**VPNs**) consist of lines that are leased to a single company, thus ensuring excellent security (Figure 14.21). VPNs transport data over the Internet, but offer encryption and additional security measures to ensure that only authorized users have access to the network and its data.

On Command Corporation provides in-room TV services to hotels around the world. The company uses a VPN to provide fast customer service and support. On Command spends the same amount of money on its VPN as on its old dedicated connection, but receives 24 times the bandwidth.

FIGURE 14.21 Blue Ridge Networks is a leading provider of secure virtual private network services.

FIGURE 14.22 Computer-based training can be an effective way to get up to speed on new technology.

COMPUTER-BASED AND WEB-BASED TRAINING

Computer-based training (**CBT**) is a form of computer-based education that uses multimedia, animation, and programmed learning to teach new skills. CBT has typically been used to train people how to use computer applications, because it enables students to learn by actually using the application (Figure 14.22). The tutorials included with many software applications are a form of CBT.

In the past, enterprises didn't like to invest the personnel, time, and money necessary to develop CBT programs to train employees on new applications. However, CBT has become a viable option for enterprises due to the increased speed and power of newer PCs as well as the availability of commercial CBT programs. CBT has an added advantage for enterprises: It is not usually time or place dependent. This means that the training is available whenever an employee has the time to access a computer terminal or workstation.

Web-based training (**WBT**) is basically CBT implemented via the Internet or an intranet. Computers must be equipped with a Web browser to take advantage of traditional Web-based training methods, such as instant messaging, discussion forums, and chat tools, in addition to more advanced applications, such as live Web broadcasts with streaming audio or video and videoconferencing.

Enterprises often use Web-based training to educate employees about a new application, program, or system. WBT is often run by a facilitator or trainer; however, it can also be self-paced and involve only the trainee.

TELECONFERENCING

Teleconferencing is when two or more people, separated by distance, use telecommunications and computer equipment to conduct business activities. Enterprises use teleconferencing to gain a competitive advantage by cutting costs and facilitating enterprisewide communications.

Large enterprises or small office/ home office (SOHO) businesses seeking to employ teleconferencing should consider professional-grade or PC-based teleconferencing systems. Professional-grade teleconferencing requires enterprises to own, purchase, or rent dedicated conferencing equipment or to contract with a company or service provider that offers these services. (Figure 14.23). One type of teleconferencing service is when each caller dials the teleconference number, provides a pass code, and is then connected with the other callers. Teleconferencing isn't limited to just voice communications, however.

FIGURE 14.23 Teleconferencing allows many people in many locations to share the convenience of a common connection.

Teleconferencing services can be used to send data and video as well.

PC-based solutions offer a number of benefits over professional-grade systems, such as lower cost and easier installation and maintenance. Many enterprises find it well worth the time and money to implement PC-based systems. Most companies immediately begin to reap the rewards of lower long-distance phone bills and higher productivity. They also can cut travel budgets because participants don't need to be physically present at meetings. The biggest drawback to the successful implementation of teleconferencing is that the video portion requires lots of bandwidth. Other concerns include poor video quality, real-time transmission delays, lack of access to facilities or equipment, and potential threats to privacy.

techtv™

For more information on video teleconferencing, go to **www.prenhall.com/ cayf2006**

FIGURE 14.24
Enterprises experience numerous benefits by allowing employees to telecommute.

Destinations

To learn more about workflow management, visit the Workflow Management Coalition's home page at **www.wfmc.org**

TELECOMMUTING

Due to the burgeoning home network market, many large and small enterprises are giving their employees the option of telecommuting. **Telecommuting** refers to using telecommunications and computer equipment to work from home while still being connected to the office (Figure 14.24). The home system must be able to connect to the company computer system to communicate with and transfer data to and from other employees.

Two million Americans telecommuted to work in 1990. By 2000, more than 30 million were doing so at least part-time. However, not all jobs lend themselves to telecommuting. Enterprises whose employees must serve or greet the public (bank tellers, waitstaff, office receptionists, and so on) are not candidates for telecommuting.

Studies have shown that enterprises experience various benefits by allowing employees to telecommute, including productivity gains, lower employee turnover, and reduced costs for office space. One major disadvantage of telecommuting is the enterprise's lack of direct supervision over a telecommuting employee's workload.

Telecommuters experience a variety benefits, including no commuting, flexible hours, more family time, and savings on car expenses (gas, tolls, parking, and so on) and work clothes. Disadvantages include the lack of social interaction and the difficulties of keeping the work and home environments separate. Societal benefits from telecommuting include fuel conservation and less air pollution.

A vital technology for enterprises with telecommuters is teleconferencing. Thanks to inexpensive software and Webcams, telecommuters can attend important meetings they may otherwise have missed. Programs such as NetMeeting enable telecommuters to communicate, interact, and share applications with co-workers. CUseeMe and iVisit are Web-based services that provide simultaneous chat and video capabilities for multiple users. To use either of the sites, you must first download and install their software. CUseeMe also offers additional functions, such as file transfer, application sharing, or online whiteboards. The program offered by iVisit does not offer these additional functions, but is significantly less expensive (Figure 14.25).

Telecommuting would be nearly impossible without broadband Internet service. With a high-speed Internet connection, telecommuters can talk with others in real-time or record video messages to attach to e-mails.

FIGURE 14.25 Web-based services such as (**a**) CUseeMe and (**b**) iVisit can provide telecommuters with simultaneous chat and video capabilities.

WORKGROUP COMPUTING

Another technology that enterprises are using for competitive advantage is workgroup computing. **Workgroup computing** occurs when all of the members of a *workgroup*—a collection of individuals working together on a task—have specific hardware, software, and networking equipment that enables them to connect, communicate, and collaborate. **Groupware** is software that provides computerized support for the information needs of these workgroups. Most groupware applications include e-mail, videoconferencing tools, group-scheduling systems, customizable electronic forms, real-time shared applications, and shared information databases.

The first successful groupware product, Lotus Notes, was designed to run on client/ server systems. Newer groupware products, such as Microsoft Exchange and new versions of Lotus Notes, run on intranets and extranets (Figure 14.26). These groupware applications enable collaboration between geographically separated workgroups and even between group members who work for other organizations, such as affiliated research labs.

A groupware application such as Microsoft Exchange can quickly determine the optimum time for a meeting, locate an open room, send a notice asking for the meeting, and then coordinate responses to show who has confirmed that they will be at the meeting. Groupware also facilitates

workflow automation. **Workflow automation** is the process of sending documents and data to the next person who needs to see them. For example, a master document may be shared among a group and then all of the group's comments can be collectively edited by the author of the document. Consider the case of an engineer at a firm who prepares a proposal for an external contract. The proposal goes to the engineer's supervisor for review and approval. The document may need to be seen by several other people before it's finally approved and sent.

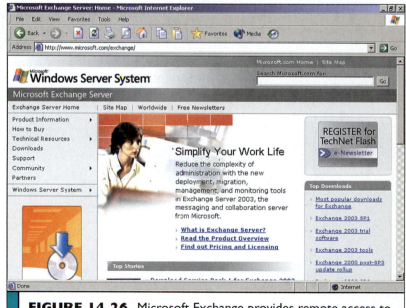

FIGURE 14.26 Microsoft Exchange provides remote access to e-mail and contacts.

What You've Learned

ENTERPRISE COMPUTING

- Enterprise computing is the use of technology, information systems, and computers within an organization or business. Personal computing is the use of technology by an individual for business or personal activities.

- Business processes are activities that have an identifiable output and a value to the organization's customers. These activities can be viewed as a series of links in a chain along which information flows within the organization. At each link, value is added in the form of the work performed by people associated with that process, and new, useful information is generated.

- In a centralized structure, the management of technology is centered in the IT department, and everyone within the organization works with standardized technology solutions in their everyday work. In a distributed structure, users are able to customize their technology tools to suit their individual needs and wants.

- Tools commonly used in enterprise computing include enterprise resource planning (ERP), customer relationship management (CRM), sales force automation (SFA), Extensible Business Reporting Language (XBRL), application service providers (ASPs), operational support systems (OSSs), and enterprise application integration (EAI).

- A group of two or more hard drives that contain the same data is called RAID (redundant array of independent disks). CD/DVD jukeboxes are enterprise storage devices that offer multiple DVD-ROM and CD-ROM drives to store and give users network access to all of an enterprise's digital content. A storage area network (SAN) is a network of storage devices that contain nothing but a disk, or disks, to store data. Network-attached storage (NAS) is a device that offers file sharing to network users.

- Electronic data interchange (EDI) is a set of standards that specifies how to transfer data and documents between enterprises using the Internet and other networks. EDI is emerging as a popular way for companies to exchange information and to conduct business transactions.

- Teleconferencing is the conduct of an organization's business by more than two people, separated by distance, through the use of telecommunications and computer equipment. Enterprises use teleconferencing to gain a competitive advantage by cutting costs and enabling enterprisewide communications.

- Telecommuting is when an employee performs work at home while linked to the office by a telecommunications-equipped computer system. Workgroup computing occurs when all of the members of a workgroup—a collection of individuals working together on a task— have specific hardware, software, and networking equipment that enables them to connect, communicate, and collaborate.

Key Terms and Concepts

Go to **www.prenhall.com/cayf2006** to review this chapter, answer the questions, and complete the exercises.

Matching

Match each key term in the left column with the most accurate definition in the right column.

_____ 1. intranet

_____ 2. centralized

_____ 3. Web portal

_____ 4. interoperability

_____ 5. enterprise

_____ 6. distributed

_____ 7. RAID

_____ 8. storage area network

_____ 9. extranet

_____ 10. application service provider

_____ 11. Zero configuration

_____ 12. scalability

_____ 13. disaster recovery plan

_____ 14. computer-based training

_____ 15. Web-based training

a. structure in which technology is customized to individual needs

b. ability to exchange data with another computer or operating system even if it is a different brand or version

c. a network of storage devices that contain nothing but a disk, or disks, to store data

d. provides software-based services and solutions to companies that want to outsource their information technology needs

e. structure in which technology is standardized

f. a method used to network devices via an Ethernet cable that does not require configuration or administration

g. a group of two or more hard drives that contain the same data

h. instruction or special training in which the student learns by executing programs on a computer

i. a hardware or software system's ability to continue functioning effectively as demands and use increase

j. a Web site that provides online services

k. internal enterprise network based on TCP/IP protocols

l. training and/or instruction implemented via the Internet or an intranet

m. a written plan with detailed instructions that specifies an alternative computing facility to be used for emergency processing until nonoperational computers can be repaired or replaced

n. an intranet that is partially accessible to authorized outsiders

o. any large organization that utilizes computers

Multiple Choice

Circle the correct choice for each of the following.

1. What term describes the use of information technology to bring major organizational changes and cost savings?
   a. Zero configuration (Zeroconf)
   b. business process reengineering (BPR)
   c. redundant array of independent disks (RAID)
   d. electronic data interchange (EDI)

2. What type of software automates sales tasks and is often used interchangeably with CRM?
   a. enterprise application integration (EAI)
   b. scalability
   c. sales force automation (SFA)
   d. storage area network (SAN)

3. Which term describes when one person controls and uses a PC for personal or business activities?
   a. intranet
   b. extranet
   c. interoperability
   d. personal computing

4. What term describes the process of sending documents and data to the next person who needs to see it?
   a. workflow automation
   b. process automation
   c. document automation
   d. data automation

5. Which term describes activities that have an identifiable output and value to customers?
   a. scalability
   b. business processes
   c. personal computing
   d. enterprise computing

6. Which enterprise storage system stores and gives employees access to an enterprise's digital content?
   a. CD/DVD jukebox
   b. intranet
   c. operational support system (OSS)
   d. Web portal

7. Which term describes a collection of individuals working together on a task who use specific hardware, software, and networking equipment to connect, communicate, and collaborate?
   a. personal computing
   b. enterprise computing
   c. enterprise storage system
   d. workgroup computing

8. Which enterprise storage system is dedicated to file sharing but does not provide e-mail, authentication, or file management?
   a. intranet
   b. redundant array of independent disks (RAID)
   c. Extensible Business Reporting Language (XBRL)
   d. network-attached storage (NAS)

9. Which term describes an information system that integrates information and applications across all functional units in an organization?
   a. extranet
   b. electronic data interchange (EDI)
   c. enterprise system
   d. operational support system (OSS)

10. Which enterprise tool is a combination of processes, software, standards, and hardware that results in the integration of two or more enterprise systems?
    a. electronic data interchange (EDI)
    b. enterprise application integration (EAI)
    c. computer-based training (CBT)
    d. application service provider (ASP)

Fill-In

In the blanks provided, write the correct answer for each of the following.

1. _____ refers to conducting business internationally where the transaction of goods and services is transparent to the consumer.

2. A(n) _____ is a network that uses the Internet to connect distributed LANs.

3. A(n) _____ is any system component that upon failure causes a malfunction in the entire system.

4. _____ is a set of standards that enables the transfer of data between enterprises using the Internet and other networks.

5. _____ is an XML-based language used for publishing and sharing an enterprise's financial information across all computer platforms and the Internet.

6. _____ is software that provides computerized support for the information needs of workgroups.

7. A(n) _____ is a condition that gives an organization a superior position over the companies it competes with.

8. _____ is the use of technology, information systems, and computers within an organization or business.

9. _____ is when employees perform work at home while linked to the office by a telecommunications-equipped computer system.

10. _____ software combines various functions in an enterprise, such as manufacturing, sales and marketing, and finance, into a single computer system.

11. A(n) _____ provides software-based services and solutions to companies that want to outsource their information technology needs.

12. _____ is a software application that keeps track of an organization's interactions with its customers and focuses on retaining those customers.

13. RAID devices offer a high degree of _____; that is, they keep working even if one or more components fail.

14. A(n) _____ is a suite of programs that supports an enterprise's network operations.

15. A(n) _____ is a public data network that provides value-added services for companies, including end-to-end dedicated lines with guaranteed security.

Short Answer

1. Describe the advantages of a centralized technology structure to a technology manager.

2. Define groupware. Provide an example of groupware in action.

3. What is an operational support system? How does it function?

4. What is a Web portal? How does it work?

5. Explain the difference between an intranet and an extranet.

6. What is an application service provider? What types of services are provided? How might the use of an ASP help an enterprise?

Go to **www.prenhall.com/cayf2006** to review this chapter, answer the questions, and complete the exercises.

Teamwork

1. Intranets

Each team member should use his or her favorite search engine to learn more about intranets. What does an intranet do for an enterprise? Who manages it? Who uses it? How does it differ from the Internet? Collaborate on a paper that meets your instructor's specifications.

2. Enterprise Storage Systems

Have each team member choose an enterprise storage system and explain how it impacts the enterprise. Be sure to find out the system's costs, location, users, and benefits. Prepare a group presentation that summarizes each of your team's findings.

3. Customer Relationship Management

Each team member is to research customer relationship management. What benefits do customers enjoy? What are some negative effects of CRM on customers' experiences? Are there issues of privacy? Divide your team into two groups to debate the benefits and drawbacks of CRM from the enterprise perspective and from the customer perspective.

4. Teleconferencing

Each team member is to research Internet teleconferencing services. How much do different services charge? Are any of them free? What can you learn about call quality? If you used such a service, would you worry about your privacy? Should you? Why or why not? Develop a group presentation that summarizes your answers.

5. Groupware

Each team member is to interview some of your instructors to determine if they use groupware for scheduling or for participating in collaborative efforts with others. Collaborate on a paper to explain the different ways that instructors use this software.

On the Web

1. Krispy Kreme

To make between 4,000 and 10,000 dozen Krispy Kreme donuts every day, managers must have all of the necessary tools and ingredients to keep the donuts coming. Explore the company's Web site at **www.krispykreme.com** to learn more about this popular enterprise. What is a "Krispy Kreme"? Where were the most recent new store openings? Is there a Krispy Kreme in your area? Check the Franchise Info link on the site and describe briefly what you must do to investigate owning a franchise. In what areas around the globe are franchise opportunities available? Briefly explain how you would use at least three of the technology tools from this chapter in managing such an enterprise.

2. Enterprise Communications Solutions

Verizon offers enterprise solutions along with its home and business products and services. Visit **www22.verizon.com/sitemap** and locate the "Enterprise Solutions" link within the Communications section at the bottom right of the page. What are the various services that Verizon has to offer under Enterprise Solutions? Pick two and describe them. Now go back to the Communications link on the Sitemap page and choose the Business Resources link. Pick one resource to read about. Write a one-page paper that summarizes what you've learned.

3. Enterprise Systems

Use your favorite search engine to search for "enterprise systems." Follow at least three links to see what you can learn about this growing field. What is an enterprise system? How is one managed? What are the benefits of implementing one?

4. Enterprise Technology Careers

Visit **www.monster.com** and type "enterprise technology manager" as your search phrase. What can you learn about a career in enterprise technology management? Where are the jobs? What do they pay? What degrees and certifications are needed?

5. E-Business

Many online companies conduct e-business through digital storefronts. Search the Web for a company that is conducting e-business. What is the company? What is its product? How is the product distributed? Does the company have regular stores as well as a digital presence? How is shipping handled? Would you consider purchasing products from this company? Why or why not?

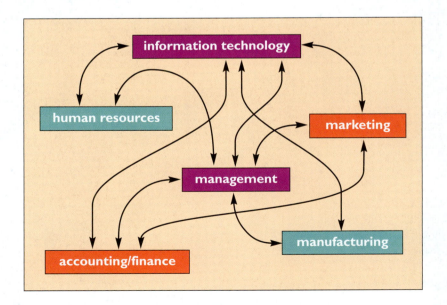

Setting Up a Video Teleconference

Why wait for expensive video phone technology to become available when you can get the same experience from your computer today at no cost? If your computer is running Windows XP and you have a broadband Internet connection, you can explore video teleconferencing technology right now using AOL Instant Messenger (AIM) (Figure 14.27).

1. Download the newest version of the AIM client from **www.aim.com**; the videoconferencing features are fairly new additions to the software.

2. Go to **www.windowsupdate.com** to verify that your version of Windows XP is up-to-date with the most recent security patches and enhancements.

3. Once the necessary software components have been installed, you're going to need a Webcam and a microphone. You can find Webcams for sale at your favorite computer store or online. Many companies sell Webcams for well under $100, and some even include built-in microphones. Popular manufacturers of Webcams include Logitech (**www.logitech.com**) and Creative Labs (**www.creative.com**). Instead of using your computer's speakers to listen to the person you are conferencing with, consider using a pair of headphones to reduce the likelihood of audio problems such as noise and feedback. You can buy headphones with a built-in microphone made specifically for videoconferencing at most computer stores.

4. Once your Webcam and microphone are installed properly, you are ready to start videoconferencing. Open an IM text chat session with the user you would like to establish the videoconference. Once connected, click the "Video" button found at the bottom of the chat window. Both you and your

"buddy" must click through several dialog boxes that warn you about the type of connection you are about to make and ask you to confirm that you really want to do this.

5. The actual videoconference connection can take a few seconds to complete, but if everything is configured properly, you should see your friend appear in a new video window and hear his or her voice in your headphones. If everything works the first time, then congratulations! If something goes wrong, such as no audio, video, or both, don't get frustrated. Videoconferencing requires many different technologies to work in concert, so don't be surprised if things don't work as planned the first few times. If you are continually experiencing problems or would like to learn more about customizing your video sessions, you should visit the AIM Web site as well as explore the AIM client's built-in help. Your Webcam's manufacturer may also have some helpful tips on its Web site.

FIGURE 14.27 You can explore video teleconferencing technology using AOL Instant Messenger (AIM).

SPOTLIGHT

Emerging

Technologies

It's easy to predict the future, the hard part is getting it right, particularly where technology is concerned. Past attempts offer examples of just how difficult it can be to predict technology. For example, in 1876, a Western Union official said, "The telephone has too many shortcomings to be seriously considered as a means of communication. The device is inherently of no value." A century later, the chairman of IBM stated that there was no reason why anyone would want a computer in his or her home.

No one can accurately predict the future of technology. However, you can keep abreast of news and learn to recognize emerging technology trends. This Spotlight looks at the trends driving contemporary computing and the potential impact of artificial intelligence (AI) as computer designers work toward creating a truly intelligent machine.

Tomorrow's Hardware: Smaller, Faster, Cheaper, and Connected

In the early days of computing, room-sized noisy machines read punched cards to perform their calculations. Today, many computers are smaller than the palm of your hand and can accomplish a wide array of tasks. But what will computers be like in the future?

NANOTECHNOLOGY AND BIOCHIPS

What would you say if someone told you that someday various products will be able to manufacture themselves or that computers will work billions of times faster than they do now? And that it will be possible to use computers to end famine and disease or to bring extinct animals and plants back to life? Or that computers will be used to make distant, uninhabitable planets more Earthlike? All of these things and more may one day be possible with nanotechnology (Figure 8A).

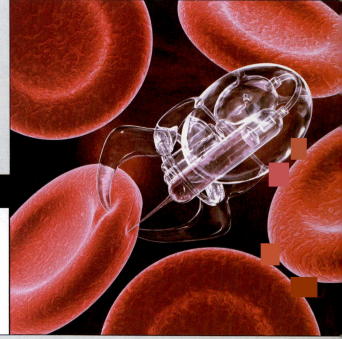

FIGURE 8A

Someday a nanoinjector may travel through your bloodstream, carrying out its mission to cure an illness or enhance your life in some way.

Merriam-Webster's Collegiate Dictionary defines **nanotechnology** as "the art of manipulating materials on an atomic or molecular scale especially to build microscopic devices." Nanotechnology is based on a unit of measure called a nanometer, which is a billionth of a meter. Today, nanotechnologists manipulate atoms and molecules to perform certain limited tasks, but someday, nanotechnology will be used to perform an array of tasks. And because of the small size of atoms and molecules, we'll be able to use them to do things we never before thought possible.

The tie between medical and corporate research in nanotechnology is already strong (Figure 8B). In fact, the first breakthroughs in nanotechnology will probably be in nanomedicine and the use of medical nanorobots. For instance, medical nanorobots may one day be able to destroy fatty deposits in the bloodstream or organize cells to restore artery walls, thereby preventing heart attacks. Nanorobots may also one day improve our immune system by disabling or ridding viruses from our bodies. Someday, doctors may use nanorobots to deliver cancer-treatment drugs to specific areas of the body.

Meanwhile, NASA has funded research to create nanoparticles and nanocapsules. Although this research will be invaluable to medical researchers, NASA hopes to use nanotechnology applications for space travel and for long-term space habitation. One of NASA's concerns is the effect of radiation on astronauts. NASA thinks that nanomedicine could perhaps be used to provide radiation protection to astronauts, to enable the self-diagnosis of disease while in space, and to deliver medication during long space missions, among other things. Nanotechnology may also be able to alter the properties of known materials, making them lighter and stronger for lengthy space flights.

Perhaps the most interesting practical use of nanotechnology is the development of the **biochip** (Figure 8C). Think of a biochip as being similar to a microprocessor, or a computer chip, with one main difference. A computer chip processes millions of computer instructions per second, whereas a biochip processes biological instructions, such as determining the number of genes in a strand of DNA.

Because the silicon-based microprocessors we know today are limited as to how fast and small they can become, researchers are looking at biochips to produce faster computing speeds. Chip makers are hoping that they will be able to integrate DNA into a computer chip to create a so-called DNA computer that will be capable of storing billions of times more data than your personal computer. Scientists are using genetic material to create nanocomputers that may someday take the place of silicon-based computers.

FIGURE 8B

The National Nanotechnology Initiative (NNI) is a U.S. government program that coordinates research and development in nanotechnology.

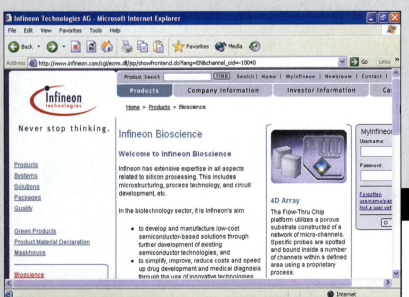

FIGURE 8C

Companies such as Infineon Bioscience are at the forefront of biochip development.

Nanotechnology sounds complex, and it is, but its possibilities and implications are truly endless. In fact, some say that nanotechnology is the most important technological breakthrough since steam power. With corporate and medical research and development on parallel "nanopaths," there may be high demand for nano-technicians in your lifetime.

Besides shrinking components through the use of nanotechnology and biochips, tomorrow's computers are affected by two laws of technology and economics: Moore's Law and Metcalfe's Law.

MOORE'S LAW AND METCALFE'S LAW

Moore's Law, predicted more than 30 years ago by Intel Corporation chairman Gordon Moore, states that microprocessors and other miniature circuits double in circuit density (and therefore in processing power) every 18 to 24 months. If Moore's Law continues until the middle of this century, computers will be 10 billion times more powerful than today's fastest machines. Storage technology shows a similar trend: steep increases in capacity and steep declines in cost.

Metcalfe's Law, predicted by Ethernet inventor Bob Metcalfe, states that the value of a computer network grows in proportion to the square of the number of people connected to it. A telephone line that connects two people is of limited value, but a telephone system that connects an entire city becomes an indispensable resource. Using Metcalfe's Law, a network connecting two people has a value of 4, but a network connecting four people has a value of 16. According to some predictions, the Internet will ultimately connect 1 billion users worldwide.

If you put these two laws together, you get a potent mixture: The computer industry is now giving us *networked* machines that double in power every 18 to 24 months.

As computers become smaller, faster, cheaper, and more interconnected, new technology will encourage the trend toward the digitization of all of the world's information and knowledge—the entire storehouse of accumulated human experience (Figure 8D).

Over the next several years, you'll see both Moore's and Metcalfe's Laws at work. Figure 8E lists the characteristics of a circa 2007 personal computer, based on the assumption that Moore's Law will remain in effect. Compare the computer of tomorrow with the computer of 1999—the difference is astounding.

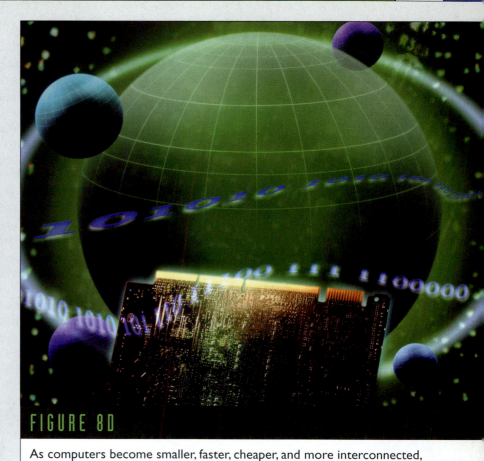

FIGURE 8D

As computers become smaller, faster, cheaper, and more interconnected, new technology will encourage the trend toward the digitization of all of the world's information and knowledge.

FIGURE 8E The Typical Personal Computer: 1999 versus 2007

Component	1999	2007
RAM	64 MB	2 GB
Processor speed (instructions per second)	400 million	14 billion
Circuit density (number of transistors)	7.5 million	250 million
Hard disk capacity	8 GB	270 GB
Average Internet connection speed (bps)	56,000	2 million

Moore's Law predicts that by 2020 all of the components of unbelievably powerful computers will be accommodated on just one tiny mass-produced silicon chip. These chips will hold superfast processors (capable of performing a trillion instructions per second), huge amounts of RAM, video circuitry—the works. And they could cost less than $500!

COMPUTERS EVERYWHERE

In light of these trends toward lower cost and miniaturization, some computer scientists are beginning to speak of ubiquitous computing. (The term *ubiquitous* means "everywhere.") With **ubiquitous computing**, computers are everywhere, even in the background, providing computer-based intelligence all around us. The realms of business, industry, science, and entertainment are employing ubiquitous computing in a number of ways.

Automated Highway Systems

Imagine that you're cruising down the freeway at 120 mph. It's foggy, and the driver of the vehicle in the next lane over has apparently fallen asleep. But you're not concerned. In fact, you're not even watching the road. Instead, you're watching television. Sound crazy? Actually, you're quite safe. You're driving a computer-equipped smart car on the next century's Automated Highway System (AHS), which, according to its proponents, will eliminate 1.2 million crashes per year, save thousands of lives, and save $150 billion in annual economic losses due to car crashes.

As you probably know, today's cars are already equipped with onboard computers that control braking and other systems. With the AHS, information will be passed between vehicles and highways via various devices and sensors that will prevent automobile collisions by electronically controlling an automobile's guidance, brakes, and steering.

According to the U.S. Department of Transportation (USDOT), there were over 43,000 highway deaths in the United States in 2003. In addition, more traffic and congestion on American highways equals lost time and money. In response, the USDOT has launched an Intelligent Transportation Systems (ITS) program to improve traffic flow and safety on America's roads.

The USDOT's ITS program has been around for 20 years. Its initiatives cover all areas of road transportation, including equipping new cars with integrated safety systems, working with state and local transportation organizations to install roadside sensor systems, and developing a national network to share data concerning weather conditions.

But could AHS actually make traffic worse in the long run? AHS is being designed to relieve congestion by moving more vehicles down existing roads in a tight, platoonlike formation. In this sense, AHS is like adding more lanes to a freeway. But adding more freeway lanes solves traffic problems only temporarily. As transportation officials in crowded urban areas have learned to their dismay, if you build more road capacity, more people drive—and they take longer trips. If AHS brings a massive expansion of road capacity, traffic will soon increase to fill this capacity, and we'll be right back to the same problem we have now: too much congestion.

Some futurists foresee a day when you'll be able to ride in an intelligent car on an intelligent highway and enjoy a safe ride with no worries about traffic jams or multi-vehicle pileups (Figure 8F). Although this may not happen for 20 or 30 years, cars and highways will continue to become safer and more efficient due to the power of automated systems.

FIGURE 8F

Singularity Watch offers futurists a free newsletter that discusses changing technologies, including information on automated highway systems.

Digital Forensics

Because computers are everywhere, they are often used to commit crimes. A new science called **digital forensics** has emerged that uses computers to fight cybercrime and computer crime. After a network or other type of attack, investigators use digital forensics tools to determine what occurred, what resources were affected, and who was responsible (Figure 8G).

In fact, digital forensics is such a hot area that a number of colleges and universities offer courses, programs, and degrees in the field. Students who take digital forensics study computer and networking technology, criminal justice, and other related fields.

Biological Feedback Devices

Biological feedback devices translate eye movements, body movements, and even brain waves into computer input. Using **eye-gaze response systems** (also called **vision technology**), quadriplegics can use this technology to control a computer by focusing their eyes on different parts of the screen. A special camera tracks the person's eye movements and moves the cursor in response.

Microsoft researchers are working on vision technology computer programs that enable computers to "see" and respond to a user's physical presence, gestures, and even certain facial expressions. Of course, Microsoft is not the only company working on this technology. Research labs around the world are trying to develop new ways for people to interact with computers that do not rely on standard input devices, such as keyboards.

In fact, vision technology is part of a larger category of research (called *perceptual user interfaces* at Microsoft) that focuses not just on vision technology, but also on speech recognition, gesture recognition, and machines that "learn."

Gesture-recognition research focuses on enabling computers to understand hand movements. As you might imagine, gesture recognition would have an obvious benefit if it could be used with American Sign Language. It will also one day play a large role in making entertainment applications, including games, more entertaining. Many hope that perceptual user interfaces will one day help physically challenged computer users control their computers with facial expressions and eye gazes. Already on the market, VisualMouse translates a user's head motions into mouse movements, allowing users to control a mouse without using their hands.

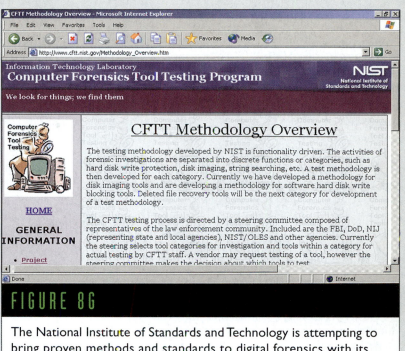

FIGURE 8G

The National Institute of Standards and Technology is attempting to bring proven methods and standards to digital forensics with its Computer Forensics Tool Testing program.

Virtual Reality

Virtual reality (**VR**) refers to immersive, 3D environments that are generated by a computer. With virtual reality, you can actually go in and explore a virtual environment (see Figure 8H).

FIGURE 8H

Where *are* you when you experience virtual reality?

Users can use helmets and sensor-equipped gloves to experience virtual reality programs. The helmet or **head-mounted display** (**HMD**), which is a helmetlike contraption or a pair of goggles, contains two miniature television screens that display the world in what appears to be three dimensions (Figure 8I). In addition to the dual monitors that display three-dimensional images, a head tracker adjusts images when you move your head to the left or right. If you turn your head, your view of the world moves accordingly. Users can use **data gloves** to touch and manipulate simulated objects. You can also use navigation controls to walk around—or fly, if you prefer—in the simulated world. You can physically explore what appears to be a complex virtual environment, even though you're really walking around a big, empty room.

The most advanced (and expensive) immersive technology to date is the **Cave Automatic Virtual Environment** (**CAVE**), which projects stereoscopic images onto walls to give the illusion of a virtual environment. To create the illusion of objects in the virtual environment, users wear special shutter glasses that alternately block the left and right eyes in synchrony with the projection sequence, which similarly alternates between the left and right stereo vision seen from the person's location. The resulting effect is so realistic that users can't tell the difference between real and simulated objects in the room unless they touch them.

On the Web, **Virtual Reality Modeling Language** (**VRML**, pronounced "vir-mal") can be used to create virtual environments online. Programmers can use VRML to define the characteristics of Web-accessible, 3D worlds. To visit a VRML site on the Web, you'll need to equip your Web browser with a VRML plug-in, such as the Microsoft VRML Viewer for Internet Explorer or WorldView (Intervista Software), a VRML plug-in for Netscape Navigator. After installing the plug-in and accessing a VRML "world" (a Web site with a .wrl extension), you can walk or fly through the 3D construct.

What's the point of virtual reality? For consumers, the answer is simple: games. Almost all of the top-selling computer games offer 3D virtual realities. But virtual reality isn't all fun and games. The military uses virtual reality systems to train fighter pilots and combat soldiers. Architects use virtual reality simulations to enable clients to preview and walk through a

FIGURE 8I

Virtual reality refers to immersive, 3D environments that are generated by computers. You can use navigation controls to walk or fly through the simulated world.

design. Surgeons can use virtual reality to learn and practice delicate and dangerous surgical techniques (Figure 8J). Manufacturers use virtual reality to analyze complex, 3D structures to make sure that they have been correctly designed and that they can be manufactured in a cost-effective way.

Wearable virtual reality devices could even affect the lives of maintenance workers. A computer on a belt could easily be connected with a display monitor concealed in an ordinary pair of eyeglasses. As the worker looks at the inside of a piece of equipment, the computer could supply a schematic. The schematic, shown on the inside of the eyeglass lens, could then be positioned over the piece of equipment. This would enable the worker to quickly pinpoint the name, purpose, and condition of each of the item's components.

This blending of virtual reality with the real world, known as **augmented reality**, is not science fiction. It's already being used by some large corporations. Taken to the next level, the schematics shown in the worker's field of vision could be interfaced with motion and position sensors so that when the worker moves his or her head, the schematics projected by the computer change to reflect the workers field of view.

New uses for augmented reality are being discovered all the time. For instance, agents for the U.S. Customs Service are using special wearable computers that utilize voice-recognition software and full-color monitors. When looking for stolen vehicles, the agents can use the computers to recall the license number of any vehicle in the United States as they stroll through parking lots or drive through traffic.

Chemical Detectors

The human nose can detect remarkably minute traces of airborne chemicals. And increasingly, so can computers. If you've visited an airport recently, you may already have been "sniffed" by a computer device designed to detect minute traces of explosives. Some travelers are asked to step into special booths that use air jets to dislodge chemicals from clothes and hands. The air is then sucked through a chemical sensor that can identify many types of explosives. A computer screen displays the results of the test and tells the operator if explosives are detected.

Tactile Displays

You've seen how computers engage our eyes and ears. What about our sense of touch? If researchers in a new field called **haptics** have their way, you'll soon be able to feel with computers as well. (The term *haptics* refers to the sense of touch.) Haptics researchers are developing a variety of technologies, including **tactile displays** that stimulate the skin to generate a sensation of contact. Stimulation techniques include vibration, pressure, and temperature changes. When used in virtual reality

FIGURE 8J

In medicine, surgeons can use virtual reality to learn and practice new techniques.

environments, these technologies enhance the sense of "being there" and physically interacting with displayed virtual objects.

It's unclear when perceptual interfaces will hit computer store shelves. But one thing is clear: Someday it will be possible for people interact with electronic devices using every one of their senses.

What if we put all of these capabilities together to develop a machine endowed with human intelligence, giving it the ability to reason, to converse in natural language (ordinary human speech), and to formulate a plan or strategy? One branch of technology is moving in that direction—artificial intelligence.

Artificial Intelligence: Toward the Smart Machine?

The goal of **artificial intelligence** (AI) is to endow computers with humanlike intelligence. AI specialists have succeeded in creating special-purpose programs that exhibit some aspects of human intelligence, but these programs are still unable to function intelligently outside the context for which they were designed. Computer scientists are sharply divided between optimists who believe that these problems will be overcome and pessimists who believe that the underlying problems are so difficult that they're impossible to solve. So let's start with an easy question—just what *is* intelligence?

Intelligence has many components:

- Learning and retaining knowledge

- Reasoning on the basis of this knowledge

- Adapting to new circumstances

- Planning (developing strategies)

- Communicating

- Recognizing patterns

However, there's no scientific consensus as to what constitutes intelligence. So how do we answer the question of whether a computer is more intelligent than the human brain?

THE COMPUTER VERSUS THE HUMAN BRAIN

How does the human brain compare with a computer? Some speculative estimates are shown in Figure 8K. Compared with computers, the human brain accepts voluminous amounts of input and stores an unbelievable amount of data. In terms of processing, the human brain excels at pattern recognition (for example, recognizing faces and understanding speech), but it's a slow calculator. In contrast, computers accept much smaller amounts of input and do a poor job of recognizing patterns, but they can calculate rapidly and produce output much faster than humans can.

So how can we tell if a computer is intelligent? British computer scientist Alan Turing created the Turing Test to measure artificial intelligence (Figure 8L). During a Turing Test, a person sits at a computer and types questions. The computer is connected to two hidden computers. At one of the hidden computers, a person reads the questions and types responses. The other hidden computer runs a program that also gives answers. If the person typing the questions can't tell the difference between the person's answers and the computer's answers, Turing says that the computer is intelligent.

By Turing's standard, computers have already passed the test of artificial intelligence. In the mid-1960s, Joseph Weizenbaum, a computer scientist at MIT, wrote a simple program called ELIZA. This program mimics a human therapist. If you type, "I'm worried about my girlfriend," the program responds, "Tell me more about your girlfriend." The program is actually very simple. If the user types a word on the program's built-in list, such as girlfriend, father, guilt, or problem, the program copies this word and puts it into the response. Even so, some people were fooled into thinking that they were conversing with a real therapist.

ELIZA doesn't fool many people for long, but today's programs are much larger and more resourceful. Many of these programs have been displayed at the Loebner Prize Competition, an annual competition designed to implement the Turing Test and award the most "human" computer. In 2000 and 2001, Richard Wallace won the prize for his work on ALICE. Short for Artificial Linguistic Internet Computer Entity, ALICE uses artificial intelligence case-based reasoning to formulate replies to comments.

Neural Networks

Neuroscientists know that the brain contains billions of interconnected brain cells called neurons

FIGURE 8K	The Human Brain as a CPU (Speculative Estimates)
Operation	**Estimated Speed or Capacity**
Input	Fast (1 gigabit per second); the human retina can achieve a resolution of approximately 127 million "pixels"
Processing	Fast for pattern recognition (10 billion instructions per second); slow for calculations (2 to 100 per second)
Output	Slow (speech: 100 bits per second)
Storage	Very large (10 terabytes), but retrieval can be uncertain

FIGURE 8L

British computer scientist Alan Turing. According to most psychologists, the Turing Test's type-and-response method is too simplistic.

(Figure 8M). One type of AI involves creating computers that mimic the structure of the human brain. Called **neural networks** (or neural nets), these computers are composed of hundreds of thousands of tiny processors that are interconnected, just like the neurons in the human brain.

Neural nets aren't programmed; they're trained. The neural net learns by trial and error, just as humans do. An incorrect guess weakens a particular pattern of connections; a correct guess reinforces a pattern. After the training is finished, the neural net knows how to do something, such as operate a robot.

Neural nets behave much the way that brains do. In fact, neural nets exhibit electromagnetic waves that are surprisingly similar to human brain waves. None of today's neural nets approach the complexity of even a farm animal's brain, but more complex neural nets are being developed.

Ordinary computers are good at solving problems that require linear thinking, logical rules, and step-by-step instructions. Neural nets are good at recognizing patterns, dealing with complexity, and learning from experience. As a result of these abilities, neural nets are emerging from laboratories and finding their way into commercial applications. Right now, banks are using neural nets to compare a customer's signature made at the bank counter with a stored signature. Neural nets can also be used to monitor aircraft engines and to predict stock market trends.

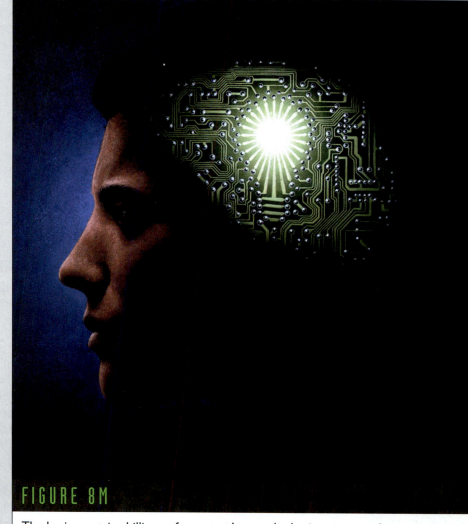

FIGURE 8M

The brain contains billions of neurons. Just as the brain connects these neurons, a neural net connects thousands of computer processing units in multiple ways.

PATTERN RECOGNITION

Imagine a computer that can see beyond the digitized image that it's recording. Computers equipped with digital cameras and **pattern-recognition software** can process digital images and draw connections between the patterns they perceive and patterns stored in a database. Pattern-recognizing computers are already used for security. For example, a new type of video surveillance camera can detect shoppers with suspicious patterns of movement and alert security personnel. Pattern-recognition software is also playing an important role in data mining, discovering previously unnoticed trends in massive amounts of transaction data.

INTELLIGENT AGENTS

You may not realize it, but you already have a helper inside your computer, one that can converse with you, understand your needs, and offer assistance. These helpers, called **intelligent agents**, can monitor conversations in newsgroups and recommend items of interest, locate human experts who can solve specific problems, help you negotiate the best price for a purchase, or scout ahead for Web pages based on your interests.

If you use Microsoft Office software, then you're probably familiar with an intelligent agent: the Office Assistant. The Office Assistant appears when a Microsoft Office program determines that you're performing a certain type of action. The Office Assistant is linked to

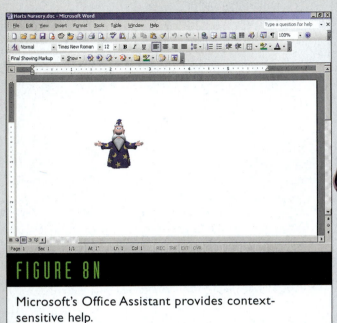

FIGURE 8N

Microsoft's Office Assistant provides context-sensitive help.

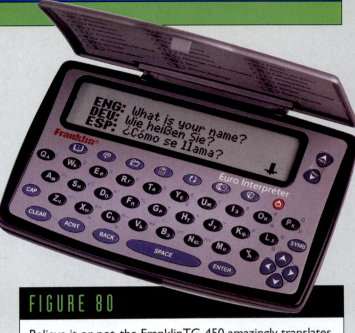

FIGURE 8O

Believe it or not, the Franklin TG-450 amazingly translates over 400,000 words and phrases in 12 languages!

Office's Help feature, so the Office Assistant can suggest formatting options and shortcuts or help you find topics in the Help library (Figure 8N).

TRANSLATION TECHNOLOGY

In the 1960s, experts confidently predicted that **machine translation**—the use of computers to translate foreign language text automatically—could be achieved quite easily. However, many problems emerged, including how to resolve ambiguity. For example, compare the word pen in the following two sentences: "My pen is in my pocket" and "Charlie is doing 25 to life in the pen." After many years of work, automatic translation software is coming closer to the dream of machine translation. The software is fast—one program can translate 300,000 words per hour—but the results can be riddled with errors. Still, the results are good enough to provide a working draft to human translators; some systems make only three to five errors for every 100 words translated.

Today, Computer Aided Translation (CAT) software can be used to translate text from one language to another. CAT technology is being used in international business to stand in when a human translator is not available. Even professional translators can use CAT tools to improve their skills.

Three major categories of CAT tools are currently available: terminology managers to handle basic word translations, automatic or machine translation (MT) tools to provide computer-aided translations, and machine-assisted human translation (MAHT) to aid professional translators. In addition to these programs, portable handheld translation devices, some as small as a credit card, help international travelers translate conversations from English to French, German, or Italian (Figure 8O). As more sophisticated translation technology emerges, someday people may be able to use CAT tools to communicate with anyone using any language.

GENETIC ALGORITHMS

Intelligence is a product of evolution through natural selection. So why not try to create artificial intelligence by creating laboratory conditions in which the most intelligent programs survive? That's the object of research on **genetic algorithms**, defined as automated program development environments in which various approaches compete to solve a problem.

According to evolutionary theory, an organism's goal is to survive and reproduce. Occasional errors in the genetic code introduce mutations, which lead to changes. Sometimes these changes are advantageous and give the organism a better chance of surviving and reproducing. Organisms with an advantageous genetic code dominate because they have more opportunities to reproduce.

Genetic algorithm research mimics nature by imitating this competition for survival. For example, researchers place a number of algorithms into a computer environment and allow them to mutate in random ways. All of the algorithms compete to try to solve a problem. Over time, one algorithm emerges as the best at tackling the problem. Where's the AI connection here? AI requires the creation of algorithms that can mimic the behavior of intelligent beings, and genetic algorithm techniques offer a new way to discover these algorithms.

STRONG AI

Although these piecemeal advances in artificial intelligence are transforming the computers and software we use every day, the decades-old dream of creating a truly intelligent computer seems as far away as ever. What's been achieved so far is a semblance of intelligence within only highly restricted areas of knowledge, such as routing parts through a factory or making airline reservations. Is the dream of true machine intelligence still alive? Proponents of **strong AI**, an area of research based on the conviction that computers will achieve an intelligence equal to that of humans, believe that it is, and that the achievement of true artificial intelligence is only decades away.

What is needed to achieve true artificial intelligence? Everyone agrees that an intelligent computer would need a high proportion of the knowledge that people carry around in their heads every day, such as the fact that Philadelphia is a city on the East Coast, and that East Coast cities can be unbearably hot in the summer. You use this type of knowledge constantly. If someone tells you, "My friend went to work in Philadelphia for the summer," you can respond, "She must not mind the heat!" But there's considerable disagreement about how this knowledge can be provided to a computer. Should humans provide such knowledge or should computers learn it on their own? One AI project, Cyc, illustrates the first approach to knowledge acquisition.

CYC

In Austin, Texas, computer scientist Douglas B. Lenat and the Cycorp company are programming a computer called Cyc (pronounced "sike," from encyclopedia) with basic facts about the world that everyone knows, such as "mountain climbing is dangerous" and "birds have feathers." The goal is to create a computer that knows as much as a 12-year-old. The challenge is that 12-year-olds know a great deal. Lenat's staff has spent more than 20 years feeding basic knowledge into Cyc—the computer now stores over 1.4 million rules and 200,000 terms—and they're still many years away from achieving their goal. Eventual goals for Cyc are to provide text and speech understanding, translation, expert systems, training simulations, games, and online advice. It will also be capable of integrating databases and spreadsheets, providing an encyclopedia, and answering questions as well as searching for documents and photos (Figure 8P).

Cyc's designers say that someday the computer will be able to learn on its own, reading material from the Internet and asking questions when it can't understand something. Already, companies are using Cyc in various capacities, and the U.S. military has invested millions of dollars in Cyc in hopes of using the computer as a military intelligence tool.

Cog and Kismet

MIT professor Rodney A. Brooks takes a different approach to computer learning, one that is based on the natural world. For example, in the natural world, intelligence evolved as organisms needed information to survive and reproduce. The path to artificial intelligence, Brooks argues, lies in creating robots that have minimal preprogrammed knowledge. The robots will then gather information on their own using massive sensory input (sight, hearing, and touch) and have artificially programmed "desires." For Brooks, intelligence isn't reasoning, but rather a set of behaviors acquired as organisms interact with their environment.

To make his point, Brooks and his students have constructed a series of impressive insectlike robots that have learned how to crawl across fields strewn with boulders (and even steal soda cans from students' desks). Their projects are Cog, a humanoid robot that has a torso, a head, and two arms, and Kismet, a "sociable humanoid robot" that can elicit emotional responses and is able to learn from and interact with humans. The big-eyed robot uses algorithms based on what we know about child development to react in a human way. According to MIT's research team, Kismet can perceive a variety of social cues from its "parent"

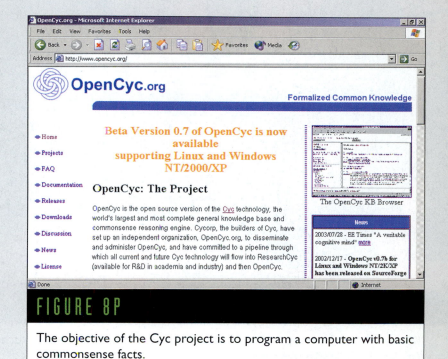

FIGURE 8P

The objective of the Cyc project is to program a computer with basic commonsense facts.

through its eyes and ears and can then deliver feedback through its facial expression, posture, and "voice."

ROBOTS

Late at night, Dottie cleans the floors in a Richmond, Virginia, office building. The work is dull and repetitive, but she doesn't mind. She's never late to work, doesn't call in sick, and doesn't even receive a salary. Dottie is a robot, created by CyberClean, a company that's going after a $50 billion industrial cleaning market. A **robot** is a computer-based device programmed to perform motions that can accomplish useful tasks. But can robots function safely? Using video sensors, Dottie observes simple rules to avoid doing any damage, such as stopping and waiting if somebody walks in front of her. When her work is finished, she returns to her charging station.

Dottie and robots like her are at the cutting edge of **robotics**, a division of the computer science field that is devoted to improving the performance and capabilities of robots. Robots are taking the place of humans in industry in many ways. In 2001, IBM conducted an experiment in which robots participated in simulated trading of commodities such as pork bellies and gold. By using specially designed algorithms, the robots performed the same tasks as human commodity brokers—and made 7 percent more money than their human counterparts!

As early as 1997, the annual market for industrial robots passed the $1 billion mark. Increasingly, robots are performing tasks such as assembly, welding, material handling, and material transport (Figure 8Q).

According to a recent estimate, more than 1 million industrial robots are in use, with more than half of them in Japan. Once found only in scientific labs, today robots paint cars for auto manufacturers, help surgeons conduct surgery, and make trips to outer space. Rock-steady surgical robots are saving lives where natural hand tremors in human surgeons could lead to fatal consequences. Robots are also exploring hazardous environments, such as the radioactive ruins of the Chernobyl Unit 4 nuclear power plant.

Robots are entering our homes, too. Can't have a pet in your dorm room? How about AIBO, the doglike "Entertainment Robot" from Sony (Figure 8R)? According to Sony, AIBO has "the five instincts of love, curiosity, movement, hunger, and sleep" as well as the "emotions of happiness, sadness, anger, surprise, fear, and dislike." How can you tell what AIBO is "feeling"? According to Sony, AIBO conveys its "feelings" through melodies, body language, and lights in its eyes and on its tail. You can even train AIBO to do tricks. Best of all, AIBO doesn't need to be house-trained!

Even more humanlike is the Japanese-made PaPeRo (short for **Pa**rtner-type **Pe**rsonal **Ro**bot) (Figure 8R). PaPeRo's colorful, rounded canister shape may not look huggable at first, but when treated with kindness, it's irresistible. PaPeRo can welcome you home after a long day, and when you're away, it wanders around looking for human companionship. If it doesn't find any, it takes a nap. PaPeRo even has the ability to recognize voice patterns; if these patterns are unfriendly, it runs away.

So where's the all-in-one personal robot that will someday mow the lawn, clean the house, and shampoo the carpets? Most experts agree that such personal robots are a decade or so away. These robots are just too expensive for consumers right now, but that will change as technology advances and market demand grows.

Researchers are also working on a robot that changes its shape to accomplish a specific task. The

FIGURE 8Q

Increasingly, robots are performing tasks such as assembly, welding, material handling, and material transport.

FIGURE 8A

Robots such as AIBO and PaPeRo are at the cutting edge of the robotics field. PaPeRo can interact with people, detect a person's presence, and even sense a person's mood and respond accordingly.

shape-changing robot has pieces that are moved around by a computer-managed algorithm. Such shape-changing robots will one day walk, crawl, carry tools, and fit into tight spaces that humans cannot.

The Future of Emerging Technology

What will the computers of the future be like? We know that they'll be fast and will have tremendous storage capacity. We are at the very beginning of an age: the Information Age. The one distinguishing feature about this age is that we know we're in it. Just think of what might have happened if people had known that they were at the beginning of the Industrial Revolution and could envision the fantastic advances to come. Think what they could have accomplished had they only known what was to happen!

Today, we know we are at the dawn of a new age. So *think*. Think about the new possibilities *every day*. Computers are your future, and they'll provide you with the means for a successful and satisfying life. Enjoy the ride!

SPOTLIGHT EXERCISES

1. Because of the enormous growth in the amount of available information, intelligent software agents have been developed to help users gather and analyze information. Visit Agentland's Web site at **www.agentland.com** to learn about this type of software. Interact with Cybelle. Find and download any of the agents that interest you. Spend at least 30 minutes exploring the site. Write a one-page paper that highlights your experience.

2. See what you can learn about automated highway systems. Begin your search at **www.itsa.org/subject.nsf/vLookupAboutITSA/What+is+ITS!OpenDocument**. Be sure to report on each of the three intelligent transportation systems areas described (ATIS, ATMA, IMS). Type "Automated Highway Systems" into your favorite search engine and browse other links that you may find. Write a short report based on your findings.

3. Investigators are using digital forensics to fight computer crime and cybercrime. Type "digital forensics" into your favorite search engine and browse at least three of the links provided. Write a one-page paper that describes what you've learned.

4. Virtual reality is a hot topic. Search the Web to learn more about virtual reality games. Is any special hardware needed? Describe your recommendations for computer components that would provide an optimum gaming experience (monitor size, video memory requirements, processor speed, and so on). Write a one-page paper that describes a virtual reality game and the ideal computer system for playing it.

5. Go to **www.ai.mit.edu/projects/humanoid-robotics-group** to learn more about robotics. Choose one of the robot names from the robot tree on the Web site. Write a one-page report that describes what the robot is meant to accomplish and your thoughts about its practical potential.

Acronym Finder

NOTE: SEE GLOSSARY FOR DEFINITIONS

3GL See third-generation language.

4GL See fourth-generation language.

ADSL See Asymmetric Digital Subscriber Line.

AGP See Accelerated Graphics Port.

AI See artificial intelligence.

ALU See arithmetic-logic unit.

ASCII See American Standard Code for Information Interchange.

ASP See application service provider.

AUP See acceptable use policy.

BIOS See basic input/output system.

BLOB See binary large object.

BMP See Windows Bitmap.

BPR See business process reengineering.

bps See bits per second.

CASE See computer-aided software engineering.

cat-5 See category 5.

CAVE See Cave Automated Virtual Environment.

CBT See computer-based training.

CD-R See compact disc-recordable.

CD-ROM See compact disc read-only memory or CD-ROM drive.

CD-RW See compact disc-rewritable.

CIS See computer information system.

CMOS See complementary metal-oxide semiconductor.

COM See Component Object Model.

CORBA See Common Object Request Broker Architecture.

CPU See central processing unit.

CRM See customer relationship management.

CRT See cathode ray tube.

CS See computer science.

CTS See carpal tunnel syndrome.

DBS See Direct Broadcast Satellite.

DNS See domain name system.

DoS See denial of service attack.

DRAM See dynamic random access memory.

DSL See Digital Subscriber Line.

DSS See decision support system.

DVD See digital video disc.

DVD-RAM See digital video disc-RAM.

DVD-ROM See digital video disc-ROM.

EAI See enterprise application integration.

EDI See electronic data interchange.

EE See electrical engineering.

EIS See executive information system.

ERD See entity-relationship diagram.

ESS See executive support system.

FAT See file allocation table.

FED See field emission display.

GIF See Graphics Interchange Format.

GPL See General Public License.

GPS See Global Positioning System.

GUI See graphical user interface.

HMD See head-mounted display.

HTML See Hypertext Markup Language.

HTTP See Hypertext Transfer Protocol.

IC See integrated circuit.

IM See instant messaging.

IP See Internet Protocol.

IS See information systems.

ISDN See Integrated Services Digital Network.

ISP See Internet service provider.

IT See information technology.

ITS See Intelligent Transportation System.

ITU See International Telecommunications Union.

JAD See joint application development.

JPEG See Joint Photographic Experts Group.

K See kilobyte.

KB See kilobyte.

L2 See level 2.

LAN See local area network.

LCD See liquid crystal display.

M See megabyte.

MB See megabyte.

MICR See magnetic-ink character recognition.

MIDI See Musical Instrument Digital Interface.

MIS See management information system.

MP3 See MPEG Audio Layer 3.

MPEG See Moving Picture Experts Group.

MUD See multiuser dungeon.

NAS See network attached storage.

NC See network computer.

NIC See network interface card.

NOS See network operating system.

OCR See optical character recognition.

OLAP See online analytical processing.

OMR See optical mark reader.

OO See object-oriented.

OOP See object-oriented programming.

OS See operating system.

OSS See operational support system.

PC See personal computer.

PCI See Peripheral Component Interconnect.

PCS See Personal Communication Service.

PDA See personal digital assistant.

PDL See page description language.

PDLC See program development life cycle.

PIM See personal information manager.

PNG See Portable Network Graphics.

PnP See Plug and Play.

PoP See point of presence.

POS See point-of-sale.

POTS See Plain Old Telephone Service.

PSTN See public switched telephone network.

RAD See rapid application development.

RAID See redundant array of independent disks.

RAM See random access memory.

RDBMS See relational database management system.

RFP See request for proposal.

RFQ See request for quotation.

ROI See return on investment.

ROM See read-only memory.

SCSI See Small Computer System Interface.

SDLC See systems development life cycle.

SDRAM See synchronous DRAM.

SET See secure electronic transfer.

SFA See sales force automation.

SOHO See small office/home office.

SONET See Synchronous Optical Network.

SPOF See single point of failure.

SQL See Structured Query Language.

SVGA See Super Video Graphics Array.

TCP See Transmission Control Protocol.

TLD See top-level domain.

TPS See transaction processing system.

UPC See universal product code.

UPS See uninterruptible power supply.

URL See uniform resource locator.

USB See universal serial bus.

VAN See value-added network.

VAR See value-added reseller.

VB See Visual Basic.

VPN See virtual private network.

VR See virtual reality.

W3C See World Wide Web Consortium.

WAN See wide area network.

WBT See Web-based training.

WLAN See wireless LAN.

WWW See World Wide Web.

XBRL See Extensible Business Reporting Language.

XML See Extensible Markup Language.

Glossary

DEFINITIONS

@ In an e-mail address, a symbol used to separate the user name from the name of the computer on which the user's mailbox is stored (for example, frodo@bagend.org). Pronounced "at."

10baseT An Ethernet local area network capable of transmitting 10 megabits of data per second through twisted-pair cabling.

100baseT See Fast Ethernet.

1394 port See FireWire port.

.NET passport A free service Microsoft introduced as part of its .NET strategy in which users create a .NET Passport profile that stores an e-mail address and a password as well as allowing the option to choose whether profile information will automatically be shared with participating Web sites to provide personalized services.

A

Accelerated Graphics Port (AGP) A port specification developed by Intel Corporation to support high-speed, high-resolution graphics, including 3D graphics.

acceptable use policy (AUP) An Internet service provider (ISP) policy that indicates which types of uses are permissible.

acceptance testing In information systems development, the examination of programs by users. See also application testing.

access point See network access point.

access speed The amount of time that lapses between a request for information from memory and the delivery of the information. Also called access time.

access time See access speed.

account On a multiuser computer system, a user information profile that includes the user's name, password, and home directory location. Unlike a profile on a consumer-oriented operating system, an account provides basic security features that prevent users from accessing or overwriting each others' files.

active monitoring In online banking, a security measure in which a security team constantly monitors the system that holds account information for the telltale signs of unauthorized access.

ActiveX control A small program that can be downloaded from a Web page and used to add functionality to a Web browser. ActiveX controls require Microsoft Windows and Microsoft Internet Explorer and are usually written in Visual Basic (VB).

Ada A programming language that incorporates modular programming principles, named after Augusta Ada Byron.

adapter 1. A circuit board that plugs into an expansion slot in a computer, giving the computer additional capabilities. Synonymous with card. Popular adapters for personal computers include video adapters that produce video output, memory expansion boards, internal modems, and sound boards. 2. A transformer that enables a computer or peripheral to work with line voltage that differs from its electrical requirements.

Add or Remove Programs An icon in a computer operating system's control panel that allows for proper installation and uninstallation of programs.

ADSL (Asymmetric Digital Subscriber Line) A type of Digital Subscriber Line (DSL) service for Internet access. ADSL enables download speeds of up to 1.5 Mbps.

adware A type of Internet spyware created by advertising agencies to collect information about computer users' Internet habits.

algorithm A mathematical or logical procedure for solving a problem.

all-in-one computer A system unit that contains all of the computer's components, including input components and the display.

alphabetic check Ensures that only alphabetical data (the letters of the alphabet) are entered into a field.

analog signal A signal sent via continuous waves that vary in strength and quality, such as those that phones and phone lines send and receive. See digital signal.

anonymity On the Internet, the ability to post a message or visit Web sites without divulging one's identity. Anonymity is much more difficult to obtain than most Internet users realize.

anonymous FTP An Internet service that enables you to contact a distant computer system to which you have no access rights, log on to its public directories, and transfer files from that computer to your own.

antivirus software A utility that checks for and removes computer viruses from memory and disks.

applet 1. A small- to medium-sized computer program that provides a specific function, such as emulating a calculator. 2. In Java, a mini-program embedded in a Web document that, when downloaded, is executed by the browser. Both leading browsers (Netscape Communicator and Microsoft Internet Explorer) can execute Java applets.

application service provider (ASP) A third-party commercial firm, nonprofit, or government entity that provides software-based services and solutions to companies that want to outsource some or almost all of their information technology needs.

application software Programs that enable you to do something useful with the computer, such as writing or accounting (as opposed to utilities, which are programs that help you maintain the computer).

application testing In information systems development, the examination of programs individually, and then further examination of the programs as they function together.

application window The area on-screen that encloses and displays a launched application.

application workspace The area within an application window that displays the document.

archive A file that contains two or more files that have been stored together for convenient archiving or network transmission.

argument set In spreadsheet programs such as Microsoft Excel, the part of a mathematical function that contains its passable parameters or variables.

arithmetic-logic unit (ALU) The portion of the central processing unit (CPU) that makes all the decisions for the microprocessor, based on the mathematical computations and logic functions that it performs.

arithmetic operations One of the two groups of operations performed by the arithmetic-logic unit (ALU). The arithmetic operations are addition, subtraction, multiplication, and division.

arrow keys See cursor-movement keys.

artificial intelligence (AI) A computer science field that tries to improve computers by endowing them with some of the characteristics associated with human intelligence, such as the capability to understand natural language and to reason under conditions of uncertainty.

artificial system A collection of components constructed by people and organized into a functioning whole to accomplish a goal.

ASCII (American Standard Code for Information Interchange) A standard computer character set consisting of 96 uppercase and lowercase letters along with 32 nonprinting control characters. Developed in 1963, ASCII was the first computer industry standard.

assembler A program that transforms source code in assembly language into machine language readable by a computer.

assembly language A low-level programming language in which each program statement corresponds to an instruction that the microprocessor can carry out.

authentication In computer security, a method of preventing unauthorized users from accessing a computer system, usually by requesting a password.

automation The replacement of human workers by machines.

autosave A software feature that backs up open documents at a user-specified interval.

auxiliary storage See storage.

B

back door A secret decoding mechanism that enables investigators to decrypt messages without first having to obtain a private key.

backbone In a wide area network (WAN), such as the Internet, a high-speed, high-capacity medium that transfers data over hundreds or thousands of miles. A variety of physical media are used for backbone services, including microwave relay, satellites, and dedicated telephone lines.

background application In a multitasking operating system, any inactive application. Compare with foreground application.

backside cache See secondary cache.

backup software A program that copies data from a secondary storage device (most commonly a hard disk) to a backup medium, such as a tape cartridge.

bad sector In magnetic storage media such as hard drives, a sector of the disk's surface that is physically damaged to the point that it can no longer store data safely.

bandwidth The amount of data that can be transmitted through a given communications channel, such as a computer network.

banner ad On the World Wide Web, a paid advertisement—often rectangular in shape, like a banner—that contains a hyperlink to the advertiser's page.

bar code reader An input device that scans bar codes and, with special software, converts the bar code into readable data.

BASIC Acronym for Beginner's All-Purpose Symbolic Instruction Code. An easy-to-use high-level programming language developed in 1964 for instruction.

basic input/output system (BIOS) Read-only memory (ROM) built into the computer's memory that contains the instructions needed to start the computer and work with input and output devices.

batch processing A mode of computer operation in which program instructions are executed one after the other without user intervention. Batch processing uses computer resources efficiently but is less convenient than interactive processing, in which you see the results of your commands on-screen so that you can correct errors and make necessary adjustments before completing the operation.

baud rate The maximum number of changes that can occur per second in the electrical state of a communications circuit. An early modem's data transfer rate may have been given in baud, but a modem's data transfer rate is now correctly measured in bits per second (bps).

beta version In software testing, a preliminary version of a program that is widely distributed before commercial release to users who test the program by operating it under realistic conditions.

binary digit See bit.

binary numbers A number system with a base (radix) of 2, unlike the number systems most of us use, which have bases of 10 (decimal numbers), 12 (feet and inches), and 60 (time). Binary numbers are preferred for computers for precision and economy. Building an electronic circuit that can detect the difference between two states (high current and low current, or 0 and 1) is easy and inexpensive; building a circuit that detects the difference among 10 states (0 through 9) is much more difficult and expensive. The word *bit* derives from the phrase binary digit.

biological feedback device A device that translates eye movements, body movements, and brain waves into computer input.

biometric authentication A method of authentication that requires a biological scan of some sort, such as a retinal scan or voice recognition.

bit Short for binary digit, the basic unit of information in a binary numbering system.

bit-mapped graphics Images formed by a pattern of tiny dots, each of which corresponds to a pixel on the computer's display. Also called raster graphics.

bits per second (bps) a measurement of data transmission speed. In personal computing, bps rates frequently are used to measure the performance of modems and serial ports.

BLOB (binary large object) In databases, a data type for very large objects, such as an entire spreadsheet file or a picture file, that may be several megabytes or more in size.

blue screen of death A feared error message with a blue background that appears when Microsoft Windows NT has encountered an error condition; typically resolved only by system rebooting.

Bluetooth A trademarked personal area network (PAN) technology, conceived by cell phone giant Ericsson and named after a 10th-century Viking, that allows computers, mobile phones, printers, and other devices within a certain range of each other to communicate automatically and wirelessly.

Boolean search A database or Web search that uses the logical operators AND, OR, and NOT to specify the logical relationship between search concepts.

boot To start the computer. See cold boot and warm boot.

booting The process of loading the operating system to memory.

boot disk See emergency disk.

boot sector virus A computer virus that copies itself to the beginning of a hard drive, where it is automatically executed when the computer is turned on.

bots Miniprograms capable of carrying out a variety of functions on the Internet, such as greeting newcomers to Internet chat groups.

branch control structure See selection control structure.

branch prediction A technique used by advanced CPUs to prevent a pipeline stall. The processor tries to predict what is likely to happen.

broadband Refers to any transmission medium that transports high volumes of data at high speeds, typically greater than 1 Mbps.

broken link On the World Wide Web, a hyperlink that refers to a resource (such as a sound or a Web page) that has been moved or deleted. Synonymous with dead link.

browser See Web browser.

bubble-jet printer See inkjet printer.

bug A programming error that causes a program or a computer system to perform erratically, produce incorrect results, or crash. The term *bug* was coined when a real insect was discovered to have fouled up one of the circuits of the first electronic digital computer, the ENIAC. A hardware problem is called a glitch.

build-or-buy decision In the development of information systems, the choice of building a new system within the organization or purchasing it from an outside vendor.

bus See data bus.

bus topology The physical layout of a local area network that does not use a central or host computer. Instead, each node manages part of the network, and information is transmitted directly from one computer to another.

business process reengineering (BPR) The use of information technology to bring about major changes and cost savings in an organization's structure. Also called reengineering.

business processes Activities that have an identifiable output and value to the organization's customers.

business skills Skills such as teamwork, project management skills, communication skills, and business savvy.

business-to-business (B2B) e-commerce A type of e-commerce where one business provides another business with the materials and supplies it needs to conduct its operations.

byte Eight bits grouped to represent a character (a letter, a number, or a symbol).

C

C A high-level programming language developed by Bell Labs in the 1970s. C combines the virtues of high-level programming with the efficiency of assembly language but is somewhat difficult to learn.

C++ A flexible high-level programming language derived from C that supports object-oriented programming but does not require programmers to adhere to the object-oriented model.

cable modem A device that enables a computer to access the Internet by means of a cable TV connection. Some cable modems enable downloading only; you need an analog (POTS) phone line and an analog modem to upload data. The best cable modems enable two-way communications through the cable TV system and do not require a phone line. Cable modems enable Internet access speeds of up to 1.5 Mbps, although most users typically experience slower speeds due to network congestion.

cache memory A small unit of ultra-fast memory used to store recently accessed or frequently accessed data, increasing a computer system's overall performance.

call center A computer-based telephone routing system that automatically connects credit card authorization systems to authorization services.

callback system A method of network control that serves as a deterrent to system sabotage by verifying the user ID, password, and telephone number of the individual trying to access the system.

carpal tunnel syndrome (CTS) A painful swelling of the tendons and the sheaths around them in the wrist due to injury caused by motions repeated thousands of times daily (such as mouse movements or keystrokes).

case control structure In structured programming, a logical construction of programming commands that contains a set of possible conditions and instructions that are executed if those conditions are true.

category 5 (cat-5) A type of twisted-pair cable used for high-performance digital telephone and computer network wiring.

cathode ray tube (CRT) A vacuum tube that uses an electron gun to emit a beam of electrons that illuminates phosphorus on-screen as the beam sweeps across the screen repeatedly.

Cave Automated Virtual Environment (CAVE) A virtual reality environment that replaces headsets with 3D glasses and uses the walls, ceiling, and floor to display projected three-dimensional images.

CD/DVD Jukebox An enterprise storage device that offers multiple DVD-ROM and CD-ROM drives to store and give users network access to all of an enterprise's digital content.

CD-R Compact disc-recordable storage media that cannot be erased or written over once data has been saved; they're relatively inexpensive.

CD-R drives Compact disc-recordable devices that can read standard CD-ROM discs and write data to CD-R discs.

CD-ROM See compact disc read-only memory.

CD-ROM drive A read-only disk drive that reads data encoded on compact discs and transfers this data to a computer.

CD-RW Compact disc-rewritable storage media that allows data that has been saved to be erased or written over.

CD-RW drive A compact disc-rewritable drive that provides full read/write capabilities using erasable CD-RWs.

cell 1. In a spreadsheet, a rectangle formed by the intersection of a row and a column in which you enter information in the form of text (a label) or numbers (a value). 2. In telecommunications, a limited geographical area in which a signal can be broadcast.

cell site In a cellular telephone network, an area in which a transmitting station repeats the system's broadcast signals so that the signal remains strong even though the user may move from one cell site to another.

cellular telephone A radio-based telephone system that provides widespread coverage through the use of repeating transmitters placed in zones (called cells). The zones are close enough so that signal strength is maintained throughout the calling area.

centralized structure When technology management is centered in the IT department, and everyone within the organization works with standardized technology solutions in their everyday work.

central processing unit (CPU) The computer's processing and control circuitry, including the arithmetic-logic unit (ALU) and the control unit.

certification An endorsement of professional competence that is awarded on successful completion of a rigorous test.

channel In Internet Relay Chat (IRC), a chat group in which as many as several dozen people carry on a text-based conversation on a specific topic.

character Any letter, number, punctuation mark, or symbol produced on-screen by the press of a key or a key combination.

character code An algorithm used to translate between the numerical language of the computer and characters readable by humans.

check-screening system A computer system used in point-of-sale (POS) terminals that reads a check's account number and accesses a database of delinquent accounts.

chip An integrated circuit (IC) that can emulate thousands or millions of transistors.

chipset A collection of supporting components that are all designed to work together smoothly on a computer motherboard.

ciphertext The result of applying an encryption key to a message.

circuit switching A type of telecommunications network in which high-speed electronic switches create a direct connection between two communicating devices. The telephone system is a circuit-switching network.

citing sources Providing enough information about the source of information you are using so that an interested or critical reader can locate this source without difficulty.

class In object-oriented (OO) programming, a category of objects that performs a certain function. The class defines the properties of an object, including definitions of the object's variables and the procedures that need to be followed to get the object to do something.

click-and-mortar In electronic commerce, a retail strategy in which a Web retail site is paired with a chain of local retail stores. Customers prefer this strategy because they can return or exchange unwanted goods more easily.

clickstream The trail of links left behind to reach a particular Web site.

client 1. In a client/server network, a program that runs on users' computers and enables them to access a certain type of data. 2. On a computer network, a program capable of contacting the server and obtaining needed information.

client/server A method of organizing software use on a computer network that divides programs into servers (programs that make information available) and clients (programs that enable users to access a certain type of data).

client/server computing A software application design framework for computer networks in which software services are divided into two parts, a client part and a server part.

client/server network A computer network in which some computers are dedicated to function as servers, making information available to client programs running on users' computers.

Clip Organizer In Microsoft Office, a repository of clip art and images that can be inserted into a document or presentation.

clipboard See Office clipboard.

Clipper Chip A microprocessor that could encrypt voice or data communications in such a way that investigators could still intercept and decode the messages.

clock speed The speed of the internal clock of a microprocessor that sets the pace at which operations proceed in the computer's internal processing circuitry.

cluster On a magnetic disk, a storage unit that consists of two or more sectors.

CMOS (complementary metal-oxide semiconductor) A special type of nonvolatile memory used to store essential startup configuration options.

coaxial cable A high-bandwidth connecting cable in which an insulated wire runs through the middle of the cable.

COBOL (Common Business-Oriented Language) An early, high-level programming language for business applications.

code The written computer instructions that programmers create.

code of conduct A set of ethical principles developed by a professional association, such as the Association for Computing Machinery (ACM).

codec Short for compression/decompression standard. A standard for compressing and decompressing video information to reduce the size of digitized multimedia files. Popular codecs include MPEG (an acronym for Motion Picture Experts Group), Apple's QuickTime, and Microsoft's AVI.

cold boot A system start that involves powering up the computer. Compare with warm boot.

collision In local area networks (LANs), a garbled transmission that results when two or more workstations transmit to the same network cable at exactly the same time. Networks have means of preventing collisions.

command A user-initiated instruction that tells a program which task to perform.

command-line user interface In an operating system, a variety of user interface that requires users to type commands one line at a time.

commercial software Copyrighted software that must be paid for before it can be used.

Common Object Request Broker Architecture (CORBA) In object-oriented (OO) programming, a leading standard that defines how objects can communicate with each other across a network.

communications The high-speed movement of data within and between computers.

communications channel (also referred to as links) In communications, the path through which messages are passed from one location to the next.

communications device Any hardware device that is capable of moving data into or out of the computer.

compact disc read-only memory (CD-ROM) A standard for storing read-only computer data on optical compact discs (CDs), which can be read by CD-ROM drives.

compact disc-recordable (CD-R) A "write-once" optical storage. Once you've recorded on the disc, you can't erase the stored data or write over the disc again. You can play the recorded CD on most CD-ROM drives.

compact disc-rewritable (CD-RW) A read/ write optical storage technology that uses a CD-R drive to record data on CD-RW discs. You can erase the recorded data and write new data as you please. Most CD-ROM drives can read the recorded data. CD-RW drives can also write to CD-R discs, but you can write to CD-R discs only once.

CompactFlash A popular flash memory storage device that can store up to 128 MB of digital camera images.

compatible The capability to function with or substitute for a given make and model of computer, device, or program.

compatible computers Computer systems capable of using the same programs and peripherals.

competitive advantage A condition that gives an organization a superior position over the companies it competes with.

compiler A program that translates source code in a third-generation programming language into machine code readable by a computer.

completeness check Determines whether a required field has been left empty. If so, the database prompts the user to fill in the needed data.

Component Object Model (COM) In object-oriented (OO) programming, a standard developed by Microsoft Corporation that is used to define how objects communicate with each other over networks.

computer A machine that can physically represent data, process this data by following a set of instructions, store the results of the processing, and display the results so that people can use them.

computer crimes Actions that violate state or federal laws.

computer ethics A new branch of philosophy dealing with computing-related moral dilemmas.

computer information system (CIS) A computer system in which all components are designed to work together.

computer network See network.

computer science (CS) A scientific discipline that focuses on the theoretical aspects of improving computers and computer software.

computer security risk Any event, action, or situation—intentional or not—that could lead to the loss or destruction of computer systems or the data they contain.

computer system A collection of related computer components that have all been designed to work smoothly together.

computer virus A program, designed as a prank or as sabotage, that replicates itself by attaching to other programs and carrying out unwanted and sometimes dangerous operations.

computer-aided software engineering (CASE) Software that provides tools to help with every phase of systems development and enables developers to create data flow diagrams, data dictionary entries, and structure charts.

computer-based training (CBT) The use of computer-assisted instruction (CAI) programs to educate adults.

conditional control structure See selection control structure.

congestion In a packet switching network, a performance interruption that occurs when a segment of the network experiences overload.

connectivity The ability to link various media and devices, thereby enhancing communication and improving access to information.

connector A component that enables users or technicians to connect a cable securely to the computer's case. A male connector contains pins or plugs that fit into the corresponding female connector.

consistency check Examines the data entered into two different fields to determine whether an error has been made.

contention In a computer network, a problem that arises when two or more computers try to access the network at the same time. Contention can result in collisions, which can destroy data.

contention management In a computer network, the use of one of several techniques for managing contention and preventing collisions.

control module In a program design tool called a structure chart, the top module or box that oversees the transfer of control to the other modules.

control structure In structured programming, a logical element that governs program instruction execution.

control unit A component of the central processing unit (CPU) that obtains program instructions and sends signals to carry out those instructions.

convergence The coming together of information technologies (computer, consumer electronics, telecommunications) and gadgets (PC, TV, telephone), leading to a culmination of the digital revolution in which all types of digital information (voice, video, data) will travel over the same network.

cookie A text file that is deposited on a Web user's computer system, without the user's knowledge or consent, that may contain identifying information. This information is used for a variety of purposes, such as retaining the user's preferences or compiling information about the user's Web browsing behavior.

cooling fan A part of the system unit that prevents components from being damaged by heat.

copy-protected software Computer programs that include some type of measure to prevent users from making unauthorized copies.

copyright infringement The act of using material from a copyrighted source without getting permission to do so.

copyright protection scheme A method used by software manufacturers to ensure that users cannot produce unauthorized copies of copyrighted software.

corporate espionage The unauthorized access of corporate information, usually to the benefit of one of the corporation's competitors.

cost/benefit analysis An examination of the losses and gains, both tangible and intangible, related to a project.

cracker A computer user obsessed with gaining entry into highly secure computer systems.

crash An abnormal termination of program execution.

cross-platform programming language A programming language that can create programs capable of running on many different types of computers.

cumulative trauma disorder (CTD) An injury involving damage to sensitive nerve tissue. See carpal tunnel syndrome.

cursor A flashing bar, an underline character, or a box that indicates where keystrokes will appear when typed. Also called insertion point.

cursor-movement keys A set of keys on the keyboard that move the location of the cursor on the screen. The numeric keypad can also move the cursor when in the appropriate mode. Also called arrow keys.

customer relationship management (CRM) Enterprise software that keeps track of an organization's interactions with its customers and focuses on retaining those customers.

custom software Application software designed for a company by a professional programmer or programming team. Custom software is usually very expensive.

cybercrime Crime carried out by means of the Internet.

cybergang A group of computer users obsessed with gaining entry into highly secure computer systems.

cyberlaw A new legal field designed to track developments in cybercrime.

cyberstalking A form of harassment in which an individual is repeatedly subjected to unwanted electronic mail or advances in chat rooms.

D

data The raw material of computing: unorganized information represented for computer processing.

data bus A high-speed freeway of parallel connections that enables the CPU to communicate at high speeds with memory.

data dependency A microprocessor performance problem in which a CPU is slowed in its functioning by the need to wait for the results of instructions before moving on to process the next ones.

data dictionary In information systems development, a collection of definitions of all data types that may be input into the system, including field name, data types, and validation settings.

data diddling A computer crime in which data is modified to conceal theft or embezzlement.

data file A named unit of information storage that contains data rather than program instructions.

data flow diagram A graphical representation of the flow of data through an information system.

data glove A device that translates hand and arm movements into computer input.

data independence In a database, the storage of data in such a way that it is not locked into use by a particular application.

data integrity In a database, the validity of the stored data; specifically, its freedom from error due to improper data entry, hardware malfunctions, or transmission errors.

data maintenance Includes procedures for adding, updating, and deleting records for the purpose of keeping a database in optimal shape.

data mart A large database that contains all the data used by one of the divisions of an organization.

data mining The analysis of data stored in data warehouses to search for previously unknown patterns.

data redundancy In a database, a design error in which the same data appears more than once, creating opportunities for discrepant data entry and increasing the chance that the data will be processed incorrectly.

data security Ensuring that the data stored in a database isn't accessible to people who might misuse it, particularly when the collected data are sensitive.

data transfer rate 1. In secondary storage devices, the maximum number of bits per second that can be sent from the hard disk to the computer. The rate is determined by the drive interface. 2. The speed, expressed in bits per second (bps), at which a modem can transfer, or is transferring, data over a telephone line.

data type In a database or spreadsheet program, a particular type of information, such as a date, a time, or a name.

data validation In a database, a method of increasing the validity of data by defining acceptable input ranges for each field in the record.

data warehouse A very large database, containing as many as a trillion data records, that stores all of a firm's data and makes this data available for exploratory analysis (called data mining).

database A collection of information stored in an organized way.

database management system (DBMS) An application that enables users to create databases that contain links from several files. Database management systems are usually more expensive than file management programs.

database program An application that stores data so that needed information can be quickly located, organized, and displayed.

database server software In a client/server database system, software that runs on a LAN and responds to remote users' requests for information.

dead link See broken link.

debugging In programming, the process of finding and correcting errors, or bugs, in the source code of a computer program.

decision support system (DSS) A program that helps management analyze data to make decisions on semistructured problems.

default In a computer program, a fallback setting or configuration value that is used unless the user specifically chooses a different one.

default value The setting in a database field that is automatically selected unless another value is provided.

deliverable In the development of an information system, the outcome of a particular phase of the systems development life cycle (SDLC).

denial of service (DoS) attack A form of network vandalism that attempts to make a service unavailable to other users, generally by flooding the service with meaningless data. Also called syn flooding.

desktop The portion of the graphical user interface (GUI) that appears after the operating system finishes loading into memory.

desktop computer A personal computer designed for an individual's use. Desktop computers are increasingly used to gain access to the resources of computer networks.

device driver A program file that contains specific information needed by the operating system so that a specific brand or model of device will function.

dialog box In a graphical user interface (GUI), an on-screen message box used to request information from the user.

digital camera A camera that records an image by means of a digital imaging system, such as a charged-coupled device (CCD), and stores the image in memory or on a disk.

digital cash system A method for using smart cards and prepaid amounts of electronically stored money to pay for small charges such as parking and tolls.

digital certificate A form of digital ID used to obtain access to a computer system or prove one's identity while shopping on the Web. Certificates are issued by independent, third-party organizations called certificate authorities (CA).

digital divide The racial and/or income disparity in computer ownership and Internet access.

digital light processing (DLP) projector A computer projection device that employs millions of microscopic mirrors, embedded in a microchip, to produce a brilliant, sharp image.

digital modem See ISDN adapter.

digital signal A signal sent via discontinuous pulses, in which the presence or absence of electronic pulses represents 1s and 0s, such as computers send and receive. See analog signal.

digital signatures A technique used to guarantee that a message has not been tampered with.

digital telephony Telephone systems using all-digital protocols and transmission, offering the advantage over analog telephony of noise-free transmission and high-quality audio.

digital video camera Camera that uses digital rather than analog technologies to store recorded video images.

digital video disc (DVD) The newest optical disc format, DVD is capable of storing an entire digitized movie. DVD discs are designed to work with DVD video players and televisions.

digital video disc-RAM (DVD-RAM) A digital video disc (DVD) format that enables users to record up to 2.6 GB of data.

digital video disc-ROM (DVD-ROM) A digital optical disc format capable of storing up to 17 GB on a single disc, enough for a feature-length movie. DVD is designed to be used with a video player and a television. DVD discs can be read also by DVD-ROM drives.

digitization The transformation of data such as voice, text, graphics, audio, and video into digital form, thereby allowing various technologies to transmit computer data through telephone lines, cables, or air and space.

Direct Broadcast Satellite (DBS) A consumer satellite technology that offers cable channels and one-way Internet access. To use DBS for an Internet connection, a modem and phone line are required to upload data.

direct conversion In the development of an information system, the termination of the current system and the immediate institution of the new system throughout the whole organization.

disaster recovery plan A written plan, with detailed instructions, specifying an alternative computing facility to use for emergency processing until a destroyed computer can be replaced.

discrete speech recognition A speech recognition technology that is able to recognize human speech only when the speaker pauses between words.

disintermediation The process of removing an intermediary, such as a car salesperson, by providing a customer with direct access to rich information and warehouse-size selection and stock.

disc A portable storage optical media, such as CD-ROM.

disk A portable storage magnetic media, such as floppy disks, that provides personal computer users with convenient, near-online storage.

disk cache A small amount of memory (up to 512 KB), usually built into the electronics of a disk drive, used to store frequently accessed data. Disk caches can significantly improve the performance of a disk drive.

disk cleanup utility A utility program that removes unneeded temporary files.

disk defragmentation A program used to read all the files on a disk and rewrite them so that files are all stored in a contiguous manner. This process almost always improves disk performance by some degree.

disk drive A secondary storage mechanism that stores and retrieves information on a disk by using a read/write head. Disk drives are random-access devices.

disk scanning program A utility program that can detect and resolve a variety of physical and logical problems related to file storage.

diskette See disk.

distributed hypermedia system A network-based content development system in which individuals connected to the network can each make a small contribution by developing content related to their area of expertise. The Web is a distributed hypermedia system.

distributed structure When technology management is decentralized and users are able to customize their technology tools to suit their individual needs and wants.

document A file created with an application program, such as a word processing or spreadsheet program.

documentation In information systems development, the recording of all information pertinent to the development of an information system, usually in a project notebook.

domain In a computer network, a group of computers that are administered as a unit. Network administrators are responsible for all the computers in their domains. On the Internet, this term refers to all the computers that are collectively addressable within one of the four parts of an IP address. For example, the first part of an IP address specifies the number of a computer network. All the computers within this network are part of the same domain.

domain name On the Internet, a readable computer address (such as www.microsoft.com) that identifies the location of a computer on the network.

domain name registration On the Internet, a process by which individuals and companies can obtain a domain name (such as www.c34.org) and link this name to a specific Internet address (IP address).

Domain Name System (DNS) The conceptual system, standards, and names that make up the hierarchical organization of the Internet into named domains.

dot-com The universe of Internet sites, especially those doing electronic commerce, with the suffix com appended to their names.

dot pitch On a monitor, the space (measured in millimeters) between each physical dot on the screen.

dot-matrix printer An impact printer that forms text and graphic images by hammering the ends of pins against a ribbon in a pattern (matrix) of dots. Dot-matrix printers produce near–letter quality printouts.

double data rate (DDR) SDRAM A type of SDRAM that can both send and receive data within a single clock cycle.

download To transfer a file from another computer to your computer by means of a modem and a telephone line. See upload.

downsizing In corporate management, a cost-reduction strategy involving layoffs to make a firm leaner and more competitive. Downsizing often accompanies technology-driven restructuring that theoretically enables fewer employees to do the same or more work.

drawing program An application program used to create, edit, and display vector graphics.

drill-down A technique used by managers to view information in a data warehouse. By drilling down to lower levels of the database, the manager can focus on sales regions, offices, and then individual salespeople, and view summaries at each level.

drive activity light A light on the front panel of most computers that signals when the hard disk is accessing data.

drive bay A receptacle or opening into which you can install a floppy drive, a CD-ROM or DVD-ROM drive, or a removable drive.

driver A utility program that is needed to make a peripheral device function correctly.

DSL (Digital Subscriber Line) A general term for several technologies that enable high-speed Internet access through twisted-pair telephone lines. Also called xDSL. See ADSL (Asymmetric Digital Subscriber Line).

DSL modem Similar to a traditional telephone modem in that it modulates and demodulates analog and digital signals for transmission over communications channels, but does so using signaling methods based on broadband technology for much higher transfer speeds.

dumpster diving A technique used to gain unauthorized access to computer systems by retrieving user IDs and passwords from an organization's trash.

DVD-R Digital video disc-recordable optical storage media that, like CD-R discs, cannot be erased or written over once data has been saved.

DVD-RAM See digital video disc-RAM.

DVD-ROM Optical storage media that can hold up to 17 GB of data.

DVD-ROM drive A read-only disk drive that reads the data encoded on DVD-ROM discs and transfers this data to a computer.

DVD+R A recordable optical storage media that enables the disc to be written to one time and read many times.

DVD+RW discs Digital video disc-read/write optical storage media that allow you to write, erase, and read from the disc many times.

DVD-RW Optical storage media on which you can write, erase, and read from the disc many times.

dynamic random access memory (DRAM) A random access memory chip that must be refreshed periodically; otherwise, the data in the memory will be lost.

E

e-book A book that has been digitized and distributed by means of a digital storage medium.

e-book reader A book-sized device that displays an e-book.

e-commerce See electronic commerce.

ECMA Script (Java Script) A scripting language for Web publishing, developed by Netscape Communications, that enables Web authors to embed simple Java-like programming instructions in the HTML text of their Web pages.

economic feasibility Capable of being accomplished with available fiscal resources. This is usually determined by a cost/benefit analysis.

e-learning The use of computers and computer programs to replace teachers and the time–place specificity of learning.

electrical engineering (EE) An engineering discipline that is concerned with the design and improvement of electrical and electronic circuits.

electronic commerce The use of the Internet and other wide area networks (WANs) for business-to-business and business-to-consumer transactions. Also called e-commerce.

electronic data interchange (EDI) A communications standard for the electronic exchange of financial information through information services.

electronic mail See e-mail.

electronic vault In online banking, a mainframe computer that stores account holders' information.

element In HTML, a distinctive component of a document's structure, such as a title, heading, or list. HTML divides elements into two categories: head elements (such as the document's title) and body elements (headings, paragraphs, links, and text).

e-mail Electronic mail; messages sent and received through the use of a computer network.

e-mail address A series of characters that precisely identifies the location of a person's electronic mailbox. On the Internet, e-mail addresses consist of a mailbox name (such as jsmith) followed by an at sign (@) and the computer's domain name (as in jsmith@hummer.virginia.edu).

e-mail attachment A computer file that is included with an e-mail message.

emergency disk A disk that can be used to start the computer in case the operating system becomes unusable for some reason.

employee monitoring When large employers routinely engage in observing employees' phone calls, e-mails, Web browsing habits, and computer files.

encapsulation In object-oriented programming, the hiding of all internal information of objects from other objects.

encryption The process of converting a message into ciphertext (an encrypted message) by using a key, so that the message appears to be nothing but gibberish. The intended recipient, however, can apply the key to decrypt and read the message. See also public key cryptography and rot-13.

encryption key A formula that is used to make a plaintext message unreadable.

end tag In HTML, the closing component of an element, such as </A>. All elements begin with a start tag; most require an end tag.

enterprise A business organization or any large computer-using organization, which can include universities and government agencies.

enterprise application integration (EAI) A combination of processes, software, standards, and hardware that results in the integration of two or more enterprise systems.

enterprise computing The use of technology, information systems, and computers within an organization or a business.

enterprise resource planning (ERP) Enterprise software that brings together various enterprise functions, such as manufacturing, sales, marketing, and finance, into a single computer system.

enterprise storage system The collection of storage within an organization. The system typically makes use of servers connected to hard disks or massive RAID systems.

enterprise systems Information systems that integrate an organization's information and applications across all of the organization's functional divisions.

entity-relationship diagram (ERD) In the design of information systems, a diagram that shows all the entities (organizations, departments, users, programs, and data) that play roles in the system, as well as the relationships between those entities.

ergonomic Describes a product that matches the best posture and functionality of the human body.

Ethernet A set of standards that defines local area networks (LANs) capable of operating at data transfer rates of 10 Mbps to 1 Gbps. About 80 percent of all LANs use one of several Ethernet standards.

Ethernet card A network interface card (NIC) designed to work with Ethernet local area networks (LANs).

ethical hacker (white hat) Hackers and crackers who have turned pro, offering their services to companies hoping to use hacker expertise to shore up their computer systems' defenses.

ethical principle A principle that defines the justification for considering an act or a rule to be morally right or wrong. Ethical principles can help people find their way through moral dilemmas.

event-driven In programming, a program design method that structures the program around a continuous loop, which cycles until an event occurs (such as the user clicking the mouse).

exception report In a transaction processing system (TPS), a document that alerts someone of unexpected developments, such as high demand for a product.

exclusion operator In database and Internet searching, a symbol or a word that tells the software to exclude records or documents containing a certain word or phrase.

executable file A file containing a script or program that can execute instructions on the computer. Program files usually use the .exe extension in the filename.

execute One of four basic operations carried out by the control unit of a microprocessor. The execute operation involves performing a requested action, such as adding or comparing two numbers.

execution cycle In a machine cycle, a phase consisting of the execute and write-back operations.

executive information system (EIS) A system that supports management's strategic planning function.

executive support system (ESS) A type of decision support system designed to provide high-level executives with information summarizing the overall performance of their organization on the most general level.

Exiting Quitting or closing down an application or program.

expansion board A circuit board that provides additional capabilities for a computer.

expansion bus An electrical pathway that connects the microprocessor to the expansion slots. Also called I/O bus.

expansion card See expansion board.

expansion slot A receptacle connected to the computer's expansion bus that accepts an expansion board.

expert system In artificial intelligence (AI), a program that relies on a database of if-then rules to draw inferences, in much the same way a human expert does.

Extensible Business Reporting Language (XBRL) Similar to XML, a language that uses standardized formatting that allows enterprises to publish and share financial information, including net revenue, annual and quarterly reports, and SEC filings, with each other and industry analysts across all computer platforms and the Internet.

Extensible Markup Language (XML) A set of rules for creating markup languages that enables Web authors to capture specific types of data by creating their own elements. XML can be used in HTML documents.

extension A three-letter suffix added to a DOS filename. The extension is often supplied by the application and indicates the type of application that created the file.

external drive bay In a computer case, a receptacle designed for mounting storage devices that is accessible from the outside of the case.

external modem A modem with its own case, cables, and power supply that plugs into the serial port of a computer.

extranet A corporate intranet that has been opened to external access by selected outside partners, including customers, research labs, and suppliers.

eye-gaze response system A biological feedback device that enables quadriplegics to control computers by moving their eyes around the screen.

F

facsimile transmission (fax) The sending and receiving of printed pages between two locations, using a telephone line and fax devices that digitize the page's image.

fair use An exception to copyright laws made to facilitate education, commentary, analysis, and scholarly research.

Fast Ethernet An Ethernet standard for local area networks (LANs) that enables data transfer rates of 100 Mbps using twisted-pair cable; also called 100baseT.

fault tolerance The ability to continue working even if one or more components fail, such as is found in a redundant array of independent disks.

fax modem A modem that also functions as a fax machine, giving the computer user the capability of sending word processing documents and other files as faxes.

fetch One of four basic operations carried out by the control unit of a microprocessor. The fetch operation retrieves the next program instruction from the computer's memory.

fiber-optic cable A network cable made from tiny strands of glasslike material that transmit light pulses with very high efficiency and can carry massive amounts of data.

field In a database, an area for storing a certain type of information.

field emission display (FED) A flat-panel display technology that uses tiny CRTs to produce each on-screen pixel.

field name Describes the type of data that should be entered into the field.

file A document or other collection of information stored on a disk and identified as a unit by a unique name.

file allocation table (FAT) A hidden on-disk table that keeps vital records concerning exactly where the various components of a given file are stored. The file allocation table is created at the conclusion of the formatting process.

file compression The reduction of a file's size so that the file can be stored without taking up as much storage space and can be transferred more quickly over a computer network.

file compression utility A program to reduce the size of files without harming the data.

file infector A computer virus that attaches to a program file and, when that program is executed, spreads to other program files.

file management program An application that enables users to create customized databases and store in and retrieve data from those databases.

file manager (My Computer in Windows, File Manager in Mac OS X, and various file management utilities in Linux) A utility program that enables you to organize and manage the data stored on your disk.

file menu In a graphical user interface (GUI), a pull-down menu that contains standard file-management commands, such as Save and Save As.

file server In client/server computing, a computer that has been set aside (dedicated) to make program and data files available to client programs on the network.

File Transfer Protocol (FTP) An Internet standard for the exchange of files between two computers connected to the Internet. With an FTP client, you can upload or download files from a computer that is running an FTP server. Normally, you need a user name and password to upload or download files from an FTP server, but some FTP servers provide a service called anonymous FTP, which enables anyone to download the files made available for public use.

filename A unique name given to a stored file.

filter In e-mail, a rule that specifies the destination folder of messages conforming to certain criteria.

filtering software A program that attempts to prevent minors from accessing adult material on the Internet.

firewall A program that permits an organization's internal computer users to access the Internet but places severe limits on the ability of outsiders to access internal data.

FireWire port An input-output port that combines high-speed performance (up to 400 Mbps) with the ability to guarantee data delivery at a specified speed, making the port ideal for use with real-time devices such as digital video cameras. Synonymous with 1394 port. FireWire is Apple Computer's name for 1394 port technology.

flame In Usenet and e-mail, a message that contains abusive, threatening, obscene, or inflammatory language.

flash memory A special type of read-only memory (ROM) that enables users to upgrade information contained in memory chips. Also called flash BIOS.

flash memory card Wafer-thin, highly portable solid state storage system that is capable of storing as much as 1 gigabyte of data. Used with some digital cameras, the card stores digitized photographs without requiring electrical power to maintain the data.

flash memory reader A slot or compartment in digital cameras and other devices into which a flash memory card is inserted.

flat file A type of file generated by a file management program. Flat files can be accessed in many different ways but cannot be linked to data in other files.

flatbed scanner A device that copies an image (text or graphics) from one side of a sheet of paper and translates it into a digital image.

flat-panel display A low-power, lightweight display used with notebook computers (and increasingly with desktop computers).

floating-point notation A method for storing and calculating numbers so that the location of the decimal point isn't fixed but floating. This allows the computer to work with very small and very large numbers.

flooding A type of antisocial behavior found on Internet Relay Chat characterized by sending repeated messages so that no one else can engage in the conversation.

floppy disk A removable and widely used data storage medium that uses a magnetically coated flexible disk of Mylar enclosed in a plastic envelope or case. Although 5.25-inch floppy disks were standard, they became obsolete due to the development of the smaller, more durable 3.5-inch disk.

floppy disk drive A mechanism that enables a computer to read and write information on a removable medium that provides a convenient way to move data from one computer to another.

flowchart In structured programming, a diagram that shows the logic of a program.

FMD-ROM (fluorescent multilayer disc–read-only memory) disc A type of high-capacity storage disc with multiple layers whose fluorescent coating allows for storage of up to a terabyte of data.

folder A graphical representation of a directory. Most major operating systems display directories as though they were file folders.

folder structure An organized set of primary and secondary folders within which to save your files.

footprint The amount of room taken up by the case on the desk.

foreground application In a multitasking operating system, the active application.

Form In the Microsoft Access database management system, the object used to collect data.

form factor A specification for mounting internal components, such as the motherboard.

format 1. A file storage standard used to write a certain type of data to a magnetic disk (also called file format). 2. To prepare a magnetic disk for first use. 3. In word processing, to choose the alignment, emphasis, or other presentation options so that the document will print with an attractive appearance.

format menu In a graphical user interface (GUI), a pull-down menu that allows you to modify such features as font style and paragraph settings.

formatting The process of modifying a document's appearance so that it looks good when printed.

Formatting toolbar In Microsoft Office, a default-loaded toolbar that includes icons for various functions, including choosing document font size and style.

formula In a spreadsheet program, a mathematical expression embedded in a cell that can include cell references. The cell displays the formula's result.

formula bar In a spreadsheet program, an area above the worksheet that displays the contents of the active cell. The formula bar enables the user to work with formulas, which normally do not appear in the cell.

Fortran An early third-generation language that enabled scientists and engineers to write simple programs for solving mathematical equations.

fourth-generation language (4GL) A programming language that does not force the programmer to consider the procedure that must be followed to obtain the desired result.

fragmentation A process in which the various components of a file are separated by normal reading and writing operations so that these components are not stored close together. The result is slower disk operation. A defragmentation utility can improve a disk's performance by placing these file components closer together.

frames In a video or animation, the series of still images flashed on-screen at a rapid rate.

frame rate In a video or animation, a measurement of the number of still images shown per second.

freeware Copyrighted software that can be freely copied but not sold.

front panel An area on the front of most computers containing various indicator lights and controls.

full backup The process of copying all files from a secondary storage device (most commonly a hard disk) to a backup medium, such as a tape cartridge.

function In spreadsheet programs such as Microsoft Excel, one of the two basic types of formulas (along with mathematic expressions). In a function, operations can be performed on multiple inputs.

function keys A row of keys positioned along the top of the keyboard, labeled F1 through F12, to which programs can assign various commands.

G

G or GB Abbreviation for gigabyte, approximately one billion (one thousand million) bytes or characters.

Gantt chart A bar chart that summarizes a project's schedule by showing how various activities proceed over time.

Gbps A data transfer rate of approximately one billion bits per second.

General Public License (GPL) A freeware software license, devised by the Open Software Foundation (OSF), stipulating that a given program can be obtained, used, and even modified, as long as the user agrees to not sell the software and to make the source code for any modifications available.

general-purpose application A software program used by many people to accomplish frequently performed tasks such as writing (word processing), working with numbers (spreadsheets), and keeping track of information (databases).

genetic algorithm An automated program development environment in which various alternative approaches to solving a problem are introduced; each is allowed to mutate periodically through the introduction of random changes. The various approaches compete in an effort to solve a specific problem. After a period of time, one approach may prove to be clearly superior to the others.

geosynchronous orbit A circular path around the Earth in which a communications satellite, for example, has a velocity exactly matching the Earth's speed of rotation, allowing the satellite to be permanently positioned with respect to the ground.

GIF (Graphics Interchange Format) A bitmapped color graphics file format capable of storing images with 256 colors. GIF incorporates a compression technique that reduces file size, making it ideal for use on a network. GIF is best used for images that have areas of solid color.

GIF animation A graphics file that contains more than one image stored using the GIF graphics file format. Also stored in the file is a brief script that indicates the sequence of images, and how long to display each image.

gigabit A unit of measurement approximately equal to one billion bits.

Gigabit Ethernet An Ethernet local area network (LAN) that is capable of achieving data transfer rates of 1 Gbps (one billion bits per second) using fiber-optic cable.

gigabit per second (Gbps) A data transfer measurement equivalent to one billion bits per second.

gigabits per second points of presence (gigaPoPs) In Internet II, a high-speed testbed for the development of next-generation Internet protocols, a point of presence (PoP) that provides access to a backbone service capable of data transfer rates in excess of 1 Gbps (one billion bits per second).

gigabyte (G or GB) A unit of measurement commonly used to state the capacity of memory or storage devices; equal to 1,024 megabytes, or approximately one billion bytes or characters.

globalization Conducting business internationally where the transaction of goods and services is transparent to the consumer.

Global Positioning System (GPS) A satellite-based system that enables portable GPS receivers to determine their location with an accuracy of 100 meters or less.

global unique identifier (GUID) A uniquely identifying serial number assigned to Pentium III processor chips that can be used by Web servers to detect which computer is accessing a Web site.

graphical MUD A multiuser dungeon (MUD) that uses graphics instead of text to represent the interaction of characters in a virtual environment.

graphical user interface (GUI) An interface between the operating system and the user. Graphical user interfaces are the most popular of all user interfaces but also require the most system resources.

graphics accelerator A display adapter (video card) that contains its own dedicated processing circuitry and video memory (VRAM), enabling faster display of complex graphics images.

graphics file A file that stores the information needed to display a graphic. Popular graphics file formats include BMP (Windows Bitmap), JPEG, and GIF.

groupware The software that provides computerized support for the information needs of individuals networked into workgroups.

H

hacker Traditionally, a computer user who enjoys pushing his or her computer capabilities to the limit, especially by using clever or novel approaches to solving problems. In the press, the term *hacker* has become synonymous with criminals who attempt unauthorized access to computer systems for criminal purposes, such as sabotage or theft. The computing community considers this usage inaccurate.

hacker ethic A set of moral principles common to the first-generation hacker community (roughly 1965–1982), described by Steven Levy in *Hackers* (1984). According to the hacker ethic, all technical information should, in principle, be freely available to all. Therefore, gaining entry to a system to explore data and increase knowledge is never unethical. Destroying, altering, or moving data in such a way that could cause injury or expense to others, however, is always unethical. In increasingly more states, unauthorized computer access is against the law. See also cracker.

handheld computer See personal digital assistant.

handling input and output One of the five basic functions of an operating system in which your computer interacts with input devices and shows you the results of its work on output devices.

haptics A field of research in developing output devices that stimulate the sense of touch.

hard copy Printed computer output, differing from the data stored on disk or in memory.

hard disk A secondary storage medium that uses several rigid disks (platters) coated with a magnetically sensitive material and housed in a hermetically sealed mechanism. In almost all modern computers, the hard disk is by far the most important storage medium. Also called hard disk drive.

hard disk controller An electronic circuit that provides an interface between a hard disk and the computer's CPU.

hard disk drive See hard disk.

hardware The physical components, such as circuit boards, disk drives, displays, and printers, that make up a computer system.

head actuator Mechanism on a floppy disk drive that moves the read/write head to the area that contains the desired data.

head crash In a hard disk, the collision of a read/write head with the surface of the disk, generally caused by a sharp jolt to the computer's case. Head crashes can damage the read/write head, as well as create bad sectors.

header In e-mail or a Usenet news article, the beginning of a message. The header contains important information about the sender's address, the subject of the message, and other information.

head-mounted display (HMD) See headset.

headset A wearable output device with twin LCD panels for creating the illusion that an individual is experiencing a three-dimensional, simulated environment.

heat sink A heat-dissipating component that drains heat away from semiconductor devices, which can generate enough heat in the course of their operation to destroy themselves. Heat sinks are often used in combination with fans to cool semiconductor components.

help menu In a graphical user interface (GUI), a pull-down menu that provides access to interactive help utilities.

help screen In commercial software, information that appears on-screen that can provide assistance with using a particular program.

help utilities Programs, such as a table of contents of frequently requested items, offered on most graphical user interface (GUI) applications.

hexadecimal number A number that uses a base 16 number system rather than a decimal (or base 10) number system.

hierarchy chart In structured programming, a program planning chart that shows the top-down design of the program and the relationship between program modules. Also called structure chart.

High Definition Television (HDTV) The name given to several standards for digital television displays.

high-level programming language A programming language that eliminates the need for programmers to understand the intimate details of how the computer processes data.

history list In a Web browser, a window that shows all the Web sites that the browser has accessed during a given period, such as the last 30 days.

home and educational programs General-purpose software programs for personal finance, home design and landscaping, encyclopedias and other computerized reference information, and games.

home page 1. In any hypertext system, including the Web, a document intended to serve as an initial point of entry to a web of related documents. Also called a welcome page, a home page contains general introductory information, as well as hyperlinks to related resources. A well-designed home page contains internal navigation buttons that help users find their way among the various documents that the home page makes available. 2. The start page that is automatically displayed when you start a Web browser or click the program's Home button. 3. A personal page listing an individual's contact information, and favorite links, and (generally) some information—ranging from cryptic to voluminous—about the individual's perspective on life.

home phone-line network (HomePNA) A linked personal communications system that works off a home's existing phone wiring, thus being easy to install, inexpensive, and fast. The acronym PNA is derived from the Home Phone Networking Alliance.

home power-line network A linked personal communications system that works by connecting computers to one another through the same electrical power outlet, thus providing the convenience of not having to locate each computer in the home next to a phone jack.

home radio-frequency (RF) network A linked personal communications system that connects computers using wireless radio signals, making computers portable throughout the house.

hot swapping Connecting and disconnecting peripherals while the computer is running.

hub In a local area network (LAN), a device that connects several workstations and enables them to exchange data.

hyperlink In a hypertext system, an underlined or otherwise emphasized word or phrase that, when clicked, displays another document.

hypermedia A hypertext system that uses various multimedia resources, such as sounds, animations, and videos, as a means of navigation as well as decoration.

hypermedia system A hypertext system that uses various multimedia resources, such as sounds, movies, and text, as a means of navigation as well as illustration.

hypertext A method of preparing and publishing text, ideally suited to the computer, in which readers can choose their own paths through the material. To prepare hypertext, you first "chunk" the information into small, manageable units, such as single pages of text. These units are called nodes. You then embed hyperlinks in the text. When the reader clicks a hyperlink, the hypertext software displays a different node. The process of navigating among the nodes linked in this way is called browsing. A collection of nodes interconnected by hyperlinks is called a web. The Web is a hypertext system on a global scale.

Hypertext Markup Language (HTML) A language for marking the portions of a document (called elements) so that, when accessed by a program called a Web browser, each portion appears with a distinctive format. HTML is the markup language behind the appearance of documents on the Web. HTML is standardized by means of a document type definition in the Standard Generalized Markup Language (SGML). HTML includes capabilities that enable authors to insert hyperlinks, which when clicked display another HTML document. The agency responsible for standardizing HTML is the World Wide Web Consortium (W3C).

Hypertext Transfer Protocol (HTTP) The Internet standard that supports the exchange of information on the Web. By defining uniform resource locators (URLs) and how they can be used to retrieve resources anywhere on the Internet, HTTP enables Web authors to embed hyperlinks in Web documents. HTTP defines the process by which a Web client, called a browser, originates a request for information and sends it to a Web server, a program that responds to HTTP requests and provides the desired information.

I

I/O bus See expansion bus.

I/O device Generic term for any input or output device.

icon In a graphical user interface (GUI), a small picture that represents a program, a data file, or some other computer entity or function.

identify theft A form of fraud in which a thief obtains someone's Social Security number and other personal information, and then uses this information to obtain credit cards fraudulently.

image editor A sophisticated paint program for editing and transforming complex bitmapped images, such as photographs.

image processing system A filing system in which incoming documents are scanned and stored digitally.

impact printer A printer that generates output by striking the page with something solid.

inbox In e-mail, a default folder that contains any new mail messages, as well as older messages that have not been moved or deleted.

inclusion operator In database or Web searching, a symbol or keyword that instructs the search software to make sure that any retrieved records or documents contain a certain word or phrase.

incremental backup The process of copying files that have changed since the last full backup to a backup medium, such as a tape cartridge.

information Processed data.

information hiding A modular programming technique in which information inside a module remains hidden with respect to other modules.

information kiosk An automated presentation system used for public information or employee training.

information overload A condition of confusion, stress, and indecision brought about by being inundated with information of variable value.

information processing cycle A complete sequence of operations involving data input, processing, storage, and output.

information system A purposefully designed system that brings data, computers, procedures, and people together to manage information important to an organization's mission.

information systems (IS) department In a complex organization, the division responsible for designing, installing, and maintaining the organization's information systems.

information technology (IT) professionals Businesspeople who work with information technology in all its various forms (hardware, software, networks) and functions (management, development, maintenance).

information technology steering committee Within an organization, the group, which generally includes representatives from senior management, information systems personnel, users, and middle managers, that reviews requests for systems development and decides whether or not to move forward with a project.

information warfare A military strategy that targets an opponent's information systems.

infrared A data transmission medium that uses the same signaling technology used in TV remote controls.

inheritance In object-oriented (OO) programming, the capacity of an object to pass its characteristics to subclasses.

inkjet printer A nonimpact printer that forms an image by spraying ink from a matrix of tiny jets.

input The information entered into a computer for processing.

input device Any device that is capable of accepting data so that it is properly represented for processing within the computer.

input/output (I/O) bus See expansion bus.

insertion point See cursor.

install To set up a program so that it is ready to function on a given computer system. The installation process may involve creating additional directories, making changes to system files, and other technical tasks. For this reason, most programs come with setup programs that handle the installation process automatically.

instant messaging (IM) system Software program that lets you know when a friend or business associate is online. You can then contact this person and exchange messages and attachments.

instruction A unique number assigned to an operation performed by a processor.

instruction cycle In a machine cycle, a phase consisting of the fetch and decode operations.

instruction set A list of specific instructions that a given brand and model of processor can perform.

intangible benefits Gains that have no fixed dollar value, such as access to improved information or increased sales due to improved customer services.

integrated circuit (IC) A semiconductor circuit containing more than one transistor and other electronic components; often referred to as a chip.

integrated program A program that combines three or more productivity software functions, including word processing, database management, and a spreadsheet.

intelligent agent An automatic program that is designed to operate on the user's behalf, performing a specific function in the background. When the agent has achieved its goal, it reports to the user.

Intelligent Transportation System (ITS) A system, partly funded by the U.S. government, to develop smart streets and smart cars. Such a system could warn travelers of congestion and suggest alternative routes.

interactive multimedia A presentation involving two or more media, such as text, graphics, or sound, and providing users with the ability to choose their own path through the information.

interface A means of connecting two dissimilar computer devices. An interface has two components, a physical component and a communications standard, called a protocol. The physical component provides the physical means for making a connection, while the protocol enables designers to design the devices so that they can exchange data with each other. The computer's standard parallel port is an example of an interface that has both a distinctive physical connector and a defining, standard protocol.

internal drive bay In a computer's case, a receptacle for mounting a storage device that is not easily accessible from outside the computer's case. Internal drive bays are typically used to mount nonremovable hard drives.

internal modem A modem that fits into the expansion bus of a personal computer. See also external modem.

internal speaker One of the components inside a computer's system unit, typically for emitting beeps and other low-fidelity sounds.

International Telecommunications Union (ITU) A branch organization of the United Nations that sets international telecommunications standards.

Internet An enormous and rapidly growing system of linked computer networks, worldwide in scope, that facilitates data communication services such as remote logon, file transfer, electronic mail, the World Wide Web, and newsgroups. Relying on TCP/IP, the Internet assigns every connected computer a unique Internet address (called an IP address) so that any two connected computers can locate each other on the network and exchange data.

Internet2 The next-generation Internet, still under development.

Internet address The unique, 32-bit address assigned to a computer that is connected to the Internet, represented in dotted decimal notation (for example, 128.117.38.5). Synonymous with IP address.

Internet appliance A device that provides much of a personal computer's functionality but at a much lower price, connects to a network, such as the Internet, and has limited memory, disk storage, and processing power.

Internet hard drive Storage space on a server that is accessible from the Internet.

Internet programs General-purpose software programs for e-mailing, instant messaging, Web browsing, and videoconferencing.

Internet Protocol (IP) One of the two core Internet standards (the other is the Transmission Control Protocol, TCP). IP defines the standard that describes how an Internet-connected computer should break data down into packets for transmission across the network, and how those packets should be addressed so that they arrive at their destination. IP is the connectionless part of the TCP/IP protocols.

Internet Relay Chat (IRC) A real-time, Internet-based chat service, in which one can find "live" participants from the world over. IRC requires the use of an IRC client program, which displays a list of the current IRC channels. After joining a channel, you can see what other participants are typing on-screen, and you can type your own repartee.

Internet service A set of communication standards (protocols) and software (clients and servers) that defines how to access and exchange a certain type of information on the Internet. Examples of Internet services are e-mail, FTP, Gopher, IRC, and Web.

Internet Service Provider (ISP) A company that provides Internet accounts and connections to individuals and businesses. Most ISPs offer a range of connection options, ranging from dial-up modem connections to high-speed ISDN and ADSL. Also provided is e-mail, Usenet, and Web hosting.

Internet telephony The use of the Internet (or of nonpublic networks based on Internet technology) for the transmission of real-time voice data.

Internet telephony service providers A long-distance voice messaging service that provides telephone service by means of the Internet or private data networks using Internet technology.

InterNIC A consortium of two organizations that provide networking information services to the Internet community, under contract to the National Science Foundation (NSF). Currently, AT&T provides directory and database services, while Network Solutions, Inc., provides registration services for new domain names and IP addresses.

interoperability The ability to work with computers and operating systems of differing type and brand.

interpreter In programming, a translator that converts each instruction into machine-readable code and executes it one line at a time. Interpreters are often used for learning and debugging, due to their slow speed.

interrupt handlers Miniprograms in an operating system that kick in when an interrupt occurs.

interrupt request (IRQ) Lines that handle the communication between input or output devices and the computer's CPU.

interrupts Signals generated by input and output devices that inform the operating system that something has happened, such as a document has finished printing.

intranet A computer network based on Internet technology (TCP/IP) that meets the internal needs of a single organization or company. Not necessarily open to the external Internet and almost certainly not accessible from the outside, an intranet enables organizations to make internal resources available using familiar Internet tools. See also extranet.

IP address A 32-bit binary number that uniquely and precisely identifies the location of a particular computer on the Internet. Every computer that is directly connected to the Internet must have an IP address. Because binary numbers are so hard to read, IP addresses are given in four-part decimal numbers, each part representing 8 bits of the 32-bit address (for example, 128.143.7.226).

IPOS cycle A sequence of four basic types of computer operations that characterize everything computers do. These operations are input, processing, output, and storage.

IrDA port A port housed on the exterior of a computer's case that is capable of sending and receiving computer data by means of infrared signals. The standards that define these signals are maintained by the Infrared Data Association (IrDA). IrDA ports are commonly found on notebook computers and personal digital assistants (PDAs).

IRQ conflict A serious system failure that results if two devices are configured to use the same IRQ but are not designed to share an IRQ line.

ISDN (Integrated Services Digital Network) A worldwide standard for the delivery of digital telephone and data services to homes, schools, and offices using existing twisted-pair wiring.

ISDN adapter An internal or external accessory that enables a computer to connect to remote computer networks or the Internet by means of ISDN. (Inaccurately called an ISDN modem.)

IT industry The industry that consists of organizations focused on the development and implementation of technology and applications.

iteration control structure See repetition control structure.

J

Java A cross-platform programming language created by Sun Microsystems that enables programmers to write a program that will execute on any computer capable of running a Java interpreter (which is built into today's leading Web browsers). Java is an object-oriented programming (OOP) language similar to C++, except that it eliminates some features of C++ that programmers find tedious and time-consuming. Java programs are compiled into applets (small programs executed by a browser) or applications (larger, standalone programs that require a Java interpreter to be present on the user's computer), but the compiled code contains no machine code. Instead, the output of the compiler is bytecode, an intermediary between source code and machine code that can be transmitted by computer networks, including the Internet.

Java Virtual Machine (VM) A Java interpreter and runtime environment for Java applets and Java applications. This environment is called a virtual machine because, no matter what kind of computer it is running on, it creates a simulated computer that provides the correct platform for executing Java programs. In addition, this approach insulates the computer's file system from rogue applications. Java VMs are available for most computers.

Jaz drive A removable drive from Iomega that can store up to 2 GB.

joint application development (JAD) In information systems development, a method of system design that involves users at all stages of system development. See also prototyping.

joystick An input device commonly used for games.

JPEG (Joint Photographic Experts Group) A graphics file format, named after the group that designed it. JPEG graphics can display up to 16.7 million colors and use lossy compression to reduce file size. JPEG is best used for complex graphics such as photographs.

K

K or KB Abbreviation for kilobyte, approximately one thousand bytes or characters.

Kbps A data transfer rate of approximately one thousand bits per second.

kernel The essential, core portion of the operating system that is loaded into random access memory (RAM) when the computer is turned on and stays in RAM for the duration of the operating session. Also called supervisor program.

key escrow The storage of users' encryption keys by an independent agency, which would divulge the keys to law enforcement investigators only on the production of a valid warrant. Key escrow is proposed by law enforcement officials concerned that encryption would prevent surveillance of criminal activities.

key field or primary key This field contains a code, number, name, or some other information that uniquely identifies the record.

key interception The act of stealing an encryption key.

key recovery A method of unlocking the key used to encrypt messages so that the message could be read by law enforcement officials conducting a lawful investigation. Key recovery is proposed by law enforcement officials concerned that encryption would prevent surveillance of criminal activities.

keyboard An input device providing a set of alphabetic, numeric, punctuation, symbolic, and control keys.

keyword In a command-line interface, words that tell the operating system what to do (such as "format" or "copy").

kilobits per second (Kbps) A data transfer rate of approximately one thousand bits of computer data per second.

kilobyte (K or KB) The basic unit of measurement for computer memory and disk capacity, equal to 1,024 bytes or characters.

kiosk A booth that provides a computer service of some type.

know-and-have authentication A type of computer security that requires using tokens, which are handheld electronic devices that generate a logon code.

knowledge base A database of represented knowledge.

knowledge management system An information system that captures knowledge created by employees and makes it available to an organization.

knowledge representation The process of eliciting rules from human experts.

L

land Flat reflective areas on an optical disc.

laptop computer A portable computer larger than a notebook computer but small enough to be transported easily. Few are being made now that notebook computers have become so powerful.

laser printer A popular nonimpact, high-resolution printer that uses a version of the electrostatic reproduction technology of copying machines.

last-mile problem The lack of local network systems for high-bandwidth multimedia communications that can accommodate the Information Superhighway.

last-mile technologies Digital telecommunications services and standards, such as coaxial cable and ISDN, that serve as interim solutions to the limitations associated with the twisted pair analog phone wiring still common in many homes and businesses.

latency In a packet-switching network, a signal delay that is introduced by the time network routers consume as they route packets to their destination.

launch To start an application program.

layer In a computer network, a level of network functionality governed by specific network protocols. For example, the physical layer has protocols concerned with the transmission of signals over a specific type of cable.

LCD monitors The thinner monitors used on notebooks and some desktop computers.

LCD projector An output device that projects a computer's screen display on a screen similar to those used with slide projectors.

leased line A permanently connected and conditioned telephone line that provides wide area network (WAN) connectivity to an organization or a business.

left pane In the My Computer primary file management utility for PCs, one of two main default windows. It displays links to system tasks, such as viewing system information. See also right pane.

legacy system A technically obsolete information system that remains in use, often because it performs its job adequately or is too expensive to replace.

level 2 (L2) cache See secondary cache.

libel A form of defamation that occurs in writing.

life cycle In information systems, the birth, development, use, and eventual abandonment of the system.

light pen An input device that uses a light-sensitive stylus to draw on-screen or on a graphics tablet or to select items from a menu.

link See hyperlink.

Linux A freeware operating system closely resembling UNIX developed for IBM-compatible PCs but also available for other platforms, including Macintosh.

liquid crystal display (LCD) A small, flat-screen monitor that uses electrical current to control tiny crystals and form an image.

listserv An automatic mailing list server developed by Eric Thomas for BITNET in 1986.

load To transfer program instructions from storage to memory.

local area network (LAN) A computer network that connects computers in a limited geographical area (typically less than one mile) so that users can exchange information and share hardware, software, and data resources.

local exchange switch A telephone system device, based on digital technology and capable of handling thousands of calls, located in the local telephone company's central office.

local loop In the public switched telephone network (PSTN), the last segment of service delivery, typically consisting of analog connections from neighborhood distribution points.

LocalTalk A protocol developed by Apple Computer that provides peer-to-peer networking among Apple Macintosh computers and Macintosh-compatible peripherals such as laser printers. LocalTalk is a low-level protocol that works with twisted-pair phone cables.

location (position) awareness A technology that uses GPS-enabled chips to pinpoint the location of a cell phone (and its user).

log in To authenticate yourself as a user with a valid account and usage privileges on a multiuser computer system or a computer network. To log in, you supply your user name and password. Also called log on.

log on See log in.

logic bomb A flaw concealed in an otherwise usable computer program that can be triggered to destroy or corrupt data.

logic error In programming, a mistake made by the programmer in designing the program. Logic errors will not surface by themselves during program execution because they are not errors in the structure of the statements and commands.

logical data type A data type that allows only a yes or no answer.

logical operations One of two groups of operations performed by the arithmetic-logic unit (ALU). The logical operations involve comparing two data items to see which one is larger or smaller.

looping See repetition control structure.

lossless compression In data compression, a method used to reduce the size of a file that enables the file to be restored to its original size without introducing errors. Most lossless compression techniques reduce file size by replacing lengthy but frequently occurring data sequences with short codes; to decompress the file, the compression software reverses this process and restores the lengthy data sequences to their original form.

lossy compression In data compression, a method of reducing the size of multimedia files by eliminating information that is not normally perceived by human beings.

low-level language A language that describes exactly the procedures to be carried out by a computer's central processing unit, such as machine or programming language.

M

M or MB Abbreviation for megabyte, approximately one million bytes or characters of information.

Mac OS Operating system and user interface developed by Apple Computer for Macintosh computers; introduced the first graphical user interface.

machine cycle A four-step process followed by the control unit that involves the fetch, decode, execute, and write-back operations. Also called processing cycle.

machine dependence The dependence of a given computer program or component on a specific brand or type of computer equipment.

machine language The native binary language consisting of 0s and 1s that is recognized and executed by a computer's central processing unit.

machine translation Language translation performed by the computer without human aid.

macro In application software, a user-defined command sequence that can be saved and executed to perform a complex action.

macro virus A computer virus that uses the automatic command execution capabilities of productivity software to spread itself and often to cause harm to computer data.

magnetic storage device In computer storage systems, any storage device that retains data using a magnetically sensitive material, such as the magnetic coating found on floppy disks or backup tapes.

magnetic-ink character recognition (MICR) system A scanning system developed by the banking industry in the 1950s. Check information is encoded onto each check before it is used to reduce processing time when the check comes back to the bank.

mainframe A multiuser computer system that meets the computing needs of a large organization.

maintenance release A minor revision to a software program, indicated by the decimal in the version number, that corrects bugs or adds minor features.

management information system (MIS) A computer-based system that supports the information needs of management.

managing applications One of the five basic functions of an operating system that enables a user to work with two or more applications at the same time.

managing memory One of the five basic functions of an operating system that gives each running program its own portion of memory and attempts to keep the programs from interfering with each other's use of memory.

markup language In text processing, a system of codes for marking the format of a unit of text that indicates only that a particular unit of text is a certain part of the document, such as an abstract, a title, or an author's name and affiliation. The actual formatting of the document part is left to another program, called a viewer, which displays the marked document and gives each document part a distinctive format (fonts, spacing, and so on). HTML is a markup language.

mass storage See storage.

math coprocessor A separate chip that frees the main processor from performing mathematical operations, usually operations involving floating-point notation.

mathematic formula In spreadsheet programs such as Microsoft Excel, one of the two basic types of formulas (along with functions). In a mathematic formula, or expression, the mathematic order of operation is followed.

maximize To enlarge a window so that it fits the entire screen.

mechanical mouse A type of mouse that uses a rotating ball to generate information about the mouse's position.

megabits per second (Mbps) In networking, a data transfer rate of approximately one million bits per second.

megabyte (M or MB) A measurement of storage capacity equal to 1,024 kilobytes, or approximately one million bytes or characters.

megapixel Type of digital camera that has a charge-coupled device with at least one million elements.

memo In databases, a data type used for large units of text.

memory Circuitry that stores information temporarily so that it is readily available to the central processing unit (CPU).

memory address A code number that specifies a specific location in memory.

memory shaving A type of computer crime in which knowledgeable thieves remove some of a computer's RAM chips but leave enough to start the computers.

menu The list of words, such as file, edit, and view, signifying categories of tasks that can be accomplished within an application.

menu bar In a graphical user interface (GUI), a rectangular bar (generally positioned near the top of the application window) that provides access to pull-down menus. On the Macintosh, an active application's menu bar is always positioned at the top of the screen.

menu-driven user interface An interface between the operating system and the user in which text-based menus show options, rather than requiring the user to memorize the commands and type them in.

Metcalfe's Law A prediction formulated by Bob Metcalfe, creator of Ethernet, that the value of a network increases in proportion to the square of the number of people connected to the network.

method In object-oriented programming, a procedure or operation that processes or manipulates data.

microcomputer A computer that uses a microprocessor as its CPU.

microphone An input device that converts sound into electrical signals that can be processed by a computer.

microprocessor See central processing unit (CPU).

Microsoft Windows Generic name for the various operating systems in the Microsoft Windows family, including, but not limited to, Microsoft Windows CE, Microsoft Windows 3.1, Microsoft Windows 95, Microsoft Windows 98, and Microsoft Windows NT.

Microsoft Windows CE An operating system for palmtop and personal digital assistant computers developed by Microsoft Corporation.

Microsoft Windows NT A 32-bit operating system developed by Microsoft Corporation for use in corporate client/server networks. The operating system consists of two components, Microsoft Windows NT Workstation (for users' systems) and Microsoft Windows NT Server (for file servers).

Microsoft Windows XP The first Microsoft operating system family that uses the same, underlying 32-bit code for all three versions (consumer, corporate desktop, and server).

microwave An electromagnetic radio wave with a very short frequency.

middleware In object-oriented programming, standards that define how programs find objects and determine what kind of information they contain.

MIDI (Musical Instrument Digital Interface) A standard that specifies how musical sounds can be described in text files so that a MIDI-compatible synthesizer can reproduce the sounds. MIDI files are small, so they're often used to provide music that starts playing automatically when a Web page is accessed. To hear MIDI sounds, your computer needs a sound card. MIDI sounds best with wavetable synthesis sound cards, which include sound samples from real musical instruments.

minicomputer A multiuser computer that meets the needs of a small organization or a department in a large organization.

minimize To reduce the size of a window so that it appears only as an icon or an item on the taskbar.

minitower case A smaller version of a system unit case designed to sit on the floor next to a desk.

mnemonic In programming, an abbreviation or a word that makes it easier to remember a complex instruction.

mobile telephone switching office (MTSO) In a cellular telephone system, the switching office that connects all of the individual cell towers to the central office and the public switched telephone network.

modeling A method by which spreadsheet programs are able to predict future outcomes.

modem Short for modulator/demodulator, a device that converts the digital signals generated by the serial port to the modulated analog signals required for transmission over a telephone line and, likewise, transforms incoming analog signals to their digital equivalents. The speed at which a modem transmits data is measured in units called bits per second, or bps. (Although bps is not technically the same as baud, the terms are often and erroneously used interchangeably.)

modifier keys Keys that are pressed to modify the meaning of the next key that's pressed.

modular programming A programming style that breaks down program functions into modules, each of which accomplishes one function and contains all the source code and variables needed to accomplish that function.

modulation protocol In modems, the communications standard that governs how the modem translates between the computer's digital signals and the analog tones used to convey computer data over the Internet. Modulation protocols are defined by ITU standards. The V.90 protocol defines communication at 56 Kbps.

module A part of a software program; independently developed modules are combined to compile the final program.

monitor A television-like device that produces an on-screen image.

Moore's Law A prediction by Intel Corp. cofounder Gordon Moore that integrated circuit technology advancements would enable the semiconductor industry to double the number of components on a chip every 18 to 24 months.

motherboard A large circuit board containing the computer's central processing unit, support chips, random access memory, and expansion slots. Also called a main board.

mouse A palm-sized input device, with a ball built into the bottom, that is used to move a pointer on-screen to draw, select options from a menu, modify or move text, and issue commands.

mousepad A clean, flat surface for moving a mouse on.

MPEG (Moving Pictures Experts Group) A set of standards for audio and video file formats and lossless compression, named after the group that created it.

MPEG Audio Layer 3 (MP3) A sound compression standard that can store a single song from an audio CD in a 3M file. MP3 files are easily shared over the Internet and are costing recording companies billions of dollars in lost royalties due to piracy.

MP2 One of several standardized audio formats for representing sounds digitally, developed by the Moving Picture Experts Group (MPEG). See Moving Picture Experts Group (MPEG) and MPEG Audio Layer 3 (MP3).

MS-DOS An operating system for IBM-compatible PCs that uses a command-line user interface.

MSN® TV An Internet service that allows customers to access the Web using a television set as a display.

multifunction devices Machines that combine printing, scanning, faxing, and copying.

multimedia The presentation of information using graphics, video, sound, animation, and text.

multimedia and graphics software General-purpose software programs for professional desktop publishing, image editing, three-dimensional rendering, and video editing.

multiplexing A technique that enables more than one signal to be conveyed on a physical transmission medium.

multitasking In operating systems, the capability to execute more than one application at a time. Multitasking shouldn't be confused with multiple program loading, in which two or more applications are present in random access memory (RAM) but only one executes at a time.

multiuser dungeon (MUD) A text-based environment in which multiple players can assume online personas and interact with each other by means of text chatting.

N

nanorobots Atoms and molecules used to perform certain tasks in nanotechnology.

nanotechnology Manipulating materials on an atomic or molecular scale in order to build microscopic devices.

native application A program that runs on a particular brand and model of processor or in a particular operating system.

natural language A human language, such as English or Japanese.

near-online storage A type of storage that is not directly available, but can be made available by a simple action such as inserting a disk.

nest In structured programming, to embed one control structure inside another.

netiquette Short for network etiquette. A set of rules that reflect long-standing experience about getting along harmoniously in the electronic environment (e-mail and newsgroups).

network A group of two or more computer systems linked together to enable communications by exchanging data and sharing resources.

network access point (NAP) A special communications device that sends and receives data between computers that contain wireless adapters.

network administrator (sometimes called *network engineers*) Computer professionals who install, maintain, and support computer networks, interact with users, handle security, and troubleshoot problems.

network architecture The overall design of a computer network that specifies its functionality at every level by means of protocols.

network attached storage (NAS) devices High-performance devices that provide shared data to clients and other servers on a local area network.

network computer (NC) A computer that provides much of a PC's functionality at a lower price. Network computers don't have disk drives because they get their software from the computer network.

network interface card (NIC) An adapter that enables a user to connect a network cable to a computer.

network layers Separate divisions within a network architecture with specific functions and protocols, allowing engineers to make changes within a layer without having to redesign the entire network.

network operating system (NOS) The software needed to enable data transfer and application usage over a local area network (LAN).

network topology The physical layout of a local area network (LAN), such as a bus, star, or ring topology, that determines what happens when, for example, two workstations try to access the LAN or transmit data simultaneously.

neural network In artificial intelligence, a computer architecture that attempts to mimic the structure of the human brain. Neural nets "learn" by trial and error and are good at recognizing patterns and dealing with complexity.

newsgroup In Usenet, a discussion group devoted to a single topic. Users post messages to the group, and those reading the discussion send reply messages to the author individually or post replies that can be read by the group as a whole.

node In a LAN, a connection point that can create, receive, or repeat a message.

nonprocedural Not tied down to step-by-step procedures. In programming, a nonprocedural programming language does not force the programmer to consider the procedure that must be followed to obtain the desired result.

nonvolatile Not susceptible to loss. If power is lost, the data is preserved.

notebook computer A portable computer that is small enough to fit into an average-size briefcase but includes nearly all peripherals commonly found on desktop computers.

nuking A type of antisocial behavior found on Internet Relay Chat characterized by exploiting bugs that cause computer crashes.

numeric check Ensures that numbers are entered into a field.

O

object 1. In object-oriented programming (OOP), a unit of computer information that contains data and all the procedures or operations that can process or manipulate the data. 2. Nontextual data. Examples of objects include pictures, sounds, or videos.

object code In programming, the machine-readable instructions created by a compiler from source code.

object-oriented database The newest type of database structure, well suited for multimedia applications, in which the result of a retrieval operation is an object of some kind, such as a document. Within this object are miniprograms that enable the object to perform tasks such as displaying graphics. Object-oriented databases can incorporate sound, video, text, and graphics into a single database record.

object-oriented (OO) programming A programming technique that creates generic building blocks of a program (the objects). The user then assembles different sets of objects as needed to solve specific problems. Also called OOP, for object-oriented programming.

Office Clipboard In Microsoft Office, a feature that temporarily stores in memory whatever has been cut or copied from a document, allowing for those items to be used within any Office application.

office suite See software suite.

offshoring The transfer of labor from workers in one country to workers in other countries.

off-the-shelf software See packaged software.

on-board video Video circuitry that comes built into a computer's motherboard.

online Directly connected to the network.

online analytical processing (OLAP) In a decision support system (DSS), a method of providing rich, up-to-the-minute data from transaction databases.

online banking The use of a Web browser to access bank accounts, balance checkbooks, transfer funds, and pay bills.

online processing The processing of data immediately after it has been input by a user, as opposed to waiting until a predetermined time, as in batch processing.

online service A for-profit firm that makes current news, stock quotes, and other information available to its subscribers over standard telephone lines. Popular services include supervised chat rooms for text chatting and forums for topical discussion. Online services also provide Internet access.

online stock trading The purchase or sale of stock through the Internet.

online storage A type of storage that is directly available, such as a hard disk, and requires no special action on the user's part to enable.

online travel reservations A rapidly growing area of e-commerce that allows consumers to use the Internet to research, book, and purchase airline flights, hotel rooms, and rental cars.

open To transfer an existing document from storage to memory.

open source software Software in which the source code is made available to the program's users.

operating system (OS) A program that integrates and controls the computer's internal functions and provides a user interface.

operational decisions Management decisions concerning localized issues (such as an inventory shortage) that need immediate action.

operational feasibility Capable of being accomplished with an organization's available resources.

operational support system (OSS) A suite of programs that supports an enterprise's network operations.

optical character recognition (OCR) Software that automatically decodes imaged text into a text file. Most scanners come with OCR software.

optical mark reader (OMR) A reader that senses magnetized marks made by the magnetic particles in lead from a pencil.

optical storage A storage system in which a storage device retains data using surface patterns that are physically encoded on the surface of plastic discs. The patterns can be detected by a laser beam.

optical storage device A computer storage device that retains data in microscopic patterns, detectable by a laser beam, encoded on the surface of plastic discs.

options Choices within an application that allow users to change defaults and to specify how they want the program to operate.

output The results of processing information, typically shown on a monitor or a printer.

output devices Monitors, printers, and other machines that enable people to see, hear, and even feel the results of processing operations.

outsourcing The transfer of a project to an external contractor.

P

packaged software Ready-to-use software that is sold through mass-market channels and contains features useful to the largest possible user base. Synonymous with off-the-shelf software and shrink-wrapped software.

packet In a packet-switching network, a unit of data of a fixed size—not exceeding the network's maximum transmission unit (MTU) size—that has been prepared for network transmission. Each packet contains a header that indicates its origin and its destination. See also packet switching.

packet sniffer In computer security, a device that examines all traffic on a network and retrieves valuable information such as passwords and credit card numbers.

packet switching One of two fundamental architectures for a wide area network (WAN); the other is a circuit-switching network. In a packet-switching network such as the Internet, no effort is made to establish a single electrical circuit between two computing devices; for this reason, packet-switching networks are often called connectionless. Instead, the sending computer divides a message into packets, each of which contains the address of the destination computer, and dumps them onto the network. They are intercepted by devices called routers, which send the packets in the appropriate direction. The receiving computer assembles the packets, puts them in order, and delivers the received message to the appropriate application. Packet-switching networks are highly reliable and efficient, but they are not suited to the delivery of real-time voice and video.

page In virtual memory, a fixed size of program instructions and data that can be stored on the hard disk to free up random access memory.

page description language (PDL) A programming language capable of precisely describing the appearance of a printed page, including fonts and graphics.

paging An operating system's transference of files from storage to memory and back.

paint program A program that enables the user to paint the screen by specifying the color of the individual pixels that make up the screen display.

parallel conversion In the development of an information system, the operation of both the new and old information systems at the same time to ensure the compatibility and reliability of the new system.

parallel port An interface that uses several side-by-side wires so that one or more bytes of computer data can travel in unison and arrive simultaneously. Parallel ports offer faster performance than serial ports, in which each bit of data must travel in a line, one after the other.

parallel processing The use of more than one processor to run two or more portions of a program simultaneously.

partition A section of a storage device, such as a hard disk, that is prepared so that it can be treated as if it were a completely separate device for data storage and maintenance.

Pascal A high-level programming language that encourages programmers to write well-structured programs, named after seventeenth-century mathematician Blaise Pascal.

passive matrix LCD An inexpensive liquid crystal display (LCD) that sometimes generates image flaws and is too slow for full-motion video. Also called dual scan LCD.

password A unique word that a user types to log on to a system. Passwords should not be obvious and should be changed frequently.

password guessing In computer security, a method of defeating password authentication by guessing common passwords, such as personal names, obscene words, and the word "password."

path The sequence of directories that the computer must follow to locate a file.

pattern recognition In artificial intelligence, the use of a computer system to recognize patterns, such as thumbprints, and associate these patterns with stored data or instructions.

PC 100 SDRAM A type of SDRAM capable of keeping up with motherboards that have bus speeds of 100 MHz.

PC card Synonymous with PCMCIA card. A computer accessory (such as a modem or network interface card) that is designed to fit into a compatible PC card slot mounted on the computer's case. PC cards and slots are commonly used on notebook computers because they offer system expandability while consuming a small fraction of the space required for expansion cards.

peer-to-peer network A computer network design in which all the computers can access the public files located on other computers in a network.

pen computer A computer operated with a stylus, such as a personal digital assistant (PDA).

peripheral A device connected to and controlled by a computer, but external to the computer's central processing unit.

PCI (Peripheral Component Interconnect) bus A type of expansion bus used with Macs and PCs to communicate with input and output devices, containing expansion slots to accommodate plug-in expansion cards.

Personal Communication Service (PCS) A digital cellular phone service that is rapidly replacing analog cellular phones.

personal computer (PC) A computer system that meets the computing needs of an individual. The term PC usually refers to an IBM-compatible personal computer.

Personal Computer Memory Card International Association (PCMCIA) card See PC card.

personal computing Any situation or setup where one person controls and uses a PC for personal or business activities.

personal digital assistant (PDA) A small, handheld computer that accepts input written on-screen with a stylus. Most include built-in software for appointments, scheduling, and e-mail. Also called palmtop.

personal firewall A program or device that is designed to protect home computer users from unauthorized access.

personal information manager (PIM) A program that stores and retrieves a variety of personal information, such as appointments. PIMs have been slow to gain acceptance due to their lack of convenience and portability.

personal productivity program Application software, such as word processing software or a spreadsheet program, that assists individuals in doing their work more effectively and efficiently.

phased conversion In the development of an information system, the implementation of the new system in different time periods, one part at a time.

photo checkout systems Used with POS terminals, a security check that accesses a database of customer photos and displays the customer's picture when a credit card is used.

photo-editing program A program that enables images to be enhanced, edited, cropped, or sized. The same program can be used to print the images on a color printer.

phrase searching In database and Web searching, a search that retrieves only documents that contain the entire phrase.

picture messaging A mobile service that allows you to send full-color pictures, backgrounds, and even picture caller IDs on your cell phone.

pilot conversion In the development of an information system, the institution of the new system in only one part of an organization. When that portion of the organization is satisfied with the system, the rest of the organization then starts using it.

pipelining A design that provides two or more processing pathways that can be used simultaneously.

pit A microscopic indentation in the surface of an optical disc that absorbs the light of the optical drive's laser, corresponding to a 0 in the computer's binary number system.

pixel Short for picture element, the smallest element that a device can display and out of which the displayed image is constructed.

plagiarism The presentation of somebody else's work as if it were one's own.

Plain Old Telephone Service (POTS) A term used to describe the standard analog telephone service.

plaintext A readable message before it is encrypted.

platform A distinct type of computer that uses a certain type of processor and operating system, such as a Macintosh or an Intel-based Windows PC.

platter In a hard drive, a fixed, rapidly rotating disk that is coated with a magnetically sensitive material. High-capacity hard drives typically have two or more platters.

plotter A printer that produces high-quality output by moving ink pens over the surface of the paper.

Plug and Play (PnP) A set of standards jointly developed by Intel Corporation and Microsoft that enables users of Microsoft Windows–based PCs to configure new hardware devices automatically. Operating systems equipped with plug-and-play capabilities can automatically detect new PnP-compatible peripherals that may have been installed while the power was switched off.

point of presence (PoP) A locality in which it is possible to obtain dialup access to the network by means of a local telephone call. Internet service providers (ISPs) provide PoPs in towns and cities, but many rural areas are without local PoPs.

point-and-shoot digital cameras Digital cameras that typically include automatic focus, automatic exposure, built-in automatic electronic flash with red eye reduction, and optical zoom lenses with digital enhancement.

point-of-sale (POS) terminal A computer-based cash register that enables transaction data to be captured at the checkout stand. Such terminals can automatically adjust inventory databases and enable managers to analyze sales patterns.

pointer An on-screen symbol, usually an arrow, that shows the current position of the mouse.

pointing device Any input device that is capable of moving the on-screen pointer in a graphical user interface (GUI), such as a mouse or trackball.

pointing stick A pointing device introduced by IBM that enables users to move the pointer around the screen by manipulating a small, stubby stick that protrudes slightly from the surface of the keyboard.

popup menu A menu that appears at the mouse pointer's position when you click the right mouse button.

port An interface that controls the flow of data between the central processing unit and external devices such as printers and monitors.

portable Able to be easily removed or inserted or transferred to a different type of computer system.

Portable Network Graphics (PNG) A graphics file format closely resembling the GIF format but lacking GIF's proprietary compression technique (which forces publishers of GIF-enabled graphics software to pay a licensing fee).

portal On the Web, a page that attempts to provide an attractive starting point for Web sessions. Typically included are links to breaking news, weather forecasts, stock quotes, free e-mail service, sports scores, and a subject guide to information available on the Web. Leading portals include Netscape's NetCenter (www.netcenter.com), Yahoo! (www.yahoo.com), and Snap! (www.snap.com).

positioning performance A measure of how much time elapses from the initiation of drive activity until the hard disk has positioned the read/write head so that it can begin transferring data.

post-implementation system review In the development of an information system, the ongoing evaluation of the information system to determine whether it has met its goals.

power-on light A light on the front panel of most computers that signals whether the power is on.

power-on self test (POST) The series of system integrity tests that a computer goes through every time it is started (cold boot) or restarted (warm boot). These tests verify that vital system components, such as the memory, are functioning properly.

power outage A sudden loss of electrical power, causing the loss of all unsaved information on a computer.

power supply A device that supplies power to a computer system by converting AC current to DC current and lowering the voltage.

power surge A sudden and sometimes destructive increase in the amount of voltage delivered through a power line.

power switch A switch that turns the computer on and off. Often located in the rear of a computer.

preemptive multitasking In operating systems, a method of running more than one application at a time. Unlike cooperative multitasking, preemptive multitasking allows other applications to continue running if one application crashes.

presentation graphics A software package used to make presentations visually attractive and easy to understand.

primary cache A small unit (8 KB to 32 KB) of ultra-fast memory included with a microprocessor and used to store frequently accessed data and improve overall system performance.

primary folder A main folder such as is created at the root of a drive to hold further subfolders. Also called top-level folder.

primary storage See online storage.

printed circuit board A flat piece of plastic or fiberglass on which complex patterns of copper pathways have been created by means of etching. These paths link integrated circuits and other electrical components.

printer An output device that prints computer-generated text or graphics onto paper or another physical medium.

privacy The right to live your life without undue intrusions into your personal affairs by government agencies or corporate marketers.

private key A decryption key.

problem A state of difficulty that needs to be resolved; the underlying cause of a symptom.

procedural language A programming language that tells the computer what to do and how to do it.

procedure The steps that must be followed to accomplish a specific computer-related task.

processing The execution of arithmetic or comparison operations on data.

processing cycle See machine cycle.

processor See central processing unit (CPU).

professional organizations (associations) IT organizations that can help you keep up with your area of interest as well as provide valuable career contacts.

professional workstation A very powerful computer system for engineers, financial analysts, and other professionals who need exceptionally powerful processing and output capabilities. Professional workstations are very expensive.

profile In a consumer-oriented operating system such as Windows 98, a record of a user's preferences that is associated with a user name and password. If you set up two or more profiles, users see their own preferences. However, profiles do not prevent users from accessing and overwriting each others' files. Compare with account.

program A list of instructions telling the computer what to do.

program development life cycle (PDLC) A step-by-step procedure used to develop software for information systems.

program maintenance In phase 6 of the PDLC, the process in which the programming team fixes program errors discovered by users.

program specification In software development, a technical description of the software needed by the information system. The program specification precisely defines input data, the processing that occurs, the output format, and the user interface.

programmer A person skilled in the use of one or more programming languages. Although most programmers have college degrees in computer science, certification is an increasingly popular way to demonstrate one's programming expertise.

programming language An artificial language composed of a fixed vocabulary and a set of rules used to create instructions for a computer to follow.

project dictionary In the development of information systems, a compilation of all terminology relevant to the project.

project notebook In the development of an information system, a place where information regarding system development is stored.

project plan A specification of the goals, scope, and individual activities that make up a project.

project proposal In phase 1 of the SDLC, a document that introduces the nature of the existing system's problem, explains the proposed solution and its benefits, details the proposed project plan, and concludes with a recommendation.

protocol In data communications and networking, a standard specifying the format of data and the rules to be followed. Networks could not be easily or efficiently designed or maintained without protocols; a protocol specifies how a program should prepare data so that it can be sent to the next stage in the communication process. For example, e-mail programs prepare messages so that they conform to prevailing Internet mail standards, which are recognized by every program involved in the transmission of mail over the network.

protocol stack In a computer network, a means of conceptualizing network architecture in which the various layers of network functionality are viewed as a vertical stack, like the layers of a layer cake, in computers linked to the network. When one computer sends a message to the network, the message goes down the stack and then traverses the network; on the receiving computer, the message goes up the stack.

protocol suite In a computer network, the collection of network protocols that defines the network's functionality.

prototyping In information systems development, the creation of a working system model that is functional enough to draw feedback from users. Also called joint application development (JAD).

providing the user interface One of the five basic functions of an operating system in which the part of the operating system that you see and interact with and by which users and programs communicate with each other is provided.

pseudocode In structured programming, a stylized form of writing used as an alternative to flowcharts to describe the logic of a program.

public domain software Noncopyrighted software that anyone may copy and use without charge and without acknowledging the source.

public key In public key cryptography, the encoding key, which you make public so that others can send you encrypted messages. The message can be encoded with the public key, but it cannot be decoded without the private key, which you alone possess.

public key cryptography In cryptography, a revolutionary new method of encryption that does not require the message's receiver to have received the decoding key in a separate transmission. The need to send the key, required to decode the message, is the chief vulnerability of previous encryption techniques. Public key cryptography has two keys: a public one and a private one. The public key is used for encryption, and the private key is used for decryption.

public key encryption A computer security process in which an encryption (or private) key and a decryption (or public) key are used to safeguard data.

public key infrastructure (PKI) A uniform set of encryption standards that specify how public key encryption, digital signatures, and CA-granted digital certificates should be implemented in computer systems and on the Internet.

public switched telephone network (PSTN) The world telephone system, a massive network used for data communication as well as voice.

pull-down menu In a graphical user interface (GUI), a named item on the menu bar that, when clicked, displays an on-screen menu of commands and options.

pumping and dumping An illegal stock price manipulation tactic that involves purchasing shares of a worthless corporation and then driving the price up by making unsubstantiated claims about the company's value in Internet newsgroups and chat rooms. The perpetrator sells the shares after the stock price goes up but before other investors wise up to the ploy.

Q

query In the Microsoft Access database management system, the object used to ask questions of the database.

query language A retrieval and data-editing language for composing simple or complex requests for data.

quoted size The front surface measured diagonally on a cathode-ray tube monitor, a figure that is greater than the viewable area, since some of the surface is hidden and unavailable for display purposes. See viewable area.

QWERTY keyboard A keyboard that uses the standard keyboard layout in which the first six letters on the left of the top row spell "QWERTY."

R

radio A wireless signaling technology that sends data by means of electromagnetic waves that travel through air and space between separate or combined transmitting and receiving devices.

RAID (redundant array of independent disks) A storage device that groups two or more hard disks containing exactly the same data.

Rambus DRAM Type of RAM that uses a narrow but very fast bus to connect to the microprocessor.

random access An information storage and retrieval technique in which the computer can access information directly, without having to go through a sequence of locations.

random access memory (RAM) Another name for the computer's main working memory, where program instructions and data are stored to be easily accessed by the central processing unit through the processor's high-speed data bus. When a computer is turned off, all data in RAM is lost.

random access storage device A storage device that can begin reading data directly without having to go through a lengthy sequence of data.

range check Verifies that the entered data fall within an acceptable range.

rapid application development (RAD) In object-oriented programming, a method of program development in which programmers work with a library of prebuilt objects, allowing them to build programs more quickly.

raster graphics See bitmapped graphics.

ray tracing A 3-D rendering technique in which color intensity on a graphic object is varied to simulate light falling on the object from multiple directions.

read To retrieve data or program instructions from a storage device such as a hard or floppy disk.

read/write The capability of a primary or secondary storage device to record (write) data and to play back (read) data previously recorded or saved.

read/write head In a hard or floppy disk, the magnetic recording and playback device that travels back and forth across the surface of the disk, storing and retrieving data.

read-only Capable of being displayed or used but not altered or deleted.

read-only memory (ROM) The part of a computer's primary storage that contains essential computer instructions and doesn't lose its contents when the power is turned off. Information in read-only memory cannot be erased by the computer.

record In a database, a group of one or more fields that contains information about something.

reengineering See business process reengineering (BPR).

refresh rate The frequency with which the screen is updated. The refresh rate determines whether the display appears to flicker.

register 1. In a microprocessor, a memory location used to store values and external memory addresses while the microprocessor performs logical and arithmetic operations on them. 2. In commercial software and shareware, to contact the software vendor and submit a form that includes personal information such as the user's name and address. Registering allows the software vendor to inform the user of important information and software updates.

registration fee An amount of money that must be paid to the author of a piece of shareware to continue using it beyond the duration of the evaluation period.

registry 1. A database that contains information about installed peripherals and software. 2. In Microsoft Windows, an important system file that contains configuration settings that Windows requires in order to operate.

relational database management system (RDBMS) A type of database software that uses the contents of a particular field as an index to reference particular records.

removable hard disk A hard disk that uses a removable cartridge instead of a sealed unit with a fixed, nonremovable platter.

repetition control structure In structured programming, a logical construction of commands repeated over and over. Also called looping or iteration control structure.

repetitive strain injury (RSI) See carpal tunnel syndrome.

Report In the Microsoft Access database management system, the object used to present data.

report generator In programming, a programming language for printing database reports. One of four parts of a database management system (DBMS) that helps the user design and generate reports and graphs in hard copy form.

request for proposal (RFP) In the development of information systems, a request to an outside vendor to write a proposal for the design, installation, and configuration of an information system.

request for quotation (RFQ) In the development of information systems, a request to an outside vendor or value-added reseller (VAR) to quote a price for specific information components.

requirements analysis A process in phase 1 of the SDLC that determines the requirements of the system by analyzing how the system will meet the needs of end users.

reset switch A switch on the front panel of most computers that can restart the computer in the event of a failure.

resolution A measurement, usually expressed in linear dots per inch (dpi) both horizontally and vertically, of the sharpness of an image generated by an output device such as a monitor or a printer.

restore To return a window to its size and position before it was maximized.

return on investment (ROI) The overall financial yield of a project at the end of its lifetime. ROI is often used by managers to decide whether a project is a good investment.

right pane In the My Computer primary file management utility for PCs, one of two main default windows. It displays the various files and drives you can choose from. See also left pane.

ring topology The physical layout of a local network in which all nodes are attached in a circle, without a central host computer.

rip and tear A confidence scam that involves convincing people that they have won a large sweepstakes prize but they cannot obtain the needed information unless they pay a fee. The prize never materializes, and the perpetrators disappear.

robot A computer-based device that is programmed to perform useful motions.

robotics A division of computer science that is devoted to improving the performance and capabilities of robots.

rot-13 In Usenet newsgroups, a simple encryption technique that offsets each character by 13 places (so that an e becomes an r, for example).

router In a packet-switching network such as the Internet, one of two basic devices (the other is a host). A router is an electronic device that examines each packet of data it receives and then decides which way to send it toward its destination.

routine (also referred to as a procedure, function, or subroutine) A section of code that executes a specific task in a program.

row In a spreadsheet, a block of cells going across the screen.

S

safe mode An operating mode in which Windows loads a minimal set of drivers that are known to function correctly.

salami shaving A computer crime in which a program is altered so that it transfers a small amount of money from a large number of accounts to make a large profit.

sales force automation (SFA) software Software that automates many of the business processes involved with sales, including processing and tracking orders, managing customers and other contacts, monitoring and controlling inventory, and analyzing sales forecasts.

satellite In data communications, a communications reflector placed in a geosynchronous (stationary) orbit.

satellite radio A type of communications technology that broadcasts radio signals back and forth between satellites orbiting more than 22,000 miles above the Earth and radio receivers on Earth.

save To transfer data from the computer's memory to a storage device for safekeeping.

save as A command that enables the user to store a document with a new name.

saving In an application software program, the process of transferring a document from the computer's temporary memory to a permanent storage device, such as a hard disk, for safekeeping.

scalability A hardware or software system's ability to continue functioning effectively as demands and use increase.

scanner A device that copies the image (text or graphic) on a sheet of paper and translates it into a digital image. Scanners use charge-coupled devices to digitize the image.

script A short program written in a simple programming language, called a scripting language.

scripting language A simple programming language that enables users to create useful programs (scripts) quickly. VBScript is one example of a scripting language.

scroll To bring hidden parts of a document into view within the application workspace.

scroll arrow An arrow appearing within the scroll bar that enables the user to scroll up or down (or, in a horizontal scroll bar, left and right) by small increments.

scroll bar A vertical or horizontal bar that contains scroll arrows and a scroll box. The scroll bar enables the user to bring hidden portions of a document into view within the application workspace.

search engine Any program that locates needed information in a database, but especially an Internet-accessible search service (such as AltaVista or HotBot) that enables you to search for information on the Internet.

search operator In a database or a Web search engine, a word or a symbol that enables you to specify your search with precision.

search utility A utility program which enables you to search an entire hard disk for a file (in Microsoft Windows it is called the Search Companion; in Mac OS it is called Find File).

secondary cache A small unit (256 K to 1 MB) of ultra-fast memory used to store frequently accessed data and improve overall system performance. The secondary cache is usually located on a separate circuit board from the microprocessor, although backside cache memory is located on the processor. Also called level 2 (L2) cache.

secondary folder See subfolder.

secondary storage See near-online storage.

sector A pie-shaped wedge of the concentric tracks encoded on a disk during formatting. Two or more sectors combine to form a cluster.

secure electronic transfer (SET) An online shopping security standard for merchants and customers that uses digital certificates.

secure mode In a Web browser, a mode of operation in which all communication to and from the server is encrypted.

seek time In a secondary storage device, the time it takes for the read/write head to reach the correct location on the disk. Seek times are often used with rotational speed to compare the performance of hard drives.

selection control structure In structured programming, a method of handling a program branch by using an IF-THEN-ELSE structure. This is more efficient than using a GOTO statement. Also called conditional or branch control structure.

sequence control structure In structured programming, a logical construction of programming commands executed in the order in which they appear.

sequential storage device A storage device that cannot begin reading data until the device has moved through a sequence of data in order to locate the desired beginning point.

serial port An input/output (I/O) interface that is designed to convey data in a bit-by-bit stream. Compare with parallel port.

server A computer dedicated to providing information in response to external requests.

setup program A utility program provided by a computer's manufacturer that enables users to specify basic system configuration settings, such as the correct time and date and the type of hard disk that is installed in the system. Setup programs are accessible by pressing a special key (such as Delete) during the computer's power-on self test (POST).

shareware Copyrighted software that may be tried without expense but requires the payment of a registration fee if you decide to use it after a specified trial period.

sheets In Microsoft Excel workbook files, the 255 sets of columns and rows intersecting at cells.

shill In an auction, an accomplice of the seller who drives up prices by bidding for an item that the shill has no intention of buying.

shoulder surfing In computer security, a method of defeating password authentication by peeking over a user's shoulder and watching the keyboard as the user inputs his or her password.

signature capture A computer system that captures a customer's signature digitally, so that the store can prove that a purchase was made.

single-lens reflex (SLR) digital camera Expensive digital camera that offers features such as interchangeable lenses, through-the-lens image previewing, and the ability to override the automatic focus and exposure settings.

single point of failure (SPOF) Any system component, such as hardware or software, that causes the entire system to malfunction when it fails.

single tasking operating system Capable of running only one application at a time.

site license An agreement with a software publisher that allows multiple copies of the software to be made for use within an organization.

slide In a presentation graphics program, an on-screen image sized in proportion to a 35mm slide.

sleep See standby.

Small Computer System Interface (SCSI) A bus standard for connecting peripheral devices to personal computers, including hard disks, CD-ROM discs, and scanners.

small office/home office (SOHO) Small businesses run out of homes or small offices—a rapidly growing market segment.

Smalltalk An early object-oriented programming language that many OO promoters believe is still the only pure OO language.

smart card A card that resembles a credit card but has a microprocessor and memory chip, enabling the card to process as well as store information.

smart tags In Microsoft Office, icons attached to items, allowing various choices for how text is treated when pasted within an application or between applications.

snapshot printer A thermal transfer printer that prints the output of digital cameras at a maximum size of 4 by 6 inches. Snapshot printers are less expensive than other thermal transfer printers.

social engineering A method of defeating password authentication by impersonating a network administrator and asking users for their passwords.

soft copy A temporary form of output, as in a monitor display.

software One of two basic components of a computer system (the other is hardware). Software includes all the instructions that tell the computer what to do.

software engineering A new field that applies the principles of mainstream engineering to software production.

software license An agreement included with most commercial software that stipulates what the user may and may not do with the software.

software piracy Unauthorized duplication of copyrighted software.

software suite A collection of full-featured, standalone programs that usually share a common command structure and have similar interfaces.

software upgrading The process of keeping a version of an application current with the marketplace, whether through patches, service releases, or new versions.

solid state storage device This device consists of nonvolatile memory chips, which retain the data stored in them even if the chips are disconnected from their current source.

sound board See sound card.

sound card An adapter that adds digital sound reproduction capabilities to an IBM-compatible PC. Also called a sound board.

sound file A file containing digitized sound that can be played back if a computer is equipped with multimedia.

sound format A specification of how a sound should be digitally represented. Sound formats usually include some type of data compression to reduce the size of sound files.

source code The typed program instructions that people write. The program is then translated into machine instructions that the computer can execute.

spaghetti code In programming, source code that contains numerous GOTO statements and is, in consequence, difficult to understand and prone to error.

spam Unsolicited e-mail or newsgroup advertising.

speaker A device that plays the computer's audio output.

specialized search engines Web location programs that index particular types of information, such as job advertisements.

speculative execution A technique used by advanced CPUs to prevent a pipeline stall. The processor executes and temporarily stores the next instruction in case it proves useful.

speech recognition The use of a computer system to detect the words spoken by a human being into a microphone, and translate these words into text that appears on-screen. Compare with speech synthesis.

spreadsheet A program that processes information in the form of tables. Table cells can hold values or mathematical formulas.

spreadsheet programs The computer equivalent of an accountant's worksheet.

spyware Internet software that is placed on a computer without the user's awareness, usually during a shareware or freeware download.

SQL Abbreviation for Structured Query Language. SQL is a standardized query language for requesting information from a database.

standalone program An application sold individually.

standard toolbar In Microsoft Office, a default-loaded toolbar that includes icons for various functions, including opening, closing, and printing files.

standby A low-power state that allows an operating system to be restored to full power quickly without going through the lengthy boot process; called sleep in the Mac OS.

star topology The physical layout of a local network in which a host computer manages the network.

start tag In HTML, the first component of an element. The start tag contains the element's name, such as <H1> or <P>.

starting the computer One of the five basic functions of an operating system in which a computer loads the operating system into the computer's RAM.

status bar An area within a typical application's window that is reserved for the program's messages to the user.

storage A general term for computer components that offer nonvolatile retention of computer data and program instructions.

storage area network (SAN) Links high capacity storage devices to all of an organization's servers, which makes any of the storage devices accessible from any of the servers.

storage device A hardware component that is capable of retaining data even when electrical power is switched off. An example of a storage device is a hard disk. Compare with memory.

storage media A collective term used to describe all types of storage devices.

store One of four basic operations carried out by the control unit of a microprocessor that involves writing the results of previous operations to an internal register.

strategic decisions Executive decisions concerning the organization's overall goals and direction.

streaming audio An Internet sound delivery technology that sends audio data as a continuous, compressed stream that is played back on the fly.

streaming video An Internet video delivery technology that sends video data as a continuous, compressed stream that is played back on the fly. Like streaming audio, streaming video begins playing almost immediately. A high-speed modem is required. Quality is marginal; the video appears in a small, on-screen window, and motion is jerky.

strong AI In artificial intelligence, a research focus based on the conviction that computers will achieve the ultimate goal of artificial intelligence, namely, rivaling the intelligence of humans.

structural unemployment Unemployment caused by advancing technology that makes an entire job obsolete.

structure chart See hierarchy chart.

structured programming A set of quality standards that make programs more verbose but more readable, more reliable, and more easily maintained. A program is broken up into manageable components, each of which contributes to the overall goal of the program. Also called top-down program design.

stylus A pen-shaped instrument used to draw on a graphics tablet or to input commands and handwriting to a personal digital assistant (PDA).

subdirectory A directory created in another directory. A subdirectory can contain files and additional subdirectories.

subfolder A folder within a folder, usually created to allow for better file organization. Also known as secondary folder.

subject guide On the World Wide Web, an information discovery service that contains hyperlinks classified by subjects in broad categories and multiple levels of subcategories.

subnotebook A portable computer that omits some components (such as a CD-ROM drive) to cut down on weight and size.

subscriber loop carrier (SLC) A small, waist-high curbside installation of the public switched telephone network that transforms local home and business analog calls into digital signals and routes them through high-capacity cables to the local exchange switch.

summary report In a transaction processing system (TPS), a document that provides a quick overview of an organization's performance.

Super Video Graphics Array (SVGA) An enhancement of the VGA display standard that can display as much as 1,280 pixels by 1,024,768 lines with as many as 16.7 million colors.

supercomputer A sophisticated, expensive computer that executes complex calculations at the maximum speed permitted by state-of-the-art technology. Supercomputers are used mostly by the government and for scientific research.

superscalar architecture A design that lets the microprocessor take a sequential instruction and send several instructions at a time to separate execution units so that the processor can execute multiple instructions per cycle.

superuser status In multiuser operating systems, a classification normally given only to network administrators, enabling them to access and modify virtually any file on the network. If intruders obtain superuser status, they can obtain the passwords of everyone on the network.

surge protector An inexpensive electrical device that prevents high-voltage surges from reaching a computer and damaging its circuitry.

swap file In virtual memory, a file on the hard disk used to store pages of virtual memory information.

swapping In virtual memory, the operation of exchanging program instructions and data between the swap file (located on the hard disk) and random access memory (RAM).

symmetric key encryption Encryption techniques that use the same key for encryption and decryption.

symptom An indication or a sign of something; an unacceptable or undesirable result.

syn flooding See denial of service (DoS) attack.

synchronous DRAM (SDRAM) The fastest available memory chip technology.

Synchronous Optical Network (SONET) A standard for high-performance networks using optical fiber.

syntax The rules governing the structure of commands, statements, or instructions given to a computer.

syntax error In programming, a flaw in the structure of commands, statements, or instructions.

synthesizer An audio component that uses FM (frequency modulation), wavetable, or waveguide technology to create sounds imitative of actual musical instruments.

system A collection of components purposefully organized into a functioning whole to accomplish a goal.

system clock An electronic circuit in the computer that emits pulses at regular intervals, enabling the computer's internal components to operate in synchrony.

system requirements The stated minimum system performance capabilities required to run an application program, including the minimum amount of disk space, memory, and processor capacity.

system software All the software used to operate and maintain a computer system, including the operating system and utility programs.

system unit A boxlike case that houses the computer's main hardware components and provides a sturdy frame for mounting and protecting internal devices, connectors, and drives.

system utilities Programs such as speaker volume control and antivirus software that are loaded by the operating system.

systems analysis A discipline devoted to the rational and organized planning, development, and implementation of artificial systems, including information systems.

systems analyst A computer professional who helps plan, develop, and implement information systems.

systems development life cycle (SDLC) An organized way of planning and building information systems.

systems engineering A field of engineering devoted to the scientific study of artificial systems and the training of systems analysts.

system utilities Programs, such as file management and file finder, that provide a necessary addition to an operating system's basic system-management tools.

T

T1 A high-bandwidth telephone trunk line capable of transferring 1.544 megabits per second (Mbps) of data.

T3 A high-bandwidth fiber-optic line capable of handling 43 megabits per second (Mbps) of computer data.

table In the Microsoft Access database management system, the object used to store data.

tablet PC A type of notebook computer that has an LCD screen that the user can write on using a special-purpose pen or stylus.

tactical decisions Middle management decisions about how to best organize resources to achieve their division's goals.

tactile display A display that stimulates the sense of touch using vibration, pressure, and temperature changes.

tailor-made applications Software designed for specialized fields or the consumer market, such as programs that handle the billing needs of medical offices, manage restaurants, and track occupational injuries.

tangible benefits In a cost-benefit analysis, benefits such as increased sales, faster response time, and decreased complaints that can be easily measured.

task pane In Microsoft Office, a feature that usually appears on the right side of an opened application window and that provides various options, such as for opening or formatting work.

TCP/IP The two most important Internet protocols. See Transmission Control Protocol and Internet Protocol.

technical skills Skills such as knowledge and experience in networking, Microsoft Windows XP, UNIX, C++, and Internet-related technologies.

technical feasibility Able to be accomplished with respect to existing, proven technology.

telecommuting Performing work at home while linked to the office by means of a telecommunications-equipped computer system.

teleconferencing A simple and secure wired voice communications application in which more than two distant people conduct business by conference call.

terabyte (T or TB) A unit of measurement commonly used to state the capacity of memory or storage devices; equal to 1,024 gigabytes, or approximately one trillion bytes or characters.

terminal An input/output device consisting of a keyboard and a video display that is commonly used with mainframe and minicomputer systems.

text messaging A mobile service, similar to using your phone for instant messaging or as a receiver and transmitter for brief e-mail messages.

thermal transfer printer A printer that uses a heat process to transfer colored dyes or inks to the paper's surface. Although thermal transfer printers are the best color printers currently available, they are very expensive.

third-generation language (3GL) A programming language that tells the computer what to do and how to do it but eliminates the need for understanding the intimate details of how the computer works.

thread 1. In multithreading, a single type of task that can be executed simultaneously with other tasks. 2. In Usenet, a series of articles on the same specific subject.

time bomb A destructive program that sits harmlessly until a certain event or set of circumstances makes the program active.

time-limited trial versions Internet-offered commercial programs capable of being used on a trial basis for a period of time, after which the software is unusable.

title bar In a graphical user interface (GUI), the top bar of an application window. The title bar typically contains the name of the application, the name of the document, and window controls.

toggle key A key on a keyboard that functions like a switch. When pressed, the function is turned on, and when pressed again, the function is turned off.

token A handheld device used to gain access to a computer system, such as an automated teller machine (ATM).

toolbar In a graphical user interface (GUI), a bar near the top of the window that contains a row of graphical buttons. These buttons provide quick access to the most frequently used program commands.

tools menu In a graphical user interface (GUI), a menu that provides access to special program features and utilities, such as spell-checking.

top-down program design See structured programming.

top-level domain (TLD) name The last part of an Internet computer address. For computers located in the United States, it indicates the type of organization in which the computer is located, such as commercial businesses (com), educational institutions (edu), and government agencies (gov).

top-level folder See primary folder.

topology See network topology.

touch screen A touch-sensitive display that enables users to input choices by touching a region of the screen.

touchpad An input device for portable computers that moves the pointer. The touchpad is a small pad in front of the keyboard that moves the pointer when the user moves a finger on the pad.

tower case A tall and deep system unit case designed to sit on the floor next to a desk and easily accommodate add-on components.

track One of several concentric circular bands on computer disks where data is recorded, similar to the grooves on a phonographic record. Tracks are created during formatting and are divided into sectors.

trackball An input device, similar to the mouse, that moves the pointer. The trackball looks something like an inverted mouse and does not require the desk space that a mouse does.

trackpad See touchpad.

trackpoint An input device on some notebook computers that resembles a tiny pencil eraser; you move the cursor by pushing the tip of the trackpoint.

tracks The concentric circular bands on a hard disk. Data is recorded in the tracks, which are divided into sectors to help keep track of where specific files are located.

trade show A periodic meeting in which computer product manufacturers, designers, and dealers display their products.

traditional organizational structure In an organization, a method used to distribute the core functions of the organization into divisions such as finance, human resources, and operations.

training seminars Computer-related training sessions, typically presented by the developer of a new hardware or software product or by a company specializing in training IT professionals in a new technology.

transaction processing system (TPS) A system that handles the day-to-day operations of a company; examples include sales, purchases, orders, and returns.

transfer performance A measure of how quickly read/write heads are able to transfer data from a hard disk to memory.

transistor A device invented in 1947 by Bell Laboratories that controls the flow of electricity. Due to their small size, reduced power consumption, and lower heat output, transistors replaced vacuum tubes in the second generation of computers.

Transmission Control Protocol (TCP) One of two basic Internet protocols (the other is Internet Protocol, IP). TCP is the protocol (standard) that permits two Internet-connected computers to establish a reliable connection. TCP ensures reliable data delivery with a method known as Positive Acknowledgment with Re-transmission (PAR). The computer that sends the data continues to do so until it receives a confirmation from the receiving computer that the data has been received intact.

trap door In computer security, a security hole created on purpose that can be exploited at a later time.

Trojan horse An application disguised as a useful program but containing instructions to perform a malicious task.

Turing test A test developed by Alan Turing and used to determine whether a computer could be called intelligent. In a Turing test, judges are asked to determine whether the output they see on computer displays is produced by a computer or a human being. If a computer program succeeds in tricking the judges into believing that only a human could have generated that output, the program is said to have passed the Turing test.

turnover line In an indentation, the second and subsequent lines.

twisted pair An inexpensive copper cable used for telephone and data communications. The term *twisted pair* refers to the braiding of the paired wires, a practice that reduces interference from electrical fields.

two-megapixel Type of digital camera that can produce sharp images at higher enlargements such as 8 by 10 inches.

U

ubiquitous computing A scenario for future computing in which computers are so numerous that they fade into the background, providing intelligence for virtually every aspect of daily life.

uninstall To remove a program from a computer system by using a special utility.

uninterruptible power supply (UPS) A device that provides power to a computer system for a short period of time if electrical power is lost.

universal product code (UPC) A label with a series of bars that can be either keyed in or read by a scanner to identify an item and determine its cost. UPC scanners are often found in point-of-sale (POS) terminals.

universal serial bus (USB) An external bus architecture that connects peripherals such as keyboards, mice, and digital cameras. USB offers many benefits over older serial architectures, such as support for 127 devices on a single port, Plug and Play, and higher transfer rates.

UNIX A 32-bit operating system that features multiuser access, preemptive multitasking, multiprocessing, and other sophisticated features. UNIX is widely used for file servers in client/server networks.

upload To send a file to another computer by means of a computer network.

URL (uniform resource locator) In the World Wide Web, one of two basic kinds of Universal Resource Identifiers (URI), a string of characters that precisely identifies an Internet resource's type and location. For example, the fictitious URL http://www.wolverine.virginia.edu/ ~toros/winerefs/merlot.html identifies a World Wide Web document (http://), indicates the domain name of the computer on which it is stored (www.wolverine.virginia.edu), fully describes the document's location in the directory structure (~toros/winerefs/), and includes the document's name and extension (merlot.html).

Usenet A worldwide computer-based discussion system that uses the Internet and other networks for transmission media. Discussion is channeled into more than 50,000 topically named newsgroups, which contain original contributions called articles, as well as commentaries on these articles called follow-up posts. As follow-up posts continue to appear on a given subject, a thread of discussion emerges; a threaded newsreader collates these articles together so readers can see the flow of the discussion.

user A person who uses a computer and its applications to perform tasks and produce results.

user ID A word or name that uniquely identifies a computer user. Synonymous with user name.

user interface The part of system software that interacts with the user.

user name A unique name that a system administrator assigns to you that you use as initial identification. You must type this name and also your password to gain access to the system.

utilities See system utilities.

V

value-added network (VAN) A public data network that provides value-added services for corporate customers, including end-to-end dedicated lines with guaranteed security. VANs, however, also charge an expensive per-byte fee.

value-added reseller (VAR) An independent company that selects system components and assembles them into a functioning system.

VBScript A scripting language used to write short programs (scripts) that can be embedded in Web pages.

vector graphic An image composed of distinct objects, such as lines or shapes, that may be moved or edited independently. Each object is described by a complex mathematical formula.

vendor A company that sells goods or services.

VGA connector A physical connector that is designed to connect a VGA monitor to a video adapter.

video adapter Video circuitry that fits into an expansion bus and determines the quality of the display and resolution of your monitor. Also called display adapter.

video capture board See video capture card.

video capture card An expansion board that accepts analog or digital video signals, which are then compressed and stored.

video card See video adapter.

video editor A program that enables you to view and edit a digitized video and to select special effects.

Video Graphics Array (VGA) A display standard that can display 16 colors at a maximum resolution of 640 pixels by 480 pixels.

video RAM (VRAM) A random access memory chip that maximizes the performance of video adapters.

videoconferencing A technology enabling two or more people to have a face-to-face meeting even though they're geographically separated.

view menu In a graphical user interface (GUI), a menu that provides access to document viewing options, including normal layout, print layout, and document magnification (zoom) options.

viewable area The front surface on a cathode-ray tube monitor actually available for viewing, which is less than the quoted size. See quoted size.

virtual memory A means of increasing the size of a computer's random access memory (RAM) by using part of the hard disk as an extension of RAM.

virtual private network (VPN) A method of connecting two physically separate local area networks (LANs) by using the Internet. Strong encryption is used to ensure privacy.

virtual reality (VR) A computer-generated illusion of three-dimensional space. On the Web, virtual reality sites enable Web users to explore three-dimensional virtual reality worlds by means of VR plug-in programs. These programs enable you to walk or "fly" through the three-dimensional space that these worlds offer.

Virtual Reality Modeling Language (VRML) A scripting language that enables programmers to specify the characteristics of a three-dimensional world that is accessible on the Internet. VRML worlds can contain sounds, hyperlinks, videos, and animations as well as three-dimensional spaces, which can be explored by using a VRML plug-in.

virus See computer virus.

vision technology See eye-gaze response system.

Visual Basic (VB) A programming language developed by Microsoft based on the BASIC programming language. Visual Basic is one of the world's most widely used program development packages.

Visual Studio .NET A suite of products that contains Visual Basic .NET, which enables programmers to work with complex objects; Visual C++, which is based upon C++; and Visual C# (pronounced "C sharp"), which is a less complex version of C++ that is used for rapid application development of Web programs.

voice recognition See speech recognition.

volatile Susceptible to loss; a way of saying that all the data disappears forever if the power fails.

W

warm boot To restart a computer that is already operating.

waterfall model A method in information systems development that returns the focus of the systems development project to a previous phase if an error is discovered in it.

waveform A type of digitized audio format used to record live sounds or music.

wavetable synthesis A method of generating and reproducing musical sounds in a sound card. Wavetable synthesis uses a prerecorded sample of dozens of orchestral instruments to determine how particular notes should sound. Wavetable synthesis is far superior to FM synthesis.

Web See World Wide Web (WWW).

Web-based training (WBT) Computer-based training implemented via the Internet or an intranet.

Web browser A program that runs on an Internet-connected computer and provides access to information on the World Wide Web (WWW).

Web cam A low-cost video camera used for low-resolution videoconferencing on the Internet.

Web-database integration The latest trend in database software, techniques that make information stored in databases available through Internet connections.

Web-enabled devices Devices that have the ability to connect to the Internet and e-book readers.

Web page A document you create to share with others on the Web. A Web page can include text, graphics, sound, animation, and video.

Web portal (portal) A Web site that provides multiple online services; a jumping off place that provides an organized way to go to other places on the Web.

Web server On the Web, a program that accepts requests for information framed according to the Hypertext Transfer Protocol (HTTP). The server processes these requests and sends the requested document.

Web site A computer that is accessible to the public Internet and is running a server program that makes Web pages available.

Web technology In application software, the capability to save files in a form that contains a Web document's underlying HTML codes, greatly facilitating file conversion.

WebTV See MSN® TV.

wheel mouse A type of mouse that has a dial that can be used to scroll through data on-screen.

whistleblowing Reporting illegal or unethical actions of a company to a regulatory agency or the press.

whiteboard A separate area of a videoconferencing screen enabling participants to create a shared workspace. Participants can write or draw in this space as if they were using a chalkboard in a meeting.

wide area network (WAN) A commercial data network that provides data communications services for businesses and government agencies. Most WANs use the X.25 protocols, which overcome problems related to noisy analog telephone lines.

Wi-fi A collection of wireless transmission standards for wireless networks.

wildcard A symbol that stands for any character or any group of characters.

window border The outer edge of a window on a graphical user interface (GUI); in Microsoft Windows it can be dragged to change the size of the window.

window controls In a graphical user interface (GUI), a group of window management controls that enable the user to minimize, maximize, restore, or close the window.

Windows Bitmap (BMP) A bitmapped graphics format developed for Microsoft Windows.

Windows Update Microsoft operating system update service that keeps your operating system up-to-date with any fixes (service patches) or protections against external environment changes.

wired Connected by a physical medium.

wireless Connected through the air or space.

wireless LANs (WLANs) Local area networks that use a radio signal spread over a seemingly random series of frequencies for greater security.

wizard In a graphical user interface (GUI), a series of dialog boxes that guide the user through a complex process, such as importing data into an application.

word processing program An office application that enables the user to create, edit, format, and print textual documents.

word size The number of bits a computer can work with at one time.

word wrapping A word processing feature that automatically moves words down to the beginning of the next line if they extend beyond the right margin.

workbook In a spreadsheet program, a file that can contain two or more spreadsheets, each of which has its own page in the workbook.

workflow automation An information system in which documents are automatically sent to the people who need to see them.

workgroup A collection of individuals working together on a task.

workgroup computing Any situation in which all of the members of a workgroup have specific hardware, software, and networking equipment that enables them to connect, communicate, and collaborate.

workstation A powerful desktop computer that meets the computing needs of engineers, architects, and other professionals who require detailed graphic displays. In a LAN, a workstation runs application programs and serves as an access point to the network.

World Wide Web (WWW) A global hypertext system that uses the Internet as its transport mechanism. In a hypertext system, you navigate by clicking hyperlinks, which display another document (which also contains hyperlinks). Most Web documents are created using HTML, a markup language that is easy to learn and that will soon be supplanted by automated tools. Incorporating hypermedia (graphics, sounds, animations, and video), the Web has become the ideal medium for publishing information on the Internet. See also Web browser.

World Wide Web Consortium (W3C) An independent standards body made up of university researchers and industry practitioners devoted to setting effective standards to promote the orderly growth of the World Wide Web. Housed at the Massachusetts Institute of Technology (MIT), W3C sets standards for HTML and many other aspects of Web usage.

worm A program resembling a computer virus that can spread over networks.

WWW See World Wide Web (WWW).

X

X.25 A packet-switching network protocol optimized for use on noisy analog telephone lines.

xDSL See DSL (Digital Subscriber Line).

XML (eXtensible Markup Language) A set of rules for creating markup languages that enables programmers to capture specific types of data by creating their own elements.

Z

Zero configuration (Zeroconf) A method for networking devices via an Ethernet cable that does not require configuration and administration.

Zip disk A removable storage medium that combines the convenience of a floppy disk with the storage capacity of a small hard disk (100 to 200 MB).

Zip disk drive A popular removable storage medium, created by Iomega Corporation, that provides 100 to 200 MB of storage on relatively inexpensive ($10 each) portable disks.

zombie A computer commandeered by a hacker to do what the hacker's program tells it to do.

Illustration Credits

CHAPTER I

Figure 1.1, top
© Tim Pannell/Corbis

Figure 1.1, bottom left
© Robert Levine/Corbis

Figure 1.1, bottom right
© Tom Stewart

Figure 1.2
© Jose Luis Peleaz/Corbis

Figure 1.3, PC
Courtesy of International Business Machines
Corporation. Unauthorized use not permitted.

Figure 1.3, Macintosh
© 2004 Apple Computer, Inc.
All rights reserved.

Figure 1.3, Notebook
Courtesy of Sony Electronics, Inc.

Figure 1.3, PDA
Courtesy of Sony Electronics, Inc.

Figure 1.5 a, b, c, d, e, f
Courtesy of International Business Machines
Corporation. Unauthorized use not permitted.

Figure 1.5h
Courtesy of Creative Labs.

Figure 1.5i
Courtesy of International Business Machines
Corporation. Unauthorized use not permitted.

Figure 1.5j
© Paul Hardy/Corbis

Figure 1.5k
Courtesy of International Business Machines
Corporation. Unauthorized use not permitted.

Figure 1.6
© Japack/Corbis

Figure 1.8
Courtesy of Intel Corporation

Figure 1.9a, Monitor
Courtesy of International Business Machines
Corporation. Unauthorized use not permitted.

Figure 1.13
Getty Images

Figure 1.14, Microcomputer
© 2004 Apple Computer, Inc.

Figure 1.14, Handheld computer
Courtesy of Hewlett-Packard

Figure 1.14, Laptop
Courtesy of International Business Machines
Corporation. Unauthorized use not permitted.

Figure 1.14, Workstation
Courtesy of International Business Machines
Corporation. Unauthorized use not permitted.

Figure 1.15, Server
Courtesy of International Business Machines
Corporation. Unauthorized use not permitted.

Figure 1.15, Minicomputer
Courtesy of Hewlett-Packard

Figure 1.15, Mainframe
Courtesy of International Business Machines
Corporation. Unauthorized use not permitted.

Figure 1.15, Supercomputer
Courtesy of Cray, Inc.

Figure 1.19
© Images.com/Corbis

Figure 1.21
© George Hall/Corbis

Figure 1.22
AP/Wide World Photos

Figure 1.23
© Reuters NewMedia/Corbis

Figure 1.24
© H. David Seawell/Corbis

Figure 1.25
© Sally Morgan, Ecoscene/Corbis

Figure 1.26
Courtesy of Wolverine

SPOTLIGHT I

Figure 1D
© 2004 Nvidia Corporate Office.
All rights reserved.

Figure 1G
© Jim Craigmyle/Corbis

Figure 1H
© Jose Luis Peleaz/Corbis

Figure 1I
Courtesy of the Software Publishers Association

Figure 1J
AFP/Getty Images

CHAPTER 2

Figure 2.1a
© 2004 Six Flags Theme Parks Inc. All rights reserved.

Figure 2.1b
© Terry Ford. All rights reserved.

Figure 2.1c
© 2004 Monster.com. All rights reserved.

Figure 2.1d
© Shopping.com. All rights reserved.

Figure 2.1e
Reprinted with permission from Britannica.com.
© 2003 by Encyclopaedia Britannica, Inc.

Figure 2.4
© America Online, Inc.

Figure 2.6a
© 2004 by Consumers Union of U.S., Inc. Yonkers, NY 10703-1057, a nonprofit organization. Reprinted with permission from the April 2004 screen capture of www.ConsumerReports.org® for educational purposes only. No commercial use or reproduction permitted. Log onto: www.ConsumerReports.org®.

Figure 2.6b
© 2004 Alternative Medicine.com. All rights reserved.

Figure 2.6c
Copyright © 2003 ABCNEWS Internet Ventures

Figure 2.7a
© University of Oregon. All rights reserved.

Figure 2.7b
© 2004 EarthCam, Inc. All rights reserved.

Figure 2.7c
Copyright © 1968-2004 Mountain News Corp.
All rights reserved.

Figure 2.9a
Screen shot(s) reprinted by permission from Microsoft Corporation.

Figure 2.9b
Copyright © NetZero, Inc. All rights reserved.

Figure 2.9c
© 2003 University of Oregon.

Figure 2.10a
Netscape browser window © 2002 Netscape Communications Corporation. Used with permission. Netscape Communications has not authorized, sponsored, endorsed, or approved this publication and is not responsible for its content.

Figure 2.10b
Screen shot(s) reprinted by permission from Microsoft Corporation.

Figure 2.11
Screen shot(s) reprinted by permission from Microsoft Corporation.

Figure 2.14
Screen shot(s) reprinted by permission from Microsoft Corporation.

Figure 2.15
© Copyright 1997-2003 Charles M. Kozierok

Figure 2.16
© Blog Search Engine. All rights reserved.

Figure 2.17
© WWW Virtual Library, 1994-2004.
All rights reserved.

Figure 2.18
©2004 Google. All rights reserved.

Figure 2.19a
© 2003 CareerBuilder

Figure 2.19b
© 2000-2003 Pearson Education, publishing as Information Please®

Figure 2.20
© 2004 by Yahoo! Inc. YAHOO! and the YAHOO! logo are trademarks of Yahoo! Inc.

Figure 2.21
© 2004 Google Inc. All rights reserved.

Figure 2.22
© 2003 Ingenta, Inc. All rights reserved.

Figure 2.24
© Dennis Novak/Image Bank/Getty Images

Figure 2.25
Screen shot(s) reprinted by permission from Microsoft Corporation.

Figure 2.26
© Firetrust Limited. All rights reserved.

Figure 2.27
Screen shot(s) reprinted by permission from Microsoft Corporation.

Figure 2.28
© Department of Educaiton and Training, Government of Western Australia. All rights reserved.

Figure 2.29
© CyberAngels. All rights reserved.

Figure 2.32
Screen shot(s) reprinted by permission from Microsoft Corporation.

SPOTLIGHT 2

Figure 2A1
© REI. All rights reserved.

Figure 2A2
© TraderOnline. All rights reserved.

Figure 2B
© Staples, Inc. All rights reserved.

Figure 2C
COPYRIGHT © EBAY INC. ALL RIGHTS RESERVED.

Figure 2D
© Shopping.com. All rights reserved.

Figure 2E
©1990-2004 Peapod, LLC. All rights reserved.

Figure 2F
© 2004 Amazon.com, Inc. All rights reserved.

Figure 2G
© 2004 Xara Group Limited. All rights reserved.

Figure 2H
Copyright © 2004 Entrepreneur.com, Inc. All rights reserved.

Figure 2I
© 2004 Webworkshop.org. All rights reserved.

Figure 2J
COPYRIGHT © EBAY INC. ALL RIGHTS RESERVED.

Figure 2K
© 2004 by Yahoo! Inc. YAHOO! and the YAHOO! logo are trademarks of Yahoo! Inc.

Figure 2L
© 2004 Expedia, Inc. All rights reserved.

Figure 2M
© Paul Barton/Corbis

Figure 2N
© BankRate.com. All rights reserved.

Figure 2O
©2004 E*TRADE Financial Corp.

Figure 2Pa
© GEICO. All rights reserved.

Figure 2Pb
Copyright © 1995-2004, The Weather Channel Interactive, Inc.

Figure 2Pc
© Copyright Homestore, Inc., 1999-2003. All rights reserved.

CHAPTER 3

Figure 3.5
© Digital Art/Corbis

Figure 3.6
© Digital Art/Corbis

Figure 3.7
Courtesy of Hewlett-Packard

Figure 3.8
© palowireless Pty Ltd. All rights reserved.

Figure 3.10
© Corbis

Figure 3.12
© NYCWireless. All rights reserved.

Figure 3.13, ISDN adapter
Courtesy of International Business Machines Corporation. Unauthorized use not permitted.

Figure 3.13, Cable modem
Courtesy of Motorola Corporation

Figure 3.14, Web-enabled pager and messaging device
Courtesy of Motorola Corporation

Figure 3.14, Web-enabled cell phone
Courtesy of Nokia

Figure 3.17
Courtesy of Nokia

Figure 3.18, Palm Pilot
© Jean Nelson/Corbis

Figure 3.18, Handspring
AP/Wide World Photos

Figure 3.18, Sharp Zaurus
AP/Wide World Photos

Figure 3.18, Blackberry
Courtesy of Blackberry

Figure 3.19
AP/Wide World Photos

Figure 3.20
© 2003 Net2Phone, Inc.

Figure 3.21
© Steve Chenn/Corbis

Figure 3.22
© 2004 EarthCam, Inc. All rights reserved.

Figure 3.23
Screen shot(s) reprinted by permission from Microsoft Corporation.

Figure 3.24
© John Feingush/Corbis

Figure 3.26
Courtesy of OnStar

Figure 3.27
© Technical Communication/Corbis

Figure 3.28
© Cheryl Raulo/Reuters/Corbis

Figure 3.29
Courtesy of Nokia

Figure 3.30
Reprinted by permission of Kensington WIFI finder

SPOTLIGHT 3

Figure 3A1
© David Young Wolf/Photo Edit

Figure 3A2
© Sky Bonillo/Photo Edit

Figure 3A3
© Charles Gupton/Corbis

Figure 3F
AP/Wide World Photos

Figure 3F
© 2004 Apple Computer, Inc. All rights reserved.

Figure 3H
Courtesy of Netgear

Figure 3Ja
Screen shot(s) reprinted by permission from
Microsoft Corporation.

Figure 3Jb
© 2004 Cisco Systems. All rights reserved.

Figure 3K
© 1995-2003 Symantec Corporation

Figure 3L
Screen shot(s) reprinted by permission from
Microsoft Corporation.

Figure 3M
© Belkin Corporation. All rights reserved.

CHAPTER 4

Figure 4.4
Screen shot(s) reprinted by permission from
Microsoft Corporation.

Figure 4.5
Screen shot(s) reprinted by permission from
Microsoft Corporation.

Figure 4.8
© Charles Gupton/Corbis

Figure 4.9a
Screen shot(s) reprinted by permission from
Microsoft Corporation.

Figure 4.9b
Screen shot(s) reprinted by permission from
Microsoft Corporation.

Figure 4.9c
Screen shot(s) reprinted by permission from
Microsoft Corporation.

Figure 4.10
Screen shot(s) reprinted by permission from
Microsoft Corporation.

Figure 4.11
Screen shot(s) reprinted by permission from
Microsoft Corporation.

Figure 4.13
Screen shot(s) reprinted by permission from
Microsoft Corporation.

Figure 4.14
Screen shot(s) reprinted by permission from
Microsoft Corporation.

Figure 4.15
© Apple Computer, Inc. All rights reserved.

Figure 4.17
© Copyright 2004 - OSDN Open Source Development
Network, Inc. All rights reserved.

Figure 4.19
Courtesy of Gateway Computers

Figure 4.19
© 2004 Apple Computers, Inc. All rights reserved.

Figure 4.20
Screen shot(s) reprinted by permission from
Microsoft Corporation.

Figure 4.21
© 2004 Symantec Corporation. All rights reserved.

Figure 4.22
Copyright © 1999-2004 SecurityFocus. All rights
reserved.

Figure 4.23
Screen shot(s) reprinted by permission from
Microsoft Corporation.

Figure 4.24
Screen shot(s) reprinted by permission from
Microsoft Corporation.

Figure 4.25
Screen shot(s) reprinted by permission from
Microsoft Corporation.

Figure 4.26
Screen shot(s) reprinted by permission from
Microsoft Corporation.

Figure 4.28
Screen shot(s) reprinted by permission from
Microsoft Corporation.

Figure 4.29
Screen shot(s) reprinted by permission from
Microsoft Corporation.

SPOTLIGHT 4

Figure 4D
Screen shot(s) reprinted by permission from Microsoft Corporation.

Figure 4E
Screen shot(s) reprinted by permission from Microsoft Corporation.

Figure 4F
Screen shot(s) reprinted by permission from Microsoft Corporation.

Figure 4G
Screen shot(s) reprinted by permission from Microsoft Corporation.

Figure 4H
Screen shot(s) reprinted by permission from Microsoft Corporation.

Figure 4I
Screen shot(s) reprinted by permission from Microsoft Corporation.

Figure 4J
Screen shot(s) reprinted by permission from Microsoft Corporation.

Figure 4K
Screen shot(s) reprinted by permission from Microsoft Corporation.

Figure 4La
Screen shot(s) reprinted by permission from Microsoft Corporation.

Figure 4Lb
Screen shot(s) reprinted by permission from Microsoft Corporation.

Figure 4M
Screen shot(s) reprinted by permission from Microsoft Corporation.

Figure 4N
Screen shot(s) reprinted by permission from Microsoft Corporation.

CHAPTER 5

Figure 5.2a
Screen shot(s) reprinted by permission from Microsoft Corporation.

Figure 5.2b
Screen shot(s) reprinted by permission from Microsoft Corporation.

Figure 5.2c
Screen shot(s) reprinted by permission from Microsoft Corporation.

Figure 5.3
Screen shot(s) reprinted by permission from Microsoft Corporation.

Figure 5.4
© Joe Madere/Corbis

Figure 5.5
Screen shot(s) reprinted by permission from Microsoft Corporation.

Figure 5.6
© PhotoWorks Inc. All rights reserved.

Figure 5.7
Adobe product screen shot(s) reprinted with permission from Adobe Systems Incorporated.

Figure 5.8
© Ulead Systems, Inc. All rights reserved.

Figure 5.9
©1995-2004 Macromedia, Inc. All rights reserved.

Figure 5.10
Screen shot(s) reprinted by permission from Microsoft Corporation.

Figure 5.11
© Tucows Inc. All rights reserved.

Figure 5.12
Reprinted with permission from Britannica.com. © 2003 by Encyclopaedia Britannica, Inc.

Figure 5.13
Screenshot of EverQuest®—used with permission of Sony Online Entertainment. EverQuest is a registered trademark of Sony Computer Entertainment America Inc. in the U.S. and/or other countries. © 2004 Sony Computer Entertainment America Inc. All rights reserved.

Figure 5.14
© Jose Paleaz/Corbis

Figure 5.15
AP/Wide World Photos

Figure 5.17
Screen shot(s) reprinted by permission from Microsoft Corporation.

Figure 5.19
Screen shot(s) reprinted by permission from Microsoft Corporation.

Figure 5.20
Screen shot(s) reprinted by permission from Microsoft Corporation.

Figure 5.21
© Tucows Inc. All rights reserved.

Figure 5.22
© BetaNews, Inc. All rights reserved.

Figure 5.23
Screen shot(s) reprinted by permission from Microsoft Corporation.

Figure 5.24
Screen shot(s) reprinted by permission from
Microsoft Corporation.

Figure 5.25
Screen shot(s) reprinted by permission from
Microsoft Corporation.

Figure 5.26
Screen shot(s) reprinted by permission from
Microsoft Corporation.

SPOTLIGHT 5

Figure 5B
Reprinted with permission of Microsoft Corporation.

Figure 5C
Screen shot(s) reprinted by permission from
Microsoft Corporation.

Figure 5D
Screen shot(s) reprinted by permission from
Microsoft Corporation.

Figure 5E
Screen shot(s) reprinted by permission from
Microsoft Corporation.

Figure 5F
Screen shot(s) reprinted by permission from
Microsoft Corporation.

Figure 5G
Screen shot(s) reprinted by permission from
Microsoft Corporation.

Figure 5H
Screen shot(s) reprinted by permission from
Microsoft Corporation.

Figure 5I
Screen shot(s) reprinted by permission from
Microsoft Corporation.

Figure 5J
Screen shot(s) reprinted by permission from
Microsoft Corporation.

Figure 5K
Screen shot(s) reprinted by permission from
Microsoft Corporation.

Figure 5L
Screen shot(s) reprinted by permission from
Microsoft Corporation.

Figure 5M
Screen shot(s) reprinted by permission from
Microsoft Corporation.

Figure 5N
Screen shot(s) reprinted by permission from
Microsoft Corporation.

Figure 5O
Screen shot(s) reprinted by permission from
Microsoft Corporation.

Figure 5P
Screen shot(s) reprinted by permission from
Microsoft Corporation.

Figure 5Q
Screen shot(s) reprinted by permission from
Microsoft Corporation.

Figure 5Ra, b, c, d, e, f
Screen shot(s) reprinted by permission from
Microsoft Corporation.

Figure 5S
Getty Images

Figure 5T
Screen shot(s) reprinted by permission from
Microsoft Corporation.

CHAPTER 6

Figure 6.4a
© 2004 Apple Computers, Inc. All rights reserved.

Figure 6.4b
Courtesy of International Business Machines.
Unauthorized use not permitted.

Figure 6.5a-b
© 2004 Apples Computers, Inc. All rights reserved.

Figure 6.6
AP/Wide World Photos

Figure 6.7
Courtesy of International Business Machines
Corporation. Unauthorized use not permitted.

Figure 6.9
Courtesy of International Business Machines
Corporation. Unauthorized use not permitted.

Figure 6.11
© Toshiba America, Inc. All rights reserved.

Figure 6.16
Courtesy of Intel Corporation

Figure 6.20
Courtesy of International Business Machines
Corporation. Unauthorized use not permitted.

Figure 6.24
© C. Mark Lawrence/Corbis

Figure 6.25a-c
Courtesy of Intel Corporation

SPOTLIGHT 6

Figure 6A
Courtesy of International Business Machines
Corporation. Unauthorized use not permitted.

Figure 6B
© Dell Inc. All rights reserved.

Figure 6D
Courtesy of International Business Machines
Corporation. Unauthorized use not permitted.

Figure 6E
Courtesy of Intel Corporation

Figure 6F
Reprinted by permission of Microsoft Corporation.

Figure 6G
AP/Wide World Photos

Figure 6I1
© LWA-JDC/Corbis

Figure 6I2
© Jose Luis Peleaz/Corbis

Figure 6J
© Susan Van Etten/Photo Edit

Figure 6L
Courtesy of Intel Corporation

Figure 6M
Courtesy of Isobar

CHAPTER 7

Figure 7.1
© William Whitehurst/Corbis

Figure 7-5, Trackball, stylus, pointing stick, joystick
Courtesy of International Business Machines
Corporation. Unauthorized use not permitted.

Figure 7-5, Touch screen
© Kim Kulish/Corbis Saba

Figure 7-6
Courtesy of Microsoft Corporation

Figure 7.8
AP/Wide World Photos

Figure 7.9a
Courtesy of Hewlett-Packard

Figure 7.9b
Courtesy of DocuPen

Figure 7.11
© 2004 SAMSUNG. All rights reserved.

Figure 7.12a
Courtesy of International Business Machines
Corporation. Unauthorized use not permitted.

Figure 7.12b
Getty Images/AFP

Figure 7.12c
AP/Wide World Photos

Figure 7.16
Xerox Corporation

Figure 7.17a
Courtesy of ViewSonic

Figure 7.17b
Common Photo

Figure 7.18
Courtesy of Canon Inc.

Figure 7.19, Left
AP/Wide World Photos

Figure 7.19, Middle
Getty Imgaes/AFP

Figure 7.19, Right
Getty Images/AFP

Figure 7.22, Left
Courtesy of Intel Corporation

Figure 7.22, Center
Courtesy of International Business Machines
Corporation. Unauthorized use not permitted.

Figure 7.23
© 2004 Delphi. All rights reserved.

Figure 7.24a-b
Courtesy of International Business Machines
Corporation. Unauthorized use not permitted.

Figure 7.25
Courtesy of Iomega Corporation

Figure 7.26
© Michael Keller Studio/Corbis

Figure 7.28
Courtesy of International Business Machines
Corporation. Unauthorized use not permitted.

Figure 7.29
Courtesy of SanDisk Corporation

Figure 7.30
Courtesy of Iomega Corporation

Figure 7.31
Courtesy of International Business Corporation.
Unauthorized use not permitted.

Figure 7.32
© Dantz Development Corporation.
All rights reserved.

SPOTLIGHT 7

Figure 7B
Screen shot(s) reprinted by permission from
    Microsoft Corporation.

Figure 7Ca
Courtesy of Dell Computers

Figure 7Cb
Courtesy of Ben Q. Joybee

Figure 7Cc
Creative Labs

Figure 7Cd
© 2004 Apple Computer, Inc. All rights reserved.

Figure 7D
© Olympus America Inc. All rights reserved.

Figure 7E, Left
© Stocker Mike/Corbis Sygma

Figure 7E, Right
© Franklin Electronic Publishers

Figure 7F
Courtesy of Gateway Computers

Figure 7G
Courtesy of SanDisk Corporation

Figure 7H
Courtesy of Kodak

Figure 7I
Reprinted with permission of Logitech

Figure 7J
Courtesy of Sony Corporation

Figure 7K
Courtesy of Panasonic

Figure 7L
© Corbis Sygma

Figure 7M
Courtesy of Sony Corporation

Figure 7N
AP/Wide World Photos

Figure 7O
Courtesy of RCA

Figure 7P
Reprinted by permission of TIVO®

Figure 7Q
© Roger Ressmeyer/Corbis

CHAPTER 8

Figure 8.1
© William Taufic/Corbis

Figure 8.3a
Courtesy of International Business Machines
    Corporation. Unauthorized use not permitted.

Figure 8.3c
Courtesy of International Business Machines
    Corporation. Unauthorized use not permitted.

Figure 8.3d
Courtesy of International Business Machines
    Corporation. Unauthorized use not permitted.

Figure 8.8, File server, print server, fax server
Courtesy of International Business Machines
    Corporation. Unauthorized use not permitted.

Figure 8.11
© Dantz Development Corporation.
    All rights reserved.

Figure 8.13
© Wave Communications. All rights reserved.

Figure 8.14
Copyright ©2003 SETI@home

Figure 8.17
© Chuck Savage/Corbis

Figure 8.18
Copyright © United Online, Inc. All rights reserved.

CHAPTER 9

Figure 9.1
Courtesy of the Electronic Privacy Information Center.

Figure 9.2
© Equifax Inc. All rights reserved.

Figure 9.3
© InfoUSA, Inc. All rights reserved.

Figure 9.4
© Ralph Cleavenz/Corbis

Figure 9.5
Copyright © 2003 AdDesigner.com.
    All rights reserved.

Figure 9.6
Screen shot(s) reprinted by permission from
    Microsoft Corporation.

Figure 9.7
Copyright © 2001 by Center for Democracy
    and Technology.

Figure 9.8
© 2004 The Direct Marketing Association.
    All rights reserved.

Figure 9.9
© 2004 by Yahoo! Inc. YAHOO! and the YAHOO! logo are trademarks of Yahoo! Inc.

Figure 9.10
© 2003 Anonymizer, Inc. All rights reserved.

Figure 9.11
© SpectorSoft Corporation. All rights reserved.

Figure 9.12
Copyright 1995–2004 by Randy McCall. All rights reserved.

Figure 9.13
© 2000-2004 Business Software Alliance. All rights reserved.

Figure 9.15
Copyright © 2000 Rhode Island Soft Systems, Inc.

Figure 9.16
Courtesy of Kensington Technology

Figure 9.19
© 2002 Netscape Communications Corporation. Used with permission. Netscape Communications has not authorized, sponsored, endorsed, or approved this publication and is not responsible for its content.

Figure 9.21
© Copyright 2004 Match.com, LP. All rights reserved.

Figure 9.22
© Image.com/Corbis

Figure 9.23
© Copyright Rostislav Persion 2004

Figure 9.24
Courtesy of APC

Figure 9.25
© James Leynse/Corbis

Figure 9.26a
AP/Wide World Photos

Figure 9.26b
AP/Wide World Photos

Figure 9.26C
© Corbis/Saba

Figure 9.28
© The Honeynet Project

Figure 9.31
Courtesy of the Federal Public Key Infrastructure Steering Committee

Figure 9.32
Courtesy of MIT

Figure 9.33
Courtesy of The Center for Democracy and Technology

Figure 9.34a,b
Copyright © 1998-2004 The Mozilla Organization

CHAPTER 10

Figure 10.1a
© 2004 Monster.com. All rights reserved.

Figure 10.1b
© 2004 by Yahoo! Inc. YAHOO! and the YAHOO! logo are trademarks of Yahoo! Inc.

Figure 10.1c
© 2004 Artemis HR. All rights reserved.

Figure 10.1d
Copyright 1995–2004 © ComputerJobs.com, Inc. All Rights Reserved.

Figure 10.1e
© 2004 by Dori Reuscher (http://www.certification.about.com), licensed to About, Inc. Used by permission of About, Inc., which can be found on the Web at http://www.about.com. All rights reserved.

Figure 10.2
Courtesy of the Bureau of Labor Statistics.

Figure 10.5
© Tom & Dee Ann McCarthy/Corbis

Figure 10.6
© John Feingersh/Corbis

Figure 10.7
© Lester Lefkowitz/Corbis

Figure 10.8a
Copyright © 2003–2004 MediaLive International, Inc. All Rights Reserved.

Figure 10.8b
© Mike Blake/Reuters/Corbis

Figure 10.9
© The Association for Women in Computing. All rights reserved.

Figure 10.10
© H1 BASE Incorporated. All rights reserved.

Figure 10.11
© Jose Luis Pelaez, Inc./Corbis

Figure 10.15a
© Copyright 2004 MediaTec Publishing Inc. All Rights Reserved.

Figure 10.15b
© Copyright 2003 TechSkills, LLC. All Rights Reserved.

Figure 10.16
© 2001-2002 - B2BMedia Inc.

Figure 10.17
© Electronic Frontier Foundation. All rights reserved.

Figure 14.11

Figure 14.12

Figure 14.13

Figure 14.14

Figure 14.15

Figure 14.16

Figure 14.17

Figure 14.18

Figure 14.19

Figure 14.20

Figure 14.21

Figure 14.22

Figure 14.23

Figure 14.24

Figure 14.25a

Figure 14.25b

Figure 14.26

Figure 14.27

SPOTLIGHT 8

Figure 8A

Figure 8B
Courtesy of the National Nanotechnology Initiative

Figure 8C

Figure 8D

Figure 8F

Figure 8G
Courtesy of the National Institute of Standards and Technology

Figure 8H

Figure 8I

Figure 8J
Courtesy of the Virtual Reality in Medicine Lab (VRMedLab) at the University of Illinois at Chicago.

Figure 8L
Courtesy of the Computer History Museum

Figure 8M

Figure 8N

Figure 8O
Courtesy of Franklin Co.

Figure 8P

Figure 8R

Figure 8R
Courtesy of PaPeRo

Index